W9-BEZ-398

VMware vCloud®
Architecture Toolkit (vCAT)

Technical and Operational Guidance
for Cloud Success

VMware Press is the official publisher of VMware books and training materials, which provide guidance on the critical topics facing today's technology professionals and students. Enterprises, as well as small- and medium-sized organizations, adopt virtualization as a more agile way of scaling IT to meet business needs. VMware Press provides proven, technically accurate information that will help them meet their goals for customizing, building, and maintaining their virtual environment.

With books, certification and study guides, video training, and learning tools produced by world-class architects and IT experts, VMware Press helps IT professionals master a diverse range of topics on virtualization and cloud computing and is the official source of reference materials for preparing for the VMware Certified Professional Examination.

VMware Press is also pleased to have localization partners that can publish its products into more than 42 languages, including Chinese (Simplified), Chinese (Traditional), French, German, Greek, Hindi, Japanese, Korean, Polish, Russian, and Spanish.

For more information about VMware Press, visit **vmwarepress.com**.

VMware vCloud® Architecture Toolkit (vCAT)

Technical and Operational Guidance for Cloud Success

VMware vCAT Team

vmware® PRESS

Upper Saddle River, NJ • Boston • Indianapolis • San Francisco
New York • Toronto • Montreal • London • Munich • Paris • Madrid
Cape Town • Sydney • Tokyo • Singapore • Mexico City

VMware vCloud Architecture Toolkit (vCAT)

Technical and Operational Guidance for Cloud Success

Published by Pearson Education, Inc.

Publishing as VMware Press

Library of Congress Control Number: 2013910623

ISBN-13: 978-0-321-91202-2

ISBN-10: 0-321-91202-0

Printed in the United States of America

First Printing: August 2013

Warning and Disclaimer

Every effort has been made to make this book as complete and as accurate as possible, but no warranty or fitness is implied. The information provided is on an "as is" basis. The authors, VMware Press, VMware, and the publisher shall have neither liability nor responsibility to any person or entity with respect to any loss or damages arising from the information contained in this book or from the use of any digital content or programs accompanying it.

The opinions expressed in this book belong to the author and are not necessarily those of VMware.

Corporate and Government Sales

VMware Press offers excellent discounts on this book when ordered in quantity for bulk purchases or special sales, which may include electronic versions and/or custom covers and content particular to your business, training goals, marketing focus, and branding interests. For more information, please contact:

U.S. Corporate and Government Sales
(800) 382-3419
corpsales@pearsontechgroup.com

For sales outside the United States, please contact:

International Sales
international@pearsoned.com

VMWARE PRESS PROGRAM MANAGERS
Eric Ullanderson
Anand Sundaram

ASSOCIATE PUBLISHER
David Dusthimer

AQUISITIONS EDITOR
Joan Murray

DEVELOPMENT EDITOR
Ellie Bru

MANAGING EDITOR
Sandra Schroeder

PROJECT EDITOR
Mandie Frank

COPY EDITOR
Krista Hansing
Editorial Services

PROOFREADER
Sheri Replin

INDEXER
Rebecca Salerno

EDITORIAL ASSISTANT
Vanessa Evans

DESIGNER
Chuti Prasertsith

COMPOSITOR
Trina Wurst

Contents

About the Contributors

The following product owners have led the vCAT 3.x development effort upon which this VMware Press release is based.

John Arrasjid—John Arrasjid is a Principal Architect at VMware, Inc., where he started in 2003. John is part of the Global Technology Solutions team, is a VMware Ambassador, and is part of the Field Office of the CTO. John was awarded the vExpert 2012 designation, given to the top VMware evangelists in the industry, for his work on vCAT and the VCDX program. As lead architect and chief product owner of vCAT, John has led the development and release of vCAT since 2011. In his 10 years at VMware, John has co-authored four other books; *VCDX Boot Camp, Cloud Computing with vCloud Director, Foundation for Cloud Computing with vSphere 4, and Deploying the VMware Infrastructure*. John regularly presents at VMworld, VMware Partner Exchange, VMware vForum, USENIX LISA, and other industry conferences. His VCDX Boot Camp has been taught to more than 800 individuals since 2008. John holds a bachelor of science in computer science from SUNY at Buffalo and holds VCDX, ITIL Foundations, and CSPO certifications. He is a founding member of the Elastic Sky band, developer of the original vmsnap/vmres tool, and developer of several consulting engagements for security, business continuity, and performance. Find John on Twitter at @vcdx001.

Matthew Wood—Matthew Wood is an independent technical writer. Matthew has been a senior technical writer, editor, and manager for VMware Technical Services, and he was the lead editor for the vCAT project from 2010 until 2013. Matthew works with architects and consultants to produce IP for services kits and solutions kits related to all aspects of VMware technology. He also has written original documentation for the VMware Services Software Solutions group to support tools such as VMware HealthAnalyzer and Migration Manager. Matthew has 38 years of experience working with technology companies, focusing especially on UNIX, virtualization, and applications that support enterprise IT environments.

Wade Holmes—Wade Holmes is a Staff Solutions Architect at VMware, Inc., and holds VCDX, CISSP, CCSK, and CSPO certifications. He has more than 16 years of experience planning, teaching, and presenting on the architecture, design, and implementation of complex computing environments of all scopes and sizes. Wade has presented and taught at conferences such as VMworld, SXSW, USENIX LISA, and VMware User Group meetings. Wade was awarded the vExpert 2012 designation, given to the top VMware evangelists in the industry. He holds a bachelor's degree in information technology and a master's degree in information assurance. Find him on Twitter at @wholmes; he also maintains a blog at www.vwade.com.

Joe Sarabia—Joe Sarabia is a Cloud Architect at VMware, Inc., and holds industry certifications that include VCAP-DCD, VCAP-DCA, MCSE, NCDA, ITIL, and CSPO. Joe has had various roles in the information technology field. He initially focused on operational roles in areas of organizations that consumed services from the business. About 10 years ago, Joe's role pivoted to architecting and providing services on behalf of the business for business units and end users to consume. He has spent the last several years of his career as one of the leading hybrid cloud and SDDC architects in the industry, focusing on delivering business value to the globe's largest organizations through complex software systems. Joe has particularly established himself as a thought leader in the areas of component integration and end user portal experience. Find him on Twitter at @joesarabia.

Rohan Kalra—Rohan Kalra is a Business Solutions Architect who brings more than 14 years of IT service management consulting experience, including global operations process re-engineering for Fortune 500 clients (EMC, Kellogg's, Banco Santander, Goldman Sachs, Ricoh, and more). Rohan led the creation and release of operational readiness related IP assets available through VMware's professional services, partner channels, and Accelerate Strategy teams. Formerly an executive technology adviser at Accenture, he led the development of operational readiness and governance components of its next-generation infrastructure solution blueprint, focused on cloud computing and delivery of IT as a Service. Rohan holds ITIL and CSPO certifications. Find him on Twitter at @kalrarohan.

Rupen Sheth—Rupen Sheth is a Senior Solutions Engineering Manager on the Global Services team at VMware, Inc., where he is responsible for monetizing and scaling the Software Defined Data Center (SDDC) portfolio of solutions and services. Rupen holds VCDX, ITIL, CSPO, and TOGAF certifications. He has extensive experience in delivering enterprise business and virtualization/cloud solutions through the effective application of information technology, process management, and coordination and management of multidisciplinary teams. Rupen started as a consultant at VMware and now leads a team of solution architects responsible for SDDC solutions and services kits that are used by VMware field and partners worldwide. Rupen has presented and taught at VMworld, VMware Partner Exchange, and USENIX conferences. Find him on Twitter at @rupensheth.

Ian Perez-Ponce—As Senior Product Manager for VMware's vCloud Hybrid Service, Ian is responsible for service-creation and monetization efforts for the company's Infrastructure as a Service (IaaS) cloud solutions portfolio. With more than 14 years of service provider and information technology experience, Ian helps define VMware's premium hybrid cloud service strategy and oversees the development of the vCloud Service Provider partner ecosystem. Find him on Twitter at @iperezponce.

Christophe Decanini—Christophe Decanini is a Consulting Architect at VMware, Inc., where he started in 2007; currently, he is the technical lead for cloud orchestration. Based in Gland, Switzerland, Christophe is a global resource supporting customers in their orchestration and automation needs. He has presented orchestration solutions at conferences such as VMworld and is the main contributor on the www.vcoteam.info blog and in the official VMware Orchestrator community. Christophe was awarded the vExpert designation in 2011, given to the top VMware evangelists in the industry. He has 18 years of experience in IT automation and holds a bachelor's degree in computer science. Find him on Twitter at @vCOTeam.

Burke Azbill—Burke Azbill has been working in IT since the mid-1990s and for VMware since 2007. He has been an active member of the VMworld Hands On Labs and a leading contributor to the vCenter Orchestrator community with both his own blog (www.vcoteam.info) and his contributions to the Official VMware Orchestrator blog and the community in the VMware forums. Burke was awarded the vExpert designation in 2011 and 2012, given to the top VMware evangelists in the industry. His industry certifications include MCP+I, MCSE, MCSD, CNE, CCA, LPIC-1, and VCP. Find him on Twitter at @TechnicalValues.

Michael Haines—Michael Haines is a Senior Cloud Networking and Security Architect and Engineer for the Global Services Engineering team at VMware, Inc. He leads the security architecture and development of VMware's cloud solutions for service providers, enterprise customers, and partners throughout Europe and Asia Pacific. Michael is responsible for providing deep technical expertise and interfacing directly with Engineering and Product Management to support and develop current and future vCloud products and initiatives. He is also involved in prototyping vCloud solutions and frequently presents on VMware's vCloud vision. This includes presentations at VMworld, where he also acts as one of the Security Lab captains. Michael is the co-author of the following publications: *Cloud Computing with VMware vCloud Director, LDAP in the Solaris Operating Environment: Deploying Secure Directory Services, and Deploying LDAP in the Enterprise: Sun BluePrints Publications.* Find him on Twitter at @michaelahaines.

Dave Richey—Dave Richey holds a degree from Harvard and has developed software training materials for more than a decade, including a full curriculum for Mac programmers. He draws on his experience in software development and technical management to edit technical documentation at VMware, Inc., in the fields of virtualization and cloud computing.

Ben Lin—Ben is a Staff Systems Engineer for the Networking and Security Business Unit (NSBU) at VMware, Inc. He holds VCDX3/4/5 certifications and actively participates in VCDX panels and development activities. Ben graduated from the University of California, Berkeley with a bachelor of science in electrical engineering and computer science. Ben co-authored the book *Cloud Computing with VMware vCloud Director* and was closely involved with cloud designs and deployments since the inception of vCloud Director. He is also co-author of VCDX Boot Camp. He regularly presents at conferences such as VMworld, VMworld Europe, Partner Exchange, USENIX LISA, USENIX HotCloud, and vForum. Find him on Twitter at @blin23.

Christopher Knowles—Chris Knowles is a Staff Architect within the Global Center of Excellence (CoE) at VMware, where he works on hybrid cloud and Software Defined Datacenter architecture and integration. Within the CoE, Chris translates complex business requirements into real-world highly integrated infrastructure solutions. Chris leads the VMware LiVefire program, which enables VMware specialists and industry partners to deliver these advanced solutions in the field. When not balancing work and life with his wife, Erin, and two boys, Evan and Spencer, Chris is a regular speaker at VMworld and other industry events. Find him on Twitter at @sugeknowles.

Thomas Kraus—Thomas Kraus works as a Solution Architect in the VMware Networking and Security Business Unit (NSBU) at VMware, Inc., where he helps VMware's largest customers rationalize, understand, and deploy network virtualization and Software Defined Datacenters. Thomas is primarily focused on the architecture, troubleshooting, and optimization of complex cloud environments, with a focus on automation and integration. In addition to being a VCDX, his relevant certifications are RHCE and NetApp SVAP. Find him on Twitter at @tkrausjr.

David Hill—David Hill is an experienced entrepreneur, IT consultant, and architect who has worked in the IT industry for more than 16 years on projects across the public sector and financial institutions. David joined VMware in 2010 and is a Senior Solutions Architect in the Professional Services Engineering (PSE) team. There he develops cutting-edge technology best practices, design guidelines, and intellectual property for the company and partners. David holds VCP 3/4/5 and VCAP-DCD4 certifications. David is the author and owner of the cloud technical blog www.virtual-blog.com. Find him on Twitter at @davehill99.

This book is dedicated to our families, friends, co-workers, customers, and partners. With you, we have found the time, energy, and enthusiasm to raise the bar and produce something to educate many on the concepts, technology, and operations for cloud computing and the software-defined data center.

—The vCAT Team

"Design is the fundamental soul of a human-made creation that ends up expressing itself in successive outer layers of the product or service."

—Steve Jobs

"I am constantly thinking about new and simple approaches to solving problems. As Albert Einstein said, 'Any intelligent fool can make things bigger and more complex. It takes a touch of genius to move in the opposite direction'. vCAT is a huge enabler for your service-oriented transformation efforts."

—Rupen Sheth, VCDX, ITIL, TOGAF certified

Acknowledgments

The vCATs

vCAT 3.1 Team members

Chief Product Owner

John Yani Arrasjid, Principal Architect

Project Leadership Team

Matthew Wood, Wade Holmes, Joe Sarabia, Rohan Kalra, Nira Metcalf, John Callaghan, Donna Colborn

Product Owners

John Arrasjid, VCDX
Burke Azbill
Christophe Decanini
Michael Haines
David Hill
Wade Holmes, VCDX
Rohan Kalra
Chistopher Knowles
Thomas Kraus, VCDX
Ian Perez-Ponce
Joe Sarabia
Rupen Sheth, VCDX
Matthew Wood

vCAT team logo concept by Catherine Arrasjid

Technical Publications

Matthew Wood, David Richey,
Patrick Carri, Barbara Weinstein

Project Management

John Callaghan, Donna Colborn

Marketing & Web

Nira Metcalf, Kathleen Tandy, Adam Souza

Contributors

Deji Akomolafe
Richard Anderson
Kalen Arndt
Richard Benoit
Bill Call
Philip Callahan
Chris Colotti, VCDX
Aidan Dalgleish, VCDX
Massimo Re Ferre
Greg Herzog, VCDX
Bill Keenan
Kevin Lees
Ben Lin, VCDX
Matthew Meyer, VCDX
Hugo Phan, VCDX
Prasad Pimplaskar
Mahesh Rajani, VCDX
Tom Ralph, VCDX
Alan Renouf
Rawlinson Rivera, VCDX
Heman Smith
Timo Sugliani
Andy Troup
Raman Veeramraju

Sponsors

Scott Bajtos, Michael "Dino" Cicciarelli, Carl Eschenbach, Pat Gelsinger, Dr. Stephen Herrod, Paul Maritz, Ray O'Farrell, Raghu Raghuram, Rajagopal Ramanujam, Matthew Stepanski, Dan Smoot, Paul Strong, Yvonne Wassenar

The vCATs

Past vCAT Team members

The following are individuals who have worked on past releases of the vCloud Architecture Toolkit. This includes releases 1.6, 2.0, 2.0.1, and 3.0. Current vCAT 3.1 members have also participated in developing past releases.

As with the current vCAT team, we recognize the value in everyone's contribution, the dedication, and the sacrifices made to deliver this highly used resource.

As of pre-release, vCAT has had over 100,000 downloads used by architects, administrators, operators, consumers, customers, consultants, and vendors.

Product Owners

David Baldwin
Russel Callan
Pang Chen, VCDX
Chris Colotti, VCDX
Aidan Dalgleish, VCDX
Michael DiPetrillo
Ford Donald
Massimo Re Ferre
Jason Karnes
Kevin Lees
Ben Lin, VCDX
Mahesh Rajani, VCDX
Kamau Wanguhu, VCDX

Project Management

Darrel Carson
Bernie Clarke
Mary Toman
John McGinn
Monte Kingstone
Jamal Abdul Kadar

Marketing

Suzanne Ambiel

Contributors

Jason Carolan
Andrew Hald, VCDX
Jeremy Hunt
Randy Keener
Hany Michael
Phillippe Michel
Alex Mittell
Srinivas Muthu
Dushyanth Nataraj
Chirag Patel
Melanie Spencer
John Stanford
Hugo Strydom
Ben Thomas
Patrick Thomas
TJ Vatsa

Foreword

One thing I've learned in my career is that architecture really matters. Bad implementations can be thrown away, but architectures last a long time—sometimes forever! Having a framework and set of principles to both guide and enable innovation can determine success, and a lack thereof almost certainly signals failure. An example I'm intimately familiar with is Intel's x86 architecture. Putting the right framework in place has allowed the X86 design team to continue to create value and introduce new innovations to hundreds of millions of users to this day.

The VMware vCloud Architecture Toolkit (vCAT) serves a similar role for VMware. It provides the best of best practices that guide customers in assembling and operating a Cloud-capable, modern platform based on the Software Defined Data Center (SDDC).

The insight behind the software-defined strategy is that cloud-scale economics and agility require a radically simpler and more flexible approach to managing the hardware, network, storage, and security elements of the data center. This kind of agility requires that every technology layer be software defined and automatable. Networking, storage, compute, and security need to be abstracted, pooled, and made reconfigurable through instructions that are not bound to physical hardware. In a word, they need to be virtualized. VMware is applying its virtualization engineering capability to all the physical layers of the datacenter and extending these capabilities across multiple clouds. This gives our customers the most choice and control in how they deliver IT.

This latest vCAT release guides our customers in moving configuration management, policy management, and provisioning into the software layer. This simplifies the challenges companies increasingly face as software development and IT teams work together and the line between their roles becomes less distinct. vCAT also now supports *hybrid cloud deployments on partners' clouds or on the VMware Hybrid Cloud Service so that customers can deploy workloads on hardware they rent or own.* vCAT can also guide customers in laying the foundation for Desktop as a Service and Platform as a Service.

vCAT and other VMware reference architectures are developed as part of the VMware Validated Architecture program. Our engineering, support, and other technical teams review and validate these reference architectures in our labs and directly through our customers' deployments.

Each day, our customers and our partners come to depend more on VMware technology. This is both exciting and humbling for our company. As VMware continues to play a more central role in the IT industry, we've recognized the need to provide deep technical guidance that helps our customers realize success. We also recognize that our customers need to support existing investments and want to have the option to choose the best technology for their needs. To this end, we've created a way for other industry players to extend vCAT and integrate their products into the SDDC architecture. This also allows partners to publish their own vCAT-compatible blueprints and design templates that guide our mutual customers in implementation and operation of solutions that incorporate those products. We believe that vCAT will continue to provide necessary and extensible architectural blueprints for the IT industry as it transitions to a software-defined approach to computing.

I heartily recommend this reference as a roadmap for anyone tasked with simplifying IT infrastructure and as an indispensable guide for those developing Software Defined Data Centers and vSphere/vCloud solutions.

Pat Gelsinger

Chief Executive Officer, VMware

Preface

"Technical skill is mastery of complexity, while creativity is mastery of simplicity."

Erik Christopher Zeeman

"What is to be sought in designs for the display of information is the clear portrayal of complexity. Not the complication of the simple; rather, the task of the designer is to give visual access to the subtle and the difficult—that is, revelation of the complex."

Edward Tufte

This book represents the work of more than 100 architects, consultants, administrators, engineers, project managers, technical editors, partners, and customers over multiple releases starting in 2010. A handful of people built the 1.x releases. For the 2.x release, approximately 72 individuals spent nearly 1,200 hours to produce 600 pages of content across eight documents. The 3.x releases saw about 42 individuals spend approximately 1,400 hours to produce 750 pages of content across nine documents. In your hands, you hold a compendium of these individual components in a single book format.

vCAT was created first as a reference architecture based on a limited set of use cases. The current release supports multiple use cases and, as such, has turned into a reference architecture toolkit that is part of a series titled VMware Validated Architectures (VVA).

The following sections present information on the owners of the product sections and a list of the contributors involved in the vCAT project since its inception. Approximately 50% of the development team holds VCDX certification. This material is thus not only a reference for SDDC and vCloud, but also a reference for those planning to achieve VCAP and VCDX certification.

You will notice our internal logo, a black cat on a white cloud. Catherine Arrasjid created this graphic to represent the project and the team of vCATs, as we are affectionately called. Our marketing team digitized it, and has become our internal team mascot.

It has been my pleasure to work on these releases—and to work with such an exceptional team of individuals, who are all recognized in the industry in their fields of specialization.

I want to call out the value of vCAT beyond just the cloud space. As you hear more about the Software Defined Data Center (SDDC) and related Software Defined components in networking, security, storage, and other areas, vCAT can provide the guidance you need. vCAT includes many of the components of SDDC—so what do you need to be aware of? We hope to include that in an addendum to vCAT that provides extensions in the SDDC area. Software Defined Networking and Security cover the areas currently represented by vCloud Networking and Security. Software Defined Storage will add relevant components on virtualization of storage. We expect a few other areas to come as the SDDC space continues to evolve.

VMware Validated Architectures, similar to vCAT, are designed to be easily integrated with third-party reference architectures. You will find references to these on the vendor sites. The goal is to allow ease of plug-and-play with other solutions, VMware, and third-party offerings.

As of publication, the vCAT site at www.vmware.com/go/vcat has more than 200,000 accesses and more than 100,000 downloads. These downloads were created by architects, administrators, operators, developers, project managers, solutions architects, and managers. The feedback has shown how vCAT is used and turned up suggestions to improve what we are producing. If you have input on improving this material, send your suggestions to IPfeedback@vmware.com. Please note that this book is printed in black and white to minimize cost and allow for wider adoption. Color versions of the original documentation in electronic and PDF format can be found at www.vmware.com/go/vcat in the Document Center tool.

We want to thank all participants on this project, with a special callout to our stakeholders who have supported this project and recognize the value it provides to our customers.

As you peruse this material, start by reading the Introduction, a guide to the material included in this book.

I wish you the best in your design and deployment of cloud and software-defined datacenters.

John Yani Arrasjid, VCDX-001

Principal Architect

VMware vCloud Architecture Toolkit R3.1 Release Notes

VMware vCloud Architecture Toolkit R3.1 Release Notes

The VMware® vCloud® Architecture Toolkit (vCAT) provides modular components so that you can design a vCloud reference architecture that supports your cloud use case. It includes design considerations and design patterns to support architects, operators, and consumers of a cloud computing solution based on VMware technologies.

For additional vCAT supporting material, visit the vCloud Architecture Toolkit page at vmware.com (www.vmware.com/go/vCAT). This is also where updates to vCAT will be posted.

vCAT 3.1 Documentation Packages

The following vCAT 3.1 packages are available:

- PDF package (~25MB)
- Documentation Center package (~50MB)

PDF Package

The PDF package is a zipped package that contains PDFs of all the documents in the toolkit. Use WinZip or a similar application to unzip the package, and use a PDF reader such as Adobe Reader to display and read the documents. You can print hard-copy documents from the PDFs.

Documentation Center Package

For a video overview on the Documentation Center packaging of vCAT, see the SME videos at www.vmware.com/go/vcat.

The documentation center package is a zipped package that contains a complete online help system that you can use to view all the documents in the toolkit from an easy-to-use interface. It offers powerful features such as the capability to search through the collection of vCAT documents, display a pregenerated PDF of a document, and, when served from a web server, access Google Translate to translate displayed pages into dozens of languages.

The vCAT 3.1 Documentation Center is also served from a website on vmware.com.

Browsers

The documentation center works with the following browsers:

- Google Chrome (preferred)
- Safari
- Internet Explorer (Search operates differently. Click the magnifying glass to search, enter a search term in the resulting text field, and press Enter or click Go).
- Firefox (works well except with Google Translate)

Installing the Documentation Center

The Documentation Center package is large, so it is recommended that you download the package over a high-speed link.

To install and display the vCAT 3.1 documentation center:

1. Download and unzip the package.
2. Double-click the index.html file to run it.
3. Allow blocked content, if prompted.

Offline Versus Online Capabilities

- If you install the Documentation Center package on your machine, you can use the toolkit offline. For example, you can install it on your laptop computer and review the documents while you are not connected to the Internet.
- If you install the Documentation Center package on a web server, the interface provides additional capabilities, such as access to Google Translate.
- The Documentation Center also optimizes the display for mobile devices. For example, using Safari on an iPad to access the documentation center works well.

Using the Documentation Center

- Click the folder icon to toggle display of the navigation pane on or off.
- Enter text in the search field and click the search icon (magnifying glass) to search for it. This is a client-side search implementation that can be used online or offline. It does not allow Boolean expressions.

If the documentation center is served from an Internet-connected web server, click the globe to display Google Translate. Select the language you want and click Translate. Each page is translated as it is displayed.

- Click a document in the navigation pane to display the sections in the document. Click a section to display content.
- Click the Page Forward or Page Back arrows to move from page to page.
- Click the Print icon to print the selected page to a printer.
- Select any document section and click the PDF icon to view a pregenerated PDF for the selected document. You can print the entire document from the PDF.
- Click the Email (envelope) icon or the link by the logo to send feedback to ipfeedback@vmware.com. The URL of the currently displayed page is automatically populated in the email Subject line.

vCAT 3.1.1 Changes and VMware Press Book Release

This book release combines all separate documents for vCAT 3.1 into one document. Each chapter in this book represents the nine separate documents. When we reference separate sections, see the associated chapter in the book format. We have not made specific updates to these release notes, to allow the material here and the material in Document Center to be synchronized.

There are several updates in this book that will apply to the updated web release.

- General
  - Updated graphics and screenshots.
  - Updated SSO material throughout.
- Chapter 1, Introduction:
  - Removed references to VMware Service Manager.
- Appendix D
  - Removed references to VMware Service Manager.

vCAT 3.1 Changes

For vCAT 3.1, most documents received additional edits, and graphics were improved for many figures. Content was updated as follows:

- *Chapter 1, Introduction:*
  - Links to brief video presentations were added for each document and topic area.
  - Figure 1.3 was updated.
- *Chapter 2, Service Definitions*:
  - The service offering examples were changed because of allocation model changes in vCloud Director 5.1.1.
  - Minor updates were made to the other service offering examples.
  - Other minor edits include the following:
    - The technology-mapping diagram was updated to show VMware vCloud Automation Center™.
    - vCloud API changed to VMware APIs.
    - VMware vCenter Operations Management Suite™ components are enumerated.
- *Chapter 3, Architecting a VMware vCloud*:
  - Information was added about vCloud Automation Center (a component of the vCloud Suite).
  - Section 3.8, "Multisite Considerations," was updated.
  - Allocation models guidance was updated.
  - Information about VMware metering was updated in Section 3.6, "vCloud Metering."
  - Hybrid vCloud considerations were updated in Section 3.9, "Hybrid vCloud Considerations."
- *Chapter 4, Operating a VMware vCloud*: Information was added about organizational structure and its evolution for vCloud in Section 4.5, "Organizing for vCloud Operations."
- *Chapter 5, Consuming a VMware vCloud*:
  - Updates were made to reflect the new network terminology in vCloud Director 5.1.
  - The text was updated to reflect new storage capabilities in vCloud Director 5.1.
  - Section 5.3.2, "vCloud Director Allocation Models," was updated to reflect changes in vCloud Director 5.1.

- Updates and clarifications were made to Section 5.4.3, "Working with Catalogs."
- Updates were made to Section 5.5.1.3, "vApp Migration," to reflect new capabilities in vCloud Director 5.1.
- Updates were made to Section 5.6.3 "What's New in the vCloud 5.1 API."

- *Chapter 6, Implementation Examples*: The following sections were extensively updated with the latest available information:
    - Section 6.3, "Organization Virtual Datacenter Examples"
    - Section 6.4.5, "VXLAN ORG Network for Disaster Recovery"
    - Section 6.7.3, "Implementing Signed Certificates from a Certificate Authority"
- *Chapter 7, Workflow Examples*: No content changes were made.
- *Chapter 8, Software Tools*: No content changes were made.
- *Chapter 9, Cloud Bursting*: No content changes were made.

Security information in Appendix B, "Security," was updated.

vCAT 3.0 Changes (Previous Release)

This section provides information on the changes that were made for the vCAT 3.0 release.

New documents were added to the toolkit, and in two cases, multiple documents were consolidated into one guide. Information about new components has been added, and information about other components has been updated.

New and Consolidated Documents

Workflow Examples, *Software Tools*, and *Cloud Bursting* are new documents with all new content.

The *vCAT 2.x Public VMware vCloud Service Definition* and *Private VMware vCloud Service Definition* have been consolidated into one *Service Definitions* document that covers public, private, and hybrid cases.

The vCAT 2.x documents, *Public VMware vCloud Implementation Examples, Private VMware vCloud Implementation Examples, and Hybrid Use Cases*, have been consolidated into one document titled *Implementation Examples* that covers public, private, and hybrid use cases. Many new implementation examples are provided.

New and Updated Components

vCAT 3.0 provided new and expanded coverage for architects, operators, and consumers.

- VMware vSphere®
- VMware vCloud Director®
- VMware vCenter™ Operations Management Suite™ (new):
  - VMware vCenter Chargeback Manager™
  - VMware vCenter Operations Manager™ (new)
  - VMware vCenter Infrastructure Navigator™ (new)
  - VMware vCenter Configuration Manager™ (new)
- VMware vCloud Networking and Security™ (formerly VMware vShield™):
  - VMware vCloud Networking and Security Edge™
  - VMware vCloud Networking and Security App™ (new)
  - VMware vCloud Networking and Security Data Security™ (new)
  - VMware vShield Endpoint™ (new)
- VMware vCloud Connector™
- VMware vCenter Orchestrator™
- VMware vSphere Service Manager™—Cloud Provisioning (new)
- VMware vCenter Site Recovery Manager™ (new)
- VMware vFabric™ RabbitMQ™ (new)
- VMware vFabric Application Director™ (new)
- VMware vFabric Application Performance Manager™ (new)
  - VMware vFabric Hyperic® (new)
  - VMware vFabric AppInsight™ (new)

VMware vCloud Networking and Security

VMware vShield has been renamed to VMware vCloud Networking and Security™. Note the following changes:

- VMware vShield Edge™ is now VMware vCloud Networking and Security Edge.
- VMware vShield App™ is now VMware vCloud Networking and Security App.
- VMware vShield Manager™ is now VMware vCloud Networking and Security Manager™.

The vCAT documents usually refer to vCloud Networking and Security, but some links to reference documents might still link to vShield documents on vmware.com. The vShield documents are being updated to reflect the new name.

Known Issues

Firefox generally works with the vCAT Documentation Center, but Google Translate does not work properly.

Providing Feedback

The usefulness of this architecture toolkit depends on feedback from customers and our network of partners. Send all feedback and IP submissions to ipfeedback@vmware.com.

From the documentation center interface, you can click the link next to the logo or click the Email (envelope) icon to send feedback.

Reader Services

Visit our website at www.informit.com/title/9780321912022 and register this book for convenient access to any updates, downloads, or errata that might be available for this book.

CHAPTER 1
Introduction

IN THIS CHAPTER

1.1 Overview

A *reference architecture* is an architecture template solution that addresses one use case in a particular domain. The VMware® vCloud® Architecture Toolkit (vCAT) provides modular components and documents to support multiple use cases, including design considerations and design patterns to support architects, operators, and consumers of cloud computing solutions based on VMware technologies.

vCAT is the first of several VMware Validated Architectures (VVA) VMware has released for customers, partners, vendors, and our internal teams. As a VVA, vCAT is supported by VMware and our support organization.

vCAT is vendor agnostic, but it does share vendor details when providing implementation examples. Vendors provide information about the use of their products with vCloud, including integration with vCAT, on the VMware Solutions Exchange (https://solutionexchange.vmware.com/store).

vCAT design guidelines cover multiple use cases. Instead of referring to *best practices* (a term subject to misinterpretation because best practices depend on use cases and are subject to many variables, including change over time), vCAT provides *design guidelines*. Architects must determine which design guidelines apply to the requirements, constraints, and characteristics of their projects and chosen technologies. When using the toolkit, consider the use case that best applies to your situation, and choose the design guidelines that support your design implementation.

This document covers the following topics:

- The vCAT documentation set
- Cloud computing and the VMware vCloud
- The journey to a mature vCloud implementation

For additional vCAT supporting material, visit the vCloud Architecture Toolkit page on vmware.com (www.vmware.com/go/vCAT). This is also where updates to vCAT are posted.

1.2 Using the vCAT Documentation Set

The vCloud Architecture Toolkit provides a set of documents to support the design of complex, integrated reference architectures for architects, operators, and consumers. Figure 1.1 shows the documents, and Table 1.1 briefly describes them.

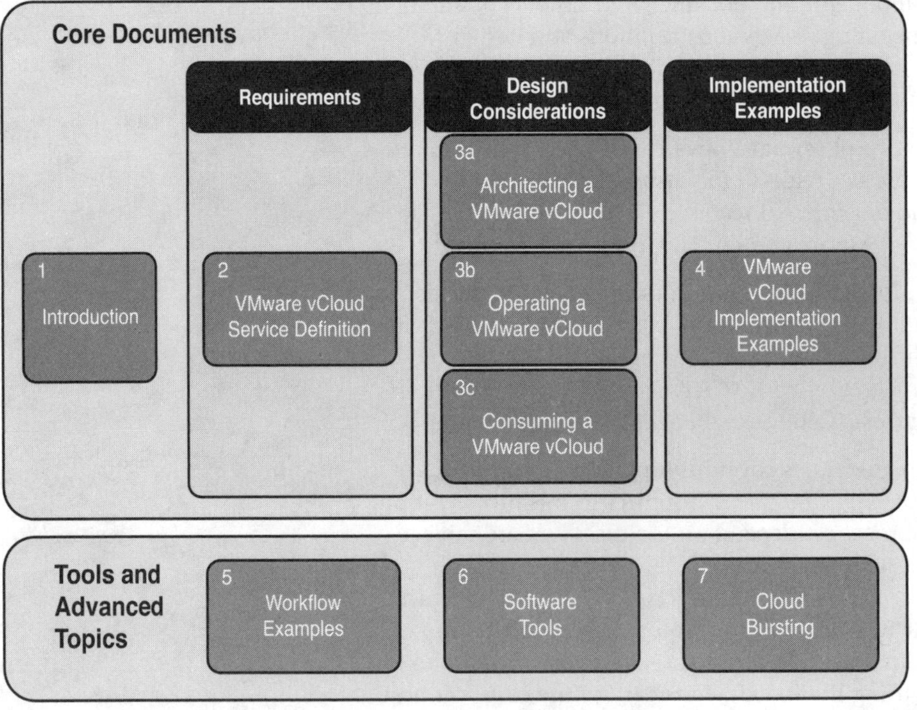

FIGURE 1.1 VMware vCloud Architecture Toolkit document map

Table 1.1 shows check marks in the first column to represent existence of an online video providing a brief presentation (<10 minutes) about a document and topic area.

TABLE 1.1 VMware vCloud Architecture Toolkit Documents

Video	Document	Description	Audience
	Release Notes	Includes information about the VMware Architecture Toolkit, toolkit packages, how to use the documentation center, and information about changes since the vCAT 3.0 release.	All
✓	*Introduction*	Covers the following topics: ▶ A brief summary of vCAT documents ▶ Suggested reading order, depending on audience or role ▶ Introduction to cloud computing and basic cloud computing requirements and definitions	All
✓	*Service Definitions*	Discusses service definition lifecycles, including specific considerations for private, public, and hybrid vCloud instances, and examples of service offerings designed to help you create service definitions that meet specific business objectives.	All
✓	*Architecting a VMware vCloud*	Details design considerations for architecting and building a VMware vCloud, including the basis for a reference architecture and guidance on requirements for implementing a VMware vCloud infrastructure.	Architects, IT operations
✓	*Operating a VMware vCloud*	Introduces high-level operational areas and discusses the evolution to support vCloud dynamics. Provides information about operational procedures, roles and responsibilities, setup, management, and monitoring of a vCloud. Also covers VMware management tools that support vCloud operations.	Architects, IT operations
✓	*Consuming a VMware vCloud*	Answers consumer questions such as the following: ▶ How do I handle the application lifecycle in a vCloud? ▶ How do I protect my workloads? ▶ How do I guarantee that workload resource requirements are met? Provides the consumer's perspective.	Architects, IT operations, consumers, end users
✓	*Implementation Examples*	Provides examples of how to build a vCloud.	Architects

Video	Document	Description	Audience
✓	*Workflow Examples*	Provides a description of useful scripts and workflows for VMware vCenter™ Orchestrator™. Other examples use technologies such as PowerCLI. Includes references to where these scripts can be found.	Architects, IT operations
✓	*Software Tools*	Includes information about software that can benefit architects and operators. Provides information about freely available technologies that have been created and used to assist in vCloud design, deployment, and operations. Also includes information about several powerful tools that are available only as part of a service engagement with VMware Professional Services or a VMware partner.	Architects, IT operations
✓	*Cloud Bursting*	Provides the theory behind autoscaling an enterprise cloud environment by using multiple cloud locations, including those owned by an enterprise and/or a service provider. This theory leverages VMware technologies but applies to other cloud technologies as well. This material is based on VMware field experience with customers and service providers.	Architects

Table 1.2 lists the typographical conventions used in all vCAT documents.

TABLE 1.2 Document Typographical Conventions

Emphasis	Emphasizes information, introduces new terms, and identifies document and workflow names.
`Command`	Identifies system commands, filenames, and Registry keys.
`Code`	Indicates code snippets and scripts.
User Interface	Identifies UI objects such as tabs, buttons, and field labels with bold text.
Hyperlink	Uses blue, underlined text to indicate an active link (URL).
Note, Caution	Notes contain information related to the topic that is of possible interest to the reader. Cautions highlight important information on potential problems or actions that might cause unexpected results. A Caution alerts the user and indicates the possibility of significant data loss.

1.2.1 Recommended Reading Order

The documents can be read in the order shown in the document map or in the order recommended for a particular audience or role, such as one of the following:

- *vCloud providers* who offer the vCloud infrastructure and services. An *architect* has overall control over how a solution is designed and implemented in the environment.
- *vCloud operators* who are responsible for operation of the cloud. *Operators* are involved with the day-to-day running and administration of the vCloud environment. They need to understand operational procedures and how the vCloud components fit together.
- *vCloud consumers* who use cloud provider resources for application deployment. A consumer (organization or individual) is someone who consumes vCloud resources. Consumers want to run their workloads in the vCloud environment without concern for the underlying infrastructure or day-to-day administration.

Table 1.3 identifies the recommended documents for each role.

TABLE 1.3 vCAT Audience Reading Guidelines

VMware vCloud Architecture Toolkit (vCAT) Reading Recommendations	Architect	Admin/ Operator	Consumer
Introduction	✓	✓	✓
Service Definitions	✓	✓	✓
Architecting a VMware vCloud	✓	✓	
Consuming a VMware vCloud	✓	✓	✓
Implementation Examples	✓		
Workflow Examples	✓	✓	
Software Tools	✓	✓	
Cloud Bursting	✓		

1.3 Cloud Computing and VMware vCloud

Cloud computing leverages the efficient pooling of an on-demand, self-managed, virtual infrastructure that is consumed as a service. VMware vCloud is the VMware solution for cloud computing that enables delivery of *Infrastructure as a Service* (IaaS). Additional "as a Service" reference architectures can be layered on top of a VMware vCloud built using vCAT.

1.3.1 VMware vCloud Requirements

According to the National Institute of Standards and Technology (NIST), the key components of a cloud are on-demand self-service, broad network access, resource pooling, rapid elasticity, and measured service. VMware aligns with the definition of *cloud* as elastic, lightweight entry and exit, available over Internet protocols, and running on a shared infrastructure.

A cloud always starts with a shared, virtual infrastructure. If any resource is dedicated to only one customer, you have a *managed hosting platform*, not a cloud infrastructure. Similarly, it is not considered a cloud if the cloud administrator or service provider must perform manual procedures to provision cloud resources following a consumer request. This is why workflow automation and orchestration are included as part of a vCloud solution.

The VMware vCloud blueprint follows these basic NIST requirements as the foundation for an IaaS cloud:

- A cloud must be built on a *pooled, virtual infrastructure*. Pools include not only CPU and memory resources, but also storage, networking, and associated services.
- The cloud should provide *application mobility between clouds,* allowing the consumer to enter and leave the cloud easily with existing workloads. The ability to use existing consumer tools to migrate workloads to or from the cloud is highly desirable. Mobility of workloads between clouds requires cross-cloud resource management.
- The cloud should be *open and interoperable*, allowing the consumption of cloud resources over open, Internet-standard protocols. Access to cloud resources does not require any other specific network protocols or clients.
- Cloud consumers should pay only for resources they consume or commit to consuming.
- The cloud should be a secure, trusted location for running cloud consumer workloads.
- Cloud consumers should have the option and capability to protect their cloud-based workloads from data loss.
- Cloud consumers are not responsible for maintaining any part of the shared infrastructure and do not need to interact with the cloud provider to maintain the infrastructure. They are not responsible for storage and network maintenance, ongoing cloud infrastructure patches, or business continuity activities. The cloud should be available to run high-availability workloads, and any faults occurring in the cloud infrastructure should be transparent to cloud consumers as a result of *built-in availability, scalability, security, and performance guarantees.*

1.3.2 VMware Alignment to Standards

VMware continues to develop technologies that align with evolving cloud standards as defined by NIST and other global standards organizations.

vCloud solutions focus on the following areas:

- **People:** People who develop solutions, architect the design, operate the implementation, and consume the resources. (See *Operating a VMware vCloud* and *Consuming a VMware vCloud.*)
- **Process:** Processes for architects, operators, and consumers.
- **Technology:** Alignment with successful design, deployment, and integration considerations. VMware technologies address the relevant areas within the standards.

Standards are still evolving for private, public, community, hybrid, and other types of clouds. vCAT focuses on the most common core design areas. The technology is the same, but operations and vCloud resource consumption vary according to the type of vCloud, the type of vCloud provider, and specific consumer requirements.

- *A private vCloud* is operated by an organization and secured behind a firewall.
- *A public vCloud* is generally accessible to users on the Internet.
- *A community vCloud* is a specific public vCloud use case in which access is limited to specified groups that share a common set of requirements.
- *A hybrid vCloud* is characterized by a connection among multiple vCloud instances. Typically, a bridge between two private vCloud instances has a dedicated and secured connection. The underlying network resides behind an Internet-facing firewall.

As cloud computing continues to evolve, many cloud definitions will arise. The information in this toolkit is a valuable aid in support of your vCloud projects, regardless of your chosen definition.

1.3.3 vCloud Definitions

vCAT uses the terms *private vCloud, public vCloud,* and *hybrid vCloud,* based on a specific set of definitions that NIST provides.

- Private cloud:

  A private vCloud (also known as an *internal vCloud*) operates on private networks, where a single company maintains accessible resources behind the firewall. In many cases, all the tenants share one legal entity. For example, a university might offer IaaS to its medical and business schools, or a company might do the same for various groups or business units. The private vCloud can be managed by the enterprise and hosted on-premises or operated on a dedicated infrastructure provided by a vCloud service provider or systems integrator. In any case, a private vCloud must conform to the organizational security constraints.

- Public cloud:

  A public vCloud offers IT resources as a service through external service providers and is shared across multiple organizations or the Internet. This can be viewed as a vCloud infrastructure that one organization operates and that multiple, legally separated organizations use.

  A public vCloud is provisioned for open access and might be owned, managed, and operated by one or more entities.

  A public vCloud provider might also support a private, community, or hybrid vCloud.

- Hybrid cloud:

  A hybrid vCloud combines the benefits of the private and public vCloud, with flexibility and choice of deployment methods.

  A hybrid vCloud consists of multiple, linked vCloud infrastructures. These distinct vCloud infrastructures can be private, community, or public; but they must meet a set of requirements that the providers define and the consumers agree to. Connecting these vCloud instances requires data and application mobility, as well as management.

  When load-balancing between vCloud instances (*cloud bursting*), use a consistent monitoring and management approach when migrating an application or data workload. For the theory behind cloud bursting, see the *Cloud Bursting* document.

- Community cloud:

  A community vCloud is a specific public vCloud use case in which the cloud is shared, and typically owned, by a group of organizations with a common set of requirements. In many cases, the organizations also include some level of legal separation. Community vCloud resources are shared, with some parts under central control and other parts with defined autonomy. A vCloud built for government, education, or healthcare is an example of a community vCloud.

  A community vCloud can be offered by a traditional service provider, by a member of the community, or by a third-party vendor and hosted on one or more sites. It can be placed on-premises at one or more of the organizations' sites, off-premises at a vCloud provider site, or both on- and off-premises.

1.3.4 Solution Area to Technology Mapping

When considering various technology solutions for your vCloud architecture, evaluate the solution and operational requirements to provide justification for the proposed solution. As VMware continues to develop Software Defined Data Center (SDDC) technologies, we will update the matching Infrastructure as a Service component. Figure 1.2 shows the categories of design considerations for building both a cloud and the underlying SDDC, with the related product technology that is used.

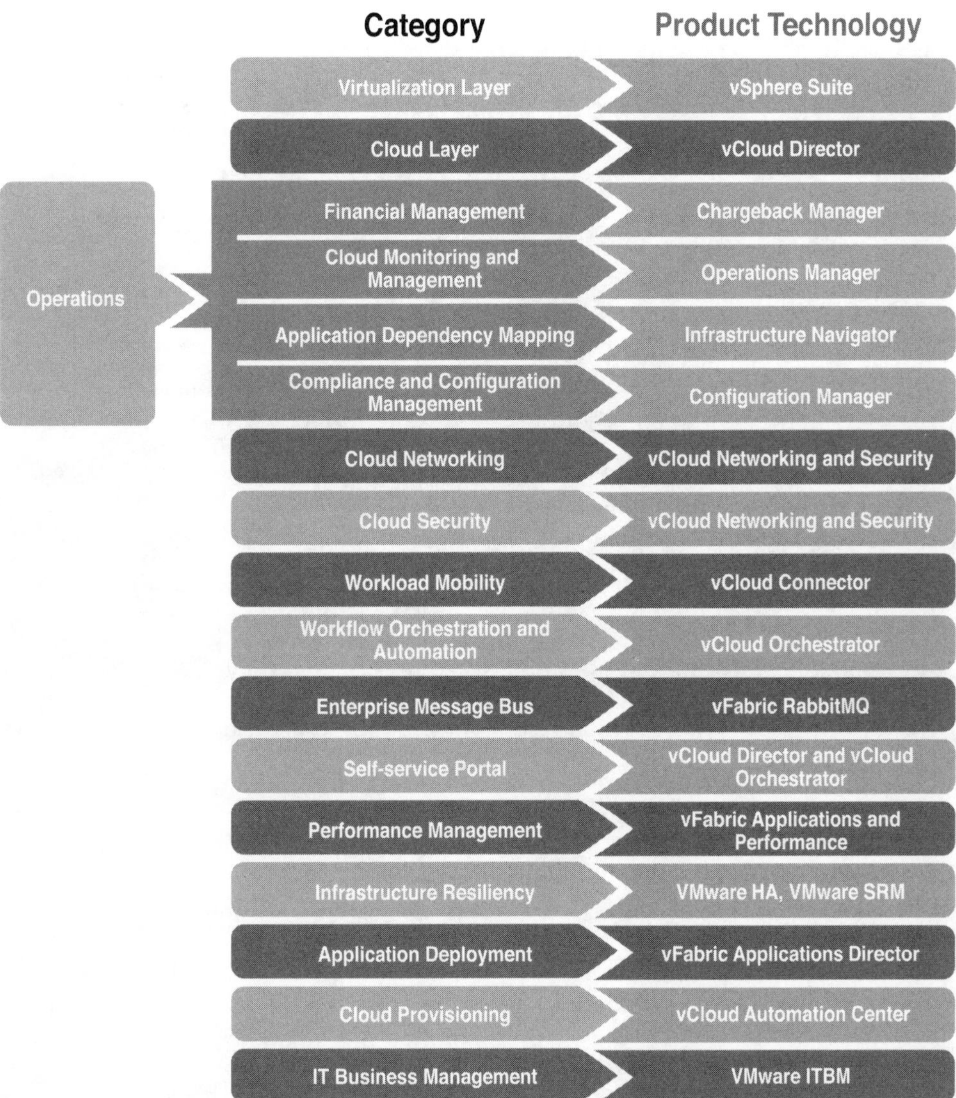

FIGURE 1.2 Technology areas

Figure 1.3 shows the technologies this vCAT release covers.

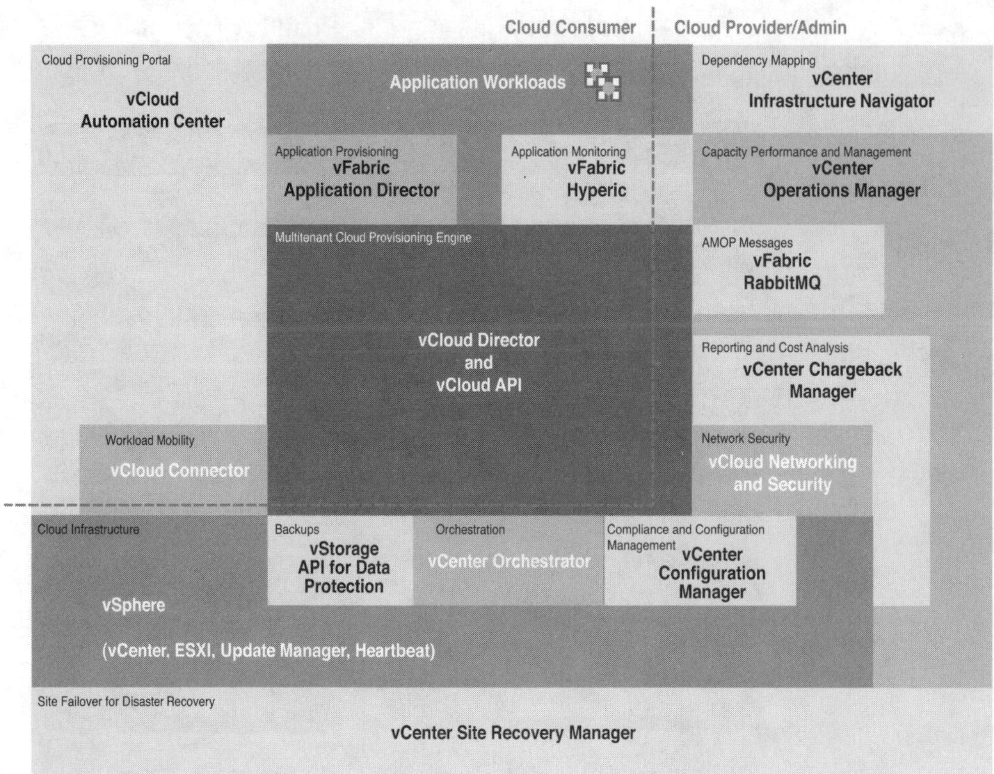

FIGURE 1.3 Technology areas in vCAT

NOTE

Except for the gray components, components that touch each other are integrated.

1.3.4.1 VMware Professional Services

VMware offers professional services that align with vCloud use cases. These range from a proof of concept (POC) that might be used as a demonstration environment, to a production deployment that requires management, workflow automation, compliance enforcement, and validation. The following services are available:

- **VMware vCloud POC Jumpstart Service:** Provides knowledge transfer workshops and hands-on product installation, configuration, and use demonstrations for the vCloud solution.

- **VMware vCloud Accelerator Service:** Rapidly delivers a functioning VMware vCloud implementation suitable for deploying applications in a limited-scale preproduction environment. If all prerequisites are met, this service engagement can be completed in fewer than 30 business days.
- **VMware vCloud Design and Deploy Service:** Provides a comprehensive architectural design for VMware vCloud that addresses the customer's unique business requirements and operational demands, helping to pave the way to vCloud computing. This service is designed for enterprises that have a well-established, vSphere-based virtualization strategy for production workloads and that are ready to take the next step toward building their production vCloud infrastructure.
- **VMware Operational Readiness for Cloud Computing Service:** Offers a four- to six-week engagement in which VMware consultants examine existing operational practices to evaluate performance across more than 150 attributes in five key areas. They uncover unknown or hidden barriers to success and highlight areas in which additional focus on people or process can deliver increased productivity, streamline operations, and improve overall vCloud solution results.

Services can be combined or customized to meet your specific requirements.

1.4 Journey to a Mature vCloud Implementation

At every stage in the processes leading to a mature vCloud implementation, financial transparency, process maturity, organizational setup, and technology implementation are critical factors for success.

VMware defines three stages on the journey to a mature vCloud: Standardize, Service Broker, and Strategic Partner. Figure 1.4 depicts these, and the following sections describe them.

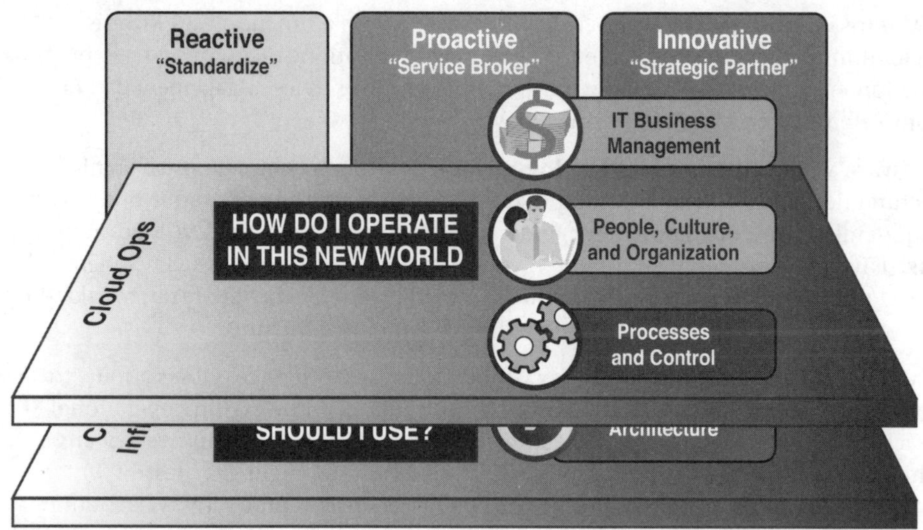

FIGURE 1.4 Journey states in vCAT

1.4.1 Stage 1: Standardize

Stage 1 often coincides with a more mature server virtualization environment, and the focus is on creating a working vCloud solution with an on-demand service catalog end users can directly access. The service catalog provides rapid deployment services for non-business-critical, development, and test environments, as well as for externally sourced applications. Implementing the service catalog promotes cloud acceptance by business users and also outlines a long-term vCloud implementation strategy with planning for operational and organizational change. The following capabilities are important for this stage:

- **Financial model and measurement:** Awareness and understanding of the costs of assets and underlying infrastructure capacity.
- **People and organization:** Specialized but shared roles for managing virtualized environments.
- No explicit virtualization Center of Excellence established.

NOTE

See "Organizing for vCloud Operations" in *Operating a VMware vCloud* for information about the Center of Excellence.

- **Process and control:**
  - IT processes are adapted for virtualization but are largely manual, with specific, customized interprocess integration.
  - The focus is on limited, continuous improvement.

- **Tools and technology:**
  - Online, self-service capability for development and test provisioning
  - Online, self-service capability for Software as a Service (SaaS)–based applications
  - Operational tools defined for virtualization environments
  - Some business workloads run in a virtualized environment, whether internal or provided by third parties

1.4.2 Stage 2: Service Broker

Stage 2 is the first service-driven stage for a vCloud. At this stage, IT has transformed from traditional models and is focused on delivering business services within a vCloud environment. This represents a cultural shift within the organization. To be successful, it requires enhanced IT operational maturity, an optimized IT organizational structure, and supporting cloud-management tools.

The term *service broker* implies that IT is organized at this stage to source internally and externally, such as adding external infrastructure capacity or providing access to vendor-based SaaS applications. The business is not necessarily aware of how the services are made available, but dramatically decreased development and provisioning times support business needs with increased quality of service and greater agility.

This stage focuses on the following goals:

- Gaining alignment and buy-in from key business stakeholders
- Creating service governance, lifecycle and service design, and development processes
- Providing service-based financial transparency
- Automating and integrating tools and technology in internal and external systems

Key capabilities for this stage include the following:

- Financial model and measurement:
  - Using usage metering and cost showback
  - Applying granular costing of underlying infrastructure assets
  - Educating IT customers about paying for services as an operating expense
  - Changing from project-based budgeting to demand-based budgeting
- People and organization: Establishing the Center of Excellence with dedicated, experienced, and knowledgeable staff
- Process and control:
  - Fully integrated IT operational processes adapted for virtualization and vCloud
  - Agile-based service design and development processes established
  - Service-level financial transparency

- Tools and technology:
  - Services defined and offered through an online consumer portal for self-service access to the service catalog
  - vCloud-level disaster recovery
  - Blueprint and policy-driven service development and provisioning
  - Purpose-built management tools for proactive vCloud operations

1.4.3 Stage 3: Strategic Differentiator

This stage is the final stage for a mature cloud. At this point, a highly efficient, scalable cloud with hybrid capability is available for an organization. IT is delivered as a service. Automated, policy-driven governance and control applies across the vCloud environment, with zero-touch operations supported by predictive and self-healing operational tool capabilities. True application mobility and device-independent access is available. The vCloud is considered to be the de facto model within the organization. The term *strategic differentiator* implies that IT has changed roles and become a business differentiator by increasing agility, resulting in faster time to market; increasing efficiency, resulting in reduced costs; and increasing reliability, resulting in dramatically increased quality of service. The following are key capabilities for this stage:

- Financial model and measurement:
  - Usage-based pricing and chargeback for services provided to business customers
  - Service demand–based budgeting
  - Priced catalog of service offerings
- People and organization: The Center of Excellence manages all elements of infrastructure, end-user, and application operations.
- Process and control:
  - Optimized, integrated, and fully automated IT processes that enhance business agility and efficiency
  - Continuous process, service, and performance improvements based on predictive capabilities
- Tools and technology:
  - Full hybrid capabilities
  - Tools that support single-pane-of-glass management across private and public vCloud environments
  - Service-level disaster recovery
  - Tools that support automated corrective actions for self-healing

CHAPTER 2
Service Definitions

IN THIS CHAPTER

2.1 Introduction

Businesses face constant pressure to introduce products and services rapidly into new and existing marketplaces, while users expect services to be easily accessible on demand and to scale with business growth. Management demands these services at a fair price. These pressures and demands all require information technology (IT) to become more service oriented. They also make it more important than ever for IT to improve its strategy to deliver services with the agility that businesses now expect. Cloud computing is central to a better IT strategy.

Virtualization has reduced costs and increased server efficiency, often dramatically, but it does not, by itself, deliver the level of automation and control required to achieve the efficiencies or agility associated with cloud computing. Cloud computing offers the opportunity to further improve cost efficiency, quality of service, and business agility. It enables IT to support a wide range of changing business objectives, from deployment of new tools, products, and services to expansion into new markets. Cloud computing transforms IT from a *cost center* into a *service provider.*

The VMware® vCloud® Suite is the VMware solution for cloud computing.

This book provides the information you need to create a service definition for an organization that provides Infrastructure as a Service (IaaS) resources for private, public, and hybrid vCloud instances. This book has the following goals:

- Acquaint you with what to consider when creating a service definition
- Provide examples that act as a starting point to create a service definition for service offerings that meet specific business objectives

2.1.1 Audience

This document is intended for those involved in planning, defining, designing, and providing VMware vCloud services to consumers. The intended audience includes the following roles:

- Providers and consumers of vCloud services
- Architects and planners responsible for driving architecture-level decisions
- Technical decision makers who have business requirements that need IT support
- Consultants, partners, and IT personnel who need to know how to create a service definition for their vCloud services

2.1.2 Deployment Model

Figure 2.1 illustrates several deployment models for cloud computing.

- For enterprises, the focus is on private and hybrid vCloud environments.
- For service providers, the focus is on public and hybrid vCloud environments.

FIGURE 2.1 Deployment models

The following are the commonly accepted definitions for cloud computing deployment models:

- **Private vCloud:** The vCloud infrastructure is operated solely for an organization and can be managed by the organization or a third party. The infrastructure can be located on-premises or off-premises.
- **Public vCloud:** The vCloud infrastructure is made available to the general public or to a large industry group and is owned by an organization that sells vCloud services.
- **Hybrid vCloud:** The vCloud infrastructure is a composite of two or more vCloud instances (private and public) that remain unique entities but are bound together by standardized technology. This enables data and application portability, such as *cloud bursting* for load balancing between vCloud instances. With a hybrid vCloud, an organization gets the advantages of both, with the capability to burst into the public vCloud when needed while maintaining critical assets on-premises.

- **Community vCloud:** Several organizations share the vCloud infrastructure. This infrastructure supports a specific community that has shared concerns, such as mission, security requirements, policy, and compliance considerations. It can be managed by the organizations or a third party and can be located on-premises or off-premises.

This book covers the following private, public, and hybrid vCloud deployment models:

- **Private vCloud:** Enterprise IT as a provider of vCloud services to consumers
- **Hybrid vCloud:** Enterprise IT as a consumer of public vCloud services, extending its own private capacity
- **Public vCloud:** Service provider IT as a provider of vCloud services to a number of enterprise consumers

The book does not cover community vCloud service definition considerations and examples.

2.1.3 Service Model

The National Institute of Standards and Technology (NIST) specifies three service layers in a cloud, as Figure 2.2 shows. VMware defines these service layers as follows:

- **Software as a Service (SaaS):** Business-focused services are presented directly to the consumer from a service catalog.
- **Platform as a Service (PaaS):** Technology-focused services are presented for application development and deployment to application developers from a service catalog.
- **Infrastructure as a Service (IaaS):** Infrastructure containers are presented to consumers to provide agility, automation, and delivery of components.

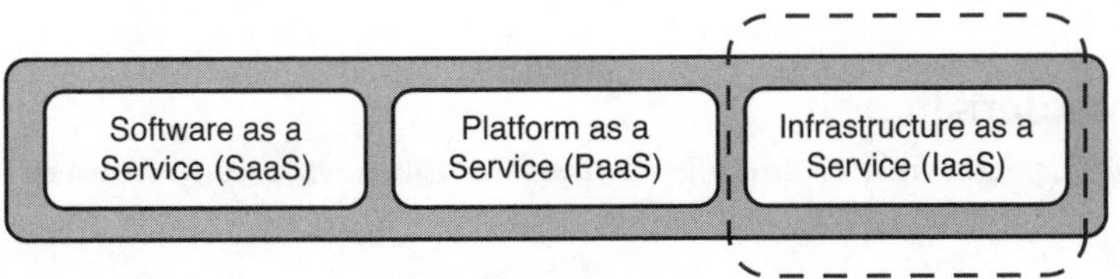

FIGURE 2.2 Service models

The service model for the service definition in this document is primarily IaaS, for an organization to provide Infrastructure as a Service to consumers of vCloud services through a catalog of predefined infrastructure containers. The IaaS service layer serves as a foundation for additional service offerings, such as PaaS, SaaS, and Desktop as a Service (DaaS).

2.1.4 Technology Mapping

vCloud services are delivered by the capabilities of the VMware technologies in the VMware vCloud Suite, as Figure 2.3 shows. The VMware vCenter™ Operations Management Suite™ includes the following technologies:

- VMware vCenter Operations Manager™
- VMware vCenter Chargeback Manager™
- VMware vCenter Configuration Manager™
- VMware vCenter Infrastructure Navigator™

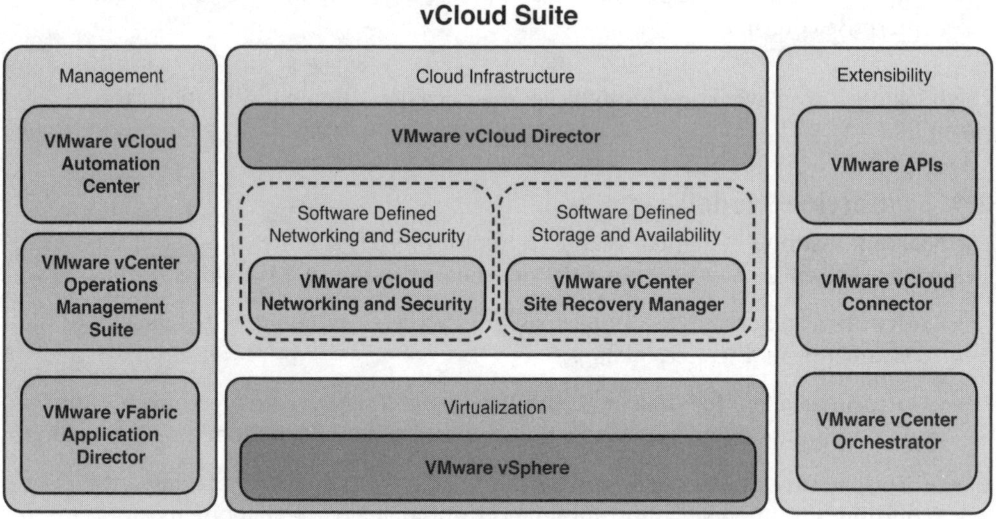

vCloud Suite

Management
VMware vCloud Automation Center
VMware vCenter Operations Management Suite
VMware vFabric Application Director

Cloud Infrastructure
VMware vCloud Director
Software Defined Networking and Security
VMware vCloud Networking and Security
Software Defined Storage and Availability
VMware vCenter Site Recovery Manager

Virtualization
VMware vSphere

Extensibility
VMware APIs
VMware vCloud Connector
VMware vCenter Orchestrator

FIGURE 2.3 Technology mapping

2.1.5 Service Characteristics

The National Institute of Standards and Technology defines the following essential cloud service characteristics:

- **Broad network access:** Capabilities are available over the network and accessed through standard mechanisms that promote use by heterogeneous thin client or thick client platforms.
- **Rapid elasticity:** Capabilities can be provisioned to scale out quickly and to be released rapidly—in some cases, automatically. Rapid elasticity enables resources to both scale out and scale in quickly. To the consumer, the capabilities available for provisioning often appear to be unlimited and can be purchased in any quantity at any time.

- **Measured service:** Cloud systems automatically control and optimize resource usage by leveraging a metering capability at some level of abstraction appropriate to the type of service. Resource usage can be monitored, controlled, and reported, providing transparency for both the provider and the consumer of the utilized service.
- **On-demand self-service:** A consumer can unilaterally automatically provision computing capabilities as needed without requiring human interaction with each service's provider.
- **Resource pooling:** The provider's computing resources are pooled to serve multiple consumers, using a multitenant model with different physical and virtual resources dynamically assigned and reassigned according to consumer demand. A sense of location independence results because the subscriber generally has no knowledge of or control over the exact location of the provided resources, but the subscriber might be able to specify location at a higher level of abstraction.

Figure 2.4 illustrates the relationships among service characteristics and how they all relate to resource pooling.

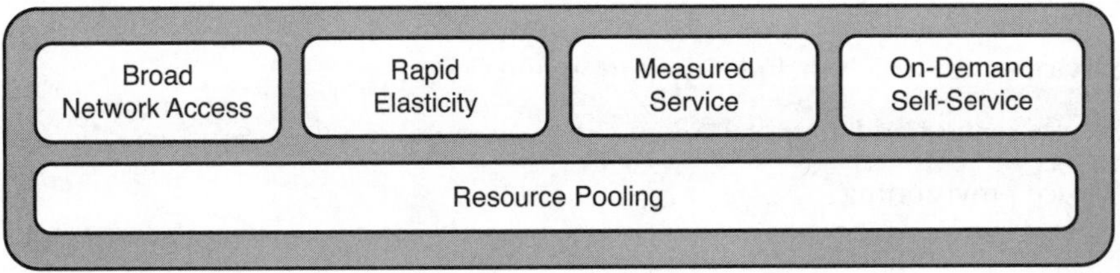

FIGURE 2.4 Service characteristics

To deliver business solutions using vCloud services, the vCloud infrastructure must have the following additional essential characteristics:

- **Standardized:** Homogeneous infrastructure delivered as software services across pools of standard x86 hardware. Homogeneity eliminates unnecessary complexity caused by operating system silos and the redundant tools and skill sets associated with them. It also eliminates costly, special-purpose hardware and enables a single, scalable approach to backup and recovery.
- **Holistic:** A platform optimized for the entire datacenter fabric, providing comprehensive infrastructure services capable of supporting any and all applications. A holistic infrastructure can support any workloads, with complete flexibility to balance the collective application demands, eliminating the need for diverse technology stacks.
- **Adaptive:** Infrastructure services are provided on demand, unconstrained by physical topology and dynamically adapting to application scale and location. The infrastructure platform configures and reconfigures the environment dynamically, based on collective application workload demands, enabling maximum throughput, agility, and efficiency.

- **Automated:** Built-in intelligence automates provisioning, placement, configuration, and control, based on defined policies. Intelligent infrastructure eliminates complex, brittle management scripts. Less manual intervention equates to scalability, speed, and cost savings. Intelligence in the infrastructure supports vCloud-scale operations.
- **Resilient:** A software-based architecture and approach compensates for failing hardware, providing failover, redundancy, and fault tolerance to critical operations. Intelligent automation provides resiliency without the need for manual intervention.

2.1.6 Service Development Approach

The approach for defining and designing vCloud services should have the following characteristics:

- Involves all necessary stakeholders.
- Documents business drivers and requirements that can be translated into appropriate service definitions.
- Takes a holistic view of the entire service environment and service lifecycle, including:
  - Service setup, which includes definition and design
  - Service request and approval
  - Service provisioning
  - Service consumption
  - Service management and operations
  - Service transition and termination

  A conscious awareness of what consumers of the service and the provider of the service experience at each stage of the service lifecycle must be taken into account, to create the necessary service definition elements for the consumer-facing service-level agreement (SLA) and internal-facing operational-level agreement (OLA) criteria.
- Defines the service scenarios and use cases.
- Represents the service to understand its components, interactions, and sequences of interrelated actions.
- Defines the users and roles involved with or interacting with the services so that the services created are user-centric.
- Defines the service contract (SLA) for the services and service components in the following areas:
  - Infrastructure services
  - Application/vApp services

- Platform services
- Software services
- Business services
- Defines service quality for these areas:
  - Performance
  - Availability
  - Continuity
  - Scalability
  - Manageability
  - Security
  - Compliance
  - Cost and pricing
- Defines the business service catalog and supporting IT service catalog

2.1.7 Concepts and Terminology

The key terms and service concepts are defined as follows:

- **Service:** A means of delivering value to consumers by facilitating outcomes that they want to achieve, without the ownership of specific costs or risks.
- **vCloud:** A model for enabling ubiquitous, convenient, on-demand network access to a shared pool of configurable resources that can be provisioned rapidly and released with minimal management effort.
- **vCloud service provider (or provider):** An entity that provides vCloud services to consumers.
- **Consumer or customer:** Someone who consumes vCloud services and defines or agrees to service-level targets.
- **Service-level target:** A commitment that is documented in a service-level agreement. Service-level targets are based on service-level requirements and are needed so that the vCloud service design is fit for its purpose. Service-level targets should be *SMART* (Specific, Measurable, Actionable, Realistic, Time-bound) and are usually based on key performance indicators (KPIs).
- **Service-level agreement (SLA):** An agreement between a service consumer and the service provider that measures the quality and performance of the available services. The SLA is the entire agreement that specifies what service is to be provided, how it is supported, time, locations, cost, performance, and responsibilities of the parties involved.

- **Service-level objective (SLO):** A negotiated document that defines the service to be delivered to the consumer, with one or more key performance indicators (KPIs). It provides a clear understanding of the nature of the service being offered, focusing on the contribution of the service to the business value chain. SLOs are specific, measurable characteristics of the SLA, such as availability, throughput, frequency, response time, or quality.
- **Operational-level agreement (OLA):** An agreement internal to the service provider that details the interdependent relationships among the internal support groups of an organization working to support an SLA.
- **VMware vCloud Suite:** The suite of VMware technologies that provide the solution for vCloud computing.
- **VMware vCloud Services or vCloud Services:** vCloud computing services built with the VMware vCloud Suite.

2.2 Service Definition Considerations

Service definition is an important aspect of service design and management. It enables both the consumer and the service provider to know what to expect (or not to expect) from a service. Clearly defined services help customers understand the scope, limitations, and cost of service offerings.

Take the following considerations into account when developing a service definition. They are common to both private and public service definitions unless otherwise noted:

- Service objectives
- Use cases
- User roles that interact with the service
- Consumption model
- Service metering, reporting, and pricing
- Service offering details (infrastructure, applications)
- Other features that vary by offering type (backup, type of storage, availability, performance, continuity)

2.2.1 Service Objectives

Understanding the service objectives is an essential first step. Service objectives must address the specific business challenges. The following are examples of service objectives for vCloud services:

- Deliver a fully operational private or public vCloud infrastructure with hybrid capability
- Provide secure multitenancy for vCloud infrastructure consumers

- Provide compliance controls and transparency for the service
- Maintain IT control of access to the system and resources
- Provide differentiated tiers of scale to align with business needs
- Allow for metering of the service for cost distribution
- Establish a catalog of common infrastructure and application building blocks
- Provide the following service offerings:
    - Basic (pay for resources used)
    - Committed (allocated resources)
    - Dedicated (reserved resources)
- Support a minimum of 1,500 virtual machines across the three service offerings, and have a plan to grow to a minimum of 5,000 virtual machines
- Provide workload mobility between vCloud instances, allowing the consumer to enter and leave the vCloud easily with existing workloads
- Provide a direct connection to the external network for applications with upstream dependencies
- Provide an isolated network for applications that need to be isolated
- Provide open, interoperable, and Internet-standard protocols for consuming vCloud resources
- Provide for workload redundancy and data protection options

2.2.2 Use Cases

The use cases in Tables 2.1 through 2.5 represent business problems (some general and some industry-specific) that can be addressed with vCloud services and represented by a service definition.

TABLE 2.1 Example: Use Case 1

Use Case UC_01	
Name	**Modernization**
Problem Statement	Existing business services, processes, and legacy applications do not allow business to stay competitive.
Description	Modernization of business services, processes, and legacy applications
Requirements/Goal	Modernize infrastructure to make it service oriented ▶ Modernize applications ▶ Modernize business processes to improve speed to market
Risks	▶ Lost competitiveness and opportunities to support introduction of products and services in new or existing markets ▶ Increasing investment in maintaining legacy applications

TABLE 2.2 Example: Use Case 2

Use Case UC_02	
Name	**Increased business capacity and scale rapidly**
Problem Statement	The business is unable to scale up its operation because IT cannot scale up capacity rapidly to support the business.
Description	IT needs to be able to scale proactively to support seasonal and periodic business demand.
Requirements/Goal	▶ Give consumers access to scale capacity on demand ▶ Enable IT to scale up, down, in, or out to support business demand ▶ Scale within a short cycle of days to meet projected demand ▶ Scale to off-premises capacity
Risks	▶ Lost revenue due to lack of capacity ▶ Lost customers from underperforming business services

TABLE 2.3 Example: Use Case 3

Use Case UC_03	
Name	**Rapid provisioning of development and test services**
Problem Statement	The business cannot develop new products and services rapidly because IT takes too long to provision development and test infrastructure.
Description	IT needs to be able to provide on-demand self-service provisioning of development and test infrastructure to support the business in rapidly developing new products and services.
Requirements/Goal	▶ Give developers and test users access to a catalog of IT infrastructure that they can rapidly provision and use ▶ Self-service provisioning, with necessary approvals ▶ Reduce time to market for products and services
Risks	▶ Products and services that are late to market, resulting in lost customers and market share

TABLE 2.4 Example: Use Case 4

Use Case UC_04	
Name	**Security and compliance assurance**
Problem Statement	The business is concerned about putting critical financial applications and data on vCloud services.
Description	IT must be able to provide secure business services for financial applications and data, which should have controlled access and be separate from other users of the vCloud services.

Use Case UC_04	
Name	**Security and compliance assurance**
Requirements/Goal	▶ Provide compliance controls and transparency for the service ▶ Provide network isolation for applications that must be isolated
Risks	▶ Security and compliance breach

TABLE 2.5 Example: Use Case 5

Use Case UC_05	
Name	**Business market launch**
Problem Statement	The business has insufficient resources and capacity to respond rapidly to marketplace needs, including seasonal events, although new opportunities have been identified.
Description	IT must be able to move at the speed of the business by rapidly providing the necessary infrastructure and services so that new applications, products, and services can be launched rapidly.
Requirements/ Goal	▶ Provide rapid service provisioning to support product and service launches ▶ Give consumers access to a catalog of IT infrastructure that they can rapidly provision and use ▶ Self-service provisioning with necessary approvals ▶ Reduce time to market for products and services
Risks	▶ Products and services that are late to market, resulting in lost customers and market share ▶ Lost opportunity cost

2.2.3 User Roles

Several user roles apply to everyone who interacts with an enterprise vCloud service. Some roles are defined in the access model of the enterprise's private vCloud service at the provider level and at the consumer level. In addition, levels of privilege granted to predefined roles have an important impact on how users interact with the enterprise's vCloud service.

Table 2.6 provides a sample of the users and roles required for the enterprise vCloud solution.

TABLE 2.6 User Roles and Rights Example

User Role	Needs	Rights
Provider Cloud Administrator	One (minimum)	Highest-level enterprise vCloud provider administrator; has superuser privileges

User Role	Needs	Rights
Provider Catalog Author	As needed	Provider user who creates and publishes new catalogs
Consumer Organization Administrator	One per organization	Administrator over systems and users in the organization
Consumer Organization Author	One or more, as needed	User role that allows vApp and catalog creation, but no infrastructure management
Consumer Organization User	One or more, as needed	User role that allows a consumer organization user to use vApps created by others

2.2.4 Metering and Service Reporting

For vCloud environments, resource metering and service reporting are essential for calculating service costs. They also play an important role in accurately measuring consumer usage and shaping consumer behavior through chargeback policies. Enterprises might not necessarily have the same cost pressures for an enterprise private vCloud as for a public vCloud service provider. The requisite chargeback procedures or policies might not exist. An alternative to chargeback is *showback,* which tries to raise awareness of the consumption usage and cost without involving formal accounting procedures to bill the usage back to the consumer's department.

Table 2.7 provides examples of workload virtual machine sizing and costing.

TABLE 2.7 Workload Virtual Machine Sizing and Costing Examples

Virtual Machine Type	Sizing	Storage	Cost Model	
Extra large	8 vCPU, 8GB RAM (can offer up to 32 vCPU and 1TB RAM)	400GB	Provision cost ($)	Operate cost ($/mo)
Large	4 vCPU, 8GB RAM	200GB	Provision cost ($)	Operate cost ($/mo)
Medium	2 vCPU, 2GB RAM	60GB	Provision cost ($)	Operate cost ($/mo)
Small	1 vCPU, 1GB RAM	30GB	Provision cost ($)	Operate cost ($/mo)

2.2.5 Security and Compliance

Security and compliance continue to be concerns for enterprise subscribers seeking to adopt vCloud services. Most regulations and mandates in the industry, such as SOX, PCI DSS, and HIPAA/HITECH, have two general areas of requirements: transparency and control.

2.2.5.1 Compliance Definition

Transparency enables vCloud consumers to know who has accessed what data, when, and where. Payment Card Industry (PCI) requirement #10.3 is a good example of the need for transparency. It states that logs must contain sufficient detail for each event to be traced to a source by user, time, and origin.

Control gives vCloud consumers a necessary component of compliance by limiting access, based on a particular role and business need. Who can access, configure, and modify a vCloud environment; what firewall ports are open; when to apply patches; and where the data resides are common concerns from auditors. Cloud consumers—especially enterprise subscribers—believe that you can outsource responsibility, but you can't outsource accountability. As evidenced in the PCI Security Standards Council *Assessor Update: July 2011*, active Qualified Security Assessors (QSA) have the ultimate responsibility for their client's assessment and the evidence provided in the Report on Compliance. Both vCloud consumers and their auditors retain final accountability for their compliance and enforcement.

By design, vCloud services are intended to address common security and compliance concerns with transparency and control by doing the following:

- Facilitating compliance through ISO 27001 certification and/or SSAE 16, SOC 2 reporting, based on a standard set of controls
- Providing compliance logging and reports to service subscribers, for full visibility into their hosted vCloud environments
- Architecting the service so that subscribers can control access to their vCloud environments

2.2.5.2 Compliance Controls

For enterprise subscribers to feel secure and safe in the vCloud services domain, and to have the information and visibility into the service needed for their own internal audit requirements, providers of vCloud services must actively pursue one of the following certifications as part of their general service availability plans:

- ISO 27001 certification, which certifies that security management processes are in place and have a relevant subset of the ISO 27001 controls, as specified by the *VMware Compliance Architecture and Control Matrix*
- SSAE 16, SOC 2 report, based on the same relevant set of controls

VMware can provide documented guidance on how to meet the standard set of compliance controls, but providers are directly responsible for achieving ISO 27001 and/or SSAE 16, SOC 2 certification status for their service environments through a third-party audit. vCloud providers should make compliance certification types and status available so that subscribers understand what standards both the hosting environment and the services have been audited against.

2.2.5.3 Compliance Visibility and Transparency

Log management is often built into many of the compliance frameworks, such as ISO 27002, HIPAA/HITECH, PCI DSS, and COBIT. Enterprise subscribers not only need visibility into their private vCloud instances, but they also demand that providers give them visibility into their public vCloud environments. For example, enterprise subscribers must collect and archive logs and reports related to user activities and access controls such as firewalls.

To meet the requirements of being compliant with the controls, providers must enable reasonable visibility and transparency into their vCloud service architecture for subscribers. To accomplish this, service providers should collect and maintain logs for periods of 6 and 12 months for relevant components of the vCloud service and should be able to provide pertinent logs back to individual vCloud subscribers on an as-needed basis. Service providers should also maintain and archive logs for the underlying multitenant hosting infrastructure, based on the same 6- and 12-month periods. In the event of an audit, service providers should be able and willing to provide these logs to an auditor and/or individual subscriber. In general, vCloud service providers should have logs covering the following components of a subscriber's environment and should keep them readily available for subscriber access for periods of up to 6 and 12 months:

- VMware vCloud Director®
- VMware vCloud Networking and Security Edge™

The VMware vCloud Suite is based on a set of products that have been used in many secure environments. Products such as VMware vCloud Director and VMware vCloud Networking and Security™ generate a set of logs that give subscribers visibility into all user activities and firewall connections. VMware provides the necessary blueprints and best practices so that providers can best standardize and capture these sets of logs and provide subscribers with the capability to access them.

In addition to logs, service providers should provide basic compliance reports to their subscribers so that they understand all the activities and risks in their vCloud environment. VMware provides design guidelines in this area so that vCloud service providers can meet common enterprise subscriber requirements. Service providers are responsible for logging their vCloud services as well as their subscriber environments. These capabilities should be implemented and validated before any vCloud service is made generally available.

2.2.5.4 Compliant and Secure Architecture

All vCloud services offer a secure platform. VMware vSphere, a core building block, offers a secure virtualization platform with EAL4+ and FISMA certifications. vCloud Director, a vCloud delivery platform, offers secure multitenancy and organization isolation. The vCloud Suite enables enterprises to exercise the defense-in-depth security best practice. The platform offers both per-organization firewalls and per-vApp firewalls, and all organizations are isolated with their own Layer 2 networks. Access and authentication can optionally be performed against an enterprise organization's own directory using LDAP or Active Directory; the enterprise can thus self-manage its user base and provide role-based access according to its own policies.

2.2.6 Capacity Distribution and Allocation Models

To support the service offerings, determining the infrastructure's capacity and scalability is important. The following models determine how the resources are allocated:

- **Pay as you go:** No upfront resource allocation; resources are reserved on demand per workload.
- **Allocation pool:** A percentage of resources is reserved with overcommitment.
- **Reservation pool:** All resources are reservation guaranteed.

To determine the appropriate standard units of resource consumption, the vCloud service provider can analyze current environment usage, user demand, trends, and business requirements. Use this information to determine an appropriate capacity distribution that meets business requirements. If this information is not readily available, predicting the infrastructure capacity can be difficult because it depends on the expected customer uptake and usage of the workloads. However, understanding the infrastructure capacity required, based on an estimate of the different allocation models and capacity distribution of the workloads, is useful. The capacity distribution and resulting infrastructure resources allocated can be adjusted based on utilization and demand.

The following example distributes capacity based on 50% of the virtual machines for the reservation pool allocation model and 50% of the virtual machines for the pay as you go model. The reservation pool model is applied to small, medium, and large pools, with a respective split of 75%, 20%, and 5%. Therefore, *small* represents 37.5% of the total, *medium* represents 10% of the total, and *large* represents 2.5% of the total number of virtual machines in the environment.

Table 2.8 lists the virtual machine count for the various resource pools supporting the two example allocation models for the virtual datacenters.

TABLE 2.8 Definition of Resource Pool and Virtual Machine Split

Type of Resource Pool	Total Percentage	Total Virtual Machines
Pay as you go	50%	750
Small reservation pool	37.5%	563
Medium reservation pool	10%	150
Large reservation pool	2.5%	37
Total	100%	1,500

The following virtual machine distribution is used in the service capacity planning example:

- 45% small virtual machines (1GB, 1 vCPU, 30GB of storage)
- 35% medium virtual machines (2GB, 2 vCPU, 40GB of storage)
- 15% large virtual machines (4GB, 4 vCPU, 50GB of storage)
- 5% extra-large virtual machines (8+GB, 8+ vCPU, 60GB of storage)

Table 2.9 lists some examples of workload virtual machine sizing and utilization.

TABLE 2.9 Workload Virtual Machine Sizing and Utilization Examples

Virtual Machine Type	Sizing	CPU Utilization	Memory Utilization
Small	1 vCPU, 1GB RAM	10%–15% average	Low (10%–50%)
Medium	2 vCPU, 2GB RAM	20%–50% average	Moderate (50%–75%)
Large	4 vCPU, 4GB RAM	>50% average	High (more than 90%)
Extra large	8 vCPU, 8GB RAM (can offer up to 32 vCPU and 1TB RAM)	>50% average	High (more than 90%)

2.2.7 Applications Catalog

Supply a list of suggested applications and vApps that the private and public vCloud should provide to the consumers. The goal is to help consumers accelerate the adoption of the vCloud service. The vApp templates provided to the consumers can be compliant based on the security policies and also must take license subscription into consideration.

Application workloads generally fall into the following categories:

- **Transient:** A transient application is used infrequently, exists for a short time, or is used for a specific task or need. It is then discarded. This type of workload is appropriate for a pay as you go consumption model.
- **Highly elastic:** An elastic application dynamically grows and shrinks its resource consumption as it runs. Examples include a retail application that sees dramatically increased demand during holiday shopping seasons and a travel-booking application that expands rapidly as the fall travel season approaches. This *bursty* type of workload is appropriate for an allocation consumption model.
- **Steady state:** A steady state application tends to run all the time in a predictably steady state. This type of workload is appropriate for a reservation consumption model.

Table 2.10 illustrates the types of applications in a service catalog, by category.

TABLE 2.10 Applications Catalog Example

Application Type	Application Description
Operating systems	▶ Microsoft Windows Server ▶ RHEL ▶ Centos ▶ SUSe Linux Enterprise Server ▶ Ubuntu Server

Application Type	Application Description
Infrastructure applications	▶ Databases: ▶ Microsoft SQL Server ▶ Oracle Database ▶ MySQL ▶ Distributed data management: VMware vFabric™ GemFire® ▶ Web/application servers ▶ Microsoft IIS ▶ VMware vFabric tc Server ▶ Apache Tomcat ▶ IBM WebSphere Application Server ▶ Simple n-tier applications ▶ Two-tier application with a web front end and database back end ▶ Three-tier application with web, processing, and database ▶ Enhanced three-tier application with added monitoring ▶ Load balancer
Application frameworks	▶ Tomcat/Spring ▶ JBoss ▶ Cloudera/Hadoop
Business applications	▶ Microsoft SharePoint ▶ Microsoft Exchange ▶ VMware Zimbra®

2.2.8 Interoperability

Interoperability aspects of the service definition should list the areas in which the solution must integrate and interact with external systems. For example, a chargeback capability of the solution might need to interoperate with financial and reporting systems. Alternatively, interoperability between vCloud instances built to the vCloud API standards might be required.

2.2.9 Service-Level Agreement

A service-level agreement (SLA) is a negotiated contract or agreement between a vCloud service provider and the consumer that documents the services, service-level guarantees, responsibilities, and limits between the two parties.

General guidelines for vCloud service providers require that any service offering made available carry a comprehensive SLA guarantee that is equal to or exceeds three 9s (99.9%) for availability and reliability, and includes special considerations for overall service performance and customer support handling and responsiveness. An SLA can be either a negotiated contract or a standard contract between a vCloud provider and subscriber that defines responsibilities and limitations associated with the services:

- Availability (uptime)
- Backups (schedule, restore time, data retention)
- Serviceability (time to respond, time to resolution)
- Performance (application performance, network performance)
- Compliance (regulatory compliance, logging, auditing, data retention, reporting)
- Operations (user account management, metering parameters, response time for requests)
- Billing (reporting details, frequency, history)
- Service credits or penalties

Although detailed guidance on how to calculate the level of availability and performance for all vCloud service elements is beyond the scope of this document, it is anticipated that service providers have an SLA framework in place that can be leveraged or augmented to support vCloud services.

SLA guarantees should extend to all facets of a provider's vCloud hosting infrastructure and individual service domains (for example, compute, network, storage, Layer 4–7 services, and management/control plane) that directly support vCloud services. Adherence to SLA requirements should also factor in the resiliency of the management framework, consisting of API and UI accessibility for service subscribers.

2.3 Service Offering Examples

Service offerings and their inherent virtual datacenter constructs provide an effective means of creating service differentiation within a broader vCloud service landscape. They deliver consistent service levels that invariably align with unique business use case requirements, as presented by individual tenants in either a private or public vCloud setting. The service offerings presented in this section serve as a reference for building a differentiated IaaS service model. They also try to address the full spectrum of enterprise workload requirements observed in the vCloud services market today.

The following is a summary of these service offerings:

- **Basic:** Based on the pay as you go allocation model. This service offering lends itself to quick-start pilot projects or test and development application workloads that typically do not require persistent resource commitments or upfront resource reservations.
- **Committed:** Based on the allocation pool allocation model. This service offering gives consumers a minimum initial commitment of resource capacity, plus the added capability to burst above that minimum if additional infrastructure capacity is available at the time of need. The level of minimum commitment, expressed as a percentage of overall capacity per resource type, provides an extra layer of assurance to consumers who seek deterministic performance levels for their application workloads.

- **Dedicated:** Based on the reservation pool allocation model. This service offering gives consumers reserved resource capacity up front, fully dedicated by individual tenant. The level of resource guarantee (always set to 100%) gives customers a higher degree of service assurance than the Committed service offering, along with additional layers of security and resource control for their application workloads.

Because of often unpredictable business demands and the elastic nature of vCloud service consumption models, it is not unreasonable for providers of private or public vCloud instances to seed a service environment with a single service offering type and adapt that service over time, given proper business justification. This approach is not only common, but also recommended, regardless of the number of service offering examples made available for consideration.

To help decide which service offering makes the most sense for a particular set of business use cases, refer to the key service attributes summarized in Table 2.11. The following sections give additional details and reference examples for each service offering.

TABLE 2.11 Service Offering Matrix Example

	Basic Service Offering	Committed Service Offering	Dedicated Service Offering
Allocation Model	Pay as you go	Allocation pool	Reservation pool
Control Plane (Management)	Shared, multitenant	Shared, multitenant	Shared, multitenant
Cluster Resources	Shared, multitenant	Shared, multitenant	Dedicated, single tenant
Unit of Consumption	vApp	Aggregate resource capacity allocated	Aggregate resource capacity reserved
Resource Allocation Settings (per Organization Virtual Datacenter)	—	▶ CPU (GHz) ▶ Memory (GB) ▶ Storage (GB)	▶ CPU (GHz) ▶ Memory (GB) ▶ Storage (GB)
Resource Guarantee Settings	▶ % of CPU ▶ vCPU speed ▶ % of memory ▶ % of storage	▶ % of CPU ▶ vCPU speed ▶ % of memory ▶ % of storage	▶ 100% of CPU ▶ 100% of memory ▶ 100% of storage
Limits (per Organization Virtual Datacenter)	Maximum number of virtual machines CPU (GHz) Memory (GB)	Maximum number of virtual machines CPU (GHz) Memory (GB)	Maximum number of virtual machines CPU (GHz) Memory (GB)
Reporting/ Billing Frequency	Per use	Monthly	Monthly or annually

	Basic Service Offering	Committed Service Offering	Dedicated Service Offering
Metering Frequency	Hourly	Hourly	Hourly
Service Availability	99.95%	99.99%	99.99%
Target Workloads	Test and development	Tier 2 and 3 production	Tier 1 production
Application Workload Examples	▶ Short-term or bursty workloads ▶ QA testing ▶ Integration testing ▶ New software version testing ▶ Short-term data analytics	▶ Static web content servers ▶ Lightly used app servers ▶ Active Directory servers ▶ Infrastructure servers (DNS, print, file) ▶ Small/medium database servers ▶ Short-term content collaboration ▶ Staging sites	▶ Exchange and SharePoint servers ▶ Large database servers (high IOPS) ▶ PCI-related servers ▶ HPC workloads ▶ SaaS production applications ▶ CRM, EDA, ERP, and SCM applications ▶ Financial applications (high compliance)

2.3.1 Service Offering—Basic

The Basic service offering is based on the pay as you go allocation model in vCloud Director. It gives subscribers instant, committed capacity on demand through access to a shared management control plane in a multitenant service environment. Resource commitments for CPU (GHz), memory (GB), and storage (GB) are committed only when virtual machines or vApps are instantiated within the target organization virtual datacenter in vCloud Director. This service is designed for quick-start pilot projects and test and development application workloads that do not typically require persistent resource commitments or upfront resource reservations.

2.3.1.1 Service Design Parameters

As part of the design process for the Basic service offering, providers should give special consideration to key service settings and values in vCloud Director that can impact service performance and consistency levels for a subscriber's organization virtual datacenter. Given the pay as you go allocation model employed in this service, certain circumstances might arise that result in subscribers overcommitting resources over time. If not properly managed, these circumstances can negatively affect performance for all application workloads. Table 2.12 provides an example of these key service settings, values, and justifications.

TABLE 2.12 Resource Allocation Settings Example—Basic Service Offering

Resource Type	Value Range	Sample Setting	Justification
CPU allocation	Variable (GHz), based on physical host capacity	50GHz	The maximum amount of CPU available to the virtual machines running in the target organization virtual datacenter (taken from the supporting provider virtual datacenter).
CPU resources guaranteed	0%–100%	0%	The percentage of CPU resources that are guaranteed to a virtual machine running within the target organization virtual datacenter. This option controls overcommitment of CPU resources.
vCPU speed	0–8GHz	1GHz	This value defines what a virtual machine or vApp with one vCPU consumes at most when running within the target organization virtual datacenter. A virtual machine with two vCPUs consumes a maximum of twice this value.
Memory resources guaranteed	0–100%	75%	The percentage of memory that is guaranteed to a virtual machine running within the target virtual datacenter. This option controls overcommitment of memory resources.
Maximum number of virtual machines	1–unlimited	Unlimited	A safeguard that allows control over the total number of vApps or virtual machines a subscriber can create within the target virtual datacenter.

In this example, the minimum vCPU speed setting is configured as 1GHz (1000MHz), with a memory resource guarantee of 75%. CPU resource guarantees and limitations on the maximum number of virtual machines supported per tenant are optional and can be implemented at the provider's discretion. The provider can use the combination of these settings to change overcommitment from aggressive levels (for example, resource guarantees set to <100%) to more conservative levels (for example, resource guarantees always set to 100%), depending on SLAs in place or fluctuating service loads.

2.3.1.2 Resource Allocation and Catalogs

The pay as you go resource allocation model enables providers to deliver high levels of flexibility in the way resources are allocated, through published vApp catalogs in vCloud Director. vApp catalogs further enable providers to publish standard application images and predefined resource profiles that subscribers can customize, based on a given set of application workload requirements.

Table 2.13 provides an example of different sizing combinations that can be included in a vApp catalog with the Basic service offering.

NOTE

vCPU quantity is based on a multiple of 1GHz, as in the example in Table 2.12. Any quantity of memory or vRAM assigned from Table 2.13 is reserved at 75%. The provider can govern subscribers' capability to select specific quantities of resources, such as vCPU, memory, and storage for a given virtual machine or vApp dynamically, as necessary. However, providers should first implement a pricing model commensurate with the range of scale for each resource type.

TABLE 2.13 Basic Service Offering Catalog Example

vApp Instance Size	vCPU/GHz	OS Bit Mode	Memory[1] (MB)	Storage[2] (GB)	Bandwidth[3] (MBps)	Cost
Extra small	1.0/1GHz	32-/ 64-bit	500–100,000	10–2,000	Variable	Set by provider
Small	1.0/1GHz	32-/ 64-bit	500–100,000	10–2,000	Variable	Set by provider
Medium	2.0/2GHz	64-bit	500–100,000	10–2,000	Variable	Set by provider
Large	4.0/4GHz	64-bit	500–100,000	10–2,000	Variable	Set by provider
Extra large	8.0/8GHz	64-bit	500–100,000	10–2,000	Variable	Set by provider

1 *Virtual memory allocation can be customized for all virtual machine instances from small through extra large. The range provided takes into account the maximum amount of memory that can be allocated per virtual machine or vApp in vCloud Director.*

2 *Storage allocations can be selected individually and are customizable for all virtual machine instances from small through extra large, based on individual subscriber requirements. The range provided takes into account the maximum amount of storage that can be allocated per virtual machine or vApp in vCloud Director.*

3 *Ingress/egress bandwidth allocation can be customized for all virtual machine instances from Small through Extra Large, based on individual subscriber requirements and the Internet service capabilities available at the provider.*

The maximum virtual machine instance size is derived from the maximum amount of vCPU and the maximum amount of memory that a physical host has available in the environment. Although the supported ranges for memory and storage in Table 2.13 indicate configuration maximums for a vSphere and vCloud Director environment, these ranges differ for different providers, given the variance in hosting architectures and physical infrastructure designs.

2.3.1.3 Service Metering

Subscribers to the Basic service offering are charged over time for the aggregate amount of resources consumed across their virtual machine and/or vApp inventory for a given organization virtual datacenter. The minimum standard time interval for billing and metering purposes is typically one hour. However, providers who have the means to do so are permitted to meter and charge subscribers for resource consumption on a subhourly basis. If subscribers opt to change the size of their virtual machine or vApp instances after initial setup, pricing changes retroactively, defaulting to the higher charge rate of either the new or the initial vCPU or memory setting. This is referred to as the *stepping function*—the virtual machine charge always steps up to the next instance size, measured by memory or vCPU, whichever charge rate is higher.

Charges for resource consumption typically begin when the virtual machine is deployed, with limited exceptions for certain resource types such as storage, which may be reserved in advance without immediate use. It is important for providers to understand how different resource states, such as *provisioned* and *reserved,* can be used to determine a chargeable event in a service billing scheme.

Table 2.14 lists the most common event triggers and resource states for vCloud Director. Columns marked with an X signify that the resource type is considered consumed when a virtual machine or vApp is in the associated state; corresponding charges then apply. These are meant to be illustrative only. Providers should rely on their own internal cost models and metering schemes for billing or showback.

TABLE 2.14 vCloud Director Event Triggers and States

API Operation	UI Operation	vCPU	RAM	Network (vNIC)	Storage
Instantiate/ compose	Add/new				X
Deploy	Start			X	X
Power on		X	X	X	X
Reset	Reset	X	X	X	X
Suspend (vApp)	Suspend				X
Suspend (virtual machine)				X	X
Shut down					X
Reboot		X	X	X	X
Power off	Stop			X	X
Undeploy					X
Delete	Delete				
Expire/deploy					X
Expire/storage (mark)					X
Expire/storage (delete[1])					

[1] *The Delete or Expire/storage state means that all resources have been both deactivated and decommissioned, and no further charges should be applied at that point.*

2.3.2 Service Offering—Committed

The Committed service offering is based on the allocation pool allocation model in vCloud Director. It guarantees subscribers a minimum resource commitment through access to a shared management control plane in a multitenant service environment. Resource commitments for CPU (GHz), memory (GB), and storage (GB) are specified by capacity allocation for each tenant organization virtual datacenter, with a percentage guarantee for each resource type. This minimum guarantee provides deterministic performance for hosted workloads while offering tenants the capability to burst over the minimum guarantee level if additional infrastructure capacity is available.

2.3.2.1 Service Design Parameters

As part of the design process for the Committed service offering, providers should pay special consideration to key service settings and values in vCloud Director that can affect service performance and consistency levels for a subscriber's organization virtual datacenter. Despite use of the allocation pool allocation model in this service, circumstances can result in subscribers overcommitting resources over time. If not properly managed, these circumstances can negatively affect performance for all application workloads. Table 2.15 provides an example of these key service settings, values, and justifications.

TABLE 2.15 Resource Allocation Settings Example—Committed Service Offering

Allocation Type	Value Range	Sample Setting	Justification
CPU allocation	Variable (GHz), based on physical host capacity	50GHz	The maximum amount of CPU available to the virtual machines running in the target organization virtual datacenter (taken from the supporting provider virtual datacenter) and the percentage of that resource guaranteed to be available to them.
CPU resources guaranteed	0%–100%	75%	
vCPU speed	0–8GHz	1GHz	This value defines what a virtual machine or vApp with one vCPU consumes at most when running within the target organization virtual datacenter. A virtual machine with two vCPUs consumes a maximum of twice this value.
Memory allocation	Variable (MB) based on physical host capacity	100GB	The maximum amount of memory available to the virtual machines running in the target organization virtual datacenter (taken from the supporting provider virtual datacenter) and the percentage of that resource guaranteed to be available to them.
Memory resources guaranteed	0%–100%	75%	
Maximum number of virtual machines	1–unlimited	Unlimited	A safeguard that allows control over the total number of vApps or virtual machines a subscriber can create within the target virtual datacenter.

In this example, the CPU allocation setting serves as a block or aggregate limit for the entire target organization virtual datacenter and has been configured as 50GHz (50,000MHz). The CPU guarantee or reservation is dynamically changed as new virtual machines are powered on in the organization virtual datacenter. The value of the CPU guarantee is equal to the CPU resources guarantee (75%) multiplied by the vCPU speed (1GHz), multiplied by the number of powered-on virtual machines, if this is less than the CPU allocation (50GHz) of the organization virtual datacenter.

The memory allocation setting also serves as a block, or aggregate, limit for the entire target organization virtual datacenter and has been configured as 100GB. The memory guarantee or reservation is dynamically changed as new virtual machines are powered on in the organization virtual datacenter. The value of the memory guarantee is equal to the memory resources guarantee (75%) multiplied by the memory of the powered-on virtual machines, if this is less than the memory allocation (100GB) of the organization virtual datacenter.

2.3.2.2 Resource Allocation and Catalogs

The allocation pool allocation model in the Committed service offering enables providers to aggregate resources in bulk, with a minimum upfront capacity guarantee for target service subscribers whose workloads demand more stringent service levels for capacity availability and performance. Similar to the Basic service offering, this service tier provides equal or better flexibility in the way resources are allocated through published vApp catalogs in vCloud Director. Subscribers gain flexibility through entitlements to create their own custom and private vApp catalogs, as well as to use any public catalogs and standard application images that the provider makes available.

Table 2.16 provides an example of different sizing combinations that can be included in a Committed service offering (virtual datacenter) catalog. Values in the CPU Guarantee and Memory Guarantee columns reflect a 75% resource guarantee listed in the example in Table 2.15. Depending on the customizable sizing options made available by a provider of this service, subscribers might be able to specify nonstandard combinations of resources such as CPU, memory, and storage types and quantities. It is still recommended, however, that providers first implement a pricing model commensurate with the range of scale for each resource type.

TABLE 2.16 Committed Service Offering Catalog Example

Virtual Datacenter Instance Size	CPU Allocation (GHz)	CPU Guarantee (GHz)	Memory Allocation (GB)	Memory Guarantee (GB)	Storage Limit[1] (GB)	Bandwidth[2] (MBps)	Cost
Small	10GHz	7.5GHz	20GB	15GB	Variable	95th percentile	Set by provider
Medium	25GHz	18.75GHz	50GB	37.5GB	Variable	95th percentile	Set by provider
Large	50GHz	37.5GHz	100GB	75GB	Variable	95th percentile	Set by provider
Extra large	100GHz	75GHz	200GB	150GB	Variable	95th percentile	Set by provider

[1] *Storage allocations can be selected individually and customized for all virtual datacenter sizes from small through extra large, based on individual subscriber requirements.*

[2] *Ingress/egress bandwidth allocation can be customized for all virtual machine instances from small through extra large, based on individual subscriber requirements and the Internet service capabilities of the provider.*

2.3.2.3 Service Metering

Subscribers to the Committed service offering are charged for the minimum amount of resource capacity guaranteed over time for a given organization virtual datacenter, as negotiated at the point of sale. The time interval used for billing and metering purposes for the amount of guaranteed capacity can vary based on actual service terms the provider sets, but it is most often based on a monthly subscription period, with a minimum enrollment term set to longer than one month. When available, burst capacity can be consumed without specific terms and obligations, but the provider must determine whether additional charges are incurred for short-term bursting or temporary scale-out operations on behalf of the subscriber.

Subscribers whose workload requirements have consistently grown beyond their initial resource capacity guarantee should have the option to move into the next band of guaranteed capacity without being penalized in price. In fact, providers are encouraged to offer a progressive discount structure that incentivizes active subscribers to consume greater amounts of the Committed service offered as needed, with minimal disruption to service contract terms or operations.

Charges for resource consumption under the Committed service offering typically start when the target organization virtual datacenter has been fully provisioned and made available to the subscriber, with limited exceptions for certain resource types, such as storage, which can be reserved up front without immediate use.

2.3.3 Service Offering—Dedicated

The Dedicated service offering is based on the reservation pool allocation model in vCloud Director. It gives subscribers of this service tier fully dedicated resources up front through access to a shared management control plane in a multitenant service environment. In contrast to all other service offerings referenced in this document, the Dedicated service offering delivers premium levels of performance, security, and resource management by reserving 100% of physical CPU (GHz), memory (GB), and storage (GB) resource capacity for each target organization virtual datacenter. This enables subscribers of the service to exercise granular control of resource commitment by specifying reservation, limit, and priority settings for individual virtual machines.

2.3.3.1 Service Design Parameters

As part of the design process for the Dedicated service offering, providers should give special consideration to key service settings and values in vCloud Director that can impact service performance and consistency levels for a subscriber's organization virtual datacenter. Although the reservation pool allocation model in this service provides stricter controls over the segmentation of resources allocated than the other models, circumstances can still arise that result in subscribers overcommitting resources over time. This situation can result in negative performance or availability implications, whether for subscribers' application workload environment; for their service settings, values, and justifications; or for both. Table 2.17 provides an example of these key service settings, values, and justifications.

TABLE 2.17 Resource Allocation Settings Example—Dedicated Service Offering

Allocation Type	Value Range	Sample Setting	Justification
CPU allocation	Custom	76.8GHz	The amount of CPU resources reserved for this organization virtual datacenter (taken from the supporting provider virtual datacenter and assigned resource cluster)
Memory allocation	Custom	1024GB	The amount of memory resources reserved for this organization virtual datacenter (taken from the supporting provider virtual datacenter and assigned resource cluster)
Maximum number of virtual machines	1–unlimited	Unlimited	A safeguard that allows control over the total number of vApps or virtual machines created by a subscriber within the target virtual datacenter

In this table, the CPU allocation setting serves as a block or aggregate limit for the entire target organization virtual datacenter and has been configured as 76.8GHz (76,800MHz). Of this 76.8GHz resource allocation, 100% of total CPU capacity is marked by default as reserved and guaranteed. The memory allocation setting also serves as a block or aggregate limit for the entire target organization virtual datacenter and has been configured as 1024GB. Of this 1024GB resource allocation, 100% of total memory capacity is also marked by default as reserved and guaranteed. This implies zero resource overcommitment by the provider for both compute and memory capacity. It also requires that the underlying provider virtual datacenter and associated physical resource clusters be 100% dedicated to each subscriber, to avoid any resource contention. The provider can use the combination of these settings to adjust CPU and memory capacity as necessary, but the need to throttle back overcommitment for this service offering does not apply.

2.3.3.2 Resource Allocation and Catalogs

Using the reservation pool allocation model in the Dedicated service offering enables providers to aggregate resources in bulk, with a 100% upfront physical capacity guarantee for target service subscribers whose workloads demand the most stringent service levels for capacity availability, performance, and security isolation. Similar to the Committed service offering, this service tier provides equal flexibility in how resources are allocated through published vApp catalogs in vCloud Director. Subscribers are entitled to the same privileges for creating their own custom and private vApp catalogs, in addition to use of any public catalogs and standard application images that the provider makes available.

Table 2.18 provides an example of different sizing combinations that can be included in a Dedicated service offering (virtual datacenter) catalog. Values in the CPU Capacity Reserved and Memory Capacity Reserved columns imply a 100% dedicated resource guarantee up front. Depending on the customizable sizing options that a provider of this service makes available, subscribers might be able to specify nonstandard combinations of resource types, such as CPU, memory, storage, and quantities. It is still recommended, however, that providers first implement a pricing model commensurate with the range of scale for each resource type.

TABLE 2.18 A Dedicated Service Offering Catalog

Virtual Datacenter Instance Size	Compute Nodes Reserved[1]	CPU Capacity Reserved[2] (GHz)	Memory Capacity Reserved[3] (GB)	Storage Limit[4] (GB)	Bandwidth[5] (MBps)	Cost
Small	2–4	9.6–19.2GHz	512–1024GB	Variable	95th percentile	Set by provider
Medium	4–8	19.2–38.4GHz	1024–2048GB	Variable	95th percentile	Set by provider
Large	8–16	38.4–76.8GHz	2048–4096GB	Variable	95th percentile	Set by provider
Extra large	16–32	76.8–153.6GHz	4096–8192GB	Variable	95th percentile	Set by provider

[1] *The compute node form factor can be either blade servers or rackmount servers. This example assumes a generic (x86) dual-processor blade server.*

[2] *CPU capacities in this example are based on each compute node having dual Intel 2.4GHz Xeon E7-2870 processors.*

[3] *Memory capacities in this example are based on each compute node having 256GB of physical memory.*

[4] *Storage allocations can be selected individually and customized for all virtual datacenter sizes from small through extra large, based on individual subscriber requirements.*

[5] *Ingress/egress bandwidth allocation can be customized for all virtual machine instances from small through extra large, based on individual subscriber requirements and the Internet service capabilities available at the provider.*

Although resources assigned at the organization virtual datacenter layer in the Dedicated service offering are fully reserved and dedicated, subscribers to the service are entitled to control resource overcommitment through reservation and limit settings for each individual virtual machine. Table 2.19 provides an example of how these resource allocation settings might be configured.

TABLE 2.19 Resource Allocation Settings per Virtual Machine

Resource Type	Priority	Reservation	Limit
CPU	▶ Low (500 shares) ▶ Normal (1,000 shares) ▶ High (2,000 shares) ▶ Custom	Custom (GHz) per virtual datacenter allocation	▶ Unlimited ▶ Maximum (custom)
Memory	▶ Low (1,280 shares) ▶ Normal (2,560 shares) ▶ High (5,120 shares) ▶ Custom	Custom (GB) per virtual datacenter allocation	▶ Unlimited ▶ Maximum (custom)

2.3.3.3 Service Metering

Similar to subscribers to the Committed service offering, subscribers to the Dedicated service offering are charged for the full amount of resource capacity guaranteed over time for a given organization virtual datacenter, as negotiated at the point of sale. The time interval used for billing and metering purposes for the amount of guaranteed capacity can vary based on actual service terms the provider sets, but it is most often based on a monthly subscription period, with a minimum enrollment term set to longer than one month.

Subscribers whose workload requirements have consistently grown beyond their initial resource capacity guarantee should have the option to move into the next band of reserved capacity without being penalized in price. Again, providers are encouraged to offer a progressive discount structure that incentivizes active subscribers to consume greater amounts of the Dedicated service offered as needed and with minimal disruption to service contract terms or operations.

Charges for resource consumption under the Dedicated service offering typically start when the target organization virtual datacenter has been fully provisioned and made available to the subscriber, with limited exceptions for certain resource types, such as storage, which can be reserved up front without immediate use.

CHAPTER 3

Architecting a VMware vCloud

IN THIS CHAPTER

3.1 Overview

This chapter provides guidance in architecting an Infrastructure as a Service (IaaS) cloud based on the VMware® vCloud® Suite. The vCloud Suite dramatically simplifies IT operations, delivering enhanced agility and better economics. At the heart of the suite are a set of *software-defined datacenter* services. These represent the application of the virtualization principles of pooling, abstraction, and automation to the domains of storage, networking, security, and availability.

The vCloud Suite components addressed in this guide include VMware vSphere®, VMware vCloud Director®, VMware vCloud Networking and Security™ (formerly vShield), the VMware vCenter™ Operations Management Suite™, VMware vFabric™ Application Director™, VMware vCenter Site Recovery Manager™, and VMware vCloud Connector™. Simplifying the delivery of resources to end users requires the architectural integration and coordination of these components. Both service providers and enterprises can use the design guidelines, with some variations depending on the point of view.

This chapter, combined with a service definition, can help you evaluate the design considerations for architecting a vCloud solution. Use the following vCloud chapters together throughout the lifecycle of a VMware vCloud computing implementation.

- This chapter provides design guidelines, design considerations, and design patterns for constructing a vCloud environment from its constituent components.
- Chapter 4, "Operating a VMware vCloud," includes design guidelines and considerations for operating and maintaining a vCloud environment. It covers the people, process, and technology involved in running a vCloud environment.
- Chapter 5, "Consuming a VMware vCloud," covers the various considerations for the consumer when choosing to leverage vCloud computing resources.

Additionally, Chapter 6, "Implementation Examples," provides modular examples that show how to use VMware component software to implement a vCloud instance.

3.1.1 Audience

This chapter is for people involved in planning, designing, and implementing VMware vCloud solutions. The target audience is architects, engineers, and IT professionals who have achieved VMware Certified Professional (VCP) or higher certification and are familiar with VMware products. The reader is assumed to be familiar with vSphere and vCloud concepts.

3.1.2 Scope

This chapter includes design guidelines, design considerations, and design patterns for building a vCloud instance.

3.1.3 Chapter Topics

The rest of this chapter is divided into the sections listed in Table 3.1, with applicable appendixes at the end of the book.

TABLE 3.1 Document Topics

Section	Description
Section 3.2, "vCloud Architecture"	Introduces the core concepts of the vCloud solution stack
Section 3.3, "vCloud Management Architecture"	Describes the components required to build a vCloud solution
Section 3.4, "Resource Group Architecture"	Provides guidance for configuring resources reserved for end-user workloads
Section 3.5, "vCloud Resource Design"	Offers design guidelines for partitioning and delivering vCloud resources relative to customer requirements
Section 3.6, "vCloud Metering"	Covers how to meter and charge for resources with VMware vCenter Chargeback Manager™ (a component of the VMware vCenter Operations Management Suite)
Section 3.7, "Orchestration and Extension"	Provides information about extending vCloud Director automation through orchestration

Section	Description
Section 3.8, "Multisite Considerations"	Covers multisite considerations
Section 3.9, "Hybrid vCloud"	Provides information about extending vCloud Director into the hybrid vCloud model
Appendix A: "Availability"	Provides design considerations for availability
Appendix B: "Security"	Provides design considerations for security
Appendix C: "vCloud Suite Disaster"	Provides design considerations for disaster recovery
Appendix D: "vCloud Director Upgrade"	Provides design considerations for upgrading to vCloud Director 5.1

3.2 vCloud Architecture

Cloud computing is a model that allows ubiquitous, convenient, on-demand network access to a shared pool of configurable computing resources. vCloud resources are provisioned rapidly and released with minimal management effort.

The VMware vCloud suite delivers a complete, integrated cloud infrastructure suite that simplifies IT operations while delivering the best service-level agreements (SLAs) for all applications. The vCloud Suite includes the entire set of vCloud infrastructure capabilities: virtualization, software-defined datacenter services, policy-based provisioning, disaster recovery, application management, and operations management.

The vCloud solution encompasses the vCloud Suite along with an architecture defined in the *VMware vCloud Architecture Toolkit* (vCAT) and a set of recommended guidelines for organization, process design, and instrumentation. These all feed a CIO scorecard enabled by the VMware IT Business Management (ITBM) product suite. It is an all-encompassing approach to maximizing the benefits of the software-defined datacenter.

Architecting a VMware vCloud focuses on the IaaS layer, detailing use of the vCloud Suite to extend the capabilities of the vSphere virtualization platform.

3.2.1 Technology Mapping

The VMware vCloud Solution is an open and modular architecture that offers choice and flexibility for running applications in public and private vCloud instances. vCloud Director implements the vCloud API, which provides compatibility, interoperability, and extensibility with other vCloud instances. VMware vCloud Automation Center™ extends vCloud Networking and Security, virtualizes the network, and creates agile, extensible, secure logical networks that meet the performance and scale requirements of virtualized applications and data. The vCenter Operations Management Suite provides the capabilities necessary to achieve an integrated approach to performance, capacity, and configuration across a vCloud infrastructure.

A vCloud architecture provides a conceptual framework to support primary business requirements, determine system functions, organize elements into distinct components, and define boundaries and connections. The focus is on clearly defined goals, analysis, and design decisions that cut through the complexity in today's technology.

Figure 3.1 shows the components of the vCloud Suite solution stack.

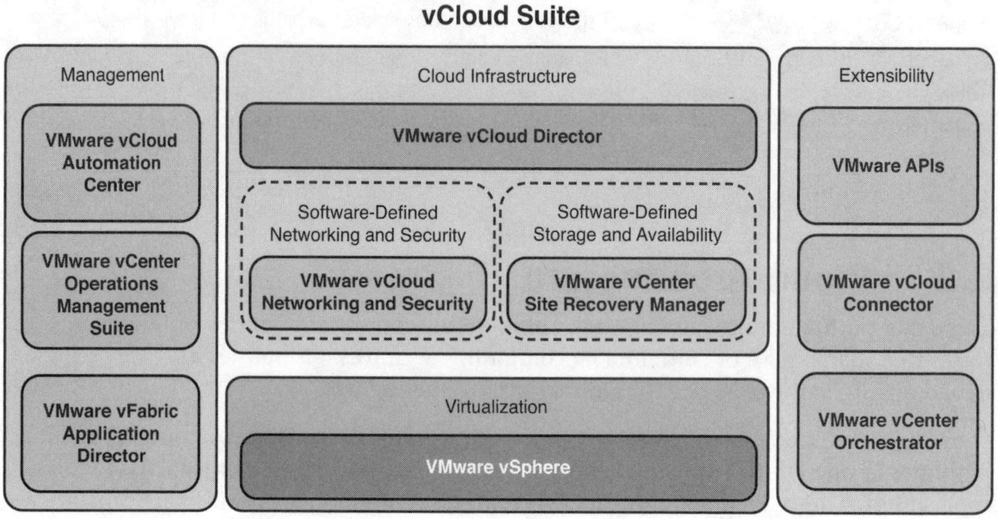

FIGURE 3.1 Technology mapping

3.2.2 vCloud Suite Components

Table 3.2 describes the components that comprise the vCloud Suite.

TABLE 3.2 vCloud Components

vCloud Component	Description
VMware vCloud Director vCloud API	Layer of software that abstracts virtual resources and exposes vCloud components to consumers. This includes: ▶ vCloud Director server (also referred to as a cell) ▶ vCloud Director database VMware vCloud API, used to manage vCloud objects programmatically.
VMware vCloud Automation Center	Enables rapid deployment and provisioning of vCloud services across private and public vClouds, physical infrastructures, hypervisors, and public vCloud providers through a secure self-service portal.

vCloud Component	Description
VMware vSphere	Virtualization platform providing abstraction of physical infrastructure layer for vCloud. This includes: ▶ vSphere hosts ▶ VMware vCenter Server™ ▶ vCenter Server database
VMware vCloud Networking and Security	Decouples network and security from the underlying physical network hardware through software-defined networking and security. This includes: ▶ VXLAN support ▶ vCloud Networking and Security Edge™ gateway ▶ vCloud Networking and Security App™ and vCloud Networking and Security Data Security™ ▶ vCloud Networking and Security Manager™
VMware vCenter Operations Management Suite	Provides predictive capacity and performance planning, compliance and configuration management, dynamic resource metering, cost modeling, and report generation using the following components: ▶ vCenter Operations Manager™ ▶ vCenter Configuration Manager™ ▶ vCenter Infrastructure Navigator™ ▶ vCenter Chargeback Manager™
VMware vFabric Application Director	Part of the VMware vFabric Cloud Application Platform family of products that provide automated provisioning of application infrastructure.
VMware vCenter Orchestrator™	Enables the automation of provisioning and operational tasks across VMware and third-party applications using an open and flexible plug-in architecture.
vCloud Connector	VMware vSphere Client™ plug-in that enables users to connect to vClouds based on vSphere or vCloud Director and manage them through a single interface.

Figure 3.2 shows the relationships among vCloud Suite components. Components that touch are integrated with each other.

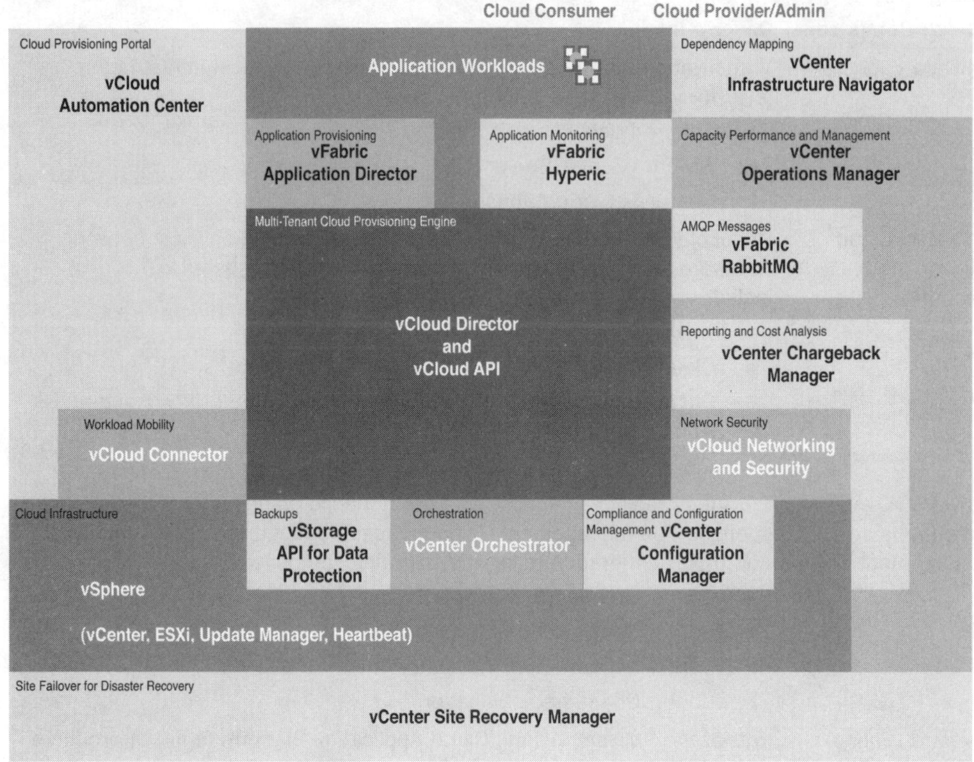

FIGURE 3.2 vCloud Suite components

3.2.3 vCloud Infrastructure Logical Design

When architecting a VMware vCloud infrastructure logical design, VMware recommends using a *building* block approach to provide a scalable, resilient architecture. The following top-level logical building blocks segregate resources that are allocated for management functions from resources dedicated to user-requested workloads (see Figure 3.3).

- **vSphere virtual management cluster:** Contains the core and optional components and services needed to run the vCloud instance. This includes core vCloud components such as VMware vCenter Server, vCloud Director, vCenter Chargeback Manager, and vCenter Orchestrator; and optional components such as the vCenter Operations Management Suite and vFabric Application Director.

- **Resource group:** Represents vCloud-dedicated resources for end-user consumption. Each resource group consists of vSphere clusters (vSphere hosts managed by a vCenter Server) and is under the control of vCloud Director. vCloud Director can manage the resources of multiple resource groups.

Separate management and resource clusters are important for the following reasons:

- **Separation of duties:** A vCloud infrastructure typically has at least two types of administrator: infrastructure (vSphere) administrator and vCloud administrator. Separating the virtual management cluster from resource groups allows separation of duties and enforcement of administrative boundaries, limiting the actions that can be performed in the vSphere clusters of a resource group.

  An administrator should not perform the following actions on a resource group through the vSphere Client:

    - Editing virtual machine properties
- Renaming virtual machines
- Disabling VMware vSphere Distributed Resource Scheduler™ (DRS)
- Deleting or renaming resource pools
- Changing networking properties
- Renaming datastores
    - Changing or renaming folders

  This is not an exhaustive list, but it covers some of the detrimental actions a vCenter administrator could perform on a vCloud resource group.

- **Resource consumption:** Virtual machines deployed into resource groups that are not managed by vCloud Director consume resources that are allocated for a particular vCloud virtual datacenter. This skews the resource utilization and consumption metrics available to the vCloud.
- **Scalability and configuration maximums:** Having separate vSphere clusters to manage compute resources that end users consume increases resource group scalability. A vCloud environment must conform to vSphere scalability and configuration maximums. Having dedicated resource group vSphere clusters means that management workloads do not affect the scalability of vCloud user resources.
- **Availability:** A virtual management cluster allows the use of VMware vSphere high availability (HA) and DRS to provide enhanced availability to all management components. A separate management cluster enables this protection in a granular fashion to satisfy management-specific SLAs. It also increases upgrade flexibility because management cluster upgrades are not tied to resource group upgrades.
- **Denial-of-service attacks or intensive provisioning:** Having separate management clusters and resource groups keeps this type of activity on the resource groups from affecting management component availability.
- **Disaster recovery facilitation:** Having separate management clusters and resource groups simplifies design and implementation of vCloud disaster recovery. The vCloud disaster recovery solution uses a vSphere cluster managed by vCenter Site Recovery Manager that contains the vCloud infrastructure management components. For more information, see Appendix C, "vCloud Suite Disaster Recovery."

- **Support and troubleshooting:** Running management components in large clusters that contain mixed resource and management components makes it difficult to diagnose issues with the management components. To facilitate troubleshooting and problem resolution, place the management components in a small and manageable cluster.
- **Separation of management components from managed resources:** Separation helps prevent inadvertent changes through the vSphere Client to entities created with vCloud Director.

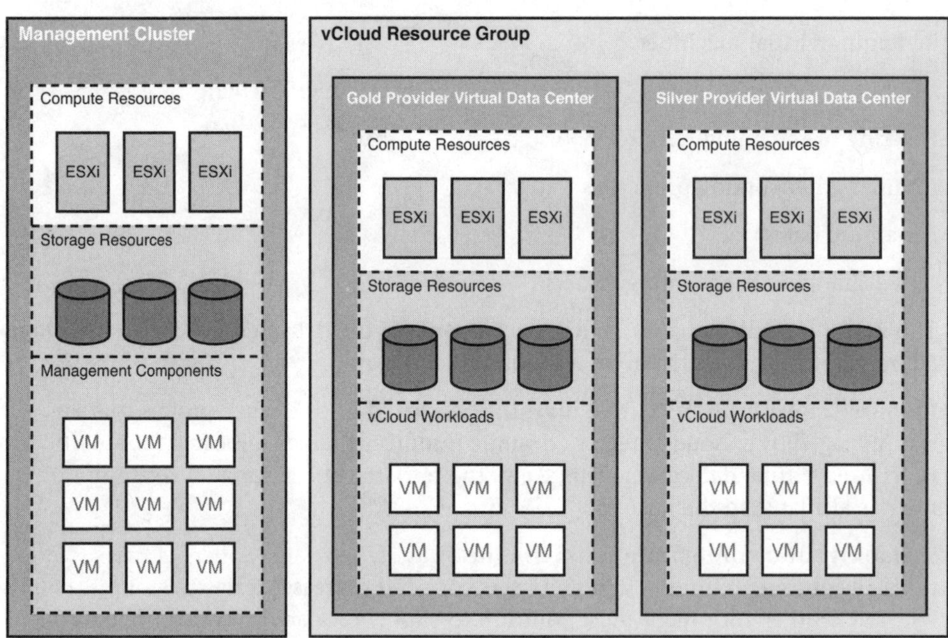

FIGURE 3.3 vCloud logical architecture overview

Achieving economies of scale means scaling vCloud resources in a consistent and predictable manner. Follow recommended practices when deploying the underlying vSphere infrastructure and other vCloud components.

3.3 vCloud Management Architecture

The design and architecture of the vCloud management infrastructure is critical to support availability and scalability of the vCloud solution.

3.3.1 Management Cluster

The management cluster hosts the necessary vCloud infrastructure components. Separating infrastructure components from resources used for end-user workloads improves manageability of the vCloud infrastructure. Figure 3.4 shows the management cluster separate from the resource groups that run the workloads.

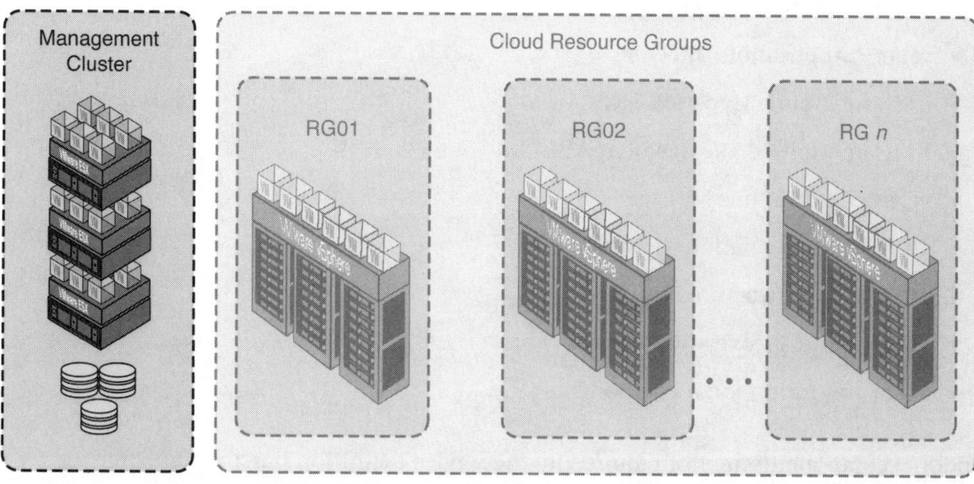

FIGURE 3.4 vCloud management cluster

Core management cluster components include the following:

- vCenter Server or VMware vCenter Server Appliance™
- vCenter Server database
- vCloud Director cells
- vCloud Director database
- vCloud Networking and Security Manager (one per resource group vCenter Server)
- vCenter Chargeback Manager
- vCenter Chargeback database
- VMware vCenter Update Manager™
- vCenter Orchestrator
- VMware vCloud Networking and Security Edge gateway appliances deployed by vCloud Director through vCloud Networking and Security Manager as needed, residing in the resource groups, not in the management cluster

The following management cluster components are optional:

- VMware vCenter Server Heartbeat™
- vCloud Automation Center
- vCloud Connector
- VMware vFabric RabbitMQ™
- vFabric Application Director
- VMware vFabric Hyperic® HQ
- VMware vSphere Management Assistant
- vCenter Operations Manager
- vCenter Configuration Manager
- vCenter Infrastructure Navigator
- vCenter Site Recovery Manager
- Databases for optional components

Optional components are not required by the service definition but are highly recommended to increase the operational efficiency of the solution.

The management cluster can also include virtual machines or have access to servers that provide infrastructure services such as directory (LDAP), timekeeping (NTP), networking (DNS, DHCP), logging (syslog), and security. See Chapter 2, "Service Definitions," for detailed sizing considerations.

Component databases, if running on the same platform, can be placed on the same properly sized database server. For example, the databases that vCloud Director, vCenter Server, and vCenter Chargeback Manager use can run on the same database server with separate database instances for each component.

Both the management cluster and resource groups reside at the same physical site to provide a consistent level of service. This minimizes latency issues that might arise in a multisite environment if workloads move between sites over a slower or less reliable network. See Section 3.8, "Multisite Considerations," for factors associated with connecting vCloud instances at different sites.

3.3.1.1 Component Sizing

Table 3.3 lists the requirements for each of the components that run in the management cluster. The following recommendations scale to accommodate the number of virtual machines and organizations listed in the private or public service definitions.

TABLE 3.3 Component Requirements for a Management Cluster

Item	vCPU	Memory	Storage	Networking
vCenter Server	2	4GB	20GB	1GigE
Database server	4	16GB	100GB	1GigE
vCloud Director cell 1	2	4GB	30GB	1GigE
vCloud Director cell 2	2	4GB	30GB	1GigE
vCenter Chargeback Manager	2	4GB	30GB	1GigE
vCloud Networking and Security Manager	2	8GB	8GB	100Mb
Total	14	40GB	218GB*	4GigE*

** Numbers rounded up or down do not affect overall sizing.*

The database server hosts databases for vCenter Server, VMware vCenter Single Sign-On, vCloud Director, and vCenter Chargeback Manager. Use different users and instances for each database based on VMware design guidelines. VMware vCloud Director 5.1 supports both Oracle and Microsoft SQL Server databases.

To facilitate file transfers in a multicell environment, a shared storage volume must be configured and made accessible to all cells in a vCloud Director server group. The necessary volume size varies based on the expected number of concurrent uploads. Following an upload, the vApp data moves to the designated organization virtual datacenter, and the data no longer resides on the NFS volume. The recommended starting size for the NFS transfer volume is 250GB. Transferred images can be large, so monitor this volume and increase the size, if necessary.

For additional installation prerequisites, see the *vCloud Director Installation and Upgrade Guide* in the vCloud Director documentation (www.vmware.com/support/pubs/vcd_pubs.html).

3.3.2 Compute Layer

The management cluster (see Figure 3.5) compute layer encompasses the CPU, memory, and hypervisor technology components. Follow vSphere design guidelines when configuring and sizing compute resources.

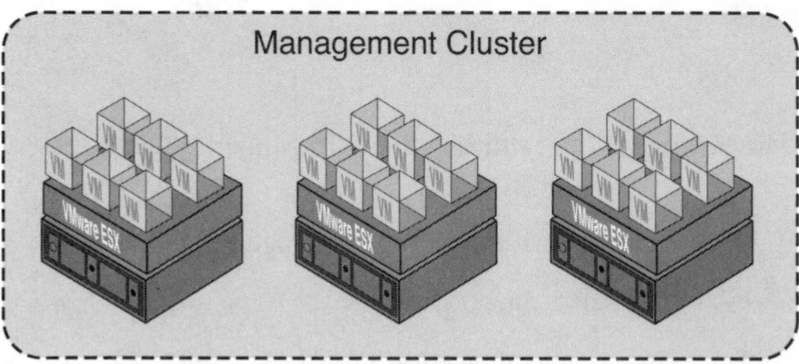

FIGURE 3.5 Three-host management cluster

Use a three-host cluster to support vCloud management components. Add hosts if the management cluster becomes resource constrained.

Enable VMware vSphere High Availability and DRS on the management cluster to provide availability for all management components. For vSphere HA, use the Percentage As Cluster Resources Reserved admission control policy in an n+1 fashion instead of defining the number of host failures a cluster can tolerate or specifying failover hosts. This allows management workloads to run evenly across the hosts in the cluster without the need to dedicate a host strictly for host failure situations. For higher availability, you can add a host for an n+2 cluster.

The vCloud Director–managed vCenter Server instances play an integral role in end-user, self-service provisioning by handling all virtual machine deployment requests from vCloud Director. VMware recommends increasing the availability of vCenter Server using solutions such as VMware vCenter Server Heartbeat.

VMware vSphere Fault Tolerance can be used for continuous virtual machine protection only if all FT requirements are met. vCenter Site Recovery Manager can protect components of the management cluster against site failure. See Appendix C for details.

vCloud Director 5.1 supports vSphere 5.0 and later. Deploy vSphere 5.1, if possible, to take advantage of the new features. Some functionality in vCloud Director requires specific features and requires particular vSphere editions. For example, automated deployment of vCloud networks requires a distributed switch, which VMware vSphere Enterprise Plus Edition™ supports.

3.3.3 Network Layer

The following design guidelines apply to network configuration for the management cluster:

- Separate network traffic logically for security and load according to traffic type (management, virtual machine, VMware vSphere vMotion®, FT, IP storage).
- Implement network component and path redundancy.
- Implement network speeds of least 1GigE to 10GigE, if possible.
- Standardize on VMware vSphere Distributed Switch™ across all clusters, including the management cluster.

3.3.4 Storage Layer

Use vSphere storage design guidelines where applicable for the management cluster. Examples include the following:

- Configure redundancy at the host (connector), switch, and storage array levels.
- Give all hosts in a cluster access to the same datastores.
- Enable VMware vSphere Storage APIs—Array Integration (VAAI).
- Use single-initiator storage fabric zoning for vSphere hosts.

3.3.5 vCenter Linked Mode

vCenter linked mode provides a *single pane of glass* to allow a common administrative state to manage multiple vCenter instances. With linked mode configured, users can view and manage the inventories of all participating vCenter Server systems. Tasks invoked on a linked mode object are executed by the vCenter Server that manages the corresponding resource. Linked mode in the vCloud Director context allows viewing of all vCenter Servers that manage vCloud resources.

vCloud Director maximums for powered-on virtual machines and registered virtual machines are substantially less than the vCenter linked mode maximums. The number of linked mode objects in a vCloud environment does not reach the linked mode maximums unless multiple vCloud instances are involved.

Additional considerations include the following:

- The vCenter Server appliance does not support linked mode.
- A vCenter instance can link only with other vCenter instances of the same version. Keep this in mind when upgrading all vCenter Server instances in a vCloud instance.
- Upgrading a linked vCenter instance breaks the link, and the instance becomes independent.

3.3.6 Cell Load Balancing

vCloud Director cells are stateless front-end processors for the vCloud instance. Each cell self-manages various functions among cells while connecting to a central database. The cell manages connectivity to the vCloud and provides API and UI endpoints, or clients.

To improve availability and scale, implement a vCloud Director server group with multiple vCloud Director cells. A multicell configuration requires load balancing or content switching of the front-end portal. Load balancers present a consistent address for services, regardless of the underlying responding node. They can spread session load across cells, monitor cell health, and add or remove cells from the active service pool. The cell architecture is not a true cluster because no failover takes place from one cell to another.

Any load balancer that supports SSL session persistence with network connectivity to the public-facing Internet or internal service network, such as the vCloud Networking and Security Edge gateway, can perform load balancing of vCloud Director cells. See the general design guidelines regarding performance, security, and manageability when deciding to share or dedicate load-balancing resources.

NOTE

SSL offloading does not work with virtual machine remote console (VMRC) proxy connections.

See Appendix A, "Availability Considerations."

3.3.7 vCenter Operations Manager

An embedded adaptor handles integration between vCloud Director and vCenter Operations Manager. The vCloud Director Adapter discovers and creates the mapping for the following vCloud entities:

- Organization
- Provider virtual datacenter
- Organization virtual datacenter
- vApp

After the mapping is performed, vCloud Director objects can be incorporated into vCenter Operations dashboards. Optionally, the adapter can import change events related to vCloud entities.

For details on installing and configuring the adapter, see the *VMware vCloud Director Adapter Installation and Configuration Guide* (ftp://ftp.integrien.com/VCOPS-VMware_Product_Adapters/VMware-vCD/vCloud-Director-Adapter-Install-and-Config-Guide.pdf).

3.4 Resource Group Architecture

A *resource group* (see Figure 3.6) is a set of resources dedicated to end-user workloads and managed by a single vCenter Server. vCloud Director manages the resources of all attached resource group vCenter Server instances. All provisioning tasks are initiated through vCloud Director and are passed down to the appropriate vCenter Server instance.

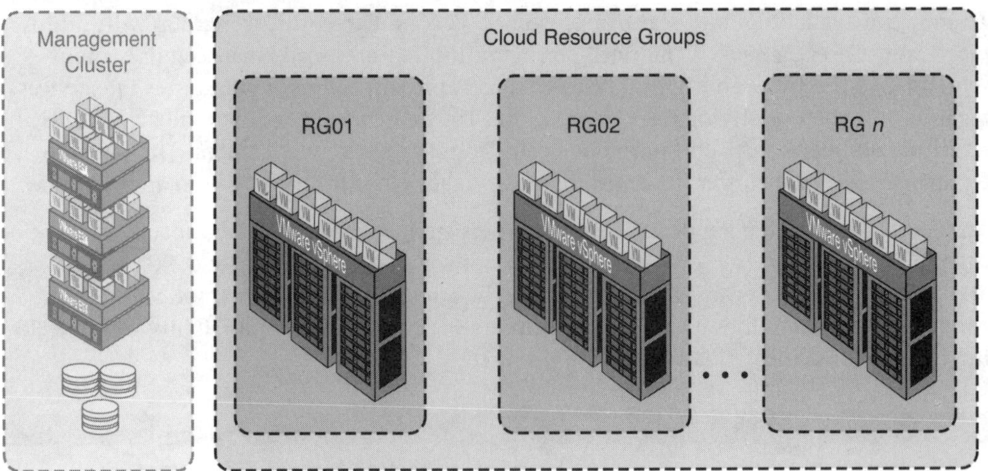

FIGURE 3.6 vCloud resource groups

Provisioning resources in standardized groupings provides a consistent approach for scaling vCloud environments. A separate vCenter Server instance is recommended to manage cloud resource groups. At a minimum, place all vCloud resource workloads in a separate cluster if you are using a single vCenter Server to manage both management components and cloud resource groups.

CAUTION

Do *not* make changes to resource group objects using the vSphere Client. Changing the state of vCloud Director–created objects using the vSphere Client can cause unpredictable side effects because vCloud Director owns these objects.

3.4.1 Compute Resources

Configure resource group vSphere hosts per vSphere design guidelines. Enable vSphere HA appropriately to protect against host and virtual machine failures.

The shift to Fault Domain Manager (FDM)–based HA in vSphere 5 is transparent to vCloud Director. The total number of hosts in an HA/DRS cluster remains at 32, so cluster sizing guidelines for vCloud environments do not change. FDM requires a single master host instead of five primary nodes for legacy HA. If the master host fails, the remaining slave hosts select a new master.

The eight hosts per cluster limitation for fast provisioning (linked clones) and VMFS datastores does not apply to vSphere 5.1–backed resource groups. Fast provisioning on VMFS5 datastores supports up to 32 hosts.

Provider virtual datacenters represent a service offering. When building clusters, group similar servers together (based on number of hosts, number of cores, amount of memory, CPU type) to support differentiation of compute resources by capacity or performance.

3.4.1.1 Stateless ESXi

Stateless ESXi refers to running VMware ESXi™ software on a host entirely in memory, with no local persistence data. Centralizing management of the host state enables consistent configuration over large sets of similar hosts and rapid provisioning of vSphere hosts. This helps improve operational efficiency in large-scale vCloud environments.

Stateless ESXi requires VMware vSphere Auto Deploy™, a deployment server that applies the image profile and host profile to the PXE-booted hosts. Install vSphere Auto Deploy on a standalone host or on the vCenter Server instance. vSphere Auto Deploy is installed by default on the vCenter Server virtual appliance. Install VMware vSphere PowerCLI™ in a location that vCenter and vSphere Auto Deploy can both reach. The host profile is essential to the stateless environment because every reboot of a server clears the host of any local configuration data.

Configure all stateless vSphere hosts for DHCP. The DHCP server requires configuration changes to direct the vSphere host to a TFTP server. The server can be a separate DHCP server or can be the organization's DHCP server. The vCenter Server virtual appliance includes DHCP and TFTP services.

Identify an image profile to use for vCloud hosts. This can be a profile stored in a public depot or a zipped file stored locally. If using host profiles, save a copy of the host profile to a location accessible by vSphere Auto Deploy, and add rules to the rules engine using VMware vSphere® ESXi™ Image Builder CLI.

Figure 3.7 shows the autodeploy steps during initial boot.

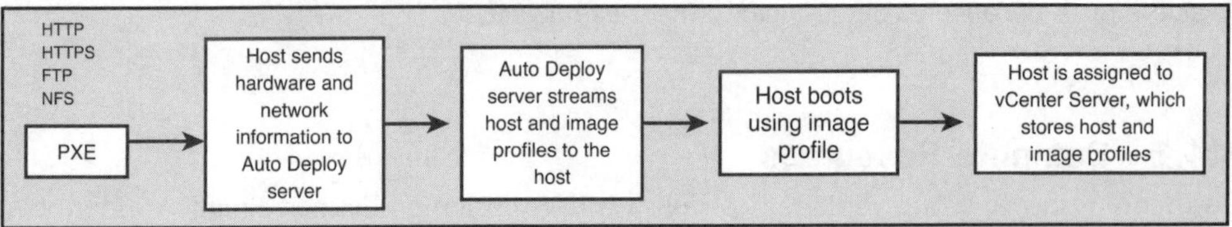

FIGURE 3.7 Auto Deploy first boot

vCloud Director can manage stateful or stateless vSphere hosts. If you choose the stateless option, add the vCloud Director vSphere Installation Bundle (VIB) (which contains the agent) to the image profile. The vCloud Director VIB loads automatically when the host boots up. For preparation and unpreparation of stateless hosts, vCloud Director configures the agent using a host profile with an associated answer file.

If the host is rebooted, the appropriate image profile is reloaded when the host starts back up. vCloud Director detects the state change, and the configuration is pushed again to the host.

If using stateless mode, avoid creating designs that require host-specific configuration. When converting a prepared stateful host to stateless, unprepare hosts before the conversion.

3.4.2 Network Resources

For the vCloud resource groups, configure networking with vSphere design guidelines in mind. Increase the number of vSphere Distributed Switch ports per host to the maximum of 4,096, to improve the scale at which vCloud Director can dynamically create port groups for vCloud networks. For more information about increasing this value, see the *vCenter Server and Host Management Guide* in the VMware vSphere documentation (www.vmware.com/support/pubs/vsphere-esxi-vcenter-server-pubs.html).

Increase the maximum transmission unit (MTU) size to 1600 for all physical network devices and vSphere Distributed Switches in the transport network to support VXLAN or vCloud Director network isolation. Failure to increase the MTU size causes packet fragmentation, negatively affecting throughput of end-user workloads.

Section 3.5, "vCloud Resource Design," covers vCloud networking considerations.

3.4.2.1 I/O Controls

vCloud Director offers the following controls to guard against the misuse of resources by consumers:

- Quotas for running and stored virtual machines determine how many virtual machines each user in the organization can store and power on in the organization's virtual datacenters. The quotas act as the default for all new users added to the organization.
- Limits for resource-intensive operations prevent consumers from affecting all users in an organization and provide a defense against denial-of-service attacks.
- Limit the number of simultaneous VMRC connections for performance or security reasons.

3.4.2.2 IPv6

Internet Protocol version 6 (IPv6) is the latest version of IP addressing, designed to succeed IPv4 as the standard protocol for the Internet. A key driver for transitioning to IPv6 is the much larger supported address space of 2^{64} addresses, as opposed to the 2^{32} addresses for IPv4.

The following vCloud Director components are required to support IPv6:

- Static IP pools
- DHCP server
- Static IP assignments
- NAT rules
- Firewall rules

The following vSphere infrastructure components support IPv6:

- vCenter Server
- ESXi
- vSwitches (standard and distributed)
- VMkernel
- vSphere vMotion
- Virtual machines (guest customization available for Windows and Linux)

vSphere virtual machines support IPv6 addressing and can be configured with the following components:

- Static IPv6 address
- Autoconfigure, using a prefix announcement from a router

- DHCP, from a DHCP6 server
- Local network addresses, for internal communication

vCloud Network and Security Edge does not currently support IPv6. Virtual machines that vCloud Director manages using IPv6 can communicate only to endpoints that are not behind vCloud Network and Security Edge devices. Virtual machines that communicate on the same directly attached vApp or organization virtual datacenter network can use IPv6. To communicate with the outside world using IPv6, connect the organization's virtual machines to a direct external organization virtual datacenter network.

Many destinations do not currently support IPv6, so operate virtual machines in dual-stack IPv4 and IPv6.

If the underlying physical infrastructure does not support IPv6, another option is to establish a *6-to-4 tunnel* using a router to provide connectivity into an IPv6 vCloud. Terminate the tunnel on a relay router that has a pure IPv6 interface as well as an IPv4 interface to move traffic between the two environments.

vCloud Director does not support IPv6 addressing for the cell network interfaces.

3.4.2.3 Virtual eXtensible LAN (VXLAN)

Virtual eXtensible LAN (VXLAN) is an IETF-submitted protocol that uses an encapsulation mechanism to enable Layer 2 overlay on Layer 3 networks. VXLAN supports elastic virtual datacenters across different networks.

VXLAN is designed to be deployed seamlessly on existing networks, requiring few changes on the physical network. VXLAN requires deployment of IP multicast across the physical network infrastructure by enabling IGMP (v1, v2, and v3) snooping on physical switches and PIM for multicast routing.

3.4.2.4 vCloud Networking and Security Edge

VMware vCloud Networking and Security Edge is a virtual firewall router that provides the perimeter security needed to support multitenancy. vCloud Networking and Security Edge devices deploy automatically when routed or isolated organization or vApp networks are created from vCloud Director. For vApp networks, vCloud Networking and Security Edge devices dynamically deploy and undeploy based on the power state of the vApp.

The license for vCloud Networking and Security Edge that is included with vCloud Director does not include features such as SSLVPN and load balancing capabilities, which are part of the fully licensed VMware vCloud Networking and Security Advanced Edition.

3.4.2.5 vCloud Networking and Security App

VMware vCloud Networking and Security App is a hypervisor-based, vNIC-level application firewall that controls and monitors all flows between virtual machines in a virtual datacenter. Firewall policies can be applied to vCenter security groups, which are custom containers created through the vCloud Networking and Security Manager UI. Container policies allow the creation of mixed trust zone clusters without requiring an external physical firewall. vCloud Networking and Security App also supports classic five tuple firewall rules.

3.4.2.6 vShield Endpoint

VMware vShield Endpoint offloads antivirus functions to a hardened security virtual machine supplied by partners such as Trend Micro. vShield Endpoint uses VMware endpoint security (EPSEC) APIs to access the file system to scan and remediate viruses. This removes the need for agents in the guest operating system and prevents antivirus storms from consuming CPU cycles during scanning or antivirus update activities. Offloading antivirus functions provides enhanced security because a malware attack often begins by disabling antivirus agents. The efficient antivirus architecture of vShield Endpoint provides antivirus as a service for large-scale vCloud environments.

3.4.2.7 vCloud Networking and Security Data Security

VMware vCloud Networking and Security Data Security™ provides visibility into sensitive data stored within your organization's virtualized and vCloud environments. Violations data that vCloud Networking and Security Data Security reports can provide information needed to protect sensitive data and achieve regulatory compliance.

NOTE

Currently, vCloud Director 5.1 is not integrated with vCloud Network and Security App, vCloud Networking and Security Data Security, or vShield Endpoint. Using these features in conjunction with vCloud Director requires careful design of the vCloud infrastructure.

3.4.3 Storage Resources

Designing storage resources for vCloud differs from the traditional vSphere approach. Platform features such as VMware vSphere Storage DRS™ and storage profiles assist in balancing workloads across storage resources, enabling providers to offer differentiated storage. This allows the provisioning of flexible pools of storage resources while maintaining consistent performance for end users. Users can choose the right storage tier for a particular type of workload.

VMware recommends the following when designing storage resources:

- Perform a current state analysis for storage usage and trends.
- Define the range of storage SLAs needed and appropriate pricing models.
- Create multiple storage profiles in vSphere, based on SLAs, workloads, and cost.
- Map storage profiles to the provider virtual datacenter.
- Select a subset of storage profiles supplied by the provider virtual datacenter to the organization virtual datacenter.
- Design for optimal availability (redundant paths from vSphere hosts to storage fabric).
- Deploy modular and scalable physical storage.
- Monitor storage usage and trends using capacity analysis tools.
- Use storage performance tools to tune vApp storage workloads.

vCloud Director supports tiering storage within a virtual datacenter using storage profiles. Configure shared storage and storage profiles in the resource groups per vSphere design guidelines.

Datastore sizing considerations include both capacity and performance:

- Datastore capacity considerations:
  - What is the optimal size for datastores based on the physical storage and vCloud workload expectations?
  - What is the average vApp size × number of vApps × spare capacity? For example, *average virtual machine size* × *number of virtual machines* × *(1+ % headroom)*.
  - What is the average virtual machine disk size?
  - On average, how many virtual machines are in a vApp?
  - What is the expected number of virtual machines?
  - How much reserved spare capacity is needed for growth?
  - Will expected workloads be transient or static?
  - Is fast provisioning used?
- Datastore performance considerations:
  - Will expected workloads be disk intensive?
  - What are the performance characteristics of the associated cluster?

NOTE

vCloud Director does not support raw device mapping (RDM).

3.4.3.1 Storage Tiering

Storage tiering in vCloud Director 5.1 is enabled on a per-virtual-machine basis through storage profiles:

- Authoring, renaming, and deletion of storage profiles is performed through vSphere.
- Storage profiles can be added, disabled, or removed at the provider virtual datacenter level.
- All available storage profiles across selected clusters are listed at provider virtual datacenter creation.
- Organization virtual datacenter storage profiles are based on a subset of storage profiles supplied by the provider virtual datacenter.

- Each organization virtual datacenter has an associated default storage profile.
- All virtual machines have an associated storage profile that defaults to the organization virtual datacenter storage profile.
- Virtual machine placement is based on storage profiles.

Other entities that support storage profiles include these:

- Templates
- Media
- Independent disks

Support for OVF storage profiles:

- vSphere does not export storage profile association when exporting a virtual machine to OVF.
- vCloud Director template download exports a template virtual machine's default instantiation profile.
- vCloud Director template upload applies the OVF-specified template virtual machine's default instantiation profile.

Disks independent of virtual machine have these characteristics:

- Are associated with an organization virtual datacenter storage profile
- Allow selection of datastore to place the disk accounts for storage profile
- Can have their storage profile changed
- Are allowed to be on a different storage profile than the virtual machine to which the disk is attached

The following vSphere changes affect vCloud Director storage profiles:

- Changed datastore labels
- Deleted storage profiles
- Changed virtual machine storage profile association
- Virtual machine migration to a new datastore using VMware vSphere Storage vMotion

Storage profile compliance checks are performed in these cases:

- When initiated through the REST API
- When automatically performed at set time intervals
- When a storage profile in use by an organization virtual datacenter is deleted in vCenter

- When a virtual machine is migrated using vSphere Storage vMotion

Noncompliance shows up in the form of system alerts on the virtual machine.

3.4.3.2 vSphere Storage vMotion

vSphere Storage vMotion enables live migration of virtual machine disk files between and across shared storage locations. Relocating vApp disks is possible using the vCloud API or the vSphere Client if the following conditions apply:

- The target datastore is part of the same organization virtual datacenter as the vApp.
- All virtual disks for an individual virtual machine are migrated to the same datastore.
- The vCloud API is used to initiate vSphere Storage vMotion for linked clones to preserve the linked clone state.

CAUTION

Do not invoke vSphere Storage vMotion migration of linked clones using the vSphere Client because doing so might cause undesirable effects such as the inflation of delta disks. A vSphere Storage vMotion operation involving a datastore *and* host might fail.

3.4.3.3 Storage I/O Control

Storage I/O control (SIOC) manages storage resources across hosts through storage device latency monitoring and disk shares that are enforced at the datastore level. Preventing imbalances of storage resource allocation during times of contention protects virtual machine performance in highly consolidated, virtualized environments.

Enabling SIOC on all datastores in a cluster results in lower worst-case device latency by maintaining a balance between workload isolation/prioritization and storage I/O throughput. For more information, see Storage I/O Control Technical Overview and Considerations for Deployment (www.vmware.com/files/pdf/techpaper/VMW-vSphere41-SIOC.pdf).

SIOC does not support raw device mapping (RDM) or datastores with multiple extents. If you are using datastores backed by arrays with automated storage tiering, validate compatibility with SIOC.

3.4.3.4 vSphere Storage APIs—Array Integration

vSphere Storage APIs—Array Integration (VAAI) is a set of protocol interfaces between ESXi and storage arrays. These ESXi extensions enable storage-based hardware acceleration by allowing vSphere to pass storage primitives to supported arrays.

In vCloud environments, cloning and snapshot operations stemming from provisioning tasks can quickly overwhelm the system. VAAI improves storage task execution times, network traffic utilization, and CPU host utilization during heavy storage operations.

For block-based storage systems, array integration extensions are implemented as T10 SCSI–based commands. Devices that support the T10 SCSI standard do not require a VAAI plug-in to offload storage functions such as full copy, block zeroing, and locking.

Hardware acceleration for NAS is enabled through the installation of vendor plug-ins. VAAI NAS plug-ins are developed by storage vendors and validated by VMware.

vCloud Director 5.1 supports the following offload through VAAI integration:

- **Block (FC, iSCSI):** Full-copy offload to array (ESXi 4.1 or later, with supported storage array firmware listed in the *VMware Compatibility Guide*)
- **NFS:** Full-copy offload to array (ESXi 5.0 or later only, with vendor-supplied VIB [Virtual Infrastructure Bundle] installed on ESXi server)
- **NFS:** Linked clone offload to array for storage arrays supporting clones of clones

See the *VMware Compatibility Guide* (www.vmware.com/resources/compatibility/search.php) for more details.

3.4.3.5 vSphere Storage DRS

vSphere Storage DRS provides initial placement and ongoing balancing recommendations for datastores in a vSphere Storage DRS-enabled *datastore cluster*. A datastore cluster represents an aggregation of datastore resources, analogous to clusters and hosts.

- vCloud Director 5.1 supports vSphere Storage DRS when using vSphere 5.1 hosts. vSphere Storage DRS also supports fast provisioning (linked clones) in vCloud Director 5.1.
- vSphere Storage DRS continuously balances storage space usage and storage I/O load, avoiding resource bottlenecks to meet service levels and increase manageability of storage at scale.
- vCloud Director 5.1 recognizes storage clusters. The member datastore clusters are visible in vCloud Director but cannot be modified from vCloud Director.
- vCloud Director 5.1 utilizes vSphere Storage DRS for initial placement of virtual machines.
- vCloud Director uses vSphere Storage DRS to manage space utilization and I/O load balancing. vSphere Storage DRS can help rebalance virtual machines, media, and virtual machine disks within the storage pod.
- As in vCloud Director 1.x, vCloud Director 5.1 determines optimal placement between datastore clusters and standalone datastores across all vSphere instances assigned within vCloud Director.
- The REST API has a new VIM object type, named `DATASTORE_CLUSTER`. The datastore properties now include the member datastore list when the VIM object type is `DATASTORE_CLUSTER`.

3.4.3.5.1 vSphere Storage DRS and Fast Provisioning

- vSphere Storage DRS supports fast provisioning in vCloud Director.
- vSphere Storage DRS supports linked clones only with vCloud Director 5.1.
- vCloud Director 5.1 does not support linked clone configurations that span datastores.
  - vSphere Storage DRS does not recommend placement of a linked clone that would span datastores from the base disk.
  - vSphere Storage DRS migrates a clone to a datastore containing a shadow virtual machine and relinks the clone to the existing shadow virtual machine.
- Linked clones can be migrated between VMFS3 and VMFS5 and are supported in vSphere Storage DRS. The format conversions are handled automatically at the platform level.
- The logic for migrating a virtual machine is influenced by factors such as the following:
  - Amount of data being moved
  - Amount of space reduction in the source datastore
  - Amount of additional space on the destination datastore
- Linked clone decisions also depend on whether the destination datastore has a copy of a base disk or whether a shadow virtual machine must be instantiated:
  - Putting a linked clone on a datastore without the base disk results in more space used on the datastore, as opposed to placing the clone on a disk where a shadow virtual machine already exists.
  - During the initial placement, vSphere Storage DRS selects a datastore that contains a shadow virtual machine so that placement results in maximum space savings. If necessary, initial placement recommendations can include evacuating existing virtual machines from the destination datastore.
- If a datastore that already contains the base or a shadow virtual machine is not available, vCloud Director makes a full clone to create a shadow virtual machine in a selected datastore and then makes linked clones in the selected datastore.
- The latest model in vSphere Storage DRS takes linked clone sharing into account when calculating the effects of potential moves.
- Linked clones and virtual machines that are not linked clones can reside on the same datastores.

3.4.3.5.2 vSphere Storage DRS Limitations

- vCloud Director does not support the creation, deletion, or modification of storage pods. These tasks must be performed at the vSphere level.
- vCloud Director does not support member datastore operations.
- Enabling vSphere Storage DRS for the datastore clusters used with vCloud Director is not supported if vSphere hosts are pre–vSphere 5.1.

3.4.4 vCloud Resource Sizing

Resource sizing for a vCloud depends on the corresponding service definition. A private vCloud service definition might not explicitly call out a required number of workloads to support. In this case, use the initial sizing for a public vCloud as guidance.

For a public vCloud, initial sizing for the vCloud consumer resources can be difficult to predict because of a lack of data points on expected consumer uptake. The provider is also not aware of existing usage statistics for vCloud workloads.

The sizing examples in the next sections come from Chapter 2 and can assist with the initial sizing of the vCloud environment.

NOTE

Contact your local VMware representative for detailed sizing of your vCloud environment.

3.4.4.1 Public vCloud Sizing Example

The service definition states that 50% of the virtual machines use the reservation pool model and 50% use the pay as you go allocation model. The model is applied to small, medium, and large pools with a respective split of 75%, 20%, and 5%. Therefore, *small* represents 37.5% of the total, *medium* represents 10% of the total, and *large* represents 2.5% of the total number of virtual machines in the environment.

Table 3.4 lists the virtual machine counts for the various virtual datacenters. The total virtual machine count of 1,500 reflects the specifications outlined in Chapter 2 for the public vCloud service definition. Change this total to reflect your own target virtual machine count.

TABLE 3.4 Definition of Resource Pool and Virtual Machine Split

Type of Resource Pool	Total Percentage	Total Virtual Machines
Pay as you go	50%	750
Small reservation pool	37.5%	563*
Medium reservation pool	10%	150
Large reservation pool	2.5%	37*
Total	100%	1,500

NOTE

Some total virtual machine values are rounded up or down because of percentages.

Chapter 2 also calls out the distribution for virtual machines in the vCloud, with 45% small, 35% medium, 15% large, and 5% extra large. Table 3.5 shows the total amount of CPU, memory, storage, and networking needed.

TABLE 3.5 Memory, CPU, Storage, and Networking

Item	# of Virtual Machines	Percent	vCPU	Memory	Storage	Networking
Small	675	45%	675	675GB	40.5TB	400Gb
Medium	525	35%	1,050	1,050GB	31.5TB	300Gb
Large	225	15%	900	900GB	54TB	400Gb
Extra Large	75	5%	600	600GB	4.5TB	200Gb
Total	1500	100%	3,225	3,225GB	130.5	1,300Gb

Before determining your final sizing numbers, refer to VMware design guidelines for common consolidation ratios. Table 3.6 shows what the final numbers might look like using typical consolidation ratios seen in field deployments.

TABLE 3.6 Example Consolidation Ratios

Resource	Before	Ratio	After
CPU	3,225	8:1	403 vCPUs
Memory	3,225GB	1.6:1	2,016GB
Storage	130.5TB	2.5:1	52TB
Network	1,300Gb	6:1	217Gb

Sixteen hosts with the following configuration can support the required capacity:

- Socket count: 4
- Core count: 6
- Hyperthreading: Yes
- Memory: 144GB
- Networking: Dual 10GigE

These calculations do not consider storage consumed by consumer or provider templates, nor do they take into account the resources consumed by vCloud Networking and Security Edge appliances. A vCloud Networking and Security Edge device backs each private organization virtual datacenter network and external routed organization virtual datacenter network.

The following are specifications for each vCloud Networking and Security Edge appliance:

- **CPU:** 1 vCPU compact, 2 vCPU large
- **Memory:** 256MB compact, 1GB large
- **Storage:** 200MB compact, 256MB large
- **Network:** 1GigE (this is already calculated in the throughput of the workloads and should not be added again)

3.4.4.2 vCloud Maximums

Scalability in vCloud infrastructures reflects the capability of the platform to manage increasing numbers of vCloud consumers and workloads with minimal impact on manageability, performance, and reliability. From the consumer's perspective, scalability refers to the capability to consume infrastructure resources responsively, on demand.

When designing for scale, consider the maximums of the vCloud platform and the underlying vSphere platform. vCloud Director 5.1 requires vSphere 5.1 and has many platform improvements and enhancements. vCloud Director also introduces a number of features that can impact scalability, including fast provisioning, extensions, SQL Server support, third-party distributed switch integration, and UUIDs.

vCloud Director web console maximums are the primary constraint, followed by vSphere platform maximums. The choice of the vCloud Director database platform (Oracle or SQL Server) can result in slight performance differences.

Table 3.7 lists vCloud maximums based on a 10-cell configuration.

TABLE 3.7 vCloud Maximums

Constraint	Limit	Explanation
Virtual machines per vCloud Director	30,000	Maximum number of virtual machines that can be resident in a vCloud instance
Powered on per vCloud Director	10,000	Number of concurrently powered-on virtual machines permitted per vCloud instance
Virtual machines per vApp	128	Maximum number of virtual machines that can reside in a single vApp
Hosts per vCloud Director	2,000	Number of hosts that a single vCloud instance can manage
vCenter Servers per vCloud Director	25	Number of vCenter servers that a single vCloud instance can manage
Users per vCloud Director	10,000	Maximum number of users supported by a single vCloud instance.
Concurrent users per vCloud Director	1,500	Maximum number of current uses that can be logged into a single vCloud instance
Organizations per vCloud Director	10,000	Maximum number of organizations that can be created in a single vCloud instance

Constraint	Limit	Explanation
vApps per organization	3,000	Maximum number of vApps that can be deployed in a single organization
Virtual datacenters per vCloud Director	10,000	Maximum number of virtual datacenters that can be created in a single vCloud instance
Datastores per vCloud Director	1,024	Number of datastores that a single vCloud instance can manage
Networks per vCloud Director	10,000	Maximum number of logical networks that can be deployed in a single vCloud instance
Routed networks per vCloud Director	2,000	Maximum number of routed networks that can be deployed in a single vCloud instance
Catalogs per vCloud Director	10,000	Maximum number of catalogs that can be created in a single vCloud instance
Media items per vCloud Director	1,000	Maximum number of media items that can be created in a single vCloud instance

See *Configuration Maximums for VMware vSphere 5.1* in the VMware vSphere documentation (www.vmware.com/support/pubs/vsphere-esxi-vcenter-server-pubs.html), and read the VMware Knowledge Base article *vCloud Director 5.1 Configuration Maximums* (http://kb.vmware.com/kb/2036392) for more information on configuration maximums.

3.5 vCloud Resource Design

Resource design for vCloud involves examining requirements to determine how best to partition and organize resources. With the commoditization of infrastructure resources, the capability to scale these fungible units up and down becomes increasingly important.

When designing for vCloud, keep in mind that the ultimate consumers of the product are the end users of system. End users have a varying range of technical skills and experience, typically less than that of the architects and administrators of the vCloud environment. To encourage the use of vCloud computing as an effective tool, simplify user decision points wherever possible. If complexity is unavoidable, document all required steps to guide the end users.

Taking a top-down approach to vCloud design necessitates understanding the new abstractions introduced in the vCloud API and how they map to traditional vSphere objects.

3.5.1 vCloud Director Constructs

vCloud Director introduces logical constructs to facilitate multitenancy and provide interoperability between vCloud instances built to the vCloud API standard.

Figure 3.8 shows the abstraction mapping for vCloud Director.

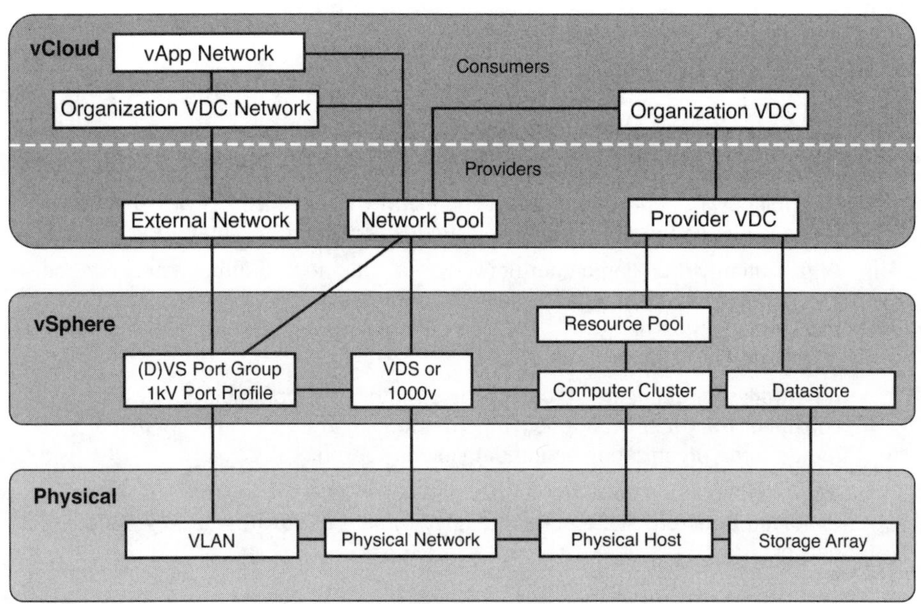

FIGURE 3.8 Physical, virtual, and vCloud abstraction mapping

Table 3.8 describes the logical constructs for vCloud Director.

TABLE 3.8 vCloud Director Constructs

Construct	Definition
Organization	The unit of multitenancy that represents a single logical security boundary. An organization contains users, virtual datacenters, and networks.
Provider virtual datacenter	A grouping of compute and storage resources from a single vCenter Server. A provider virtual datacenter consists of a single resource pool and one or more datastores. Multiple organizations can share provider virtual datacenter resources.
Organization virtual datacenter	A subgrouping of compute and storage resources allocated from a provider virtual datacenter and assigned to a single organization. A virtual datacenter is a deployment environment where vApps can be instantiated, deployed, and powered on. An organization virtual datacenter allocates resources using one of the following models: ▶ Pay as you go ▶ Reservation pool ▶ Allocation pool
Catalog	A repository of vApp templates and media available to users for deployment. Catalogs can be published to all organizations in the same vCloud environment.

3

Construct	Definition
vApp	A container for a software solution in the vCloud, and the standard unit of deployment for workloads in vCloud Director. vApps contain one or more virtual machines, have power-on operations, and can be imported or exported as an OVF.
External network	External networks provide external connectivity to organization virtual datacenter networks and are backed by port groups configured for Internet accessibility.
Organization virtual datacenter network	Organization virtual datacenter networks are instantiated through network pools and bound to a single organization. Organization virtual datacenter networks map to a vSphere port group and can be isolated, routed, or directly connected to an external network.
vApp network	A network that connects virtual machines within a vApp, deployed by a consumer from a network pool. vApp networks can be directly connected or routed to an organization virtual datacenter network.
Network pool	A network pool is a collection of isolated Layer 2 virtual networks available to vCloud Director for the automated deployment of private and NAT-routed networks.

Use the vSphere Client to observe how creating entities through vCloud Director translates into vCenter Server tasks.

3.5.2 Organizations

Organizations are the unit of multitenancy within vCloud Director and represent a single logical security boundary. Each organization contains a collection of end users, computing resources, catalogs, and vCloud workloads. For a public vCloud, vCloud Director organizations typically represent different customers. In a private vCloud, organizations can map to different department or business units. Each department or business unit might have multiple environments, such as development and production.

Organization users can be local users or can be imported from an LDAP server. LDAP integration can be specific to an organization or can inherit the system LDAP configuration defined by the vCloud system administrator. For information about how to configure LDAP, see the *vCloud Director Installation and Upgrade Guide* (www.vmware.com/support/pubs/vcd_pubs.html). Create a local organization administrator for each organization to mitigate loss of administrative control from LDAP authentication or connectivity issues.

The name of the organization, specified when the organization is created, maps to a unique URL that allows access to the UI for that organization. For example, an organization named Company1 maps to `https://<hostname>/cloud/org/Company1`. Use a standard naming convention for organization names; avoid using special characters or spaces because they can affect the URL in undesirable ways.

Use system defaults for most of the other organization settings, with the exception of leases, quotas, and limits. The service definitions have no specific requirements for these values—set them as needed.

3.5.2.1 Administrative Organization

A common design guideline is to create an administrative organization to provide a sandbox for system administrators and maintain a master catalog of vApp templates published to all other organizations in the vCloud environment. Users in an organization typically consume resources by deploying vApps from a predefined catalog. The master catalog provides a global library of standardized vApp templates to promote reusability of common assets built to provider standards.

Administrators assigned to the administrative organization are responsible for creating standardized gold master vApp templates for inclusion in the master catalog. Place nonfinalized vApps in a nonpublished internal catalog.

Configure the administrative organization to allow catalog publishing. Create a pay as you go organization virtual datacenter to minimize the amount of resources reserved.

3.5.2.2 Standard Organizations

Create an organization for each tenant of the vCloud, with the following considerations:

- Do not allow the organization to publish catalogs.
- Use leases, quotas, and limits that meet the provider's requirements.

3.5.2.3 Policies

Policies govern end-user behavior in vCloud environments. When creating an organization, specify policies for the total number of running and stored virtual machines according to the following definitions:

- *Running VM quota* refers to the maximum number of powered-on virtual machines.
- *Stored VM quota* refers to the maximum number of all virtual machines, including powered-off virtual machines.

Lease policies govern the persistence of vApps and vApp templates in an organization virtual datacenter. Specify the maximum length of time vApps can run and be stored in the organization virtual datacenters, according to the following definitions:

- The *maximum runtime* lease specifies the amount of time vApps can run before vCloud Director automatically stops them.
- The *storage lease* specifies the amount of time vApps or vApp templates are stored before vCloud Director automatically performs storage cleanup.

Lease policies can also be set to never expire. When any option for storage lease except the Never Expire option is selected, the storage is automatically cleaned up. Storage cleanup options include the following:

- **Permanently Deleted:** After the lease expires, the vApp or vApp template is automatically deleted.
- **Moved to Expired Items:** Flags the vApps or vApp templates for deletion. Items move to the Expired Items view, where they are unusable unless the lease is renewed.

3.5.3 Provider Virtual Datacenter

The *virtual datacenter* is a new construct that represents the standard container for a pool of compute and storage resources. Two types of virtual datacenters exist: provider and organization. Provider virtual datacenters consists of resource pools and datastores from a single vCenter Server. When creating a provider virtual datacenter, observe the following guidelines:

- Define the standard units of consumption. Variance in virtual datacenter allocations decreases manageability. Look at existing trends to determine common container sizes.
- Resource pools can map to a single provider virtual datacenter.
- If enough capacity exists, map the root resource pool of the cluster to provider virtual datacenters. This simplifies resource management. If the cluster expands, the backed provider virtual datacenter automatically grows as well. This is not the case if a standard resource pool is used. Multiple parent-level resource pools can add unnecessary complexity and lead to unpredictable results or inefficient use of resources if the reservations are not set appropriately.
- Create multiple provider virtual datacenters to differentiate computing levels or performance characteristics of a service offering. An example of differentiating by availability is n+1 for a bronze provider virtual datacenter versus n+2 for a silver provider virtual datacenter.
- One or more datastores can be attached to a provider virtual datacenter. Multiple provider virtual datacenters can share the same datastore. For isolation and predictable storage growth, do not attach the same datastore to multiple provider virtual datacenters.
- Storage tiering is not possible within a provider virtual datacenter. Instead, supply tiered pools of storage through multiple provider virtual datacenters.
- As the level of expected consumption increases for a given provider virtual datacenter, add hosts to the cluster from vCenter Server and attach more datastores.
- As the number of hosts backing a provider virtual datacenter approaches the halfway mark of cluster limits, implement controls to preserve headroom and avoid reaching the cluster limits. For example, restrict the creation of additional tenants for this virtual datacenter and add hosts to accommodate increased resource demand for the existing tenants.
- If the cluster backing a provider virtual datacenter has reached the maximum number of hosts, create a new provider virtual datacenter associated with a separate cluster.

See Chapter 2 for guidance on provider virtual datacenter sizing. Consider the following:

- Expected number of virtual machines
- Size of virtual machines (CPU, memory, storage)

In some cases, a "special-purpose" provider virtual datacenter dedicated to a single workload type might be needed. Special use case provider virtual datacenters are an example of what makes vCloud computing so flexible and powerful. The primary driver behind the need for a special-purpose virtual datacenter is to satisfy the license restrictions imposed by software vendors stipulating that all the processors that *might* run specific software must be licensed for it, regardless of whether they actually *are* running that software.

To keep licensing costs down while meeting the EULA requirements of such software vendors, create a purpose-specific provider virtual datacenter backed by the minimum number of CPU sockets needed to achieve performance requirements. Create a corresponding organization virtual datacenter per tenant, and provide descriptive naming to guide users to deploy workloads accordingly.

3.5.3.1 Elastic Virtual Datacenter

Rapid elasticity is a primary characteristic of vCloud computing. It involves quickly adding and releasing resources based on customer usage demands. vCloud Director supports compute elasticity by allowing provider virtual datacenters to span multiple clusters and by providing automatic placement of vApps. Aggregating capacity across multiple clusters into a single shared buffer offers potential for greater efficiency and utilization of the hardware. Figure 3.9 shows the use of vMotion across cluster boundaries in an elastic virtual datacenter.

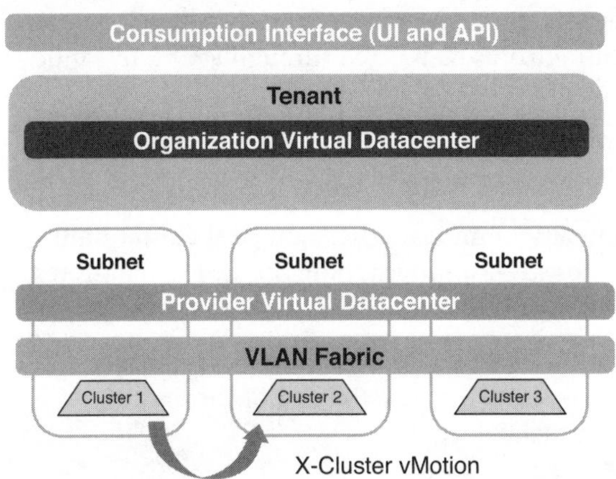

FIGURE 3.9 Elastic virtual datacenters

Expansion of a provider virtual datacenter can occur in the following scenarios:

- Creation of an organization virtual datacenter
- Increase in the size of an organization virtual datacenter
- Power-on of a virtual machine or vApp
- Resumption or unsuspension of a virtual machine or vApp

The requested operation succeeds if enough nonfragmented compute capacity exists in the underlying provider virtual datacenter and if network requirements are met.

The primary resource pool is the resource pool used in the initial creation of the provider virtual datacenter. Reservation pool virtual datacenters are bound to the primary resource pool and cannot draw resources from multiple resource pools. After creating a provider virtual datacenter, system administrators can add resource pools through the web console or vCloud API. Adding the resource pools allows the virtual datacenter to draw resources from multiple sources.

The following are considerations for an elastic virtual datacenter:

- The datacenter can support pay as you go and allocation pool organization virtual datacenter types.
- Elasticity is limited to a single vCenter datacenter. A provider virtual datacenter can draw resources from resource pools created in the same vCenter datacenter as the primary resource pool.
- Existing provider virtual datacenters and organization virtual datacenters are upgraded to elastic automatically after upgrading to VMware vCloud Director 5.1.
- Organization virtual datacenters expand automatically in response to user consumption. Pay as you go grows as needed, and allocation pool grows to the allocated size.
- Clusters in a provider virtual datacenter can connect to a common network, which can be the same network or different networks connected through a VXLAN fabric.
- Newly added resource pools might connect to datastores that have not been added to the provider virtual datacenter. Add all visible datastores to the provider virtual datacenter.
- Use elastic virtual datacenter functionality to mitigate the eight-host cluster limit for fast provisioning on VMFS3 datastores. (Fast provisioning on VMFS5 datastores supports up to 32 hosts.)
- Do not add extra resource pools from the same compute cluster if it is already backing a provider virtual datacenter. Instead, increase the size of the existing resource pool that is mapped to the virtual datacenter.
- vCloud Director places the vApp in the resource pool with the most available constrained capacity.

3.5.4 Organization Virtual Datacenters

An organization virtual datacenter allocates resources from a provider virtual datacenter and makes it available for use for a given organization. Multiple organization virtual datacenters can share the resources of the same provider virtual datacenter.

Network pools provide network resources to organization virtual datacenters. When creating an organization virtual datacenter, select a network pool and specify the maximum allowable number of provisioned networks to allow users to self-provision vApp networks.

3.5.4.1 Allocation Models

Organizations can draw resources from multiple organization virtual datacenters using one of the resource allocation models: reservation pool, allocation pool, or pay as you go.

3.5.4.1.1 Reservation Pool Model

Reservation pool resources allocated to the organization virtual datacenter are completely dedicated. All guarantees are set to 100%. Reservation pool virtual datacenters map to resource pools with the reservations set equivalent to the limits. Figure 3.10 shows a reservation pool split between two tenants.

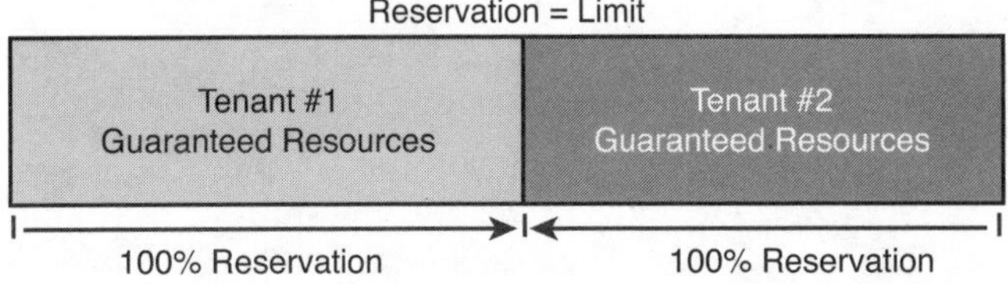

FIGURE 3.10 Reservation Pool

3.5.4.1.2 Allocation Pool Model

An allocation pool is a pool of allocated resources with a certain percentage of resources guaranteed. When an organization virtual datacenter is created using the allocation pool model (see Figure 3.11), a dynamic resource pool is instantiated. This resource pool automatically adjusts available resources as new workloads are powered on, based on the values specified within the virtual datacenter. Each value has a direct impact on how the related resource pool dynamically changes as new virtual machines are deployed. The following values are required when defining the size of an organization virtual datacenter:

- **CPU Allocation:** The maximum amount of CPU resources available to the virtual machines running within the organization virtual datacenter.
- **CPU Resources Guaranteed:** The percentage of CPU resources guaranteed to be available to the running virtual machines.
- **vCPU Speed:** The maximum speed in GHz that each vCPU can consume. A virtual machine with two vCPUs can consume twice this value.
- **Memory Allocation:** The maximum amount of memory available to the virtual machines running within the organization virtual datacenter.
- **Memory Resources Guaranteed:** The percentage of the memory resources guaranteed to the running virtual machines.

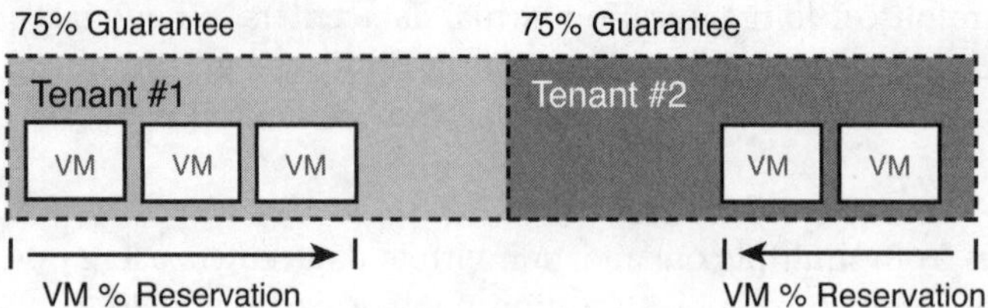

FIGURE 3.11 Allocation Pool

An organization virtual datacenter is created with the following values:

- CPU allocation = 100GHz
- CPU resources guaranteed =75%
- vCPU speed = 1GHz
- Memory allocation = 100GB
- Memory resources guaranteed = 75%

After the organization virtual datacenter is created, a corresponding resource pool is created. Unlike versions of vCloud Director earlier than version 5.1, a reservation is not initially set on the resource pool. The resource settings are dynamically changed as each new virtual machine is powered on within the organization virtual datacenter. The following formulas calculate resource pools reservations as virtual machines are deployed.

- CPU resources guaranteed × vCPU speed × # of virtual machine CPUs allocated = CPU reservation
- CPU allocation = CPU limit
- Memory resources guaranteed × Virtual machine memory allocated = Memory reservation

Using the example values, when a virtual machine with 1 vCPU and 2GB memory is powered on, the corresponding resource pool is updated based on the values defined at the organization virtual datacenter. In this example, the resource pool is dynamically set with the following values:

- CPU reservation = 750MHz.
- CPU limit = organization virtual datacenter CPU allocation.
- Memory reservation = 1536MB. This corresponds to 1 vCPU at 1GHz and 2GB memory with a 75% guarantee.

NOTE

A memory limit is not required because it not possible for a virtual machine to consume more memory than it is allocated.

When an additional virtual machine with the same configuration is powered on, the resource pool is again updated. In this example, the resource pool is set to the following configuration:

- CPU reservation = 1500MHz
- CPU limit = organization virtual datacenter CPU allocation
- Memory reservation = 3000MB

This corresponds to 2 vCPUs at 2GHz and 4GB memory with a 75% guarantee.

As additional virtual machines are deployed, the resource pool is dynamically updated until 100 vCPUs (100GHz) or 100GB of memory is allocated. After the CPU or memory allocation is reached, vCloud Director prohibits powering on additional virtual machines.

In vCloud Director 5.1.1, the CPU limit applied to the resource pool is set to the same value as the allocation of the virtual datacenter. This allows an organization virtual datacenter that has only a single virtual machine to consume as much as possible. In this case, it would be limited to the core speed of the physical CPU because a 100GHz physical core currently is not available. As additional virtual machines are powered on, only the reservation changes on the resource pool. The limit remains equal to the virtual datacenter allocation. After the allocation is reached, vCloud Director prevents new virtual machines from powering on.

3.5.4.1.2 Pay As You Go Model

The pay as you go model (see Figure 3.12) provides the illusion of an unlimited resource pool. This model maps to a subresource pool with no configured reservations or limits. Resources are committed only when vApps are deployed in the organization virtual datacenter.

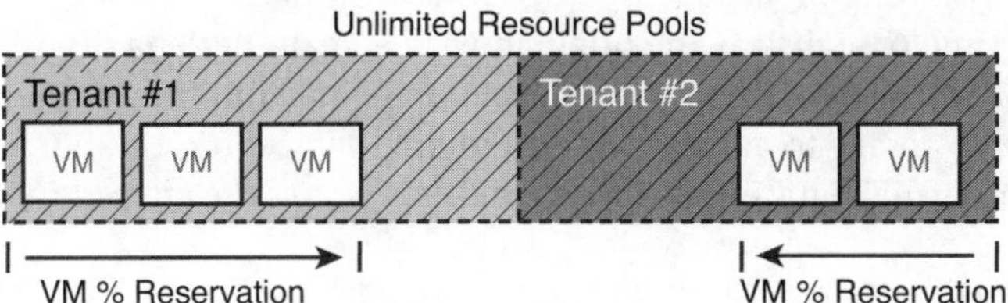

FIGURE 3.12 Pay As You Go

When an organization virtual datacenter is created, vCenter Server creates child resource pools with corresponding resource reservations and limits under the resource pool representing the organization virtual datacenter.

For each vCloud tenant, review the applicable service definition to determine the number and types of organization virtual datacenters to create. Consider expected use cases, workload types, future capacity, and the maximum number of virtual machines per organization virtual datacenter.

Use prescriptive naming for organization virtual datacenters to guide expected user behavior. All users in an organization can view all allocated organization virtual datacenters.

NOTE

vCloud Director 5.1 introduces the capability to limit the resources allocated within a pay as you go organization virtual datacenter through CPU and memory resource limits. Previous versions of vCloud Director allowed capping only the number of virtual machines.

3.5.4.1.4 Mixed Allocation Models in a Provider Virtual Datacenter

A single provider virtual datacenter mapped to the cluster level can be configured with multiple allocation models for consumers based on their functional requirements. Creating a provider virtual datacenter model (pay as you go) does not guarantee that the same settings are applied across the organization virtual datacenter. The model changes the vSphere resource distribution in a similar manner to using multiple allocation models.

3.5.4.2 Thin Provisioning

Thin provisioning allows oversubscription of datastores by presenting a virtual machine with more capacity than is physically allocated. For applications with predictable capacity growth, thin provisioning can provide an efficient way of allocating capacity. When using thin provisioning, additional management processes are required. Configure vCenter Server alarms to issue an alert when approaching an out-of-space condition, and allow sufficient time to source and provision additional storage.

Thin provisioning is an option when configuring organization virtual datacenters. vApps created after enabling thin provisioning use thin-provisioned virtual disks.

3.5.4.3 Fast Provisioning

Fast provisioning allows rapid provisioning of vApps through vSphere 5 linked clone technology. A linked clone uses the same base disk as the original, with a chain of delta disks to keep track of the differences between the original and the clone. By default, fast provisioning is enabled when allocating storage to an organization virtual datacenter. Disabling fast provisioning on organization virtual datacenters means that full clones are created for subsequent vApp deployments.

Fast provisioning benefits include the following:

- **Increased elasticity:** The capability to quickly provision vApps from a catalog using linked technology allows vCloud applications to scale up as needed.
- **Increased operational efficiency:** Use of linked clones typically results in significant improvement in storage utilization.

Fast provisioning includes the components:

- **Linked clone:** Virtual machine created as a result of a copy operation, leveraging a redo-log-based linked clone from the parent.
- **Shadow VM:** Full copy of the primary virtual machine used as the source for linked clone creation. A shadow virtual machine allows cross-datastore provisioning and is transparent to end users. Shadow virtual machines are created for vApp templates only, not for MyCloud vApps.

During fast provisioning, vApp files can reside on the same virtual datacenter as the primary virtual machine or a different virtual datacenter. The choice of destination virtual datacenter impacts fast provisioning deployment based on the associated datastores and vCenter Server instances, as shown in Table 3.9.

TABLE 3.9 Linked Clone Deployment

Source vCenter	Target vCenter	Source Datastore	Target Datastore	Shadow VM
VC1	VC1	DS1	DS1	Not created until linked clone depth limit is reached (default = 31)
VC1	VC1	DS1	DS2	Created on DS2 and registered on VC1
VC1	VC2	DS1	DS1	Created on DS1 and registered on VC2
VC1	VC2	DS1	DS2	Created on DS2 and registered on VC2

Both source and target virtual datacenters have fast provisioning enabled. Linked clones created from VC1 use the primary virtual machine as the base disk. Linked clones created from VC2 use the shadow virtual machine as the base disk.

The following are considerations for fast provisioning:

- Separate the datastores reserved for fast provisioning from the datastores reserved for full clones to improve performance and manageability.
- Fast provisioning requires vSphere 5.x.
- vSphere Storage DRS with vCloud Director 5.1 supports fast provisioning.
- vSphere Storage DRS determines datastore selection when using VMware vCenter 5.1.
- Provisioning time is nearly instantaneous when provisioning to the same datastore.
- Using VMFS5 datastores removes the 8-host limit for fast provisioning (32-host maximum).
- Using VMFS3 datastores enforces an eight-host limit for fast provisioning.
- Provisioning a virtual machine to a different datastore triggers the creation of shadow virtual machines if one does not already exist on the target datastore.

- Shadow virtual machines are full copies of the source virtual machines, which factors into sizing considerations for preprovisioning shadow virtual machines across datastores.
- Storage array caching can boost linked clone performance. Ample storage array cache greatly benefits an environment that uses linked clones.
- Although no limit governs the width of a tree, datastores can fill up if a tree gets too wide. Use cross-datastore linked clones to mitigate this issue.
- The maximum linked clone chain length is 30. Further clones of the vApp result in full clones.
- Shadow virtual machines are treated differently from normal virtual machines and can be referenced through the vCloud API by the `SHADOW_VM` entity type.
- Invoke vSphere Storage vMotion migration of linked clones only through the vCloud API (`Relocate_VM` call). The target virtual datacenter must have visibility to the datastore that contains the source disks.
- Do not invoke vSphere Storage vMotion operations on linked clones through the vSphere Client; doing so consolidates the linked clones and might result in inconsistent behavior.

3.5.4.4 vApp Placement

During vApp deployments, the vCloud Director virtual machine storage placement algorithm works as follows:

1. For fast provisioning–enabled virtual datacenters, identify a datastore that contains a base disk. If a base disk for the virtual machine exists, place a virtual machine on that datastore. The following conditions apply if the target datastore is reaching yellow or red disk thresholds.
   - If a base disk exists but the target datastore exceeds the red threshold, look for a normal or yellow-threshold datastore. If no suitable datastores are available, the operation fails.
   - If a base disk exists but the target datastore exceeds the yellow threshold, look for a datastore that has not reached its yellow threshold. If none exists, deploy on the target datastore if capacity is sufficient.
2. If no base disk exists, place the virtual machine on the datastore with the most available capacity that does not exceed the yellow threshold.

Figure 3.13 charts the vApp placement algorithm that the vCloud Director Placement Engine uses.

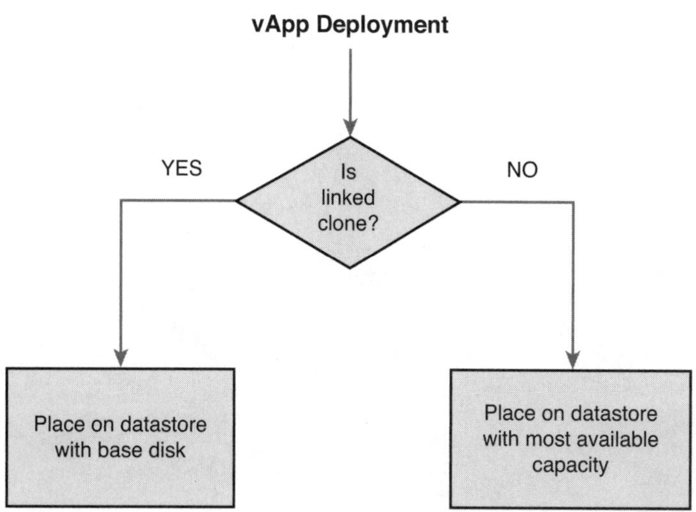

FIGURE 3.13 vCloud Director Placement Engine vApp placement algorithm

vApp creation fails if the vApp contains multiple virtual machines that cannot fit on a single datastore in the target virtual datacenter. Consider the following scenario:

- Virtual datacenter1:
  - Datastore1: 20GB free space
  - Datastore2: 30GB free space
- vApp1:
  - VM1: 30GB
  - VM2: 30GB

Because the total size required for vApp1 exceeds the maximum available capacity of all datastores, the vApp deployment task fails. To mitigate this risk, follow VMware design guidelines for datastore utilization through proactive monitoring and storage maintenance.

When vCenter 5.1 is used in combination with vCloud Director 5.1, the vCenter 5.1 vSphere Storage DRS datastore placement engine is used in lieu of the vCloud Director placement engine when datastore clusters are available as a deployment target. Figure 3.14 displays the workflow.

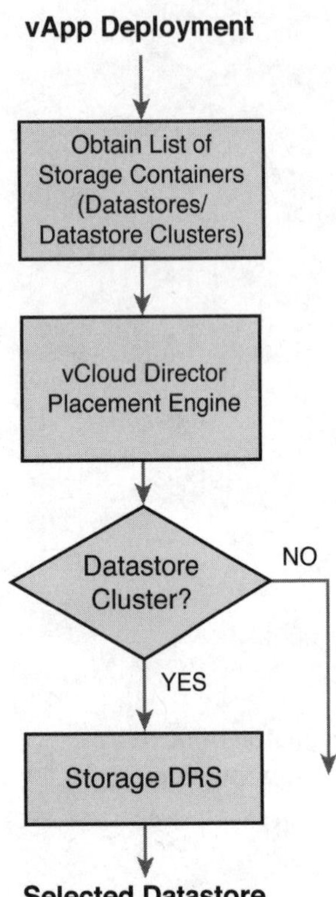

FIGURE 3.14 vCloud Director storage placement

3.5.4.5 Public vCloud Considerations

The public service definition requirements (see Table 3.10) used in this example are taken from Chapter 2.

TABLE 3.10 Public vCloud Virtual Datacenter Requirements

Requirements
Three different service offerings are required: Basic (pay as you go), Committed (allocation pool), and Dedicated (reservation pool).
The vCloud infrastructure supports a minimum of 1,500 virtual machines across the three service offerings.
Split the reservation pool into small, medium, and large pools with a split of 75%, 20%, and 5%.

The service definitions are as follows:

- The *Basic* service offering uses the pay as you go allocation model, allowing customers to vary their resource usage while being charged for the resources that they consume.

- The *Committed* service offering uses the allocation pool model, which specifies a resource container size that has a certain percentage reserved.
- The *Dedicated* service offering uses the reservation pool model because this offering requires dedicated and guaranteed resources for the consumer.

The service definition has specific requirements for the maximum number of virtual machines each organization can have, based on size. Refer to the public service definition for the maximum virtual machine count for each virtual datacenter type.

The service definition provides detailed and descriptive guidance on how much a provider should charge for each service tier. Chargeback integrates with vCloud Director to provide metering and cost calculation functionality. For more information, see the User's Guide in the vCenter Chargeback Manager documentation (www.vmware.com/support/pubs/vcbm_pubs.html).

Best Practices and Troubleshooting Guide (www.vmware.com/support/pubs/vcbm_pubs.html) describes recommended practices around vCloud Director and vCenter Chargeback integration to accommodate instance-based pricing (pay as you go), reservation-based pricing, and allocation-based pricing.

3.5.4.6 Private vCloud Considerations

The private service definition requirements (see Table 3.11) used in this example are from service definitions.

TABLE 3.11 Private vCloud Virtual Datacenter Requirements

Requirements
Three different service offerings are required: Basic (pay as you go), Committed (allocation pool), and Dedicated (reservation pool).
The vCloud infrastructure supports a minimum of 1,500 virtual machines across the three service offerings.
Split the reservation pool into small, medium, and large pools with a split of 75%, 20%, and 5%.

Each organization virtual datacenter has a specified storage limit except when using the pay as you go allocation model, for which the storage limit can be unlimited. For this example, no storage limit is set because the static storage values that are provided for individual virtual machines limit the number of virtual machines in the organization. To improve storage efficiency, enable thin provisioning on organization virtual datacenters.

3.5.5 vCloud Networking

Workloads for vCloud consumers require network connectivity at the following levels:

- External networks connect vApps to outside networks. An external network maps to a vSphere port group with external connectivity.

- Internal or routed networks are used to facilitate communication between virtual machines within a vCloud instance. These are backed by vCloud Director network pools.
- Network design complexity depends on vCloud workload requirements. A vApp with a large number of upstream dependencies is more complex to deploy than a vApp with a self-contained application.
- vCloud Director coordinates with vCloud Networking and Security Manager to provide automated network security for a vCloud environment. vCloud Networking and Security Edge gateway devices are deployed during the provisioning of routed or private networks. Each vCloud Networking and Security Edge gateway runs a firewall service that allows or blocks inbound traffic to virtual machines that are connected to a public access organization virtual datacenter network. The vCloud Director web console exposes the capability to create five-tuple firewall rules that consist of source address, destination address, source port, destination port, and protocol.

3.5.5.1 External Networks

An external network provides connectivity outside an organization through an existing, preconfigured vSphere port group. These can be a standard port group, distributed port group, or third-party distributed switch port group construct such as the Cisco Nexus 1000V port profile.

In a public vCloud, external networks can provide access through the Internet to customer networks, typically using VPN or MPLS termination. Before creating external networks, provision the requisite number of vSphere port groups with external connectivity.

3.5.5.2 Network Pools

Network pools contain network definitions used to instantiate private or routed organization and vApp networks. Networks created from network pools must be isolated at Layer 2.

The following types of network pools are available:

- vSphere port group–backed network pools are backed by preprovisioned port groups, distributed port groups, or third-party distributed switch port groups.
- Virtual eXtensible LAN (VXLAN) network pools use a Layer 2 over Layer 3 MAC in UDP encapsulation to provide scalable, standards-based traffic isolation across Layer 3 boundaries (requires a distributed switch).
- VLAN-backed network pools are backed by a range of preprovisioned VLAN IDs. For this arrangement, all specified VLANs are trunked into the vCloud environment (requires a distributed switch).
- vCloud Director Network Isolation–backed (VCD-NI) network pools are backed by vCloud isolated networks. A vCloud isolated network is an overlay network uniquely identified by a fence ID that is implemented through encapsulation techniques that span hosts and provides traffic isolation from other networks (requires a distributed switch).

Table 3.12 compares the options for a network pool.

TABLE 3.12 Network Pool Options

Consideration	vSphere Port Group Backed	VXLAN Backed	VLAN Backed	vCloud Network Isolation Backed
How it works	Requires that isolated port groups be created and exist on all hosts in the cluster	▶ Maps multicast address to a VXLAN segment ID for isolation ▶ Tunnels virtual machine–to–virtual machine traffic over a Layer 3 network by a VTEP (ESXi hosts) ▶ Achieves node learning is done through multicast, not broadcast	▶ Uses a range of available VLANs dedicated for vCloud ▶ Has network isolation that relies on inherent VLAN isolation	Creates an overlay network (with fence ID) within a shared transport network
Advantages	—	▶ Does not rely on VLAN IDs for isolation ▶ Works over any Layer 3 multicast-enabled network ▶ Has no "distance" restrictions; managed by multicast radius	▶ Offers the best network performance ▶ Allows vCloud Director to create port groups as needed	▶ Offers scalability to create thousands of networks per transport network ▶ Is more secure than the VLAN-backed option due to vCloud Director enforcement ▶ Allows vCloud Director to create port groups as needed

Consideration	vSphere Port Group Backed	VXLAN Backed	VLAN Backed	vCloud Network Isolation Backed
Disadvantages	▶ Requires manual creation and management of port groups ▶ Makes it possible to use a port group that is not actually isolated	Requires end-to-end multicast	▶ Has limited VLANs (4,096 maximum) ▶ Requires used VLANs to be configured on all associated physical switches ▶ Scoped to a single virtual datacenter and vCenter Server	Requires overhead to perform encapsulation

3.5.5.2.1 vSphere Port Group–Backed Considerations

- Use standard or distributed virtual switches.
- vCloud Director does not automatically create port groups. Manually provision port groups for vCloud Director to use ahead of time.

3.5.5.2.2 VXLAN-Backed Considerations

- Distributed switches are required.
- Configure the MTU to be at least 1600 at ESXi and on the physical switches, to avoid IP fragmentation.
- Map the guest MTU size to accommodate the VXLAN header insertion at the ESXi level.
- Use explicit failover or "route based on IP hash" as the load-balancing policy.
- If VXLAN transport is traversing routers, multicast routing must be enabled (PIM—BIDIR or SM).
  - More multicast groups are better.
  - Multiple segments can be mapped to a single multicast group.
  - If VXLAN transport is contained to a single subnet, IGMP Querier must be enabled on the physical switches.
  - Use BIDIR-PIM where available so that any sender can be a receiver as well. If BIDIR-PIM is not available, use PIM-SM.

- If VXLAN traffic is traversing a router, enable proxy ARP on the first-hop router.
- Use five-tuple hash distribution for uplink and interswitch LACP.

3.5.5.2.3 VLAN-Backed Considerations

- Distributed switches are required.
- vCloud Director creates port groups automatically as needed.

3.5.5.2.4 vCloud Network Isolation-Backed Considerations

- Distributed switches are required.
- Increase the MTU size of network devices in the transport VLAN to at least 1600, to accommodate the additional information needed for VCD-NI. The information includes all physical switches and vSphere Distributed Switches. Failure to increase the MTU size causes packet fragmentation, negatively affecting network throughput performance of vCloud workloads.
- Specify a VLAN ID for the VCD-NI transport network (optional, but recommended for security). If no VLAN ID is specified, it defaults to VLAN 0.
- The maximum number of VCD-NI-backed network pools per vCloud instance is 10.
- vCloud Director automatically creates port groups on distributed switches as needed.

3.5.5.3 vCloud Networking and Security Edge Gateway

vCloud Networking and Security Edge gateways provide external network connectivity to vCloud consumers. The gateways are first-class entities that are associated with an organization virtual datacenter. They cannot be shared across other organization virtual datacenters. Each has up to 10 interfaces and can be connected to multiple external networks.

3.5.5.4 Organization Virtual Datacenter Networks

Organization virtual datacenter networks provide network connectivity to vApp workloads within an organization. Users in the organization connect to outside networks through external organization virtual datacenter networks, similar to how users in an organization connect to a corporate network that is uplinked to an Internet service provider. During creation, you can specify whether organization virtual datacenter networks are specific to a virtual datacenter or shared with all the organization's virtual datacenters (as in vCloud Director 5.1).

Connectivity options for organization virtual datacenter networks include the following:

- External direct-connect organization virtual datacenter network
- External routed organization virtual datacenter network
- Internal isolated organization virtual datacenter network

Internal and routed organization virtual datacenter networks are instantiated through network pools by vCloud system administrators. Organization administrators do not have the capability to provision organization virtual datacenter networks, but they can configure network services such as firewall, NAT, DHCP, VPN, load balancing, and static routing.

3.5.5.4.1 Direct

In a directly connected external organization virtual datacenter network, the vApp virtual machines are in the port group of the external network. IP address assignments for vApps follow the external network IP addressing (see Figure 3.15).

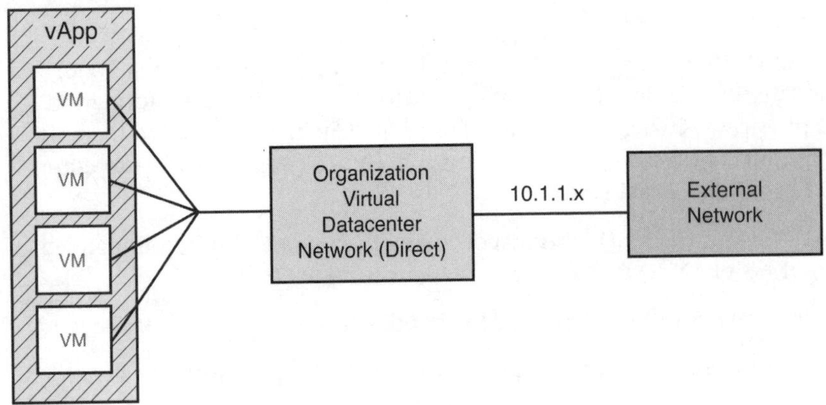

FIGURE 3.15 External organization virtual datacenter network (Direct)

3.5.5.4.2 Routed

A routed external organization virtual datacenter network is protected by a vCloud Networking and Security Edge device that provides DHCP, firewall, NAT, VPN, and static routing services. The vCloud Networking and Security Edge device connects to the organization virtual datacenter network and the external network port groups (see Figure 3.16).

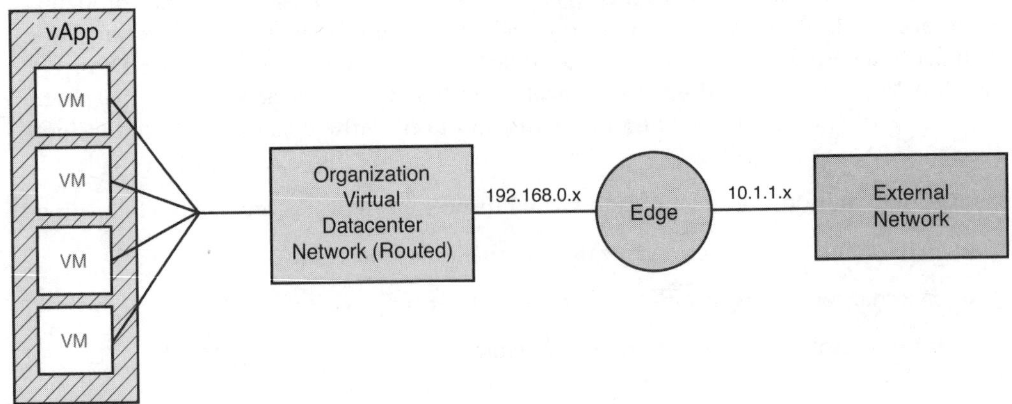

FIGURE 3.16 External organization virtual datacenter network (routed)

3.5.5.4.3 Isolated

An internal organization virtual datacenter network is isolated from all other networks (see Figure 3.17).

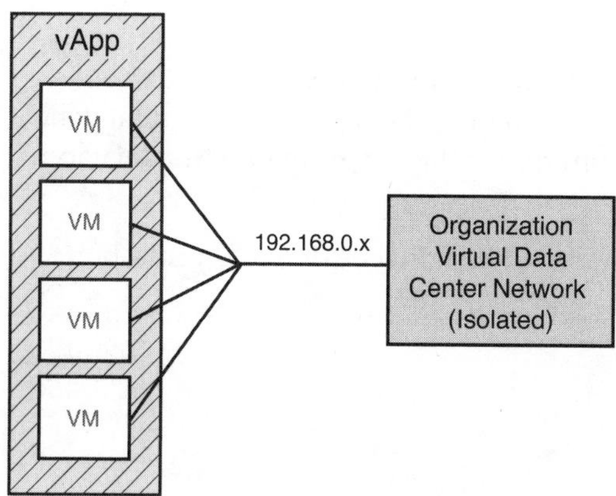

FIGURE 3.17 Internal organization virtual datacenter network (isolated)

3.5.5.5 vApp Networks

vApp networks are created by vCloud consumers and connect multiple virtual machines in a vApp. vApp networks separate vApp virtual machines from the workloads in the organization virtual datacenter network. The effect is similar to placing a router in front of a group of systems (vApp) to shield the systems from the rest of the corporate network. vApp networks are instantiated from a network pool and consume vSphere resources while the vApp is running.

Connectivity options for vApp networks include the following:

- **Direct:** vApps connect directly to the organization virtual datacenter network.
- **Fenced:** Identical virtual machines can exist in different vApps. A virtual router provides isolation and proxy ARP.
- **Routed:** A new network is defined. A virtual router provides NAT and firewall functionality.
- **Isolated:** Communication is restricted to the virtual machines in the vApp. No connection exists to an organization virtual datacenter network.

vApp networks are created as follows:

- By manually create vApp networks using the Add Network Wizard. Connecting the vApp network to an organization virtual datacenter network creates a routed connection, with configurable NAT and firewall services.

- By fencing a vApp directly connected to an external or organization virtual datacenter network. Choosing the Fence option associates an implicit vApp network to the vApp. Firewall and NAT services are configurable on a fenced network.

3.5.5.5.1 Direct

Connecting virtual machines in a vApp directly to an organization virtual datacenter network places vApp virtual machines in the port group of the organization virtual datacenter network. IP address assignments for vApps follow the organization virtual datacenter network IP addressing scheme.

Figure 3.18 shows a vApp network directly connected to a direct external organization virtual datacenter network.

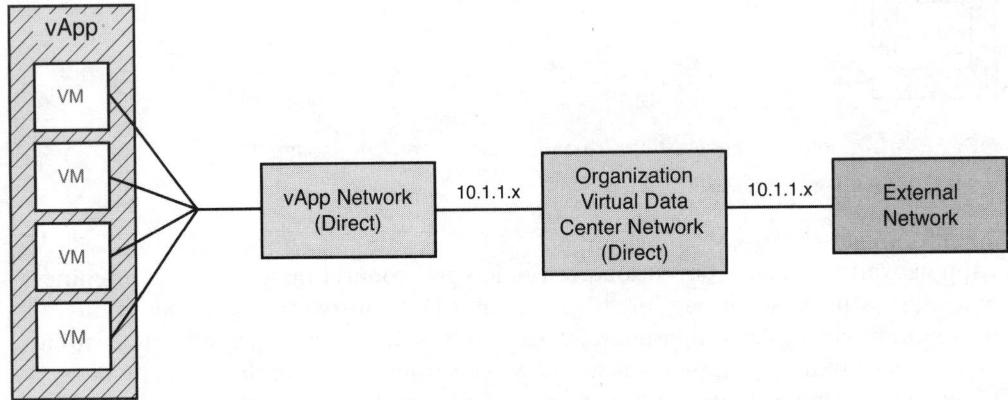

FIGURE 3.18 vApp network (direct) for organization virtual datacenter network (direct)

Figure 3.19 shows a vApp network directly connected to a routed external organization virtual datacenter network. vCloud Networking and Security Edge provides DHCP, firewall, NAT, and static routing services to the organization virtual datacenter network.

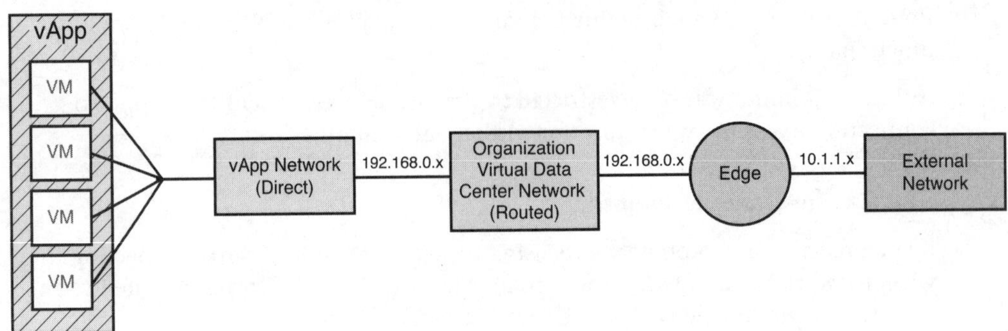

FIGURE 3.19 vApp network (direct) for organization virtual datacenter network (routed)

Figure 3.20 shows a vApp network directly connected to an isolated organization virtual datacenter network. A vCloud Networking and Security Edge automatically deploys only if using DHCP services.

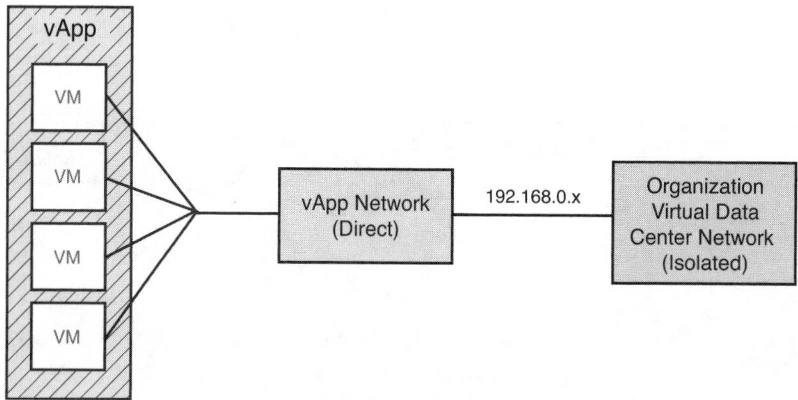

FIGURE 3.20 vApp network (direct) for organization virtual datacenter network (isolated)

3.5.5.5.2 Fenced

For a fenced network, the external and internal IP subnet is the same, with proxy ARP used to move traffic. vCloud Networking and Security Edge provides the network fencing functionality for vCloud environments. The option to fence a vApp is available if the vApp directly connects to an organization virtual datacenter network.

Depending on the organization virtual datacenter network connection, NAT or double NAT might take place for incoming or outgoing traffic from a vApp network perspective. The following scenarios describe single and double NAT situations.

Figure 3.21 illustrates a scenario in which a vApp network connected to a direct organization virtual datacenter network is fenced.

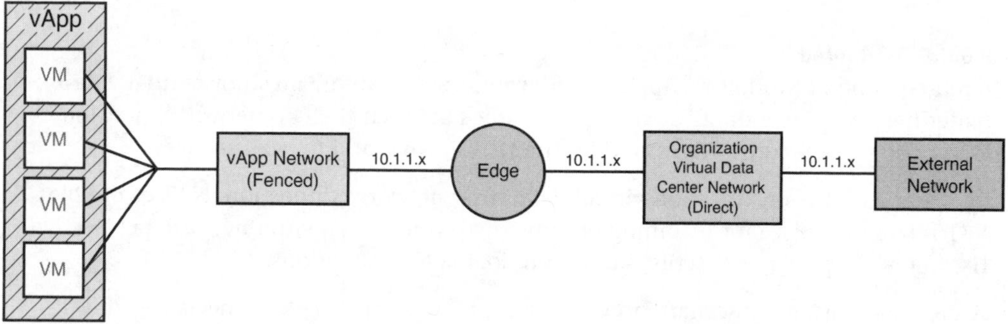

FIGURE 3.21 vApp network (fenced) for organization virtual datacenter network (direct)

If you are fencing a vApp network connected to a routed organization virtual datacenter network, double NAT occurs with two vCloud Networking and Security Edge instances deployed. Figure 3.22 illustrates this scenario.

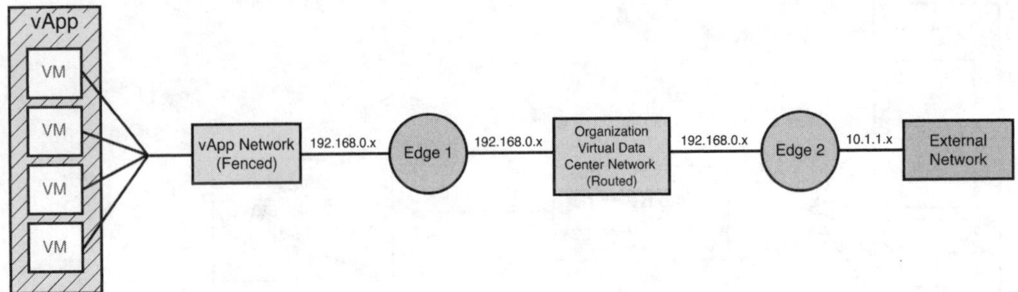

FIGURE 3.22 vApp network (fenced) for organization virtual datacenter network (routed)

Figure 3.23 shows a fenced vApp network connected to an isolated organization virtual datacenter network. Only one NAT exists.

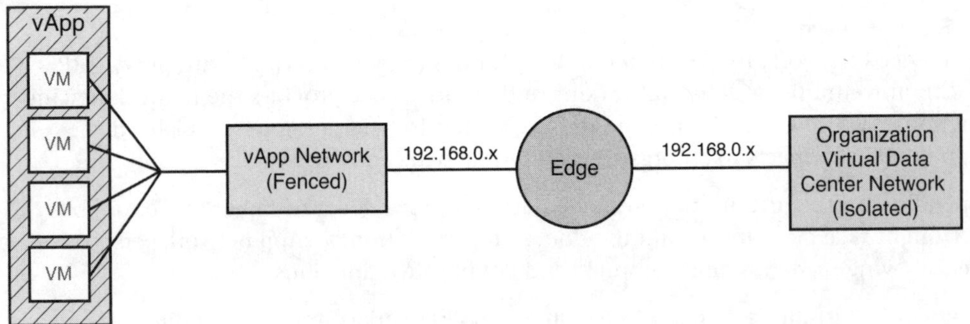

FIGURE 3.23 vApp network (fenced) for organization virtual datacenter network (isolated)

3.5.5.5.3 Routed

A routed vApp network is a vApp network connected to an organization virtual datacenter network where the IP address space differs between the two networks. A vCloud Networking and Security Edge provides the DHCP, NAT, and firewall services.

Depending on the organization virtual datacenter network connection, NAT or double NAT might take place for incoming or outgoing traffic from a vApp network perspective. The following scenarios describe single and double NAT situations.

Figure 3.24 illustrates a scenario in which a routed vApp network connects to a direct organization virtual datacenter network.

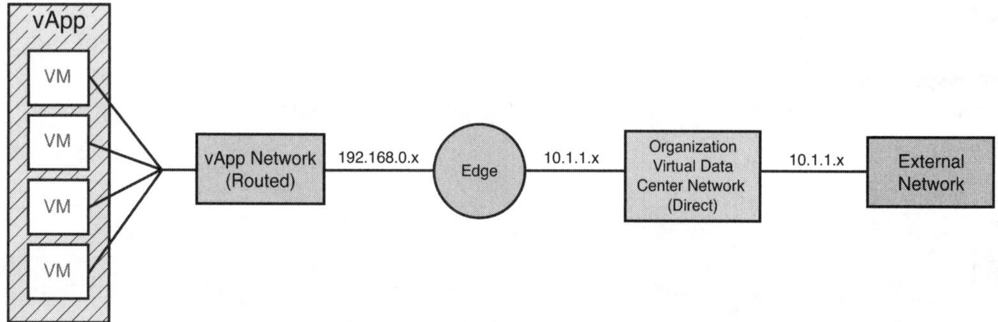

FIGURE 3.24 vApp network (routed) for organization virtual datacenter network (direct)

If a routed vApp network connects to a routed organization virtual datacenter network, double NAT occurs with two vCloud Networking and Security Edge instances deployed. Figure 3.25 illustrates this scenario.

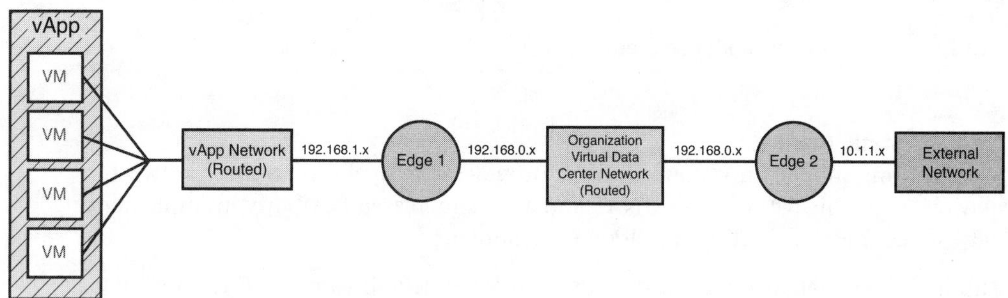

FIGURE 3.25 vApp network (routed) for organization virtual datacenter network (routed)

Figure 3.26 shows a routed vApp network connected to an isolated organization virtual datacenter network.

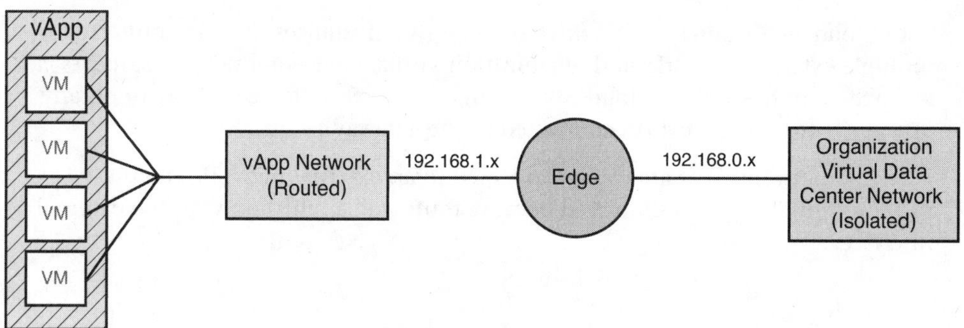

FIGURE 3.26 vApp network (routed) for organization virtual datacenter network (isolated)

3.5.5.5.4 Isolated

A vApp network configured to None is completely isolated, and the virtual switch of the corresponding port group is the endpoint for this network. This network is isolated on Layer 2, and only intra-vApp communication is possible (see Figure 3.27).

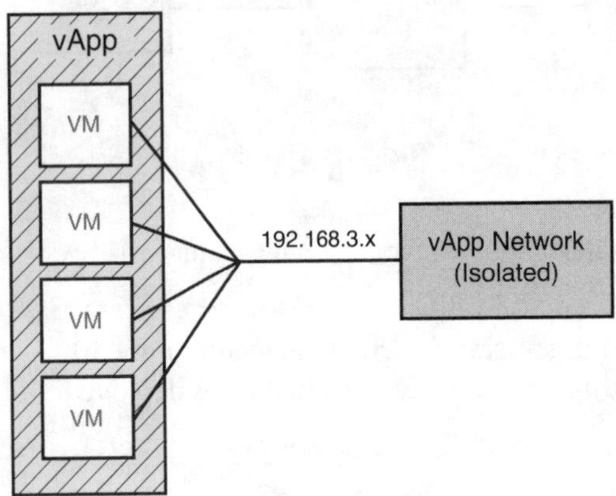

FIGURE 3.27 vApp network (isolated)

3.5.5.6 Static Routing

Static routing support in vCloud Director provides the capability to route between network segments without using NAT and allows increased flexibility in implementing network connectivity within a vCloud environment.

Although most networks have a directly connected default gateway, it is possible for networks to have more than one route (for example, when using multiple interfaces on vCloud Networking and Security Edge devices). Static routing provides a way to manually configure routing tables so that traffic can be forwarded to these remote networks while still using the default gateway for all remaining traffic.

In vCloud Director, static routing can be configured at both the routed organization virtual datacenter network level and the vApp network level.

- For vCloud Networking and Security Edge gateway instances that are connected to multiple external networks and organization virtual datacenter networks, routes can be applied on the entire vCloud Networking and Security Edge gateway or on any one of the external networks connected to the gateway.
- For vApp networks that are route-connected to an external network, the static routing configuration is simplified because routes are applied only on the external interface.

3.5.5.7 Static Routing Organization Virtual Datacenter Network Use Cases

The following use cases demonstrate the different options for static routing with vCloud Director.

3.5.5.7.1 Accessing Network Resources on an External Network

This use case (see Figure 3.28) applies to scenarios that have a requirement for connectivity to network resources through a different next-hop address than the default external gateway. An example involves access to a remote management network through a VPN or proxy, or by accessing services in another organization.

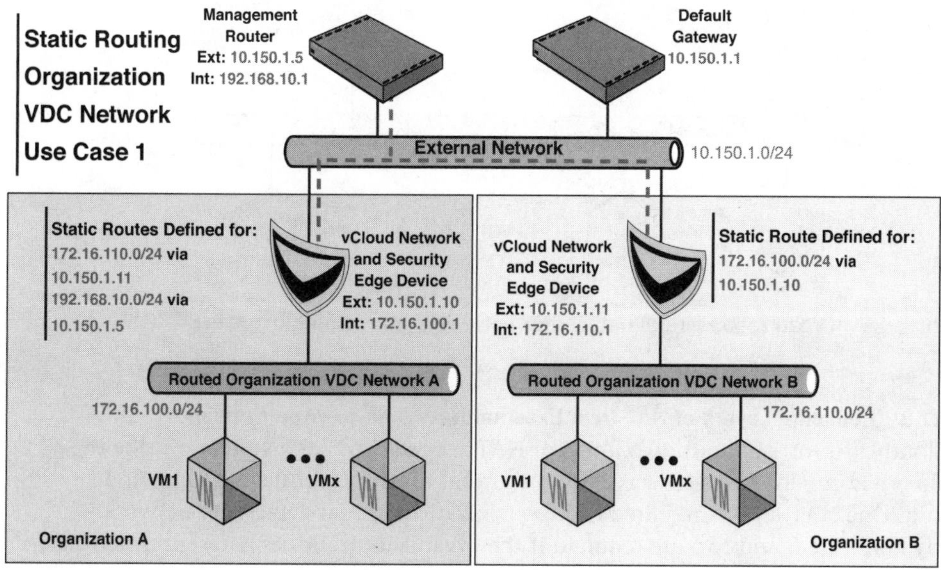

FIGURE 3.28 Organization virtual datacenter network static routing use case 1

3.5.5.7.2 Enabling vApp Networks Connected to an Organization Virtual Datacenter Network to Communicate Directly

This use case (see Figure 3.29) allows virtual machines connected to different vApp networks (in a common organization virtual datacenter network) to communicate without NAT. This configuration reduces the operational overhead of maintaining port forwarding or IP translation NAT rules for connectivity within the organization.

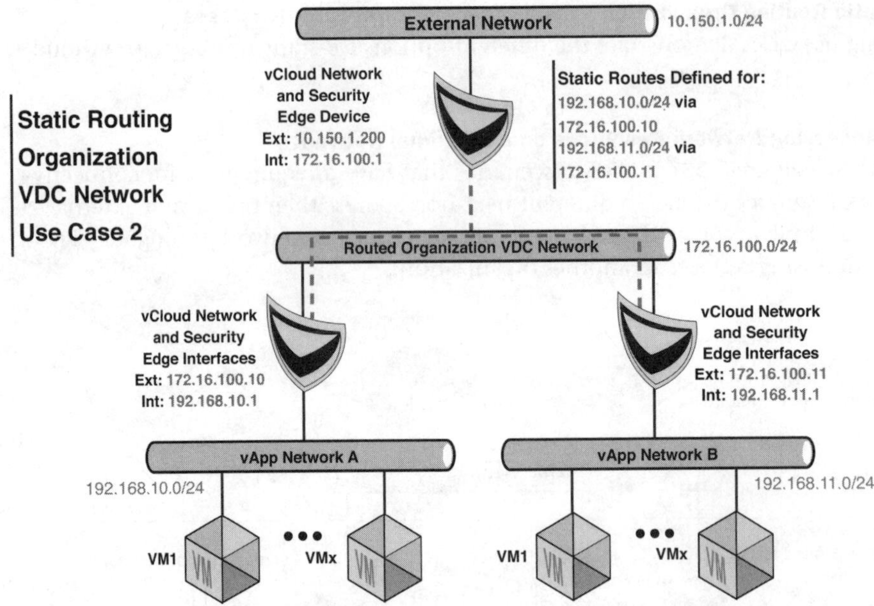

FIGURE 3.29 Organization virtual datacenter network static routing use case 2

3.5.5.7.3 Reducing Layers of NAT from External Networks to vApp Networks

In vCloud Director 1.0, up to two levels of NAT are required for a system outside the vCloud environment to access services on a virtual machine connected to a vApp network. One NAT level is required if the organization virtual datacenter network is directly connected, and two are required if the organization virtual datacenter network is routed. Static routing significantly simplifies connectivity to external systems required for services such as monitoring and patch management, or for integration into centralized services such as authentication and logging. Because these routing capabilities are delivered through vCloud Networking and Security Edge, the self-service firewall management is still maintained. This is important in private vCloud deployments where networks are typically flatter to support the centralized services, and static routing is an alternative to directly connecting virtual machines to the external networks.

3.5.5.8 Static Routing vApp Network Use Cases

3.5.5.8.1 Enabling vApp Networks Connected to an Organization Virtual Datacenter Network to Communicate Directly

This scenario provides connectivity similar to the use case in Figure 3.30.

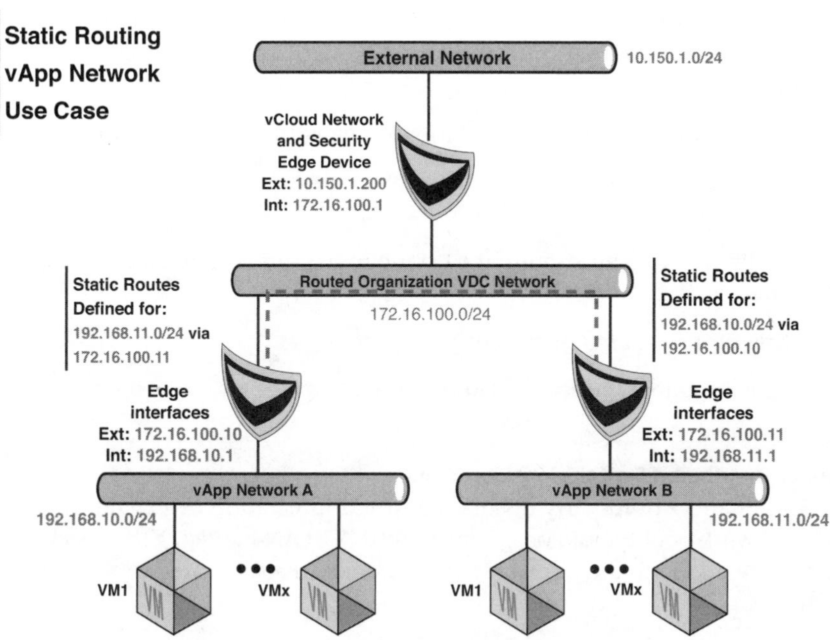

FIGURE 3.30 vApp network static routing use case

If vApp level static routing is configured, enable Always Use Assigned IP Addresses Until This vApp or Associated Networks Are Deleted so that the next-hop addresses for static routes does not change while vApps are powered off.

An overlap arises between organization virtual datacenter network use case 2 (see Figure 3.29) and the vApp network use case, so it is important to understand the advantages and disadvantages of both configurations:

- Applying static routes at the organization virtual datacenter network consolidates management to a common view but requires all traffic to pass through the organization's vCloud Networking and Security Edge device.
- vApp network static routes allow traffic to flow directly between the vApps that provide the highest performance.
- Static routing at the vApp network layer supports scenarios in which the organization virtual datacenter network is directly connected.

Although providing connectivity between vApps without address translation is required, VMware recommends that you apply static routes in the vApp network vCloud Networking and Security Edge device. Unlike NAT, static routing does not support overlapping network ranges. If there are plans to leverage static routing within the vCloud environment, allocated IP addresses for organization and vApp networks must be unique.

The static routing and NAT features are not mutually exclusive and can be used together. For example, NAT can provide external connectivity, while static routing permits direct access to other vApps within an organization.

Consider the following limitations when using static routing with vCloud Director:

- Static routing is supported only with vCloud Networking and Security Edge 5.0 (or later).
- Static routing is limited to a maximum of 64 static routes per vCloud Networking and Security Edge device.
- Dynamic routing protocols are not currently supported.
- Static routing does not apply to fenced vApps.

3.5.5.9 Third-Party Distributed Switch Considerations

vCloud Director 5.1 enhances third-party distributed switch integration by extending support for all the network pool types. Port group–backed, VXLAN-backed, VLAN-backed, and VCD-NI-based network pools are available for creation with a supported third-party distributed switch.

3.5.6 Networking—Public vCloud Example

The public service definition requirements (see Table 3.13) used in this example are from Chapter 2.

TABLE 3.13 Public vCloud Network Requirements

Requirements
Pool of eight public routable IP addresses for each tenant
Minimum of one routed organization virtual datacenter network protected by a firewall service
Capability to create up to 10 vApp networks

3.5.6.1 External Networks

All service tiers use a shared public Internet connection. When establishing the external network, do the following:

- Map to a vSphere port group that is configured for Internet connectivity.
- Provide the network configuration details, including subnet mask, default gateway, and DNS.
- Reserve the static IP address range available for this network. vCloud Director automatically assigns IP addresses to devices directly connecting to external networks.
- Give the network a descriptive name, such as Shared-Internet.

For sizing purposes, create an IP address pool large enough to support Internet connectivity for all organizations in the vCloud. The estimated number of organizations for 1,500 virtual machines is 25, so provide at least 25 IP addresses in your static IP pool. Each organization requires at least eight public IP addresses to allow inbound access to virtual machines.

3.5.6.2 Network Pools

Each organization in a public vCloud requires individual private networks. vCloud Director instantiates isolated Layer 2 networks using network pools.

Create a single vCloud Director VXLAN network pool for all organization virtual datacenter network deployments. VXLAN requires the use of a distributed switch.

Network pools handle the automated creation of organization virtual datacenter networks and vApp networks. A minimum of 12 networks is required in the network pool per organization, with 10 reserved for vApp networks and 2 used for organization virtual datacenter networks. Given the estimate of 25 organizations, the network pool should contain at least 300 networks. vCloud Director creates auto-expandable static port groups for organization and vApp networks. The maximum number of networks in a network pool is limited to 10,000 direct connect vCloud datacenter networks or 2,000 routed vCloud datacenter networks. Figure 3.31 shows an example of using a public vCloud network.

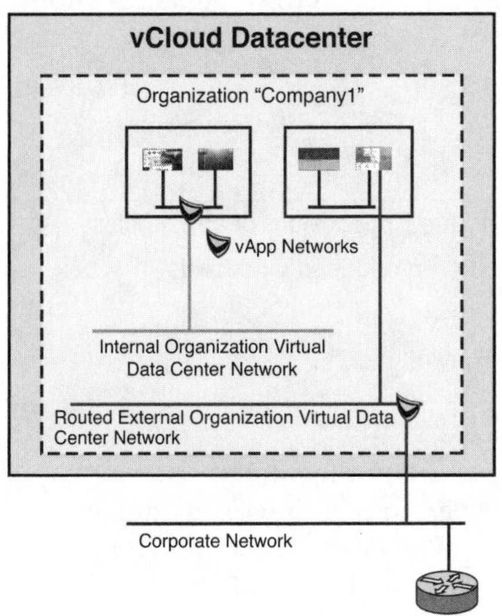

FIGURE 3.31 Example of public vCloud networking

3.5.6.3 Organization Virtual Datacenter Networks

Create two different organization virtual datacenter networks for each organization: one routed external organization virtual datacenter network and one internal organization virtual datacenter network. The Create Organization Network Wizard provides the option of creating these two organization virtual datacenter networks in one workflow. When naming an organization virtual datacenter network, start with the organization name and a hyphen—for example, Company1-Internet.

The routed external organization virtual datacenter network uses vCloud Networking and Security Edge for firewall and NAT services to isolate organization traffic from other organizations that share the same external provider network. Both the external organization virtual datacenter network and the internal organization virtual datacenter networks are instantiated from the previously established vCloud Director Network Isolation network pool. Each organization virtual datacenter network requires network configuration settings and a pool of IP addresses. Because both networks are private networks, you can use RFC 1918 addresses for each static IP address pool. The static IP address pool can be as large as desired. Typically, an RFC 1918 class C is used.

The last step is to add external public IP addresses to the vCloud Networking and Security Edge configuration on the external organization virtual datacenter network. Using the Configure Services interface, add eight public IP addresses to an external organization virtual datacenter network. The IP addresses listed come from the external network static IP address pool.

3.5.7 Networking—Private vCloud Example

The private service definition requirements (see Table 3.14) used in this example are from Chapter 2.

TABLE 3.14 Private vCloud Network Requirements

Requirements
vApps require a direct connection to the external network due to upstream dependencies.
An isolated network is needed for development, test, and preproduction workloads.
Users have the capability to self-provision networks.

3.5.7.1 External Networks

Private vCloud networking requirements tend to vary based on the primary use cases driving the project. Enterprises that act as service providers to their internal customers tend to have comparable network requirements to that of a public vCloud. Enterprises that use vCloud for development or preproduction environments have different requirements.

Enterprises commonly require direct connections from inside the vCloud environment into the networking backbone. This is analogous to "extending a wire" from the network switch that contains the network or VLAN to be used all the way through the vCloud layers into the vApp. Each organization in the private vCloud has an internal organization virtual datacenter network and a direct-connect external organization virtual datacenter network.

Figure 3.32 shows an example of using a private vCloud network.

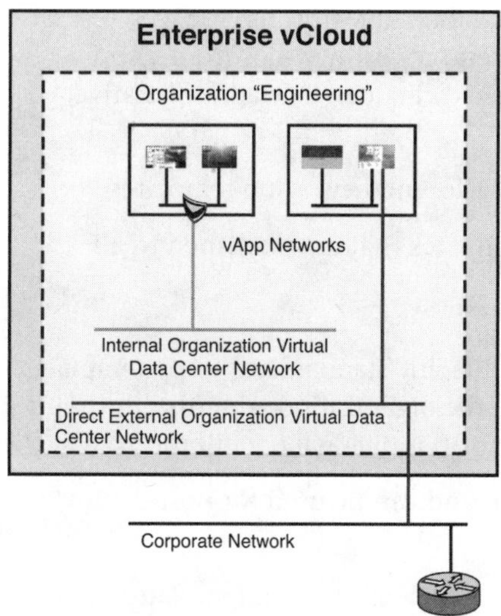

FIGURE 3.32 Example of private vCloud networking

At least one external network is required for external organization virtual datacenter networks to access resources outside vCloud Director—the Internet for public vCloud deployments and an internal (local) network for private vCloud deployments.

To establish this network, use the New External Network Wizard and specify external network settings and static IP address ranges. For the static IP address pool, a good starting range is 30 reserved IP addresses for static assignment.

3.5.7.2 Network Pools

The requirements call for one internal organization virtual datacenter network and the capability for consumers to create private vApp networks. No minimum number of vApp networks is defined, but typically organizations start with around 10. Size the network pool to be the number of organizations multiplied by 11. VMware recommends setting the maximum number of networks per network pool to 2,000 routed or 10,000 direct-connect networks.

3.5.7.3 Organization Networks

At least one organization external network is required to connect organization vApps to other vApps and/or the networking layers beyond the private vCloud.

To accomplish this, create an external organization virtual datacenter network using the Create Organization Network Wizard, and select Direct Connection from the drop-down menu. vApps that connect to this organization virtual datacenter network are dropped directly on the vSphere port group that corresponds to the external network.

Implementing routed networking can add complexity to the network design. For more information on adding network options, see the *vCloud Director Administrator's Guide* in the VMware vCloud Director documentation (www.vmware.com/support/pubs/vcd_pubs.html).

Catalogs are the primary deployment mechanism in vCloud Director, serving as a centralized repository for vApp templates and media. Users self-provision vApps from vApp templates located in internal catalogs or global published catalogs. The administrative organization virtual datacenter has two catalogs:

- **Internal catalog:** Acts as the staging area for developing new vApp templates
- **Master catalog:** Contains gold master vApp templates that are published to all organizations

Organizations leverage the published master catalog to deploy standardized vApp templates. Each organization also has a private catalog created by the organization administrator. This private catalog is used to upload new vApps or media to an individual organization.

Guest customization changes the identity of the vApp and can be used for post-deployment steps, such as joining vApps to domains.

No additional configuration requirements exist for the catalogs or vApp templates in this vCloud architecture. Refer to the private or public service definition for a full list of recommended templates. vApp templates usually include base operating system templates with no applications installed, or application-specific vApp templates.

3.5.8 vApp

A *vApp* is a container for a distributed software solution and is the standard unit of deployment in vCloud Director. It has power-on operations, consists of one or more virtual machines, and can be imported or exported as an OVF package. Although similarly named, VMware vSphere vApps™ and vCloud vApps have subtle differences. For example, vCloud vApps can contain additional constructs such as vApp networks but do not offer the resource controls found in vSphere vApps.

3.5.8.1 General Design Considerations

The following are general design considerations for vApps:

- Use a default of one vCPU unless requirements call for more (such as a multi-threaded application).
- Always install the latest version of VMware Tools™.
- Deploy virtual machines using default shares, reservations, and limits settings unless a clear requirement exists for doing otherwise.
- For virtual network adaptors, use VMXNET3 if supported.
- Secure virtual machines as you would physical machines.
- Virtual hardware versions 7, 8, and 9 are supported, depending on the vSphere host version backing the hosts in the provider virtual datacenter. Virtual hardware version 9 is supported in vSphere 5.1.

- Verify that the virtual machine virtual hardware version matches the highest required version within the provider virtual datacenter. The highest version chosen is the highest available with the provider virtual datacenter.
- Use standard virtual machine naming conventions.

3.5.8.1.1 Virtual Hardware Version 9

vCloud Director 5.1 exposes the highest version of virtual hardware available in the provider virtual datacenter. Users can choose the virtual hardware version desired, up to the latest version supported by the provider virtual datacenter for their organization virtual datacenter. vSphere 5.1 supports the use of virtual hardware version 9.

Virtual hardware version 9 provides capabilities to vCloud vApps such as Windows 8 XP mode, 64-bit nested virtualization, and CPU-intensive workloads.

- **Windows 8 XP mode:** XP mode allows a virtualized XP instance to run for compatibility with older applications that do not natively run on Windows 8. Users who need to run XP mode in Windows 8 must choose an organization virtual datacenter that is backed by a provider that allows version 9 virtual hardware. After specifying virtual hardware version 9, the user must also enable the Nested HV feature.
- **64-bit nested virtualization:** Hyper-V and virtualized ESXi nested virtualization can be helpful for nonproduction use cases such as training and demonstration environments. Virtualized Hyper-V or virtualized ESXi running nested 64-bit virtual machines requires virtual hardware version 9 with the Nested HV feature enabled.
- **CPU-intensive workloads:** Users who need to run an extremely CPU-intensive workload in a virtual machine that requires 32 to 64 vCPUs must use virtual hardware version 9.

3.5.8.2 Differences Between vSphere and vCloud Director vApps

An OVF section is an XML fragment that contains data for a specific function, such as resource settings, startup and shutdown sequence, or operating system type. The following is the general format of an OVF section:

```
<myns:MyOvfSection ovf:required="true or false">
 <Info>A description of the purpose of the section</Info>
 ... section specific content ...
</myns:MyOvfSection>
```

Because vCloud Director does not currently support all the OVF sections that vSphere supports, the following sections of the vSphere vApp OVF representation are not visible to vCloud Director:

- `AnnotationSection`
- `DeploymentOptionSection`
- `InstallSection`

- ProductSection
- ResourceAllocationSection

vCloud Director and vSphere support all other OVF sections. When vCloud Director ignores a section, vSphere might interpret the contents differently than if it was a native vSphere vApp. This can result in differences in behavior when operating the imported vApp in a virtual datacenter. vCloud Director removes the ignored OVF sections during a vApp download.

3.5.9 Snapshots

vCloud Director 5.1 provides full support for snapshot functionality. This section discusses snapshots, the impact they have on the underlying infrastructure, and the considerations to take into account before enabling snapshot functionality in a vCloud environment.

3.5.9.1 Snapshot Architecture

A snapshot preserves the state and data of a virtual machine at a specific point in time:

- The state includes the virtual machine's power state (powered on, powered off, suspended).
- The data includes all the files that make up the virtual machine.

Snapshots work by creating delta copies (point in time) of the specified virtual machine files. Figure 3.33 provides a high-level illustration of how the process works.

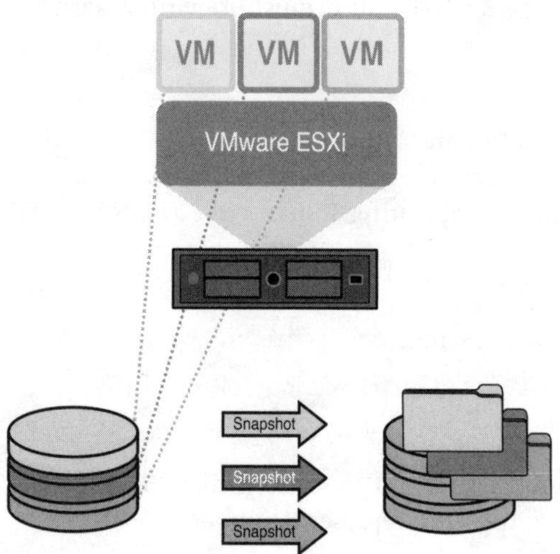

FIGURE 3.33 Snapshot processing

Each snapshot consists of the following files, where <vm> is the name of the virtual machine and <number> identifies the specific snapshot:

- <vm>-<number>.vmdk and <vm>-<number>-delta.vmdk

  A collection of .vmdk and -delta.vmdk files for each virtual disk is connected to the virtual machine at the time of the snapshot. These files are referred to as *child disks, redo logs*, or *delta links*. Child disks can later become parent disks for future child disks. From the original parent disk, each child constitutes a redo log that points back from the present state of the virtual disk, one step at a time, to the original one.

NOTE

The <number> value might not be consistent across all child disks from the same snapshot. The filenames are chosen based on filename availability.

- <vm>.vmsd

  The .vmsd file is a database of the virtual machine's snapshot information and the primary source of information for the snapshot manager. The file contains line entries that define the relationships between snapshots, as well as the child disks for each snapshot.

- <vm>Snapshot<number>.vmsn

  These files record the memory state at the time of the snapshot.

3.5.9.2 Snapshot Use Cases

The following are primary use cases for using snapshots in a vCloud environment:

- Production backups
- Development/test environments
- Third-party backup integration

3.5.9.2.1 Production Backups

Do not use snapshots as a long-term production backup solution. A snapshot is a copy of files stored within the same datastore. If the datastore is lost, the virtual machine and snapshot are also lost. However, snapshots do allow consumers to quickly take temporary near-line backups of the current virtual machine state, to mitigate risk during change management windows and then quickly restore when needed to return to a previous configuration.

3.5.9.2.2 Development and Test Environments

Snapshots allow easy in-place upgrades with minimal risk and are an excellent solution for version control when a vCloud environment is used for development. Developers can make changes to the virtual machine and then, if a failure occurs, can easily roll back to the previous version (state).

3.5.9.2.3 Third-Party Backup Integration

Some backup vendors use snapshots to create a copy of the virtual machine and then export the snapshots to a storage location outside the vCloud infrastructure. For more information, see the individual vendor solution briefs on the VMware Solutions Exchange (https://solutionexchange.vmware.com/).

3.5.9.3 Design Considerations

This section describes the design considerations to take into account when enabling snapshot functionality in a vCloud environment.

3.5.9.3.1 Security

Consumers must have the user right `vAPP_Clone` to create snapshots.

3.5.9.3.2 Storage

For each snapshot, the total consumed disk space includes the sizes of the files needed to capture the state of the virtual machine at the time of the snapshot (for example, hard disk and memory).

For example:

vmdk file + Memory size = Total consumed disk space

Figure 3.34 illustrates this.

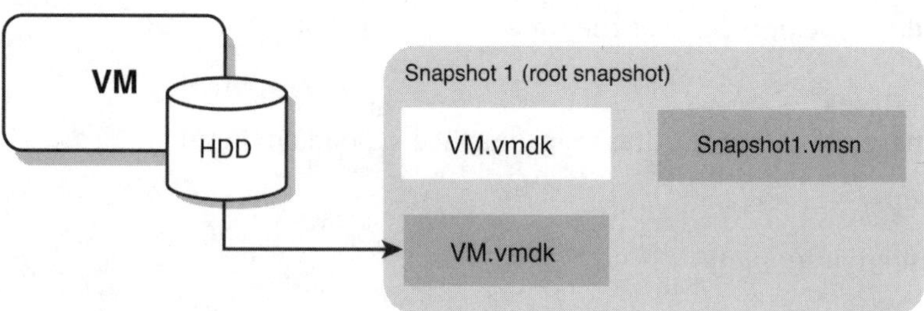

FIGURE 3.34 Snapshot sizing

vCloud administrators must take into account the number of consumers they will permit to take snapshots. Because a vCloud virtual machine can create only one snapshot, this calculation is relatively easy.

Datastore free space monitoring is critical to the success of any vCloud environment, and even more so in an environment that allows snapshots. Allowing multiple virtual machines and snapshots to consume a datastore can impact consumers' capability to start their virtual machines. To mitigate this, consider using vSphere Storage DRS, which allows for the redistribution of virtual machines if a datastore violates a free space threshold. However, vSphere Storage DRS is not a replacement for careful datastore sizing and monitoring because it does not stop a snapshot from writing to the datastore when performing migrations.

3.5.9.3.3 Performance

To reduce the impact of storage performance issues when creating snapshots, configure the storage array that serves the vCloud infrastructure to support VAAI. VAAI provides hardware-assisted locking. Hardware-assisted locking allows offloading of the lock mechanism to the arrays and does so with much less granularity than for an entire LUN. Therefore, the VMware cluster can provide significant scalability without compromising the integrity of the VMFS shared storage pool metadata.

3.5.9.4 vCloud Director Snapshot Characteristics

vCloud Director 5.1 snapshot capabilities include the following:

- One snapshot per virtual machine is permitted.
- NIC settings are marked read-only after a snapshot is taken.
- Editing of NIC settings is disabled through the API after a snapshot is taken.
- To take a snapshot, the user must have the `vAPP_Clone` user right.
- Snapshot storage allocation is added to Chargeback.
- vCloud Director performs a storage quota check.
- REST API support is provided to perform snapshots.
- The snapshot can include virtual machine memory.
- Full clone is forced upon copy or move of the virtual machine, resulting in the deletion of the snapshot (shadow VMDK).

3.5.10 Storage Independent of Virtual Machines

The use of independent disks with vCloud Director 5.1 allows updates of virtual machines without impacting the underlying data. For example, you can detach the data disk from the existing virtual machine, delete the existing virtual machine, re-create the virtual machine, and reattach the original disk. This feature is a key enabler to enhance the deployment of a Cloud Foundry PaaS cloud within a vCloud environment.

3.5.10.1 Independent Disk Architecture

The independent disk feature consists of the following:

- A database schema to represent independent disks in vCloud Director and their associated backing in vSphere
- A set of methods that implement the external vCloud Director API by manipulating the database schema and invoking the VIM API
- A set of event handlers invoked by the VC Listener (Inventory Service) that allows vCloud Director to keep track of relevant vCenter Server activity (for example, vSphere Storage vMotion initiated by vSphere Storage DRS, or the vSphere Client)

Virtual disks in vSphere do not necessarily have unique IDs. For example, when a virtual disk is cloned (virtual machine clone) in vSphere, the new virtual machine receives a unique ID, but the disk IDs are reused. Also, the vSphere disk ID might be changed at any point using the vSphere API, which would break the vCloud Director reference pointer if it were the unique ID.

Therefore, vCloud Director generates and uses its own identifier for independent disks, persisted in the vCloud Director database. vCloud Director does not currently have the API infrastructure to support adding the vCloud Director disk ID to the disk metadata in the VMDK files.

A disk becomes detached in vCenter when a virtual machine using that disk is deleted in vCloud Director, but the disk must be saved for future virtual machines. Because detached disks are not known objects in vSphere, features such as vSphere Storage DRS cannot be used to migrate the detached independent disks. To aid in this situation, vCloud Director creates a virtual machine shell for each detached virtual disk and attaches the disks to the new shell. If the independent disk must be attached to a new virtual machine, the shell is deleted.

If a delete action takes place before an attach action, vCloud Director performs a check to verify that the disk is attached to a virtual machine object before completing the delete request, to avoid inadvertently deleting the independent disk.

If actions are taken against the vCenter (through the UI or API), certain update actions are either safe or unsafe to perform:

- vSphere Storage vMotion or virtual machine relocate actions are safe actions to perform. vCenter updates vCloud Director with the revised locations of the disk files.
- Disk add and disk remove actions and the associated disk locations are unknown to vCloud Director and, therefore, are unsafe to perform.

3.5.10.2 Design Considerations

Independent disk limitations and usage considerations are as follows:

- Only SCSI controller types are supported.
- The disk size counts against the organization virtual datacenter quota.
- If the class of storage is not specified, the organization virtual datacenter default is used.
- If you delete a virtual machine, the independent disk is first detached from the virtual machine.
- When exporting a virtual machine with an independent disk, the disk is not tagged to identify that its source was an independent disk.

- The following operations cannot be performed if the virtual machine currently has an attached independent disk:
  - Clone vApp
  - Copy vApp virtual machine
  - Capture vApp to catalog
  - Move virtual machine
  - Change owner
- When using the elastic virtual datacenter feature and allowing a provider virtual datacenter to span multiple clusters, it might be necessary to move an independent disk to a different datastore to attach it to a virtual machine in a different cluster. To avoid such a move, use the `locality` argument to create a disk in the destination cluster for the virtual machine (not necessarily on the same datastore).
- The scalability maximum for this feature is one independent disk per virtual machine, up to the maximum number of virtual machines for vCloud Director.

3.5.11 vApp Load Balancing

vApp load balancing is used to increase availability through redundancy, increase throughput, minimize response time by redirecting to servers based on load or proximity, and avoid overloading resources.

3.5.11.1 Background

The vCloud Director environment is compatible with traditional IP-based load balancing schemes. You can even run multicast-based load balancing schemes with some caveats. Global load balancers can also be used with vCloud Director–hosted virtual machines because back-end servers do not need any special configuration options.

VMware vCloud Director 5.1 offers options for self-service load balancing using the vCloud Networking and Security Edge built-in load balancer.

3.5.11.2 Load Balancing Architecture Options

In a vCloud Director environment, various options exist for implementing load-balanced vApps. Differences in architecture are based on the type of load balancer. Use cases include the following:

- External hardware-based load balancer
- Third-party virtual appliance load balancer
- vCloud Networking and Security Edge used as a load balancer

vApp Load Balancing Examples

This section provides examples for each type of load balancer use case.

3.5.11.3.1 Example: External Hardware-Based Load Balancer Appliance

Third-party hardware load balancers provide options to control exactly how the load is to be balanced or distributed. Load balancers are not restricted to web traffic only—they can often be configured to handle arbitrary protocols. When you have esoteric workloads that you need to put behind a load balancer, these hardware boxes are still the most feature-rich option available.

In a vCloud Director environment, the most straightforward way to use hardware load balancers is to put the back-end (load to be balanced) virtual machines on a directly attached organization virtual datacenter network that is shared with the back-end connection of the load balancer. This is usually thought of as a DMZ network. The load balancing logic is contained in the load balancer, and the virtual machines based on vCloud Director are used as pure compute resources.

In Figure 3.35, the DMZ network is a vApp or organization virtual datacenter network that is bridged to the external network. The public network can be any physical networking that routes to the client location.

When evaluating the use of hardware-based load balancers, weigh the higher per-port cost against the availability of multiprotocol support and other advanced load-balancing options.

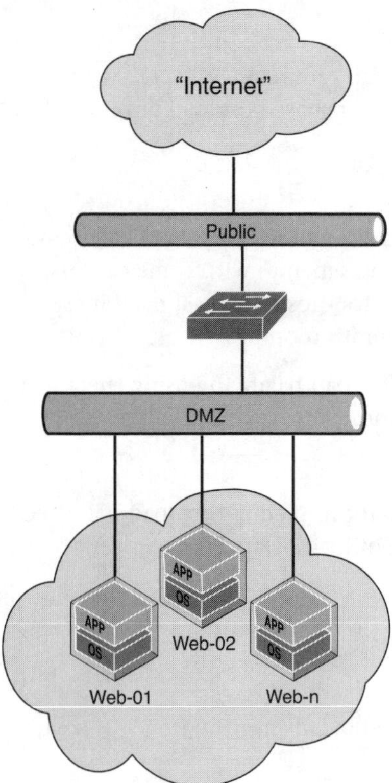

FIGURE 3.35 Hardware-based load balancer

3.5.11.3.2 Example: Third-Party Virtual Appliance As a Load Balancer

Many third-party virtual load balancers are available, with varying degrees of multiprotocol support and advanced features. The third-party configuration works with all virtualization-supported networking protocols that the virtual load balancer supports.

When using a virtual appliance as a load balancer, protect the security of the vApp workloads upstream by using a firewall. In this configuration, vCloud Director does not provide security or isolation for the back-end workloads other than what the load balancer provides.

In Figure 3.36, the DMZ network is an isolated vApp or organization virtual datacenter network, and the public network is a vApp or organization virtual datacenter network that is bridged to an external network capable of routing to clients.

A major advantage in running a virtual appliance instead of a hardware appliance is that the network port can scale up to the bandwidth that is available on the vSphere host (usually 10Gbps per port). In some implementations, having up to 10Gbps of bandwidth available is a significant advantage over the bandwidth available with a physical appliance. Hardware appliances usually are limited to 1Gbps ports.

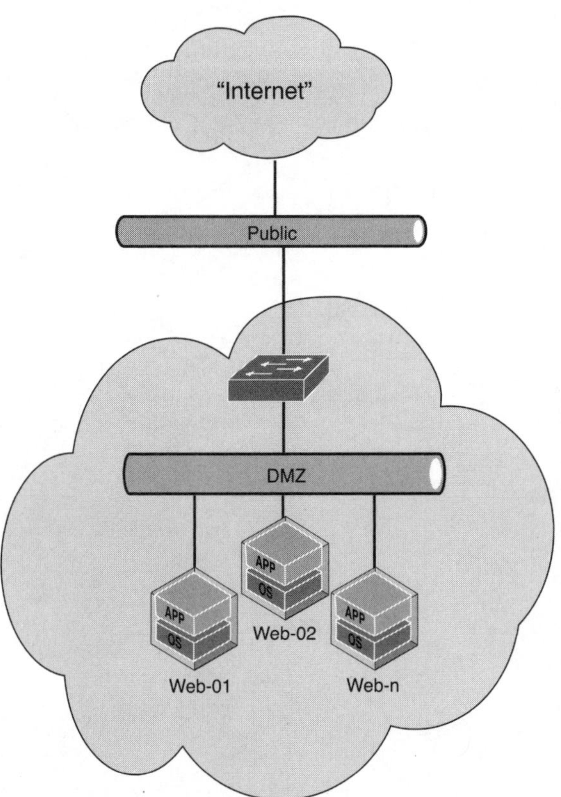

FIGURE 3.36 Third-party virtual load balancer

3.5.11.3.3 Example: vCloud Networking and Security Edge As a Load Balancer

vCloud Network and Security Edge offers basic HTTP (port 80) and HTTPS (port 443) load balancing and can be used for applications that need one or both of these protocols. vCloud Networking and Security Edge can be used to load-balance vCloud Director cells and the basic web server configuration.

vCloud Networking and Security Edge currently has limited load-balancing advanced features, such as SSL termination and stickiness. If advanced features are critical to the operation of the application being load-balanced, consider evaluating a third-party virtual or physical load-balancing appliance.

In Figure 3.37, vCloud Networking and Security Edge provides the load-balancing functionality and firewall needed to secure the vApp workloads.

As in the third-party virtual appliance as a load balancer example, the DMZ network should be an isolated vApp or organization virtual datacenter network, but the public network should be a vApp or organization virtual datacenter network that is bridged to the external network that routes to client locations.

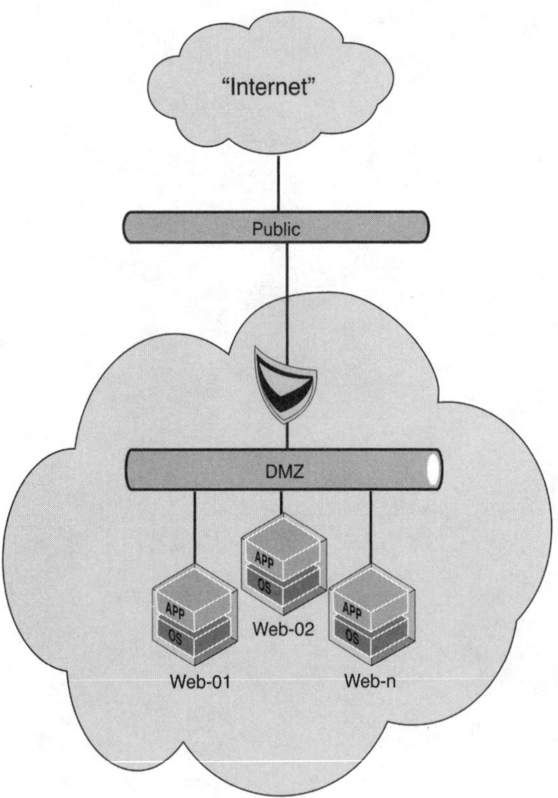

FIGURE 3.37 vCloud Networking and Security Edge as a load balancer

3.5.11.4 Load Balancing Design Implications

VMware vSphere high availability protects against physical host failures and restarts failed virtual machines using a third-party load-balancing virtual appliance or the solution based on vCloud Networking and Security Edge. This affords about 99.9% uptime for the load balancing functionality (based on vSphere HA availability numbers).

You can improve availability for the load balancer by running it in native high availability mode. This affords the edge an almost instantaneous failover, with session preservation.

3.6 vCloud Metering

For vCloud environments, resource metering is essential to accurately measure consumer usage and shape consumer behavior through chargeback policies. VMware vCenter Chargeback Manager provides the metering capability to enable cost transparency and accountability in vCloud environments.

When running a private vCloud, enterprises do not necessarily have the same cost pressures as a public vCloud service provider. Required chargeback procedures or policies might not exist. An alternative to chargeback is *showback*, which attempts to raise awareness of consumption usage and cost by showing the consumer what the services would cost without involving formal accounting procedures to bill the usage back to the consumer's department.

Chargeback provides cost transparency and accountability to align consumer behavior with the actual cost of the consumed resources. Without showback or chargeback, consumers are not aware of the actual cost of the resources they consume and thus have little incentive to change their consumption patterns. vCloud computing resources can be easily spun up, and with the exception of deployment policies that dictate resource leases, no disincentives or penalties exist to curb excessive use. Metering exposes heavy or demanding users who could monopolize vCloud resources.

3.6.1 vCenter Chargeback Manager

vCenter Chargeback Manager provides the metering capability to measure, analyze, and report on resources used in private and public vCloud environments. vCloud providers can configure and associate various pricing models to vCloud Director entities. The cost transparency enabled by vCenter Chargeback allows vCloud providers to validate and adjust financial models based on the demand for resources.

3.6.1.1 vCenter Chargeback Manager Architecture

The vCenter Chargeback Manager is based on a Windows server that runs the vCenter Chargeback web application, load balancer, and data collector services. Services can run on separate servers for scalability and resiliency. The server can be virtual or physical and has the following recommended specifications:

- 2.0GHz or faster Intel/AMD x86 processor
- 4GB or more RAM

- 3GB disk storage
- 1Gbps Ethernet adapter

vCenter Chargeback Manager instances can be clustered together to provide improved performance and availability for the user interface. A cluster configuration leverages the Apache load balancer, which is bundled with the Chargeback software. All instances in a cluster must run the same version of Chargeback. A Chargeback cluster can include up to three Chargeback servers. Sizing for chargeback instances in a cluster depends on the number of simultaneous users.

Load balancing is active/active. Each user request, whether it comes from the user interface or an API, routes through the load balancer. The load balancer forwards the request to a Chargeback instance in the cluster based on the number of requests currently serviced by each instance in the cluster. With multiple instances, Chargeback also load-balances the report-processing load by leveraging the internal Quartz scheduler. If the load-balancer service terminates, the Windows service can be restarted. The built-in load balancer cannot be replaced with a third-party load balancer. All Chargeback instances in a cluster connect to the same Chargeback database.

If the load-balancer service becomes unavailable, the Chargeback Manager application does not work. If the Tomcat server on a cluster instance terminates, the load balancer redirects requests to other cluster instances.

For a load-balanced session, *stickiness* is enabled. The session always sticks to one vCenter Chargeback server. If multiple sessions are in use, the following algorithm applies:

1. The load balancer uses the number of requests to find the best worker.
2. Access is distributed according to the `lbfactor` (it is the same for all the servers in the cluster) in a sliding time window.

For more information, see *The Apache Tomcat Connector—Reference Guide* (http://tomcat.apache.org/connectors-doc/reference/workers.html) for the following properties:

- `sticky_session = 1` (true)
- `method = R`

Figure 3.38 shows a vCenter Chargeback cluster.

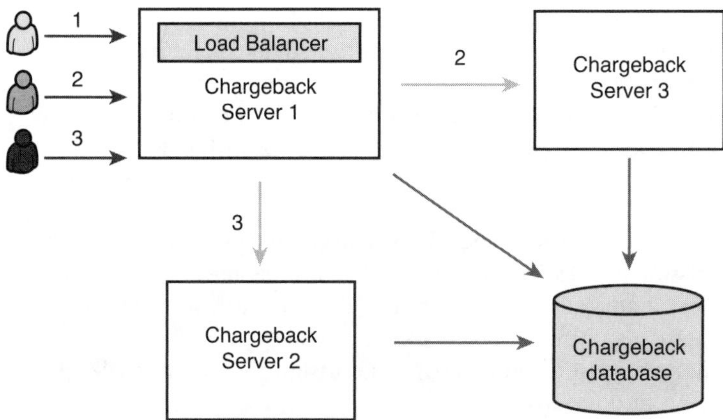

FIGURE 3.38 vCenter Chargeback cluster

Multiple Chargeback environments (separate vCenter Chargeback Manager and database) can work with a single vCloud Director instance, but this increases the load on the vCloud Director instance.

The vCenter Chargeback Database stores organization hierarchies, cost/rate plans, and global chargeback configuration data. Supported databases include Microsoft SQL Server Express, Microsoft SQL Server, and Oracle. Database partitioning helps to improve the performance of vCenter Chargeback Manager. vCenter Chargeback Manager does not support the database (DB2 or PostgreSQL) included in the vCenter appliance.

3.6.1.2 Data Collectors

vCenter Chargeback Manager integration with vCloud Director is handled through data collectors:

- **Chargeback Manager data collector:** Connects to vCenter Server to gather virtual machine metrics. Add all vCenter Servers imported into vCloud Director to Chargeback Manager to see virtual machine–level details. Virtual machines are absent in the vCloud hierarchies until their respective vCenter Servers are registered with Chargeback.

- **vCloud data collector:** Connects to the vCloud Director instance using the vCloud API and monitors all vCloud Director chargeback-related events. The vCloud data collector populates the Chargeback Manager database with vCloud hierarchies and allocation unit information.

- **vCloud Networking and Security Manager data collector:** Connects to vCloud-associated vCloud Networking and Security Manager instances to collect network statistics for networks included in the vCloud hierarchy.

Install additional vCloud Director or vCloud Networking and Security Manager data collectors on separate servers for increased availability. Multiple data collectors act in an active/passive configuration. When one instance terminates, the other instance takes ownership and starts processing. A Chargeback Manager environment can have multiple vCloud data collectors but can connect to only one vCloud Director instance.

3.6.1.3 User Roles

The default superuser role has access to the entire Chargeback application. The administrator role has access and permissions to resources that the superuser assigns. Similarly, users created in less privileged roles by administrators are visible only to those administrators. For example, administrator A1 does not have access to users created by administrator A2. With this in mind, administrators must carefully create and assign roles and privileges. This also extends to LDAP users and groups.

3.6.2 Maximums

Table 3.15 lists maximums for Chargeback Manager.

TABLE 3.15 Maximums

Constraint	Limit	Explanation
vCenter Servers in a Chargeback system	10	Maximum number of vCenter Servers that a single Chargeback system supports
vCenter Servers per data collector	5	Maximum of vCenter Servers that a single Chargeback data collector supports
Virtual machines per data collector	15,000	Number of virtual machines that a single Chargeback data collector supports
Virtual machines/entities in a Chargeback system	35,000	Maximum number of entities per Chargeback system
Virtual machines/entities per hierarchy	1,000	Maximum number of entities per Chargeback hierarchy
Hierarchies in a Chargeback system	5,000	Maximum number of hierarchies per Chargeback system
Concurrent reports (~3,000 pages) per Chargeback system	5	Maximum number of concurrent reports per Chargeback system

3.6.3 Cost Calculation

To track resource metrics for vCloud entities, vCenter Chargeback Manager sets allocation units on vCloud hierarchies based on the parameters of the allocation model configured in vCloud Director. Allocation units are variables associated with chargeback metrics that represent the allocated size of the resource. Table 3.16 lists these allocation units.

TABLE 3.16 vCloud Hierarchy Allocation Units

Entity	Pay As You Go	Allocation Pool	Reservation Pool
Organization virtual datacenter	None	▶ CPU ▶ Memory ▶ Storage	▶ CPU ▶ Memory ▶ Storage
vApp	None	None	None
Virtual machine	▶ vCPU ▶ Memory ▶ Storage	▶ vCPU ▶ Memory ▶ Storage	▶ vCPU ▶ Memory ▶ Storage
Template	Storage	Storage	Storage
Media file	Storage	Storage	Storage
Independent Disk	Storage	Storage	Storage
Network	▶ DHCP ▶ NAT ▶ FirewallCount of networks	▶ DHCP ▶ NAT ▶ FirewallCount of networks	▶ DHCP ▶ NAT ▶ FirewallCount of networks

3.6.3.1 Pricing Models

Installing vCloud and vCloud Networking and Security Manager data collectors creates default cost models and billing policies that integrate with vCloud Director and vCloud Networking and Security Manager. Billing policies control costs assessed to resources used. Default vCloud billing policies charge based on allocation for vCPU, memory, and storage. Cost time intervals include hourly, daily, weekly, monthly, quarterly, half-yearly, or yearly.

Instead of modifying default billing policies and pricing models, make copies and modify the duplicates. For more information, see the User's Guide in the vCenter Chargeback Manager Documentation (www.vmware.com/support/pubs/vcbm_pubs.html).

Rate factors allow the scaling of base costs for a specific chargeable entity. Example use cases include the following:

- **Promotional rate:** A service provider offers new clients a 10% discount. Instead of modifying base rates in the cost model, apply a 0.9 rate factor to reduce the base costs for client by 10%.
- **Rates for unique configurations:** A service provider decides to charge clients for special infrastructure configurations using a rate factor to scale costs.

VM instance pricing assigns a fixed price to a hard bundle of vCPU and memory. Virtual machine instance matrixes are linked with a pricing model. The pricing model includes the hierarchy selection criteria, a fixed pricing table, and a default fixed price. Selection criteria options include name pattern matching, custom attribute matching, or no criteria.

VM instance uses a step function—if there is no entry for a particular virtual machine size, the charge is based on the next larger instance size.

vCenter Chargeback Manager 2.5 introduces VM instance pricing for all allocation models. Use VM instance pricing to create a fixed-price matrix for different virtual machine bundles.

3.6.3.2 Reporting

Chargeback can generate cost, usage, and comparison reports for hierarchies and entities. Match the entity or hierarchy with the appropriate cost model when generating reports.

The Chargeback API can export reports to XML. Developers can use XSLT to transform the raw XML into a format that the customer's billing system supports. Reports run from the Chargeback user interface are available in PDF and XLS format. Create service accounts with read-only privileges to run reports from the UI or Chargeback API.

3.7 Orchestration and Extension

The vCloud environment consists of several components that expose web services. A vCloud orchestration platform can tie services together into a logical workflow. VMware has different management applications supporting workflow process definition and execution.

- vCenter Orchestrator is a technical orchestration authoring platform within vCenter that enables administrators to automate repetitive tasks by creating workflows that leverage extensive integrations with VMware and third-party vCloud components. See Chapter 7, "Workflow Examples," for detailed examples of orchestrated workflows.
- vFabric Application Director automates the deployment of multitier applications to the vCloud. vFabric Application Director can simplify virtual machine template management by providing a catalog of services used to install, configure, and start software services on virtual machines. vFabric Application Director uses the vCloud API to issue provisioning requests to a vCloud provider and can be deployed in public, private, and hybrid vCloud environments.
- VMware Service Manager™ is a configurable ITIL platform that features service desk, automated configuration and change management, IT asset management, self-service, and request fulfillment. As part of the service request, it supports a configurable portal using high-level business workflow modeling for approvals, notifications, and tasks integration.

3.7.1 vCloud API

The vCloud API provides an interface for managing resources in vCloud instances and is the cornerstone of federation and ecosystem support. All current federation tools communicate with the vCloud environment through the vCloud API. It is important that a vCloud environment expose the vCloud API to vCloud consumers.

The vCloud API can be used to facilitate communication to vCloud resources using a user interface other than the vCloud Director web console. For example, provisioning portals communicate with vCloud Director using the vCloud API.

Currently, vCloud Director is the only software package that exposes the vCloud API. In some environments, vCloud Director is behind another portal or in a location that is not accessible to the vCloud consumer. In this case, use an API proxy or relay to expose the vCloud API to the end consumer.

Because of the value of the vCloud API, some environments might want to meter and charge for API usage. VMware also recommends protecting the vCloud API through audit trails and API inspection. In some cases, vCloud providers might want to extend the vCloud API with new features.

To assist with the vCloud API use cases, the vCloud provider might want to implement an API proxy. The vCloud API is a REST-based service that contains XML payloads. For this reason, any suitable XML gateway can be used as a proxy for the vCloud API. Several third-party solutions on the market today excel in XML gateway services. VMware collaborates with some of these vendors to develop joint guidance on how to deploy their solutions in a vCloud Director environment. For the latest information on these efforts and collateral, contact your local VMware vCloud specialist.

For more information about the vCloud API and SDKs, visit the developer communities at http://communities.vmware.com/community/vmtn/developer/forums/vcloudapi.

3.7.2 Cloud Provisioning with vFabric Application Director

vFabric Application Director is an entry point into the vCloud for creating and deploying multitier applications. vFabric Application Director consumes vCloud resources by defining a vCloud *provider* that is associated with a vCloud Director organization and associated catalogs.

- vFabric Application Director uses the vCloud API and requires access to the vCloud Director servers to issue provisioning requests.
- vFabric Application Director has a catalog of services that define how to install, configure, and start services on a virtual machine.
- vFabric Application Director can assemble virtual machines and services into a multitier application that is deployed to a vCloud provider.

3.7.2.1 Simplifying vApp Template Management

Catalog services can be constructed for each software component that is normally installed on virtual machines that are deployed to the vCloud environment. Consider a virtual machine as a collection of software packages and services running on a guest operating system. Most software components fit into a layered model where administrative duties might fall to different departments for maintaining software at each layer.

In Figure 3.39, multiple layers of software and services define the characteristics of the virtual machine. By creating services for each component in the vFabric Application

Director catalog, each department can maintain a service component in the catalog. This simplifies base virtual machine template creation and the management process because the templates need to contain only the base operating system and appropriate patch level. All other services can be installed, configured, and started by vFabric Application Director.

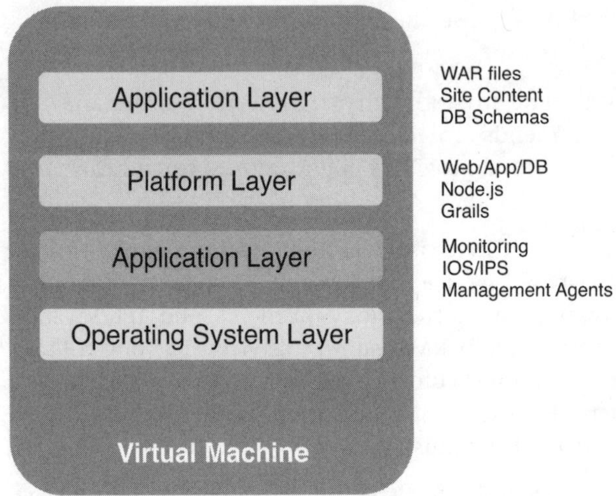

FIGURE 3.39 Software component layers

3.7.2.2 Simplifying vApp Template Management

To build a multitiered vApp, vFabric Application Director uses a blueprint to construct a vCloud vApp that contains multiple virtual machines. Each virtual machine in the vApp can be based on different vApp templates, and each virtual machine can be customized by the services selected from the vFabric Application Director catalog.

In Figure 3.40, a three-tiered application consisting of a presentation (web) tier, application tier, and database tier is modeled in vFabric Application Director as a blueprint. At deployment time, vFabric Application Director creates a corresponding vApp in the vCloud provider based on the virtual machine templates specified in the blueprint.

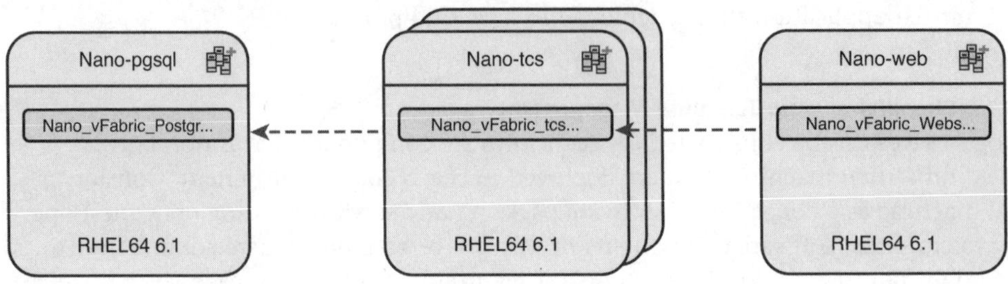

FIGURE 3.40 Three-tiered application modeled in vFabric Application Director

3.7.2.3 Guest Customization and the vFabric Application Director Agent

Virtual machine templates that vFabric Application Director consumes must have the vFabric Application Director agent installed. The interaction works as follows:

1. Upon first boot, virtual machines deployed by vFabric Application Director in the vCloud provider environment go through the vCloud guest customization process.
2. At the end of guest customization, the vFabric Application Director agent on each deployed virtual machine initiates contact with the vFabric Application Director server and downloads the latest version of the agent software.
3. The agent downloads the service scripts and creates environment variables that correspond to properties created in the service or blueprint.
4. Service scripts can then be executed to install, configure, and start software on each deployed virtual machine.

The vFabric Application Director agent in each virtual machine establishes the connection to the vFabric Application Director server. This reduces the complexity of firewall management.

3.7.2.4 vCloud Networks and vFabric Application Director

When provisioning a vApp, vFabric Application Director does not create any vApp internal networks. Application Director connects provisioned vApps directly to a vCloud organization virtual datacenter network. This removes the capability to provision fenced vApps with vFabric Application Director. Properties can be dynamically updated at deployment time, so service scripts can be written to modify relevant configuration parameters for software being installed or configured.

As an example, a property can be created to acquire the IP address of a new virtual machine at deployment time. A service script can use this IP address property to properly configure an application based on the new IP address of the newly provisioned virtual machine. This property can be exposed across multiple services and across multiple virtual machines deployed by vFabric Application Director through dependency mapping in the blueprint.

- vFabric Application Director–deployed vApps that are directly connected to an organization virtual datacenter network must allow for the agent service in each virtual machine to contact the vFabric Application Director server.
- vFabric Application Director does not connect a vApp to an isolated organization virtual datacenter network because that removes the agent's capability to contact the vFabric Application Director server.
- vFabric Application Director connects vApps only to an organization virtual datacenter network that is direct or routed to an external network.

3.7.2.5 Building a Software Repository

Building a central software repository or depot simplifies the service-development process. Locate the software repository in the same environment or datacenter as the target vCloud provider where vFabric Application Director–provisioned applications are deployed.

Data downloads from the software repository can be large in complex deployments, so consider bandwidth and latency between the software repository and provisioned virtual machines.

vFabric Application Director can optionally place content on a provisioned virtual machine using a special *content* type property. To support this feature, the software repository must allow HTTP access for file downloads. Other access methods require service authors to write their own methods to retrieve data from a software repository.

3.7.2.6 Design Implications

vFabric Application Director server is supported only when deployed to an environment based on vCloud Director. Often the vCloud environment on which vFabric Application Director is deployed is the same environment where applications are being provisioned. Because vFabric Application Director uses the vCloud API to issue provisioning requests, the vFabric Application Director server must be capable of issuing API calls to the vCloud Director servers that are managing the vCloud environment. This has the following security implications for some consumers:

- In public vCloud deployments, vCloud consumers often have access to only one vCloud organization. In this scenario, the vFabric Application Director vCloud provider organization is the same as the organization housing the vFabric Application Director server. If access to multiple organizations is available, it might be beneficial to deploy the vFabric Application Director server and software repository to one organization and have provisioned workloads deployed to another organization. Network access must be available from the deployed virtual machines to the vFabric Application Director server and software repository.
- In private vCloud deployments, deploy the vFabric Application Director server to a vCloud organization designated for management systems. This provides isolation for administrative purposes and can simplify Chargeback administration. The software repository can also be deployed to the management organization. vCloud providers can be defined in vFabric Application Director based on organization separation policies. Network access must be available from the deployed virtual machines to the vFabric Application Director server and software repository.
- In a hybrid vCloud deployment, the vFabric Application Director server might not be local to the vCloud provider where applications are deployed. vFabric Application Director uses the vCloud API to make provisioning requests to the vCloud provider. The agent installed in each vFabric Application Director–provisioned virtual machine must also be capable of establishing a network connection to the vFabric Application Director server. VMware recommends locating the software repository in the same environment or datacenter as the target vCloud provider because of bandwidth and latency considerations.

- Deploying vFabric Application Director servers into a vSphere environment is not currently a supported configuration.

3.7.3 vCloud Messages

vCloud messages provides the capability to connect vCloud Director with external systems (see Figure 3.41). vCloud Director can be configured to post notifications or messages to AMQP-based enterprise messaging brokers. vCloud messages provide visibility through nonblocking and blocking notifications, allowing for end-to-end integration.

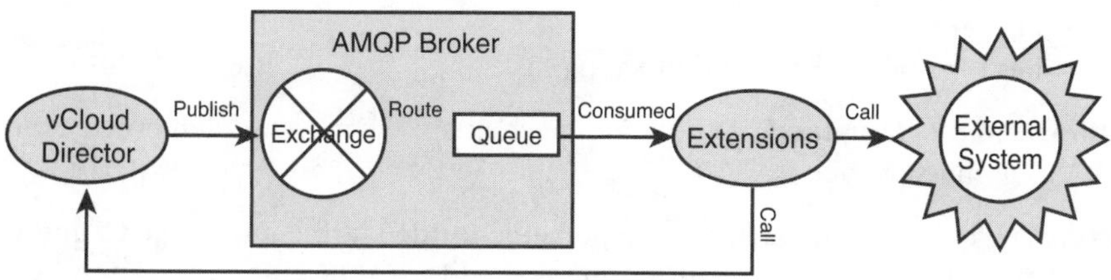

FIGURE 3.41 vCloud messages

3.7.3.1 Message Publication

The system administrator can configure vCloud Director to enable the publication of messages for all event notifications or for specific blocking tasks:

- Notifications are published on user-initiated events (for example, creation, deployment, and deletion of a vApp) and system-initiated events (for example, vApp lease expiration) that contain the new state of the corresponding vCloud Director entity.
- Blocking tasks suspend long-running operations started as a task before publishing messages and wait until a system administrator approves or rejects the request.

Message publication is enabled for operations started in the vCloud Director UI or vCloud API.

vCloud Director publishes notification messages to an Advanced Message Queuing Protocol (AMQP) exchange (requires AMQP version 0.9.1 supported by vFabric RabbitMQ version 2.0 and later).

3.7.3.2 Routing

The AMQP broker uses routing as an effective way to filter vCloud notification messages and dispatch them to different queues for one or multiple extensions.

The exchange routes notifications to its bound queues according to their queue routing key and exchange type. The vCloud notification messages routing key has the following syntax format:

```
<operationSuccess>.<entityUUID>.<orgUUID>.<userUUID>.<subType1>.<subType2>...
  <subTypeN>.[taskName]
```

3.7.3.3 Extension

An extension is a script or an application that has the following capabilities:

- Subscribes to an AMQP queue for receiving new messages
- Triages the received messages
- Processes messages into operations (internal or external calls)
- Calls the vCloud API to get more information on the objects involved in an operation and takes action on blocked tasks

3.7.3.4 Design Considerations

The following applies for notifications and blocking tasks:

- Notifications and blocking tasks are separate mechanisms that are implemented over the same AMQP message bus.
- When a task is blocked, an extension is responsible for delivering a message to query the status of the related object or take action on the blocked task.
- `Resume`, `Progress` (that was made), `Abort`, and `Continue` are valid calls against a blocking task.
- Configure the timeout for a blocking task globally in vCloud Director.
- You can abort a waiting blocking task directly from the VMware vCloud Director UI.

3.7.4 vCenter Orchestrator

vCenter Orchestrator is a system for assembling operational workflows (see Figure 3.42). The primary benefit of vCenter Orchestrator is to coordinate multiple systems to achieve a composite operation that would have otherwise required several individual operations on different systems. See Chapter 2 for detailed examples of orchestrated workflows.

In general, if an operation uses only one underlying system, consider providing direct access to that system for efficiency and reduction of complexity. In a vCloud environment, vCenter Orchestrator can automate highly repetitive tasks to avoid manual work and errors.

vCenter Orchestrator consists of the following applications:

- **vCenter Orchestrator Client:** Enables the workflow developer to create, assemble, test, and package workflows, actions, policies, resources, and configurations.
- **vCenter Orchestrator Server Web Configuration:** Runs as an independent application side by side with a web front end to allow administrators to configure the vCenter Orchestrator Server and its plug-ins and perform maintenance operations.
- **vCenter Orchestrator Server:** Provides runtime orchestration service, including its interfaces and its pluggable adapters.

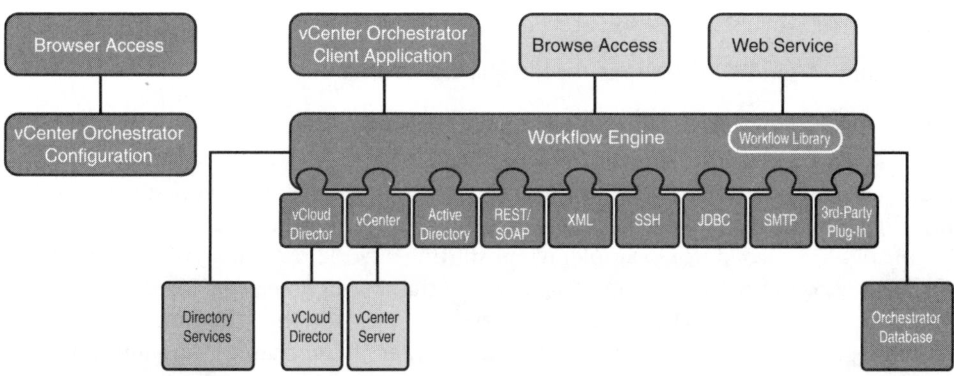

FIGURE 3.42 vCenter Orchestrator architecture

vCenter Orchestrator has a plug-in framework, and plug-ins are available for vCenter Server, vCloud Director, and vCenter Chargeback. This enables vCenter Orchestrator to orchestrate workflows at the VIM API, VIX API, vCloud API, and Chargeback API levels.

Orchestration use cases include the following:

- vCloud administration operations
- Organization administration operations
- Organization consumer operations

3.7.4.1 Design Considerations

Depending on the overall architecture and how orchestration is used, orchestrating a vCloud can require one or more vCenter Orchestrator servers. vCenter Orchestrator manages vCloud Director and vCenter using their web services.

vCenter Orchestrator can manage a variable number of hosts per plug-in. Actual limits are subject to a number of determining factors, such as bandwidth, number of objects, and concurrent workflows. For example, a single vCenter Orchestrator can manage the following:

- Multiple vCloud Director hosts
- Multiple vCenter hosts
- Multiple other host types (UCSM, REST, SOAP, vCenter Update Manager)

NOTE

Plug-ins designed for a given version are designed to work for the same version of the product. If managing a mix of host versions, keep the plug-in version at the earliest common version for backward compatibility (for example, use plug-in 5.1 if managing a mixed vCloud Director 1.5 and vCloud Director 5.1 environment). Avoid mixing host versions, where possible—if versions are mixed, the operations need to be thoroughly tested. Using the latest version of a plug-in to support an older version of the product is not supported.

3

Multiple vCenter Orchestrator servers can manage the following:

- The same vCloud Director host (or load-balanced cells)
- The same vCenter server

vCloud Director uses a stateless RESTful web service. No session is maintained between vCloud Director and vCenter Orchestrator—this minimizes resource usage on both servers. When updates are needed (for example, when starting a workflow using vCloud Director objects), the resources used are proportional to the number of objects updated. This involves sending several HTTP GET/PUT/POST/DELETE requests to the vCloud Director server and, upon reply, creating or updating objects in vCenter Orchestrator. Using multiple sessions (*per user* mode in the plug-in configuration) multiplies the number of objects. vCloud Director can be load-balanced to avoid having a single point of failure and using too many resources on a single cell.

vCenter uses a stateful SOAP web service that supports a large service definition and advanced mechanisms, such as a notification service, that vCenter Orchestrator uses extensively. Sessions are continually maintained between vCenter and vCenter Orchestrator. This has an important impact on resource consumption on both servers even when there is no workflow activity.

The session activity and associated resource consumption on both servers is proportional to the number of objects loaded in the vCenter Orchestrator vCenter inventory that multiply the number of sessions opened. For this reason, configure the vCenter plug-in using a shared session instead of a session per user, and limit the number of vCenter Orchestrator servers that manage a single vCenter. Workflow activity also consumes resources for objects that are not in the inventory cache.

Additional considerations include the following:

- vCenter Orchestrator 5.1 introduced new per-node maximums of 20 vCenter Server instances, 1280 vSphere hosts, and up to 35000 virtual machines in inventory.
- vCenter Orchestrator scalability can be increased with the use of the VMware vCenter Orchestrator Multi-Node Plug-In. See the Multi-Node Plug-In blog (http://blogs.vmware.com/orchestrator/2012/01/vco-multi-node-plug-in.html) for more information.
- If a vCenter Orchestrator is overloaded by a large level of objects to manage, attempt to tune the server for higher scalability. Alternatively, design the solution to use different vCenter Orchestrator instances that manage different vCenter Servers, or connect to a large vCenter using different vCenter Orchestrator instances that are configured with accounts to access different zones of vCenter.

3.7.4.2 Scalability

When configuring vCenter Orchestrator to run numerous concurrent workflows, it is necessary to understand how the Orchestration engine works.

The vCenter Orchestrator Workflow Engine default configuration allows for running up to 300 concurrent workflows. When the running queue exceeds this number, the workflows are placed in an execution queue and moved back to the running queue as soon as one or more workflows have completed an execution run. Completed workflow states can be completed successfully, failed, canceled, or "passivated" (waiting-for-signal state). The execution queue has a default size of 10,000 workflows. If the execution queue size is exceeded, the workflow engine marks subsequent workflows as failed.

A running workflow consumes at least one running thread (either running the workflow or updating the workflow state) and from 1MB to a few megabytes of memory (varies depending on the number of enabled plug-ins and plug-in objects). Limiting the number of workflows allows allocation of threads and memory, with the maximum depending on the JVM settings, the operating system, and the underlying hardware.

To change the default value, change the following properties in the `Orchestrator\appserver\server\vmo\conf\vmo.properties` configuration file:

- `com.vmware.vco.workflow-engine.executors-count`
- `com.vmware.vco.workflow-engine.executors-max-queue-size`

NOTE

VMware recommends following the guidelines in the rest of this chapter before increasing the default settings for the concurrent workflows because doing so requires expanding the resources for the vCenter Orchestrator Java virtual machine, the host operating system, the host virtual machine, and possibly the vCenter Orchestrator Database.

Each active plug-in has an impact on the workflow engine performance. A plug-in loads classes, runs update threads, logs information to disk, provides objects to the scripting engine, and maintains the inventory. Even if the plug-in is unused, it consumes resources and increases the memory footprint of each running workflow. Disable all plug-ins that are not in use to increase the workflow engine capacity.

3.7.4.3 Workflow Design

Workflow design affects duration and use of resources. The following are design guidelines for workflow design:

- **Effective scripting:** Use scripting development design guidelines to avoid unnecessary and highly resource-demanding operations such as active wait loops, repetitive expensive calls to the same resources, and ineffective algorithms. Perform extensive testing on a vCenter Orchestrator test server before running new or updated workflows on a production system.
- **Workflow threading control:** Having many distinct running workflows increases the amount of resources are used.
- Workflows started individually and workflows started using the Asynchronous Workflow or Nested Workflow palette elements run in different workflow instances.

- A subworkflow in a master workflow still runs within the same workflow instance but uses fewer resources. Link the workflows in higher-level workflows instead of calling individual workflows in sequence.
- **Reduce the number of waiting workflows:** If the reason for the high concurrency is a high number of workflows waiting on external systems, the following methods can help avoid consuming resources while waiting:
  - The Wait Until date workflow palette element and the `System.Sleep()` methods keep the workflow in a running state in the execution queue. Even if the thread is in Sleep mode, it still consumes memory. For long-running workflows, these can be replaced by the `waiting timer` or `waiting event` palette elements. Using one of these elements passivates the workflow execution and saves its state in the vCenter Orchestrator database. The workflow is then removed from the running queue, and memory is freed. The vCloud Director library's long-running workflows make extensive use of the waiting event palette element.
  - When workflow activity must be suspended until a determined time, programmatically schedule a workflow task.

Although they save active resources, each passivation and activation consumes CPU resources and database access. The following are design guidelines for using the waiting timer or waiting event:

- Do not trigger a large number of these at the same time.
- Do not set very short timers in loops.

3.7.4.4 Solution Guidelines

In addition to the server configuration and the workflow design, you must have a well-controlled overall solution that includes the upper management layers and the orchestrated systems.

- **Misuse of orchestration:** An orchestration engine provides automation and integration to manage complex cross-domain processes. It provides several facilities for versatility, resiliency, and auditing that would be excessive for simple operations that do not require this level of service. Do not use vCenter Orchestrator to replace single calls to the vCloud Director API.
- **Control of the workflows:** The systems calling a vCenter Orchestrator should have a workflow throttling mechanism adjusted according to tested maximums for vCenter Orchestrator to avoid resource starvation.
- **Load balancing:** If maximums are exceeded, it might be necessary to design the system to load-balance the workflows across different vCenter Orchestrator servers.
- **Orchestrated systems bottleneck:** Use vCenter Orchestrator workflows to prevent starting too many operations at once on the orchestrated systems. Design this

logic to support the defined load. Expose the parameters that have an influence on the started workload as configuration elements to be adjusted by the orchestration administrator (a parameter that determines the number of vApp clones to be processed in parallel).

3.7.4.5 Orchestrator Client

The vCenter Orchestrator Server has a client application to develop workflows and actions. During server installation, install the client on the same system as the server. In production environments, the local installation of the client software is used only in emergency cases when a matching client is not available through developer workstations.

Have developers install the client on their workstations to connect to their test or development servers on the same LAN. If connecting to a remote server, use Remote Desktop to run the client from the same LAN.

3.7.4.6 vCloud Director Plug-In

When specifying the Host field of the plug-in, the value must be the same as the value the vCloud Director server specifies. This value is determined as follows:

- If a value is specified under vCloud Director Administration—Public Addresses—External REST API Base URI, use this value in the plug-in configuration. For example, using a load-balanced vCloud Director requires changing the public address to the one specified for the virtual server in the load balancer configuration. Verify that forward and reverse DNS are working for the specified address.
- If a hostname or fully qualified domain name (FQDN) is specified, verify that forward and reverse DNS are working, and use the FQDN in the plug-in configuration.
- If no hostname is specified and the vCloud Director server is configured only to use an IP address, use the same IP address for the plug-in configuration.

NOTE

Failure to configure the plug-in as specified results in undesired effects.

After specifying the `Host` field, choose a strategy for managing the user logins. The available options are Share a Unique Session and Per User Session.

- When Share a Unique Session is configured, a single session is created between vCenter Orchestrator and vCloud Director based on the configured organization and credentials. The vCenter Orchestrator user inherits the rights of those credentials for any workflow executed. From an auditing perspective, a shared session shifts the auditing responsibility from vCloud Director to vCenter Orchestrator. The workflows developed for such integration must have an appropriate level of logging set up to meet the organization's audit requirements.

- When Session Per User is configured, the user authenticated in vCenter Orchestrator is used to authenticate in vCloud Director. This creates a session for each user between vCenter Orchestrator and vCloud Director that is associated with an inventory based on this user role and permissions. This requires having the organization use an LDAP host synchronized with the LDAP host configured in vCenter Orchestrator.

Also consider the following:

- For organizations that use different LDAP hosts, one dedicated instance of vCenter Orchestrator is required per organization.
- Multiple sessions can strain CPU, memory, and bandwidth.

In addition, an organization setting is required. The organization defines the scope of the operations that vCenter Orchestrator can perform:

- `SYSTEM` is set when requiring create, read, update, and delete access to all organizations and to their associated virtual infrastructure resources.
- A specific organization is set when restricting create, read, update, and delete access to all elements that belong to the given organization.

The most common use cases for the plug-in usually correspond to one of the following scenarios:

- As a public or private vCloud provider using a vCenter Orchestrator server as part of the vCloud management cluster:
    - Tasks such as managing provider resources and on-boarding new organizations require system-level administrative permission to vCloud Director. This scenario uses Share a Unique Session, an organization set to `SYSTEM`, and the system administrator credentials.
    - Use Session Per User if the administrative tasks require different roles and permissions. In this case, the `SYSTEM` organization must be set up to synchronize with the vCloud provider LDAP host that is configured with vCenter Orchestrator.

If configuring more than one vCloud Director connection, use a combination of shared session and per-user session to grant vCenter Orchestrator workflows users the shared access session permissions for the configured organization. For example, if the plug-in is set with a system-shared session and a requirement exists to grant vCenter Orchestrator users access to a given organization, have both connections use Session Per User and set permissions differently for the sessions, to avoid all users having wide access to all organizations.

- As a public vCloud tenant of one or more organizations, using vCenter Orchestrator in the tenant premise or as part of the organization vApps:

  - For organization administrative tasks, use Share a Unique Session with organization administrator credentials. If administering more than one organization, one new vCloud Director Connection can be added per organization.
  - Configure the plug-in as Session Per User for delegating workflows operations tasks that are not covered by the vCloud Director interface to organization users who have different roles and permissions. In this configuration, set up the organization to synchronize with the tenant LDAP host configured in vCenter Orchestrator.

- As a private vCloud organization tenant using a vCenter Orchestrator server as part of the vCloud management cluster, and a single LDAP host.

  The vCloud provider configures a new connection using this specific organization and Session per User. Set up the organization to synchronize with the LDAP host that is configured with vCenter Orchestrator. All other organizations configured in other connections also synchronize with the same LDAP HOST server.

3.7.5 vCenter Orchestrator Examples

Orchestration brings automation to vCloud administration, organization administration, and self-service consumer operations.

3.7.5.1 vCloud Administration Orchestration Examples

The following examples highlight the value of vCenter Orchestrator to the vCloud system administrator. The following use case focuses on infrastructure management and the resource provisioning process.

- A provider wants to begin working with a new customer. The main steps are to add a new organization, users (possibly from LDAP), networks, virtual datacenters, and catalogs. The provider might also want to schedule a recurring chargeback report for billing and send an email notification to tenants, advising them that their vCloud environment is ready.
- A tenant requests additional external network capacity. The provider wants to automate the creation of the network, which includes name generation, identification, and allocation of available VLAN and IP address range; configuration of the network switch and vCloud perimeter firewall; creation of the external network in vCenter; and allocation of the external network to the tenant's organization.

3.7.5.2 Organization Administration Orchestration Examples

Operational tasks within the tenant's organization can also benefit from automation. The following examples address vApp lifecycle management, such as vApp creation, configuration, maintenance, and decommission.

- Virtual machines are created in an environment using Active Directory to identify services such as authentication and printing. After deployment, the virtual machine must join the Active Directory domain. It is usually preferable to use an organization unit (OU) other than the default Computers container. vCenter Orchestrator can create the virtual machine's computer account in the proper OU before virtual machine deployment so that that the computer account name is unique and resides in the proper OU. Similarly, when the virtual machine is decommissioned, vCenter Orchestrator can remove the entry in the OU as part of the same workflow.

- An organization administrator wants to manage recurring updates to a software package or configuration element across several virtual machines in a single operation. A workflow can accept a list of systems and a source for the software or configuration as parameters and then perform the update on each system.

3.7.5.3 vCloud Consumer Operation Orchestration Examples

vCloud consumer operations are tasks that the organization administrator wants to offload to a self-service operation. Performing the operation as a vCenter Orchestrator workflow provides an easy way to expose the operation to a customer through the built-in portal or a customized portal that leverages the web services API. Many operations in this category can be satisfied directly through the vCloud Director web console. However, some operations affect multiple systems or fit better into a customer portal. These operations are natural candidates for an orchestration workflow. vCloud consumers do not have visibility into orchestration components, so the vCloud provider must initiate the workflow using the vCenter Orchestrator Client unless the provider creates a portal to serve as a front end to vCenter Orchestrator.

Example use cases include resetting user account passwords on virtual machines using the VIX plug-in, placing a load-balanced service into maintenance mode (stopping the service, removing it from the load-balancing pool, and disabling monitors), loading certificates into virtual machines, and deploying instances of custom applications from the organization's catalog.

vCenter Orchestrator can be used to create custom workflows at the vCloud API and vSphere levels. Other vCloud provisioning solutions frequently have built-in workflow functionality that integrates with vCloud Director through the vCloud API and is an alternative to vCenter Orchestrator.

See the VMware vCenter Orchestrator documentation (www.vmware.com/support/pubs/orchestrator_pubs.html) for additional information on installation, configuration, and workflow development. Also see Chapter 2 for detailed examples of orchestrated workflows.

3.7.5.4 Using Orchestrator As a vCloud Director Extension

vCenter Orchestrator fully supports consuming blocked tasks and notifications messages, callbacks, and calls to external systems by way of vCloud Director, AMQP, and other specific product plug-ins (see Figure 3.43).

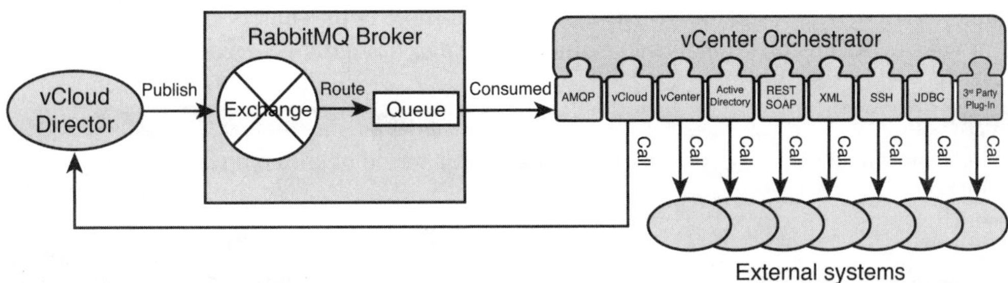

FIGURE 3.43 vCenter Orchestrator as a vCloud Director extension

The AMQP plug-in comes with workflows and requires a one-time setup. Provide values for the following:

- **Add a broker:** Add an AMQP broker by providing hostname and credentials.
- **Declare an exchange:** Declare an exchange for the configured broker.
- **Declare a queue:** Declare a queue for vCenter Orchestrator workflows.
- **Bind:** Bind a queue to an exchange by providing a routing key.
- **Subscribe to queues:** Allow vCenter Orchestrator to receive message updates on new messages.

Restarting the vCenter Orchestrator server automatically saves and reloads the configuration.

The plug-in supports adding a policy element of type `subscription` that has an `onMessage` trigger event. A policy can be set up to start a workflow processing new messages.

Workflows are provided to triage and process the message to output vCloud Director objects. These can provide all the information necessary for audit purposes and for designing custom logic before calling external systems. External systems are called in two ways:

- Specific vCenter Orchestrator plug-in adapters such as vCloud Director, vCenter, Update Manager, and Active Directory
- Generic plug-in adapters such as REST, SOAP, XML, SSH, and JDBC

vCloud Director workflows can abort, resume, or fail blocked task objects. See Chapter 4, "Operating a VMware vCloud," for example workflows using vCloud messages.

3.8 Multisite Considerations

Initial vCloud Director deployments were targeted at traditional test and development, scale-out infrastructure, and Tier 3 workloads where advanced infrastructure features were typically not required. As customers started to adopt vCloud Director for a different set of workloads, a new set of requirements arose. One of these requirements is the capability to deploy vCloud Director to manage resources that span more than a single site.

NOTE

Multisite hybrid vCloud scenarios (defined as a combination of private and public cloud resources) are not discussed.

This section provides guidelines and discusses various options, limitations, and supported scenarios to deploy vCloud Director in a distributed scenario that focuses on a specific vCloud distributed model. The goal is to take a private or public vCloud instance and describe the options for stretching it across multiple locations; this model takes a single vCloud Director instance with two or more vCloud Director cells and determines how the different components can be deployed separately in different locations. From a vCloud Director perspective, this is considered a single vCloud. Figure 3.44 illustrates this concept.

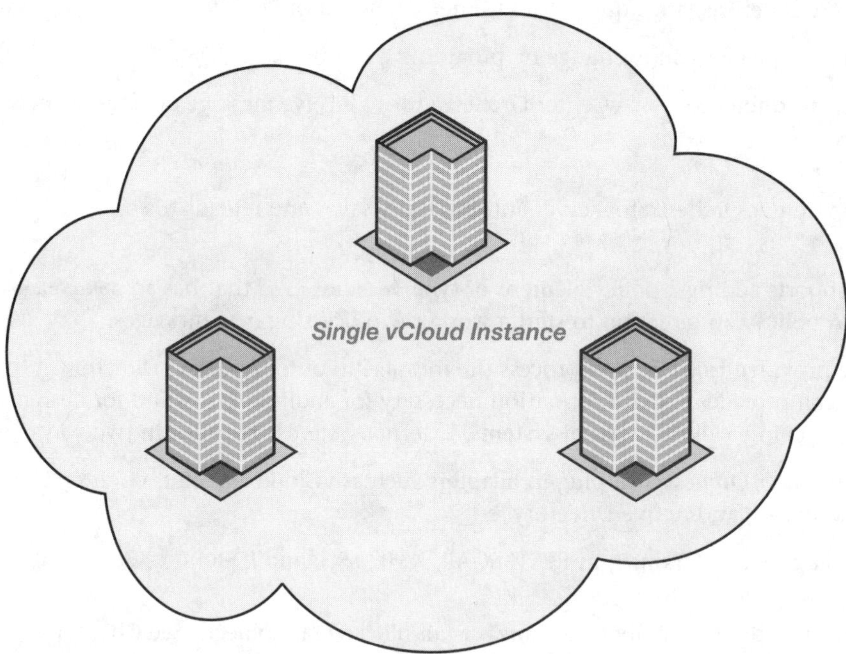

FIGURE 3.44 Single vCloud, multiple sites

Additional models enable enterprise customers and service providers to create a single vCloud that spans multiple remote sites. One of the alternative models is to deploy traditional vCloud Director instances in each of the available locations and layer an additional level of management on top of them to create a single entry point into dispersed vCloud instances. This additional layer can be implemented with an additional software layer such as VMware vCloud Automation Center. Figure 3.45 illustrates this concept.

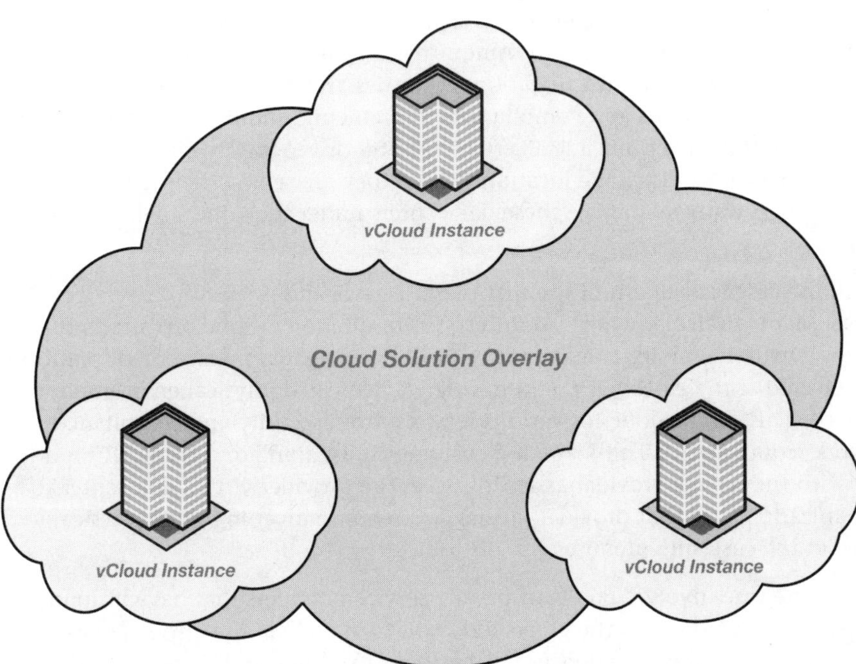

FIGURE 3.45 Multiple vCloud instances tied together

3.8.1 Multisite Availability Considerations

Various distributed scenarios can enable vCloud capacity to be spread across different premises located around the world. Some of the distributed design options lead to resiliency advantages. Others might be prerequisites for DR scenarios (however, these are more of an implicit outcome of distributing the compute farm than an explicit design goal).

Creating a distributed vCloud model is foundationally required but is not sufficient to address high availability and disaster recovery for vCloud workloads. The focus of this section is on how to distribute resources, not how to make workloads highly available on those resources.

3.8.2 Distributed Cloud Deployments Use Cases

The following are some major use cases for spanning a vCloud across multiple locations (other use cases are possible.):

- **Better and more uniform usage and management of distributed resources:** Many customers and service providers want to build one single vCloud that contains resources that are distributed across cities, countries, and continents. That is the way they operate their IT. They prefer to install and operate one vCloud out of the box than build two or more vCloud instances that would require additional integration.

- The second use case is similar to the first, but the business driver is different. Although customers and service providers distribute resources because that is how they operate as a global company, in some situations, the service providers require that the resources be distributed in various countries and geographies. This is because of data regulations and compliance requirements, and because their customers cannot take their assets outside a certain country or geography. In this case, service providers must distribute locations where they are selling their services. These service providers want to manage these datacenters under the same single vCloud umbrella.
- The third use case is a variant of the first two use cases and is specific to service providers. Many service providers are interested in offering vCloud services to their customers where the service is managed centrally on a shared management platform but is delivered at the customer premise, where a dedicated physical environment is deployed. This can be done for various reasons, from security and compliance to network requirements. Think about a customer subscribing to a public vCloud service, with the service provider assigning an entire provider virtual datacenter to that organization, and that provider virtual datacenter happening to be physically deployed at the customer premises.
- The fourth use case involves public or private service providers that have vCloud consumers distributed across the globe and want to guarantee the lowest possible latency and best possible experience. The best way to achieve this is to move the user workloads and the systems where they run physically as close as possible to the consumer. These service providers also want to manage these resources as a single vCloud.
- The fifth use case is to provide a mechanism to allow end users to consume resources that are physically distributed in different locations for increased resiliency. When the resiliency of the end-user workload is managed at the application level, the end users can instantiate loosely coupled virtual machines in standalone provider virtual datacenters distributed at remote locations, thus achieving scalability and resiliency. In this case, the end user is responsible for managing the resiliency of the application.
- The sixth use case enables a vCloud provider to increase resiliency of end-user workloads by failing them over to different sites if anything fails at the datacenter where the workload is originally instantiated. In this scenario, application resiliency is achieved through recovery mechanisms implemented at the infrastructure level, not at the application level. This is a resiliency service that the vCloud administrator offers to the end user regardless of the application resiliency attributes.

This section focuses on describing the various options for stretching standalone compute resources in different locations under the governance of a single vCloud.

3.8.3 Multisite Terminology

This section uses the following terminology:

- **Distributed vCloud:** The generic concept of spreading vCloud resources and components across different locations
- **Location:** A physical location, a building, or an entire physical datacenter with LAN connectivity, where vCloud components are deployed
- **Single Site vCloud:** A vCloud that spans one or more locations that are connected with MAN connectivity
- **Multisite vCloud:** A vCloud that spans one or more locations that are connected with WAN connectivity

Figure 3.46 shows the distributed vCloud deployment options.

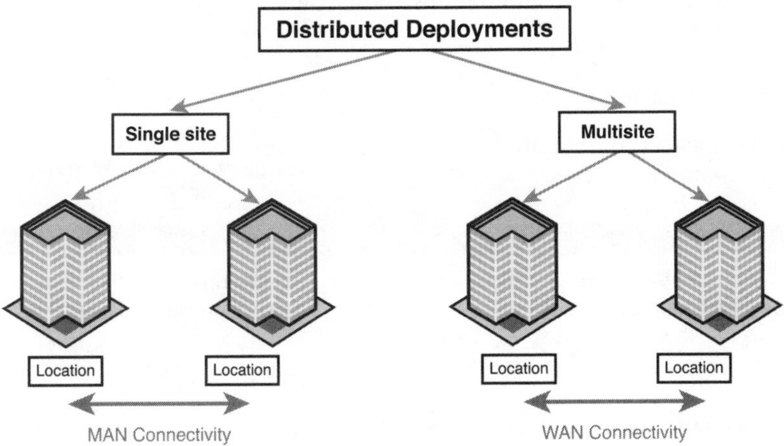

FIGURE 3.46 Distributed deployment options

Historically, a vCloud Director deployment was supported only in a single site or in a single location. However, this statement led to some confusion because it is not very deterministic. In fact, it is not unusual to find connectivity between different locations at large corporations that is better than the connectivity in a single site at smaller organizations.

For this reason, this statement is clarified with a more deterministic approach. A *single site* is considered to be any local or distributed IT deployment where connectivity between any of the deployed components has a latency round-trip time (RTT) of 20 milliseconds (or less).

This does not call out bandwidth requirements. This is because bandwidth is more of a problem from the perspective of an end-user experience than it is from a functional perspective. We assume that bandwidth in a MAN scenario is sufficient to not cause connectivity problems. However, we realize that, depending on the usage patterns of the vCloud, a relatively low bandwidth can result in higher response time for the user. The vCloud architect is responsible for planning according to the expected result and projected usage patterns.

These network characteristics are referred to as *MAN connectivity*. A single-site deployment is on in which one or more locations are used to host all the vCloud Director components, and the RTT connectivity within a location or across two or more locations is less than 20ms.

- If the vCloud Director deployment has all the components that fall within these connectivity characteristics, it is considered to be a single site and the deployment is fully supported.
- If the distributed vCloud Director deployment has components that fall outside these network characteristics, it is a *multisite* implementation.

3.8.4 Deployment Options

A vCloud platform can be distributed in an infinite number of ways. This is because of the number of vCloud components that must be deployed and the various connectivity options.

The following options lead to different combinations and layouts:

- Connectivity between locations (MAN/WAN)
- Network layer (Layer 2/Layer 3)
- End-user workload clusters configurations (stretched/separate)

NOTE

The combination of some of these options might not be viable. For example, a vSphere stretched cluster configuration requires it is deployable only in conjunction with a Layer 2 stretched network.

Figure 3.47 shows the scenarios covered later in this section.

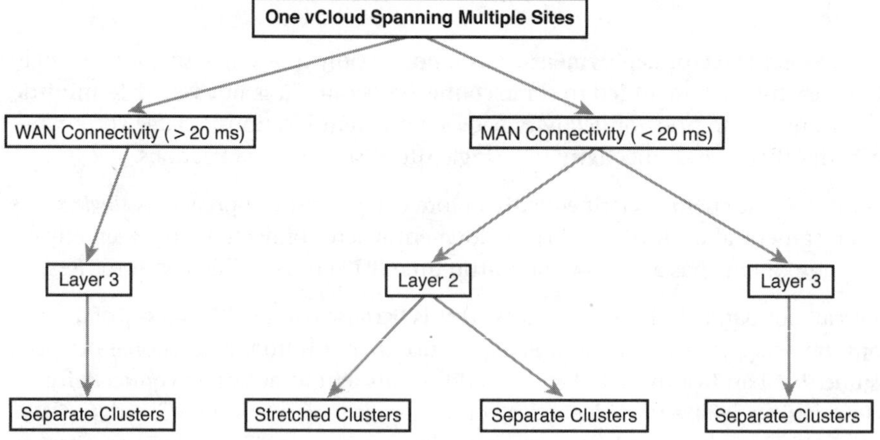

FIGURE 3.47 Summary of deployment scenarios

Table 3.17 shows a slightly different view of the same options.

TABLE 3.17 Summary of Deployment Scenarios

Connectivity	Network Layer	Clusters Configuration
MAN	Layer 2	Stretched clusters
MAN	Layer 2	Separate clusters
MAN	Layer 3	Separate clusters
WAN	Layer 3	Separate clusters

Figures 3.48–3.51 show the logical architecture of the four different deployment models.

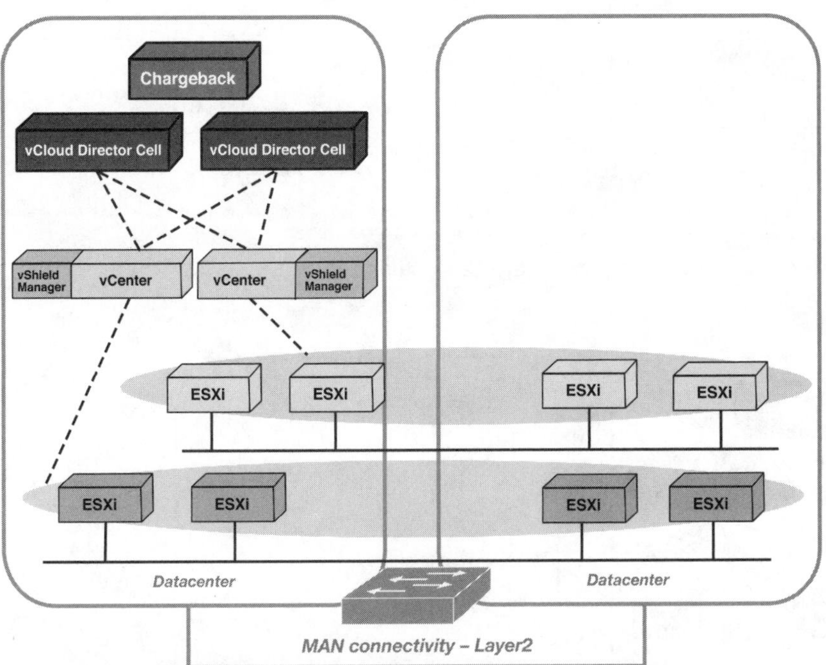

FIGURE 3.48 MAN connectivity—stretched Layer 2 clusters

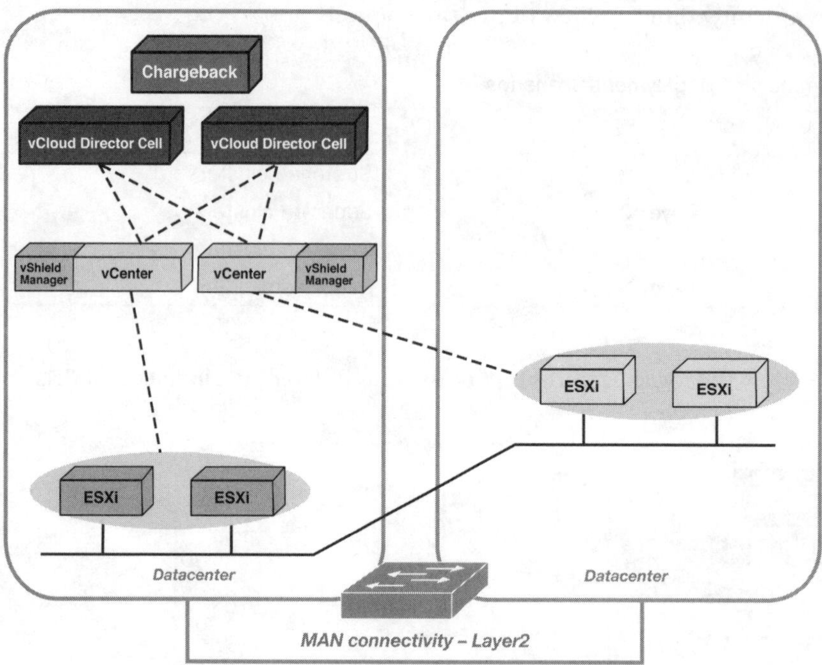

FIGURE 3.49 MAN connectivity—separate Layer 2 clusters

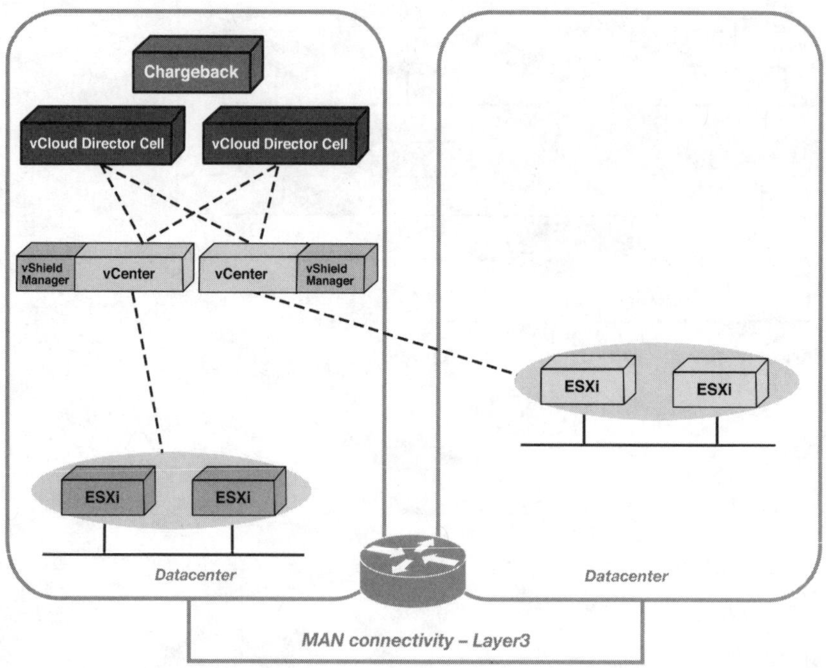

FIGURE 3.50 MAN connectivity—separate Layer 3 clusters

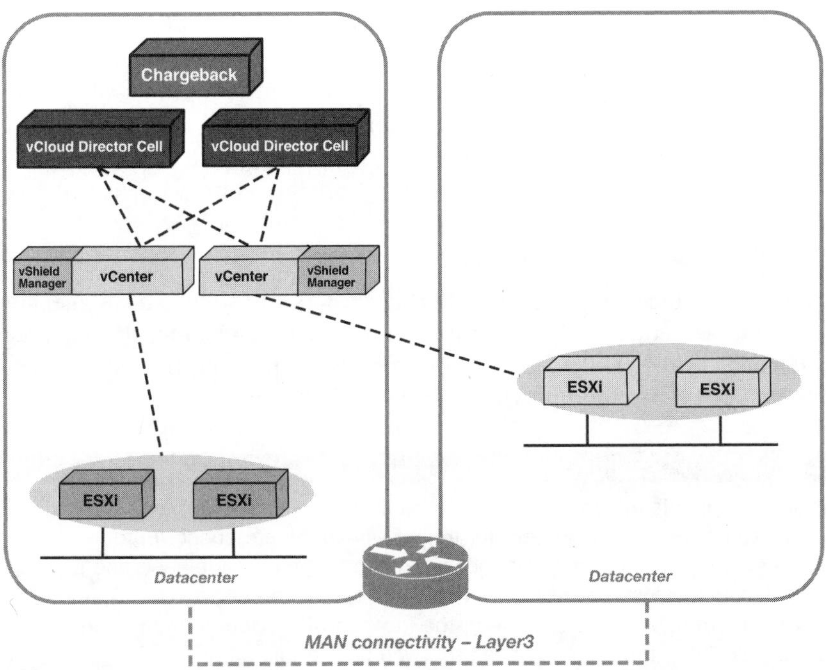

FIGURE 3.51 WAN connectivity—Layer 3 clusters

NOTE

Although the diagrams show two vCenter Servers managing two different clusters, the same concepts apply with a single vCenter that manages two clusters. For convenience, vCenter servers are always shown located close to the vCloud Director cells and far from the ESXi hosts. The same supportability considerations apply when the vCenter servers are located close to the ESXi hosts and far from the vCloud Director cells.

3.8.5 Supportability Considerations for Single-Site Deployments

VMware supports vCloud Director 5.1 in MAN scenarios (as described in Section 3.8.3, "Multisite Terminology"). Some supportability considerations are as follows:

- All provider workloads, with the exception of vCenter Server and vCloud Networking and Security Manager instances, must be deployed in a single location.
- Clusters backing provider virtual datacenters can be deployed in different locations if connectivity between locations has latency requirements as described in Section 3.8.3, "Multisite Terminology." Minimize the likelihood of a path failure across datacenters that might partition the provider workloads.
- vCenter Server and vCloud Networking and Security Manager instances managing and servicing clusters in distributed locations can be deployed either close to the

vCloud Director core components (vCloud Director cells and vCloud Director database) or close to the clusters they manage.

Architects implementing a single-site vCloud across different locations should deploy the various components with consideration given to sensitive operations such as vApp copies so that the deployment is fully optimized and the architecture takes into account network chokepoints (especially in terms of bandwidth) that can exist even in a MAN scenario. This has to do more with optimization than supportability.

Stretched clusters (which include stretched vSphere DRS clusters and stretched storage) are fully supported when implemented with the storage vendor–neutral guidance documented in this section. Stretched clusters (which require 10ms or lower latency) can enable increased flexibility in both tenant and provider workload placement.

NOTE

The generic single-site considerations in this section apply to tenant deployments that have latency within 20ms. Stretched clusters for tenant workloads are supported only when sites have latency within 5ms or 10ms (depending on the vSphere release and underlying storage technology used). At 5ms or 10ms latency (depending on the vSphere release and underlying storage technology used), the location of provider infrastructure components is more flexible. It is recommended that you do the following:

- Follow this guidance for any single-site deployment within 20ms.
- Follow specific recommended guidance for vCloud Director deployments on top of vSphere stretched clusters within 10ms (these practices are dictated by the underlying storage solution supporting the stretched cluster and could override the vendor-neutral stretch cluster recommended practices in this chapter).

See the VMware vCloud Blog article "Stretched vCloud Director Infrastructure" (http://blogs.vmware.com/vcloud/2013/01/stretched-vcloud-director-infrastructure.html) for more information.

3.8.6 Multisite Supportability Considerations

VMware does not currently support distributed vCloud Director 5.1 deployments in multisite scenarios. Instantiating provider virtual datacenters that are located across a WAN is not possible (as described in Section 3.8.3, "Multisite Terminology").

Figure 3.52 summarizes the supportability options, with associated constrains and requirements.

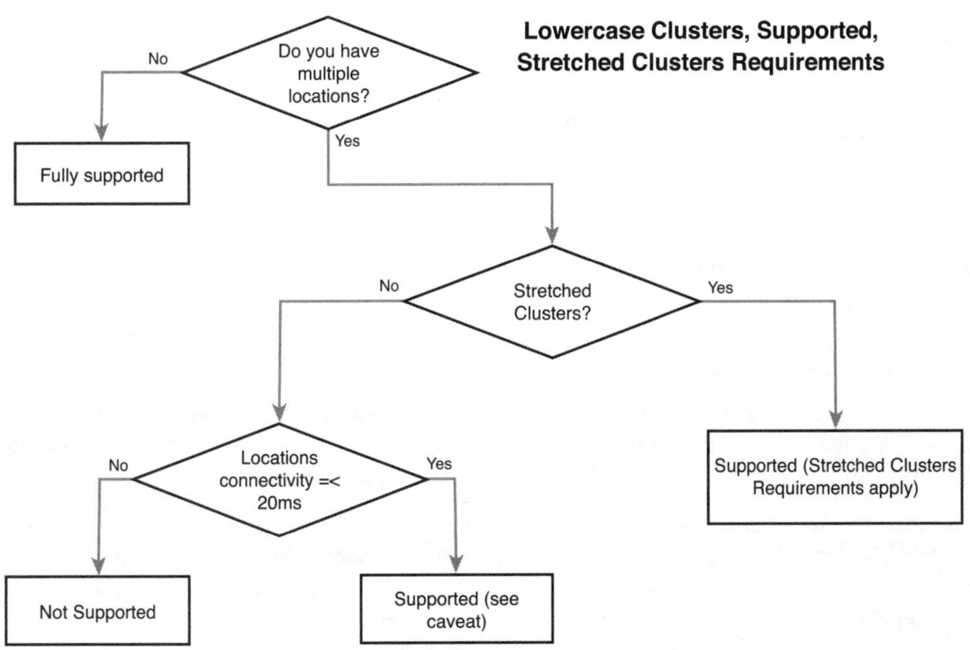

FIGURE 3.52 Supportability flowchart

3.9 Hybrid vCloud Considerations

A hybrid vCloud incorporates a combination of vCloud instances and can include both on- and off-premises resources (see Figure 3.53). Applications can be located on-premises, off-premises, or a combination of both. Enterprises with an existing private vCloud can choose or be required to provide and manage public vCloud resources in a secure and scalable way. Connectivity between different vCloud instances that enables data and application portability indicates a hybrid vCloud solution.

NOTE

This section focuses on workload mobility within a hybrid vCloud enabled by vCloud Connector. It does not discuss the hybrid vCloud governance enabled by vCloud Automation Center.

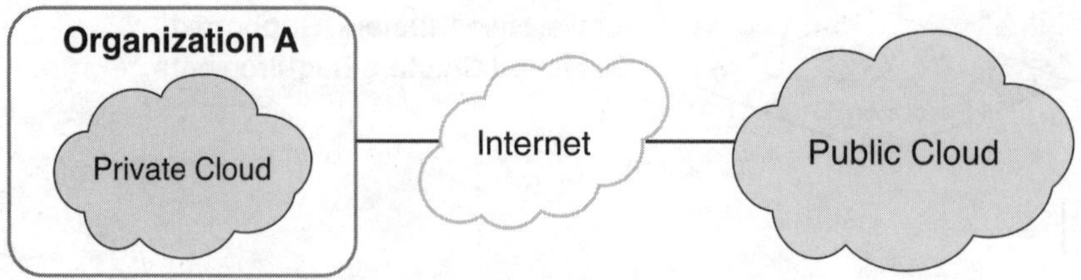

FIGURE 3.53 Hybrid vCloud example

3.9.1 vCloud Connector

With the emergence of cloud computing, private enterprises must manage multiple vCloud instances, both private and public. Given these public and private options, ease of migrating workloads between vCloud instances becomes increasingly important.

vCloud Connector enables users to connect to vCloud instances based on vSphere or vCloud Director and manage them under a single interface. Through the vCloud Connector interface, users can view, copy, and operate workloads across internal datacenters and private or public vCloud instances.

vCloud Connector provides point-to-point reliable transfers between vCloud instances by using a checkpoint restart mechanism. If a transfer between nodes fails, vCloud Connector can restart the task and continue the copy from where it stopped instead of having to start at the beginning of the file, as a standard HTTP upload requires. vCloud Connector also uses HTTPS so that transfers are secure.

vCloud administrators install vCloud Connector, but both administrators and end users can use it to view and manage workloads. vCloud Connector is delivered as a virtual appliance with the UI instantiated as a web client.

3.9.1.1 vCloud Connector Placement

Workload copy operations use the vCloud Connector appliance as an intermediary, so you must consider network latency and bandwidth between vCloud instances. For some use cases, running multiple instances of vCloud Connector across multiple vCenter Server instances might be preferable, to avoid network latency or excessive bandwidth consumption. Figure 3.54 shows the vCloud Connector 2.0 transfer path.

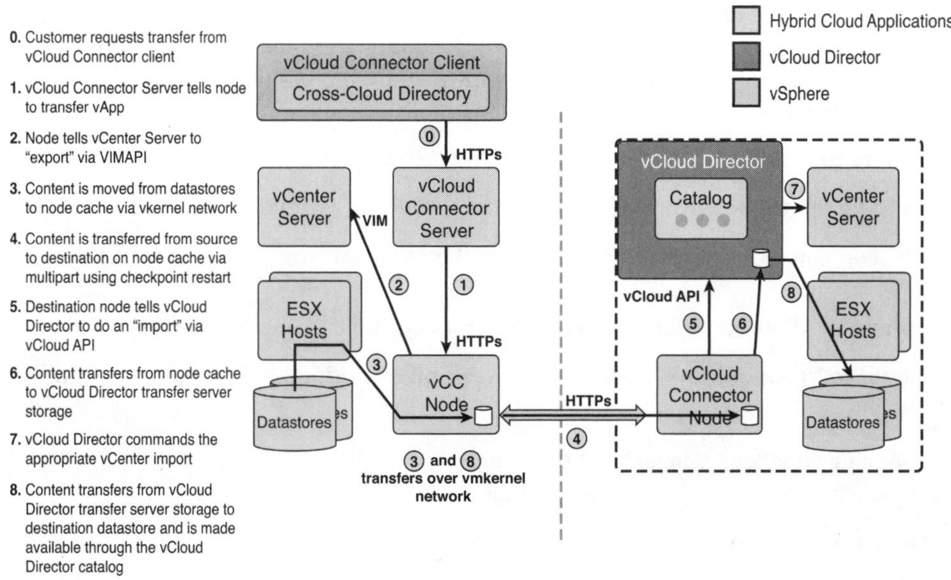
0. Customer requests transfer from vCloud Connector client
1. vCloud Connector Server tells node to transfer vApp
2. Node tells vCenter Server to "export" via VIMAPI
3. Content is moved from datastores to node cache via vkernel network
4. Content is transferred from source to destination on node cache via multipart using checkpoint restart
5. Destination node tells vCloud Director to do an "import" via vCloud API
6. Content transfers from node cache to vCloud Director transfer server storage
7. vCloud Director commands the appropriate vCenter import
8. Content transfers from vCloud Director transfer server storage to destination datastore and is made available through the vCloud Director catalog
vCloud Connector Client
Cross-Cloud Directory
HTTPs
vCenter Server
VIM
vCloud Connector Server
ESX Hosts
HTTPs
vCC Node
Datastores
3 and 8 transfers over vmkernel network
HTTPs
Hybrid Cloud Applications
vCloud Director
vSphere
vCloud Director
Catalog
vCenter Server
vCloud API
ESX Hosts
vCloud Connector Node
Datastores

FIGURE 3.54 vCloud Connector basic transfer path

Figure 3.55 shows the vCloud Connector architecture.

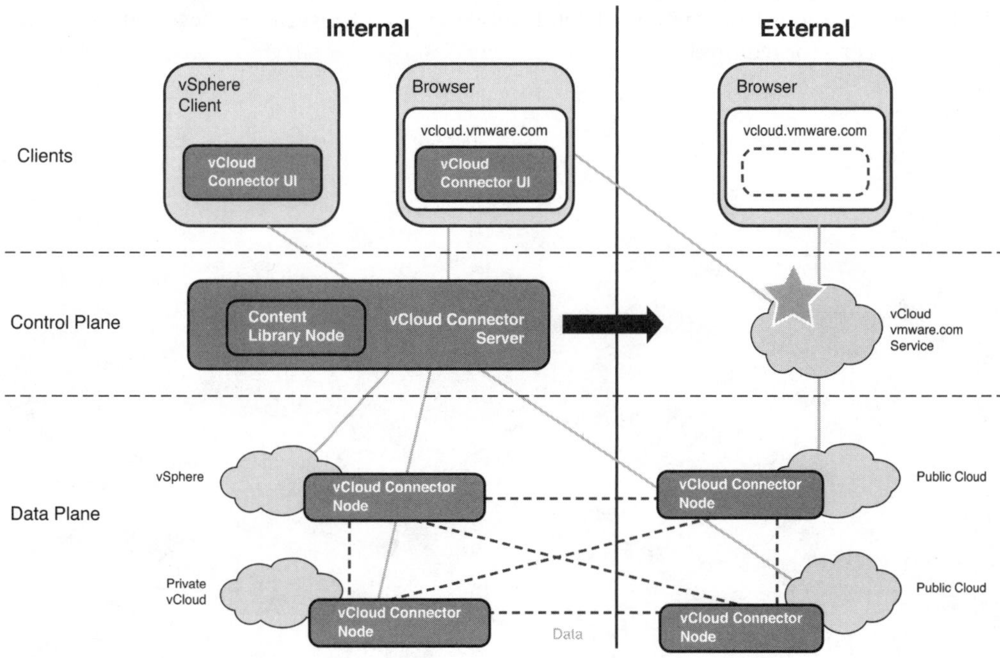
Internal
External
Clients
vSphere Client
vCloud Connector UI
Browser
vcloud.vmware.com
vCloud Connector UI
Browser
vcloud.vmware.com
Control Plane
Content Library Node
vCloud Connector Server
vCloud vmware.com Service
Data Plane
vSphere
vCloud Connector Node
Private vCloud
vCloud Connector Node
Data
vCloud Connector Node
Public Cloud
vCloud Connector Node
Public Cloud

FIGURE 3.55 vCloud Connector architecture

3.9.1.2 vCloud Connector Example Usage Scenarios

vCloud Connector can support a number of workload migration use cases involving virtual machines, virtual machine templates, vApps, and vApp templates. The following migrations are possible:

- **vSphere to vCloud:**
  - Migrate vSphere workloads into private or public vCloud instances
  - Populate vCloud Director with templates from vSphere
- **vSphere to vSphere:** Balance workloads across multiple vSphere instances
- **vCloud to vCloud:** Move workloads between private or public vCloud providers

3.9.1.3 Additional vCloud Connector 2.0 Features

vCloud Connector has the following additional features:

- **Datacenter extension:**
  - Layer 2 extension from the existing enterprise network to a public vCloud over a secure SSL VPN tunnel. Figure 3.56 shows this.
  - Capability to move a virtual machine from an enterprise network (vSphere or vCloud Director) to the public vCloud and retain the same IP and MAC addresses.
  - Version 5.1 of vSphere, vCloud Networking and Security Manager, and vCloud Director required.

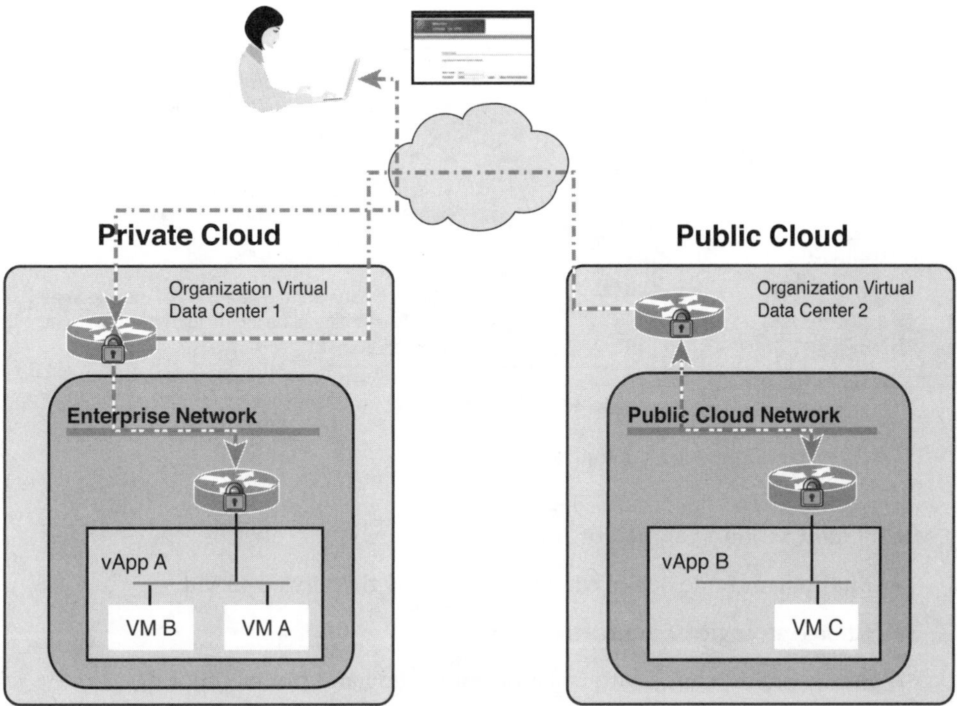

FIGURE 3.56 vCloud Connector datacenter extension

- **Content sync:**
  - Public vSphere folder, or private or public vCloud catalog
  - Subscription to the published folder or catalog from one or more vSphere instances, or private or public vCloud instances
  - New or modified templates in the published folder or catalog automatically copied to the subscribing vCloud instances that leverage the vCloud Connector secure transfer mechanism
  - Folders and catalogs kept synchronized across vCloud instances
  - Support for vSphere 4.x (and later) and vCloud Director 1.5 (and later)

Figure 3.57 shows the workflow for vCloud Connector content synchronization.

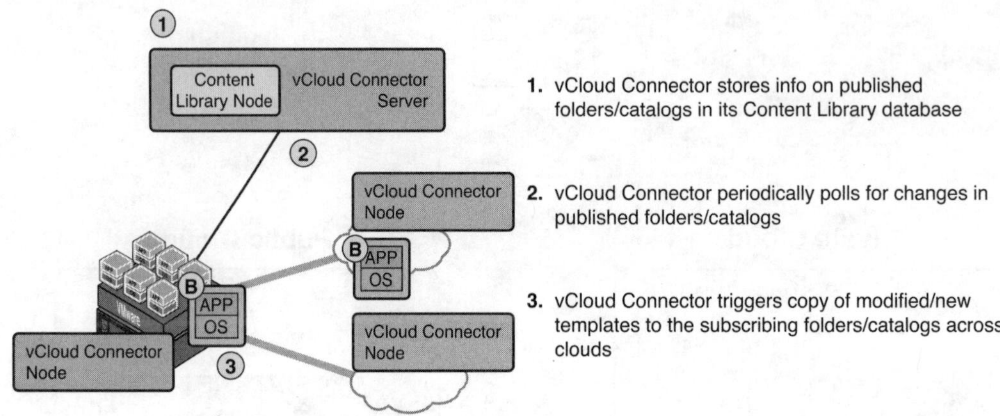
1
Content Library Node
vCloud Connector Server
2
vCloud Connector Node
B
APP
OS
B
APP
OS
vCloud Connector Node
vCloud Connector Node
3
1. vCloud Connector stores info on published folders/catalogs in its Content Library database
2. vCloud Connector periodically polls for changes in published folders/catalogs
3. vCloud Connector triggers copy of modified/new templates to the subscribing folders/catalogs across clouds

FIGURE 3.57 vCloud Connector content sync

- **Multitenant vCloud Connector node:**
  - Multitenant node deployed and managed by the service provider
  - Choice of single or multitenant node
  - Secure multitenancy with isolation for logging and troubleshooting
  - Support for vCloud Director 1.5 (or later)

Figure 3.58 shows multitenancy within a vCloud Connector setup.

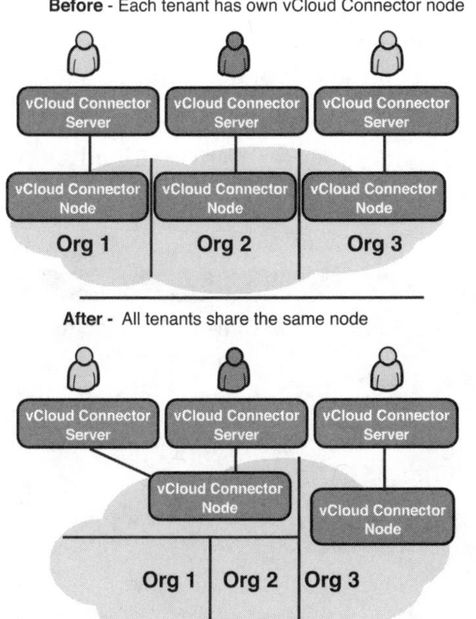

- Multitenant node deployed/managed by service provider
- Choice of single or multitenant node
- Secure multitenancy with isolation for logging and troubleshooting
- Ease of vCloud Connector adoption helps customers get to hybrid cloud faster
- Support for vCloud Director 1.5+

FIGURE 3.58 vCloud Connector multitenant vCloud Connector node

3.9.1.4 vCloud Connector Limitations

vCloud Connector has the following restrictions:

- Currently, there is no way to have predefined vCloud instances display in vCloud Connector. User must manually add all vCloud instances that they intend to access to vCloud Connector. No vCloud instances are defined by default.
- Traffic to and from the vCloud Connector appliance is not WAN-optimized, so migrating workloads over WAN links is not ideal even if sufficient bandwidth exists. Avoid traversing WAN links where possible by installing vCloud Connector appliances in optimal locations. Currently, there is no way to limit which vCloud instances can be added to a vCloud Connector instance, so instruct users to use only the proper vCloud Connector instance for their needs.
- The transfer process caches virtual machines in two different storage locations. To facilitate successful transfers, size the vCloud Connector staging storage and vCloud Director transfer storage appropriately. The staging storage is 40GB by default, so the largest virtual machine vCloud Connector can transfer around 40GB.
- vCloud Connector is designed to give a consistent view of workloads across multiple vCloud instances and migrate those workloads. vCloud Connector cannot perform all the operations vCloud Director can handle, so use the vCloud Director web console to manage workloads.

- All workload transfers are cold migrations. Power off vApps and virtual machines before migration. Hot migrations are currently not available. Also, vApp networking configuration must be modified before powering on the virtual machines.
- vCloud Connector can handle up to 10 concurrent transfers. Subsequent requests are queued. The maximum number of vCloud connections for a single vCloud Connector is five (vCloud Director or vSphere).

NOTE

vCloud Connector 1.5 does not support the vCloud 5.1 Suite. vCloud Director 5.1 requires vCloud Connector 2.0 or later.

3.10 References

For additional information, see the documents listed in Table 3.18.

TABLE 3.18 Reference Documentation

Topic	Document
vCloud Director	*vCloud Director Security Hardening Guide* (www.vmware.com/files/pdf/techpaper/VMW_10Q3_WP_vCloud_Director_Security.pdf) Go to the VMware vCloud Director documentation site for the following vCloud Director documentation (www.vmware.com/support/pubs/vcd_pubs.html): ▶ *vCloud Director Installation and Configuration Guide* ▶ *vCloud Director Administrator's Guide* *What's New in VMware vCloud Director 1.5 Technical Whitepaper* (www.vmware.com/resources/techresources/10192)
vCloud Automation Center	Go to the VMware vCloud Automation Center documentation site for the following vCloud Automation Center documentation (www.vmware.com/support/pubs/vcac-pubs.html): ▶ *vCloud Automation Center Installation Guide* ▶ *vCloud Automation Center Reference Architecture* ▶ *vCloud Automation Center Operating Guide* ▶ *vCloud Automation Center Self-Service Portal* ▶ *vCloud Automation Center Extensibility Guide* *What's New in VMware vCloud Automation Center 5.1* (www.vmware.com/resources/techresources/10340)
vCloud API	Go to the VMware vCloud Director documentation site for the following vCloud Director documentation (www.vmware.com/support/pubs/vcd_pubs.html): ▶ *vCloud API Specification* ▶ *vCloud API Programming Guide*

Topic	Document
vSphere	VMware vSphere 5 documentation: (www.vmware.com/support/pubs/vsphere-esxi-vcenter-server-pubs.html) *What's New in VMware vSphere 5.1* (www.vmware.com/files/pdf/products/vsphere/vmware-what-is-new-vsphere51.pdf) *Performance Best Practices for VMware vSphere 5.0* (www.vmware.com/resources/techresources/10199) *VMware vCenter Server 5.1 Database Performance Improvements and Best Practices for Large-Scale Environments* (www.vmware.com/files/pdf/techpaper/VMware-vCenter-DBPerfBestPractices.pdf)
vCloud Networking and Security	*Administration Guide* (www.vmware.com/support/pubs/vshield_pubs.html) VMware vCloud Networking poster (www.vmware.com/files/pdf/techpaper/VMware-vCloud-Networking-Poster.pdf) *VXLAN Performance Evaluation on VMware vSphere 5.1* www.vmware.com/files/pdf/techpaper/VMware-vSphere-VXLAN-Perf.pdf) *Replacing Default vCenter 5.1 and ESXi Certificates* (www.vmware.com/files/pdf/techpaper/vsp_51_vcserver_esxi_certificates.pdf)
vCenter Chargeback	▶ *vCenter Chargeback User's Guide* ▶ (www.vmware.com/support/pubs/vcbm_pubs.html)
vCenter Orchestrator	vCenter Orchestrator Developer's Guide (www.vmware.com/pdf/vco_410_developers_guide.pdf) VMware vCenter Orchestrator Administration Guide (www.vmware.com/pdf/vco_410_admin_guide.pdf) vCenter Server 4.1 Plug-In API Reference for vCenter Orchestrator 6 (www.vmware.com/support/orchestrator/doc/vco_vsphere41_api/index.html)

CHAPTER 4

Operating a VMware vCloud

IN THIS CHAPTER

4.1 Overview

This chapter offers practical, operations-focused guidelines to help you implement a VMware® vCloud®. Based on the *vCloud Operations Framework,* the guidelines have the near-term goal of supporting Infrastructure as a Service (IaaS) within a comprehensive, service-focused, operational framework. The long-term goal for IT operations is full implementation of IT as a Service (ITaaS), so this chapter also discusses many considerations with ITaaS in mind. These guidelines should be useful to both service providers and enterprises.

The following vCloud chapters are designed to be used together throughout the lifecycle of a VMware vCloud computing implementation. In combination with a service definition, these chapters provide a comprehensive view of VMware vCloud computing:

- Chapter 3, "Architecting a VMware vCloud," provides design guidance, design considerations, and design patterns for *constructing* a vCloud environment from its constituent components.
- Chapter 4, "Operating a VMware vCloud," includes design guidance and considerations for *operating and maintaining* a vCloud environment. It covers the people, process, and technology involved in running a vCloud environment.
- Chapter 5, "Consuming a VMware vCloud," covers considerations for *consumers* who choose to leverage vCloud computing resources.

Additionally, Chapter 6, "Implementation Examples," provides modular examples that show how to use VMware component software to implement a vCloud. Chapter 7, "Workflow Examples," and Chapter 8, "Software Tools," also provide useful information for IT operations.

NOTE

Detailed implementation procedures for installing a vCloud are available in the VMware vCloud product documentation (www.vmware.com/support/pubs/vcd_pubs.html).

4.1.1 Audience

This chapter is intended for IT personnel who are involved in the IT business, service, operations, and infrastructure governance, along with operational control, for one or more instances of vCloud delivering cloud services. The reader is assumed to be familiar with IT service management principles and VMware vSphere® and vCloud concepts.

4.1.2 Scope

This chapter focuses on operating a vCloud from the perspectives of organizational structure, service management, operations management, and infrastructure management.

4.2 Cloud Computing

Cloud computing leverages the efficient pooling of on-demand, self-managed virtual infrastructures, which are consumed as services. Figure 4.1 illustrates key cloud computing principles and service layers.

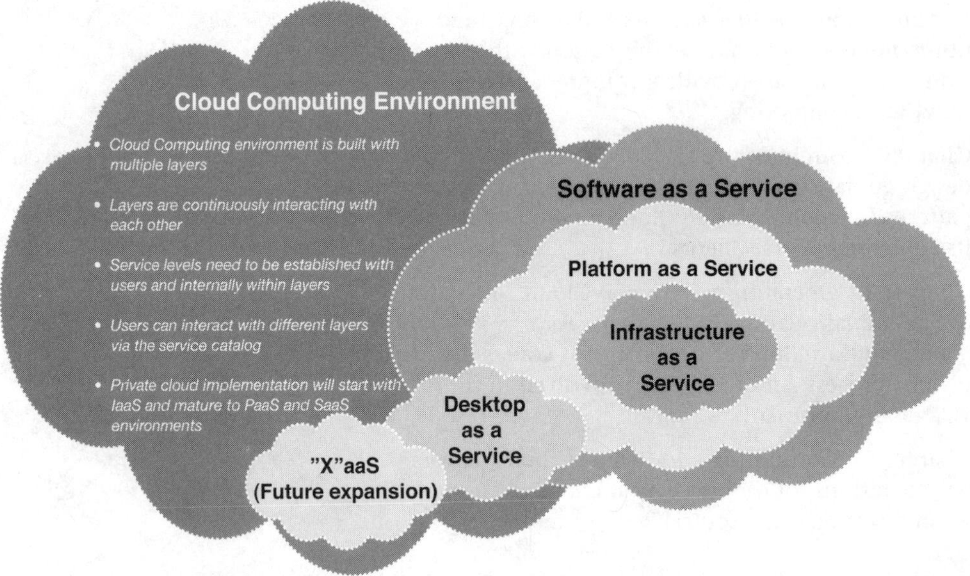

FIGURE 4.1 Cloud computing layers

The National Institute of Standards and Technology (NIST) specifies three service layers in a cloud. VMware defines the following service layers:

- **Software as a Service (SaaS):** Business-focused services presented directly to users in a service catalog
- **Platform as a Service (PaaS):** Technology-focused services for application development and deployment presented directly to application developers through a service catalog
- **Infrastructure as a Service (IaaS):** Infrastructure containers for better agility, automation, delivery of components, and related purposes

Additional service layers are expected to become available as other services, such as Desktop as a Service, are developed.

Companies adopt cloud computing to improve quality of service, business agility, and operating cost efficiency.

- **Quality of service:** Standardized and automated service offerings, with associated availability levels and service management, help promote quality of service. Customers can provision a reliable vCloud service with predictable service levels to get the service they need, as they need it, within expected timeframes. To provide standardized, repeatable service, IT must introduce operational efficiencies and control the underlying infrastructure and applications.
- **Business agility:** A proactive, service-driven model helps IT provide and manage services, which are added to a service catalog to facilitate end-user self-service. IT retains control of the environment (for example, by protecting against oversubscription). Providing the reliable, dynamic services expected from a vCloud requires automation of complex, time-consuming, error-prone tasks. This model reduces IT lag, improving business agility and increasing speed to market.
- **Increased cost efficiency:** The key to increased cost efficiency is reduction of operational expenses. The current operational cost and burden of managing IT—approximately 70% operational expenses (OpEx) and 30% capital expenses (CapEx)—must change, especially as IT becomes more service driven. IT operational processes for vCloud computing must be enhanced by automation and the use of tools for management, compliance, and process governance. IT organizational structures must be optimized to support vCloud operations and management.

4.2.1 vCloud Operations Framework

An IT organization's adoption of IT as a Service (ITaaS) in a vCloud is evolutionary: The people, processes, and tools continue to evolve over time. The organizational structure and critical processes that support the adoption of ITaaS via vCloud computing are defined by the underlying VMware vCloud Operations Framework (VOF), as Figure 4.2 shows.

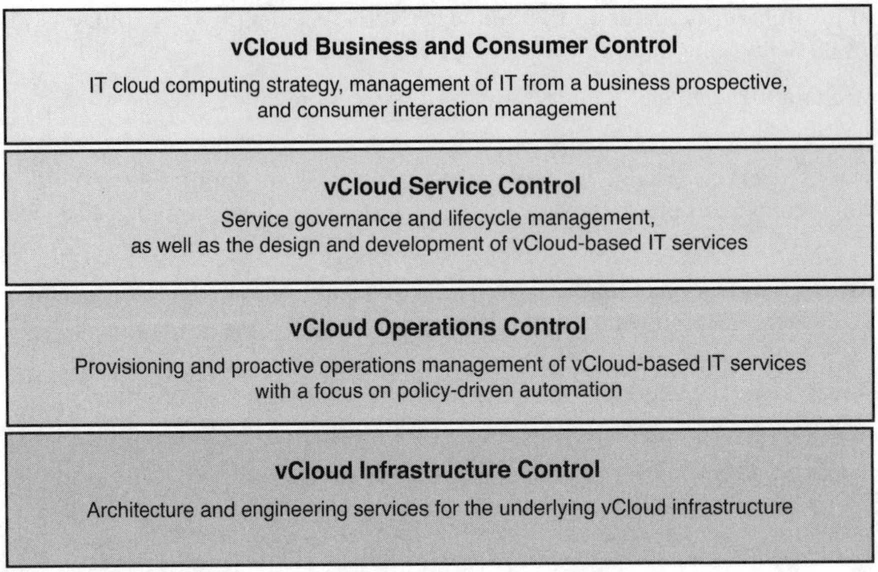

FIGURE 4.2 vCloud Operations Framework

The vCloud Operations Framework consists of the following layers:

- **vCloud Business and Consumer Control:** Addresses business-driven strategy in the context of consumer-driven requirements and demand for vCloud services, management of IT from a business perspective, and consumer interaction management.
- **vCloud Service Control:** Converts the consumer-driven requirements and demand, supported by business drivers, into vCloud service definitions. It also manages service development, creates service-level agreements (SLA), reports SLA compliance results back to the business and its consumers, and manages the lifecycle of services included in the service portfolio.
- **vCloud Operations Control:** Defines, deploys, and executes vCloud operations-related processes and supporting tools, and proactively manages the operations and delivery of vCloud services, with an emphasis on policy-driven automation.
- **vCloud Infrastructure Control:** Architects and deploys the underlying vCloud infrastructure on which the services are offered, provisioned, and run.

As Figure 4.3 shows, all these layers are required for support of IaaS, PaaS and SaaS services.

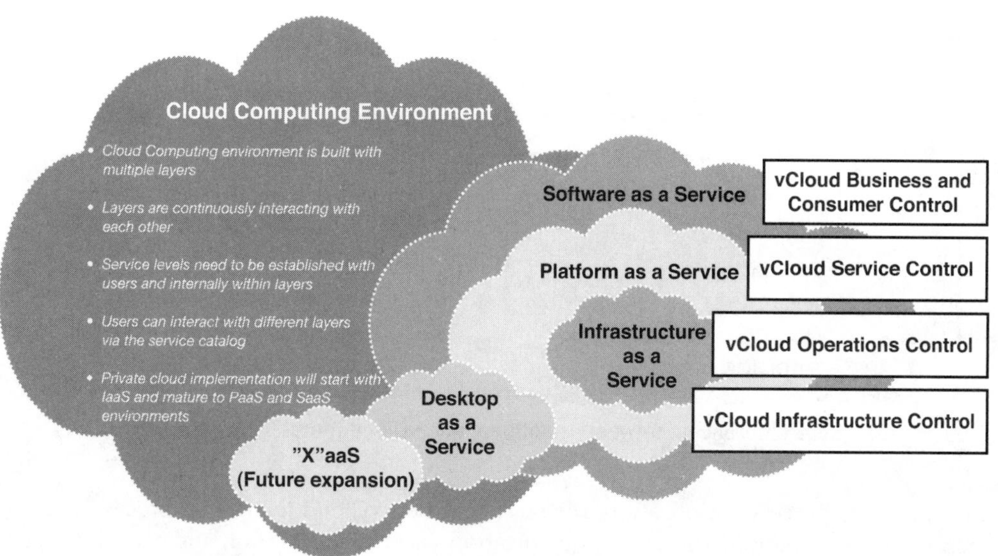

FIGURE 4.3 vCloud Operations Framework mapped to service layers

4.3 Process Maturity for vCloud Operations

Cloud computing is changing how resources are shared and consumed. Instead of relying on dedicated machines and workloads, vCloud relies on pooling and sharing of resources that are dynamic in nature. Within vCloud environments, new models are needed to effectively evaluate process maturity.

4.3.1 Traditional versus Maturity Models Specific to VMware

Traditional process maturity scales (ITIL, COBIT, CMM based) focus solely on optimizing processes in the physical world and are not capable of assessing the maturity of vCloud operations environments. Assessing process maturity in a vCloud environment requires a new scale.

Figure 4.4 represents the core differences between a traditional scale and a maturity scale based on VMware vCloud.

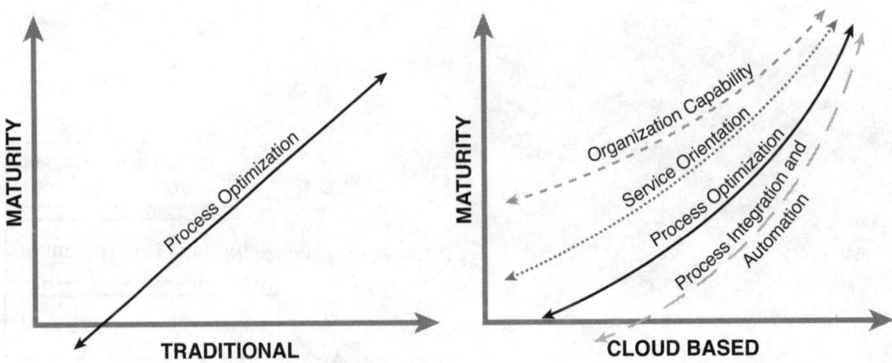

FIGURE 4.4 Core differences between traditional and vCloud maturity scales

In addition to process optimization, the scale based on vCloud focuses on process integration and automation, and on the organization's service orientation and capabilities, instead of on process optimization. The resulting maturity scale includes these elements:

- *Organization capability* is a measure of an organization's capability to use resource allocation, resource knowledge, and organizational setup to support vCloud operations.
- *Service orientation* is a measure of an organization's maturity and capability to align IT services with business user needs.
- *Process optimization* focuses on establishing and enforcing consistent, repeatable, and documented processes throughout an organization. On the maturity scale based on vCloud, process optimization is extended to the virtualization and vCloud computing stacks. In addition, process refinement is anticipated and planned for, to keep up with dynamic nature of the vCloud computing.
- *Process integration and automation* measures the evolution of traditional IT processes and their adoption for vCloud.

4.3.2 Process Maturity Scale Specific to VMware

Figure 4.5 shows the process maturity scale based on VMware vCloud. Organizations move from left to right on this scale over time, with the final goal of delivering IT as a Service (ITaaS) within a vCloud.

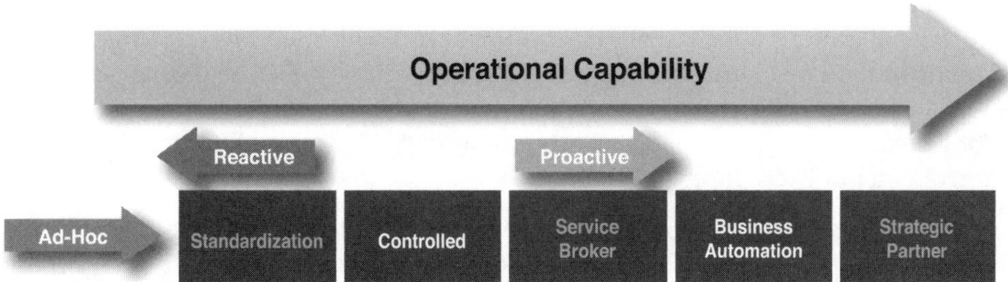

FIGURE 4.5 vCloud process maturity scale

Table 4.1 describes the process maturity scale states.

TABLE 4.1 Process Maturity Scale Legend

Maturity Level	Description
Standardization Level 1	Basic operational processes and tools are adapted for core virtualization, but not for vCloud computing. Processes objectives are defined, but activities are performed manually.
Defined/Controlled Level 2	Limited operational processes and tools are adapted for vCloud computing. Processes objectives are documented, and organization roles and responsibilities are defined. Limited, automated integration with existing IT processes (change, configuration, others) takes place.
Service Broker Level 3	Complete operational control is established over processes and tools, and a vCloud COE is in place. The organization is more service driven and offers services directly to business users through a service catalog. Operational processes are service focused and proactive. Service, design, and development procedures are clearly defined.
Business Automation Level 4	Automated process-management policies and operational controls are in place. Organization focus moves toward business agility—critical business services are offered through the vCloud with complete operational control. Detailed measurements and metrics are automatically collected and available for consumption. An expanded COE is established to support vCloud operations.
Strategic Partner Level 5	Operational control is automated and policy driven. Automated self-healing operations remediate errors and maintain quality of service. All processes are integrated, and the organization can consistently achieve ITaaS objectives and satisfy business demands.

4.3.3 Evolution of vCloud Operations

The following sections address how the people, processes, and tools that comprise the VMware vCloud Operations Framework evolve as an IT organization adopts ITaaS in a vCloud.

4.3.3.1 People

IT organizational evolution for vCloud computing begins with the VMware design guideline for virtualization operations: *Create a Center of Excellence (COE)*. The COE is central to successful operation of a virtualized environment, and it is essential for vCloud operations. For a detailed description of a COE, see Section 4.5.2.1, "vCloud Infrastructure Operations Center of Excellence."

Initially, the COE is the focal point for architecting, engineering, and administering the vCloud infrastructure. As vCloud computing takes on a more prominent role and purpose-built management tools mature, the organization adopts an increasingly service-driven approach. This paves the way for the next phase of the vCloud operations evolution, in which the focus shifts from the vCloud infrastructure to the services offered through it.

In the second phase, the COE includes responsibilities for current and new roles focused on the following:

- Construction of service offerings
- Service provisioning management
- Proactive operations management
- Integration and automation management

At this point, automation capabilities begin to drive increased operational efficiency, which leads to increased productivity and frees people up to work on other value-add initiatives. Meanwhile, improved management tool capabilities enable greater visibility into the infrastructure, applications, and user experience, all of which help to identify problems before they can lead to unacceptable performance or outages.

Eventually, purpose-built management tools and automation of business-aligned services progress to the point at which vCloud operations evolve from proactive service operation to predictive, policy-driven, end-to-end, vCloud-based service operation. Discrete operational and functional roles evolve into COE roles and skill sets that are focused on management tools and automation capabilities. Operational domain knowledge remains essential but now supplements deep management tools and automation expertise.

4.3.3.2 Process

As the IT organization continues to evolve, the maturity of vCloud management tools and automation drives vCloud process governance and implementation.

Initially, vCloud computing uses the same operational process approach as virtualization. This approach is effective while pilot studies are conducted and the vCloud is used for development and testing. At this stage, results depend on the maturity of the operational processes themselves, their integration with broader enterprise operational processes, and how successfully the combination has been adapted for virtualization. Maturity levels of the operational processes range from those characterized as reactive and immature—those still based on operating a physical infrastructure—to more mature processes adapted for the unique capabilities of virtualization.

As the IT organization evolves and becomes more service driven, operational processes must become more proactive and service focused. This requires implementing management tools that are purpose-built for vCloud and process automation. Traditional, discrete operational process and functional areas continue to exist, but management tools and automation begin to support some process consolidation and efficiency gains.

At this stage, the vCloud operational model cannot be CMDB driven. Instead, multiple federated configuration-management systems need to manage and interact with each other to support the dynamic nature of a vCloud. vCloud operational processes focus on delivering consumer-facing or infrastructure-related services; both are subject to the same service governance and lifecycle management, while blueprint and policy drive their design development.

The nature of vCloud computing forces proactive operations and management:

- Optimal performance and reliability of the vCloud requires enhanced performance management.
- Capacity management relies increasingly on forward-looking demand projections so that resources can be in place before users need them.
- IT financial management can no longer be project driven—it must become resource investment driven.

These factors position IT vCloud operations for the next phase, in which the company expands the vCloud environment and migrates business-critical services to it.

As vCloud management tools and underlying automation mature, the IT organization evolves from proactive to predictive operations and management. Operational process and functional areas are consolidated as management tools provide more intelligent, end-to-end operational capabilities. Configuration and compliance management become policy driven, with automated drift remediation and built-in auditability. Operations management can now be based on predictive analytics, with automated remediation reducing the number of incidents and/or systemic problems. Consumer-facing services that are deployed for subsequent on-demand self-service provisioning, automatically deployed infrastructure, and resource access supplemented by transparent bursting to an external vCloud provider can all use fully automated provisioning. The ultimate goal of *zero-touch* operations is now within reach.

4.3.3.3 Tools

Management tools must mature to support the evolution of vCloud operations. VMware envisions a dramatic change in vCloud operational processes over time based on the evolution of vCloud management tools, an increasing focus on policy-driven automation, and management tool maturity. For example:

- Proactive operations move to predictive operations that directly impact how event, incident, problem, availability, and performance management are realized.

- Configuration management moves from being CMDB based to adopting a more virtualized, on-demand approach in which configuration and relationship information is collected by multiple, federated configuration-management systems that independently manage and interact with each other, and provide data to management tools as required.
- Service offering development evolves from static and discrete vApp-based development to dynamic, blueprint-based and policy-based vApp construction.

These capabilities, along with increases in operational efficiency, process and functional area consolidation, and zero-touch operations, all depend on the evolution of vCloud management tools and a focus on policy-driven automation.

4.4 Changing Role of Information Technology Organizations

IT is undergoing tremendous change. Modern mobile devices such as tablets and smartphones are replacing traditional desktop and laptop platforms, and business users now expect on-demand accessibility of services on mobile platforms. Internal IT organizations are also seeing growing competition from external service providers. *Shadow IT* (IT solutions built and used inside organizations without official approval) continues to grow because some business needs are not serviced internally. The business expects IT to deliver services that do the job well for a fair price today, not six months from now. These trends make it necessary to rethink, reshape, and reimagine the function of IT and its relationship to business.

4.4.1 IT and Business Relationship

The relationship between IT and business must become more service driven, with IT in the role of the preferred supplier and business as the consumer. As the supplier, IT is responsible for providing services when they are needed. The following core IT disciplines apply to this relationship:

- Provisioning focuses on providing on-demand services while responding rapidly to changing business needs.
- IT economics focuses on increasing efficiency and reducing IT costs, optimizing CapEx and OpEx expenditures for the IT organization, and maintaining the expected quality of service.

4.4.2 Rethink IT

IT must move toward *IT as a Service* (ITaaS). IT organizations must become more service oriented, aligning IT services to business-consumable services that must be available on-demand and must be capable of scaling with business growth.

Becoming a service orientation is transformational for an IT organization. The first step in the transformation, server virtualization, has already been taken. Virtualization facilitates resource sharing, and IT organizations are investigating other initiatives to further enhance this capability:

- Implementing a comprehensive vCloud strategy
- Automating infrastructure management and operations
- Virtualizing business-critical applications
- Building new, modern applications for a post–personal computer era

Cloud computing is critical to the success of the ITaaS model. For VMware, it is a logical follow-up to virtualization. A VMware vCloud enables IT to realize cost-effective pooling and sharing of resources without increasing overall IT complexity and costs. vCloud models also allow for a consistent, repeatable architectural approach that reduces support costs.

In this new model, IT moves to a more proactive role, that of an effective business partner that seeks to meet business objectives. The IT supplier and business consumer come together to focus on better quality of delivered services, using negotiated service-level agreements and a process of continuous improvement. This enhances communication between IT and business, improving transparency, flexibility, and cost visibility.

4.5 Organizing for vCloud Operations

A transformative aspect of vCloud computing is its impact on the IT organization. By definition, vCloud computing provides on-demand service delivery and requires a service-driven IT organization. From an organizational perspective, delivering a service based on vCloud impacts all layers of the VMware vCloud Operations Framework: vCloud Business and Consumer Control, vCloud Service Control, vCloud Operations Control, and vCloud Infrastructure Control. It also directly impacts the relationships of these entities with other organizational teams within IT and with customers, who are the key IT shareholders.

4.5.1 Organizational Overview

vCloud Operations focuses on two organizing concepts, vCloud Tenant Operations and vCloud Infrastructure Operations, as well as their relationships to application development, the Network Operations Center (NOC), and customers. (See Figure 4.6.)

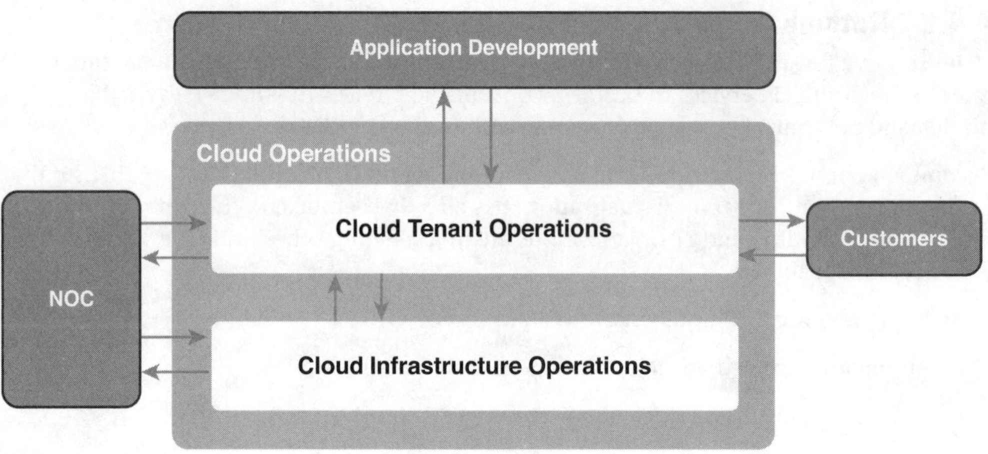

FIGURE 4.6 vCloud organizational overview

In non-vCloud environments, application development is responsible for designing, developing, integrating, and testing a company's custom applications and databases, and integrating and testing third-party applications. It fills the same role in a vCloud environment. The difference is that the vCloud environment promotes an agile approach to development, coupled with modern Platform as a Service–based tools and a tighter relationship to vCloud operations (specifically, vCloud Tenant Operations). Section 4.5.3, "vCloud Tenant Operations," discusses this relationship. Multiple application development teams can interact with vCloud Tenant Operations.

For vCloud computing, the design guideline for the Network Operations Center (NOC) is to become a center for proactive vCloud monitoring, event management, and remediation. From an organizational perspective, the requirement is to add vCloud-specific subject matter experts (SMEs) and begin migrating Tier 2 support responsibilities to the NOC. Instrumenting the NOC with purpose-built vCloud management tools is critical to achieving this. The NOC interacts with vCloud Tenant Operations and vCloud Infrastructure Operations for Tier 3 support as needed. Section 4.5.2, "vCloud Infrastructure Operations," and Section 4.5.3, "vCloud Tenant Operations," discuss this interaction.

vCloud Tenant Operations is responsible for managing end-customer organization relationships and governing, developing, releasing, provisioning, and operationally managing the services offered on the vCloud computing infrastructure. Organizationally, it represents the vCloud Service Control layer of the vCloud Operations Framework and the vCloud Operations Control layer as it relates to the offered services. Service offerings can include applications that an application development team provides.

vCloud Infrastructure Operations is responsible for architecting, engineering, deploying, and operationally managing the underlying logical and physical vCloud computing infrastructure.

4.5.2 vCloud Infrastructure Operations

vCloud infrastructure management encompasses the vCloud Operations Control and vCloud Infrastructure Control layers of the vCloud Operations Framework. It is responsible for architecting, engineering, deploying, and operating the underlying vCloud infrastructure. In VMware terms, the underlying vCloud infrastructure is defined as VMware vCloud Director®, its supporting components such as VMware vCloud Networking and Security™ and VMware vCenter Chargeback™, and the VMware vSphere and the physical infrastructure.

The vCloud Operations Control layer defines operating the vCloud infrastructure. This layer includes the functional operational areas that affect or are most affected by vCloud. They are divided into the following categories:

- Proactive operations management:
    - Change management
    - Configuration and compliance management
    - Capacity management
    - Performance management
    - Access and security management
    - Availability and continuity management
    - Monitoring, event, incident, and problem management
    - Analytics, trending, and metrics
- Integration and automation management

The vCloud Operations Control layer applies to the vCloud infrastructure and to vCloud service operations. For more information, see Section 4.5.3, "vCloud Tenant Operations."

vCloud Infrastructure Operations benefits considerably by reorganization. Traditional infrastructure operations consist of operational functional domains overlaying siloed infrastructure domains with little cross-domain interaction, unless interaction is required for a particular project or deployment. Infrastructure virtualization provides the most recent and compelling opportunity for the infrastructure management component of infrastructure operations to break from this traditional approach by creating a Center of Excellence (COE).

4.5.2.1 vCloud Infrastructure Operations Center of Excellence

The vCloud Infrastructure Operations Center of Excellence (COE) model is an extension of the VMware Center of Excellence model. Many organizations of various sizes have used the VMware Center of Excellence model to facilitate the adoption of VMware technology and to simplify the complexity of managing a VMware virtual infrastructure.

The vCloud Infrastructure Operations COE model defines cross-domain vCloud Infrastructure Operations management accountability and responsibility within team roles across an organization. These team roles enable an organization to consistently measure, account for, and improve vCloud infrastructure operations management.

The COE model further extends operations by including many of the responsibilities previously reserved for the traditional operations team. As vCloud-specific infrastructure operations tools advance, they (combined with automated remediation capabilities) reduce the need for dedicated operations roles. Roles evolve to have a deeper relationship to tools and associated operations. For example, instead of having an Availability Management role, availability management capabilities are built into the infrastructure architecture using a tool such as the VMware vCenter Operations Management Suite™ to proactively monitor availability. Automated remediation scripts help resolve anomalies before services are affected.

The vCloud Infrastructure Operations COE is a focused "virtual" team of vCloud infrastructure operations specialists and related functional groups that together form a vCloud Infrastructure Operations COE ecosystem (see Figure 4.7). The ecosystem serves as the focal point for all decisions and actions involving vCloud infrastructure operations.

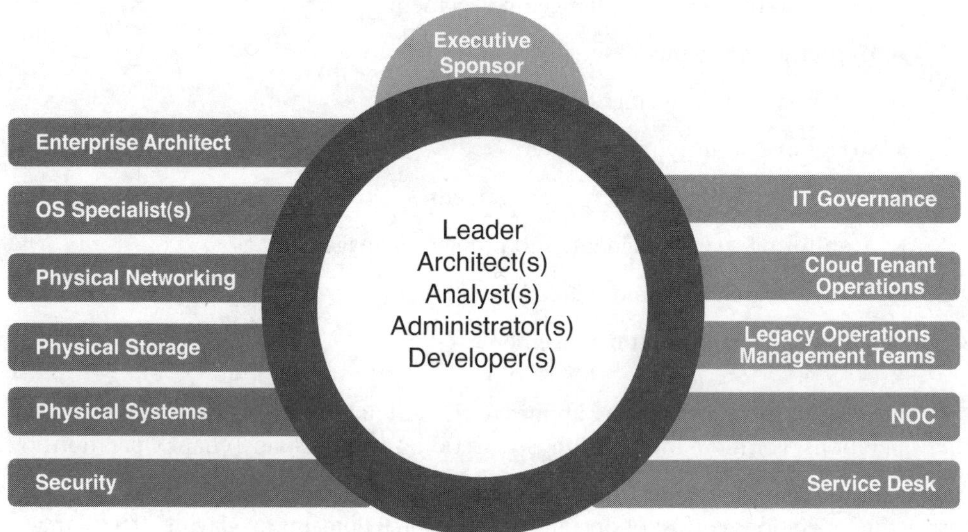

FIGURE 4.7 vCloud Infrastructure Operations Center of Excellence ecosystem

vCloud Infrastructure refers both to internally provided vCloud infrastructure and to infrastructure provided by an external vCloud provider. The following sections describe the primary roles for members of the vCloud Infrastructure Operations COE core team.

4.5.2.1.1 Executive Sponsor

- Provides clear messaging, leadership, and guidance to the entire IT organization and affected organizations about the vCloud Infrastructure Operations COE.
- Drives the cross-domain alignment required to establish a successful, functioning vCloud Infrastructure Operations COE extended team. This level of sponsorship is important for breaking down organizational barriers and mandating integrated

process design and implementation across the affected organizations. Cross-domain alignment and integrated process implementation are required to sustain a vCloud infrastructure at the level needed to support service offerings based on vCloud and associated service levels.

4.5.2.1.2 vCloud Infrastructure Operations COE Leader

Figure 4.7 refers to this function as Leader.

- Provides leadership and guidance to vCloud Infrastructure Operations COE members.
- Has a direct line of communication to the executive sponsor.
- Works with vCloud Tenant Operations regarding the planned vCloud-based service offering portfolio and any portfolio changes.
- Is responsible and accountable for making sure that the vCloud infrastructure can support service offerings based on vCloud and service levels.
- Actively promotes awareness of the impact of the vCloud infrastructure on service offerings and service level support and delivery.
- Facilitates integration of the vCloud infrastructure—for example, for change management—into existing traditional IT operations management processes, as needed.
- Coordinates and assists with planning cloud infrastructure initiatives.
- Provides guidance to Change Management for changes related to the vCloud infrastructure. Might authorize low-risk, low-impact changes to the vCloud infrastructure. Lobbies on behalf of the vCloud Infrastructure Operations COE for preapproved changes.
- Facilitates development and maintenance of vCloud infrastructure capacity forecasts.
- Manages the acquisition and installation of vCloud infrastructure components.
- Maintains management-level relationships with the vCloud Infrastructure Operations COE ecosystem teams.
- Is involved in managing vendor relationships for vCloud infrastructure components.
- Is involved in managing provider relationships with external vCloud providers.

4.5.2.1.3 vCloud Infrastructure Operations COE Architect

Figure 4.7 refers to this function as Architect(s).

- Is responsible for including operational considerations in vCloud infrastructure architecture and design
- Is responsible for developing and maintaining vCloud infrastructure architecture and design documents and blueprints

- Works closely with storage and network groups to architect and design vCloud infrastructure extensions
- Works with enterprise architects to make sure that the vCloud infrastructure architecture is aligned with company architectural standards and strategies
- Is responsible for architecting and designing the vCloud layer in support of the planned service offering portfolio based on vCloud and any portfolio changes
- Is responsible for working with the IT security team to make sure any architecture or design decisions address security and compliance
- Is responsible for architecting and designing solutions for vCloud infrastructure integration points with ecosystem team systems
- Provides subject matter expertise to support build, configuration, and validation processes
- Maintains awareness of VMware software patches and their impact on the environment
- Develops and maintains operational guidelines for the maintenance and support of the vCloud infrastructure
- Mentors and provides subject matter expertise to vCloud Infrastructure Operations COE core and ecosystem team members
- Assists with Tier 3 support to resolve issues related to vCloud infrastructure
- Develops software and hardware upgrade plans
- Develops and maintains the availability policy for the vCloud infrastructure, consistent with operating-level agreement (OLA) requirements

4.5.2.1.4 vCloud Infrastructure Operations COE Analyst

Figure 4.7 refers to this function as Analyst(s).

- Is responsible for developing and maintaining the vCloud infrastructure capacity forecast
- Is responsible for the day-to-day capacity and resource management of the vCloud infrastructure
- Works with the IT security team to make sure that the vCloud infrastructure aligns with IT security and compliance policies; assists in developing automated compliance policies
- Initiates requests for new vCloud infrastructure components
- Assists with Tier 3 support for issues related to vCloud infrastructure capacity and performance
- Assists with the change-management process as applied to the vCloud infrastructure
- Is responsible for maintaining the vCloud infrastructure asset-management data

- Is responsible for tracking and analyzing vCloud infrastructure performance, usage, and other operational analytics
- Is responsible for validating billing metering data collected for the service offerings based on vCloud

4.5.2.1.5 vCloud Infrastructure Operations COE Administrator

Figure 4.7 refers to this function as Administrator(s).

- Deploys and configures vCloud infrastructure components
- Executes the validation plan when deploying new infrastructure components
- Works with vCloud Infrastructure Operations COE ecosystem team members to configure vCloud infrastructure components
- Is responsible for auditing vCloud infrastructure component configuration consistency
- Develops and maintains vSphere and vCloud internal user access roles
- Creates, configures, and administers vCloud provider-related components, such as vCloud Networking and Security, vCenter Chargeback, and vCloud-specific operational management tools
- Works with the IT security team to implement vCloud-related security and compliance policies
- Determines maintenance windows for the vCloud infrastructure consistent with operating-level agreement requirements
- Provides Tier 3 support of the vCloud infrastructure
- Tests and installs vCloud infrastructure patches
- Verifies that the vCloud infrastructure is correctly instrumented for monitoring and logging purposes
- Is responsible for working with developers and other teams to implement any required vCloud integration with external systems
- Works with developers to implement workflows that impact the vCloud infrastructure

4.5.2.1.6 vCloud Infrastructure Operations COE Developers

Figure 4.7 refers to this function as Developer(s).

- Works with COE ecosystem teams to implement any required vCloud integration with other applications
- Develops, tests, and deploys vCloud-impacting automation workflow
- Evangelizes and mentors vCloud COE ecosystem teams about vCloud integration and automation

- Develops and maintains vCloud integration and automation workflow documentation
- Works with vCloud COE members and the ecosystem team to establish integration and automation monitoring
- Works with vCloud COE members and the ecosystem team to establish automated event remediation wherever possible and appropriate
- Provides Tier 3 vCloud integration and automation workflow support

Because these roles and responsibilities require unique skills, a different person should fill each role. With the exception of the vCloud Infrastructure Operations COE Leader, the number of people taking on each role depends on the scale and scope of the vCloud infrastructure.

4.5.2.2 Role of vCloud Infrastructure Operations COE in Standardization

In a traditional organization, multiple business units drive IT. The business unit (BU) controls IT funding, and each BU can enforce separate infrastructure policies and procedures. This approach leads to disjointed architectures and a lack of standardization. IT groups that support such an environment struggle to achieve agreed-upon operating levels, leading to end-user frustration, IT support inefficiencies, and possibly even financial liability.

The implementation of a vCloud changes this scenario. A vCloud is built as a shared resource that requires enforcement of consistent standards across the entire IT organization. To define and enforce these standards, all infrastructure policies and procedures associated with the vCloud should be driven by the vCloud Infrastructure Operations COE team instead of by BUs. This shift poses a significant challenge for organizations that try to move into a vCloud-appropriate infrastructure operating model. The vCloud Infrastructure Operations COE needs to negotiate with different business groups and rely on executive sponsorship and support during the transition to vCloud. More rigorous standards need to apply across the whole organization.

One recommended approach is to align vCloud Tenant Operations with the organization's phased development approach, adding a *vCloud-first policy* during the analysis and design phase for all new projects. Other recommendations include running vCloud Tenant Operations–driven assessments on applications that are being considered for migration to the vCloud. Assessments determine gaps and set expectations with business units on expected changes. The key to success is the capability to balance agility to meet business needs with stringent enforcement of defined standards within the vCloud.

4.5.2.2.1 Layers of Standardization

The vCloud is a shared resource running on infrastructure supported by the vCloud Infrastructure Operations Center of Excellence and core infrastructure teams. Whereas the vCloud Infrastructure Operations COE sets standards for the vCloud, core infrastructure teams might develop standards for the infrastructure that supports the vCloud. For example, the storage team might create standards for how new logical unit number (LUN) storage is presented for vCloud consumption. This layer of abstraction allows the storage team the flexibility to choose the most cost-effective SAN vendor and, if required, support a multivendor environment.

4.5.2.2.2 Measurement with Industry Benchmarks

vCloud technology is evolving at a rapid pace. After a vCloud is established within an organization, a continuous improvement cycle needs to be set up with annual reviews to make sure that the organization's vCloud is not lacking any current industry standards or benchmarks. The vCloud Infrastructure Operations COE is responsible for running this assessment and presenting the results, including recommendations for remediation, back to the leadership team.

4.5.3 vCloud Tenant Operations

vCloud Tenant Operations is central to governing, developing, and providing vCloud service offerings. It incorporates the Service Control layer of the vCloud Operations Framework and the Consumer Management component of the IT Business and Consumer Control layer. It also includes an Operations Control layer specifically applied to services. Figure 4.8 shows a high-level view of Tenant Operations and its ecosystem.

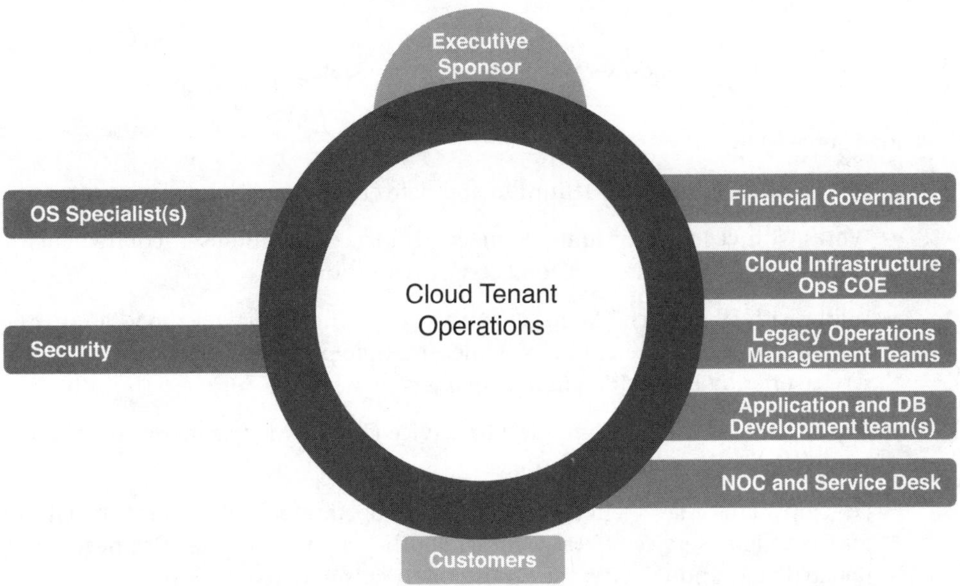

FIGURE 4.8 Tenant Operations

The following roles and responsibilities are involved in vCloud Tenant Operations:

- vCloud Service Leader:
  - Provides leadership and guidance to vCloud Tenant Operations members
  - Has a direct line of communication to the executive sponsors
  - Maintains a working relationship with the vCloud Infrastructure Operations leader

- Actively promotes awareness of tenant operations team to end-user organizations
- Maintains management-level relationships with the tenant operations ecosystem teams
- Assigns vCloud Service Offering responsibilities to service owners

- Customer Manager:
  - Is responsible for establishing and maintaining a working relationship with end-user organizations.
  - Determines and collects business requirements for end-user organization service offerings. Works with the designated vCloud Service Owner to translate the business requirements into a vCloud Service Definition.
  - Works with end-user organizations to understand project service offering demands.
  - Is responsible for end-user organization issue escalation.
- vCloud Service Owner:
  - Is responsible for overall definition and delivery of the vCloud service offering.
  - Works with vCloud Consumer Management to collect end-user requirements and translate them into a vCloud service definition.
  - Works with IT Financial Management to determine a price for the vCloud service offering and determine whether multiple prices are appropriate if the service offering is provided in multiple service tiers.
  - Provides the required information to Service Catalog Management, to correctly set up the service catalog offering.
  - Develops service-level agreements (SLA) and operating-level agreements (OLA) for the vCloud service offerings for which they are responsible. Also negotiates updated SLAs and OLAs as the service offering is updated.
  - Leads development and enhancement efforts and works with vCloud Service Architects on the vCloud service offerings.
  - Is responsible for Tier 3 support and escalations for the vCloud service offerings.
  - Makes sure that the service levels are met through corresponding OLAs with vCloud Infrastructure Operations.
  - Regularly monitors and reports on service level attainment for the vCloud service offerings.

- vCloud Service Portfolio Manager:
  - Develops and maintains vCloud Service Portfolio policy, including criteria for acceptance and rejection.
  - Manages the portfolio of vCloud services and works with IT management to develop the vCloud service offering strategy that determines what services are included in the portfolio. Makes sure that the service offering strategy aligns with the IT strategy.
  - Proactively identifies potential vCloud service offerings based on demand information gathered from vCloud Consumer Managers or other sources, such as requests coming in through the service desk.
- vCloud Service Catalog Manager
  - Manages the vCloud service offering catalog and makes sure that all the information contained in the catalog is accurate and up-to-date
  - Maintains the consumer self-service catalog portal information
- vCloud Service Architect
  - Defines a vCloud service offering based on the requirements provided by the vCloud service owner after it is determined that the service offering is to be included in the vCloud Service Portfolio
  - Translates vCloud business requirements into technical requirements that can be used to architect a vCloud service offering
- vCloud Service Developer:
  - Works with the vCloud Service Architect to understand technical requirements for the vCloud service offering
  - Works with the application development team to incorporate custom or third-party applications into vCloud service offerings as needed
  - Develops new vCloud service offering components into blueprints, or constructs blueprints from existing vCloud service offering components for automatic provisioning
  - Develops and maintains vCloud service offering blueprint documentation
  - Works with the vCloud Service Analyst and application development to define service monitoring
  - Works with the vCloud Service Analyst and application development to establish automated event remediation wherever possible and appropriate
  - Works with the vCloud Service Analyst and application development to make sure security, operations, and chargeback metering capabilities are built into vCloud service offerings

- Provides support for Tier 3 vCloud service offerings
- Develops service-related and service integration workflows
- Develops customizations for and maintains the online consumer self-service catalog capability

- vCloud Service QA:
  - Develops test plans, and tests and accepts services as ready for release to production, regardless of whether the services were developed in-house or by third parties, or are SaaS-based. Also performs post-release validation of services.
  - Develops test plans, and tests and accepts service-related and service integration workflows as ready for release to production. Also performs post-release validation.
  - Develops test plans, and tests and accepts online consumer self-service catalog capabilities as ready for release to production. Also performs post-release validation.
  - Is responsible for making sure that service desk personnel are trained to support the services that are put into production.
- vCloud Service Analyst:
  - Develops and maintains service capacity forecasts.
  - Is responsible for the day-to-day capacity and resource management of services.
  - Works with the IT security team to verify that services align with IT security and compliance policies. Assists in developing automated compliance policies.
  - Initiates requests for new or expanded service capacity.
  - Assists with Tier 3 support for issues related to tenant-deployed services.
  - Monitors and analyzes service performance, availability, usage, and other operational analytics.
  - Verifies that the NOC can support released services.
  - Works with the service QA to release services into production and coordinates any required change management. This responsibility decreases over time as the release process is automated and services consisting of previously released components are considered preapproved from a change management perspective.
- vCloud Service Administrator:
  - Administers tools vCloud Tenant Operations use to govern, develop, and operate services.

- Administers customer vCloud environments.
- Administers customer vApps and applications contained in vApps, if offered as a service. This is not usually applicable for development and test customers.

Either a single person or multiple people can satisfy these roles and responsibilities. The decision to employ one or multiple people depends on the number of vCloud service offerings. For a new vCloud environment, initial staffing should include the following roles and responsibilities:

- A single Consumer Manager.
- A single vCloud Service Portfolio Manager who is also responsible for vCloud Service Catalog management.
- One or more vCloud Service Owners, each responsible for conducting vCloud service development and working with other teams to make sure that the agreed-upon vCloud service levels for their vCloud service offering or suite of vCloud service offerings are maintained. The number of vCloud Service Owners depends on the number and complexity of the services to be offered, as well as the rate of service offering change.
- A single vCloud Service Architect.
- One or more vCloud Service Developers, depending on the number and complexity of the services to be offered and the rate of service offering change.

4.5.3.1 Relationship to Application Development

vCloud Tenant Operations interacts with application development teams from the following perspectives:

- Application development team as a customer
- Service development
- Production operations

The application development team is a customer of vCloud Tenant Operations. It uses a service that can provide virtual resources for deploying a development environment or a service in the form of PaaS. vCloud Tenant Operations monitors the environment for availability and is also involved in the release of the application as a service in the vCloud environment.

For service development, vCloud Tenant Operations interacts with an application development team if a custom application is needed to provide the service. Application development is seen as a partner (as well as a customer) in the service development process. vCloud Tenant Operations works with application development to make sure the application is properly instrumented for meaningful monitoring, security, and metering (for showback or chargeback). In addition, the teams work closely together to release the service into production.

The final perspective is production operations. In this case, vCloud Tenant Operations interacts with an application development team, if needed, in a Tier 3 support capacity.

4.5.4 Evolution of Organizational Structure for vCloud

The traditional IT organizational structure must evolve to support a model based on vCloud.

4.5.4.1 Traditional Organization Structure

Figure 4.9 shows an example of a traditional organization structure.

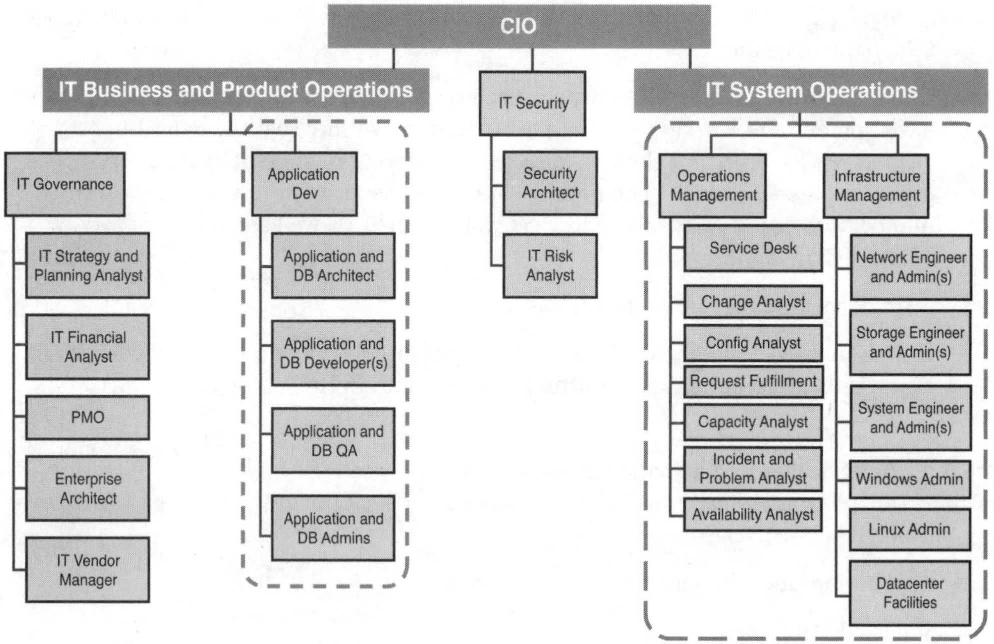

FIGURE 4.9 Traditional organization structure

This structure represents a traditional organization with two core groups: application development and infrastructure. The application development team focuses on application creation, and the infrastructure team focuses on management of hardware resources and daily operation of components. This model applies for most VMware customers, but there is limited focus on the cloud services. VMware associates this model with the reactive state in the vCloud capability model.

The traditional organization has limited focus on cloud management. Responsibilities for supporting the vCloud are typically handled by the roles that manage the physical and virtual world. This organizational structure has limitations and needs to evolve to fully realize the benefits of a cloud.

4.5.4.2 Organization Structure Focused on vCloud

Figure 4.10 shows an example of how the organization structure might evolve to support and effectively manage a vCloud.

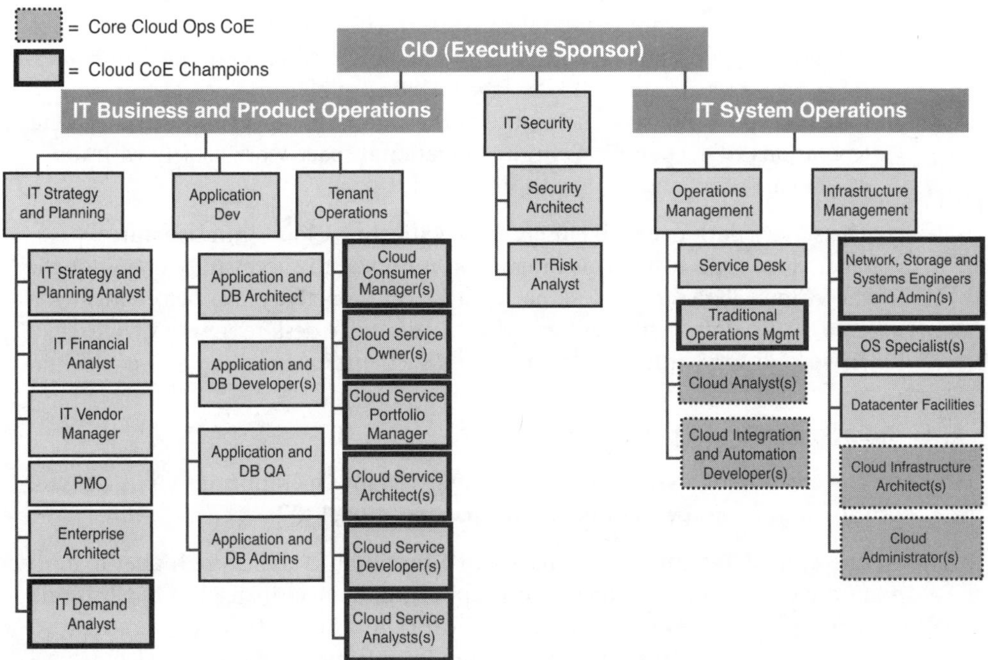

FIGURE 4.10 Organization structure focused on vCloud

The organizational structure based on vCloud represents a modern organization focused on vCloud with three core groups: application development, Tenant Operations, and Infrastructure Operations. The following describes how the model based on vCloud is different from the traditional model.

- IT System Operations:
  - The organizational model based on vCloud includes creating a focused group, the vCloud Infrastructure Operations Center of Excellence (COE), to support and manage vCloud infrastructure and operational components.
  - Under Infrastructure Management, a focused vCloud Infrastructure Operations COE champion role is added within the core infrastructure and operating system groups. The infrastructure-focused vCloud champions are responsible for pooling core physical infrastructure components to support the vCloud platform. The operating system group aligned vCloud champions work with the focused vCloud Infrastructure Operations COE to manage and maintain operations system standards for autodeployment packages within the vCloud.

- vCloud COE champions also act as the liaison between their respective groups and the vCloud Infrastructure Operations COE team. The goal is enhanced communication and alignment to support vCloud agility.
- Under Operations Management, the traditional operations management process teams allocate vCloud COE Infrastructure Operations champions' roles focused on operational governance and process automation. The standard ITSM processes are still valid, but they need to evolve and become proactive to support the dynamic nature of the vCloud. The vCloud Infrastructure Operations COE champions in the operational space work closely with the vCloud architect and analyst to support this goal.
- The service desk needs to closely work with the vCloud Infrastructure Operations COE team. This interaction is critical to successfully operationalize the vCloud. The service desk needs to act on proactive alerts before incidents occur. This alignment requires a dedicated service desk representative to take on vCloud Infrastructure Operations COE champion roles.

- IT Business and Product Operations:
  - The creation of a service-focused vCloud Tenant Operations group is a significant shift from the traditional organization model.
  - The vCloud Tenant Operations group is essential to achieving higher maturity in the cloud because it focuses on supporting services instead of applications. Services are at the core of the vCloud concept. vCloud Tenant Operations moves the overall organization to a service mindset; the primary IT objectives are to manage and maintain services offered in the vCloud.

4.6 vCloud Business and Consumer Control

The vCloud Business and Consumer Control layer deals with an organization's overall IT vCloud computing strategy, management of IT from a business prospective, and consumer interaction management.

4.6.1 Introduction to IT Business Management

IT Business Management (ITBM) is part of the top two service layers of the vCloud Operations Framework: Business and Consumer Control and Service Control (see Figure 4.3). ITBM addresses the business-driven strategy, as well as consumer-driven requirements and demand for vCloud services to be offered. It offers IT executives the visibility and control required to run IT as a business. In addition, it simplifies and automates the strategic business aspects of IT service delivery by optimizing the customer-specific cost elements and service-level requirements that directly influence IT service value.

4.6.1.1 ITBM Process Components

The ITBM layer is divided into the following major subcomponents:

- **IT Governance:** Focuses on financial transparency, with the capability to collect, model, and report costing data aligned to IT services. This subject area includes the following:
  - IT Financial Management
  - Demand Management and Budget Planning
  - IT Risk Management
  - IT Vendor Management
  - Accounting and Billing
- **Consumer Management:** Aligns IT services with customer requirements and makes sure that the customer catalog satisfies business requirements. It is responsible for managing customer expectations and providing customers with control and governance across the IT service portfolio. This subject area includes the following:
  - Consumer Service Catalog Management
  - Consumer Management and Reporting
- **Service Governance and Lifecycle Management:** Provides the methodology and control over the proposal, acceptance or rejection decision, definition, and end-to-end disposition of services and service offerings, along with governance and control over the quality of services available. This subject area includes the following:
  - Service Portfolio Management
  - Service Level Management
- **Service Design and Development:** Provides methodology and structure for the creation of new IT services. It enhances cost efficiency by reviewing service costs, chargeback, and metering as part of the development cycle. It also adds agility and speed when creating services by adding appropriate blueprints, and it allows for bundling and tiering of IT infrastructure resources. This subject area includes the following:
  - Infrastructure Architecture and Engineering Services
  - Service Chargeback and Metering

4.6.1.2 VMware Product Alignment

VMware addresses ITBM with the following products to help customers:

- **vCenter Chargeback:** End-to-end cost reporting solution for virtual environments that leverages integration with vSphere and vCloud Director.
- **VMware IT Business Management Suite:** Set of SaaS business applications that automate key processes for IT business management. Through its proactive planning, billing, and cost optimization capabilities, ITBM provides the visibility and

predictability that enable stakeholders to improve value and align spending with business goals. It also automates the core financial processes needed to easily plan, charge, and optimize the cost and value of IT. The ITBM suite includes these components:

- **IT Costing:** Maps the connections between IT services and their underlying cost drivers using an intuitive graphical approach that enables total cost of ownership (TCO) and unit cost tracking
- **IT Demand Management and Budget Planning:** Facilitates accurate, fact-based IT budgeting, planning, and forecasting
- **IT Showback and Chargeback:** Gives business units visibility into IT costs and alternatives, including fully itemized billing and chargeback
- **IT Cost Optimization:** Automatically identifies potential areas for ongoing cost reduction, such as candidates for virtualization and consolidation, storage tiering, SLA reduction, end of life, deferral of upgrades, and support reduction
- **Vendor Manager:** Provides a control and optimization mechanism for vendor agreements that proactively governs contractual commitments
- **SLA Manager:** Sets, tracks, and reports on SLAs, key performance indicators (KPIs), and key value indicators (KVIs) for services, vendors, and customers, and performs root cause and business impact analysis at all levels

4.6.1.2.1 Relationship Between Chargeback and ITBM Suite

vCenter Chargeback collects virtualization and vCloud cost data by integrating with vSphere and vCloud Director. It then provides cost data to the ITBM suite for inclusion in cost models.

Both products are connected by the vCenter Chargeback Connector, which scans vCenter Chargeback for a specific hierarchy and creates a report schedule to generate cost reports for this hierarchy on a daily basis. The connector also retrieves both generated and archived reports and provides the cost data for each virtual machine in the hierarchy to the IT Business Management Suite.

Based on the cost data collected by the connector, the IT Business Management Suite populates detailed analysis reports in its cost model and CIO dashboard. This integration provides visibility to CIOs across all IT assets and enables them to easily identify cost reduction opportunities by comparing virtualization, vCloud, and physical costs.

4.6.1.2.2 Cost Models

The ITBM Suite provides out-of-the-box (OOTB) cost models. A *cost model* is a multitiered set of allocation rules that map the financial relationships from the general ledger up to the business units within the organization. The relationships reveal which entities drive the cost of other entities.

The *cost browser* provides a simple way for users (typically the IT finance administrator) to create and modify a cost model that defines the cost relationships in their business structure. Cost models can be modified periodically by adding or deleting elements and changing dependencies to reflect the current contributory relationships between cost object types.

The OOTB cost model does not necessarily reflect all financial aspects of a fully mature IT organization. Instead, it provides immediate value to typical IT organizations and introduces design guidance for object types and common allocation rules that allocate cost end to end from the general ledger to the business units. If needed, the model can be enhanced to reflect any organization cost structure and data sources.

4.6.1.2.3 Integration with vCloud

Using the ITBM Suite, the customer gains unprecedented visibility and transparency across all IT components (physical, virtual, and vCloud). The ITBM Suite enables automatic tracking and processing of IT cost and service data across the organization. ITBM dashboards provide a 360-degree view of what IT services cost to deliver and the service levels that are provided. This visibility enables IT to run like a business and helps IT executives make fact-based decisions.

4.7 vCloud Service Control

vCloud Service Control deals with service governance and lifecycle management, and the design and development of vCloud-based IT services.

4.7.1 vCloud Service Governance and Lifecycle Management

The purpose of vCloud Service Governance and Lifecycle Management is to implement a standard methodology and control over the proposal, acceptance or rejection decision, definition, and end-to-end disposition of services and service offerings. It also provides governance and control over the quality of available services. Elements include Service Portfolio Management, Catalog Management, and Service Level Management.

4.7.1.1 Service Portfolio and Catalog Management

The purpose of the *service portfolio* is to accept or reject service proposals and maintain the overall catalog of services, whether rejected, under development, deployed, or retired. A primary responsibility of Service Portfolio Management is to verify that the services accepted for development and deployment align with the strategic and business requirements of the organization and its customers. This includes continuous review to allow adjustment of services due to new requirements and retirement of existing services due to lack of demand or replacement with a newer service.

The purpose of a *service catalog* is to maintain the active set of services. Active services are those under development or currently offered to customers for use in the vCloud environment. In this context, the service catalog is part of the overall service portfolio (as opposed to the consumer service catalog, from which customers deploy service offerings). The tool that supports the service portfolio and contains the service catalog provides a mechanism for automatically populating the consumer self-service catalog from the service offerings defined in the service catalog as part of the service offering release process. Regular reviews of the service catalog should be performed and adjustments made in line with feature changes in future releases of vCloud Director, vSphere, or other supporting products.

4.7.1.1.1 vCloud Service Catalog Components

The service catalog for the vCloud that vCloud Director supports offers service components to the end customer. At a minimum, the service catalog must define the following:

- **Organization container:** The *container* for the customer's IaaS, with attributes that hold basic, default service configuration information. Typically, only one organization container is purchased per customer.
- **Organization virtual datacenters:** The boundaries for running the virtual machines within the IaaS service, configured with sizing information based on the customers' requirements, with an appropriate SLA assigned to them. A minimum of one organization virtual datacenter is required for a customer to offer a service. Additional organization virtual datacenters can be requested, if required.

In addition to these core vCloud components, an organization can establish a standard set of offerings within the vCloud service catalog to provide customers with vApps (standardized groupings of preconfigured virtual machines) and media (installable software packages).

After being accepted into the service portfolio, the service and constituent service offerings should be defined with at least the following components:

- Service description
- Service requirements
- Service-level agreements
- Support terms and conditions
- Service lifecycle considerations
- Projected demand information for capacity planning
- Pricing and chargeback requirements
- Compliance requirements (regulatory and otherwise)
- Security requirements
- Monitoring and other operational requirements

Including pricing and chargeback, compliance, security, and operational requirements in the service definition is critical because these are core considerations during the service design and development process.

4.7.1.1.2 Service Types

Service types include business user services and technology services.

- **Business user services:** Defined as Software as a Service (SaaS) offerings, these services are generally directly consumed by users and are available as part of the organization's enterprise service catalog.

- **Technology services:** Defined as Infrastructure as a Service (IaaS) or Platform as a Service (PaaS), these technology services are not consumed directly by users, but they enable infrastructure automation that enhances an IT organization's capability to provide business user services.

4.7.1.1.3 Service Interrelationships

For optimal vCloud business user services, all types of technology services must be seamlessly integrated, usually with a workflow engine named the *orchestration layer*. Invoking a business user service can automatically trigger one or more technology services. The rules governing these workflows need to be preconfigured and preapproved for control. They are also needed to provide an agreed-to level of service to the business user. This agreed-to level of service is known as a *service-level agreement* (SLA).

4.7.1.1.4 vCloud Service Catalog Evolution

To improve the vCloud service catalog process and help realize vCloud benefits, as many service offerings as possible should be made available to users through automated provisioning.

In the virtualization world, the initial process for procurement of virtual machines generally follows the model that is applied to physical infrastructure. Although it is effective, it is not the most efficient mechanism for providing services, and vCloud benefits cannot be fully realized unless the process is changed. Figure 4.11 gives a logical representation of the evolution of the vCloud service catalog from this current state to the desired end state.

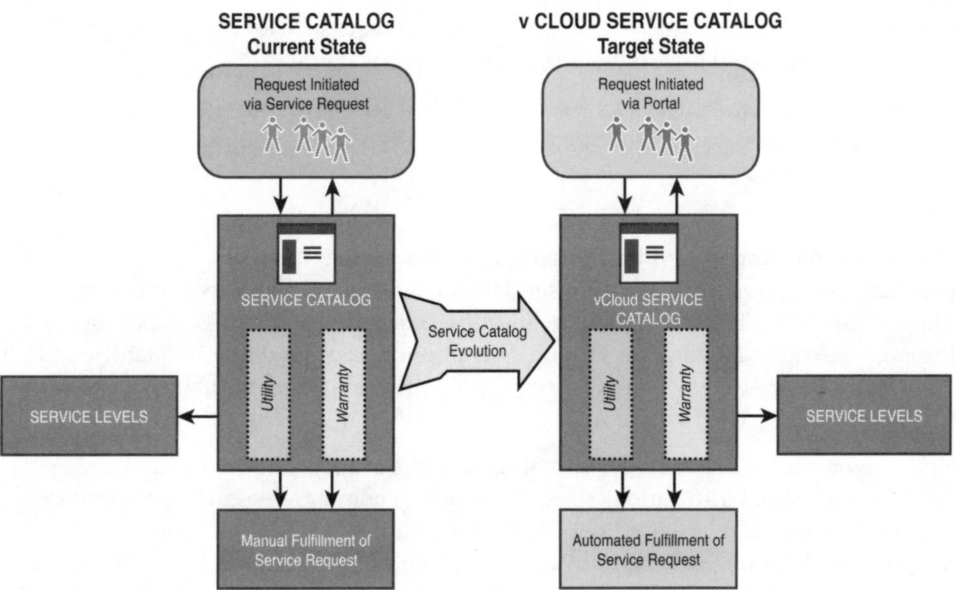

FIGURE 4.11 Service catalog evolution

In the service catalog current state, when a new service is requested, a service request is submitted to select and provision an offering from the service catalog. In addition to the utility (vApp or organization virtual datacenter) to be provided to the customer, the request includes the required service level provided by the virtual datacenter in which the vApp is to be provisioned, as well as any built-in availability features within the vApp itself. After the service is ordered, the end customer must wait for staff to fulfill the service request for the virtual machines to provide the service to be provisioned.

To satisfy the self-service, on-demand attribute of vCloud computing, the customer should be able to connect to a portal, select the required service offering, and have it automatically provisioned. This removes the need for manual selection from the service catalog and also removes delay in the provisioning processes. Figure 4.11 shows this process as the vCloud service catalog target state.

vCloud Director provides the capability to manage these requests from the service catalog. For vApps, an organization administrator can determine who within the organization has rights to request and provision vApps and thus provide end-to-end self-service. With vCloud Director, the user can select and provision the vApp and also specify the organization's virtual datacenter in which it is to be deployed. Because organization virtual datacenters are associated with provider virtual datacenters, the user is essentially selecting the required level of service.

To transition to the target state vCloud service catalog:

1. Continue with the service request process until the vCloud service catalog is available on the portal.
2. Enable IT staff to perform vCloud service catalog requests with automated provisioning on behalf of the user, including required approvals.
3. Add the capability for users to access the vCloud service catalog and request services that result in automated provisioning of the corresponding vApps, including required approvals.

4.7.1.1.5 Standardization of vCloud Offerings into the Service Catalog

Standardization of service offerings is essential to achieving a scalable, cost-efficient vCloud environment. Typically, compute resource-based service offerings (CPU, memory, and storage) provide a baseline for vCloud consumption and should be standardized as much as possible, regardless of whether they apply to organization virtual datacenters or vApps (and their associated virtual machines).

Compute resources for organization virtual datacenters available in the service catalog should be standardized into various sizes. The required compute resource configurations vary depending on the selected vCloud Director allocation model (allocation pool, pay as you go, or reservation pool) because attributes such as CPU speed and CPU or memory guarantee vary. Combining these two components means that the service catalog can offer differently sized organization virtual datacenters for each type of allocation model.

Similarly, to create a vApp catalog item (public or organization), standardization should be used as possible. From a compute resource point of view, standard-sized virtual machines should be created to use in a *pick list* of machines for vApp creation. These standardized virtual machines can vary in resource size for CPU, memory, and storage (for example, Standard, Standard Plus, Advanced, Premium, and Premium Plus). Because a vApp consists of one or more individual virtual machines, the appropriately sized virtual machines can be selected from the pick list during the vApp catalog creation process.

In addition to the basic compute offerings of the virtual machines within the vApps, it is necessary to develop the service catalog to include vApp software configurations. These can be basic groupings of compute resources and can be expanded over time to offer more advanced services. Table 4.2 shows sample vApp offerings.

TABLE 4.2 Sample vApp Offerings

vApp	Configuration
2-Tier Standard Compute	1x Standard RHEL Web virtual machine 1x Standard Windows Server 2008 Application virtual machine
3-Tier Standard Compute, Advanced Database	1x Standard RHEL Web virtual machine 1x Standard RHEL application virtual machine 1x Advanced MySQL Database virtual machine
3-Server Standard Plus Compute (not necessarily tiered)	3x Standard Plus Windows Server 2008 Application virtual machine

4.7.1.1.6 Establish Service Levels for vCloud Services in the Service Catalog

To provide an appropriate level of service for the vCloud customers' requirements, services should be further differentiated by their corresponding service levels. Service levels can be defined with availability and recoverability attributes such as Recovery Time Objective (RTO), Recovery Point Objective (RPO), and incident response times. The attributes can be applied to the different components within the service catalog.

It is possible to design for different service levels for the virtual machines contained in a vApp. For example, a vApp could contain multiple web servers to provide resilience in the event of server failure, and thus a lower RTO for the service.

Virtual datacenters provide abstracted physical and virtual resources. Different service levels can be defined by using (or not using) the underlying hardware technology (such as server capabilities, storage array technologies, storage protocols, and replication) and virtualization technology (HA, DRS, VMware vSphere vMotion®, and others).

Combined, vApps and the capabilities of the virtual datacenters on which they can be deployed offer the capability to create a powerful and extensive vCloud service catalog.

4.7.1.2 Service Level Management

Service Level Management defines the service-level agreement (SLA) associated with a vCloud service offering or a tier of service, negotiates corresponding operating-level agreements with the service provider to support the SLAs, and regularly monitors service levels and reports on results.

4.7.1.2.1 Definition of Service-Level Agreement

A *service-level agreement* (SLA) is a predetermined agreement between the service consumer and the service provider that measures the quality and performance of the available services. SLAs can be of many types, from those that measure pure service availability to those that measure response time for service components and process workflows as experienced by users.

Services run at every layer of the vCloud stack, so service consumers might be business users or internal IT groups who access the vCloud primarily for technology and infrastructure services. SLAs for base technology services that business users do not consume directly but are needed to make sure that downstream operations and infrastructure components support the business users' SLAs are referred to as *operational-level agreements* (OLAs).

4.7.1.2.2 vCloud Layers and SLAs

A typical vCloud computing environment consists of multiple layers (IaaS, PaaS, SaaS, and possibly others). The customer chooses how to implement the vCloud stack based on business requirements. Options include creating a private vCloud, using a public vCloud provider, or creating a hybrid vCloud model with both private and public vCloud resources. The enabler for this flexibility is an organization's capability to guarantee availability and performance at every vCloud layer. Signing SLAs externally with service providers or, for a private vCloud, creating SLAs with internal user organizations and supporting OLAs with the IT organization, achieves this.

4.7.1.2.3 Example

Figure 4.12 shows an example use case for an organization with an IaaS layer hosted by a public vCloud provider and the PaaS and SaaS layers maintained internally.

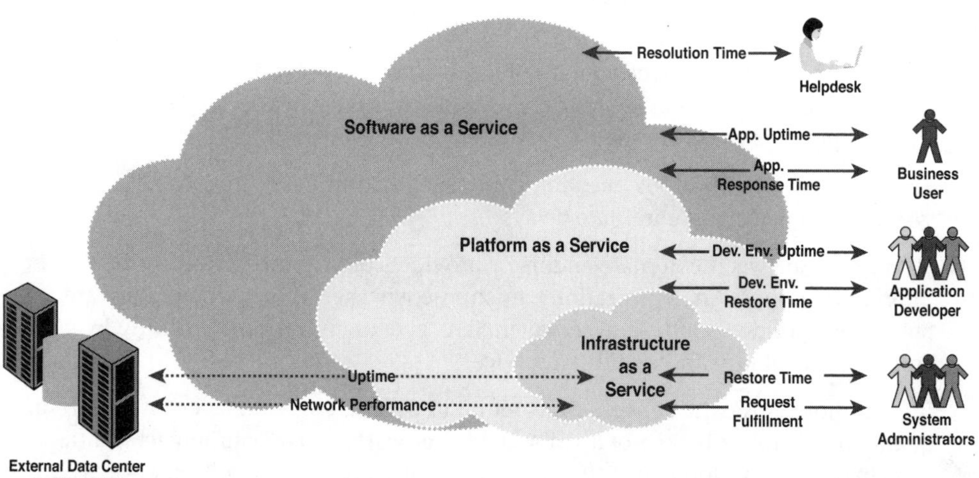

FIGURE 4.12 Example organization with public vCloud IaaS and private vCloud PaaS/SaaS layers

The SLAs shown are for illustration purposes only and are a subset of the total number of SLAs created within an organization in such a case.

The example includes the following SLAs:

- IaaS layer:
    - Uptime/availability SLA signed with the external vCloud service provider
    - Network performance SLA signed with the external service provider
    - Request fulfillment SLA—measure of response time for provisioning and access configuration requests
    - Restore time SLA
- PaaS layer:
    - Uptime/availability SLA for development environment
    - Uptime/availability SLA for critical development environment components
    - Restore time SLA for development environment
- SaaS layer:
    - Uptime/availability SLA specific to an application
    - Application response time SLA—measure of how the application is performing for the business users
    - Time to resolution SLA—time to recover an application in case of a failure

Given this example, the following are some key conclusions:

- SLAs, OLAs, and KPIs are relevant at all levels within a vCloud stack. These agreements are required to provide efficiency and accountability at every layer, for both external providers and internal IT groups.
- These SLAs, OLAs, and KPIs need to be managed within every layer to help isolate systemic problems and eliminate delays.
- SLAs can be between external vendors or providers of vCloud services, or between internal IT groups. An organization can choose whether to implement a private, public, or hybrid vCloud. At every layer, SLAs give organizations flexibility by guaranteeing availability and quality of service.
- Interrelationships exist between SLAs set up at different vCloud layers. A change in quality of service or breach of an SLA at a lower vCloud layer can impact multiple SLAs in a higher vCloud layer. In the example, if a breach of a performance SLA results in the external vCloud provider's incapability to support OS performance needs, the breach has a ripple effect at the SaaS layer, decreasing application performance and response time for business users.
- SLAs need to be continuously managed and evaluated to maintain quality of service in a vCloud. Business needs are continuously evolving, resulting in changing vCloud business requirements. SLAs must be continuously updated to reflect current business requirements.

Consider the impact of adding another 1,000 users to a particular application so that the application becomes mission critical. SLAs supporting the application might need to be updated to provide increased uptime and availability. This might lead to increased demands at the IaaS layer, so SLAs with the external IaaS provider might also have to be expanded.

4.7.1.2.4 vCloud SLA Considerations

vCloud SLA considerations include the following:

- **Uptime/availability SLA:**
  - To what timeframe does the SLA pertain? Timeframes are generally divided into tiers depending on business criticality (9 to 5, 24 by 7).
  - Are maintenance windows (for configuration changes, capacity changes, and OS and application patch management) included or excluded from availability SLAs?
  - Do multi–virtual machine vApps need to be treated as a single entity from an SLA perspective?
- **End user response time SLA:** This is generally focused on overall user experience, measuring response time from local and major remote sites to get a representative view. Measurement is implemented with remote simulators and by running automated robotic scripts.

- **Recovery (system, data) SLA:** What recovery time objectives and recovery point objectives need to be met?
    - Are backups required?
    - Is high availability required?
    - Is fault tolerance required within the management cluster?
    - Is automated disaster recovery failover required within certain time parameters?
- **Privacy SLA (data security, access and control, compliance):**
    - Do data privacy requirements (encryption, others) exist?
    - Are there regulatory requirements?
    - Are specific roles and permission groups required?
- **Provisioning SLA:** Are there provisioning time requirements?
- **SLA penalties:**
    - How are SLA penalties applied?
    - Are they applied as service credits?
    - What legal liabilities apply, and how are they covered?
    - Is there a termination for cause clause in the SLA?
    - What defines an outage, and who bears the burden of claim?
    - What is the track record for delivering on SLAs? These SLA considerations should be applied to external service providers.

4.7.1.3 Roles and Responsibilities

The following are primary roles associated with Service Governance and Lifecycle Management:

- Service Portfolio Manager
- Service Catalog Manager
- Service Owner
- Service Level Manager

4.7.1.3.1 Service Portfolio Manager

The Service Portfolio Manager role is the gatekeeper for accepting proposed services and constituent service offerings into the overall portfolio of vCloud services. Responsibilities include the following:

- Developing service/service offerings analysis and acceptance criteria
- Reviewing and accepting or rejecting service proposals
- Continuously reviewing the overall portfolio of services for applicability and demand
- Providing initial service/service offering demand information for vCloud capacity planning
- Authorizing a service owner to define and develop, or retire, a service or service offering

4.7.1.3.2 Service Catalog Manager

The Service Catalog Manager role manages the "active" service catalog component of the overall service portfolio. The active service catalog contains the definitions for those service/service offerings currently either under development or available to consumers for deployment. Responsibilities include the following:

- Maintaining information about services and service offerings contained in the active service catalog
- Verifying that service and service offering information is accurate and complete, and providing it to consumers through the consumer self-service portal

4.7.1.3.3 Service Owner

The Service Owner role has end-to-end responsibility for defining, developing, maintaining, and decommissioning a specific service or set of services and their component service offerings. Responsibilities include the following:

- Translating business requirements into a service definition
- Defining service/service offering composition details, pricing, service levels, support terms and conditions, operational considerations, and any service-specific compliance requirements
- Working with the Service Architect to translate the service definition into service design and development technical details
- Managing development, deployment, update, and retirement of the services and service offerings
- Tracking demand and service requests for service updating and retirement

4.7.1.3.4 Service Level Manager

The Service Level Manager role establishes and maintains SLAs, and reports on service level attainment. Responsibilities include the following:

- Developing service-level agreements for customers
- Tracking and reporting on service level attainment
- Developing operating-level agreements with the service provider in support of SLAs

4.7.1.3.5 Staffing Considerations

As with most vCloud operations-related roles, staffing depends on scale. Initially, a single person can fill the Service Portfolio and Service Catalog Manager roles. As the number of services and service offerings and the activities involving them increase, the Service Portfolio Manager and Service Catalog Manager roles might each require a person. The same is true for the Service Owner and Service Level Manager roles.

4.7.2 vCloud Service Design and Development Management

The purpose of vCloud Service Design and Development Management is to implement a standard methodology with governance and control across all service development groups within an organization. This area focuses on design and architecture consistency, cost transparency, and service metering based on consumption. It includes subareas for service development, service showback, and metering management.

4.7.2.1 Service Development Management

The process for Service Development Management enforces a structured approach to maintain quality and consistency during service development. The following sections describe the main process components.

4.7.2.1.1 Service Requirements

The Service Requirements process manages the interaction between the service development teams and the business user during development of new services. A clear communication channel is set up, and a standard service definition document template is created and used to capture business requirements. Continuous review takes place, and signoffs occur after every significant service development phase. This function requires analysis time for alignment with the Service Portfolio process. Business scenario and use cases are developed, and a cost-benefit analysis is completed before service development begins.

Focus areas include the following:

- Involvement of all necessary stakeholders
- Documentation of business drivers and requirements that can be translated into appropriate service definitions and SLAs
- Clear definition of operational requirements, along with alignment with appropriate service tiers
- Definition of business scenarios and use cases
- Definition of the business users and roles that interact with services development so that user-centric services are created

- Workflow representation of the service to understand the components of the service, interactions, and sequence of interrelated actions
- Cost-benefit analysis (internal versus external)

4.7.2.1.2 Service Requirements—Initiation Workflow

Figure 4.13 shows a sample service initiation workflow for creating a new service and the roles that are involved in the process.

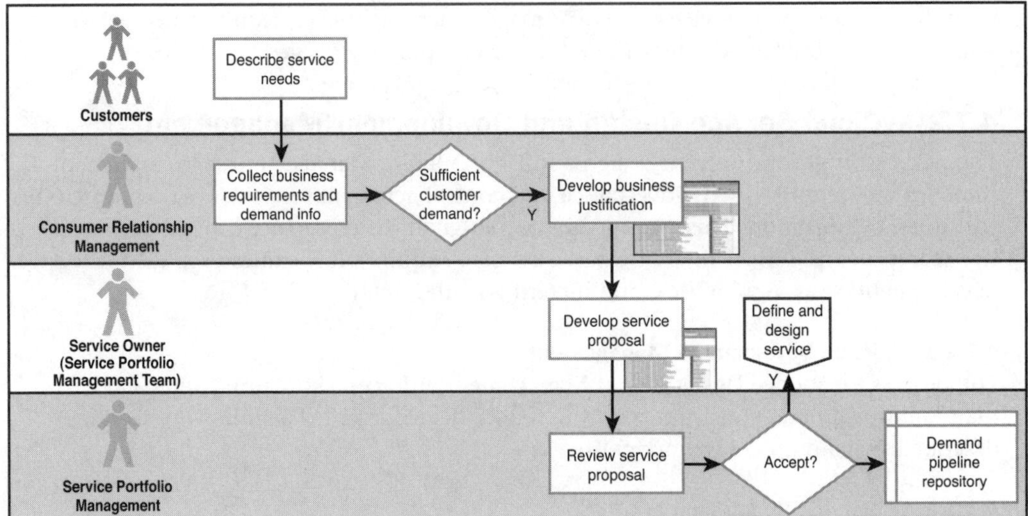

FIGURE 4.13 Service requirements workflow

See Section 4.5, "Organizing for vCloud Operations," for more information about the organization and roles.

4.7.2.1.3 Service Design

The Service Design process focuses on creating consistent architecture and design for new services. This function is responsible for creating architecture blueprints and service templates for rapid service creation.

Key focus areas:

- High-level design representation of the service, to understand its components, interactions, and sequence of interrelated actions and expected SLAs
- Integration and alignment with the service portfolio and catalog process areas
- Integration and alignment with the service showback and metering process
- Business user signoff on service design

4.7.2.1.4 Service Design—Workflow

Figure 4.14 shows a sample service design workflow and the roles that are involved in the process.

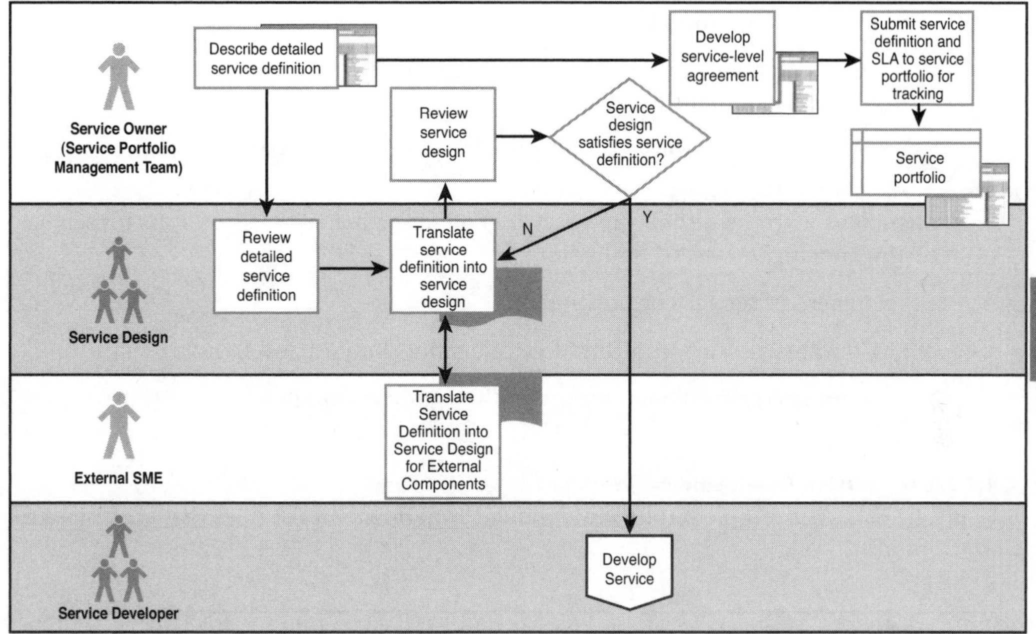

FIGURE 4.14 Service design workflow

Refer to Section 4.5, "Organizing for vCloud Operations," for more information about the organization and roles.

4.7.2.1.5 Service Development

The Service Development process focuses on developing the services and aligning service development methodologies for an organization. This function requires speed and agility to respond quickly to changing business needs. This function also manages and controls the overall service development environment, platforms, and tools used in the overall service development process.

Key focus areas:

- Agility and rapid response
- Definition of service development methodology (in general, Agile development is recommended)
- Integration and alignment with other operational process areas:
  - Performance SLAs (application response time, bandwidth including burst, time to respond, time to resolution)

- Availability SLAs (uptime, backup, restore, data retention)
- Continuity SLAs (RPO, RTO)
- Scalability
- Manageability (user account management, supportability)
- Security (application/data access, management/control access, user accounts, authentication/authorization)
- Compliance (regulatory compliance, logging, auditing, data retention, reporting)

- Alignment with the service showback and metering management process for service costing, pricing, metering, and billing
- Development of service controls:
    - Continual service reporting, service quality analysis, and trending
    - Automated remediation scripts and integration workflows

4.7.2.1.6 Service Development—Workflow

Figure 4.15 shows a sample service development workflow and the roles that are involved in the process.

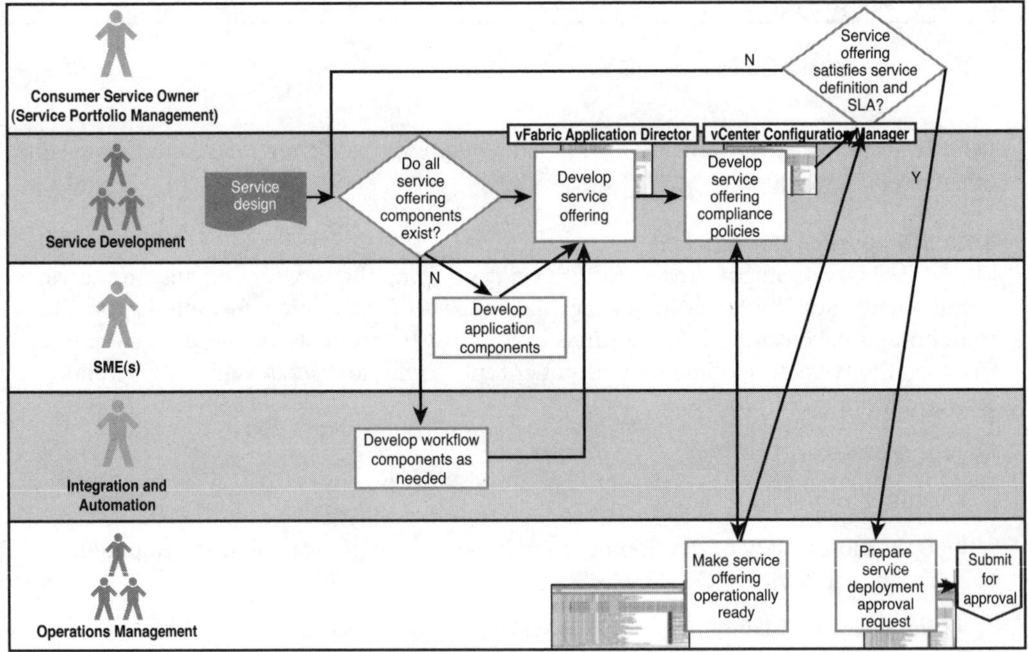

FIGURE 4.15 Service development workflow

See Section 4.5, "Organizing for vCloud Operations," for more information about the organization and roles.

4.7.2.1.7 Common Service Development Characteristics

The following are common service development characteristics of a vCloud service:

- **On-demand self-service:** A vCloud service needs to be designed and developed to allow for on-demand provisioning via a service catalog that uses automated workflows with minimal human interaction from the service's provider side.
- **Service mobility:** Services should be designed to be accessible from multiple end-user computing mobility platforms, such as tablets, phones, and other thin or thick end-user platforms.
- **Resource pooling:** Services should designed to use pooled computing resources, not bound to physical infrastructure. There should be a sense of location independence—the service consumer generally has no control or knowledge over the exact location of the provided resources.
- **Rapid elasticity:** Services should be capable of using the vCloud elastic and bursting feature to support high-utilization timeframes. Services should be designed to automatically scale and release computing resources.
- **Measured service:** Services must be designed with capability to leverage metering capability based on service consumption. This is critical to make the service a viable business investment for the service provider. This feature is at the heart of the service showback and metering process.

4.7.2.2 Service Showback and Metering

The service showback and metering process provides a mechanism for calculating service costs for end users. The short-term goal is to raise awareness of costs based on service consumption usage. For an organization in an initial maturity state, no formal accounting procedures and billing are involved, but as the maturity within the organization increases, the service showback and metering process integrates with the IT business control layer and supports automated IT chargeback.

Key focus areas:

- **Early alignment during the service design and development process:** Showback enables service subscribers to see costs associated with service usage. Showing the cost of consumption is the first step toward moving an organization to IT chargeback, in which consumers pay for services they consume.
- **Showing and calculating true service costs:** Service costing is complex in a vCloud because services are designed to run on pooled resources and have inherent elasticity features. The key to success is understanding and aligning to vCloud cost models, and being able to break down individual service component costs and understand their interrelationships.

4.8 vCloud Operations Control

vCloud Operations Control deals with provisioning and proactive operations management of IT services based on vCloud, with a focus on policy-driven automation.

4.8.1 Provisioning Management

In IT, generally, and in vCloud, *provisioning* typically refers to one of the following:

- Provisioning virtual machines or vCloud components (vApps, business applications, services) as a result of a consumer request
- Provisioning the underlying infrastructure that supports virtualization or vCloud platforms

Provisioning resulting from a consumer request is evolving in vCloud computing. A primary goal when implementing a vCloud computing environment is to lower ongoing OpEx costs. Provisioning that results from a consumer's request is an activity from which significant OpEx savings can be realized. Savings are realized by the following:

- Providing a self-service portal through which a consumer can make requests from a service catalog
- Automating the resulting provisioning process to satisfy the consumer's request

4.8.1.1 Consumer Self-Service Portal

From a consumer perspective, vCloud computing is driving the following new expectations:

- Self-service
- Flexibility and granularity of choices
- Instant gratification
- On-demand services

A private or public vCloud provider can meet these expectations by providing an online consumer self-service capability. For a private vCloud, this capability is deployed internally. When using a public vCloud, consumers might have access to the public vCloud self-service, online service catalog. By providing access, the provider expects to benefit by being able to deliver vCloud services quickly and inexpensively, while still maintaining control over the process. The consumer's expectations are met by automating the provisioning process.

Initially, the online, self-service capability must provide an easy way for the consumer to provision resource-based services in the form of vApps. Ultimately, this must be extended to offer self-service access to any and all IT services, whether as a wholly contained development environment, Software as a Service–based applications, or applications for mobile devices. Providing this addresses consumer expectations regarding flexibility and granularity of choices.

The online, self-service portal should provide the capability to do the following:

- Get secure access
- View available services, costs, and service tiers
- Request vApps and other services based on organizational maturity
- Obtain any required approvals through automated workflows
- Track request status
- View items successfully provisioned
- Perform tasks such as start, stop, and add capacity (at least this minimal set)
- Receive notifications
- Decommission items
- View basic consumption reports
- View the health of provisioned items

4.8.1.2 Provisioning Process Automation

Automating the provisioning process to satisfy consumer requests is a key element in meeting custom expectations and enables the provider to realize OpEx savings. Initially, process automation applies to vApp provisioning, but provisioning of other IT services can also be automated.

Automated vApp provisioning consists of the following:

- An automated vApp provisioning process that handles the entire lifecycle of a vApp
- Automated interaction between the vApp provisioning process and other required processes and associated systems

Figure 4.16 illustrates an example vApp provisioning process that can be fully automated.

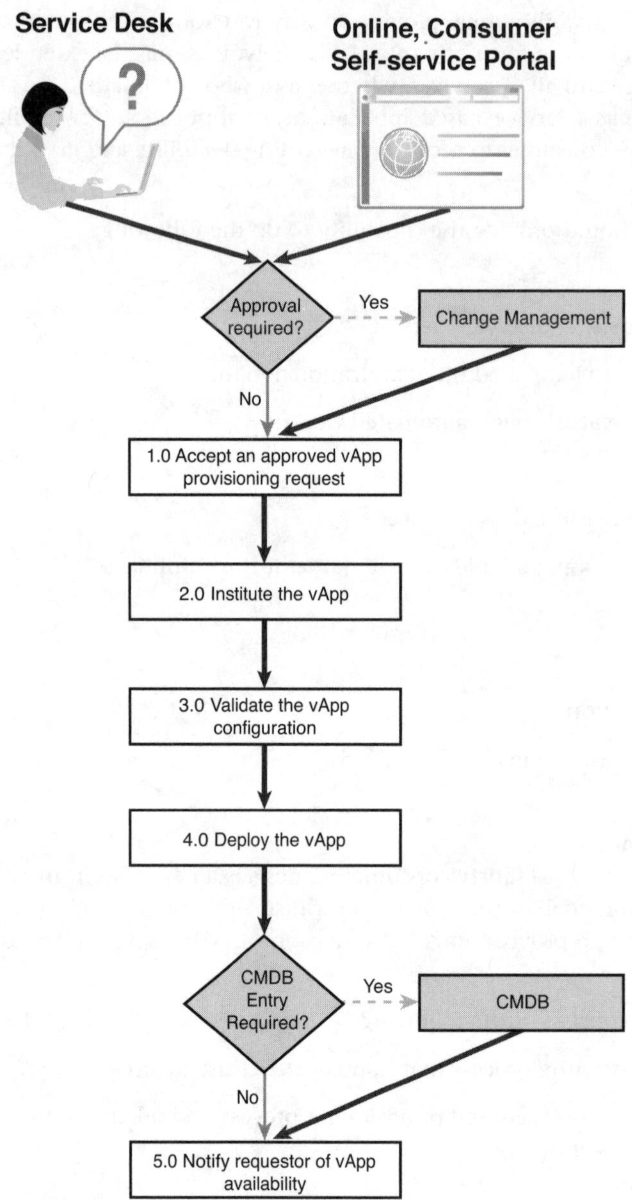

FIGURE 4.16 Provisioning workflow

This vApp provisioning process can be fully automated using VMware vCenter Orchestrator™. The vCenter Orchestrator plug-in directly supports automating the following tasks:

- Instantiating the vApp
- Validating the vApp configuration
- Deploying the vApp

Additional vCenter Orchestrator standard protocol plug-ins (email, SOAP, HTTP REST) and VMware partner application plug-ins provide the mechanisms for automating integration with Change Management and Configuration Management, and with other third-party applications and systems as needed. For information regarding Orchestrator plug-ins, see www.vmware.com/products/datacenter-virtualization/vcenter-orchestrator/plugins.html.

OpEx savings are realized by automating what were previously a set of manually executed steps typically driven by work queues. After automating, a process that previously took days or weeks might take only minutes or hours. In addition to OpEx savings, consumer satisfaction increases as their expectation of instant gratification is met.

4.8.1.3 Provisioning Process Analyst

After provisioning processes are automated, a provisioning process analyst role is needed. Provisioning process analyst responsibilities include the following:

- Working with service development to understand the provisioning implications of new services to be offered
- Providing Integration and Automation Management with requirements for workflow implementation, modification, maintenance, and integration with systems in other process areas
- Working with Service Level Management to understand operating-level requirements for vApp provisioning
- Working with monitoring to properly instrument the provisioning process, create thresholds, and implement monitoring
- Working with Release Management on coordination and validation:
    - Provisioning of workflow releases
    - Updates to existing service catalog entries that affect the provisioning process
    - New service offerings added to the service catalog

Staffing levels for the provisioning process analyst role depends on the following factors:

- Number of distinct service offerings
- Rate of service releases
- Provisioning operating agreements tied to service-level agreements

Whether a part-time or full-time provisioning process analyst or multiple analysts are needed depends on the use and stability of the automated provisioning process and any related operating-level agreements tied to service-level agreements. In most cases, a part-time or, at most, a single full-time analyst is sufficient. Additional OpEx savings can be realized through IT role consolidation. After the provisioning process is automated, the provisioning process analyst responsible for provisioning management should maintain the automation workflows and integration points with other applications. With the appropriate skills and training, this role can be shared with other roles that have integration and automation activity responsibilities.

Cloud computing drives customer expectations toward increased agility and choice and requires less time to deliver. By providing an online consumer self-service portal backed by an automated service provisioning processes, providers can realize OpEx savings and satisfy consumers' expectations.

4.8.2 Capacity Management

Capacity Management focuses on providing vCloud capacity to meet both existing and future needs in support of vCloud service offerings.

For the vCloud provider, the goal of capacity planning is to provide sufficient capacity within the vCloud infrastructure to meet the current and future needs of the services offered to customers. Sufficient reserve capacity must be maintained in the vCloud infrastructure to prevent virtual machines and vApps from contending for resources under normal circumstances, thus breaching agreed service levels.

The vCloud provider components must manage the following:

- Management cluster that contains all the components used to create and manage the vCloud
- Resource clusters that provide resources to the vCloud consumers

The sizing of the management cluster is generally predictable, but consideration needs to be given to the number of vCloud Director cells and the size of the vCloud Director, vCenter, and Chargeback databases. Additionally, if VMware vCenter Operations products are used, the storage required for vApps needs to be considered because it can be substantial in large environments. Initial sizing guidelines for the management cluster are provided in Chapter 3.

Usage can be unpredictable for vCloud consumer resources such as vApps and organization virtual datacenters. To size consumer resources, estimate the initial capacity required and use vCloud Capacity Management techniques, which predict future usage needs based upon past usage trends.

Capacity planning is required to make sure that the vCloud resources supplied to the tenant are used appropriately, are available when required, and expand or contract depending on current and future demand.

4.8.2.1 Capacity Management Process Definition and Components

Historically, capacity management is usually performed when the system is implemented and covers the capacity requirements for the entire lifetime of the system. This creates significant waste during the system's early life because the excess capacity is not required until later, if at all. Potential exists for significant waste during the system's entire lifecycle because of many other factors, including overestimation of usage or early retirement from technology evolution.

Even with virtualization, ensuring that sufficient capacity is readily available is always a concern. Virtualized environments manage capacity by reducing the contention for resources, usually by reducing the ratio of virtual machines to hosts. This approach wastes resources as low ratios are adopted.

To make a vCloud implementation successful, resource waste must be avoided. The capacity-management process must become proactive, with adjustments to capacity configuration as conditions change. It is not sufficient to "set it and forget it." Focusing on proactive capacity management makes it possible to increase the density of virtual machines on hosts. This enables the provider to realize the cost benefits of implementing a vCloud without compromising the services that run on it.

Figure 4.17 illustrates a high-level, proactive capacity-management process. This process is applicable to both vCloud providers and tenants.

Although the proactive capacity-management process appears the same as the traditional capacity-management process, the dynamic nature of the vCloud requires that the proactive process be more agile and rely less on manual intervention. Manual capacity management might be appropriate in a physical infrastructure or during early virtualization adoption stages, but only tooling and automation can provide the proactive capacity-management required for the vCloud.

Long-term capacity issues should be identified early so that the vCloud service is not impacted. With appropriate tooling, early warning is possible. Historical capacity usage behavior can be identified and combined with known future demand to provide a vCloud capacity forecast.

Short-term capacity breaches also need to be identified early so that remediation can be put in place to keep from compromising vCloud SLAs.

With this short-term and long-term knowledge, automation can help make the required resources available in the appropriate environment. For short-term breaches, automation can help identify underused resources in one environment and temporarily transfer them to an environment that is under-resourced. For long-term capacity issues, the automated provisioning process for new resources is predictable and well defined. This makes it possible to provision new resources such as hosts, clusters, or organization virtual datacenter capacity as required, without service breaches.

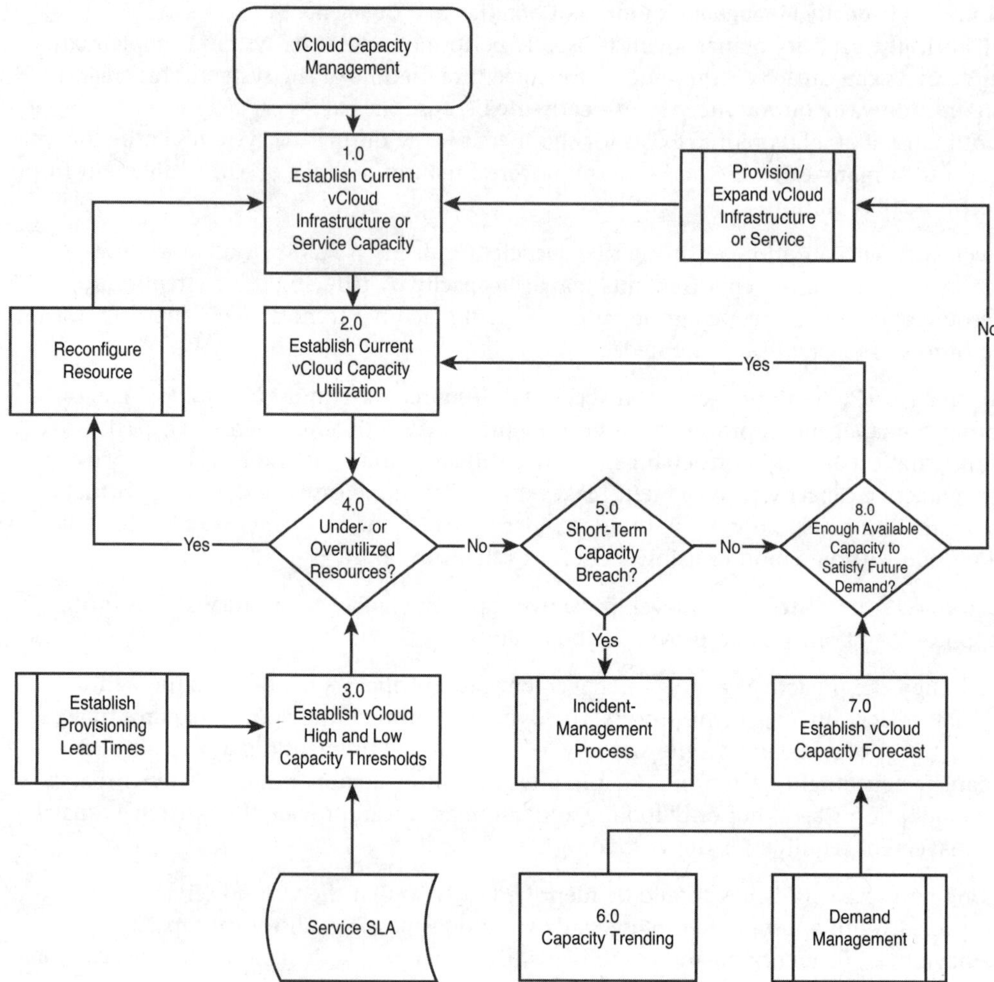

FIGURE 4.17 High-level proactive capacity management process

From a high level, capacity management involves the following:

1. Determining current capacity reserves
2. Forecasting new requirements
3. Planning for additional capacity

Continuous improvement activities are critical to extracting the most value from the vCloud infrastructure. Results can be achieved through simple, periodic planning activities supported by regular capacity augmentation and operational day-to-day activities.

4.8.2.2 Process Evolution for vCloud Capacity-Management Operations

To provide robust capacity management, automate and remove the need for manual intervention wherever possible. Capacity management takes time and effort to evolve, so work on maturing processes in stages instead of trying to do everything in a single step.

Initially, the challenge is to document and maintain capacity-management processes, policies, and methods. Any tools used to assist with vCloud capacity must be carefully selected and suitable for the purpose. All capacity-management roles and responsibilities should be clearly defined.

Over time, vCloud organizations mature and become more vCloud service focused. Tool automation is introduced so that incorrectly sized vCloud components can be easily identified and adjusted with minimal manual interaction. Evaluate automation possibilities to identify other capacity scenarios that can be made more efficient. Specific vCloud KPI metrics should be identified and reported to key stakeholders. Short- and long-term capacity plans should become ingrained within the organization.

To fully integrate capacity management into the vCloud service offering, implement automated capacity-management remediation to stabilize the environment and make sufficient capacity available for services. The COE should be responsible for end-to-end vCloud Capacity Management using highly optimized capacity-management tools and processes.

4.8.2.3 Process Automation and Tool Alignment and Integration

Capacity Management cannot depend on manual processes and activities in a vCloud. Given its ever-changing nature, effective management of vCloud capacity requires an up-to-date view of usage and available capacity of services and infrastructure. Manual processes and most capacity tools cannot provide real-time capacity data.

vCloud providers must provide the capacity for vCloud consumers required to meet the agreed-to SLAs. For the provider to realize ROI, some level of resource sharing is required. Intelligence must be built into Capacity Management tools so that the dynamic usage of the vCloud environment is better understood and any recurring usage behavior is clear. There must be a view of the vCloud customer's environment and virtual datacenters to understand the capacity provisioned, the demand for the resources, and any recurring resource usage behavior.

To provide agile capacity management, it is important that no other process impact the delivery of additional capacity. For example, the change-management process must be closely aligned with the provisioning process so that additional capacity can be rapidly put in place. Capacity provisioning can be at an infrastructure layer (hosts, storage, and vSphere) and at a service layer (new virtual datacenters, additional capacity to existing virtual datacenters). If the change-management process involves lengthy change tickets and CAB attendance, some of the benefits of the vCloud are lost. A lengthy change-management process can delay the introduction of additional capacity into the vCloud, which, in turn, could negatively impact the vCloud consumer's services and associated SLAs.

You must understand the impact of each vCloud Director allocation model on the underlying vSphere infrastructure before effective Capacity Management can be implemented.

Otherwise, it is not be possible to understand how the organization virtual datacenters and virtual machines can use the available capacity.

Each vCloud Director organization virtual datacenter has an underlying vSphere resource pool that supports it and provides the resources to all the virtual machines in the deployed vApps. The configuration of an organization virtual datacenter has a direct relationship to the configuration of the vSphere resource pool and the virtual machines in it. For example, percent guarantees in vCloud Director translate to reservations in the underlying vSphere components. The relationship between vSphere reservations and vCloud guarantees varies depending on the selected vCloud Director allocation model.

Using VMware vCenter Operations Manager™—part of the VMware vCenter Operations Management Suite—makes it possible to understand the complexity in vCloud implementations because the vSphere adapter provides specific vSphere metrics and an analysis of their impact on the environment. The *Risk badge* (see Figure 4.18) in the vCenter Operations vSphere UI provides vSphere Capacity Management functions.

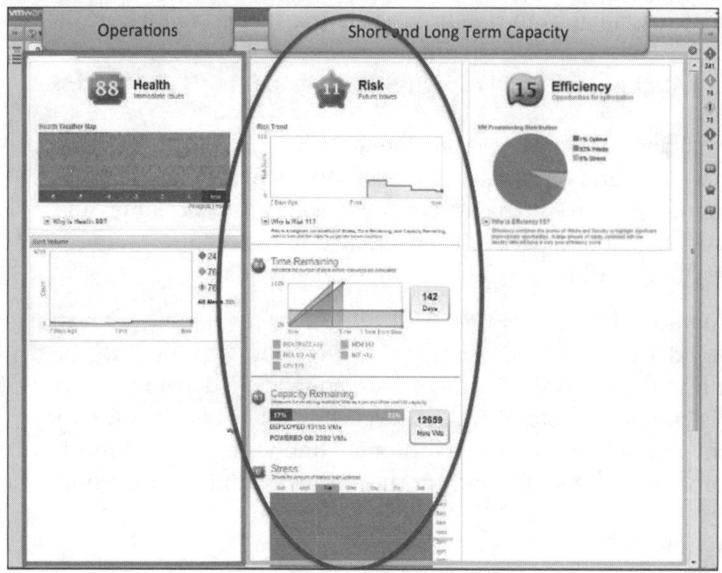

FIGURE 4.18 vCenter Operations Capacity Management in the vSphere UI

In vCenter operations, the analytics functionality analyzes the current and past usage patterns of resources in a vCloud environment, and what-if scenarios help establish future capacity requirements.

The VMware design guideline states that a provider virtual datacenter should be supported by an entire vSphere cluster. Then you can view the capacity information for the provider virtual datacenter in the vCenter Operations vSphere UI by selecting the underlying vSphere cluster.

Because vCenter operations can connect to multiple vCenter instances using the same adapter, you can manage the capacity of multiple resource provider virtual datacenters and the management cluster in a single implementation—provided that the implementation remains within the sizing guidelines for vCenter operations.

4.8.2.4 Roles and Responsibilities for Capacity Management

The vCloud Center of Excellence (COE) model supports capacity management of the vCloud services and the supporting infrastructure. Depending on the size and vCloud maturity of the vCloud organization, the primary capacity management responsibility lies with either the COE analyst or, for smaller organizations, a dedicated Capacity Management individual or team. The primary responsibility is to maintain an accurate and up-to-date capacity-management plan and forecast. Achieve this by granting access to the capacity data and metrics by using appropriate capacity health-monitoring tools such as vCenter Operations.

Automation is essential for capacity management of the vCloud, and the COE analyst, COE developer, and capacity management champion are responsible for making sure that the capacity-management tools and processes for this automation work effectively. Validate effectiveness by auditing the data used in the capacity forecasts and the tools used for the capacity plan. The ultimate goal is to automate as much as possible with minimal administrative interaction.

For more information about vCenter operations, see the latest VMware vCenter Operations Management Suite documentation (www.vmware.com/products/datacenter-virtualization/vcenter-operations-management/technical-resources.html).

4.8.3 Performance Management

This section focuses on addressing vCloud performance issues in support of vCloud service offerings. For a vCloud provider, the goal of performance management is to avoid or quickly resolve performance issues in the vCloud infrastructure and meet the performance requirements for the services offered to consumers. Monitoring is required for the VMware vCloud infrastructure to prevent agreed-upon services levels from being breeched.

Although performance management is performed in the context of normal event, incident, and problem management, it is specifically called out in a vCloud environment because of its importance in persuading potential vCloud users that concerns about additional layers of virtualization and the vCloud have been addressed and that their SLAs will continue to be met. In a traditional physical environment, servers are typically oversized to such a degree on dedicated hardware that performance issues are unlikely to occur. In a shared vCloud environment, users must feel confident that the provided services will meet their needs.

4.8.3.1 Performance Management Process Definition and Components

The high-level event, incident, and problem processes for performance management in Figure 4.19 apply for both vCloud providers and tenants. These processes look the same as any traditional Performance Management process. However, the dynamic nature of the vCloud and the drive to reduce OpEx means that the process has to be more agile and must rely less on manual intervention. Manual performance management might be appropriate for physical infrastructure world and early virtualization adoption stages, but only tooling and automation can provide the level of performance management required for the vCloud.

At a high level, the objectives of event, incident, and problem processes for performance management are to automate as much as possible and maximize the number of tasks that can be performed by Level 1 operators (instead of Level 2 administrators or Level 3 subject matter experts [SME]). The following are possible ways to handle events, incidents, or problems, listed in order of preference:

1. **Automated workflows:** These workflows are totally automatic and can be initiated by predefined events or support personnel.
2. **Interactive workflows:** These workflows require human interaction and can be initiated by predefined events or support personnel.
3. **Level 1 support:** Operators monitor systems for events. They are expected to follow runbook procedures for reacting to events, which might include executing predefined workflows.
4. **Level 2 support:** Administrators with basic technology expertise handle most routine tasks and execute predefined workflows.
5. **Level 3 support:** SMEs for the various technologies handle the most difficult issues and are also responsible for defining the workflows and runbook entries that allow Level 1 operators and Level 2 administrators to handle more events and incidents. Section 4.8.4, "Event, Incident, and Problem Management," describes this in more detail.

4.8.3.1.1 Event Management Process for Performance Management

As Figure 4.19 shows, performance events are generated in multiple ways:

- **vCenter Operations Manger Early Warning Smart Alerts:** These alerts arise when multiple metrics show a change in behavior. Level 2 administrators typically review them to determine whether an incident has occurred.
- **vCenter Operations Manager Key Performance Indicator (KPI) Smart Alerts:** These alerts result from anomalous behavior from predefined KPIs or Super Metrics. Because these alerts are more specific, they are more readily automated with workflows.
- The Service Desk receives a call from a user to report a performance issue.
- The Level 1 operator receives an alert from the monitoring system regarding a performance issue.

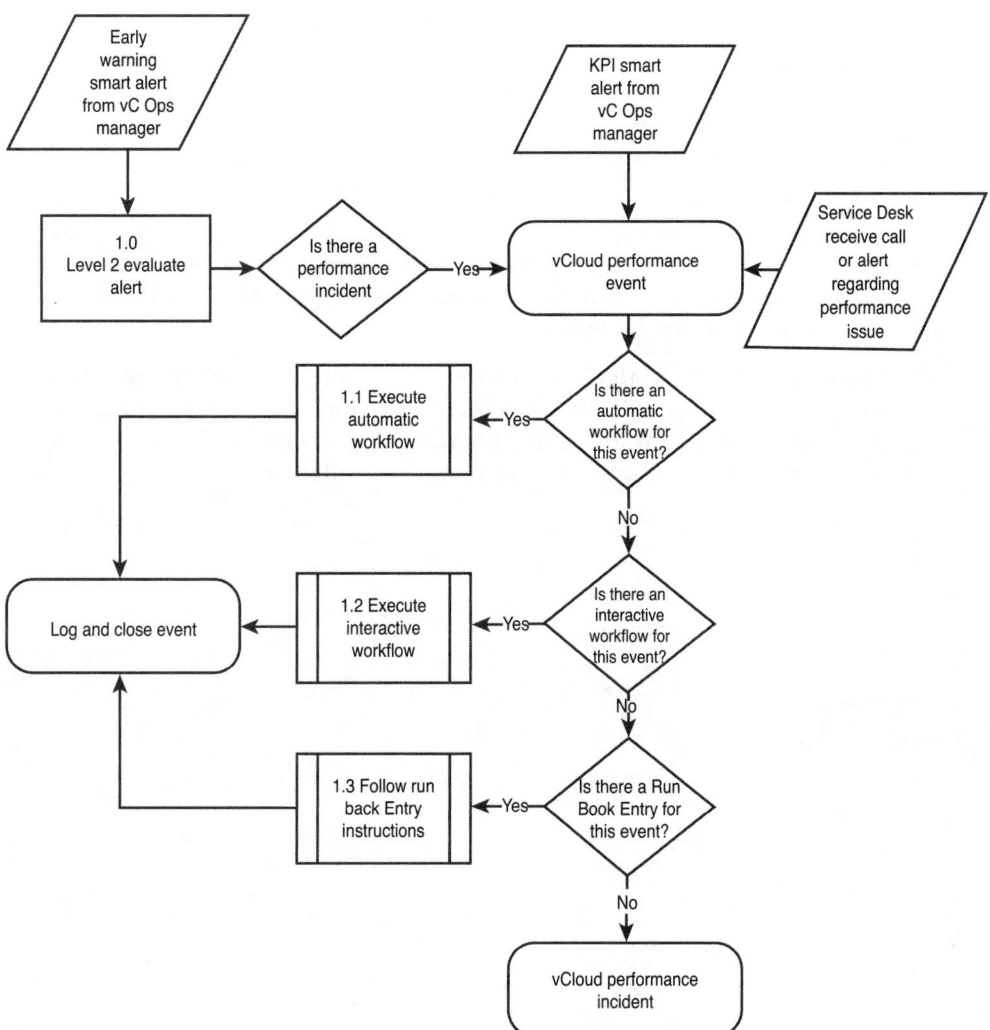

FIGURE 4.19 High-level event-management process for performance

If a performance event is identified as a known issue, it might trigger a predefined action such as an automated workflow, interactive workflow, or runbook procedure. If the event does not have a definition, it becomes an incident that a Level 2 administrator or Level 3 SME must resolve.

4.8.3.1.2 Incident Management Process for Performance Management

As Figure 4.20 shows, performance incidents are resolved in different ways, depending on how they are generated.

- **Lack of tenant capacity:** When a tenant's capacity is fully used, events can be triggered depending on how the tenant's lease is defined. If the tenant purchased a *bursting* capability, additional resources can be added at a premium cost if they are in excess of their base usage. If bursting has not been purchased or is not available, the tenant should be notified that their capacity is fully used.
- **Lack of provider capacity:** This should never happen if the design guidance for proactive capacity management is established and effective. If capacity is fully used, the service provider must either add more capacity or move capacity around to address the issue. This condition should be reported to Capacity Management and can result in SLA breaches for tenants.
- **Hardware or software failure:** Performance issues can be the result of software or hardware error such as host failures, configuration errors, bad software updates, or other repairable issues. If insufficient redundancy is built into the overall vCloud, these types of errors can also result in SLA breaches for tenants.

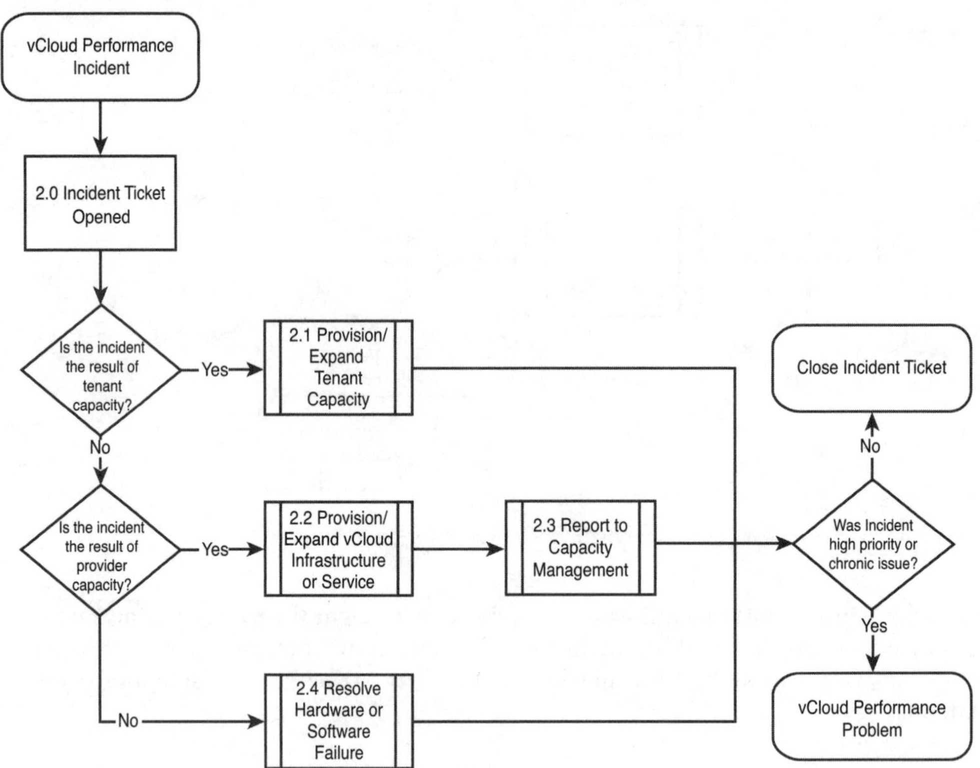

FIGURE 4.20 High-level incident management process for performance

If the incident is high priority or a chronic issue, turn it over to Problem Management for further analysis.

4.8.3.1.3 Problem Management Process for Performance Management

As Figure 4.21 shows, the primary goal of Problem Management is to identify the root cause of a problem. After the root cause is identified, develop and implement an action plan to avoid the problem in the future.

- The preferred method is to fix the root cause so that the problem never occurs again.
- If the problem cannot be eliminated, workflows and runbook entries must be defined so that the problem can be quickly resolved if it occurs again. KPIs and Super Metrics can be defined to help identify an issue before it becomes a problem.

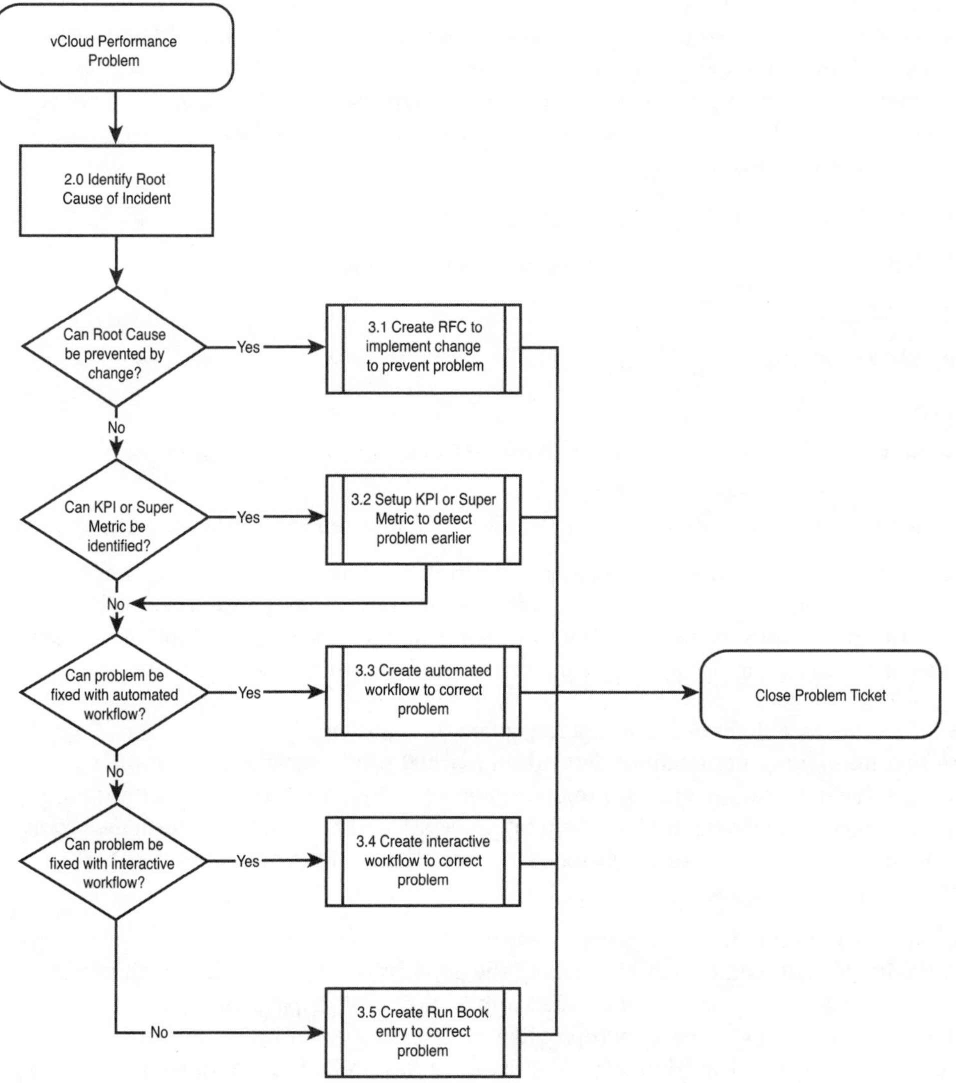

FIGURE 4.21 High-level problem-management process for performance

Process Evolution for Cloud Operations

To provide a robust performance-management process, automate and remove the need for manual intervention wherever possible. Evolving the performance-management process takes time and effort. Work on maturing processes in stages instead of trying to do everything in a single step.

Initially, the challenge is to document and maintain the performance-management processes, policies, and methods. Any tools used to assist with vCloud Performance Management must be carefully selected and suitable for the purpose. All performance-management roles and responsibilities should be clearly defined.

Over time, vCloud organizations mature and become more vCloud service focused. Tool automation is introduced so that performance issues can be easily identified and rectified with minimal manual interaction. Evaluate automation possibilities to identify other performance scenarios that can be made more efficient. Better metrics and event coverage are necessary for all aspects of an application, including the capability to collect performance metrics for the following:

- Components (appliances, operating systems, devices)
- Middleware (databases, web servers, Java, messaging)
- Applications
- Virtualization
- vCloud
- Services, including active and/or passive end-user experience monitoring

Specific vCloud KPI metrics should also be identified and reported to key stakeholders.

To fully integrate performance management into the vCloud service offering, implement automated performance remediation to stabilize the environment and provide satisfactory performance for services. The COE is responsible for end-to-end vCloud Performance Management using highly optimized performance-management tools and processes.

4.8.3.2 Process Automation and Tool Alignment/Integration

Performance management cannot depend on manual processes and activities in a vCloud. Given its dynamic nature, effective management of vCloud performance requires tooling and instrumentation to be in place. Manual processes and traditional performance tools that focus primarily on up or down status cannot provide the required level of performance data.

For effective performance management, you must understand the impact of *metric coverage*. Having instrumentation at all levels of the application stack enables much better insight into the overall performance of an application. This is particularly true with *end-user experience monitoring*, which provides information to administrators about the consumer experience. Traditionally, administrators have relied on component-level monitoring to approximate a service's availability or performance. This approach provides only partial results and rarely identifies actual performance problems.

To solve this problem, an analytics tool is needed to analyze more than just the up or down status of traditional monitoring tools. An analytics tool enables an administrator to see the relative performance of a system based on dynamically generated baselines. By using VMware vCenter Operations Manager (part of the VMware vCenter Operation Management Suite), this level of detail in vCloud implementations is understood and can be instrumental in revealing more complex performance-management issues.

4.8.3.3.1 Event Management

A key feature of vCenter Operations Manager is the capability to establish dynamic baselines on millions of metrics within an organization's environment. These baselines also take into account time of day, day of week, and other cyclical patterns to understand normal behavior. The baselines are then used to determine early warning smart alerts if too many metrics start behaving abnormally at the same time. If KPIs or Super Metrics have been defined to capture known problem areas, KPI smart alerts that have associated automated or interactive workflows can be triggered. Figure 4.22 shows the custom user interface used for vCenter Operations Manager event management.

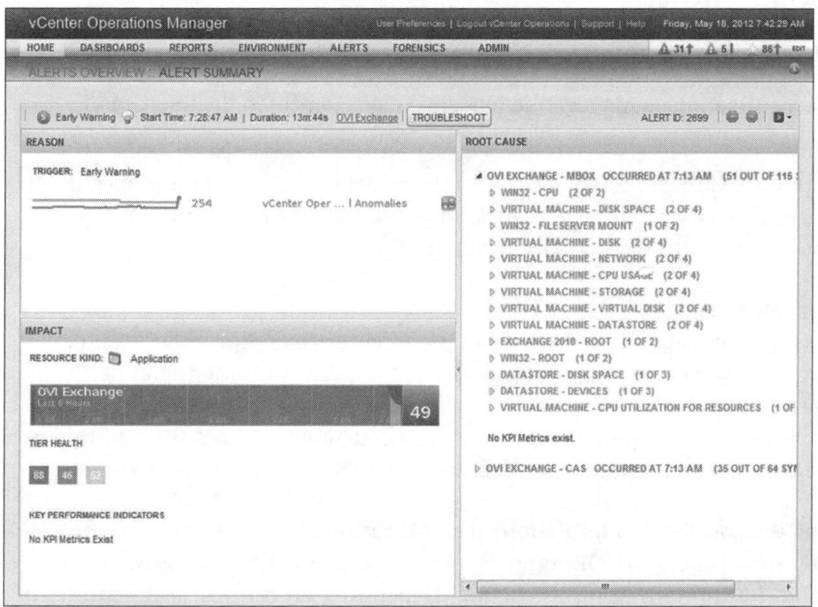

FIGURE 4.22 vCenter Operations Manager event management within the custom UI

4.8.3.3.2 Incident Management

When a performance incident is identified, an administrator can use vCenter Operations Manager to locate the responsible underlying system. The Health badge can provide insight into performance-management incidents (see Figure 4.23).

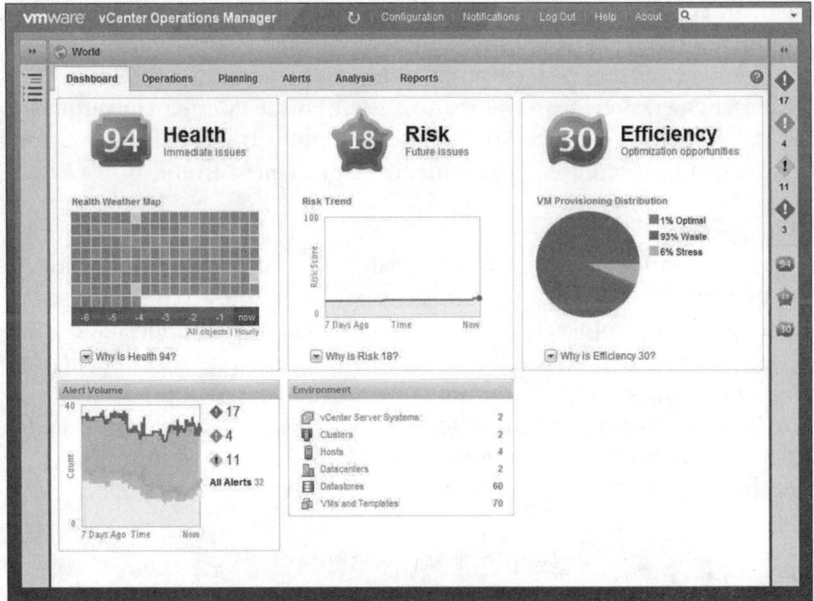

FIGURE 4.23 vCenter Operations Manager performance management in the vSphere UI

The vCenter Operations Manager analytics capability analyzes the current and past usage patterns of resources in a vCloud environment and provides users with both a high-level and detailed view of the health of their environment.

4.8.3.3.3 Problem Management

After an incident is resolved, an administrator can use vCenter Operations Manager to identify the responsible system and the root cause of the issue. Examining the underlying system that was responsible for a performance issue can expose the relationship to other tiers within an application, any smart alerts that are associated with it, and the performance history of affected components. This process can help identify the root cause of the issue.

4.8.3.4 Roles and Responsibilities for Performance Management

The vCloud Center of Excellence (COE) model supports performance management for vCloud services and the supporting infrastructure. Depending on the size and maturity of the vCloud organization, the primary performance management responsibility lies with either COE analyst or administrator for smaller organizations, or with a dedicated performance management individual or team within the COE. The primary responsibility is to address performance issues and quickly mitigate them when they arise. This is achieved by granting access to the performance data and metrics by means of appropriate performance health–monitoring tools such as vCenter Operations Manager.

Automation and instrumentation are essential for vCloud Performance Management, and the COE analyst, COE developer, and performance management champion must be responsible for making sure that the performance-management tools and processes for this automation are working effectively. Validation should be conducted by auditing the data used in the performance forecasts and the tools used for the performance plan. The goal is to automate this process as much as possible, with minimal administrative interaction.

For information on vCenter Operations, see the latest VMware vCenter Operations Management Suite documentation (www.vmware.com/products/datacenter-virtualization/vcenter-operations-management/technical-resources.html).

4.8.4 Event, Incident, and Problem Management

Traditionally, *Event, Incident, and Problem Management* focused on monitoring the services offered from the vCloud and on minimizing impact from unplanned events. Restoring service as rapidly as possible and preventing repeat events from affecting services were also core functions. Today there is an increased emphasis on reducing vCloud OpEx cost and increasing reliability. This can be achieved by increasing automation, allowing operators to handle more routine tasks, and proactively detecting and eliminating incidents before they impact end users.

Event Management focuses on how to categorize and handle outputs from monitoring and analytics tools. Based on predefined rules, inputs to event management are called *events*. They can be associated with a variety of possible actions, ranging from suppression, to triggering an automatic workflow, to triggering an incident to be created in the case of a performance incident or an actual outage.

Incident Management focuses on how to handle performance incidents or outages. Such occurrences are referred to as *incidents*. The primary focus of incident management is to manage the incident until it is resolved. Recurring incidents or incidents that are high priority can be referred to Problem Management for further investigation.

Problem Management focuses on identifying root causes for recurring and high-priority incidents. After a root cause has been identified, a plan of action is generated that, ideally, repairs the underlying problem. If the problem cannot be fixed, additional monitoring and event management handling might be implemented to minimize or eliminate future occurrences of the problem.

One of the main benefits of implementing a vCloud environment is to lower ongoing OpEx costs. A key to realizing this goal is vCloud Event, Incident, and Problem Management process automation that consists of the following:

- Automating responses to events when possible
- Creating highly automated workflows to other events where some operator input is required as part of decision support
- Creating runbook entries, workflows, and automations so that operators (instead of administrators or subject matter experts) can handle many more events
- Automating interaction between the vCloud Event, Incident, and Problem Management process and other required processes and associated systems
- Identifying, instrumenting, and developing key performance indicators (KPIs) that can develop workflows and automations

4.8.4.1 Event, Incident, and Problem Management Process Definition and Component

The following must be in place for successful vCloud event, incident, and problem management:

- Monitoring of the vCloud environment
- An event-management system, such as a Manager of Manager (MoM), for applying rules to events that can launch workflows or route events to the appropriate support teams
- A ticketing system and methodology so that various support teams are allocated tickets in an efficient manner
- Defined incident priorities and severities
- Well-understood roles and responsibilities
- The capability to view KPI status

Figure 4.24 shows the overall Event, Incident, and Problem Management process and the interrelationship among the components. All three subject areas are shown together because they are intrinsically linked. Event Management feeds into Incident Management, which feeds into Problem Management. Problem Management then feeds back into Event Management to complete the cycle. Because IT is ever evolving and changing, Event, Incident, and Problem Management must be continually updated to keep pace.

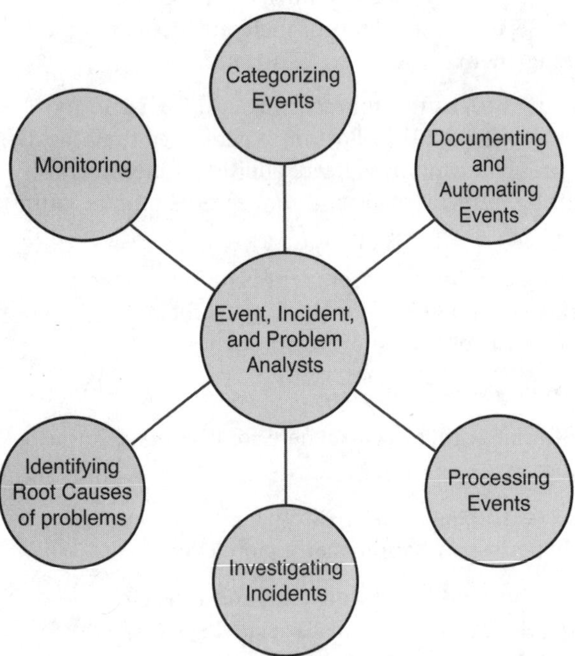

FIGURE 4.24 High-level Event, Incident, and Problem Management processes

One of the first steps in Event Management is to monitor components and services. Events can then be fed into an Event Management system, such as a MoM, and metrics can be fed into an analytics engine, such as vCenter Operations Manager, for processing.

A key component of Event Management is event categorization. After an event is categorized, rules and documentation such as runbooks and workflows can be developed to handle the event the next time it occurs. This proactive approach leads to fewer new incidents and reduces the duration and severity of the outages and performance incidents that do occur.

Core process areas of Incident Management include managing support tickets by determining priority and impact, handling customer communications, facilitating technical and management communication (including phone bridges), and closing out tickets.

When an incident is recurring or high priority, it is sent to Problem Management to identify the root cause. After a root cause is identified, a solution is developed either to fix the problem or to establish monitoring or event handling to eliminate the problem or reduce the severity the next time the problem occurs.

4.8.4.2 Process Evolution for vCloud Operations

To provide a robust event, incident, and problem management process, automate and remove the need for manual intervention wherever possible. Evolving the process takes time and effort—work on maturing processes in stages instead of trying to do everything in a single step.

Initially, the challenge is to document and maintain the performance-management processes, policies, and methods. Any tools used to assist with vCloud Event, Incident, and Problem Management must be carefully selected and suitable for the purpose. All Event, Incident, and Problem Management roles and responsibilities should be clearly defined.

Over time, vCloud organizations mature and become more vCloud service focused. As a result, automated responses and analytics are necessary to help vCloud providers provide the required levels of service. As the analytics engine better understands the vCloud environment, rapid identification of events that could become incidents enables fixes to be put in place before services are affected. Initially, the fixes are manual, but with maturing processes in place, tool automation can be introduced so that future incidents can be easily identified and rectified with minimal manual interaction. Automation possibilities must be evaluated to identify other event, incident, and problem scenarios that can be made more efficient. Specific cloud KPI metrics should be identified and reported to key stakeholders.

4.8.4.3 Process Automation and Tool Alignment/Integration

The vCloud Event, Incident, and Problem Management processes depend on tooling. If the appropriate tools are not in place, it is difficult to manage and operate the environment while sustaining the required service levels. Traditionally, event, incident, and problem management has relied heavily on tooling; in a vCloud, the scope of the required tools increases. This is the result of additional vCloud requirements, such as a greater need for early warning for impending incidents and a higher level of automation. For early warnings, increased functionality of the tools (for example, smart alerts, dynamic thresholds, and intelligent analytics) helps fulfill this requirement. For a higher level of automation, additional tools, such as vCenter Orchestrator, are required.

To realize the vCloud benefits of reliability and lower OpEx costs, it is not sufficient to merely interpret events to highlight incidents and problems. It is also necessary to establish how incidents can be more efficiently identified, how remediation can be put in place quickly, and how to identify the root cause to prevent the problem from happening again.

Because the vCloud resources and services supplied to vCloud customers are based on underlying vSphere resources, it is possible to use tools that manage and monitor at the vSphere level.

As Figure 4.25 shows, vCenter Operations Manager can provide an up-to-date understanding of the health of the vSphere environment as it relates to the vCloud provider virtual datacenters.

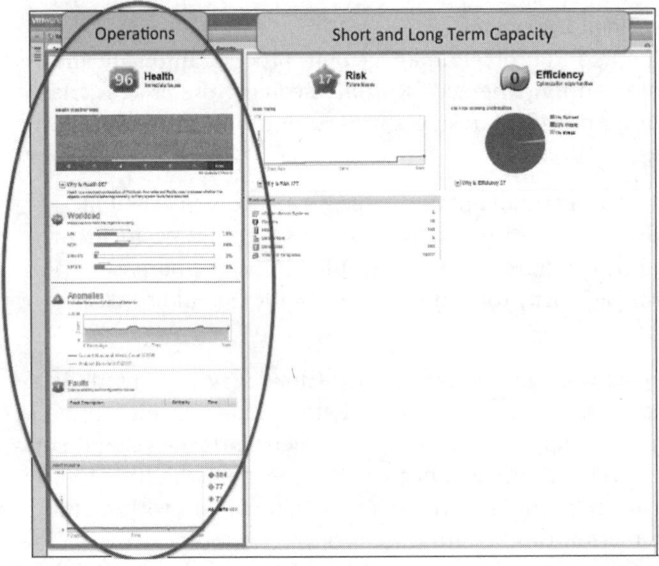

FIGURE 4.25 vCenter Operations Manager Event and Incident Management

The Health badge shows a score that indicates the overall health of the selected object. The object can be a vCenter instance, vSphere datacenter, cluster, host, or datastore. The monitoring mechanism provides proactive analysis of the performance of the environment and determines when the health of the object reaches a level that indicates an incident might be about to occur. To enforce effective management, the vCloud NOC can be provided with a dashboard that shows key metrics that indicate the health of the environment.

The score shown for the Health badge is calculated from the following sub-badges:

- **Workload:** Provides a view of how hard the selected object is working
- **Anomalies:** Provides an understanding of metrics that are outside their expected range
- **Faults:** Provides detail on any infrastructure events that might impact the selected objects availability

For faults, active vCenter events or alerts are used. These can include host hardware events, virtual machine FT and HA issues, vCenter health issues, cluster HA issues, and so on. The vCenter alerts are supplied through the vSphere adapter into vCenter Operations Manager and can identify root cause. Additionally, vCenter Operations Manager generates alerts if a sub-badge score hits a predefined value.

The events or alerts appear as faults, as Figure 4.26 shows.

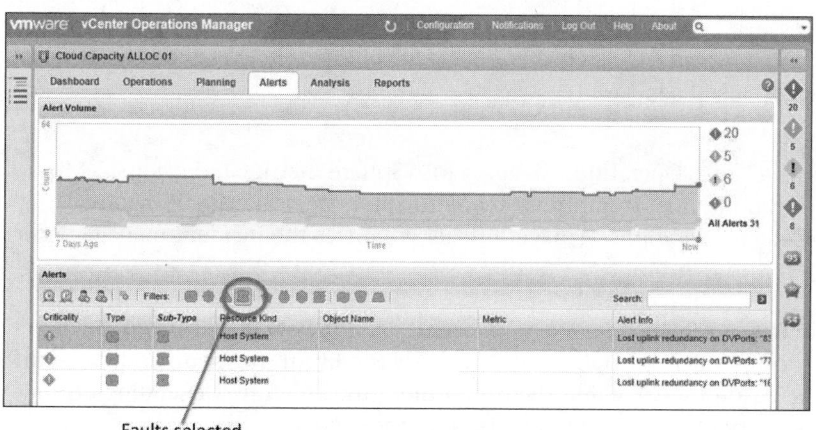

FIGURE 4.26 vCenter Operations Manager faults

Any fault can be selected to gain further information. In Figure 4.27, the event is associated with a host and indicates that an uplink has been lost.

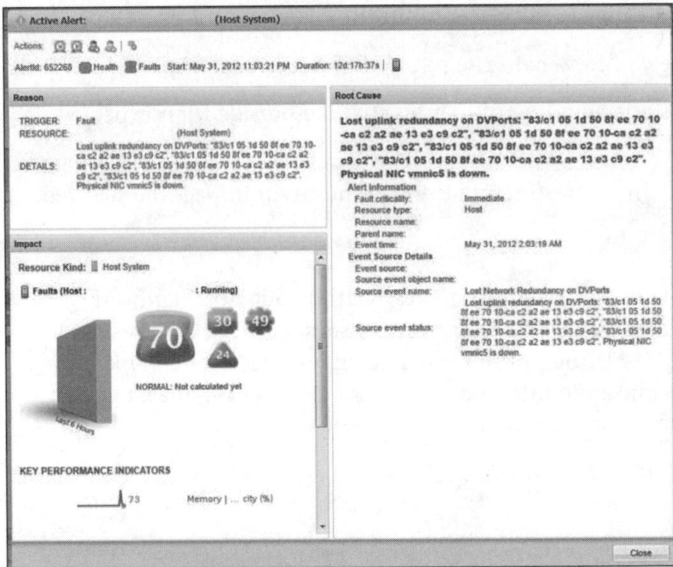

FIGURE 4.27 vCenter Operations alert

In addition to using vCenter Operations Manager for vSphere metrics and events, VMware vFabric™ Hyperic® can provide operating system and application metrics. Providing these metrics to vCenter Operations Manager further enhances the incident management toolset.

4.8.4.4 Roles and Responsibilities for Event, Incident, and Problem Management

The vCloud Center of Excellence (COE) model supports the Event, Incident, and Problem Management of the vCloud services and the supporting infrastructure. Depending on the size and vCloud maturity of the vCloud organization, the model for managing events, incidents, and problems is based on several levels for larger organizations. Each of these levels has an escalation path to the next level, until SMEs are required to help resolve incidents or problems.

1. Initial responsibility for any incident lies with the Level 1 Service Desk or operations center, such as a NOC. There, the intention is to resolve as many incidents as possible. KPIs are used for measurement.

2. Typically, a NOC with a general level of vCloud knowledge and skill provides Level 2 support.

3. Level 3 support comes from the vCloud COE subject matter experts (SMEs), as well as other technology specialists that provide resources and knowledge of the vCloud environment, such as network, storage, and security. Refer to Section 4.5.2.1, "vCloud Infrastructure Operations Center of Excellence," for more information about the COE.

The COE analyst works with the Event Management analyst so that event routing rules, runbook entries, and workflows that define event handling are well defined and accurate. They implement additional monitoring for events that indicate an incident has occurred and define event routing rules, runbook entries, and/or workflows to handle known events. They need to understand the monitoring implications of new Event Management rules, automations, and workflows. They also need to provide requirements for automation and workflow implementation, modification, maintenance, and integration with other systems. In addition, they work to categorize events for promotion to a workflow or support queue.

Specific to Incident Management, the COE analyst and administrator work with the Incident Management analyst so that event routing rules, runbook entries, and workflows defining event handling are well defined and accurate. They identify recurring or high-priority incidents that Problem Management needs to examine for root cause analysis. They also work with the infrastructure and application teams to categorize, manage, and resolve incidents, and they work with the service desk to communicate status of incidents.

The COE analyst works with the Problem Management analyst to identify recurring or high-priority problems that need root cause analysis and assist in identifying the root cause. They implement monitoring, event routing rules, runbook entries, and/or workflows to handle problem events. They also develop a plan to address the root cause of a problem, which might include a permanent solution or might require a workaround that is coordinated with Event Management.

For information about vCenter Operations Manager, refer to the latest VMware vCenter™ Operations Management Suite documentation (www.vmware.com/products/datacenter-virtualization/vcenter-operations-management/technical-resources.html).

For information about VMware vFabric Hyperic, see the latest product documentation (http://support.hyperic.com/display/DOC/HQ+Documentation).

4.8.5 Configuration and Compliance Management

vCloud differs from traditional virtualization in its increasing reliance on automation, increased scale, and dynamic workload management. It is the equivalent of moving from a handcrafted workshop to a fully automated assembly line with the benefits of speed, reliability, and volume. To realize this goal, all the components that constitute the vCloud must be interchangeable and secure. This can be achieved through *Configuration and Compliance Management.*

Configuration Management focuses on defining and maintaining information and relationships about a vCloud and its components and services. This might involve a Configuration Management Database (CMDB) to store data centrally or a Configuration Management System (CMS) to federate data across multiple repositories. Another aspect of configuration is to maintain a record of the single source of truth for each piece of data and coordinate the exchange of data with external systems.

In contrast with Configuration Management, *Compliance Management* focuses more on maintaining corporate vCloud provider or tenant standards for systems that might include compliance standards such as PCI, SOX, or HIPPA. In addition to security settings and firmware, software, and patch levels, Compliance Management is concerned with change management, user access, and network security.

Together, Configuration and Compliance Management validate that configuration settings, firmware, software, and patch versions all follow predetermined standards and policies set by the controlling organization, which can be the vCloud provider, the tenant, or the subtenants.

A major goal of implementing a vCloud is to lower ongoing OpEx costs. To realize this goal, promote and maintain standardization of as many components as possible while maintaining a high level of security and compliance. The following practices are necessary to realize maximum OpEx savings:

- Automated provisioning of interchangeable components that meet vCloud provider or tenant standards and compliance policies
- Ongoing validation that standards and compliance policies are maintained over time
- Ongoing validation that the underlying vCloud infrastructure meets standards and compliance policies (*trusted cloud*)
- Ongoing reporting of noncompliant systems
- Ongoing remediation of noncompliant systems
- Tracking and propagating relationships between components to enhance impact analysis and troubleshooting of the vCloud
- Work with existing CMDB, CMS, or other vCloud provider or tenant data sources to understand where the sources of truth are for exchanging data with the rest of the organization

4.8.5.1 Configuration and Compliance Management Process Definition and Components

For effective configuration and compliance management, the following must be in place:

- Configuration and compliance tools to capture the current state of the vCloud environment
- Automation and workflow tools to detect, report, and remediate noncompliant systems
- A CMDB, CMS, or other corporate data schemas to identify where the single sources of truth exist within a vCloud provider or tenant organization
- Defined vCloud provider or tenant standards and compliance policies
- Defined vCloud provider or tenant Change Management policies for compliance remediation
- Defined vCloud provider or tenant access policies for user access and level of rights
- Defined vCloud provider or tenant network security policies

- Well-understood roles and responsibilities
- Capability to capture, record, and view KPI statistics

Figure 4.28 shows a high-level view of the Configuration and Compliance Management process.

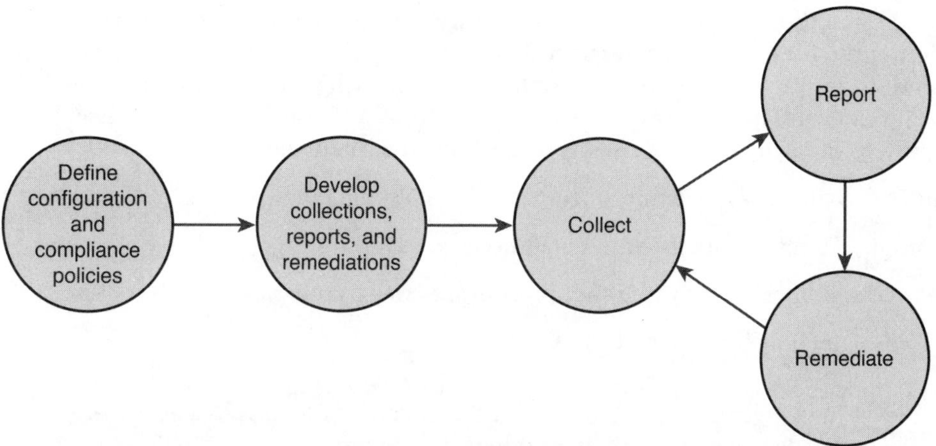

FIGURE 4.28 High-level Configuration and Compliance Management process

The process involves the following steps:

1. Define the standards and compliance policies. This is an ongoing process that must be updated as new components are developed and compliance policies evolve. Goals must be established for level of compliance and time to remediate.
2. Develop content for the following areas:
    - Collections to validate compliance
    - Reports to show levels of compliance
    - Automations and runbook entries to remediate noncompliance
3. As part of a regular cycle, gather information about the following:
    - Configuration settings for standardization and hardening
    - Firmware, software, and patch levels
    - Status and completeness of change records, especially for systems subject to compliance regulations
    - User access records such as rights allowed, logins, failed logins, commands used, and others
    - Network access records such as firewall rules, denied access, and so on

4. Evaluate the results and generate reports that show the level of compliance for each area.

5. Remediate if noncompliance is detected. Depending on the type of noncompliance and any impacted service levels, different levels of urgency might apply.

4.8.5.2 Process Evolution for vCloud Operations

To provide a robust Configuration and Compliance Management process, automate and remove the need for manual intervention wherever possible. People, process, and tools must be in place to support the overall process. Evolving the Configuration and Compliance Management process takes time and effort—work on maturing processes in stages instead of taking on the challenge as a whole in a single step.

Initially, the challenge is to define, document, maintain the following.

- **People:** All roles, responsibilities, and necessary skill sets
- **Processes:** Interactions with other processes, as well as other personnel
- **Tools:** Functionality required

Over time, vCloud organizations mature and become more vCloud service focused. As a result, automated collections, reports, and remediation are necessary to help vCloud providers meet the required levels of standardization and compliance. These efforts are initially manual, but as processes mature, tool automation can be introduced and expanded so that future standards and compliance policies can be implemented with minimal manual interaction. Automation possibilities must be evaluated to identify other configuration and compliance scenarios that can be made more efficient.

Configuration and Compliance Management processes should also include collection and reporting of specific vCloud KPIs to key stakeholders showing the overall state of the environment. Examples might include percent of noncompliant configuration items or services, time to remediate noncompliant systems, or percent of services made compliant through automated remediation.

4.8.5.3 Process Automation and Tool Alignment/Integration

The configuration and compliance processes for vCloud depend on tooling. The appropriate tools must be in place to effectively manage and operate the environment while sustaining the required service levels. Traditionally, Configuration and Compliance Management has been mostly manual, with few tools used. In a vCloud, additional tools are required due to additional requirements, such as a greater need for standardization and compliance, and a higher level of automation.

The following products are available to assist with process automation:

- **vCloud Director:** As the core of the vCloud, this is the single source of truth for all the vCloud components. vCloud Director manages all the vCloud relationships, including provider virtual datacenters, organization virtual datacenters, and vCloud networks and storage.

- **vSphere:** While vCloud Director provides a level of abstraction from the vSphere virtualization layer, vSphere provides the single source of truth for configuration and relationship information about the virtualization components that support the vCloud, such as hosts, virtual switches, and datastores. vSphere configuration information is usually not referred to directly for configuration and compliance management, but is used in other tools.
- **VMware vCenter Configuration Manager™:** Collects and validates configuration, software, and patch information for the vCloud infrastructure and the vCloud service components. It also remediates configuration settings and software and patch levels.
- **VMware vCenter Infrastructure Navigator™:** Collects and stores relationships between the virtual machines that make up and interact with an application or service.
- **VMware vCloud Networking and Security Manager™, VMware vCloud Networking and Security App™, and VMware vCloud Networking and Security Edge™:** Manages vCloud network policies, configurations, and settings.
- **vCenter Orchestrator:** Collects information, generates reports, and remediates issues through automated workflows. vCenter Orchestrator is the preferred method for interfacing with systems outside the VMware ecosystem.

For more information about these tools, see the latest documentation at www.vmware.com/products.

This suite of products is required to varying degrees, depending on whether configuration and compliance is from a provider or tenant perspective.

Tenants have visibility of all components in their domain but might not have visibility into components that make up a service that has been provided to them. For example, a public vCloud tenant will probably not have a view into the vSphere virtual infrastructure within the provider's environment. For this example, the scope of configuration and compliance management is limited to the virtual datacenter instance.

A vCloud provider will probably not have any view inside the components that it has provided to a tenant. This also applies to tenants who provide services to subtenants. For example, a Value Added Reseller (VAR) who buys an organizational virtual datacenter from a vCloud provider would not have visibility into the virtual machines that it resells to its customers.

A provider offers a vCloud service with infrastructure that might meet a certain level of compliance (for example, PCI or SOX), which would be reflected in the service level offered to its tenants. It is the provider's responsibility to make sure that this service level is adhered to and that all the components remain compliant (possibly including services consumed from other providers). It is each tenant's responsibility to make sure that the infrastructure and services built on top also adhere to the same compliance level.

4.8.5.4 Roles and Responsibilities for Configuration and Compliance Management

The COE model supports Configuration and Compliance Management for vCloud services and the supporting infrastructure. Refer to Section 4.5.2.1, "vCloud Infrastructure Operations Center of Excellence," for more information about the COE.

Depending on the size and maturity of a vCloud provider or tenant organization, the staffing levels for the roles described in this section can range from a single individual in a smaller organization who performs multiple roles, up to a team that performs a single role in a large organization.

In the vCloud environment, the COE analyst role (for vCloud providers) and the vCloud Service Analyst role (for vCloud tenants) are responsible for overseeing the running of the following core Configuration and Compliance Management processes: Responsibilities include the following:

- Defining vCloud configuration and compliance standards
- Developing collections to validate compliance
- Developing reports showing compliance levels
- Developing remediation
- Collecting and reporting Configuration and Compliance Management KPIs
- Coordinating integration with CMDB, CMS, or other data sources
- Overseeing collections
- Producing reports of compliance
- Coordinating remediation efforts
- Assisting in developing automated compliance policies

When required, the enterprise Configuration and Compliance Management analyst role works with the COE analyst or service analyst on the following tasks:

- Reviewing configuration and compliance standards and policies
- Assisting with the development of the collections, reports, and remediation

4.8.6 Orchestration Management

Orchestration Management is responsible for gathering and understanding service orchestration workflow requirements; managing their development, testing, and release; and interacting with the COE to integrate infrastructure-related automation workflows.

4.8.6.1 Orchestration Management Definition

Orchestration Management is the process responsible for governance and control over orchestration workflows and the resulting automation within the vCloud. The goal of Orchestration Management is to understand the impact of orchestration workflows on an organization's vCloud, on those who approve or benefit from the orchestration, and on the interrelations between orchestration and traditional IT service management processes.

4.8.6.2 Value of Orchestration Management in a vCloud

Orchestration capabilities contribute greatly to making a vCloud dynamic and to vCloud agility, elasticity, and self-healing properties.

Along with the benefits, elasticity raises some risks. A successful vCloud implementation must focus on delivering consistent quality of services. Orchestration Management adds the layer of control required to achieve consistency in a vCloud. Control also includes the capability to protect and secure the vCloud. Unwarranted actions in a vCloud cannot be tolerated, so orchestration workflows and actions must be tightly controlled.

The following sections provide information about how to control orchestration in a vCloud. Orchestration is a relatively new feature, and as organizations mature in their management of vCloud environments, the role of Orchestration Management becomes more important.

4.8.6.2.1 Orchestration Workflow Creation Control in a vCloud

Before implementing orchestration workflows in a vCloud environment, answer the following questions:

- Who approved the orchestration workflow?
- Why is it needed?
- What impact does the orchestration workflow have on the vCloud environment?
- Who needs to be informed when the workflow is executed?

Answer these questions for all orchestration workflows that are built into the vCloud. VMware recommends that the following teams be involved during development of orchestration workflows:

- The Orchestration Management team, which focuses on business requirements gathering and business unit negotiations
- The COE team, which focuses on technical development of workflows to facilitate the implementation of consistent standards across all orchestration workflows in the organization

Development of orchestration workflows is complex. Orchestration engages with multiple internal and external systems in a vCloud environment, so a complete development lifecycle must be followed with dedicated support from the application and business teams.

Appropriate testing should be completed at every stage of development, including unit, system, and integration testing, before moving orchestration workflows into production. As part of development testing, operational testing that includes performance and scalability scenarios for end-to-end automation processes must also be completed. In many cases, orchestration workflows themselves might be able to withstand new loads, but external or downstream systems might experience a performance impact. A clear roll-back procedure must be established for exceptions to protect against impacting production functions.

4.8.6.2.2 Orchestration Workflow Execution Control in a vCloud

A vCloud is a dynamic environment where continuous changes are made to improve the quality of the services that run on it. Orchestration plays a key part in this agility, allowing automated actions to be performed as required by vCloud. Orchestration Management focuses on vCloud impacts and maintains flexibility in the environment. VMware recommends control for the execution of orchestration workflows developed for vCloud, with error handling built into the workflows. If workflow execution issues arise, notifications need to be sent to the operations team, with appropriate escalations and tiering for alerts.

4.8.6.2.3 Orchestration Management in Relation to Change Management

As orchestration matures, complex manual tasks are automated. Prior to implementation, workflows that will lead to changes in business services that directly impact users must be analyzed in detail. The Change Advisory Board (CAB) needs to preapprove actions on production applications. Additional controls might also be set to allow for notification back to the CAB upon execution of critical business that impacts orchestration workflows. This must be done in accordance with an organization's change control policies. Business impact should be the main driver for discussion between the orchestration team and CAB. The CAB should allow more flexibility to simple orchestration actions that impact vCloud internal background operations (for example, capacity-related actions) but that do not directly impact a business application or service and might not need require approval for them.

4.8.6.2.4 Orchestration Management in Relation to Configuration Management

Orchestration can be used to provision new vApps in a vCloud. Orchestration Management needs to integrate with and provide status on new or updated configuration items to the Configuration Management System (CMS) to provide consistency. Also, the CMS can trigger autoscaling actions for vApps executed by an orchestration workflow, to provide quality of service.

Another aspect of the relationship between orchestration and configuration management is understanding the physical layer that supports the vCloud environment. In mature implementations, orchestration can interact with the Configuration Management layer to identify gaps in the physical layer and remediate as needed to maintain environment stability (for example, adding new storage capacity).

4.8.6.2.5 Orchestration Management in Relation to Security

Services based on vCloud focus on business users, enabling them to request new services directly via the service catalog. Orchestration is critical to such automation and should have an API to communicate with external systems. Orchestration adds flexibility in a vCloud. With flexibility comes a requirement to add controls so that there are no security risks or exposure for the organization. Because the orchestration workflows have access rights to multiple systems, the orchestration workflow code needs to be protected. Encryption controls such as *Set Digital Rights* management need to be enabled while moving workflow code packages within servers. Access to the orchestration servers must be limited. VMware recommends that the COE exclusively control and manage access on these servers.

4.8.6.2.6 Orchestration Management in Relation to Audit and Compliance

Orchestration workflows allow vCloud to be more dynamic. Automated actions enhance key vCloud functions such as provisioning and self-service. Although enhanced automation is highly beneficial, it poses a challenge to organizations that are bound by tight audit, regulatory, and compliance rules. VMware recommends that orchestration engines running the orchestration workflows be centralized within an organization, with centralized error handling and logging for all workflows. Reporting features that checkpoint all workflow actions must be enabled for audit compliance. Centralized orchestration engines also enhance an organization's problem management and root-cause analysis capabilities.

Some recommended orchestration management principles currently cannot be fully automated and require manual configuration actions based on individual client needs. VMware continues to improve existing libraries, and as vCloud implementations mature, more packaged orchestrations with control and governance features should be available for clients to download.

4.8.7 Availability Management

Availability Management focuses on cost-effectively meeting or exceeding the agreed-upon service-level requirements for the level of availability provided for all vCloud service offerings. Managing availability in a vCloud environment depends on VMware vCloud Director component availability and on the resilience of the underlying infrastructure. vCloud Director works transparently with VMware vCenter Server to provision and deploy virtual machines on hosts. Architecting redundancy and protecting the infrastructure components is imperative. VMware vSphere High Availability (HA) can protect provisioned virtual machines; backup tools in the guest operating system or vStorage API can also protect them.

4.8.7.1 Uptime SLAs

VMware vCloud components support a 99.9% uptime SLA out of the box. This might be sufficient for noncritical applications or applications that are inherently highly available. For vCloud, uptime SLAs typically require the following verification:

- End customer workloads are running.
- End customer workloads are accessible (via the vCloud portal, the API, and remote access protocols).

In some cases, a provider (external service provider or internal IT) might want to increase the vCloud uptime SLA. VMware can control the resiliency of only its vCloud platform components and can provide recommendations to mitigate single points of failure (SPOF) in the underlying infrastructure. A provider can eliminate SPOF by providing redundancy. For example:

- Redundant power sourced from multiple feeds, with multiple whips to racks, and sufficient backup battery and generator capacity
- Redundant network components
- Redundant storage components
    - The storage design needs to be able to handle the I/O load. Customer workloads might not be accessible under high disk latency, file locks, and so on.
    - The storage design should be tied to business continuity and disaster recovery plans, possibly including array-level backups.
- Redundant server components (multiple independent power supplies, network interface cards (NICs), and, if appropriate, host bus adaptors (HBAs)
- Sufficient compute resources for a minimum of n+1 redundancy within a vSphere high availability cluster, including sufficient capacity for timely recovery
- Redundant databases and management

Appropriate Change, Incident, Problem and Capacity Management processes must also be well defined and enforced to make sure that poor operational processes do not result in unnecessary downtime. In addition to a redundant infrastructure, everyone responsible for operating and maintaining the environment and the supporting infrastructure must be adequately trained and skilled.

For more detailed information on increasing vCloud component resiliency, refer to Appendix A, "Availability Considerations."

4.8.8 Continuity Management

Continuity Management for vCloud focuses on making sure that the service offerings based on vCloud and the infrastructure upon which they are hosted can be resumed within an agreed-upon timeframe if service is disrupted—regardless of whether the outage is at the vApp level or whether it impacts an entire vCloud environment instance. In this context, VMware defines two components to Continuity Management: Disaster Recovery (strategic), and vApp Backup and Restore (tactical).

4.8.8.1 Disaster Recovery

Disaster Recovery (DR) focuses on recovering systems and infrastructure after an incident that interrupts normal operations. A disaster can be defined as partial or complete unavailability of resources and services, including software, the virtualization layer, the vCloud layer, and the workloads running in the resource groups. Different approaches and technologies are supported, but at least two areas require disaster recovery: the management cluster and consumer resources. Different approaches and technologies are supported.

4.8.8.1.1 Management Cluster Disaster Recovery

Good practices at the infrastructure level lead to easier disaster recovery of the management cluster. This includes technologies such as HA and DRS for reactive and proactive protection at the primary site. VMware vCenter Heartbeat™ can also protect vCenter Server at the primary site. For multisite protection of virtual machines, VMware vCenter Site Recovery Manager™ (SRM) is a VMware solution that works well because the management virtual machines are not part of a vCloud instance of any type (they run the vCloud instances). For a detailed description of using SRM to provide disaster recovery solution for the management cluster, see www.vmware.com/files/pdf/techpaper/vcloud-director-infrastructure-resiliency.pdf.

Disaster Recovery operational considerations for the vCloud management cluster are the same as for a virtualized environment. A vCloud infrastructure risk assessment must be undertaken to determine the threat risk exposure and the corresponding mitigation activities. The actions necessary for executing the mitigation activities, including those for the management cluster, should be captured in a vCloud infrastructure continuity plan. After the vCloud infrastructure disaster recovery planning and technical implementation are complete, awareness building, disaster recovery training, disaster recovery testing, and review/adjustment should be considered part of ongoing vCloud operations.

VMware vCenter Site Recovery Manager 5 can perform a disaster recovery workflow test of the cloud management cluster. This can be useful to verify that the steps taken to move the cloud management stack from the protected site to the recovery site complete without fail. But the SRM test feature is only validation of the workflow, not functional testing of connectivity (because of the fencing feature that protects the production vCloud management cluster).

4.8.8.1.2 vCloud Consumer Resources Disaster Recovery

The vCloud consumer resources (workloads or vApps) can be failed over to an alternate site, but VMware vCenter Site Recovery Manager (SRM) cannot be used. Although SRM is vCenter Server aware, it is not vCloud Director aware. Without collaboration between vCloud Director and SRM, the underlying mechanisms that synchronize virtual machines cannot keep vCloud consumer resources in sync.

A solution for vCloud consumer workload disaster recovery is to use storage replication. Storage replication can replicate LUNs that contain vCloud consumer workloads from the protected site to the recovery site. Because the LUN/datastores containing vCloud consumer workloads cannot currently be managed by SRM, manual steps might be required during failover. Depending on the type of storage used, these steps can potentially be automated by leveraging storage system API calls.

Operationally, recovery point objectives support must be determined for consumer workloads and included in any consumer service-level agreements (SLAs). Along with the distance between the protected and recovery sites, this helps determine the type of storage replication to use for consumer workloads: synchronous or asynchronous.

For more information about vCloud management cluster disaster recovery, see www.vmware.com/files/pdf/techpaper/vcloud-director-infrastructure-resiliency.pdf.

4.8.8.2 Backup and Restore of vApps

Some manual backup and restore procedures are required for the vApps that are deployed into the vCloud. Traditional backup tools do not capture the required metadata associated with a vApp, such as owner, network, and organization. This results in recovery and restoration issues. Without this data, recovery must include manual steps and requires configuration attributes to be manually reentered.

Within a vCloud environment, a vApp can be a single virtual machine or a group of virtual machines, treated as one object. Backup of vApps on isolated networks must be supported. Identifying inventories of individual organizations becomes challenging based on current methods that enumerate the backup items using vSphere. vSphere uses universally unique identifiers (UUIs) to differentiate objects, whereas vCloud Director uses object identifiers.

For backing up and restoring vApps, VMware recommends the use of VMware vSphere® Storage APIs—Data Protection backup technology. This technology has no agents on guest operating systems, is centralized for improved manageability, and has a reduced dependency on backup windows.

Guest-based backup solutions might not work in a vCloud because not all virtual machines are accessible through the network. Also, virtual machines might have identical IP addresses. Therefore, backups of vCloud vApps require a virtual machine-level approach.

Use the full name and computer name fields to specify realistic names that help describe the virtual machines when deploying virtual machines (as part of a vApp). If this is not done, the generic information in these fields can make it difficult to specify individual virtual machines. vApps and virtual machines that vCloud Director provisions have a large GUID template_name. Multiple virtual machines might appear to be similar, making it difficult for a user or administrator to identify and ask for a specific virtual machine to be restored.

4.8.8.2.1 VMware Solutions

VMware Data Recovery is a solution based on vStorage APIs for Data Protection. Other storage APIs for data protection–based backup technologies are available from third-party backup vendors. Currently, because of the issue of universally unique identifiers (UUIs) versus object identifiers, Data Recovery cannot be used with VMware vCloud Director.

For backup of vCloud workloads, VMware recommends that clients validate the level of support provided by the vendor to make sure client requirements are supported. Table 4.3 provides a checklist of vCloud vApp requirements to ask vendors about.

TABLE 4.3 vCloud vApp Requirements Checklist

vApp Requirement	Detail
vStorage API Data Protection integration	▶ vStorage API Data Protection that provides change-block tracking capability to reduce backup windows. ▶ Integration to enable backup of isolated virtual machines and vApps. ▶ Integration with vStorage API Data Protection to provide LAN-free and server-free backups to support better consolidation rations for vCloud and the underlying vSphere infrastructure. ▶ Use of the virtual machine universally unique identifier (UUI) versus the virtual machine name, to support multitenancy and avoid potential name space conflicts.
vCloud Director integration	▶ Interface support for vCloud provider administrator teams. In the future, some vendors might provide consumer (organization administrator and users) access. ▶ Include vCloud metadata for the vApps. This includes temporary and permanent metadata per virtual machine or vApp. This is required to make sure that recovery of the virtual machine or vApp has all the data required to support resource requirements and SLAs.
vApp requirements	▶ Provide vApp granularity for backups. Support the backup of multitiered vApps (for example, a Microsoft Exchange vApp that has multiple virtual machines included. The backup selection of the Exchange vApp would pick up all the underlying virtual machines that are part of the main vApp). This capability is not available today, but vendors are working to develop it.

4.8.8.2.2 Challenges

Challenges associated with backing up and restoring a vCloud include the following:

- vApp naming that poses conflict issues between tenants
- vApp metadata required for recovery
- Multiobject vApp backup (protection groups for multitiered vApps)
- Manual recovery steps in the vCloud
- Support for backup of vApps on isolated networks or with no network connectivity
- Enumeration of vApps by organization for use by the organization administrator
- Enumeration of vApps by organization and provider for use by the organization provider
- User-initiated backup/recovery
- Support of provider (provider administrator) and consumer (organization administrator and user)

For more detailed information about vCloud Business Continuity, see Appendix J, "Business Continuity."

4.8.9 Access and Security Management

Access and Security Management is essential for a vCloud architecture.

4.8.9.1 Workload Isolation

Additional security controls and network functionality can be added to a vCloud platform for greater versatility in hosting enterprise applications.

Using VMware vCloud Networking and Security technology to isolate Layer 2 traffic and persistent network policies, a vApp can have a number of private, vApp-only networks that never leak outside their environment. It is possible to clone this environment indefinitely, never changing an IP address or configuration file.

When a vApp is built, firewall rules created in VMware vCloud Networking and Security Edge (Edge) can permit or restrict access from external vSphere objects or physical networks to TCP and UDP ports of the application. See Figure 4.29.

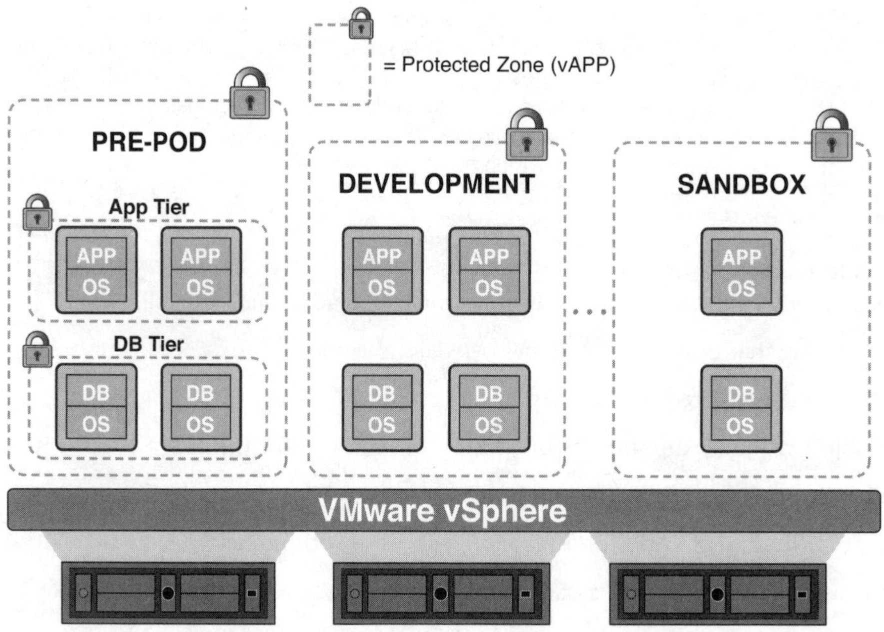

FIGURE 4.29 Workload isolation

Although the vApp is the recommended way to create the virtual infrastructure for multi-tiered applications, administrators can define security rules based on any of the following vSphere objects: datacenter, cluster, resource pool, vApp, port group, or VLANs. A rule that is created for a container applies to all resources in that container.

4.8.9.2 Access Management

Within a public or private vCloud environment, directory services must be configured for vCloud Director to enable user access to vCloud resources.

A mechanism for authorization and authentication is available within vCloud Director. Directory services based on Lightweight Directory Access Protocol (LDAP) and network authentication protocols such as Active Directory, OpenLDAP, or Kerberos v5 can be configured with vCloud Director. See the *VMware vCloud Director Administrator's Guide* (at www.vmware.com/support/pubs/vcd_pubs.html) for additional information about integrating these services with vCloud Director.

User authorization is controlled through *role-based access control* (RBAC) within vCloud Director. Careful consideration must be given to roles and responsibilities for managing vCloud Director, whether as a provider or as a tenant. The *VMware vCloud Director Administrator's Guide* contains details about permissions, roles, and settings that can be modified to fit the requirements for access control within the organization.

From a provider perspective, the system administrator role should be restricted to only individuals within the provider organization's vCloud operations team who need that level of access. Other individuals within the provider organization who require only vCloud Director organization access should use other roles. If possible, an LDAP group for the provider administrators should be created and imported into vCloud Director with the system administrator role applied to it. All users who require this level of access can then be managed through the LDAP system. The built-in admin account should not be used for vCloud administration, and the credentials must be stored securely.

From a tenant perspective, there are predefined roles. The organization administrator is the highest level of privilege, and it should be limited to individuals within the tenant organization's vCloud operations team that truly require that level of access. This can be achieved with LDAP groups by importing them so that vCloud Director roles can be applied to them. A variety of roles exist with vCloud Director for organizations, and if required, additional roles can be created with alternate privileges. A policy of *least privilege* (grant only privileges required to perform the role) should be applied to all individuals who require access to the vCloud organization, with continued use of LDAP groups to assist with managing this policy.

4.8.9.3 Log Management

Providing log data to customers is an important capability for providers offering vCloud services. The primary advantages include the following:

- **Regulatory compliance:** Aggregate log data for security review and analysis through applicable controls. Archive historical data and retrieve based on an audit window containing relevant data. Logs showing specific events such as a user authentication with a timestamp are examples of satisfactory evidence for auditors
- **Tenant requirements:** Tenants (customers or clients) should have access to logs that pertain to the use of their particular compute resources. Tenant log requirements are similar to those for a provider, but the capability to offer the data that corresponds to the specific tenant is an important capability in a vCloud environment.

- **Event correlation:** Log data can be forwarded to Security Information and Event Management (SIEM) tools for analytic analysis and correlation with unique behavioral signatures. This enables the possibility of early and possibly real-time detection of an attack, misconfiguration, and secondary capacity utilization reporting.
- **Operational monitoring:** For the automation of health and status reporting, logs can provide data that can be checked when required for state changes to applications, operating systems, and virtual machine hosts.
- **Simple troubleshooting:** Many applications and operating systems provide the capability to enable more verbose logging detail during runtime. When troubleshooting unexpected behavior, this additional detail can provide the information needed when attempting to remediate most problems.

4.8.9.3.1 Logging and Architecture Considerations

- **Redundancy:** The leading logging platform is syslog. Syslog is a UDP-based protocol, so the delivery of all log data is not guaranteed. To facilitate the integrity of log delivery over networks, try the following:
  - Design physical redundancy on logging equipment (redundant network interfaces, others).
  - Specify multiple syslog targets.
  - If only one remote syslog target is possible, configure local logging as well as one remote target.
  - Host the log targets on DRS-enabled hosts so that vCenter can manage availability of the syslog virtual machine and service.
- **Scalability:** When compared with customer-generated events, vCloud infrastructure components generate considerably less log data. However, customer components such as the vCloud Networking and Security Edge firewall generate a very high volume of logging. Logs from performance data such as IOPS, network throughput, and CPU utilization are critical, so the design guideline is to define standalone disk partitions for log collection and archiving on a collection server. Additionally, if possible, this data should be part of the vCloud monitoring solution using vCenter Operations Manager.
- **Reporting:**
  - Logs need to be available to customers in raw format from both vCloud Director and vCloud Networking and Security Edge that pertain specifically to their organization and networks.
  - Within vCloud Director, customer-specific activity is specified as an identifier for the customer's organization.
  - vCloud Networking and Security Edge applies descriptive and unique names to organization-specific traffic that SIEM products use to correlate log messages.

4.8.9.3.2 Logging as a Service

When enabling a formalized service for log collection and processing, a provider should consider offering the following types of log services to a customer:

- **Provider log management of customer logs for systems within the vCloud organization:** The customer sends logs to a provider for analysis and report generation of customer-specific events.
  - Pros:
    - Logs can be sent over a private VLAN within the provider's environment.
    - Cost savings for customer of licensing SIEM tools.
  - Cons:
    - Difficult to customize analysis and correlation to other customer-specific events.
    - Dedicated resources are required even with low utilization.
    - Billing does not follow the IaaS model because resource consumption is primarily for storage and analysis.
- **Provider forwarding logs to customer for management:** Logs from provider resources, such as network equipment, host server, and firewall appliances, are sent to the customer system for collection and analysis.
  - Pros:
    - vCloud resources are scalable and rely on distributed analysis within the customer environment.
    - The customer uses a tool of choice for analysis and reporting.
  - Cons:
    - The customer creates a duplicate copy of the infrastructure log, for audit purposes.
    - The log transmission requires network resources.
    - Due to multitenancy within the vCloud, a potentially complex implementation is required as a result of the need for a built-in intelligence engine in the log-forwarding mechanism.

4.9 vCloud Infrastructure Control

vCloud Infrastructure Control deals with architecture and engineering services for the underlying vCloud infrastructure. This layer includes infrastructure architecture services, infrastructure engineering services, and infrastructure deployment services. Operationally, the key for control and governance in these areas is to establish, document, and implement a standardized architecture vision and create consistent design principles and enterprise-wide blueprints for vCloud. Additional guidance on design principles and standards is provided in Chapters 3 and 6. The following are some key topic areas that provide operational guidance.

- Chapter 3, *Architecting a VMware vCloud*:
    - Section 3.2, "vCloud Architecture"
    - Section 3.3 "vCloud Management Architecture"
    - Section 3.6 "vCloud Metering"
    - Section 3.7 "Orchestration and Extension"
- Chapter 6, *Implementation Examples*:
    - Section 6.8, "vCloud Management and Monitoring Examples"

4.9.1 Monitoring

Monitoring the components of a vCloud Director implementation is essential to the health of a vCloud environment and is necessary to maintain capacity and meet service-level agreements. This section provides recommendations regarding what systems and associated objects to monitor, and introduces readily available tools that can be used to extract health-related metrics. This chapter does not go into details on specific limits or thresholds because they are available in the product documentation. This chapter does not attempt to provide specifics for setting up a monitoring solution because various service providers and enterprises might have very different monitoring solutions in place to be integrated.

4.9.1.1 Management Cluster

Design guidelines for monitoring the management cluster components are the same as the guidelines for monitoring vSphere components. A centralized monitoring tool such as VMware vFabric Hyperic HQ Enterprise can be used to monitor the core objects (Oracle Server, SQL Server, Active Directory Server, DNS Server, Red Hat Enterprise Linux Server, and Windows Server) that are needed to run a vCloud environment. A customer can use SNMP and SMASH to monitor the hosts on which the vCloud Director cells are installed and running, but the vCloud Director application itself cannot be monitored by SNMP or SMASH. However, SNMP can be integrated from vCenter. Alternatively, cells can be monitored through integration with a third-party monitoring platform via JMX Beans. Beyond JMX Beans monitoring, the vCloud and vSphere APIs provide component, resource, and activity metrics that can be used for health and capacity management.

4.9.1.2 Cloud Consumer Resources and Workloads

Design guidelines for monitoring the vCloud consumer resources and workloads are the same as for monitoring vSphere. However, there are additional vCloud-specific considerations for VMware vCloud Networking and Security Edge and vCloud consumer workloads.

4.9.1.2.1 vCloud Networking and Security Edge

VMware vCloud Networking and Security Edge appliances are self-contained environments that are stateless in nature. There is a "health check" API call that can be made to an edge appliance to determine whether it is functioning correctly. If the API returns negative, initiate a reboot of the edge device. At the time of reboot, configuration information is updated from the VMware vCloud Networking and Security Manager, and the edge device continues to function properly.

4.9.1.2.2 Cloud Consumer Workloads

Monitoring workloads provisioned by vCloud consumers might be desirable. vCloud Director does not provide any built-in monitoring of workloads for availability or performance. Several third-party solutions are available to monitor vSphere resources and workloads running on vSphere. However, these solutions might not work all the time when vCloud Director is in use. Isolated networking in vApps might prevent monitoring tools from acquiring the performance or availability information of a vApp. Furthermore, vApps might be provisioned and deprovisioned or power-cycled at any time by a vCloud consumer, and these actions might create false positives in the monitoring environment. Until solutions in the market are fully integrated with vCloud Director, providing detailed monitoring for vCloud consumer workloads might be difficult.

CHAPTER 5
Consuming a VMware vCloud

IN THIS CHAPTER

5.1 Overview

Cloud computing leverages the efficient pooling of on-demand, self-managed virtual infrastructure to provide resources that are consumable as a service. VMware® vCloud® is the VMware cloud solution.

Consumers consume vCloud resources. Understanding consumption requires understanding an organization's processes, constraints, and requirements. This applies both to enterprises and to service providers, with some variations depending on use cases.

This chapter serves as a reference for infrastructure architects, managers, and end users who are considering the first steps on the journey to private, public, or hybrid vCloud computing. It covers the following material:

- An approach to consuming a vCloud from the consumer's perspective
- A methodology for choosing consumption models
- Special considerations for:
  - Developing service catalogs
  - Working with VMware vCloud® vApps
  - Achieving successful interactions between enterprises and service providers

Chapter 3, "Architecting a VMware vCloud"; Chapter 4, "Operating a VMware vCloud"; and this chapter are designed to be used together throughout the lifecycle of a VMware vCloud computing implementation. Using all three documents together, in combination with a private or public service definition, helps develop a comprehensive view of VMware vCloud computing.

5.1.1 Audience

This chapter is designed for those who plan to consume vCloud resources, including architects and designers who have been trained on VMware vSphere and vCloud technologies.

Two types of consumers exist:

- **End users:** People concerned with running applications in an environment, regardless of the underlying virtualization infrastructure and vCloud layer.
- **Administrators:** IT administrators of enterprises and small businesses whose organizations might have purchased cloud computing resources from service providers to augment their in-house resources.

5.1.2 Scope

This document provides design considerations and patterns for consuming vCloud resources.

5.2 vCloud Consumption Approach

Adopting a consistent approach to vCloud resource consumption and understanding the underlying vCloud and vSphere components can provide valuable insight into design guidelines for consumption. Such an approach is especially valuable for IT administrators who manage end-user resources that are hosted at a service provider.

5.2.1 vCloud Consumer Resources

vCloud consumer resources are provided by a VMware vSphere infrastructure dedicated to hosting vCloud workloads. VMware vCloud Director® builds on vSphere hardware abstraction capabilities and introduces logical constructs, such as *virtual datacenters*, *organizations*, and *organization virtual datacenter networks*, to facilitate multitenant resource consumption.

Figure 5.1 shows the logical constructs in vCloud Director and illustrates how an organization or end user views the vCloud environment and its related constructs.

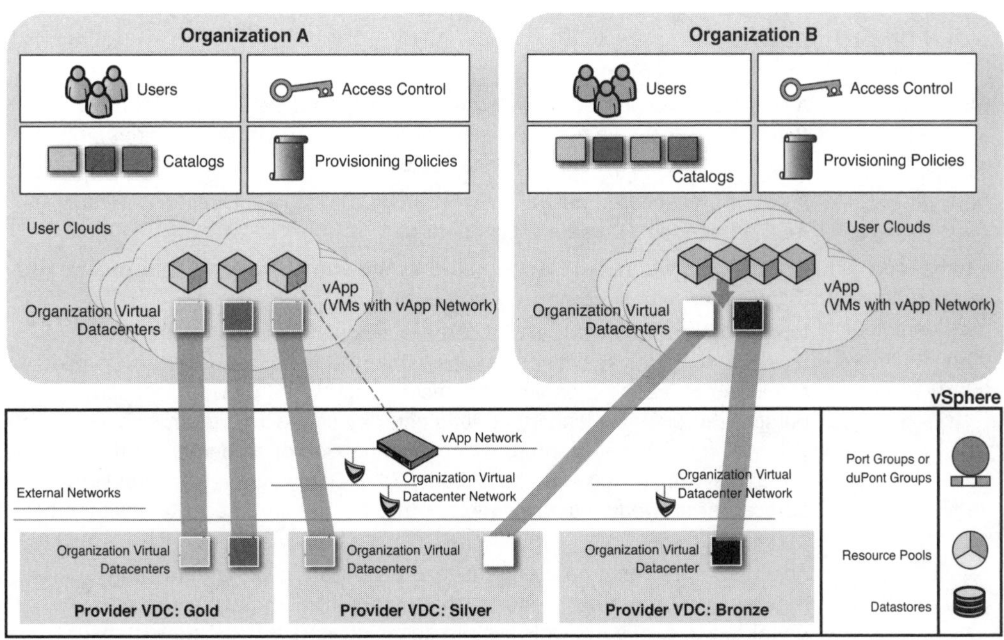

FIGURE 5.1 Mapping vCloud Director logical constructs to vSphere

Table 5.1 describes the logical constructs in vCloud Director that abstract underlying vSphere resources.

TABLE 5.1 vCloud Director Logical Constructs As Viewed by an Organization

vCloud Director Construct	Description
Organization	A unit of administration that represents a logical collection of users, groups, and computing resources. The organization also serves as a security boundary from which only users of a particular organization can deploy workloads and have visibility into deployed workloads in the vCloud.
Provider virtual datacenter	A collection of vSphere resources, such as CPU, memory, and storage, shared among tenants. This collection is usually based on business requirements.
Organization virtual datacenter	A subset of provider virtual datacenter resources assigned to an organization and backed by a VMware vCenter™ resource pool that is automatically created by vCloud Director. An organization virtual datacenter allocates resources using one of the following models: ▶ Pay As You Go ▶ Allocation Pool ▶ Reservation Pool

5

vCloud Director Construct	Description
vApp template and media catalogs	A collection of services available for consumption. Catalogs contain *vApp templates* (preconfigured containers of one or more virtual machines), media (ISO images of operating systems), or both.
Network pool	A set of preallocated networking resources that vCloud Director can draw from as needed to create virtual networks.
Internal and external organization virtual datacenter networks	Organization virtual datacenter networks are virtual networks that provide an organization with vApp network connectivity. Internal organization virtual datacenter networks are isolated networks used for connectivity between vApps within the organization virtual datacenter. External organization virtual datacenter networks provide connectivity outside the organization virtual datacenter by connecting to an existing external network, using either a direct connection or a connection routed through a vCloud Network and Security Edge Gateway. Organization virtual datacenter networks can be shared with other virtual datacenters within the organization. Administrators can create and manage organization virtual datacenter networks, but there are limits to what an organization administrator is permitted to configure. Only system administrators can create external networks.
vApp network	Virtual network contained within a vApp that facilitates network connectivity between virtual machines in the vApp. vApp networks can be connected to an organization virtual datacenter network with a direct, NAT-routed, or fenced connection to enable communication with other vApps inside or outside the organization, if the organization virtual datacenter network is connected to an external network. vApp networks are backed by network pools. Most users with access to a vApp can create and manage their own vApp networks.

5.2.2 vCloud Consumer Resource Capacity

One of the key benefits of implementing a vCloud is the capability to rapidly provision vApps into the vCloud environment. Capacity management is designed so that the vCloud infrastructure has sufficient capacity to meet the current and future needs of consumers under normal circumstances. Maintaining sufficient reserve capacity in the vCloud infrastructure typically prevents vApps from contending for resources. This mitigates the risk of breaching a service-level agreement (SLA).

Provisioning and consuming vApps reduces the capacity of the vCloud infrastructure. To provide additional capacity, vCloud providers typically implement robust management processes that make sufficient resources available to support the service-level requirements associated with vApp provisioning and performance.

As vCloud resources are consumed, additional capacity must also be added to allow for anticipated future demand while preserving sufficient capacity for near-term needs. To predict future capacity needs, analyze current capacity usage and trends to determine growth rates, and then estimate future needs based on new consumers and projects.

5.3 Choosing a vCloud Consumption Model

vCloud providers offer consumer resources to support different SLAs, costing, and sharing models.

5.3.1 Consuming vCloud Services

The following vCloud service offerings apply to both private and public vCloud, but each has a different impact on consumption. Choose the service offering that best supports your use cases.

- **Basic service offering (unreserved pay-per-use class):** Designed for quick-start pilot projects and workloads, such as software testing, that do not need reservations or guaranteed performance.
- **Committed service offering (subscription model):** Provides reserved compute resources with the capability to burst above committed levels if additional capacity is available. It offers predictable performance by reserving resources for workloads within a multitenant infrastructure while enabling access to more resources as they become available.
- **Dedicated service offering:** Provides dedicated compute resources, sometimes known as a *virtual private cloud.* It offers predictable performance by reserving dedicated resources. This service offering can help support SLAs for Tier 1 applications. Under this service offering, end users with appropriate privileges have flexibility in modifying compute allocations to the vApps and virtual machines.

Service classes are designed to help consumers move their workloads to a vCloud. Any existing VMware virtual machine or virtual application (vApp) can run with little or no modification in a public vCloud. Compatibility with existing enterprise VMware deployments is a key design objective. There is no requirement to deploy a private vCloud to realize the benefits of vCloud computing because any VMware-based virtualized infrastructure is compatible.

All vCloud consumption models are fundamentally based on vCloud Director allocation models, regardless of the name or branding attached to a given service offering.

5.3.2 vCloud Director Allocation Models

Allocation models define how resources are allocated to an organization's virtual datacenter and how resources are consumed when vApps are deployed.

Allocation models are differentiated by how resources are reserved or limited. A limit can be placed at the level of a virtual machine or a resource pool. To guarantee resources to a virtual machine or to an entire resource pool, vCloud Director sets a reservation or not, depending on the allocation models used. The following are vCloud allocation models:

- Allocation Pool
- Pay As You Go
- Reservation Pool

Figure 5.2 shows the vCloud Director screen for selecting an allocation model.

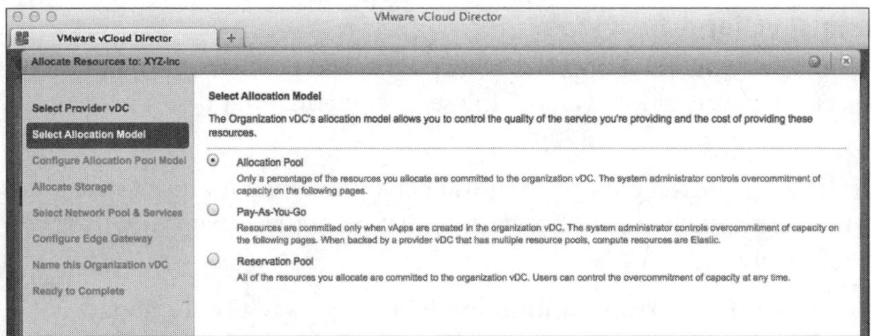

FIGURE 5.2 Allocation models

5.3.2.1 Allocation Pool

The customer is charged for the preallocation of resources to an organization virtual datacenter. A provider can charge the customer based on the allocated resources, the guaranteed resources, or a combination of the guaranteed resources and the consumption of resources beyond the guarantee. The cloud provider manages resource overcommitments by defining a guaranteed percentage of allocated resources, such as CPU, memory resources, virtual CPU speed, and an optional maximum virtual machine limit. Only the vCloud provider can expand or contract resources. The allocation pool model can consume resources from one or more resource pools, depending on the vCloud provider's configuration.

The allocation pool model enables an organization to procure resources under normal operating conditions but has the capability to *burst* for more resources when need arises. Because this model guarantees a specified percentage of the allocated resource, the remainder that is not guaranteed is shared with other tenants. This can result in resource contention.

The allocation pool model is usually a good fit for relatively steady-state workloads that occasionally surge.

5.3.2.2 Pay As You Go

The customer is charged for each running virtual machine. As with the allocation pool model, the vCloud provider manages resource overcommitments by defining a guaranteed percentage of allocated resources, such as CPU, memory resources, and a maximum number of virtual machines. The cloud provider can specify a maximum virtual CPU speed, or limit. Unlike the allocation and reservation pool models, the pay as you go model facilitates an unlimited approach to resource consumption within the constraints of the vCloud provider's physical infrastructure. As with the allocation pool model, the pay as you go model can consume resources from one or more resource pools, depending on the vCloud provider's configuration.

Typically, the pay as you go model is a good fit for transient and training environments.

5.3.2.3 Reservation Pool

As with the allocation pool and pay as you go models, the reservation pool allocation model applies charges for the preallocation of resources to an organization virtual datacenter. The fundamental difference from the allocation pool model is that the vCloud provider cannot overcommit resources because all CPU and memory resources are 100% guaranteed. However, the vCloud provider can specify a maximum number of virtual machines. Only the vCloud provider can expand or contract resources. The reservation pool is unique, in that it offers consumers full resource-management controls in the form of shares, reservations, and limits. This is similar to *vSphere resource management.*

The reservation pool represents a good fit for steady-state workloads that require guaranteed performance. To make best use of this model, you should know the customer's application profile well enough to optimize resource provisioning.

vCloud providers typically charge a premium for this type of allocation model because they cannot overcommit resources.

5.3.2.4 Storage Allocation

The allocation of storage resources is the same for all allocation models and is charged as capacity is allocated. The vCloud provider manages storage resource overcommitment by defining a maximum amount of storage that can be consumed within the organization virtual datacenter and by controlling whether storage is *thin-provisioned* (not preallocated) or *thick-provisioned* (preallocated in full).

A vCloud Director 5.1 feature provides multiple classes or tiers of storage capacity within an organization virtual datacenter. This allows an application owner to deploy a multitier application with different classes of storage for different tiers.

5.4 Organization Catalogs

An *organization catalog* is a container for vApp templates and media files. Detailed information about organization catalogs is available in the VMware vCloud Director documentation (www.vmware.com/support/pubs/vcd_pubs.html).

Figure 5.3 shows two views of a sample published catalog. The vApp templates are visible from the vApp Template tab, and the media files are visible from the Media tab.

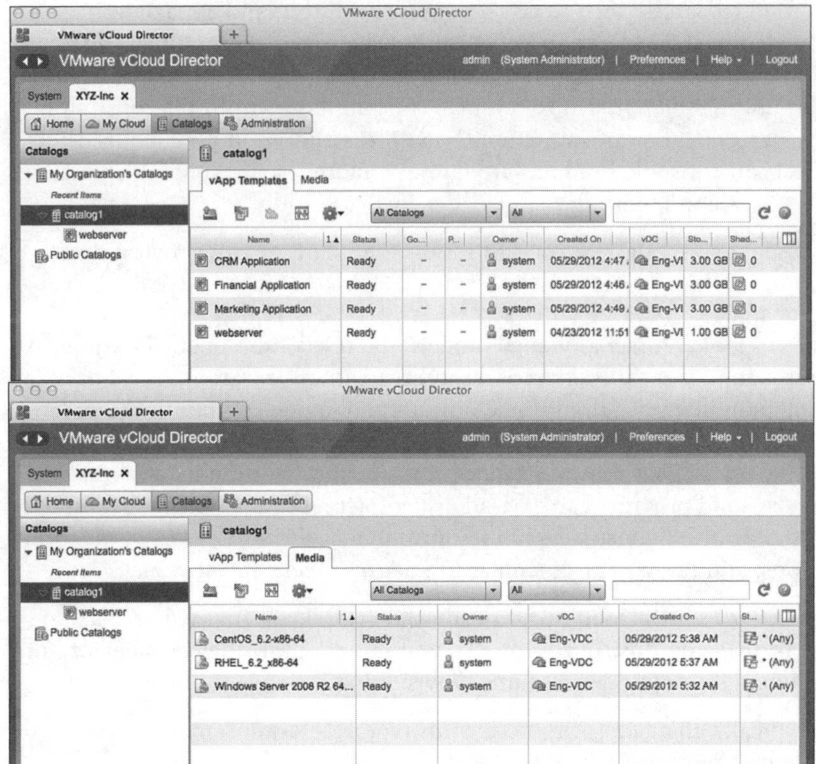

FIGURE 5.3 vApp templates and media files in a catalog

Organizations can offer the following types of service catalogs to their users or customers:

- **A vCloud service catalog:** Includes predefined vApps, virtual machines, and images (operating systems and applications) that users can deploy within an organization
- **An operational service catalog:** Includes operational features such as development of a vCloud service catalog, backup and recovery services, archival services, managed services, and migration services

The following sections focus on the vCloud service catalog and include design considerations for organizations and their virtual datacenters, as well as their service catalogs. Catalogs can grow exponentially with the permutation and combination of guest operating system versions, service packs, and patch levels, as well as any installed applications or configurations and their version levels. VMware vFabric™ Application Director™ can address the growing number of vApp templates in catalogs.

5.4.1 Understanding Catalogs

The vSphere approach to implementing cataloglike functionality helps understand the contents of a vCloud catalog and how the catalog is used. Although vSphere does not use the concept of a catalog, it achieves similar functionality with virtual machine templates and media files (ISO/FLP). The following steps outline how to build a fairly common Linux, Apache, MySQL, and PHP (LAMP) stack configuration in vSphere.

1. Gather the relevant media. In some cases, the media are readily available for download in the form of ISO files from operating system vendors. Applications might be available only as binaries, in the form of TAR, ZIP, or RPM files. You can copy binaries directly to a virtual machine with tools such as FTP or SCP, or by bundling the binaries into an ISO file. These ISO files are then typically available on a dedicated, shared datastore.
2. Create virtual machine templates with a bare guest operating system installed on each template, and clone them to create instances of virtual machines to install applications. You can use a single template to create a web server, application server, and database server. Users can mix and match templates to satisfy use case requirements.
3. After deploying virtual machines from templates, you can customize each virtual machine for its specific purpose by installing Apache/PHP, Tomcat, and MySQL software binaries, either directly or by mounting a custom ISO image.
4. After the individual virtual machines are configured, an administrator can clone them to templates for future use.

vSphere cannot transform a vApp into a template. Any modifications to a vApp require that templates be converted back to virtual machines. Only the virtual machines can be modified.

The following sections discuss how vCloud Director implements the same functionality.

5.4.1.1 Software Media Files

In a vCloud, ISO files are uploaded to a catalog, as shown in Figure 5.3. The catalog belongs to an organization that is backed by one or more organization virtual datacenters. These are then backed by provider virtual datacenters. A provider virtual datacenter comprises a collection of compute resources, including datastores. These media files might be private, public, or shared with named users.

Uploaded media files are located on the compute resource associated with the organization virtual datacenter. You can attach them to existing virtual machines or use them to install new virtual machines with a process almost identical to the vSphere procedure in Section 5.4.1.

A good catalog includes all commonly used operating systems, such as the various editions of Windows and common Linux distributions such as Red Hat, CentOS, or SUSe. Software media can consist of custom operating system builds, kickstart CDs, or software packages. No limits apply when including default operating system installation media.

5.4.1.2 vApp

In the LAMP stack example that follows, three virtual machines running a Linux guest operating system are deployed into a vSphere environment. The most efficient approach is to build and configure a single virtual machine, clone it to a template, and redeploy the same virtual machine as many times as necessary to support application requirements. Customizing the virtual machine's hardware configuration might be necessary, depending on the application.

In vCloud Director, the smallest construct is a vApp. The vApp can contain one or more virtual machines.

To create a LAMP stack:

1. Create a vApp.
2. Within the vApp, create a virtual machine with a specific guest operating system.
3. After installing the guest operating system, shut down the vApp and capture it to a catalog.
4. After capturing the vApp, create the LAMP stack by creating a new vApp.
5. Add the captured virtual machine repeatedly, as needed.
6. Install and configure the application as needed.
7. Shut down the vApp.
8. Capture the vApp again to the catalog.
9. Other users can now deploy the vApp from the catalog.

The foundation for a good catalog is a collection of commonly used configurations of virtual machines, operating systems, and applications that can be deployed as single vApps or used to build vApps that contain multiple virtual machines.

5.4.2 Populating a Catalog

Populating a catalog involves creating vApps and adding them to a catalog while considering costs associated with the catalog and vApps after they are deployed. Populating also involves determining whether the catalog should be placed in a global or organizational catalog.

5.4.2.1 Catalog Items

To populate catalog items such as vApp templates, use the vCloud Director Catalogs tab (see Figure 5.4), or add them from the My Cloud tab of a powered-off vApp.

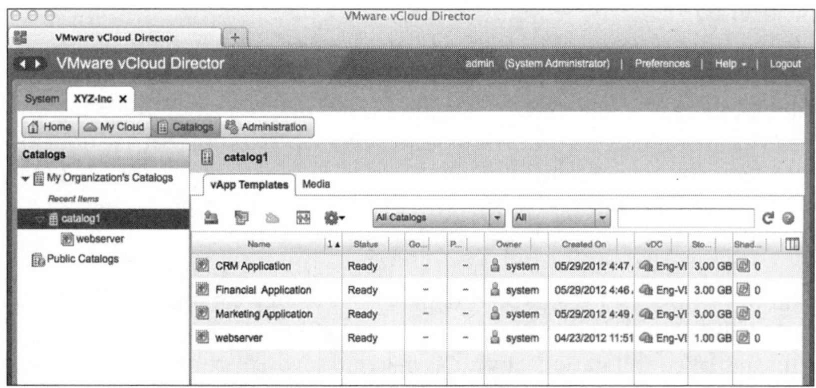

FIGURE 5.4 vCloud Director Catalogs tab

Consider the following when determining the number of vApp templates to add to the catalog:

- A need to enforce standardized virtual machine configurations
- A requirement to provide applications preconfigured as vApps
- User privileges needed to modify vApp and virtual machine configurations

The size of the anticipated user base and the level of control granted to users determines how many vApp templates to create.

The following are examples of common use cases for catalog entities:

- A vApp author, or application developer, who deploys a vApp as a development and testing platform
- A vApp user, or business user, who deploys a vApp with the latest version of an internally developed application for user acceptance testing (UAT)

5.4.2.1.1 Application Developer Use Case

Application developers are skilled in IT and require many vApp configurations with different internal virtual machine configurations and software package installation configurations. Instead of trying to predict the requirements for each developer, the infrastructure team can provide a collection of media files and basic, predefined standard vApp templates based on an existing corporate standard. Developers can then construct their own individual vApps and modify the configuration (CPU, RAM, disk) of the contained virtual machines. You might not need to create many vApp templates in advance because a single vApp template for each major guest operating system and application might be enough. No requirement exists for defining small, medium, and large hardware-based derivatives of the same vApp template because the user can edit the virtual hardware after deployment.

5.4.2.1.2 Business User Use Case

Business users are not necessarily aware of IT requirements and often do not fully understand the differences and implications of virtual machine–level hardware changes. An infrastructure team would not delegate full control to business users and, therefore, could deploy a predefined vApp configuration that meets their requirements. Because the user cannot edit the hardware after deployment, a requirement could offer a more extensive catalog, including small, medium, and large hardware-based derivatives of the same vApp template.

5.4.2.2 Cost

The cost of maintaining catalogs and vApps after deployment from a catalog is an additional consideration. Media files and vApp templates consume disk space and have associated costs, as does the actual configuration of virtual machines, which consume compute resources within a vApp. Oversize virtual machines can artificially reduce the overall capacity of an organization virtual datacenter and also have an inherent cost, depending on the allocation model and charging strategy. Given these costs, consider the following:

- Place a catalog in an organization virtual datacenter that uses lower-cost storage, such as NFS.
- Use shared and published catalogs to minimize the number of duplicated vApp templates and media files.
- Depending on the specific catalog requirements, use a catalog-only organization virtual datacenter, mapped to a lower-tier vSphere cluster that uses lower-cost datastores. If using storage profiles, use a lower-tier storage profile. Using a lower-tier vSphere cluster or a lower-tier storage profile helps provide cost-effective storage for catalog items. Reserve more expensive storage tiers to run workloads.

5.4.2.3 Global Catalog

When consuming resources from a private vCloud, the provider often populates a *global catalog* with core operating system versions and hardware configurations that align with the organization's current physical and virtual hardware standards. Often these hardware standards are derived from legacy physical server configurations or from virtual machine configurations adopted in previous server consolidation activities. Requirements to maintain consistency with physical standards tend to use chargeback mechanisms based on capital hardware, depreciation, and recurring maintenance instead of actual resource allocation costing. This is the basis for using VMware vCenter Chargeback™ with vCloud Director. As confidence in self-service catalogs increases and additional control is delegated to users, a shift to a simplified catalog becomes possible.

A public vCloud provider, on the other hand, is less likely to offer a global catalog with core operating system versions, largely because of the variance in requirements from different consumer organizations and complications associated with licensing. In some cases, a public provider might offer standard media files and standard vApp templates that are not constrained by licensing restrictions. Over time, public vCloud providers can offer more services as they try to differentiate themselves from competitors. Similarly, software vendors might look to partner with public providers to offer their applications as a service.

5.4.2.4 vFabric Application Director

VMware vFabric Application Director helps reduce the number of variations of vApp templates in a catalog. Because vFabric Application Director runs arbitrary scripts during vApp deployment, it can be scripted to install patches, service packs, applications, and third-party software. This helps reduce the number of catalog items with different variations of guest operating system versions and patch levels. It also helps reduce the number of applications and associated patch levels.

5.4.3 Working with Catalogs

When working with vCloud catalogs, consider creating, publishing, accessing, and searching catalogs, as well as how consumers interact with providers.

5.4.3.1 Browsing

To simplify catalog browsing, use a simple, logical, and methodical naming convention for media files and vApp templates. Also consider incorporating vApp template name versioning to identify patch updates and service pack updates. This enables users to quickly find templates that meet their requirements.

Figure 5.5 shows the use of the search drop-down menu to filter and narrow results. In the following example, users seek Windows vApp templates based on a keyword search for "Win." Because a logical naming convention is used, results are almost immediate.

You can search for a vApp template or media file based on Name, Status, Gold Master, Published, Owner, Created On, or Virtual Datacenter. You can specify that the search be conducted on All Catalogs, My Catalogs, or Catalogs Shared to Me.

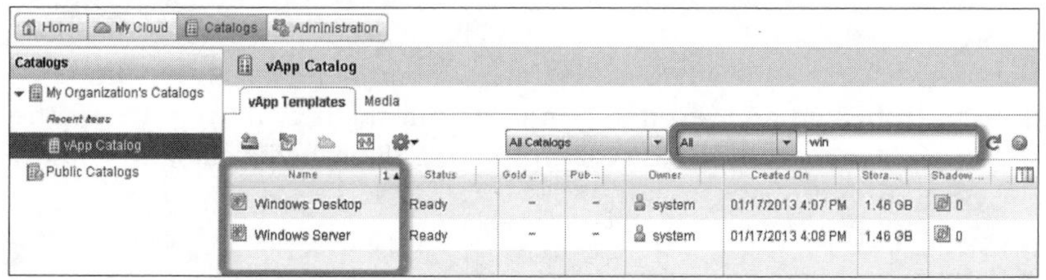

FIGURE 5.5 Browsing and searching catalogs

Use the search drop-down menu to filter and narrow your search when creating a new vApp. While adding virtual machines to a vApp, you can search for existing virtual machine configurations that are available from existing vApp templates, as shown in Figure 5.6.

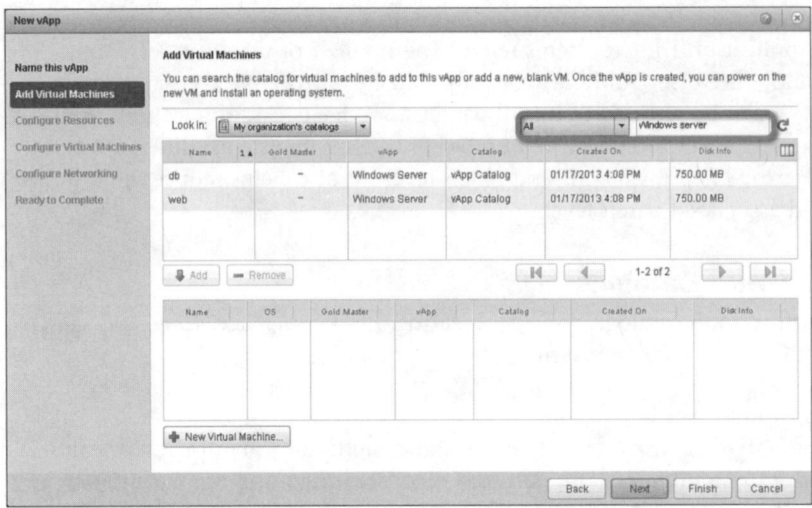

FIGURE 5.6 Browsing and searching for virtual machines during vApp creation

5.4.3.2 Catalog Access

Catalogs can be private, shared, or published. When a catalog is created, it is owned by the user who created it and is private by default. You can *share* a catalog with specific users and groups in an organization or *publish* it to all organizations within vCloud Director.

When deciding whether to share or publish a catalog, determine who should have access to the catalog and its contents. Publishing the catalog makes it accessible to all organizations, assuming that users have the View Published Catalogs permission. Sharing allows more granular access control based on users and groups within the organization where the catalog was created. The following are use case examples for a published catalog in enterprise and service provider environments.

5.4.3.3 Sharing a Catalog

The key question when deciding to share a catalog is whether you need to share catalog items with all the users in your organization or a subset. For instance, sharing a catalog could make media files available to all users in your organization. A more restricted use case might involve a group of individuals in an organization who are working on a specific application or operating system and want to share a media file among themselves.

To access a shared catalog, users need the View Private and Shared Catalogs permission. This permission is not assigned to all roles by default.

5.4.3.4 Publishing a Catalog

You can publish a catalog during the creation process, or you can select an existing catalog, right-click, and select Publish.

5.4.3.4.1 Enterprise Environment Use Case

Within an enterprise organization, it is not uncommon for the IT team to create its own smaller organizations to build and update vApp templates. These templates are then shared with other business units through the global catalog and are aligned with corporate build standards to reduce variances and support increased security.

5.4.3.4.2 Service Provider Environment Use Case

Service providers often allow individual organizations to manage their own catalogs where the service provider offers a compute resource instead of a service. Some service providers who seek to differentiate themselves or offer additional services, might publish common ISO files or basic virtual machine configurations consistent with licensing implications. Service providers might also offer published catalogs that contain applications that software vendors have developed or configured.

ISO images cannot be shared with different organizations in a published catalog. For an ISO image to be mapped to a virtual machine, the ISO image must be available in the same organization virtual datacenter as the virtual machine.

5.4.3.5 Media File Limitations

vCloud Director does not permit media file sharing outside an organization. This means that even if a catalog is published and vApp templates are available, the media files are not. To address this issue, build local organization catalogs and share those catalogs with the entire organization. All users should have the View Private and Shared Catalogs permission, but the vApp User role does not provide this permission by default.

5.4.3.6 Updating vApp Templates

A user's capability to update vApp templates and hardware and network configuration details depends on the permissions delegated to the role associated with the user's account. For example:

- **vApp User:** This role does not allow the user to reconfigure vApps or vApp templates. Users cannot modify the compute resource or disk, or view the catalog or existing vApps, unless they are shared with them. The user who owns the vApp can add and remove network interface controllers (NICs) and update the networks to which a vApp is connected.
- **vApp Author:** This role allows for the provisioning of vApps but does not permit access to published catalogs by default. The user must create virtual machines from scratch unless granted access to the published or shared catalogs. The user can update vApp and virtual machine configurations such as CPU, RAM, and networking.

The effect of these permissions can differ, depending on whether a vApp is shared or owned. For these permissions to apply, the user must *own* the vApp. When the vApp is shared, the user can be granted read only, read/write, or full control permissions.

5.4.3.7 Deploying vApps

A user's capability to deploy vApp templates depends on the user's role and the permissions delegated. For example:

- **vApp User:** This role can deploy vApps from a catalog and copy it to an alternative organization virtual datacenter.
- **vApp Author:** With the proper permissions, this role can deploy vApps and select a destination organization virtual datacenter. Following deployment, the vApp author can copy a vApp from one organization virtual datacenter to another in the same way a vApp user or the vApp author can move a vApp from one organization virtual datacenter to another. A vApp author can also add the vApp to the catalog.

5.4.3.8 Selecting Networks

The impact of using a catalog on network connectivity is subtly different, depending on whether vApp network or organization virtual datacenter network types are in use.

5.4.3.8.1 Internal vApp Networks

When a vApp containing internal vApp networks is deployed, the configuration of the internal networks is consistent with the configuration at the time the vApp was added to the catalog. The configuration, including firewall rules, is predefined and does not need to be updated. A user with the appropriate permissions can change this configuration.

The exception to this rule is when you use network address translation (NAT) with the default one-to-one mapping configuration. All virtual machines connected to the given vApp network use this NAT configuration automatically, regardless of any change you made when creating the vApp. For example, if a vApp containing three virtual machines is created and mapped to an organization virtual datacenter network with NAT, three NAT-routed IP addresses are allocated. Although it is possible to disable these IP addresses manually, as in the LAMP stack example, changes are lost when the vApp is deployed from the catalog. For the changes to remain in effect, use the port forwarding approach in which all rules are retained as they would be for firewalls.

5.4.3.8.2 Organization Virtual Datacenter Networks

For a vApp and its associated virtual machines to have connectivity outside the vApp, the virtual machines must be connected to an internal or external organization virtual datacenter network. The organization administrator usually creates and defines available organization virtual datacenter networks. When the vApp is deployed, it is automatically attached to the organization virtual datacenter network defined when it was created and uploaded to the catalog. It is also possible for the user to select which network to connect to the virtual machine.

A vApp deployed from a published catalog created in a different organization might have a different or invalid network defined, in which case the user should select a valid organization virtual datacenter network and attach the vApp.

5.5 Creating and Managing vApps

The vApp is a virtual application container and is the basic construct for workloads in a vCloud deployment. vCloud vApps are similar to vApps in vSphere, but vCloud extends the attributes of a vApp. A vSphere and vCloud Director vApp can contain one or more virtual machines. A multitiered vCloud vApp includes the attributes of each component—SLAs, role-based access controls (RBAC), and lifecycle management.

5.5.1 Migrating Workloads to a vCloud

Physical workloads cannot be directly migrated to a vCloud. However, they can be migrated after they have been initially migrated to vSphere.

5.5.1.1 Migrating Physical Workloads to vSphere

Physical machines cannot be directly migrated to a vCloud datacenter because of limitations such as device drivers, any hardware dependencies, and the static attributes of a physical system. vCloud requires virtualized workloads. Apart from the basic virtualization foundation, a fully implemented vCloud datacenter also requires availability, scalability, resource pooling, and VMware vSphere Distributed Resource Scheduler™ (DRS). The first stage of moving a physical machine to a vCloud datacenter is to virtualize it on vSphere (see Figure 5.7).

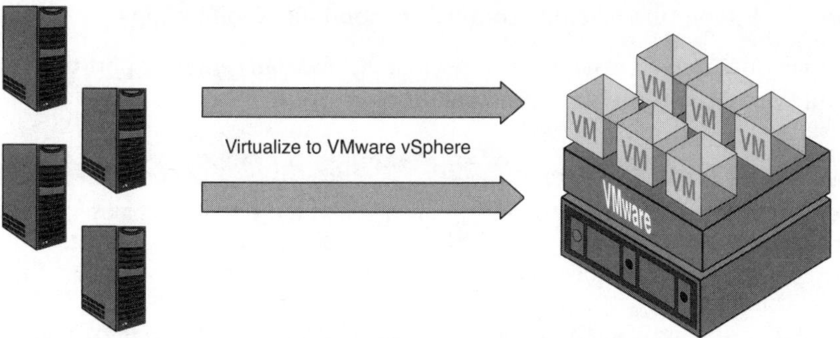

FIGURE 5.7 Migrating from a physical machine to a vSphere virtual machine

5.5.1.2 Migrating Virtual Workloads to vCloud Director

Before migrating the newly created virtual machine to the vCloud datacenter, VMware recommends that you identify a minimum period of time to monitor and optimize the virtual machine hardware for the guest operating system and guest application requirements. For many applications, an appropriate amount of time for this process is a typical full application business cycle, such as the first day through the last day of a business month. As an example, use VMware vCenter Operations Manager™ to determine whether the virtual machine is sized properly.

After the physical machine is virtualized, stabilized, and optimized to run in a virtual datacenter, you can move the virtualized workload to a VMware vCloud datacenter, as shown in Figure 5.8.

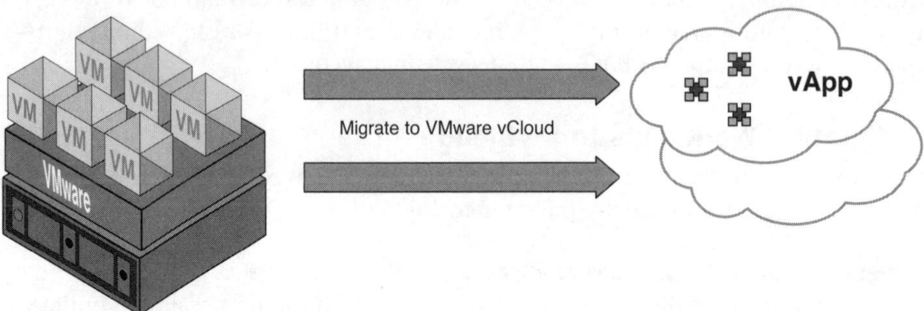

FIGURE 5.8 Migrating from a vSphere virtual machine to a vCloud vApp

In vCloud, a virtual machine is encapsulated by a vApp. A vCloud vApp is a logical entity comprising one or more virtual machines. It uses the Open Virtualization Format (OVF) to specify and encapsulate all components of a multitier application and the associated operational policies and service levels. A vCloud vApp might or might not be associated with vApp networks for intervirtual machine communication in a vCloud vApp.

To move a virtual machine from a virtual datacenter to a vCloud datacenter, export the virtual machine and then import it in OVF file format.

NOTE

If vCloud Director is attached to a vCenter server, you can import the virtual machines without having to export them.

OVF is an industry standard approved and certified by the Distributed Management Task Force (DMTF). A standard OVF package consists of the following components:

- At least one OVF descriptor with the extension `.ovf`
- Zero or one OVF manifest with the extension `.mf` (contains the SHA-1 digests of individual files in the package)
- Zero or one OVF certificate with the extension `.cert` (contains a digest of the manifest file and Base64-encoded X.509 signed certificate)
- Zero or more disk image files with extension `.vmdk` (required for VMware vCloud)
- Zero or more additional resource files, such as ISO images

Several methods enable you to convert a virtual machine or a vApp to an OVF package that by the organizations and catalogs in the vCloud datacenter can consume directly:

- Export and upload the OVF manually:
  - Use the vSphere Client™ to export the OVF file manually and select Catalogs—Upload in the vCloud UI to upload the OVF file. The user privilege required for this operation is at least catalog author, organization administrator, or system administrator.
  - Manually import directly into the vCloud from a connected vCenter instance. The virtual machine must be powered off, without any snapshots or vSphere fault tolerance enabled. Select Catalogs > Import from vSphere in the vCloud UI to import the virtual machine (see Figure 5.9). This operation requires the system administrator user privilege.

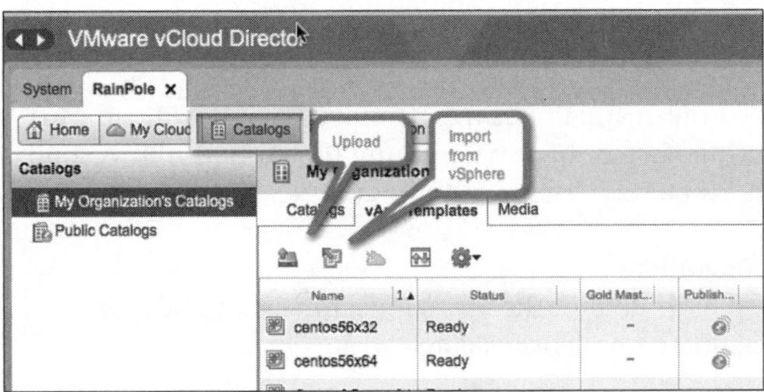

FIGURE 5.9 Manually import to vCloud

- Use a hybrid vCloud plug-in, such as VMware vCloud Connector™. The vCloud Connector virtual appliance must be installed and configured to be used with the source vCenter instance. You must also add a vCloud to vCloud Connector to manage it.

You can use any of these methods to move workloads into the vCloud, but first consider and understand the limitations imposed by the physical locations of the vCloud environments.

5.5.1.3 vApp Migration

In conjunction with vCloud Connector, a hybrid vCloud enables vApps to move between public and private vCloud services. For versions earlier than vCloud Director 5.1, some configurable vApp elements are not transported with the migration process. Keep track of what is and is not transported because you might need to reconfigure the vApp after the migration so that it functions properly. You can view the configuration parameters from two perspectives—from the vApp itself or the virtual machines within the vApp. With vCloud Director 5.1, lossless OVF export is provided to enable greater portability between vCloud environments.

NOTE

Metadata defined on vCloud entities is not transported during the migration process.

5.5.1.3.1 Migration Process

To move a vApp from vCloud A to vCloud B with the vCloud Connector:

1. Export the virtual machines in the vApp from vCloud A to an OVF.
2. Stage them on the vCloud Connector appliance with the vCloud API. The data is transferred to the vCloud Connector appliance over HTTPS.
3. Use the `HTTPS upload` command to upload the staged OVF to vCloud B.
4. Import the OVF into vCloud B's catalog or directly to an organization datacenter.

The migration process can be carried out manually using the upload and download capabilities of the vCloud Director user interface or by programming the vCloud API. vCloud Connector simplifies vApp migrations but is not required.

5.5.1.3.2 vApp Power Action Configuration

When a vApp is migrated, the vApp itself defines the virtual machine start and stop settings within the vApp. These parameters are encapsulated within the vApp:

- Start/Stop Order
- Start Action
- Start Delay
- Stop Action
- Stop Delay

All these parameters are transferred with the vApp from one vCloud to another. The configuration in vCloud A remains consistent in vCloud B.

5.5.1.3.3 vApp Network Configuration

Configuration parameters are associated with virtual machines in the migrated vApp, including network segments (vApp networks) that are private to the vApp itself in the source vCloud. Some of these configuration items are maintained during a migration; others require reconfiguration by the vApp user after migration.

vApp networks are not maintained across a vCloud migration—vApp networks that are defined in a vApp in vCloud A are *not* created and mapped to the virtual machines within the vApp in vCloud B. Assuming that vCloud A and vCloud B use the same network topology, after moving the application to vCloud B, the end user must complete the configuration process by re-creating the vApp networks as they were defined in vCloud A.

5.5.1.3.4 Hardware Configuration

Hard disk configuration and disk bus type are maintained across a vCloud migration. If a specific disk bus type is selected for a virtual machine's disk, this setting is maintained when the virtual machine migrates from vCloud A to vCloud B.

In versions earlier than vCloud Director 5.1, network interface assignments, configuration types, and network adapter types are not maintained across a vCloud migration. When the vApp is transferred, the virtual machine network interfaces revert to the default adapter type, flexible. With vCloud Director 5.1, the lossless OVF export capability preserves these settings.

IP addresses are not held across a vApp migration and must be reconfigured to the new vCloud IP addressing scheme. The end user must reconfigure all virtual machine network adapter settings for a migrated vApp.

5.5.1.3.5 Guest OS Customization

Even if Enable Guest Customization is not selected in vCloud A, it is enabled in vCloud B when the vApp is migrated, regardless of whether the virtual machine has an installed operating system and VMware Tools™.

Most password reset parameters are maintained. When the password reset parameters are configured for the virtual machine, the settings transfer from vCloud A to vCloud B. However, if the virtual machine configuration specifies a default local administrator password, this information does not transfer to vCloud B. The end user must re-enter the default password for the virtual machine.

5.5.1.3.6 Resource Allocation

Resource allocation controls set on the individual virtual machines in a vApp are maintained across a migration from vCloud A to vCloud B. However, for the settings to be used, the vApp must be deployed to a virtual datacenter that uses a reservation pool allocation model. Datacenters that use the allocation pool or pay as you go model do not support resource allocation controls.

Table 5.2 summarizes vApp parameters and indicates whether they are maintained across a migration.

TABLE 5.2 vApp Parameters

Configuration Item	Maintained?	Notes
Start/stop order	Yes	
Start action	Yes	
Stop action	Yes	
Start/stop delay	Yes	
vApp networks	No	Networks and associated configurations are lost. Networks must be redefined and NICs attached.

Configuration Item	Maintained?	Notes
NIC assignment (non-vApp network)	No	NICs must be reassigned.
Guest customization enabled	No	Check box is selected in target vCloud.
CPU hot add	No	
Memory hot add	No	
Synchronize virtual machine time	No	
Password reset	Yes	
Default password	No	Defaults to blank field in UI.
Disk bus type	Yes	
Network adapter type	No	Defaults to flexible.
Resource allocation	Yes	When vApp is deployed to reservation pool virtual datacenter.
OVF properties	Yes	Accessed through VMware Tools and used for scripting, for fetching, and for post-configuration and provisioning.

5.5.2 Using vCloud Workloads

The following sections provide examples of logging into vCloud Director, deploying a vApp, interacting with the vApp, and managing runtime and storage leases.

5.5.2.1 Logging into the vCloud Director Portal

vCloud Director requires Microsoft Internet Explorer 7.0 or later, or Mozilla Firefox 3.x or later. For advanced browser configuration options, see the *vCloud Director User's Guide* (www.vmware.com/support/pubs/vcd_pubs.html).

The following procedure provides an example of how a consumer logs into the vCloud Director portal.

To log into the vCloud Director portal:

1. Go to your organization URL (https://<vCloud-Director-IP-address>/cloud/org/<OrganizationName>/).

2. To log in, enter your username and password, as provided by your administrator (see Figure 5.10).

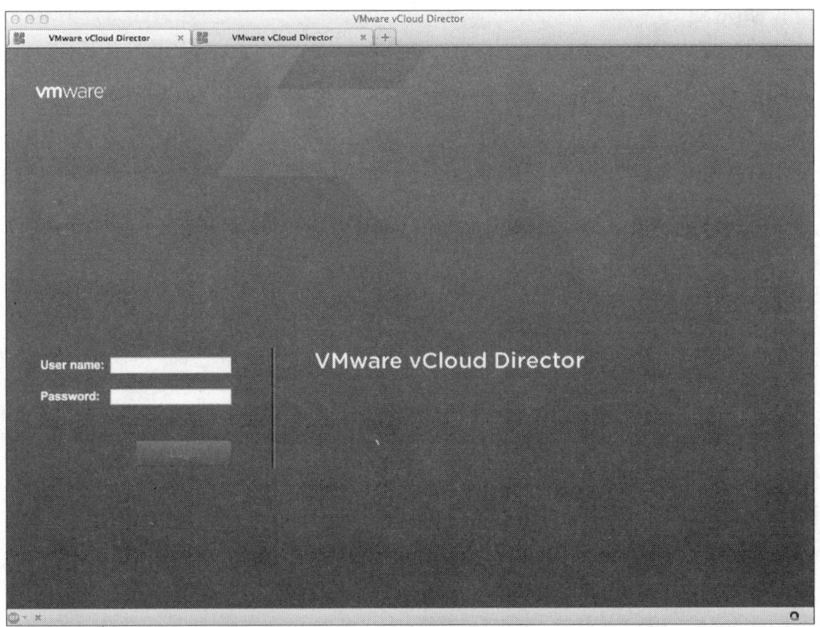

FIGURE 5.10 vCloud Director login screen

3. After you have logged in, you can perform various tasks from the main vCloud Director Home view (see Figure 5.11).

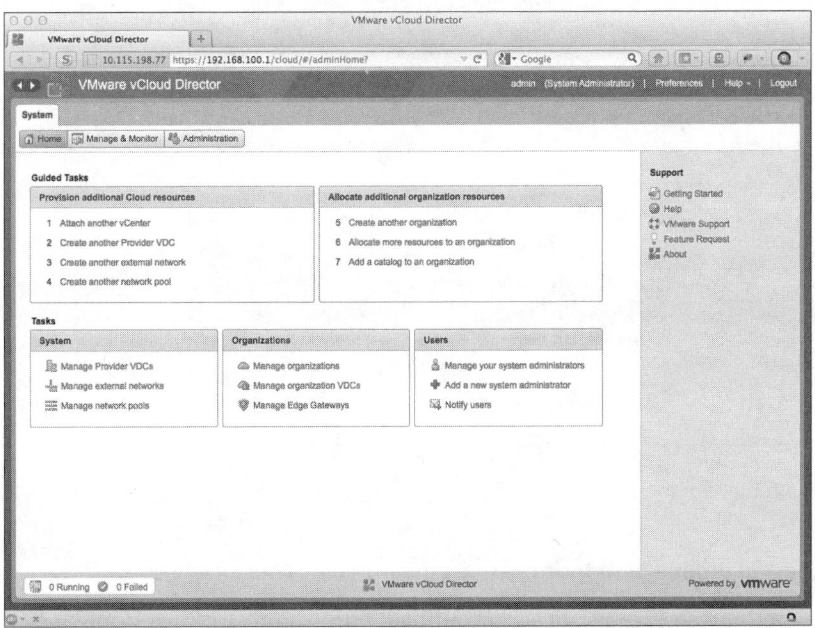

FIGURE 5.11 vCloud Director Home view

5.5.2.2 Deploying a vApp

The following procedure provides an example of how a consumer can deploy a vCloud vApp from a catalog.

To deploy a vApp from a catalog:

1. On the vCloud Director administration screen, click Add vApp from Catalog.
2. Review the available catalogs and select a vApp. (See Figure 5.12.)

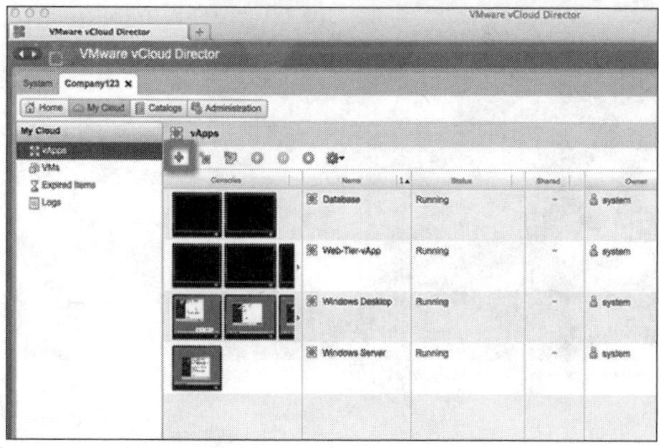

FIGURE 5.12 vApp listing for Company123

3. On the vApp Template screen (see Figure 5.13), click Next (not shown).

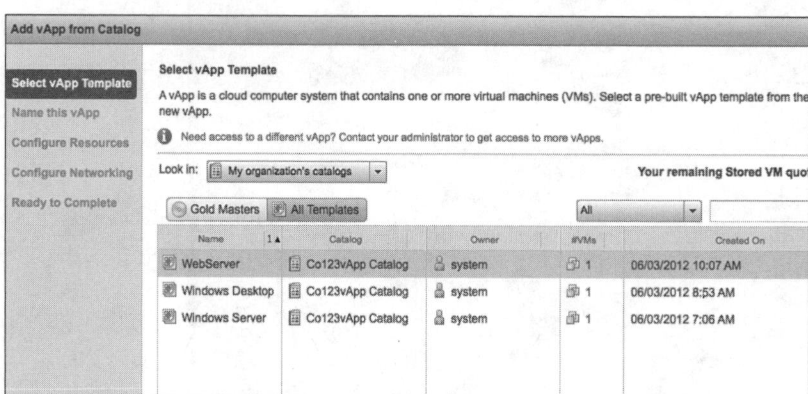

FIGURE 5.13 vApp template screen

4. Select a name and enter a description (see Figure 5.14) for your new vApp.

   Usually, runtime and storage leases are predefined, but in some cases, you might be permitted to specify a time period.

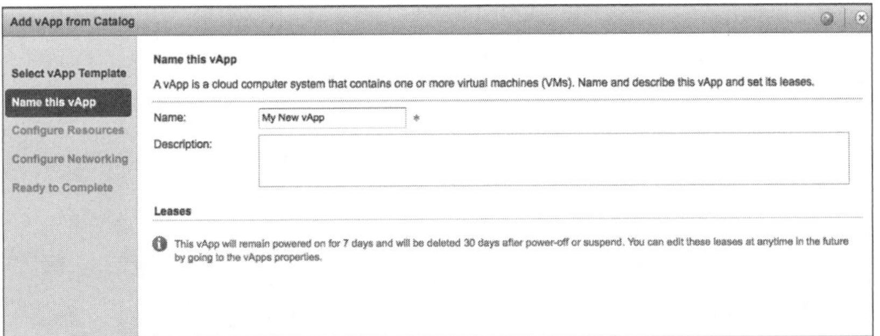

FIGURE 5.14 vApp name and description entry screen

5. Select the destination organization virtual datacenter from the Virtual Datacenter drop-down menu.
6. Select the storage profile for this vApp. This is a new feature in vCloud Director 5.1.
7. On the vApp storage configuration screen (see Figure 5.15), click Next.

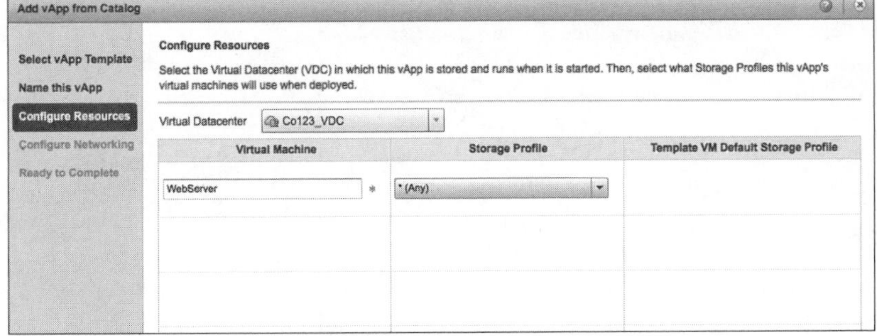

FIGURE 5.15 vApp storage configuration screen

8. Specify the full name and computer name for each virtual machine in the vApp.
9. Select the network and IP address assignment. Typically, an external or internal network is available.
10. On the vApp network configuration screen (see Figure 5.16), click Next.

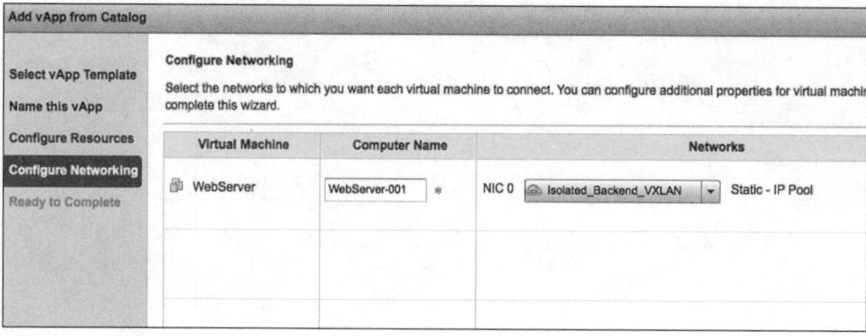

FIGURE 5.16 vApp network configuration screen

11. On the Ready to Complete screen, verify that everything is correct.
12. Click Finish.
13. The status for the requested vApp deployment displays on the main administration screen (see Figure 5.17).

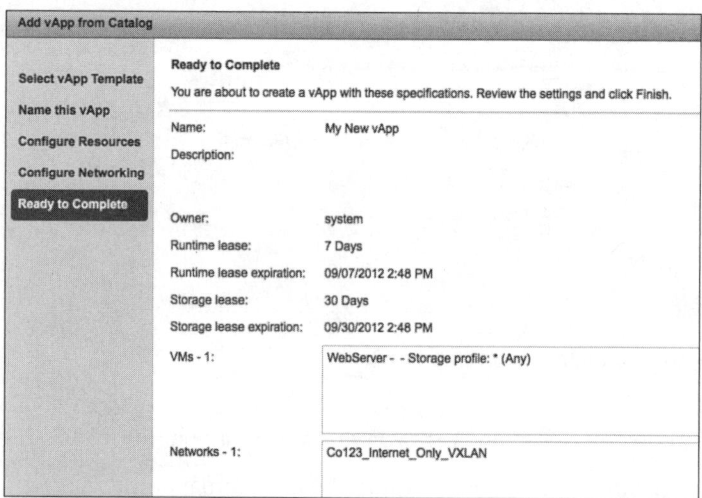

FIGURE 5.17 vApp review and confirmation screen

5.5.2.3 Interacting with the vApp

The following example illustrates the deployed vApp options available to a user and describes where and how to implement configuration changes.

To interact with the vApp:

1. From the vCloud Director Organization Administration screen, click My Cloud.
2. From the list of vApps, right-click the desired vApp to display an Actions menu (see Figure 5.18).

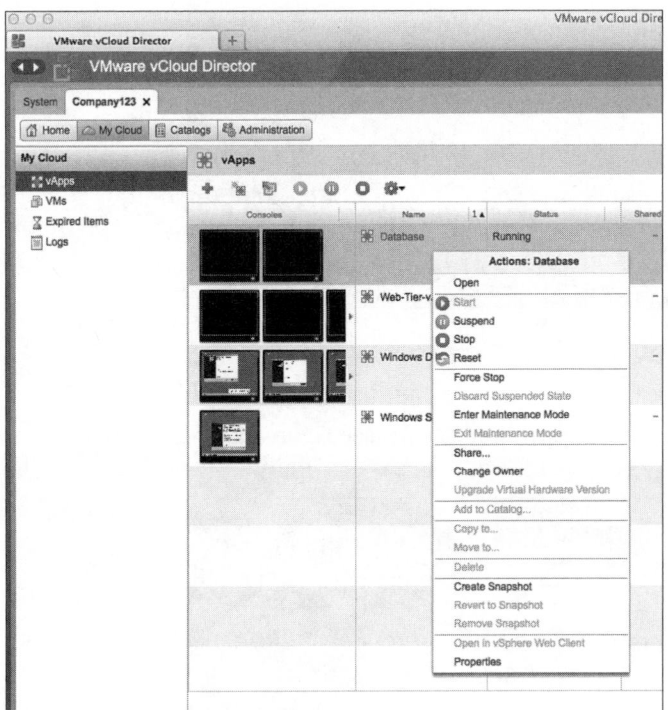

FIGURE 5.18 Selecting a vApp action

When a vApp is powered on, all virtual machines within that vApp are also powered on. You can modify this behavior by selecting Properties in the Actions menu, clicking the Starting and Stopping VMs tab, and using the drop-down menus to modify and reorder start and stop actions. Figure 5.19 shows this.

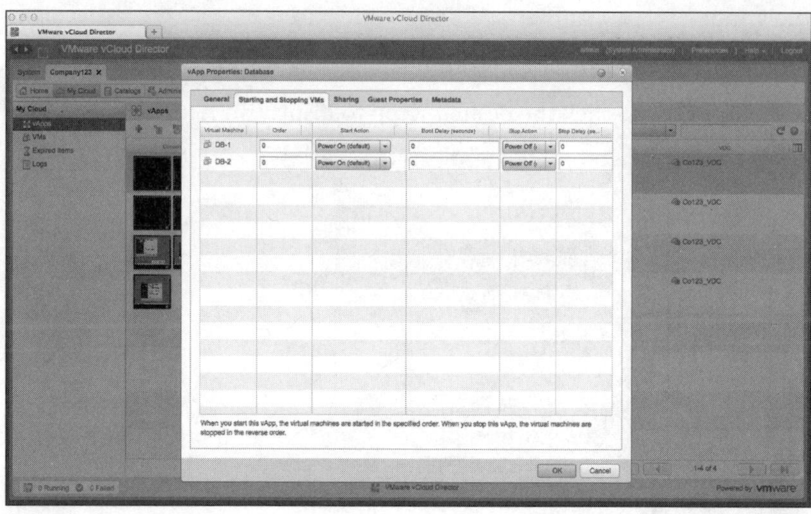

FIGURE 5.19 vApp properties

3. Under the Metadata tab, enter any arbitrary value (see Figure 5.20).

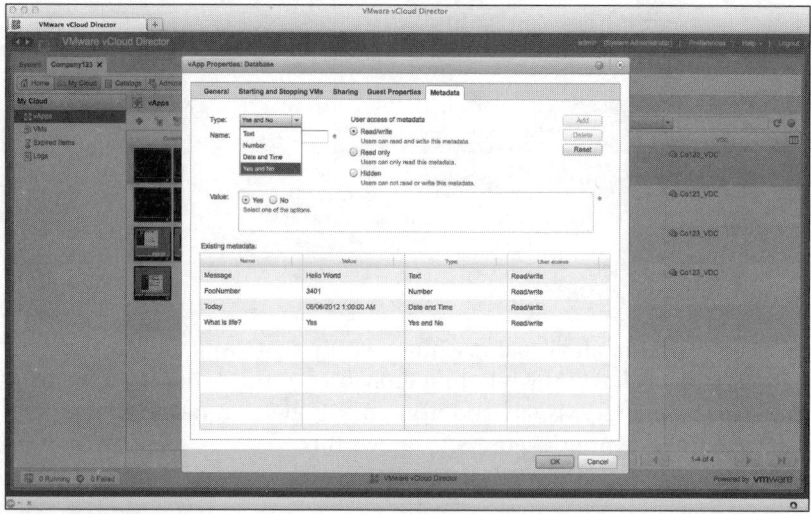

FIGURE 5.20 vApp metadata properties

4. To view a diagram of all virtual machines, see the networking details and access each virtual machine individually (see Figure 5.21).

5. Select a vApp from the vApp menu.

6. Click Open.

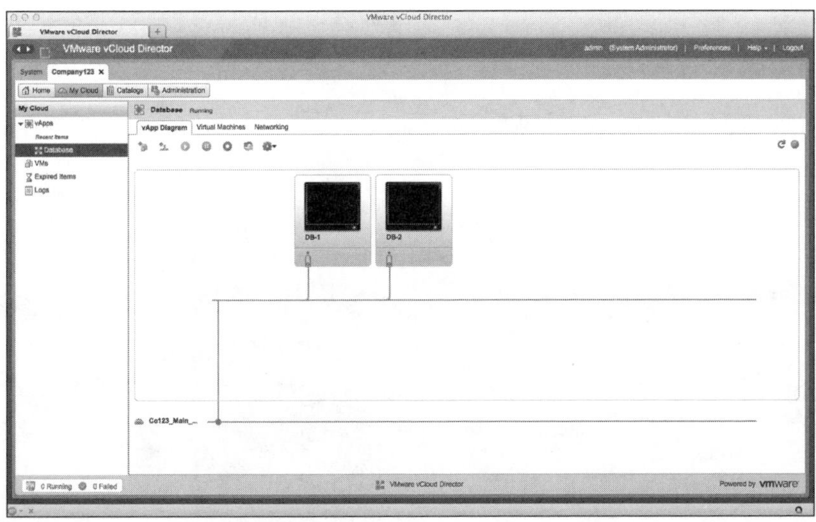

FIGURE 5.21 vApp stucture with two virtual machines

7. Click the Virtual Machines tab to gain console access to each machine.
8. Right-click the console to access virtual machine console controls.

5.5.2.4 Runtime and Storage Leases

Because vCloud is a shared environment, your administrator might specify *runtime leases* and *storage leases* to prevent you from indefinitely running your vCloud computing resources. Leases provide a level of control over an organization's storage and compute resources by specifying the maximum amount of time that vApps can run and that vApps and vApp templates can be stored. The computing and storage resources that represent your vCloud computing system expire at a point determined by your vCloud administrator and are automatically freed up for other uses at that time.

The runtime lease prevents inactive vApps from consuming compute resources. If a virtual machine is unused, it is powered down so that memory and compute resources can be used for other workloads. The storage lease functions the same way but also reclaims storage.

The vCloud administrator defines what happens when these leases expire. In the following example, the runtime lease is initially set to 14 days. The user can log in and reset to extend the lease. In this example, the user extends the lease for an additional 14 days.

As your vApp approaches the expiration date of its lease, you typically receive an expiration notice in email.

To extend the lease of a running vApp (see Figure 5.22):

1. Choose Manage vApps from the Home tab.
2. Right-click your vApp.

3. Select Properties.
4. Select Reset Leases.
5. Change the values of the leases as desired.
6. Click OK.

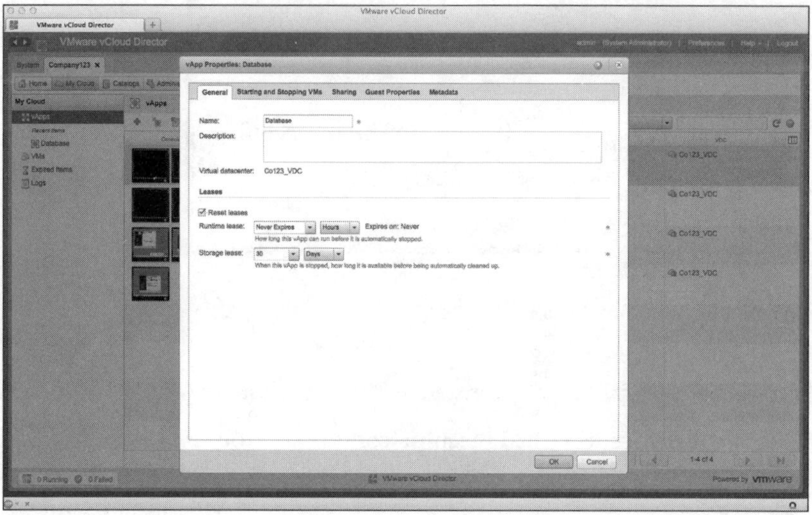

FIGURE 5.22 Extending a vApp lease

After the virtual machine is stopped when the runtime lease expires, the storage lease goes into effect. Depending on the configuration the administrator sets, the vApp is moved to an expired state or deleted.

Ask your administrator for the default options for your organization. The following quotas and limits can be applied:

- Running virtual machines quota
- Stored virtual machines quota
- Number of resource-intensive operations per user limit
- Number of resource-intensive operations per organization limit
- Number of simultaneous connections per virtual machine limit

Similarly, the running virtual machine and stored virtual machine quotas can be applied to individual users. As a user, you can find out your individual limits by clicking Administration > Users, right-clicking your user account, and selecting Properties. Scroll to the bottom to see the defined quotas. (See Figure 5.23.)

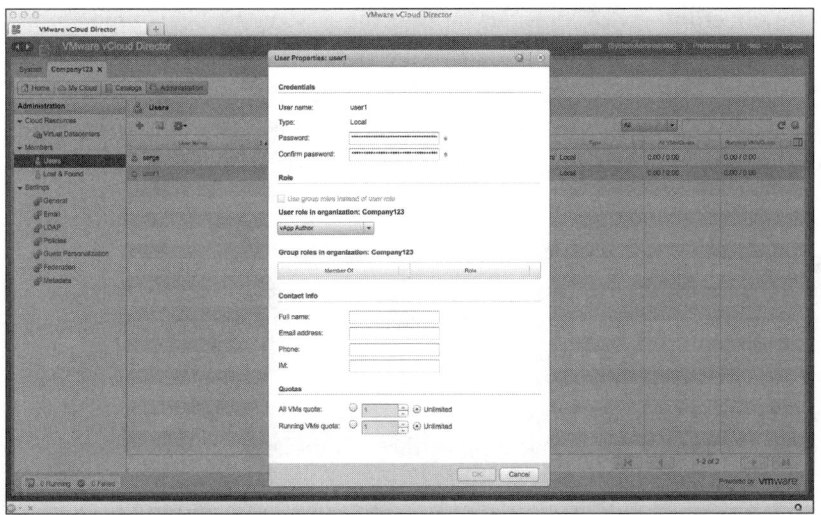

FIGURE 5.23 User properties

If your vApp is missing, the storage lease of your vApp might have expired. Contact your administrator to determine whether your vApp has expired and might be recoverable or was deleted and might not be recoverable.

5.5.3 Directory Services in vCloud

Directory services serve several purposes in vCloud Director. This discussion refers to Microsoft Active Directory, but the same considerations apply for other directory services. Directory services used with vCloud Director include authentication services in the following areas:

- **Infrastructure:** vCloud Director, vCenter, and other supporting applications that vCloud Director does not manage
- **vCloud Director Management:** Within the vCloud Director portal for the system and organization realms
- **Organizational:** Internal to an organization, including vApps contained in an organization

NOTE

For considerations that apply to running Active Directory or other clock-shift sensitive directory services within a virtual environment, see the white paper *Virtualizing a Windows Active Directory Domain Infrastructure* (www.vmware.com/files/pdf/Virtualizing_Windows_Active_Directory.pdf).

The best location for directory services depends on how the services are being used. Locations can be external to an organization, shared inside an organization, or encapsulated and distributed per vApp.

Placement can be guided based on a few key measures. Use the information in the following sections in conjunction with other reference materials to form the basis for an appropriate design.

5.5.3.1 Hosting Locations for Directory Services

When selecting the placement of directory servers in the vCloud, consider the strict availability and longevity requirements for directory service servers in balance with the applications that the deployed instance will support.

5.5.3.1.1 External to the vCloud

VMware recommends that any services that support the vCloud Director instance and infrastructure be hosted externally to the vCloud Director managed environment. Specifically, directory services should be hosted external to the vCloud and can be configured using standard procedures for virtualizing the service. Follow design guidelines for virtualizing Active Directory and other directory platforms. Using vCloud does not change these practices.

In a private vCloud architecture, directory services can be hosted external to the vCloud environment if there is no geographical separation between host platforms.

5.5.3.1.2 Within the vCloud

vCloud-hosted applications are dependent on directory service. After you determine the level of dependency, performance gains are achieved by encapsulating and distributing directory servers with dependent vApps services that are offered in the vCloud.

The expiration of runtime and storage leases for vApp hosting directory services can lead to unexpected outages for dependent applications. A solution to vApp expiration is to create a separate vCloud Director organization that has indefinite leases to host services that should not expire.

Provide for isolation between any redundant directory servers hosted within vCloud. To avoid single points of failure, it might be necessary to distribute directory servers over multiple provider virtual datacenters that do not share physical dependencies.

5.5.3.1.3 Single Sign-On

As IT systems proliferate to support business processes, users and system administrators face an increasingly complicated interface. Users typically have to sign on to multiple systems, with multiple sign-on dialogs that might involve different usernames and authentication information. System administrators must coordinate and manage user accounts within each system to maintain the integrity of security policy enforcement.

The goal of the vCloud Director 5.1 Web Single Sign-On (SSO) feature is to simplify the sign-on process to provide an authentication service that service providers and enterprise customers can use.

Access control is a key security model component because it restricts unauthorized users. It is part of what is known as the *triple A process* of authentication, authorization, and accountability. Authentication systems have traditionally been based on passwords, and many organizations now use more advanced technologies, such as tokens or biometrics. Some organizations enforce two-factor authentication.

Although knowing who should be authenticated serves as a basis of access control, authorization is also an issue. Authorization defines what access the user has and what capabilities are available. A vCloud administrator is normally authorized to perform more functions than an ordinary user. To control access to the end tenant's vCloud organization, limit authorization to only the required functions.

Single Sign-On addresses a problem common to all service providers and enterprise customers. Various systems within the service provider and enterprise likely require the user to log on to each system with different credentials. Single Sign-On addresses this problem by authenticating users once to a single authentication authority and then providing access to all other protected resources without reauthenticating. Kerberos and directory services are examples of authentication systems that can implement Single Sign-On. Before implementing Single Sign-On, consider the security implications. For example, if an attacker can authenticate as a given individual, that attacker can then access multiple systems.

Compliance requires that identities be controlled. *Risk management* involves event identification, analysis, and response mechanisms faced by a service provider or enterprise. Risk management is not only a defensive operation to minimize risk effects; it is also proactive, enabling the service provider or enterprise to take advantage of the triggering of a risk event. *Compliance* is the process of implementing procedures to meet the governance policy. Compliance requires a level of monitoring, analysis, and reporting. These elements are tied to identity management. Governance policies establish who has access to which functions in the service provider or enterprise and the conditions that are imposed on that access.

Service providers and enterprises typically request Single Sign-On functionality because they want end tenants to log into their own portals and be redirected to the vCloud Director portal without reauthenticating. Service providers also encourage Single Sign-On because it significantly decreases administrative costs by reducing password-related tasks and support. Handling authentication can be done on a centralized basis rather than a per-application basis. Single Sign-On additionally enhances security and compliance for service providers and enterprises by providing a central facility to log all system and application access.

vCloud Director and its Single Sign-On feature must be interoperable and work with the existing service provider and enterprise infrastructures. Providing interoperability greatly increases the use of the vCloud Director Single Sign-On functionality and reduces the inconvenience users experience when asked to reauthenticate.

Service providers and enterprises can offer a vCloud Director web-based portal application to enable vCloud end tenants to administer and troubleshoot identity information and perform self-service requests to add, remove, or change user roles.

5.5.4 vApp Deployment Readiness

vApp deployment readiness metrics should be assessed before deploying a vApp. These include vApp design considerations, vApp limitations inside vCloud, and vApp validation that should be performed before uploading to a vCloud service catalog.

5.5.4.1 vApp Design Considerations

A vCloud vApp differs from a vSphere vApp in the way it is instantiated and consumed in the vCloud. A vApp is a container for a distributed software solution and is the standard unit of deployment in vCloud Director. It allows power-on and -off operations to be defined and ordered, consists of one or more virtual machines, and can be imported or exported as an OVF package. A vCloud vApp can have additional vCloud-specific constructs such as networks and security definitions.

5.5.4.1.1 General Design Considerations

Some general recommendations for designing vApps include the following:

- Default to one vCPU unless requirements call for more (multithreaded application virtual machines).
- Always install the latest version of VMware Tools.
- Deploy virtual machines using default shares, reservations, and limit settings unless a clear requirement exists to avoid defaults.
- For virtual network adaptors, use VMXNET3 where supported.
- Secure virtual machines as you would physical machines.
- Use standard virtual machine naming conventions.

5.5.4.1.2 vApp and Virtual Machine Hardware Version Considerations

vSphere 5.1 supports virtual machine hardware version 9. This support is carried over to vCloud Director. For maximum configuration values, see *VMware Configuration Maximums (VMware vSphere 5.1)* (www.vmware.com/pdf/vsphere5/r51/vsphere-51-configuration-maximums.pdf). The major use cases for using hardware version 9 follow:

- **Windows 8 XP mode:** XP mode allows a virtualized Windows XP instance to run on Windows 8 for compatibility with older applications that do not run natively on Windows 8. Users running XP mode in Windows 8 must choose an organization virtual datacenter that is backed by a provider virtual datacenter with support for virtual hardware version 9. After adding support for virtual hardware version 9, you must also enable the Nested HV feature.
- **64-bit nested virtualization:** Hyper-V and virtualized VMware vSphere ESXi™ nested virtualization can be helpful for nonproduction use cases, such as training and demonstration environments. Virtualized Hyper-V or virtualized ESXi running nested 64-bit virtual machines requires virtual hardware version 9 with the Nested HV feature enabled.

- **CPU-intensive workloads:** Running a CPU-intensive workload in a virtual machine requiring between 32 and 64 vCPUs requires virtual hardware version 9.

5.5.4.1.3 Network Design Considerations

A vApp network provides network connectivity to virtual machines within a vApp. Virtual machines in a vApp use an organization virtual datacenter network to connect to the outside world or to other vApps in the organization. A vApp network is backed by a network pool unless it is directly attached to an organization virtual datacenter network that is directly attached to an external network. vApp networks are created with one of the following methods:

- **Dynamic:** Created when a vApp is directly connected to an organization virtual datacenter network and deployed in fenced mode. No opportunity exists to use the DHCP, NAT, or firewall services at the vApp network level because this network is created automatically. It is not accessible from the vCloud UI.
- **Manual:** Created and either connected to an organization virtual datacenter network in NAT mode or left isolated. DHCP, NAT, and firewall service rules can be defined manually at the vApp network level as needed.

A vApp network can be directly connected to an organization virtual datacenter network, whether routed, isolated, or connected with NAT. The following are types of vApp networks:

- **Direct:** Virtual machines in a vApp are configured to connect directly to the organization virtual datacenter network port group and are assigned IP addresses from the organization's network range.
- **NAT-routed:** vApps are protected behind a VMware vCloud Networking and Security Edge (Edge) instance that provides NAT services for outbound and inbound access.
- **Fenced:** Identical virtual machines can exist in different vApps by isolating their MAC addresses. Fenced vApps are protected behind an Edge instance with proxy Address Resolution Protocol (ARP) capabilities.
- **None:** These networks are isolated, with no external access to an organization virtual datacenter network or other vApps in the organization.

The following sections describe the most common vApp network configurations.

5.5.4.1.4 Direct—External Organization Virtual Datacenter Network

Connecting a vApp to an organization virtual datacenter network that has a *direct* connection to an external network connects the vApp directly to the external network and deploys the vApp there with the external network's IP addressing. Figure 5.24 shows an example vApp with three virtual machines using this configuration.

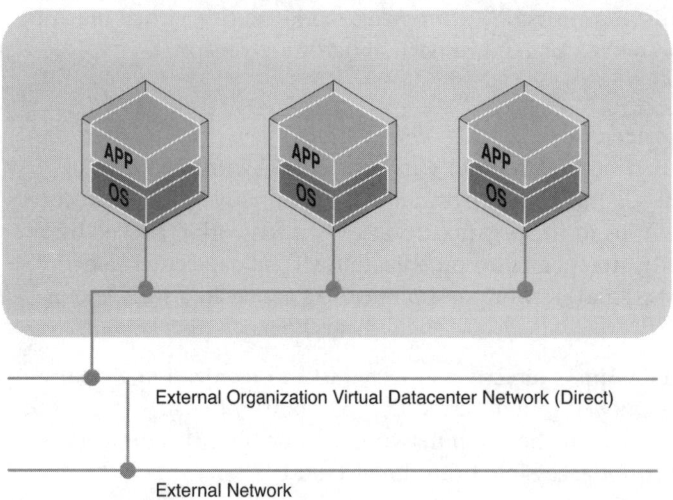

FIGURE 5.24 Direct connection to a directly connected external organization virtual datacenter network

5.5.4.1.5 Direct—External Organization Virtual Datacenter Network (Routed)

If the same example vApp with three virtual machines is connected to an organization virtual datacenter network that has a *routed* connection to an external network, the vApp is connected to an organization virtual datacenter network and is deployed there with the organization virtual datacenter network's IP addressing. The Edge Gateway device then provides a routed connection between the organization virtual datacenter network and the external network. Figure 5.25 shows this scenario.

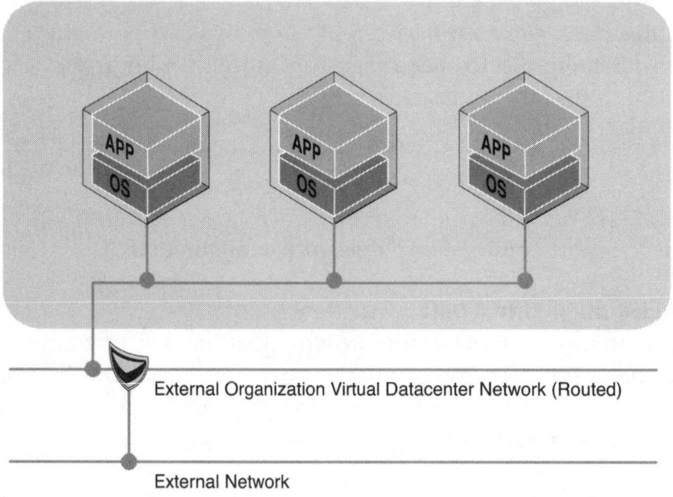

FIGURE 5.25 Direct connection to a routed external organization virtual datacenter network

5.5.4.1.6 Direct—Internal Organization Virtual Datacenter Network (Isolated)

As Figure 5.26 shows, if the same vApp is connected directly to an *isolated* organization virtual datacenter network, the vApp is deployed there with the organization virtual datacenter network's IP addressing.

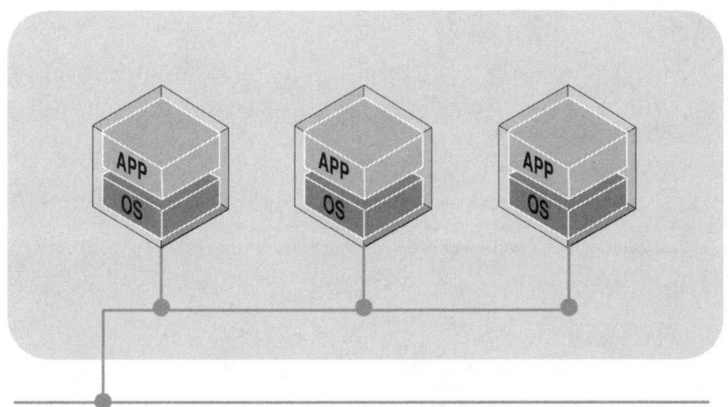

FIGURE 5.26 Direct connection to an isolated internal organization virtual datacenter network

5.5.4.1.7 Fenced—Dynamically or Manually Created

In vCloud Director, a network type is *fenced* when the virtual machines in the vApp share the same Layer 2 network as their organization virtual datacenter network. This is a special case of a NAT-routed network in which the inside and outside addresses of the Edge device are on the same Layer 2 network. In this mode, the Edge device provides proxy ARP services to the virtual machines in the vApp.

From a vApp network perspective, depending on the type of connected organization virtual datacenter network, a NAT or double NAT might occur for incoming or outgoing traffic. The following scenarios describe a double and single NAT situation.

5.5.4.1.8 NAT-Routed—External Organization Virtual Datacenter Network (Routed)

If a vApp configured with a NAT-routed vApp network is connected to an external NAT-routed organization virtual datacenter network, the deployment results in a double NAT. In this scenario, the virtual machines are connected to a NAT-routed vApp network and are deployed there with the vApp network's IP addressing. The first Edge device provides NAT between the vApp network and the organization virtual datacenter network. The second Edge device provides NAT between the organization virtual datacenter network and the external network. Figure 5.27 shows this scenario.

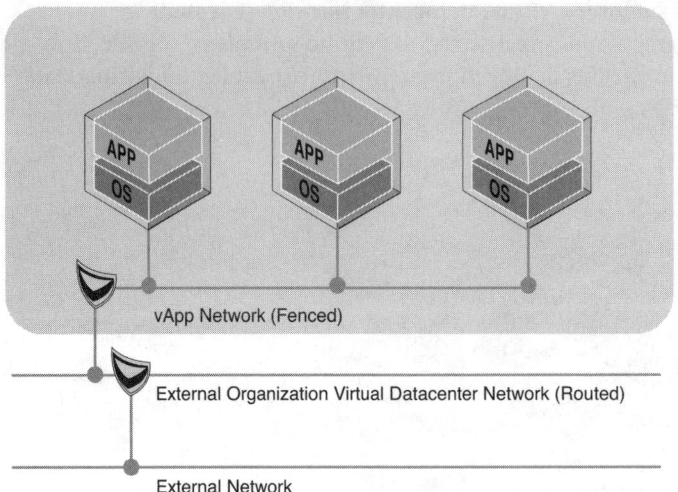

FIGURE 5.27 NAT-routed—external organization virtual datacenter network (routed)

5.5.4.1.9 NAT-Routed—Internal Organization Virtual Datacenter Network (Isolated)

If the same vApp, configured with a NAT-routed vApp network, is connected to an isolated organization virtual datacenter network, the deployment results in a single NAT. The virtual machines are connected to the vApp network and deployed with the vApp network's IP addressing. The Edge device then provides NAT between the vApp network and the organization virtual datacenter network. Figure 5.28 shows this scenario.

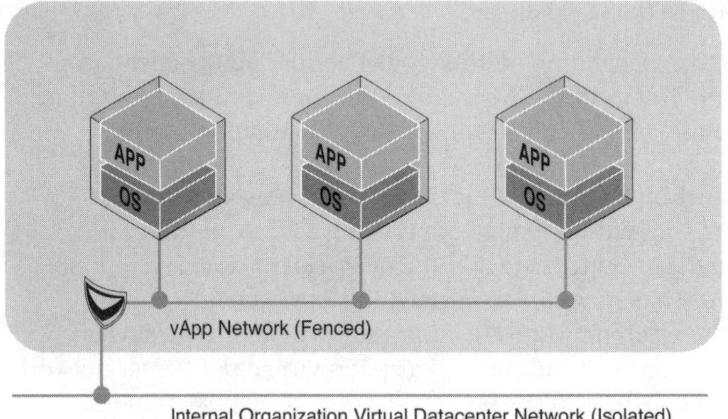

FIGURE 5.28 NAT-routed—Internal organization virtual datacenter network (isolated)

5.5.4.1.10 NAT-Routed—External Organization Virtual Datacenter Network (Direct)

Figure 5.29 shows a scenario in which a vApp is configured with a NAT-routed vApp network that is connected to an external organization virtual datacenter network. The virtual machines are connected to a NAT-routed vApp network and deployed there with the vApp network IP addressing. The Edge device provides NAT between the vApp network and the external network.

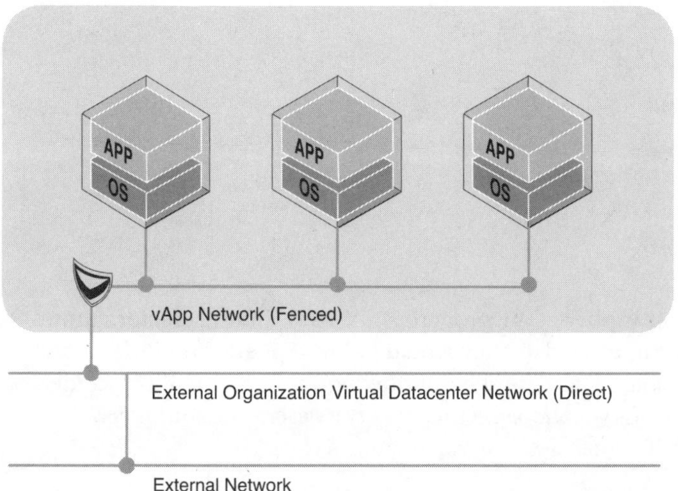

FIGURE 5.29 NAT-routed—external organization virtual datacenter network (direct)

5.5.4.1.11 Isolated vApp Network

A vApp network that is configured with no organization virtual datacenter network connectivity is completely isolated. The network is isolated at Layer 2, and no connectivity outside the vApp is possible. This configuration is usually used to build multitier applications. Figure 5.30 shows this.

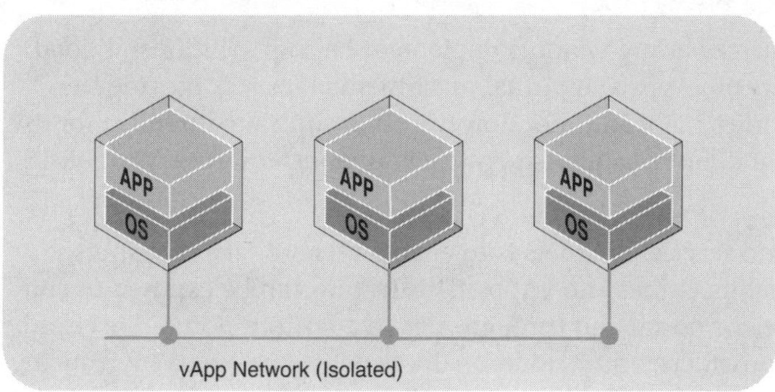

FIGURE 5.30 Isolated vApp network

5

5.5.4.2 vApp Limitations Within vCloud

vCloud Director does not support some OVF sections. Backup limitations and the nature of vCloud Director vApps render vApp backups a complex undertaking.

5.5.4.2.1 OVF Restrictions

Because vCloud Director does not currently support all the OVF sections that vSphere supports, the following sections of the OVF representation of the vSphere vApp are not carried over to vCloud Director:

- `AnnotationSection`
- `DeploymentOptionSection`
- `InstallSection`
- `ProductSection`
- `ResourceAllocationSection`

vCloud Director parses all other vSphere OVF properties. When vCloud Director ignores a section, its contents are not interpreted as they would be by vSphere, and differences in behavior could arise when you instantiate the imported vApp in a virtual datacenter. When a vApp is downloaded from vCloud Director, the OVF descriptor contains only vCloud Director–supported OVF semantics.

5.5.4.2.2 Backup Limitations

Using vCloud APIs for virtual machine backups poses some major limitations for backup of vApps, and the intricate nature of vApp constructs stored in the vCloud Director database requires additional overhead for backups and restores in case of a failure. vApp networks, whether fenced or NAT-routed, are backed by VMware vCloud Networking and Security Manager, making the situation even more complex.

A simpler approach might be to orchestrate vApp backups by using the *full clone* mechanism at scheduled intervals. An orchestration engine such as VMware vCenter Orchestrator™ makes this a reasonable alternative until this capability becomes available through the native APIs or from third-party products or plug-ins.

To help customers and third-party backup vendors implement backup solutions, vCloud Director 5.1 supports snapshots of vApps and virtual machines. Snapshots provide the capability to roll back to an earlier point in time. However, snapshots are intended for use as a temporary resiliency method, not as a permanent backup, disaster recovery, or business continuity process.

One use case for enterprises and service providers is to enable users to take snapshots before they modify their virtual machines and vApps. This feature can be exposed to end users through the vCloud Director portal and through APIs in a custom portal. This can be a value-added feature for the providers, and it additionally benefits customers by reducing the administrator overhead.

Similarly, a third-party vendor can take a snapshot immediately before taking a backup of the vApp and then delete the snapshot after the backup is complete. Customers can schedule backup windows as done in a vSphere environment.

In vCloud Director, virtual machines and vApps can have only one snapshot. Any subsequent creation of snapshots overwrites the previous one. Snapshots are supported on virtual machines and vApps, in both a powered-on or powered-off state. Reverting the snapshot restores the previous state of the virtual machines in which the snapshot was taken. However, it does not restore the network mapping and OVF properties associated with the virtual machines and vApps. While a snapshot is active, the network configuration cannot be modified. An `Undeploy` operation on vApps preserves the snapshot, but cloning and capturing to the catalog operation does not. Snapshots at the vCenter layer are automatically consolidated.

Snapshot consumers must address the following considerations:

- Storage snapshots consumed.
- Storage snapshots consumed in fast-provisioned environments.
- Snapshot management.
- Backup and recovery of vApps and virtual machines with snapshots.
- For a service provider: costs of snapshots are readily made available to the end customer.
- For an enterprise IT provider: snapshot usage affects future storage needs.

5

5.5.4.2.3 Disaster Recovery in vCloud

In vCloud Director 5.1, disaster recovery is not integrated natively with VMware vCenter Site Recovery Manager™. VMware consultants have a workaround to help enterprises protect investments in vCloud. See the following whitepapers:

- **Blog post:** *Overview of Disaster Recovery in vCloud Director* (http://blogs.vmware.com/vcloud/2012/02/overview-of-disaster-recovery-in-vcloud-director.html)
- **Whitepaper:** *VMware vCloud Director Infrastructure Resiliency Case Study* (www.vmware.com/files/pdf/techpaper/vcloud-director-infrastructure-resiliency.pdf)

5.5.4.3 vApp Validations

vCloud APIs have no prebuilt mechanism to automatically evaluate whether a vApp is ready to be uploaded to vCloud Director for consumption. One way to address this is to create a separate user, such as vApp Tester, who would be responsible for checking the validity and functionality of the vApp's readiness. The flow of events could be as follows:

1. The user, vApp Author, creates the vApp to solve a problem or business case.
2. The vApp is passed on to vApp Tester. vApp Author and vApp Tester might have access to a separate, dedicated catalog. vApp Author uploads the vApp to the catalog, and vApp Tester takes it for testing and validation.

3. After vApp Tester completes the functionality testing of the vApp and obtains the expected results, someone with appropriate credentials can upload it to a public or private catalog.

This is similar to the *test* and *dev* roles and responsibilities in a standard vSphere deployment.

5.5.4.4 vApp Lifecycle Considerations

You must understand vApp dependencies and verify that business requirements can continue to be fulfilled throughout the lifecycle.

Providing Infrastructure as a Service (IaaS) requires new approaches to workload management, which can be disruptive, but many benefits exist (see Chapter 4, "Operating a VMware vCloud," for information about proven approaches for managing vCloud environments). VMware vCloud Director supports delivery of Infrastructure as a Service.

When using vCloud Director, one common concern is the underlying network configuration implemented to support deployed vApps, particularly how the configuration impacts network connectivity outside the vCloud and the associated impact on application dependencies.

To effectively design a new vApp, you must have a detailed understanding of application behavior and external dependencies. vCloud Director leverages the Edge networking appliance, which offers DHCP, firewall, NAT, static routing, and VPN capabilities that can be configured and managed from within vCloud Director. Section 5.5.4.1 describes various scenarios that illustrate vApp network configurations with and without Edge.

Figure 5.31 shows an Edge appliance being used to fence a vApp so that it can be isolated, yet it uses NAT for connectivity to and from external resources. This configuration can present challenges for agent-based solutions, such as backup or antivirus updates.

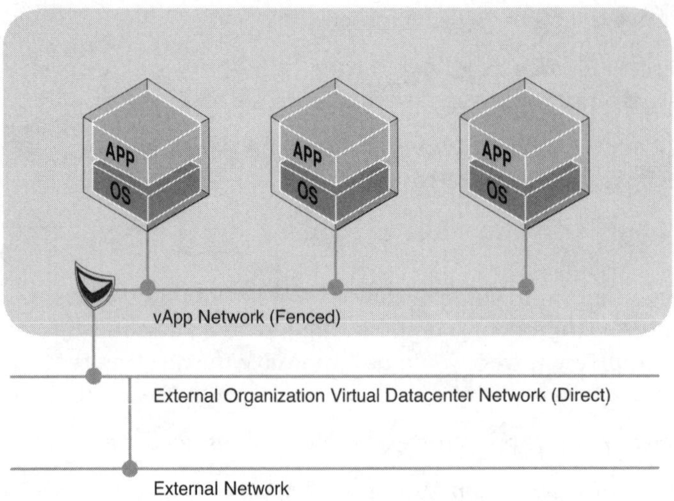

FIGURE 5.31 Sample vApp backed by a fenced network

In this example, private addressing is used behind the Edge appliance, and a single NAT address maps a single public IP address for the web-based application. Access to the vApp from outside the vCloud goes through the public IP address on port 80, which is redirected to the web server using its internal private IP address. In some cases, an application requires an agent installed on the virtual machines inside the vApp.

5.5.4.5 OVF Properties

When users migrate virtual machines from any virtualization environment to vCloud Director, the OVF format is required. vCloud Director imports virtual machine artifacts in the OVF format. Open Virtualization Application (OVA) format is not supported for importing vApps in vCloud Director. The difference between OVF and OVA, which is usually a TAR file with the same contents as several OVF files, is that OVA can have multiple virtual machines with a single metadata file.

Users can pass custom properties when importing via OVF properties. This creates opportunities for further customization of virtual machines.

The vCloud API and the user interface support OVF properties. OVF properties can take any of the following forms:

- String
- Integer
- Boolean
- String Choice
- IP
- Custom types

The guest operating system can use the following mechanisms to get these properties:

- The ISO image is mounted on the first available CD-ROM drive in the guest operating system. The properties can be read from an XML file named `ovf-env.xml` in the root directory of the mounted image. This method works even if VMware Tools is not installed.
- With VMware Tools installed, the guest operating system can access the properties by issuing a `vmtoolsd` query:

```
vmtoolsd --cmd "info-get guestinfo.ovfEnv"
```

Programs or scripts executed within the guest OS can obtain these OVF properties. This provides the potential for the following actions:

- Passing in configuration parameters
- Passing a message to a program or script, enabling dynamic behavior
- Enabling users to select from an options list to pass in information (using the String Choice property type)

5

Programs or scripts running in the guest operating system can query OVF properties at any time. One use case runs a script when the guest operating system boots. This script obtains the OVF properties and follows a set of decision paths to configure the system based on these values.

Another use case executes an automatically scheduled script or program to query the OVF properties at known intervals. If OVF properties change between iterations, the scheduled script or program can alter its behavior as the message changes.

As with the vSphere API Guest Operations (formerly the VIX API), the guest operating system does not need to be connected to a network to enable OVF properties to be read. The properties are made available to the guest OS with VMware Tools or as a file contained in an ISO image mounted on a CD-ROM drive.

The vCloud API provides calls to get and set OVF properties. It can be used to query vApp templates and instantiated vApp objects to obtain `ProductSections` that contain the `ProductSectionList`. When using the vCloud API to add, update, or remove a property, you must supply a `ProductSectionList` object.

With the vCloud Director UI, you can set OVF property values when you add a new vApp. To set properties on an instantiated vApp, vCloud Director provides tabs to configure custom properties at the vApp and virtual machine levels.

For more information on using the properties, see "Leveraging vApp & VM Custom Properties In vCloud Director" (http://blogs.vmware.com/vsphere/2012/06/leveraging-vapp-vm-custom-properties-in-vcloud-director.html).

5.5.4.6 OVF Package Upload Latency Considerations

The transfer for OVF files from client devices to a vCloud Director cell typically occurs in a WAN environment where bandwidth and network speed are limited. Considerations for transferring OVF files are discussed in more detail in the "VMware vCloud Director 1.0 Performance and Best Practices" (www.vmware.com/files/pdf/techpaper/VMW-Performance-vCloud-Director-1-0.pdf).

5.5.4.7 Relocate Existing vApps

You can choose between two primary methods for migrating a vApp between datastores within an organization virtual datacenter:

- vCloud Director-initiated vApp relocate
- VMware vSphere Storage vMotion®

Choose the method that best fits your case after considering storage efficiency and provisioning time.

5.5.4.7.1 Prerequisites

The following are prerequisites for moving a vApp between virtual datacenters:

- The target datastore and vApp must exist within the same organization virtual datacenter.

- All virtual disks for an individual virtual machine must reside within a single datastore.

NOTE

Storage configuration policies might affect capacity requirements for storing a virtual machine, and this might impact fast provisioning.

5.5.4.7.2 Use Cases

Several potential use cases exist for the migration of vApps between organization virtual datacenters:

- Planning maintenance of underlying storage
- Rebalancing storage utilization for capacity or performance management
- Upgrading or replacing a back-end storage system

5.5.4.7.3 Storage vMotion Procedure

Storage vMotion can be performed from the vSphere Client or through scripts that leverage vCenter procedures to complete the task. The following is a procedure for the migration process as performed from the vSphere Client.

To migrate a vApp:

1. Log in to the vCloud Director portal as a system administrator.
2. Find the organization that contains the vApp.
3. Open the organization.
4. Find and open the vApp.
5. Click the Virtual Machines tab.
6. Right-click the virtual machine to display the vApp VM menu.
7. Select Properties.
8. Note the value of the Name in vSphere property of the virtual machine (see Figure 5.32). Use this value to find the virtual machine in vSphere. The UUID portion is unique, but names might be duplicated within an environment.

NOTE

If this section is not visible, the logged-in user does not have vCloud Director System Administrator privileges.

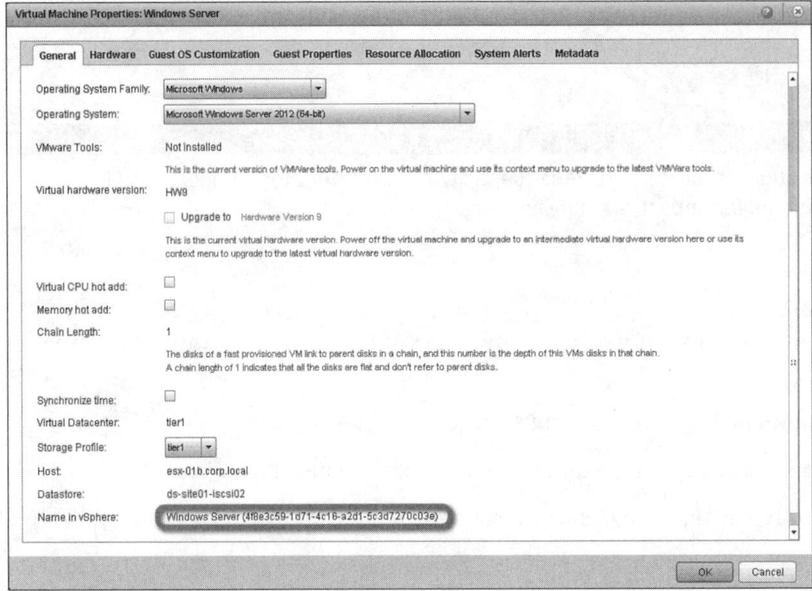

FIGURE 5.32 vSphere name for virtual machine

9. Using the vSphere Client, connect to the vCenter server that manages the host specified in the virtual machine properties.

10. Type the UUID of the target virtual machine in the inventory search panel, shown in Figure 5.33.

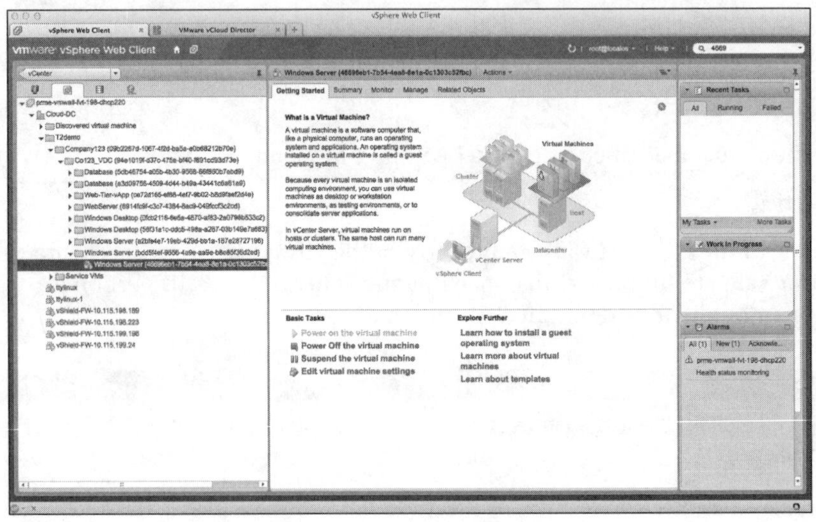

FIGURE 5.33 Selection of target virtual machine

11. Locate the virtual machine in the results list.

12. Select the virtual machine.

13. Click Inventory > Virtual Machine.

14. Select Migrate as shown in Figure 5.34.

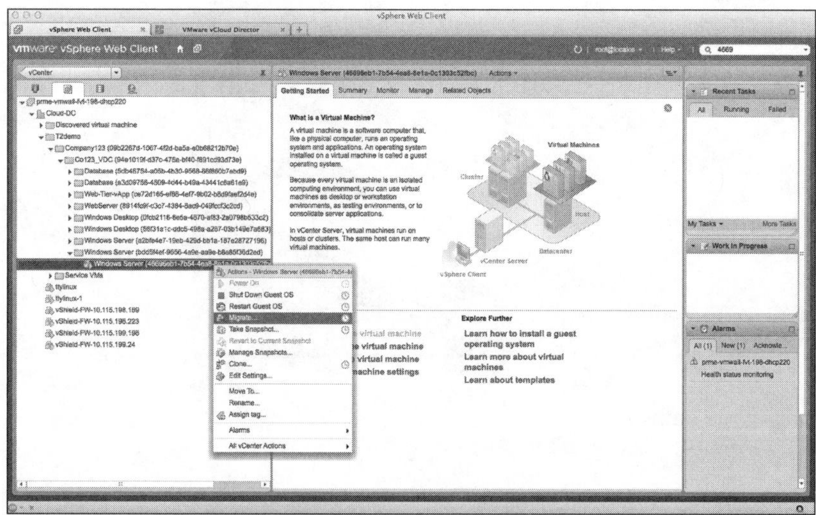

FIGURE 5.34 Selecting Migrate

15. If running vSphere 5 or later, read the Warning dialog box. Click Yes to continue (see Figure 5.35).

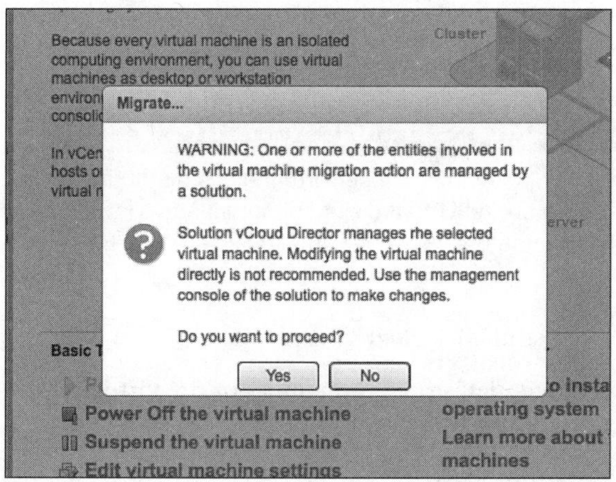

FIGURE 5.35 Migrate confirmation screen

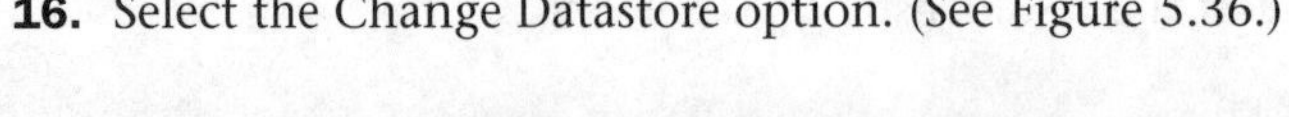

16. Select the Change Datastore option. (See Figure 5.36.)

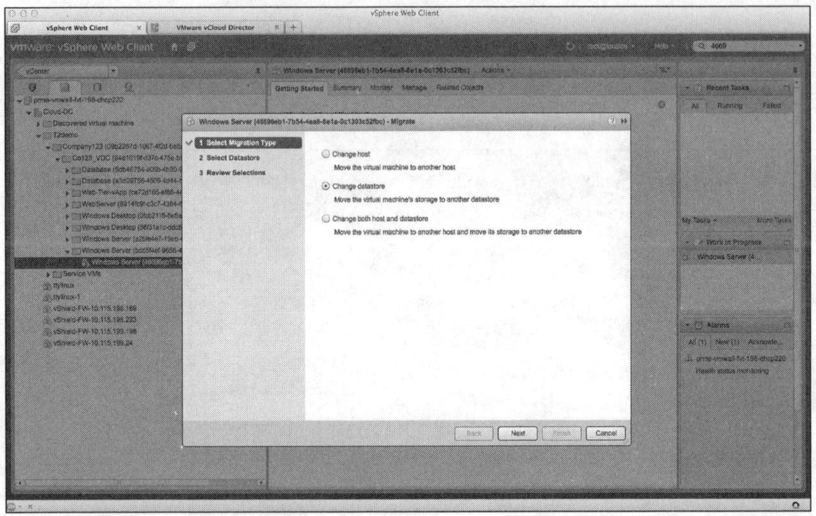

FIGURE 5.36 Changing the datastore

17. Click Next to continue.

18. Do not modify the currently assigned default resource pool selection.

CAUTION

Never use the vSphere Client to modify the virtual machine resource pool. If you are using a vSphere version earlier than vSphere 5, you must manually select the correct resource pool. The selected resource pool must match the current resource pool that contains the virtual machine.

NOTE

Configurations that have a single virtual machine using multiple virtual disks distributed over more than one datastore are not supported. All virtual disks supporting any virtual machine must be contained within a single datastore.

19. Select the target datastore from the list, and click Next to continue.

20. Before proceeding, confirm that the target datastore is a member of the virtual datacenter that contains the vApp within vCloud Director.

21. Click Finish to start the Storage vMotion process.

22. Continue to monitor the event status for progress. After the storage migration is complete, the new datastore name displays in the virtual machine properties.

5.5.4.7.4 Risks

Configuration changes at the vSphere layer do not propagate to vCloud Director. The following risks are associated with migrating vApps and virtual machines at the vSphere layer without vCloud Director involvement.

- If the virtual machine is migrated to datastores that are not assigned to the appropriate virtual datacenter management, anomalies might occur.
- If the resource pool assignment of the virtual machine is changed in the vSphere Client, abnormal behavior might result.

Changes made in vCloud Director are stored in the database. To mitigate the risks, use Representational State Transfer (REST) APIs with integrated fail-safes.

5.5.4.7.5 Impact

The virtual machine is relocated as requested between datastores. Any services the virtual machine provides are unavailable while it is stopped or suspended during the relocate event. The relocate process is performed as a clone operation. To minimize risk, a delete operation follows it.

5.5.4.8 Moving a vApp Between Organization Virtual Datacenters

The following are potential use cases for vApp migration between organization virtual datacenters:

- vApp lifecycle management
- vApp performance management
- Virtual datacenter resource management

For lifecycle management, processes can be developed to migrate a vApp between virtual datacenters. These processes serve different purposes during vApp development and promotion cycles. For example, a vApp might be initially provisioned within a development virtual datacenter. At the end of the development cycle, the vApp can be migrated or copied to a quality assurance and testing virtual datacenter. In the final stage, the vApp can be copied to the catalog for publication to users.

To migrate a vApp between virtual datacenters:

1. Log in as a user with the appropriate permissions.
2. Click the My Cloud tab.
3. Locate the vApp that requires migration.
4. If the vApp is running, stop or suspend the vApp by right-clicking and selecting Stop or Suspend.
5. After the vApp has been selected and stopped or suspended, right-click and select Move To (see Figure 5.37).

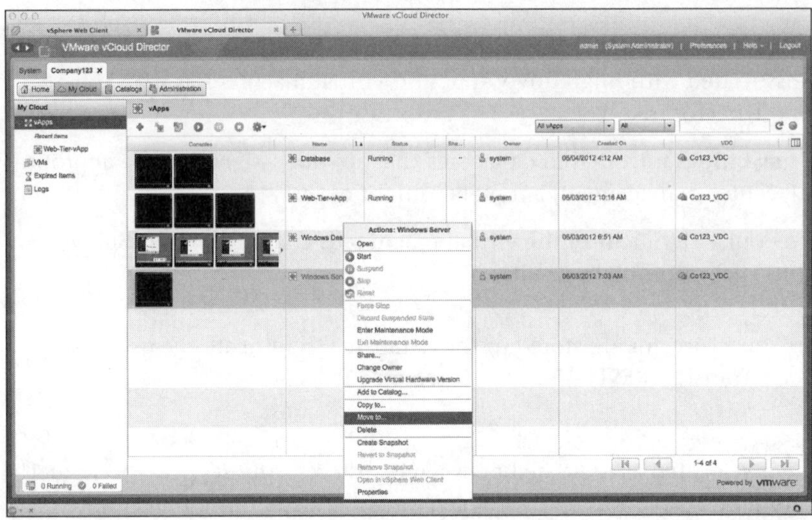

FIGURE 5.37 Selecting vApp Move To option

6. When prompted, select the target virtual datacenter from the drop-down menu and click OK (see Figure 5.38).

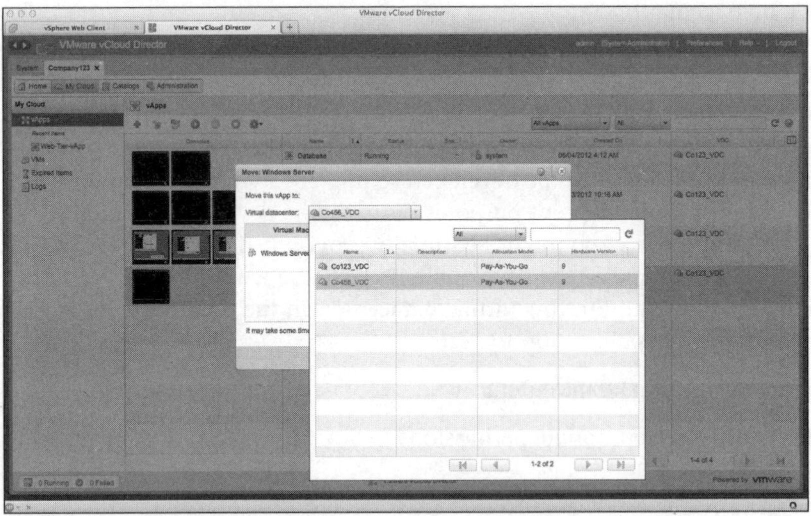

FIGURE 5.38 Target datastore for vApp being moved

7. Wait for the copy and delete operations to finish, and verify that the vApp is located in the target virtual datacenter.

8. Following migration, verify the networking requirements within the target virtual datacenter. Virtual datacenters are often defined based on physical vSphere resources, which can have networking configurations that differ from the source networks.

During the migration, virtual machines contained within the vApp are copied to new datastores. Copy time varies depending on whether the source or target organization virtual datacenter has been prepared for fast provisioning.

5.5.5 Updating vApps

You can change or reset the virtual machine MAC addresses, the CPU and memory values, and the number of vNICs. The following section describes how to change the MAC address.

5.5.5.1 Changing a Virtual Machine MAC Address

You can change the MAC address assigned to a virtual machine in a vApp. vCloud Director assigns a MAC address to all deployed vApps and virtual machines. Perform any modifications to assigned MAC addresses through the vCloud Director portal, the API, or tools that use the API. If permitted on the virtual switch, you can alternatively edit the MAC address in the guest operating system.

5

5.5.5.1.1 Prerequisites

The following are requirements for modifying the MAC address of a virtual machine:

- The virtual machine must be in a powered-off state.
- The user performing the action must have full control rights to the virtual machine.

5.5.5.1.2 Use Cases

Use cases that might require changing the MAC address of a virtual machine include the following:

- Forcing new, unique MAC address creation for guest software licensing requirements
- Preventing duplication of MAC addresses within a single network when virtual machine network connections are relocated during the lifecycle
- Assigning a MAC address based on the current vCloud Director environment for imported virtual machines

5.5.5.1.3 vCloud Director MAC Address Reset Procedure

A new MAC address can be generated quickly for any virtual machine network interface within the vCloud Director portal.

To generate a new MAC address for a virtual machine network interface:

1. Log into the vCloud Director portal as a user with rights to target the vApp virtual machine. See Figure 5.39 for the portal view.

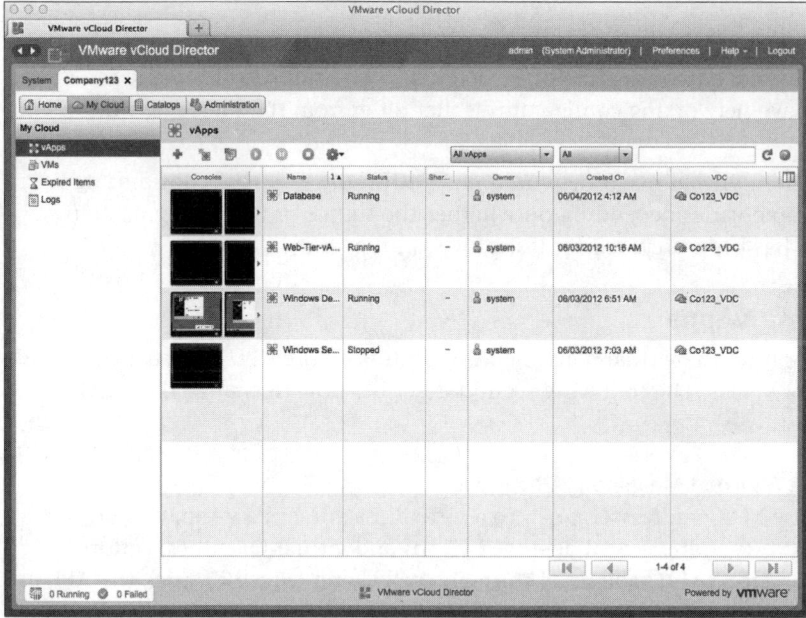

FIGURE 5.39 vCloud Director portal as seen by user with rights to the target vApp virtual machines

2. Navigate to the target vApp.
3. Right-click and select Open (see Figure 5.40).

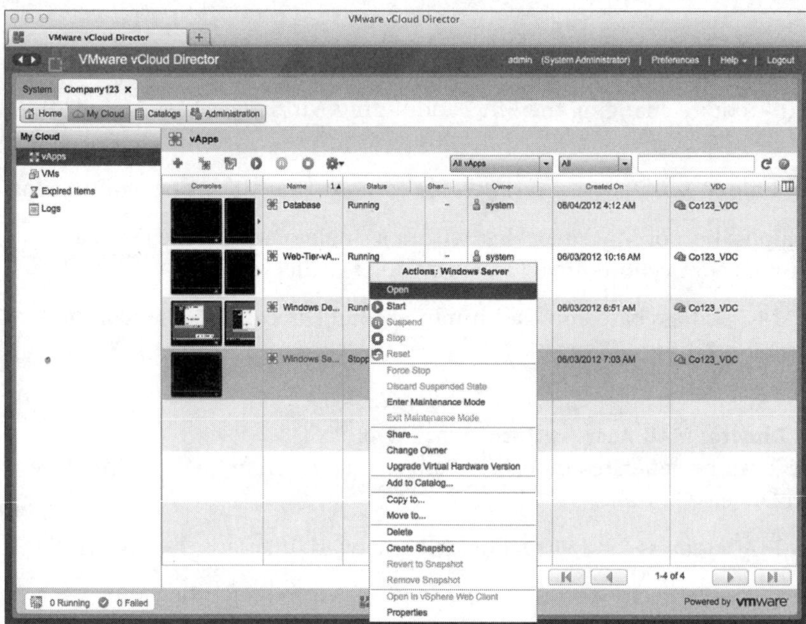

FIGURE 5.40 Opening a virtual machine

4. Open the vApp and select the target virtual machine.
5. Right-click and select Properties (see Figure 5.41).

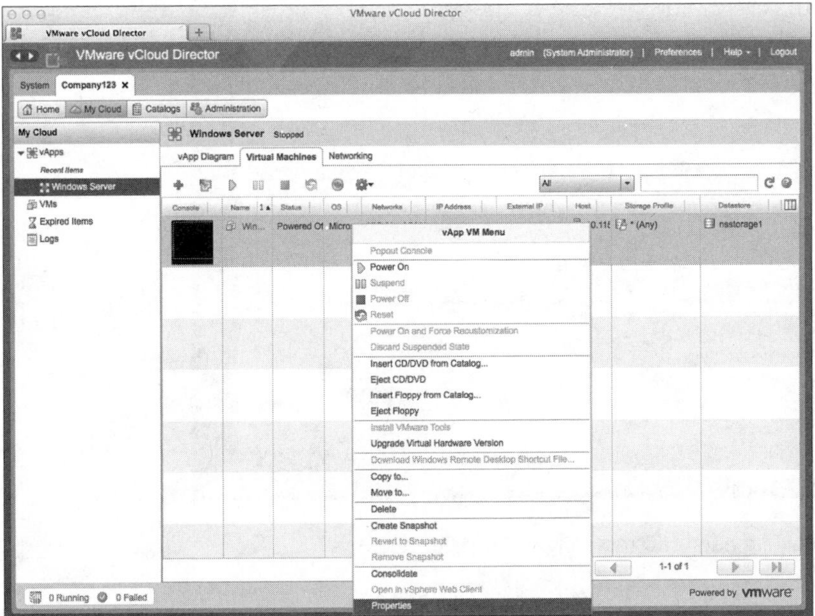

FIGURE 5.41 Opening the virtual machine properties

6. Switch to the Hardware tab, scrolling down to the NICs section, if necessary.
7. Determine which network interfaces require a new MAC address.
8. Click the drop-down menu with the MAC address.
9. Select Reset for each NIC that requires a new MAC address (see Figure 5.42).

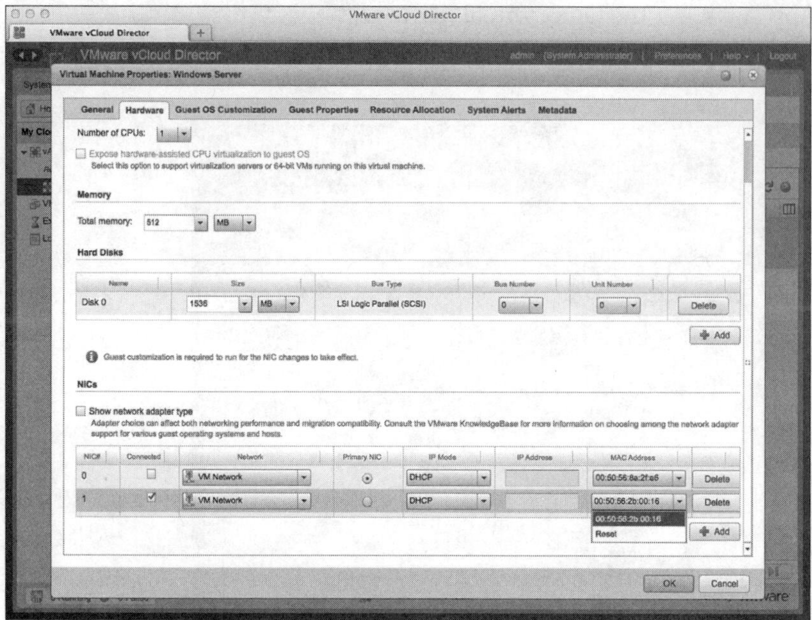

FIGURE 5.42 Resetting each NIC requiring a new MAC address

10. Select OK to activate the changes. vCloud Director assigns and configures a new MAC address within the virtual machine hardware.

11. Verify your changes by inspecting the Virtual Machine Properties NICs panel (see Figure 5.43).

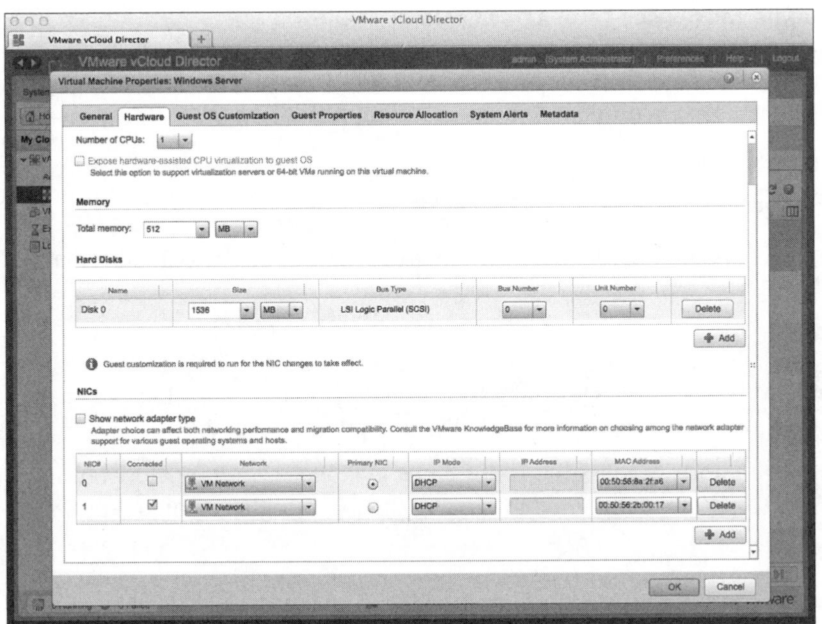

FIGURE 5.43 Verifying virtual machine NIC properties

5.5.5.2 Impact and Risks

The MAC address of the virtual machine interface selected for MAC regeneration has a new MAC address allocated based on the identity of the vCloud Director instance.

Applications and services that depend on MAC address registration might be impacted. This includes DHCP reservations and MAC address–aware software licensing.

5.5.6 Establishing Service Levels

Service-level agreements (SLAs) between consumers and providers are needed to align business requirements with offered services. This becomes increasingly important as business-critical applications move to a vCloud-based environment. Providers can be enterprises or public vCloud service providers. This section provides guidance for consumers.

5.5.6.1 Defining a Service-Level Agreement

For a service provider to optimally provide vCloud consumers with services, technology services must be seamlessly integrated. Generally, a workflow engine called the *orchestration layer* is used for this purpose. Invoking a service can automatically trigger one or more technology services. The rules governing these workflows must be preconfigured and preapproved for control, and they must provide an agreed-upon level of service to the consumer. This agreed-upon level of service is known as a *service-level agreement* and is typically defined as a predetermined agreement between the service consumer and the service provider that measures the quality and performance of available services.

5.5.6.2 vCloud Layers and Service-Level Agreements

A typical vCloud-computing environment consists of multiple layers, such as IaaS, Platform as a Service (PaaS), and Software as a Service (SaaS). Based on their business requirements, consumers have a number of options for implementing the vCloud stack:

- Creating a private vCloud
- Using a public vCloud provider
- Adopting a hybrid vCloud model in which both private and public vCloud resources are used

The capability of an organization to guarantee availability and performance at every vCloud layer enables this flexibility. Flexibility is achieved by establishing SLAs externally with service providers or by creating SLAs internally for a private vCloud.

For an organization with an IaaS layer that is hosted by a public vCloud provider but in which PaaS and SaaS layers are maintained internally, the following SLAs might apply:

- IaaS layer:
    - **Uptime and Availability SLA:** Established with the external vCloud service provider
    - **Network Performance SLA:** Established with the external vCloud service provider
    - **Request Fulfillment SLA:** Measure of response time for provisioning and access configuration requests
    - **Restore Time SLA:** Measure of response time for restoration of services
- PaaS layer:
    - **Uptime and Availability SLA:** For the development environment
    - **Uptime and Availability SLA:** For critical development environment components
    - **Restore Time SLA:** For the development environment
- SaaS layer:
    - **Uptime and Availability SLA:** Specific to an application
    - **Application Response Time SLA:** Measure of how the application performs for the business users
    - **Time to Resolution SLA:** Time to recover an application in case of failure

5.5.6.3 vCloud Considerations for Service-Level Agreements

SLAs are required to provide efficiency and accountability at every layer for both external providers and internal IT groups. Managing SLAs in every layer helps to isolate systemic problems and eliminate delays.

Interrelationships between SLAs exist at different vCloud layers. Any change in quality of the service or a breach of one of the lower vCloud layers might impact multiple SLAs at a higher vCloud layer. Using the previous example of an organization with an IaaS layer hosted by a public vCloud provider and PaaS and SaaS layers maintained internally, an SLA performance breach resulting in external vCloud providers that cannot support operating system performance needs propagates problems to the SaaS layer, decreasing application performance and response time for business users.

Business needs are continuously evolving, as are business requirements for a vCloud. SLAs must be continually updated to reflect current business requirements. In the previous example, adding a thousand new business users to a particular application likely will increase the criticality and cause the application to be deemed mission critical. This business change means that corresponding SLAs supporting the application might require revision for increased uptime and availability. This, in turn, leads to increased demands at the IaaS layer, requiring revisions to SLAs with an external IaaS provider as well.

5.6 Consuming vCloud with the API

The vCloud API is used to interact with vCloud Director from outside its native portal. The VMware vCloud API provides support for developers who build interactive clients of VMware vCloud Director using a RESTful application development style. The vCloud API clients and servers communicate over HTTP, exchanging representations of vCloud objects. These representations take the form of XML elements. HTTP GET requests retrieve the current representation of an object, HTTP POST and PUT requests create or modify an object, and HTTP DELETE requests typically delete an object.

The VMware vCloud API was designed to be supported by the ecosystem of vCloud-ready service providers and to interact with what are known as *pure virtual* resources. Any IaaS cloud architecture consists of raw hardware resources abstracted and presented to end users in the form of vCloud resources. For example, in a VMware vCloud environment, networking and datastore resources are connected to vSphere hosts in the form of switches, port groups, and storage in datastores and datastore clusters. When you build a cloud infrastructure, network and storage configuration should be transparent to the end user.

5.6.1 Characteristics of the API

Depending on desired operations and the assigned privileges, specific APIs are available.

5.6.1.1 Self-Service APIs

These are typical operations performed by an end user who consumes cloud resources:

- Creating vApps and virtual machines
- Performing power operations on vApps and virtual machines
- Listing resources available to the user
- Managing the vApp lifecycle

Typically, users never see the administration side of the vCloud API and do not have permission to use it. They use the vCloud API for automated tasks and use the graphical vCloud interface for daily tasks and operations. Independent software vendor (ISV) partners might write workflow applications to take advantage of reduced privileges and provide an interface to their customers on their custom portal. This prevents breaches from escalating to administrator privileges. The roles defined for users in the vCloud Director GUI are the same as those in the vCloud API when the same logins are used.

5.6.1.2 Administrative APIs

Administration APIs have higher privileges and access to the following vCloud Director management functions:

- Creating, updating, and deleting virtual datacenters
- Creating, updating, and deleting organizations
- Creating, updating, and deleting networks

5.6.2 API Functions

Some of the most important API functions include the following:

- **Authentication operations:** These API functions provide basic authentication over TLS/SSL. They also provide information about supported versions of the API.
- **Resource navigation operations:** APIs are REST based. Each resource is a named URI that the HTTP or HTTPS protocol uses to access and act upon resources, such as a vApp.
- **Long-running operations:** These tasks take a longer time to run, such as deploying a vApp with many virtual machines. The status of these tasks is modeled as a resource, so it can be retrieved like other resources using a URI.
- **Error reporting:** One of the key functions of the API is to report any errors that occur in vCloud Director.

5.6.3 What's New in the vCloud 5.1 API

vCloud Director 5.1 provides the following new and expanded features, and APIs have been updated accordingly:

- **Query Service:** Introduced in the vCloud 1.5 API. Useful when searching for resources. You do not have to traverse the resource tree to find specific children nodes. The query service has been expanded in the vCloud 5.1 API and includes the capability to query for metadata tags.
- **Metadata Tagging:** Expanded in the vCloud 5.1 API. Annotate vCloud resources with typed metadata that can be system defined and either hidden from or read-only for users, or user defined that is read-writable. Consumers can interact with metadata from the UI in vCloud Director 5.1; in previous releases, this feature was available only from the API.
- **API Extensions:** New in the vCloud 5.1 API. Provides the capability to extend the vCloud API to modify existing functionality or add new capabilities to the API.
- **Block Tasks and Notifications:** Introduced in the vCloud 1.5 API. This feature relates to the messages vCloud Director publishes and consumes. In blocking tasks, the system waits for a user to take an action. For example, if a manager must provide approval when a developer requests vCloud resources, a blocking task might be created. When a developer deploys a vApp, the manager is notified and must approve before proceeding with deployment.
- In notifications, also called *nonblocking events*, a message is sent to the event's Advanced Message Queuing Protocol (AMQP) broker.

5.6.4 vCloud SDK

APIs involve creating XML payloads to post and parsing an XML response. The SDK simplifies the development process. Currently, Java, .NET, and PHP have supported language bindings.

These language bindings can be downloaded from VMware vCloud API (www.vmware.com/go/vcloudapi).

5.7 Consuming vCloud with vFabric Application Director

Cloud computing is aggressively driving efficiencies in processes, compliance, and innovation in applications, and optimizing the infrastructure on which they run. Requirements vary according to who consumes the services. Application owners want the simplicity and agility to deploy platforms for development in the cloud. The platforms are fully configured environments that meet internal enterprise compliance requirements. Infrastructure owners want the capability to create self-service models for application owners.

Virtualization has matured to the point at which virtual machines can be deployment in a matter of hours; for contrast, provisioning physical servers once took weeks. When all levels of control are in place, vCloud Director provisions solutions in minutes with self-service portal capabilities and integration with third-party provisioning systems using vCloud APIs.

vFabric Application Director furthers the deployment of applications in the cloud. vFabric Application Director addresses these major challenges:

- Legacy deployments
- Proliferation of virtual machine templates and customization scripts
- Disconnected application operations

In legacy deployments, little or no automation takes place. Complex dependencies might or might not be abstracted. Maintaining those abstractions can increase overhead. The deployments might not be cloud aware, might have tighter dependency on the cloud infrastructure, and might not be flexible enough to meet developer needs in timely manner.

Permutation and combination of application and guest operating system versions in vApp templates have increased. This gives administrators enormous challenges to standardize configurations, security, and compliance.

Monitoring systems does not automatically discover applications after their deployments. This leads to long troubleshooting cycles and capacity-planning processes with little or no autoscaling capabilities for applications.

vFabric Application Director, shown in Figure 5.44, addresses many of these shortcomings. It has an architecture, model-based application deployment, integrated active application monitoring and management, and provisioning to public, private, and hybrid clouds.

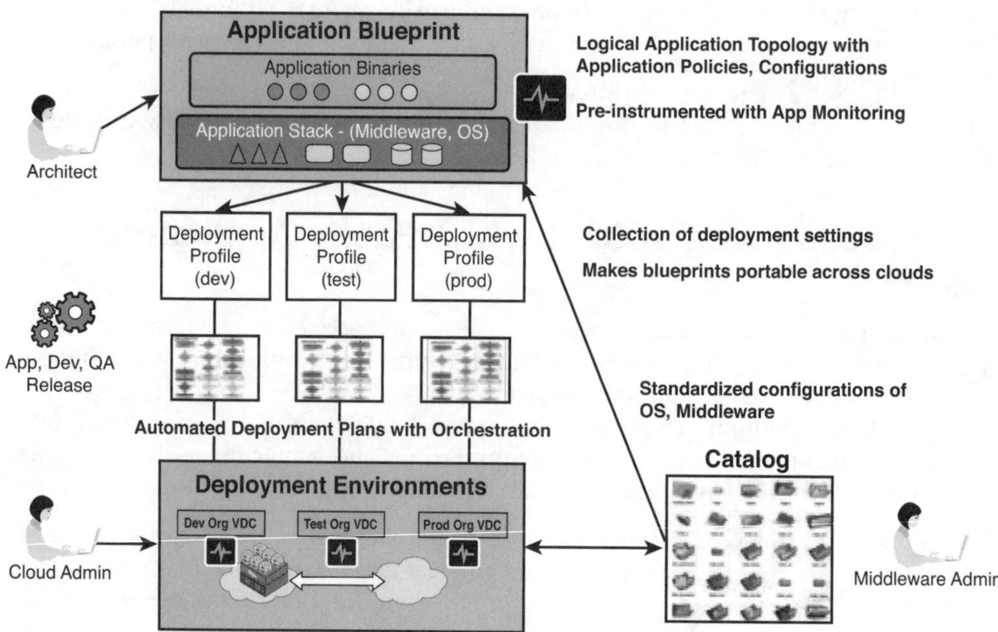

FIGURE 5.44 vFabric Application Director

5.8 References

- VMware vSphere documentation

  www.vmware.com/support/pubs/vsphere-esxi-vcenter-server-pubs.html
- VMware vCloud Director documentation

  www.vmware.com/support/pubs/vcd_pubs.html
- "Virtualizing Existing Domain Controllers"

  http://kb.vmware.com/kb/1006996
- "FSMO Placement and Optimization on Active Directory Domain Controllers"

  http://support.microsoft.com/kb/223346
- "Active Directory Replication over Firewalls"

  http://technet.microsoft.com/en-us/library/bb727063.aspx
- "How to Configure a Firewall for Domains and Trusts"

  http://support.microsoft.com/kb/179442
- "Virtualizing a Windows Active Directory Domain Infrastructure"

  www.vmware.com/files/pdf/Virtualizing_Windows_Active_Directory.pdf
- VMware vCloud Director Security Hardening Guide

  www.vmware.com/files/pdf/techpaper/VMW_10Q3_WP_vCloud_Director_Security.pdf
- "VMware vCloud Director 1.0 Performance and Best Practices"

  www.vmware.com/files/pdf/techpaper/VMW-Performance-vCloud-Director-1-0.pdf
- Active Directory Branch Office Guide Series http://technet.microsoft.com/en-us/library/cc749926.aspx www.microsoft.com/downloads/details.aspx?FamilyId=9A4C7AC3-185E-4644-9E98-4876B2A477E7&displaylang=en
- "Description of Support Boundaries for Active Directory over NAT"

  http://support.microsoft.com/kb/978772

Third-party URLs are subject to changes that VMware cannot control. You might be able to locate a third-party document by searching from their home page.

CHAPTER 6

Implementation Examples

IN THIS CHAPTER:

6.1 Overview

This chapter provides detailed examples that illustrate use of the components of the VMware vCloud Suite. The examples highlight key design decisions associated with implementing an Infrastructure as a Service (IaaS) solution. Each example is a module that can provide a baseline or component of an overall IaaS design. The examples are intended to serve as a reference for architects and engineers, and assumes familiarity with VMware products in the VMware vCloud Suite, including VMware vSphere®, VMware vCenter™, and VMware vCloud Director™.

6.1.1 Implementation Examples Structure

Use the implementation examples as a reference for a specific technology or feature in the vCloud Suite to quickly find and research an area of interest. Each example is organized as shown in Table 6.1.

TABLE 6.1 Example Layout

Section	Notes
x.x <Example Name> Deployment Models	Deployment models for this technology example (private, public, hybrid, all).
Example Components	The required software components and versions. For example: vSphere 5.1, vCloud Director 5.1.
x.x.1 Background	Background about a specific technology example and an overview that describes how it can be used.
x.x.2 Example	An example of the use of the technology or feature for a specific use case. The examples refer to the fictitious companies Company1 and Company2.
x.x.3 Design Implications	Information to consider when using the technology or feature.

For each example, see the VMware product installation and administration guides for additional information.

6.1.2 vCloud Suite Components

Table 6.2 describes the components of the VMware vCloud Suite.

TABLE 6.2 vCloud Components

vCloud Component	Description
VMware vCloud Director vCloud API	Layer of software that abstracts virtual resources and exposes vCloud components to consumers. Includes: ▶ vCloud Director Server (also referred to as a *cell*) ▶ vCloud Director Database ▶ VMware vCloud API, used to manage vCloud objects programmatically
VMware vSphere	Virtualization platform providing abstraction of physical infrastructure layer for vCloud. Includes: ▶ VMware ESXi™ hosts ▶ VMware vCenter™ Server ▶ vCenter Server database
VMware vCloud Networking and Security	Decouples network and security from the underlying physical network hardware through software-defined networking and security. Includes: ▶ VXLAN support ▶ vCloud Networking and Security Edge Gateway ▶ App and Data Security Manager

vCloud Component	Description
VMware vCenter Operations Management Suite	Provides predictive capacity and performance planning, compliance and configuration management, dynamic resource metering, cost modeling, and report generation using the following components: ▶ vCenter Operations Manager™ ▶ vCenter Configuration Manager™ ▶ vCenter Infrastructure Navigator™ ▶ vCenter Chargeback Manager™
vFabric Application Director	Part of the Cloud Application Platform family of products that provide automated provisioning of application infrastructure.
VMware vCenter Orchestrator™	Enables the automation of provisioning and operational tasks across VMware and third-party applications using an open and flexible plug-in architecture.
VMware vCloud Connector	vSphere Client plug-in that enables users to connect to vSphere-based or vCloud Director–based clouds and manage them through a single interface.

6.1.2.1 VMware vCloud Director

VMware vCloud Director further abstracts the virtualized resources presented by vSphere by providing the following logical constructs that map to the following vSphere logical resources:

- **Organization:** A logical object that provides a security and policy boundary. Organizations are the main method of establishing multitenancy and typically represent a business unit, project, or customer in a private vCloud environment.
- **Virtual datacenter:** Deployment environment in which virtual machines run.
- **Organization virtual datacenter:** An organization's allocated portion of provider virtual datacenter resources, including CPU, RAM, and storage.
- **Provider virtual datacenter:** vSphere resource groupings of compute, storage, and network resources that power organization virtual datacenters.

Figure 6.1 shows the vCloud Director abstraction layer in relation to vSphere and physical resources.

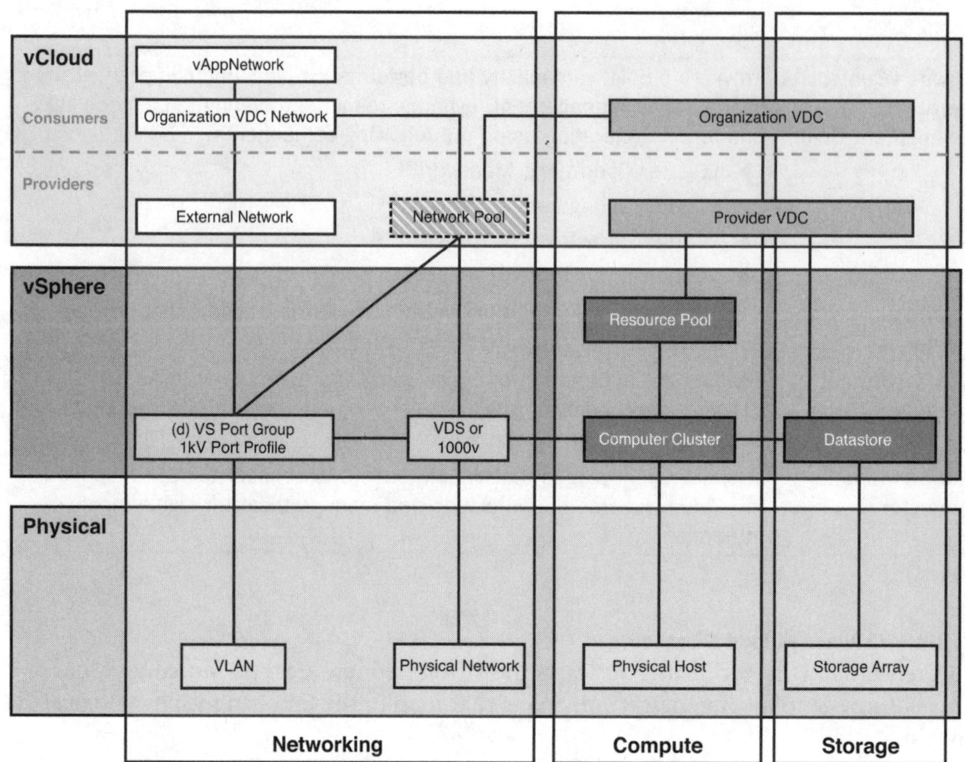

FIGURE 6.1 VMware vCloud Director abstraction layer

6.2 vCloud Cell Design Examples

The following section include design patterns for creating vCloud Director cells that are the foundation for a VMware vCloud.

6.2.1 Load-Balanced Cell Configuration

Deployment Models: Private, public, hybrid

Example Components: vCloud Director 5.1, vCloud Networking and Security Edge 5.1, vSphere 5.1

6.2.1.1 Background

A vCloud Director cell consists of Red Hat Enterprise Linux (see the *VMware Compatibility Guide* for supported versions) with installed and configured VMware vCloud Director binary files. This server becomes the portal for the vCloud Director environment, for both administrators (providers) and users (consumers) of the vCloud.

This example architecture covers the following considerations:

- Shared transfer space
- Load balancer setup
- SSL offload for certificates and SSL to cells
- Load balancer health check rules
- External URL settings in vCloud Director.

6.2.1.2 Example

This example demonstrates how to set up load-balanced vCloud Director cells. The following prerequisites align with and are explained in the setup considerations.

6.2.1.2.1 Prerequisites

- More than one vCloud Director–supported cell server (Red Hat Enterprise Linux).
- Supported network latency (in this example, <2ms RTT between vCloud Director cells). The environment must behave as though it is a single site (that is, low latency).
- Location and password of the keystore file that includes the SSL certificates for this server.
- Shared transfer storage space, mapped on each vCloud Director cell.
- Shared database instance.
- Network Time Protocol configured on each cell.
- Network load balancer device, and console and proxy health monitors.
- vCloud Director Public Addresses configuration.

6.2.1.2.2 Setup Considerations

- More than one vCloud Director cell is required. Multiple vCloud Director cells are desirable for redundancy and to provide a sufficient number of console sessions.
  - If the first vCloud Director cell is lagging because of too many console connections, adding more load-balanced cells offloads the workload between the cells by providing more console connections.
  - If the first cell becomes unavailable, users can no longer use the vCloud Director portal or console sessions. Having multiple, load-balanced cells enables user sessions to be re-established across other cells.

In this example, the customer wants to gain vCloud Director cell redundancy by load balancing the cells. There is no need to get more console access connections because of the limited number of users accessing the vCloud Director portal or vCloud Director backspace-presented virtual machine consoles.

- Network latency between the cells must be low enough to perform as though the cells reside in the same datacenter (LAN speed). Cells must have low latency between each other and also between themselves and the shared database. This provides proper communication and updates between the cells, along with the cell-to-database traffic.

  The customer is hosting all the vCloud Director cells within two adjacent racks in a datacenter. This configuration has less than a 2ms round-trip time (RTT) between the cells and corresponding services (database, vSphere, and so on).

- Certificates are generated when a vCloud Director cell is installed. See the *vCloud Director Installation Guide* for information about creating the proper certificates.

  During the creation of the certificates, the HTTP and Console IP addresses are identified, along with the keystore location and password. Record this information. The default location is `/opt/keystore/certificates.ks`.

  The customer wants to create an untrusted (self-signed) certificate using the following command. This command creates an untrusted certificate for the HTTP service in a keystore file named `certificates.ks`:

```
keytool -keystore certificates.ks -storetype JCEKS -storepass
passwd-genkey -keyalg RSA -alias http
```

Table 6.3 contains the customer-provided information used to populate the certificate as prompted during the certificate creation from the preceding command.

TABLE 6.3 Example Responses to Questions Asked During Certificate Creation

Certificate-Prompted Question	Customer Answer
What is your first and last name?	Mycloud.example.com
What is the name of your organization unit?	IT
What is the name of your organization?	Example Company Name
What is the name of your city or locality?	Tucson
What is the name of your state or province?	Arizona
What is the two-letter country code for this unit?	US

The following command adds an untrusted certificate for the console proxy to the keystore file created in the previous step:

```
keytool -keystore certificates.ks -storetype JCEKS -storepass passwd-genkey -keyalg
RSA
-alias consoleproxy
```

- For the transfer service, each server must mount an NFS or other shared storage volume at `$VCLOUD_HOME/data/transfer`, which is typically `/opt/vmware/vcloud-director/data/transfer`. This volume must have write permission for root.

NOTE

In some lab and POC environments, it is acceptable, though not recommended, to share a local NFS mount from one cell server to other cell servers. Keep in mind that if this NFS server becomes unavailable, functions and services using this share will become unavailable and copy operations in progress will fail.

- Database connection information and other reusable responses you supplied during the configuration are preserved in a file located at `/opt/vmware/vcloud-director/etc/responses.properties` on this server. Copy this file to each additional cell server before the configuration of the vCloud Director cell server software. This file is referenced during the initiation of the installation using this command:

  ```
  installation-file -r path-to-response-file
  ```

- The Network Time Protocol (NTP) must be properly configured on each vCloud Director cell. vCloud Director cells with improperly configured NTP settings can have trouble connecting to ESXi hosts, the database instance, vCloud Networking and Security Manager, and other cells. If one cell in the group does not have the correct time, and a user connects through this cell, actions will not complete correctly and many errors will occur. This because of the time stamps from that cell trying to access the load-balanced environment (other cells) and the shared database with time stamps that do not match the times of the improperly configured cell.
- A network load balancer, whether physical or virtual, must be configured to proxy the HTTP and console connections for the vCloud Director environment. This section also includes setting up the health monitoring on the load balancer for the vCloud Director environment.

To configure the HTTP portal connections:

1. Copy the SSL certificate to the load balancer for the HTTP public URL (that is, `https://mycloud.example.com`).
2. Set up the Health Monitor on the load balancer (F5 Load Balancer, in this customer example) using the following URL:

   ```
   https://<Cell_Hostname>/cloud/server_status
   ```

3. Each node can have a hostname-based cert `node1.example.com`, `node2.example.com`, and so forth.

6

To configure the console proxy connections:

1. Configure HTTPS pass-through for the console proxy connections. Each node should have the same hostname in the certificate when it is generated (that is, `http://mycloud.example.com`). For more details, see the *vCloud Director Installation and Configuration Guide*. Console connections are load balanced. Because the certificates are the same for each cell console, they must be passed through the load balancer. Otherwise, each cell would need a unique certificate in the load balancer and a certificate mismatch error would occur.

2. Set up the Health Monitor on the load balancer (F5, in this customer example) using the following URL:

   ```
   https:///sdk/vimServiceVersions.xml
   ```

3. Configure SSL persistence for the vCloud Director load balancer connections.

4. In the vCloud Director system administration section, fields exist for the vCloud Director public URL, console proxy address, and REST API base URL. If these fields are not updated with the load balancer public IP addresses/URLs, replies from the cell will reflect that of the individual cell and not that of the public URL information.

An example of configuring console proxy connections (from the *vCloud Director Installation and Configuration Guide*) is shown in Figure 6.2 and Table 6.4:

- When you create an organization, its organization URL includes the public web URL instead of the HTTP service IP address. vCloud Director also modifies the organization URLs of existing organizations.
- Remote console session tickets sent to the HTTP service IP address return the public console proxy address.
- XML responses from the REST API include the base URL, and the transfer service uses the base URL as the upload target.

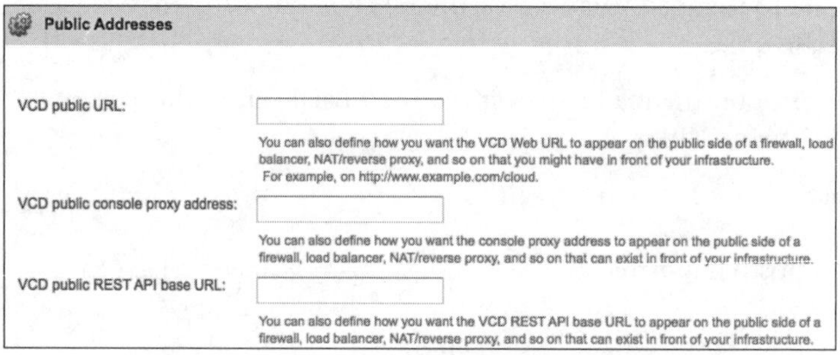

Public Addresses

VCD public URL:

You can also define how you want the VCD Web URL to appear on the public side of a firewall, load balancer, NAT/reverse proxy, and so on that you might have in front of your infrastructure.
For example, on http://www.example.com/cloud.

VCD public console proxy address:

You can also define how you want the console proxy address to appear on the public side of a firewall, load balancer, NAT/reverse proxy, and so on that can exist in front of your infrastructure.

VCD public REST API base URL:

You can also define how you want the VCD REST API base URL to appear on the public side of a firewall, load balancer, NAT/reverse proxy, and so on that can exist in front of your infrastructure.

FIGURE 6.2 Interface for entering public addresses

TABLE 6.4 Public Addresses Field Examples

Public Addresses Field	Example Data
VCD public URL	http://mycloud.example.com
VCD public console proxy address	mycloud-console.example.com
VCD public REST API base URL	mycloud.example.com

- The **VCD public URL** requires HTTPS. This address is also set in the load balancer and DNS so that users can access the vCloud Director portal using this public URL.
- The **VCD public console proxy address** does not use HTTPS. This URL is also in DNS and on the load balancer, to direct users to the appropriate cell for virtual machine console access.
- The **VCD public REST API base URL** is for users to access the load balancer environment using the REST API.

Figure 6.3 shows traffic communication between the cells and ESXi hosts.

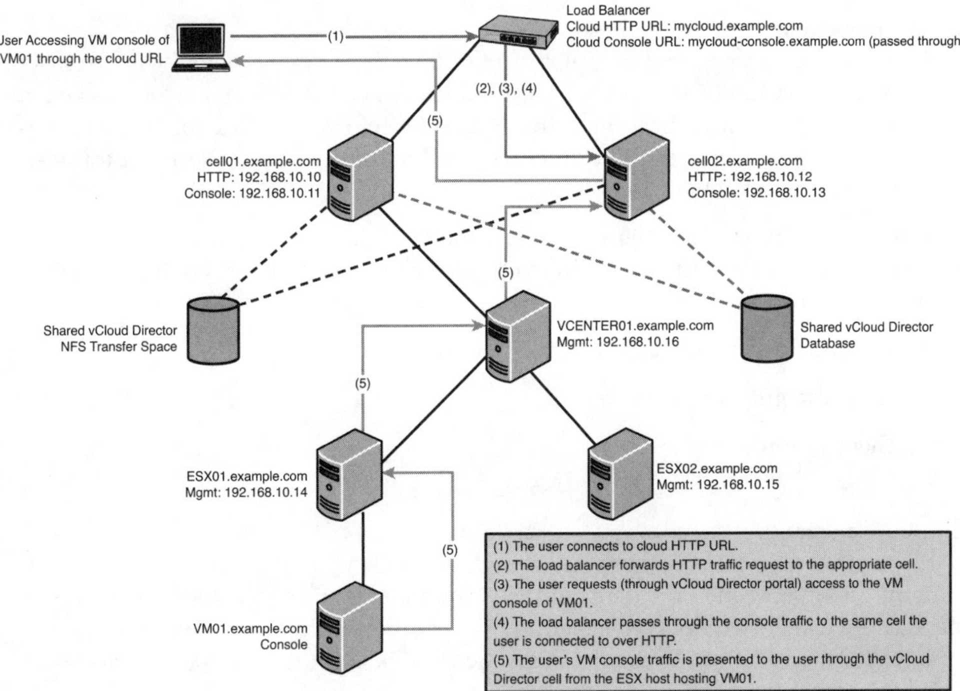

FIGURE 6.3 HTTPS and console proxy connections

To access the console of a virtual machine, vCloud Director uses the console proxy IP address of the vCloud Director cell server to connect directly (through the load balancer, in this case) to the ESXi host and attach the user to the console of the target virtual machine.

When a user connects to the vCloud Director portal, a different URL is used (also using the load balancer, in this case) and the user connects through to the HTTPS vCloud Director portal hosted on the vCloud Director cells. All actions and commands executed within the vCloud Director portal are sent directly (transparent to the end user) to the relevant vCenter Server or, in some cases, directly to the ESXi host.

All vCloud Director cells in the same vCloud must access the same vCloud Director database. Each vCloud Director cell must also be configured for the same NFS mount point, which is used as vCloud Director transfer space.

6.2.2 Secure Certificates

Deployment Models: Private, public, hybrid

Example Components: vCloud Director 5.1, vCloud Networking and Security Edge 5.1, vSphere 5.1

6.2.2.1 Background

Security is a critical component of a successful vCloud deployment. Before you can install and run VMware vCloud Director, you must implement certificates and key management for secure access and authentication to the vCloud Director server. The following example shows how to implement security features designed to safeguard data, keep out intruders, and allow access to legitimate users.

Using the SSL/TLS protocol in the vCloud environment provides secure communication between the end tenant (client) and vCloud Director cell (server). Providing secure communication requires:

- Confidentiality and privacy of communication
- Message integrity and hashing
- Authentication

6.2.2.2 Example

Regardless of whether you are a private, hybrid, or public vCloud provider, securing communication between end tenants of the vCloud portal and the vCloud Director infrastructure usually requires implementing SSL certificates from a trusted Certificate Authority (CA). The following example uses the QuoVadis CA to issue SSL certificates for vCloud Director.

This process flow in Figure 6.4 includes procedures for requesting, configuring, obtaining, and installing an SSL certificate from QuoVadis.

NOTE

QuoVadis is used for this example, but any trusted CA can be used.

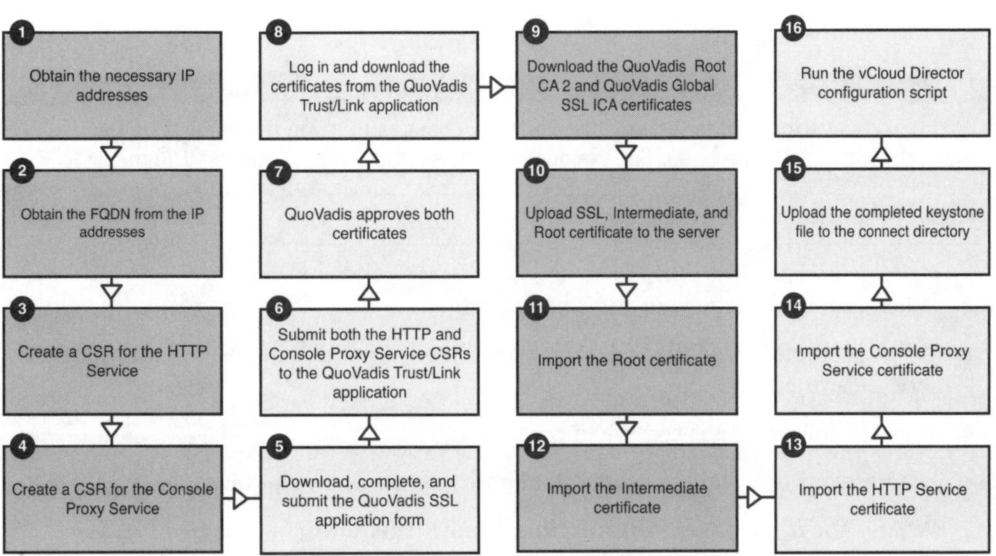

FIGURE 6.4 Requesting, configuring, obtaining, and installing an SSL certificate

6.2.2.2.1 Prerequisites for Creating the Required Certificate Signing Requests

Before creating a Certificate Signing Request (CSR), you must know the IP address and FQDN (fully qualified domain name) of your servers.

To list server information and change to the keytool directory, follow these steps:

1. From the vCloud Director cell, run `ifconfig` (8) to list the IP addresses for this server. Record the two IP addresses that correspond to the vCloud Director HTTP service interface and the Console Proxy Service interface.
2. To obtain the FQDNs, use the command `nslookup ipaddress`. Record these FQDNs, which are needed for the HTTP server and Console Proxy service SSL certificates.
3. Change your directory to `/opt/vmware/vcloud-director/jre/bin/keytool`.

`keytool` is installed along with vCloud Director by default. Alternatively, you can use `keytool` on another computer that has a Java version 6 runtime environment installed, and then import the created Java `Keystore` file onto your vCloud Director server. This example assumes that you are using the `keytool` installed on the vCloud Director server.

6.2.2.2.2 Part I: Creating the CSR for the HTTP Service

To create the CSR for the HTTP service:

1. After you have navigated to the `keytool` directory, run the command shown in the following screenshot.

```
keytool -keystore certificates.ks -storetype JCEKS -storepass password -genkey
-keyalg RSA -alias http
```

NOTE

You can change the values for variables, but any changes that you make must be used throughout the entire process. For example, if the keystore name is changed from `certificates.ks` to `mysslcertificate.ks`, you must continue to use `mysslcertificate.ks` in place of `certificates.ks`.

2. When prompted, type your first and last name.
3. When prompted, type the FQDN (fully qualified domain name) to use for the HTTP service certificate.
4. Type the following answers when prompted:

   What is your first and last name? [Unknown]: **`mycloud.mydomain.com`**

   What is the name of your organizational unit? [Unknown]: **`MyCompanyDivision`**

   What is the name of your organization? [Unknown]: **`MyCompanyLegalName`**

   What is the name of your City or Locality? [Unknown]: **`CityOfMyCompany`**

   What is the name of your State or Province? [Unknown]: **`StateOfMyCompany`**

5. Type `yes` to continue when `keytool` summarizes your entries.

```
Is CN=mycloud.quovadisglobal.com, OU=Cloud Services, O=QuoVadis Limited,
L=Hamilton, ST=Pembroke, C=BM correct? [no]:yes
```

NOTE

QuoVadis is used for this example; the information this summary displays should use your company's information.

6. Confirm that you have access to this `keystore` file by entering a password. This uses `psswrd` as an example.
7. Type the key password for `<http> psswrd` (press Enter if it is the same as the `keystore` password).

8. Run the following command to obtain your CSR This creates the `http.csr` file.

```
Keytool -keystore certificates.ks -storetype JCEKS -storepass password -certreq
  -alias -http -file http.csr
```

6.2.2.2.3 Part II: Creating the CSR for the Proxy Service

To create the CSR for the proxy service:

1. In the `keytool` directory, run the following command:

```
keytool -keystore certificates.ks -storetype JCEKS -storepass password -genkey
  -keyalg RSA -alias consoleproxy
```

2. When prompted, type the FQDN (fully qualified domain name) to use for the Console Proxy Service certificate. Use the same FQDN as for the HTTP service certificate.
3. Type the following answers when prompted:

   What is your first and last name? [Unknown]: **`mycloud.mydomain.com`**

   What is the name of your organizational unit? [Unknown]: **`MyCompanyDivision`**

   What is the name of your organization? [Unknown]: **`MyCompanyLegalName`**

   What is the name of your City or Locality? [Unknown]: **`CityOfMyCompany`**

   What is the name of your State or Province? [Unknown]: **`StateOfMyCompany`**

4. Type **`yes`** to continue when `keytool` summarizes your entries.

```
Is CN=mycloud.quovadisglobal.com, OU=Cloud Services, O=QuoVadis Limited,
L=Hamilton, ST=Pembroke, C=BM correct? [no]:yes
```

NOTE

QuoVadis, an international Certification Service Provider (CSP), is used in the summary to provide a clear example. The information this summary displays should use your company's information.

5. Confirm that you have access to this `keystore` file by entering a password. This uses `psswrd` as an example.
6. Type the key password for `<http> psswrd` (press Enter if it is the same as the `keystore` password).
7. Next, run the following command to obtain your CSR (Certificate Signing Request). This creates the `consoleproxy.csr` file.

```
Keytool -keystore certificates.ks -storetype JCEKS password -certreq -alias
consoleproxy -file consoleproxy.csr
```

6.2.2.2.4 CSR Submission and Certificate Collection from QuoVadis

At this point, you should have two separate CSRs, one for the HTTP service and one for the Console Proxy service (named `http.csr` and `consoleproxy.csr`, in this example).

To complete the SSL Certificate Request forms and get access to the QuoVadis Trust/Link system:

1. Copy both files to a computer that has Internet access.
2. Complete the QuoVadis SSL Certificate Request Forms to validate each SSL certificate request. The forms are available at www.quovadisglobal.bm/sitecore/content/Bermuda/Manage/ApplicationForms.aspx.
3. Submit the form to QuoVadis.

QuoVadis then validates your organization. After successful completion, you receive a login to the QuoVadis Trust/Link system.

6.2.2.2.5 Part I: Submitting Your CSRs

To submit your CSRs:

1. Go to https://tl.quovadisglobal.com.
2. Click SSL Subscribers.

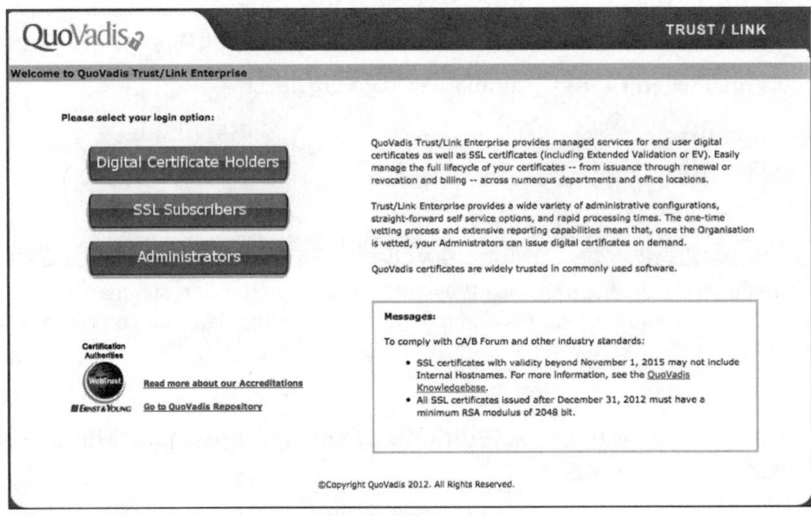

FIGURE 6.5 QuoVadis login type selection screen

3. Log in with your email address and password.

FIGURE 6.6 QuoVadis login screen

4. Click the Request Certificate link under the Subscriber Services heading in the left pane. You have only 10 minutes to complete each request.

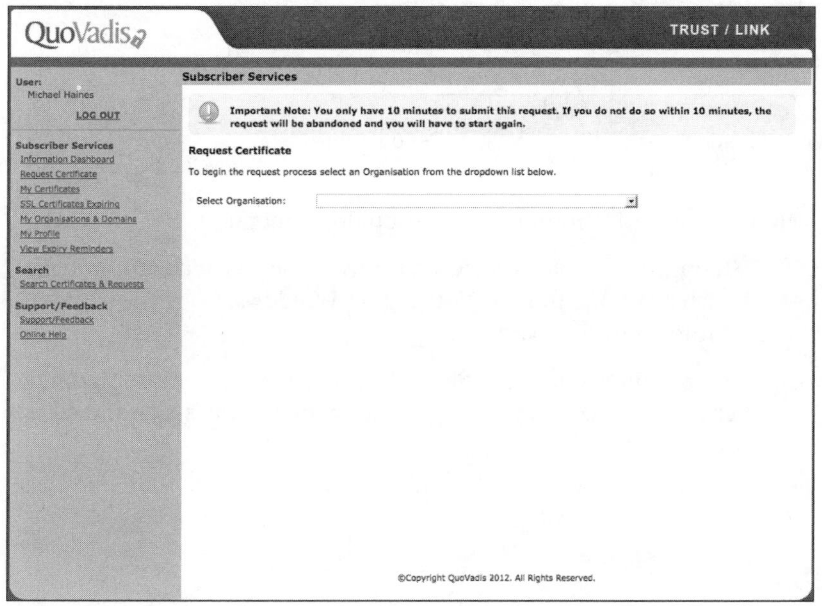

FIGURE 6.7 QuoVadis screen select subscriber services for Request Certificate

5. From the drop-down menu, select the approved organization to which you want to submit an SSL certificate.

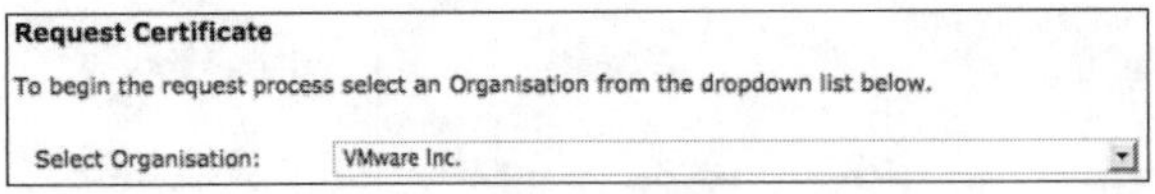

Request Certificate

To begin the request process select an Organisation from the dropdown list below.

Select Organisation: VMware Inc.

FIGURE 6.8 QuoVadis organization entry

6. Select the Policy Template that you want to use from the drop-down menu.

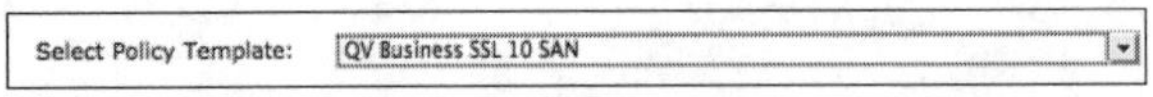

Select Policy Template: QV Business SSL 10 SAN

FIGURE 6.9 QuoVadis policy template selection

NOTE

If you do not have any policy templates to choose from, contact QuoVadis Support.

7. Select the Validity Period of the certificate.

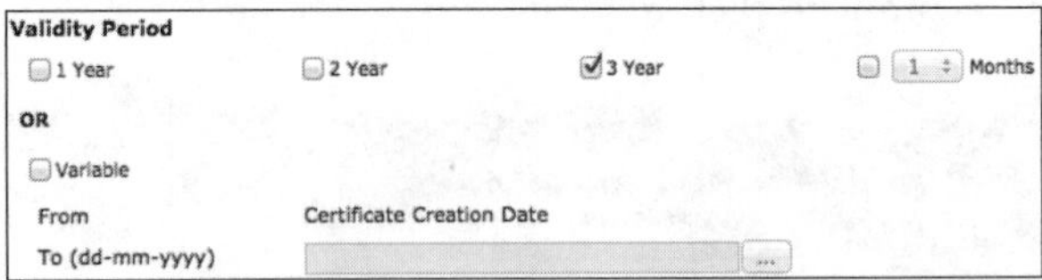

FIGURE 6.10 QuoVadis support – certificate Validity Period settings

8. Optionally, select the Server Platform from the drop-down menu.
9. Open the HTTP CSR (or the Console Proxy CSR, if this is your second run-through) using a text editor such as VI on Linux or Notepad on Windows. Copy the contents from the text editor into your Clipboard).
10. In Trust/Link, paste the contents of your CSR in the Enter Your Certificate Signing Request field, and enter all the contents of your CSR, including the `BEGIN` and `END` lines.

CSR
Enter your Certificate Signing Request: Hide Example CSR
-----BEGIN CERTIFICATE REQUEST-----
-----END CERTIFICATE REQUEST-----

FIGURE 6.11 QuoVadis CSR entry

11. Click Submit. The Validate CSR Content screen decodes and displays the CSR that you submit.
12. Verify the content of the CSR and make changes, if necessary.

Subscriber Services

Important Note: You only have 10 minutes to validate this certificate request. If you do not do so within 10 minutes, the request will be abandoned and you will have to start again.

Request Certificate - Validate CSR Content

Certificate Content

Field Name	From CSR	Updated Value	
DN Email:			optional
Common Name:	domainname.com	mycloud.quovadisglobal.com	* mandatory
Organizational Unit:			optional
Organizational Unit:			optional
Organizational Unit:			optional
Organization:	Legal Name of Organisation	VMware Inc.	* mandatory
Locality:	City associated with Org	Palo Alto	* mandatory
State:	State associated with Org	California	* mandatory
Country:	BERMUDA	UNITED STATES	* mandatory
Subject Alt DNS Name:	domainname.com	mycloud.quovadisglobal.com	* mandatory
Subject Alt DNS Name:			optional
Subject Alt DNS Name:			optional
Subject Alt DNS Name:			optional
Subject Alt DNS Name:			optional

FIGURE 6.12 QuoVadis validation screen for CSR content

13. If the certificate requires any SAN fields, enter them into the Subject Alt DNS Name fields in the Certificate Content section. If any SAN fields are added, verify that the Common Name is included as the first SAN field.

14. When you are finished, click Submit. QuoVadis reviews the details of your certificate and contacts you if anything is incorrect. Your certificate is then approved.
15. Repeat this procedure for `consoleproxy.csr`.

6.2.2.2.6 Part II: Obtaining your SSL Certificates

After the request has been approved, you receive an email informing you that your certificate is ready to download.

To obtain your SSL certificates:

1. Go to https://tl.quovadisglobal.com.
2. Click SSL Subscribers.
3. Log in with your email and password.
4. Click the My Certificates link under Subscriber Services in the left pane.
5. Click the common name of the certificate that you applied for. The status of the certificate should be Valid Certificate.
6. A summary of the certificate details displays. Click Download.
7. On the Download Your SSL Certificate page, click the Download your SSL Certificate in PEM (Base 64) format icon. Rename this file to `http.crt` (assuming that you are downloading the certificate for the HTTP service).
8. Repeat this procedure for the Console Proxy Service SSL certificate. When you obtain this file, rename this file as `consoleproxy.crt`.

6.2.2.2.7 Installing your SSL Certificates

At this point, you should have both SSL certificates for mycloud.mycompany.com, one for the HTTP Service (`http.crt`) and one for the Console Proxy Service (`consoleproxy.crt`).

To install your SSL certificates:

1. Transfer the `http.crt` and `consoleproxy.crt` files to the `keytool` folder.
2. Download the QuoVadis Root CA 2 from www.quovadisglobal.com/en-GB/QVRepository/~/media/Files/Roots/quovadis_rca2_der.ashx.
3. Download the QuoVadis Global SSL ICA from www.quovadisglobal.com/en-GB/QVRepository/~/media/Files/Roots/quovadis_globalssl_der.ashx.
4. Transfer both of these files to the `keytool` folder on the vCloud Director cell.

   The following files should be in the `keytool` folder:

   - `certificates.ks`
   - `http.crt`
   - `consoleproxy.crt`

- quovadis_rca2_der.crt
- quovadis_globalssl_der.crt

5. Run the following command to install the QuoVadis Root CA 2 certificate into the keystore file.

```
keytool -storetype JCEKS -storepass psswrd -keystore certificates.ks -import -
alias Root -trustcerts -file quovadis_rca2_der.crt
```

6. Run the following command to install the QuoVadis Global SSL ICA certificate into the keystore file:

```
keytool -storetype JCEKS -storepass psswrd -keystore certificates.ks -import -
alias intermediate -trustcacerts -file quovadis_globalssl_der_crt
```

7. Run the next two commands to install both the HTTP Services and Console Proxy Service certificates into the keystore file:

```
keytool -storetype JCEKS -storepass psswrd -keystore certificates.ks -import -
alias http -file http.crt
keytool -storetype JCEKS -storepass psswrd -keystore certificates.ks -import -
alias consoleproxy -file consoleproxy.crt
```

8. Run the following command to verify that all the certificates are imported correctly:

```
keytool -storetype JCEKS -storepass psswrd -keystore certificates.ks -list
```

9. Move the certificates.ks file to a directory of your choosing. The directory used in this example is /opt/keystore/.
10. Remove or delete the .crt files from the vCloud Director cell after you have imported the certificates into the keystore:
    - http.crt
    - consoleproxy.crt
    - quovadis_rca2_der.crt
    - quovadis_globalssl_der.crt
11. Run the configuration script to configure vCloud Director. This script is located in the /opt/vmware/vcloud-director/bin/configure directory.
12. Specify the IP addresses for both the HTTP and Console Proxy Service.
13. When requested, enter the path to the keystore file. This is the folder where you uploaded your certificates.ks file.
14. Enter the path to the Java keystore that contains your SSL certificates and private keys:/opt/keystore/certificate.ks.

6

15. Type the password to access the keystore file. Also type private key passwords for the certificates.

Please enter the password for the keystore: **psswrd**

Please enter the private key password for the 'http' SSL certificate:

Please enter the private key password for the consoleproxy SSL certificate:

16. Finish the configuration according to your setup. When the process is complete, your SSL certificate should work with vCloud Director.

6.2.2.3 Design Implications

The following are design implications for using SSL cetificates with vCloud Director.

- When using SSL certificates, it is important to understand and evaluate the different types of SSL certificates available for your specific requirement.
- In a production environment, do not configure vCloud Director to use self-signed certificates. This is a poor security practice. Self-signed certificates are digitally signed by the private key that corresponds to the public key included in the certificate, instead of having a CA sign the certificate. By self-signing a certificate, you attest that you are who you say you are. No trusted third party is involved to verify the identity of the system that owns the certificate.
- Self-signed certificates do not have a valid chain of signatures leading to a trusted root certificate. They provide a weaker form of security because, although you can verify that such a certificate is internally consistent, anyone can create one; you cannot know whether it is safe to trust the issuer or the site the certificate is coming from. Nevertheless, self-signed certificates are common. For example, vCenter installations use a self-signed certificate by default.
- The server key store should be considered highly sensitive because a compromise of the server key allows impersonation of the server and/or access to the encrypted traffic. Java keystores provide a method of securely storing private keys and their associated certificates, protected by a password. vCloud Director supports only the JCEKS format for keystore files. (Other formats that Java supports include PKCS12 and JKS. JKS is less secure, so it is not recommended.)

6.3 Organization Virtual Datacenter Examples

Understanding how to configure and set up the various allocation models is key to building out your vCloud instance. Allocation models define the way resources are allocated from the provider virtual datacenter to a vCloud Director organization virtual datacenter. They also define the way resources can be used when deploying VMware vApps™ within the vCloud Director organization's virtual datacenter. The allocation models follow:

- Pay as you go
- Reservation pool
- Allocation pool

Because allocation models are specific to a particular organization, they should be treated individually for each consumer. Although many providers use a starting template approach, allocation models are specific to a particular organization and should be configured to meet the needs of the consumer who will be using them. The provider must understand the individual consumer's requirements in the context of the available configuration options.

6.3.1 Pay As You Go Allocation Model

Deployment Models: Private, public

Example Components: vCloud Director 5.1, vCloud Networking and Security Edge 5.1, vSphere 5.1

6.3.1.1 Background

The following is an example of a vCloud provider setting up the pay as you go model based on the consumer's criteria.

6.3.1.2 Use Case

A new customer known as Company2 is requesting resources on Company1's vCloud and has asked the vCloud provider to obtain capacity in the Company1 vCloud. Company2 wants a model that provides the following:

- Paying for resources as the company uses them, and unlimited access to resources within the organization virtual datacenter.
- Very-high-performance virtual machines.
- Highest level of memory guarantees. Memory performance is a larger concern than CPU.
- Virtual machines with multiple vCPUs that have a minimum speed of at least 2GHz and some level of CPU guarantee.

The pay as you go model was chosen because it satisfies Company2's requirements and applies the resources the consumer wants the same way to each virtual machine they deploy.

6.3.1.2.1 Assumptions

The following are assumptions for this use case.

- Company1 has a single configured provider virtual datacenter.
- Networking is routed. vCloud Networking and Security gateways are deployed and configured after the organization is configured.

6.3.1.2.2 Organization Functional Requirements

- 100% memory reservation
- Agreed-to 50% CPU reservation
- Minimum CPU speed 2GHz
- Unlimited resources within the organization virtual datacenter
    - No CPU or memory quota
    - No maximum number of virtual machines
- No specific storage requirements
    - Storage is thin provisioned.
    - Fast provisioning is disabled.

Based on the requirements, Company1 will use the settings shown in Table 6.5 to configure Company2's organization.

TABLE 6.5 Company2 Pay As You Go Organization Settings

Setting	Memory Reservation
CPU Quota	Unlimited
CPU Resources Guaranteed	50%
vCPU Speed	2GHz
Memory Quota	Unlimited
Memory Resources Guaranteed	100%
Maximum Number of VMs	Unlimited

6.3.1.3 Example

Figure 6.13 shows the vCloud Director configuration for Company2's organization.

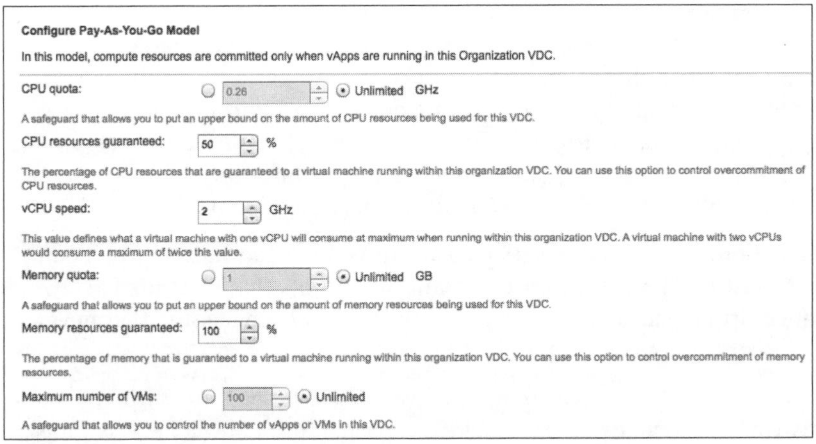

Configure Pay-As-You-Go Model

In this model, compute resources are committed only when vApps are running in this Organization VDC.

CPU quota: 0.26 Unlimited GHz

A safeguard that allows you to put an upper bound on the amount of CPU resources being used for this VDC.

CPU resources guaranteed: 50 %

The percentage of CPU resources that are guaranteed to a virtual machine running within this organization VDC. You can use this option to control overcommitment of CPU resources.

vCPU speed: 2 GHz

This value defines what a virtual machine with one vCPU will consume at maximum when running within this organization VDC. A virtual machine with two vCPUs would consume a maximum of twice this value.

Memory quota: 1 Unlimited GB

A safeguard that allows you to put an upper bound on the amount of memory resources being used for this VDC.

Memory resources guaranteed: 100 %

The percentage of memory that is guaranteed to a virtual machine running within this organization VDC. You can use this option to control overcommitment of memory resources.

Maximum number of VMs: 100 Unlimited

A safeguard that allows you to control the number of vApps or VMs in this VDC.

FIGURE 6.13 Pay as you go settings

The settings correspond to Company2's requirements:

- **CPU Quota:** Provisioning stops when the virtual datacenter has reached the configured amount. For example, if this is set to 100GHz and all virtual machines are provisioned with 1GHz CPUs, then when 100GHz worth of CPU is deployed, no more will be provisioned. This can be a combined total based on the number of vCPUs on each virtual machine.
- **CPU Resources Guaranteed:** This sets a per-virtual-machine reservation on CPU, based on a given percentage.
- **vCPU Speed:** This sets a per-virtual-machine CPU limit on the specified amount.
- **Memory Quota:** Setting a limit prevents provisioning of more virtual machines when that limit is reached.
- **Memory Resources Guaranteed:** This sets a per-virtual-machine reservation on memory, based on a given percentage.
- **Maximum Number of VMs:** This is a hard limit on the organization virtual datacenter for the total number of virtual machines that can be deployed. This can be useful to prevent overcommitment.

NOTE

The vSphere resource pool expandable reservation for both CPU and memory should be Enabled.

These settings can be changed to meet the consumer's functional requirements for performance and cost over time.

6.3.1.4 Design Implications

Because this allocation model assigns all settings on a per-virtual-machine basis, any updates to this model require a shutdown and restart of the virtual machines. Based on the selected settings, this could be considered one of the best-performing models in terms of guaranteeing the allocated virtual machine resources. This is because each virtual machine is always guaranteed its settings and can go to the root resource pool if needed. Company2 gets 100% of physical memory to all virtual machines and 50% physical CPU.

Essentially, this model provides unlimited resources within the organization virtual datacenter, so providers must be diligent in capacity planning. Company1 must proactively monitor the provider virtual datacenter for resource availability to make sure that new virtual machines can continue to be deployed and powered on.

The pay as you go model also has the capability to leverage elastic provider virtual datacenters. The pay as you go model can use this added capacity automatically and is transparent to consumers. They can continue to deploy virtual machines as long as capacity exists to meet their requirements.

6.3.2 Reservation Pool Model

Deployment Models: Private, public

Example Components: vCloud Director 5.1, vCloud Networking and Security Edge 5.1, vSphere 5.1

6.3.2.1 Background

The following is an example of a provider creating the reservation pool model based on the consumer's criteria.

6.3.2.2 Use Case

A new customer known as Company2 is requesting resources on Company1's vCloud and has asked the vCloud provider to obtain capacity in the Company1 vCloud. Company2 wants a model that provides the following:

- Defined memory and CPU resources that are consistent for billing. The customer has not yet determined the number of virtual machines it will have, but it wants consistent billing.
- A dedicated pool of resources to distribute to virtual machines as the consumer sees fit when deploying workloads. Based on the initial pool of resources requested, Company1 will also apply a total virtual machine limit to the pool to help Company2 limit overcommitment.
- No fast provisioning is done, but thin provisioning is acceptable.

Settings can be adjusted as needed to meet the needs of Company2's vApps.

Based on these requirements, the reservation pool model was chosen as the best fit to meet Company2's needs. This model provides dedicated resources to start, with control over resource allocation to the virtual machines from vCloud Director.

6.3.2.2.1 Assumptions

The following are assumptions for this use case.

- Company1 has a single configured provider virtual datacenter. Storage performance is predetermined.
- Networking will be routed. vCloud Networking and Security gateways will be deployed and configured after the organization is configured.
- The customer will control and maintain the individual virtual machine resource configurations.

6.3.2.2.2 Organization Functional Requirements

- 25GB memory
- 25GHz CPU
- 25 maximum virtual machines, determined by Company1 based on the organization sizing to prevent overcommitment
- Personal control over the individual virtual machine resource configurations
- No fast provisioning done, but thin provisioning enabled

Based on the requirements, Company1 will use the settings shown in Table 6.6 to configure the Company2's organization.

TABLE 6.6 Company2 Reservation Pool Organization Settings

Parameter	Setting
CPU Allocation	25GHz
Memory Allocation	25GB
Maximum Number of VMs	25

6.3.2.3 Example

Figure 6.14 shows the vCloud Director configuration for Company2's organization.

Configure Reservation Pool Model

In this model, you allocate resources to the organization VDC. All resources are guaranteed to the organization VDC, but users in the organization can control commitment on per-VM basis.

CPU allocation: 25 GHz (93% of available Provider vDC capacity of 26.86GHz)

The amount of CPU resources reserved for this organization VDC.

Memory allocation: 14.9 GB (100% of available Provider vDC capacity of 14.90GB)

The amount of memory resources reserved for this organization VDC.

Maximum number of VMs: 25 Unlimited

A safeguard that allows you to control the maximum number of virtual machines in this organization VDC.

The committed resources from the primary resource pool of Provider VDC, 'ProviderVDC01' using these allocation settings:

Metric	Total	Allocation	Reservation Committed	Reservation Used
CPU	33.56 GHz	57.24GHz (170.46%)	44.48GHz (132.46%)	31.78GHz (94.65%)
Memory	18.62 GB	32.76GB (175.94%)	25.69GB (137.97%)	18.86GB (101.29%)

Move your mouse over each column header to see more information.

The typical number of vApps or VMs you can expect using these allocation settings:

25 'small' VMs: 1.0 GHz CPU = 1 vCPUs * 256 MHz vCPU Rating, 512 MB RAM

12 'medium' VMs: 4.0 GHz CPU = 2 vCPUs * 256 MHz vCPU Rating, 1.0 GB RAM

6 'large' VMs: 16.0 GHz CPU = 4 vCPUs * 256 MHz vCPU Rating, 2.0 GB RAM

FIGURE 6.14 Reservation pool Settings

The settings correspond to Company2's requirements:

- **CPU Allocation:** This sets the CPU on the vSphere resource pool with a reservation and limit equal to the selected amount.
- **Memory Allocation:** This sets the memory on the vSphere resource pool with a reservation and limit equal to the selected amount.
- **Maximum Number of VMs:** This is a hard limit on the virtual datacenter for the total number of virtual machines that can be deployed. It can be useful to prevent overcommitment.

NOTE

The vSphere resource pool expandable reservation for both CPU and memory should be Disabled.

These settings can be changed to meet the consumer's functional requirements for performance and cost over time. In fact, changes to these settings can be made on the fly to increase resources. Depending on the number of vApps deployed, carefully consider the potential impact before reducing values.

6.3.2.4 Design Implications

Because this allocation model assigns all settings on a resource pool basis, updates to this model do not require a shutdown and restart of the virtual machines to pick up the changes. Based on the settings chosen, this model could be considered one of the best models because the consumer has control over how the pool of resources is divided among the virtual machines.

The provider must monitor the use of the Maximum Number of VMs setting. If this is left as unlimited and the consumer does not set any per-virtual-machine reservations, there is potential for overcommitment. In theory, a consumer can deploy more or larger virtual machines than the pool is configured for (additional resources such as memory could be paged out to satisfy the configuration). Assigning a limit to the maximum total number of virtual machines can help keep the pool within the expected size.

Huge virtual machines can be created using this model, but it is important to understand the role overhead reservations play, along with the standard per-virtual-machine reservations. Understanding the effect of these settings on vSphere is crucial for implementation.

For more information, see Chapter 13 in the book *VMware vSphere 5.1 Clustering Deepdive*, available from retailers.

6.3.3 Allocation Pool Model

Deployment Models: Private, public

Example Components: vCloud Director 5.1, vCloud Networking and Security Edge 5.1, vSphere 5.1

6.3.3.1 Background

The following is an example of a vCloud provider setting up the allocation pool model based on the consumer's criteria.

6.3.3.2 Use Case

A new customer known as Company2 is requesting resources on Company1's vCloud and has asked the vCloud provider to obtain capacity in the Company1 vCloud. Company2 wants a model that provides the following:

- A combination of the characteristics of the pay as you go per-virtual-machine settings with the pool-based aspect of the reservation pool.
- High-performing virtual machines, but the company does not want the management overhead of setting resource options for each virtual machine. The company wants to start with a set amount of resources, with a portion automatically guaranteed. It is not sure how many virtual machines it will need to deploy.
- No fast provisioning is done, but thin provisioning is acceptable.

Based on the initial pool of resources Company2 requested, Company1 will apply a total virtual machine limit to the pool to help Company2 to limit overcommitment. Company1 can adjust these settings as needed to meet more or less demand from Customer2's vApps, but some virtual machine restarts would be needed.

Based on these requirements, the allocation pool model was chosen as the best fit to meet Company2's needs. This model gives the company dedicated resources to start with, and preset guarantees are applied to each virtual machine, along with the total guarantee set in the resource pool.

6.3.3.2.1 Assumptions

The following are assumptions for this use case.

- Company1 has a single provider virtual datacenter configured. Storage performance is predetermined.
- Networking will be routed. vCloud Director will deploy vCloud Networking and Security Gateways at network creation time after the organization is configured.

6.3.3.2.2 Organization Functional Requirements

- 25GB memory with 100% guarantee. This is automatically applied to the pool and to the individual virtual machines.
- 25GHz CPU with 50% guarantee. Applied to the pool, but not to the virtual machines.
- 12 maximum virtual machines. Determined by Company1, based on the organization sizing, to prevent overcommitment.
- vCPU speed of at least 2GHz.
- No fast provisioning.

Based on the requirements, Company1 will use the settings in Table 6.7 to configure Company2's organization.

TABLE 6.7 Company2 Allocation Pool Organization Settings

Parameter	Setting
CPU Allocation	25GHz
Memory Allocation	25GB
vCPU Speed	2GHz
Maximum Number of VMs	12

6.3.3.3 Example

Figure 6.15 shows the vCloud Director configuration for Company2's organization.

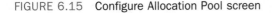

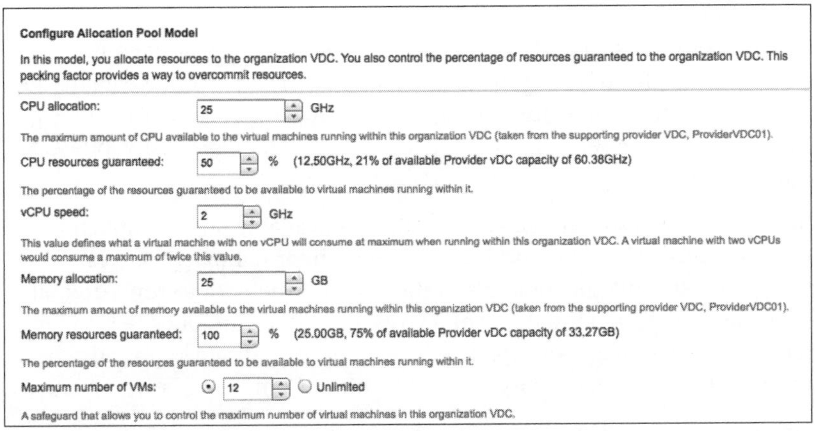

Configure Allocation Pool Model

In this model, you allocate resources to the organization VDC. You also control the percentage of resources guaranteed to the organization VDC. This packing factor provides a way to overcommit resources.

CPU allocation: 25 GHz

The maximum amount of CPU available to the virtual machines running within this organization VDC (taken from the supporting provider VDC, ProviderVDC01).

CPU resources guaranteed: 50 % (12.50GHz, 21% of available Provider vDC capacity of 60.38GHz)

The percentage of the resources guaranteed to be available to virtual machines running within it.

vCPU speed: 2 GHz

This value defines what a virtual machine with one vCPU will consume at maximum when running within this organization VDC. A virtual machine with two vCPUs would consume a maximum of twice this value.

Memory allocation: 25 GB

The maximum amount of memory available to the virtual machines running within this organization VDC (taken from the supporting provider VDC, ProviderVDC01).

Memory resources guaranteed: 100 % (25.00GB, 75% of available Provider vDC capacity of 33.27GB)

The percentage of the resources guaranteed to be available to virtual machines running within it.

Maximum number of VMs: 12 Unlimited

A safeguard that allows you to control the maximum number of virtual machines in this organization VDC.

FIGURE 6.15 Configure Allocation Pool screen

The settings correspond to Company2's requirements:

- **CPU Allocation:** This sets the CPU on the vSphere resource pool with a reservation and limit equal to the selected amount.
- **CPU Resources Guaranteed:** This is the amount of the vSphere reservation on the resource pool.
- **vCPU Speed:** This sets a per-virtual-machine CPU limit to the specified amount.
- **Memory Allocation:** This sets the memory on the vSphere resource pool, with a reservation and limit equal to the specified amount.
- **Memory Resources Guaranteed:** This is the amount of the vSphere reservation on the resource pool and on the individual virtual machines.
- **Maximum Number of VMs:** This is a hard limit on the virtual datacenter for the total number of virtual machines that can be deployed. It can be useful to prevent overcommitment.

NOTE

The vSphere resource pool that corresponds to the virtual datacenter has an expandable reservation on both CPU and has memory Disabled.

These settings can be changed to meet the consumer's functional requirements for performance and cost over time. In fact, changes to these settings can be made on the fly to increase resources. Depending on the number of vApps deployed, carefully consider the potential impact before reducing values.

6.3.3.4 Design Implications

Because this model assigns settings to both a resource pool and the virtual machines, any updates require a shutdown and restart of the virtual machines. The percentage guarantee for memory applies to every virtual machine in this virtual datacenter, similar to the pay as you go model. Additionally, the settings are applied to the resource pool in vSphere, as with the reservation pool model.

With the settings in Figure 6.15, 100% memory reservation is available on the vSphere resource pool and 50% of the CPU reservation is available. Each virtual machine created also requires a 100% virtual machine memory reservation within the pool to run. After all pool resources are assigned, no more virtual machines are allowed to run, but the settings can be adjusted. Because the resource pool expandable reservation is disabled, in most cases, VMware admission control prevents too many virtual machines from being powered on.

Lowering the percentage guarantee below 75% or even 50% can also create challenges because the resource pool gets only a fraction of the configured resources shown as Available Reservations. Virtual machines are still required to reserve those same values at power-on. When using the allocation pool model, higher values are always better, to prevent any limitations within the organization virtual datacenter.

The allocation pool model can also leverage elastic provider virtual datacenters in vCloud Director. The allocation pool model can use this added capacity automatically, without affecting Company2. The company can continue to deploy virtual machines as long as there is capacity to meet the requirements.

Understanding the effect of these settings on vSphere is crucial to implementation. As with all the allocation models, the provider needs to monitor the customer's virtual datacenters and keep the customer informed about resource usage. If a virtual datacenter runs out of resources, vCloud Director sends an error message to the customer.

6.3.4 Service Provider Performance Offerings

Deployment Models: Private, public

Example Components: vCloud Director 5.1, vCloud Networking and Security Edge 5.1, vSphere 5.1

6.3.4.1 Background

During any provider and consumer conversation, the topic of virtual machine performance arises. In some cases, this is referred to as one element of a service-level agreement (SLA). In this document, the aspect of a tenant's performance is examined in relation to the three allocation models.

NOTE

Higher performance levels are defined as guaranteeing physical resources from the provider virtual datacenter to the consumer. Actual virtual machine performance can vary, based on the application running within the virtual machine. However, guaranteeing required resource availability to a virtual machine provides the best performance.

We previously showed examples of how to create virtual datacenters based on various use cases. The intent in this case is to expand on the tenant requirements that drive decisions to the different allocation models. Thinking about allocation models in the context of performance rather than uptime or availability is just another option.

6.3.4.2 Use Case

Company1 has built a new vCloud Director environment and is working on how to present options to customers for performance-based virtual datacenters. Knowing that the vCloud Director allocation models are largely reservation based, the company wants to determine the best set of requirements and considerations to take into account when talking to customers. Company1 wants to tailor offerings to the customer's needs but has not finalized the service offerings.

6.3.4.2.1 Assumptions

The following are assumptions for this use case.

- The same provider virtual datacenter backs the various allocation models.
- Storage is currently the same within the provider virtual datacenter.
- The catalog of virtual machines will vary in size.
- An elastic virtual datacenter will be used, if needed (assuming that it can be used).

To develop a menu of options for customers, three levels of performance have been determined for each allocation model. These can be modified as customer needs change. Company1 defines performance categories as Low, Medium, and High. This is different from how virtual machine templates are defined (Small, Medium, and Large). The goal is to balance the machine configurations with the actual allocation model under which customers are running.

6.3.4.3 Example

Company1 originally set up template-based organization virtual datacenters that all provide the same consumer offering within each available model (see Table 6.8).

TABLE 6.8 Company1 Pay As You Go Offering

Parameter	Low	Medium	High
vCPU Speed	1GHz	2GHz	2.5GHz
CPU Guarantee	0%	25%	50%
Memory Guarantee	0%	50%	100%
Memory Quota	—	—	—
CPU Quota	—	—	—
Maximum Number of VMs	Unlimited	Unlimited	Unlimited

Pay as you go is an "all you can use" model, with the only restriction being the resources available in the provider virtual datacenter. The settings in Table 6.8 are assigned individually on a per-virtual-machine basis. In effect, the memory and CPU guarantees allocate physical resources to these virtual machines. Therefore, a 100% guarantee means that each virtual machine is granted 100% of its requested resources within the virtual datacenter, as represented in the case of memory for High as long as the physical resources are available. In this example, a 2.5GHz CPU with 50% CPU and 100% memory guarantee could effectively be the highest-performing virtual machine possible.

TABLE 6.9 Company1 Reservation Pool Offering

Parameter	Low	Medium	High
CPU Allocation	15GHz	25GHz	50GHz
Memory Allocation	15GB	25GB	50GB
Maximum Number of VMs	15	25	50

With the reservation pool model, the responsibility is on the consumer to assign physical resources from the pool to the virtual machines. This model effectively reserves 100% of the physical resources configured for CPU and memory from Company1's provider virtual datacenter. Other customers cannot use CPU and memory resources. Consumers do not necessarily get better performance, but the potential exists for higher-performing and lower-performing virtual machines within the consumer's organization. The consumer must decide which virtual machines will be configured for higher or lower performance within the given pool of resources. Company1 has provided resources that the consumer can allocate as desired. The levels represent the larger amounts of resources a customer has available. This increases the potential for more individual virtual machines to perform better, provided that they are configured correctly. Table 6.10 shows example settings for the allocation pool offering by Company1.

TABLE 6.10 Company1 Allocation Pool Offering

Parameter	Low	Medium	High
CPU Allocation	15GHz	25GHz	50GHz
CPU Guarantee	50% (7.5GHz)	75% (18.75GHz)	100% (50GHz)
vCPU Speed	1GHz	2GHz	2.5GHz
Memory Allocation	15GB	25GB	50GB
Memory Guarantee*	50% (7.5GB)	75% (18.75GB)	100% (50GB)
Maximum Number of VMs	15	25	50

*Memory is assigned to an individual virtual machine based on the percentage.

With the allocation pool, the available resources in the pool are determined by the guarantees assigned. Table 6.10 lists the actual available resources within the pool for the consumer to use. This is similar to the reservation pool model. Effectively, the high-performance option is truly that—it gives the pool a 100% guarantee on not only the resource pool, but also the individual virtual machines. The High option is almost a full combination of the other two models. The only real difference is that when Low or Medium is used, some virtual machines can access the extra, unreserved resources depending on the configuration.

6.3.4.4 Design Implications

High performance relates to guaranteeing physical resources in the provider virtual datacenter. Providers must keep in mind that this could mean lower consolidation ratios on the provider clusters. In all cases, Company1 has imposed a "total number of virtual machines" limit on the consumers. This is to mitigate some of the following considerations:

- **Pay as you go:** With this model, the consumer might get performance that is easier to manage, but because of its "all you can use" (within the virtual datacenter) model, Company1 must closely monitor the provider virtual datacenter. If the provider virtual datacenter is low on resources, it can affect the consumer's capability to add more virtual machines.
- **Reservation pool:** With this model, it is up to the consumer to use resources responsibly to get the desired performance within the pool. Otherwise, higher consolidation ratios can be achieved, but performance can suffer. In addition, this can affect other consumers on the same datastores because of swapping.
- **Allocation pool:** This model can mitigate some of the issues found in the reservation pool model. Because this is a hybrid of the pay as you go and reservation pool models, it handles everything if you use the high-performance configuration. By using the high-performance configuration, you get a dedicated pool that the consumer cannot grow out of (like the reservation pool). Each virtual machine in the pool gets 100% guarantee of the available resources. When the pool is completely consumed, provisioning stops.

Company1 has designed the deployment with some aspects of consumer performance in mind, not only with each allocation model, but also with levels within each model. These templates are not static—they are just a starting point. Customer requirements can drive customization and changes to these options. Company1 will bill customers for any changes required. The company feels that consumers can start with these models and modify them as needed.

NOTE

It is not possible for a consumer to change models without downtime and migration. Modifying the settings of each allocation model is possible, but some virtual machine reboots might be required.

6.4 Networking Examples

6.4.1 vApp Load Balancing with vCloud Networking and Security Edge

Deployment Models: Private, public

Example Components: vCloud Director 5.1, vCloud Networking and Security Edge 5.1, vSphere 5.1

6.4.1.1 Background

The vCloud Networking and Security Edge Gateway (Edge Gateway) introduced by vCloud Director supports and exposes a powerful load balancer to the organization administrator. This section demonstrates a simple example of its configuration.

6.4.1.2 Use Case

An organization administrator is setting up a simple *n*-tier application comprised of front-end web servers and back-end database servers. For high availability and scaling, the administrator wants to load-balance these web servers. The administrator wants to avoid using in-guest techniques and does not want to deploy additional virtual machines to deliver this load-balancing service because of the burden of having to manage additional infrastructure workloads. The administrator has decided to use the out-of-the-box load-balancing service that the Edge Gateway provides, as the easiest way to meet these needs. The administrator wants to use public IP addresses to be able to define a virtual IP that balances (round-robin) two web servers that are instantiated in an organization.

6.4.1.3 Example

The Edge Gateway is connected on one side to the vCloud Director external network, which connects directly to the Internet. It is also connected to two routed organization virtual datacenter networks. Our focus is on the network named Org-External-Routed-Internet because this is where the web servers to be load balanced are connected. Figure 6.16 shows the network device information.

TABLE 6.11 Network Device Information

Device	Location	IP/Netmask	Notes
Internet-NAT	External network	192.168.0.0/24	Class C network
	Static IP pool	192.168.0.120–130	10 public IP addresses
Org-External-Routed-Internet	Organization virtual datacenter network	10.179.3.0/24	Class C network
	Static IP pool	10.179.3.11–200	190 internal IP addresses
Edge-Gateway	COE organization	External: 192.168.0.120	Internet-NAT
		Internal: 10.179.3.1	Org-External-Routed-Internet
WebApp-01	COE organization	10.179.3.11	Guest IP address
WebApp-02	COE organization	10.179.3.12	Guest IP address

Figure 6.16 shows the components of a typical load-balancing arrangement.

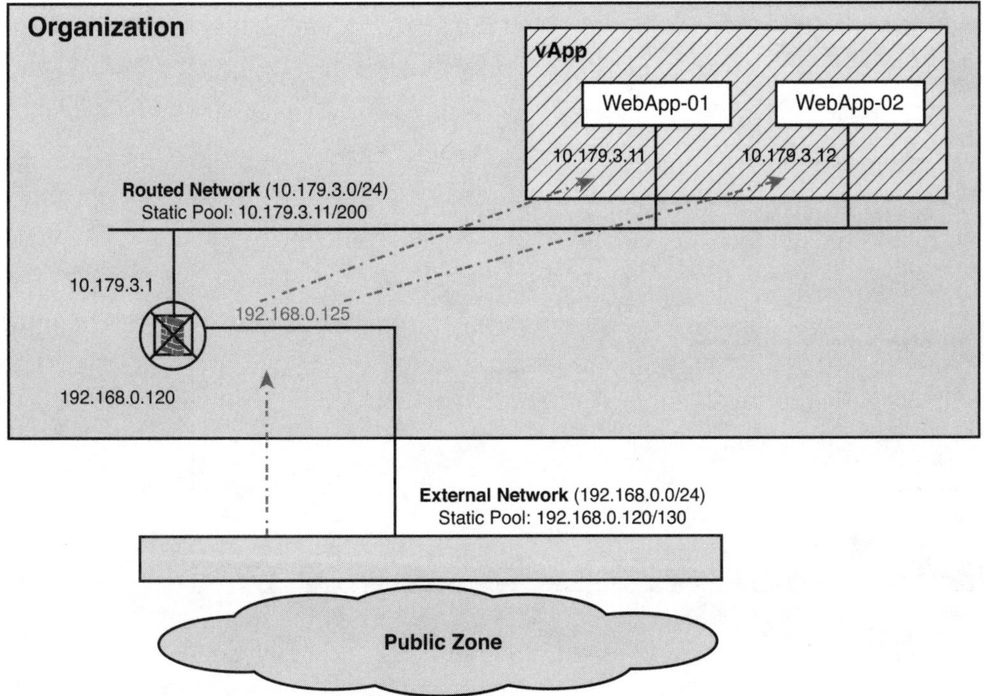

FIGURE 6.16 Graphical summary of components

To create load balancing with vCloud Networking and Security Edge:

1. To create a load-balancing rule, the organization administrator must use a public IP address from the external network that the vCloud administrator preallocated. In this example, the vCloud administrator reserved for this vCloud Networking and Security Edge instance the public IP address range 192.168.0.125–130, as indicated in the vCloud Networking and Security Edge Gateway properties. One of these reserved IP addresses will be used later as the virtual IP address.

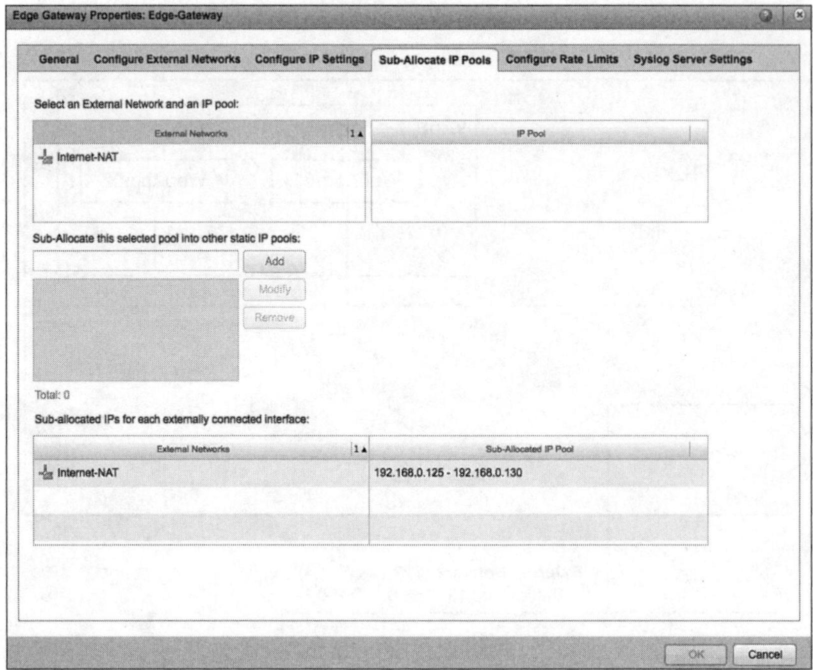

FIGURE 6.17

2. Open the vCloud Networking and Security Edge Gateway services page and click the Load Balancer tab to configure the load-balancing rule.

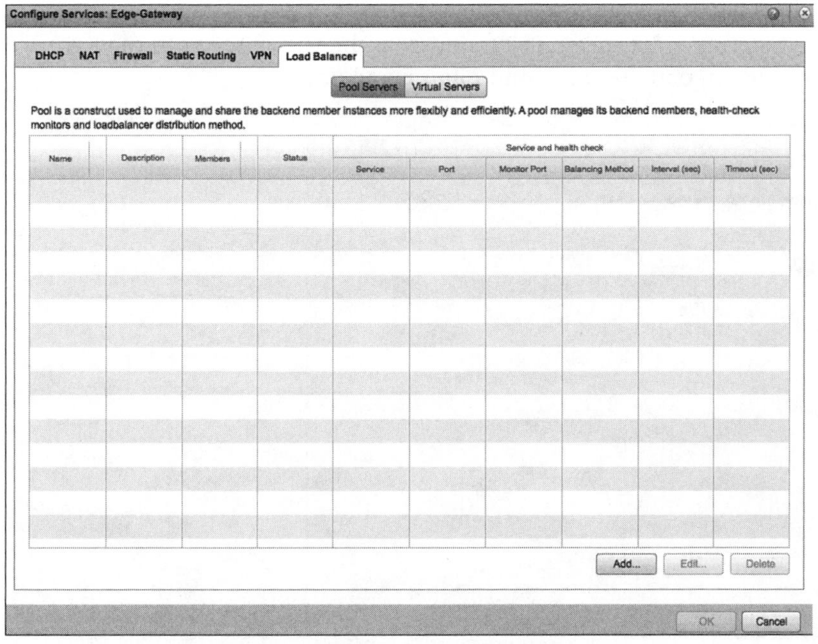

FIGURE 6.18

3. Click Pool Servers and list the web servers that are to be load balanced.

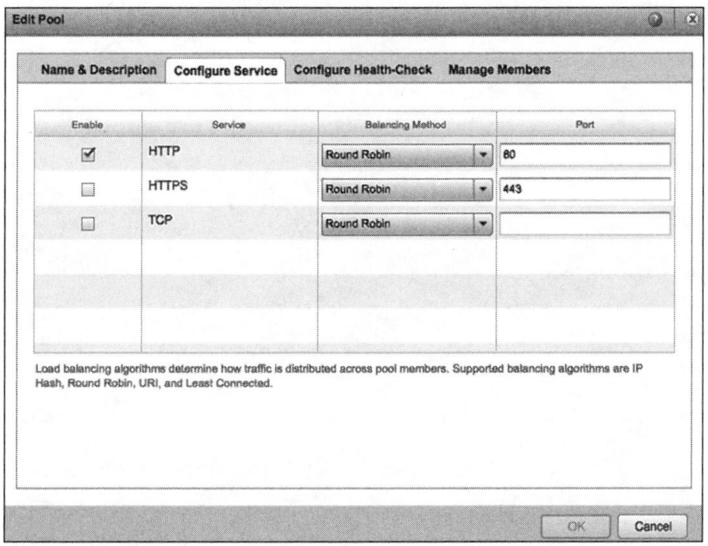

FIGURE 6.19

4. Configure the two web servers in this pool, and use the vCloud Networking and Security Edge Gateway to balance HTTP traffic from the virtual server to the web servers on destination port 80 in a round-robin manner.

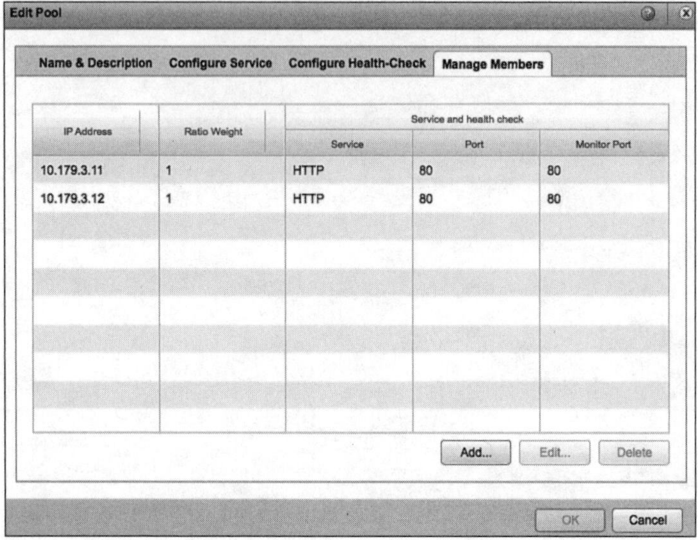

FIGURE 6.20

5. Now that a pool of servers is configured, a virtual server can be configured from the following view of the Load Balancer tab.

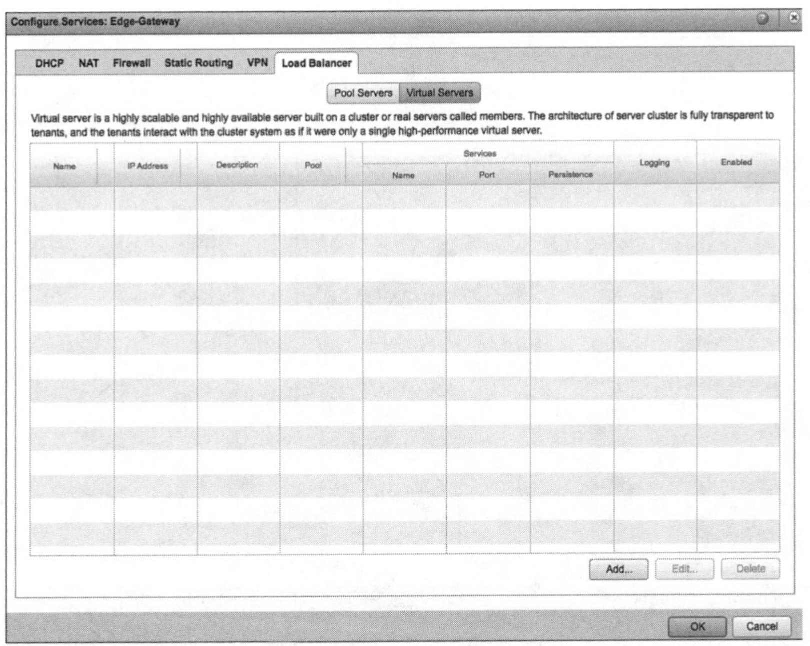

FIGURE 6.21

6. You can configure a new virtual server by selecting the previously defined pool and allowing the services you want (see Figure 6.16). This is the pool created in the previous step that contains the two front-end web servers.

   When the configuration is finalized, the new virtual server is displayed in the Load Balancer page of the vCloud Networking and Security Edge Gateway services.

Add Virtual Server

Name: WebApp-vServer *

Description:

Applied on: Internet-NAT

IP address: 192.168.0.125 *

Pool: WebApp-LB-Pool Supports (HTTP)

Services:

Enabled	Name	Port	Persistence Method	Cookie name	Cookie mode
☑	HTTP	80	None		
☐	HTTPS	443	Session Id		
☐	TCP		None		

☑ Enabled

☑ Log network traffic for virtual server

OK Cancel

FIGURE 6.22

NOTE

The 192.168.0.125 IP address used in the example is one of the public IP addresses (on the external network) assigned to this vCloud Networking and Security Edge instance. This is used to create a load balancing rule that leverages the vCloud Networking and Security Edge DNAT capabilities.

7. Confirm that the virtual server was created as intended.

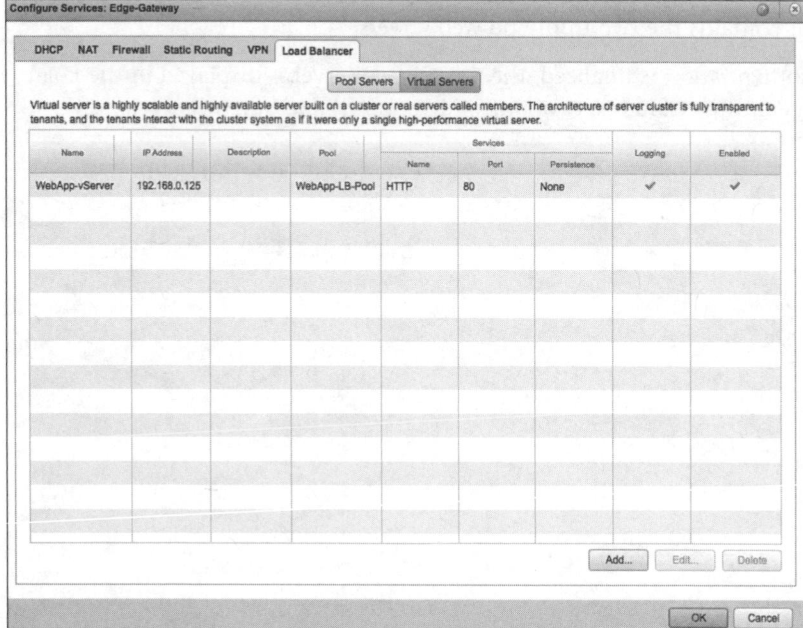

FIGURE 6.23

At this point, connecting from outside the organization to http://192.168.0.125 results in the vCloud Networking and Security Edge Gateway balancing in a round-robin manner the two web servers with IP addresses http://10.179.3.11 and http://10.179.3.11, respectively.

This load balancing configuration was done at the vCloud Networking and Security Edge Gateway level, backing the organization network. This configuration is not possible on the vCloud Networking and Security Edge device backing a vApp network.

6.4.2 Static Routing

Deployment Models: Private, public

Example Components: vCloud Director 5.1, vCloud Networking and Security Edge 5.1, vSphere 5.1

6.4.2.1 Background

The static routing functionality of vCloud Networking and Security Edge (Edge) that is exposed through vCloud Director can be used to route packets and establish communication between vApp networks that would not normally be capable of communicating. The two vApp networks can be connected to the same the virtual datacenter network or to separate organization virtual datacenter networks. Although establishing an interorganization IPsec VPN tunnel between the QE and Engineering organization would provide connectivity, using the static routing feature limits communication to specific vApp networks defined in the routing statements. This example covers specifically static routing, not NAT using Edge firewall rules to provide security and limit access to the destination IP address.

6.4.2.2 Use Case

In this static routing example, the build01.qe.vmlab.com virtual machine deployed in the QE organization must access a specific code repository server code01.eng.vmlab.com that exists in a separate engineering organization for periodic downloads of the updated software builds for testing. This testing takes place on virtual machines inside the QE organization, and the communication remains inside the internal physical network.

6.4.2.3 Example

Figure 6.24 shows an example of static routing.

6

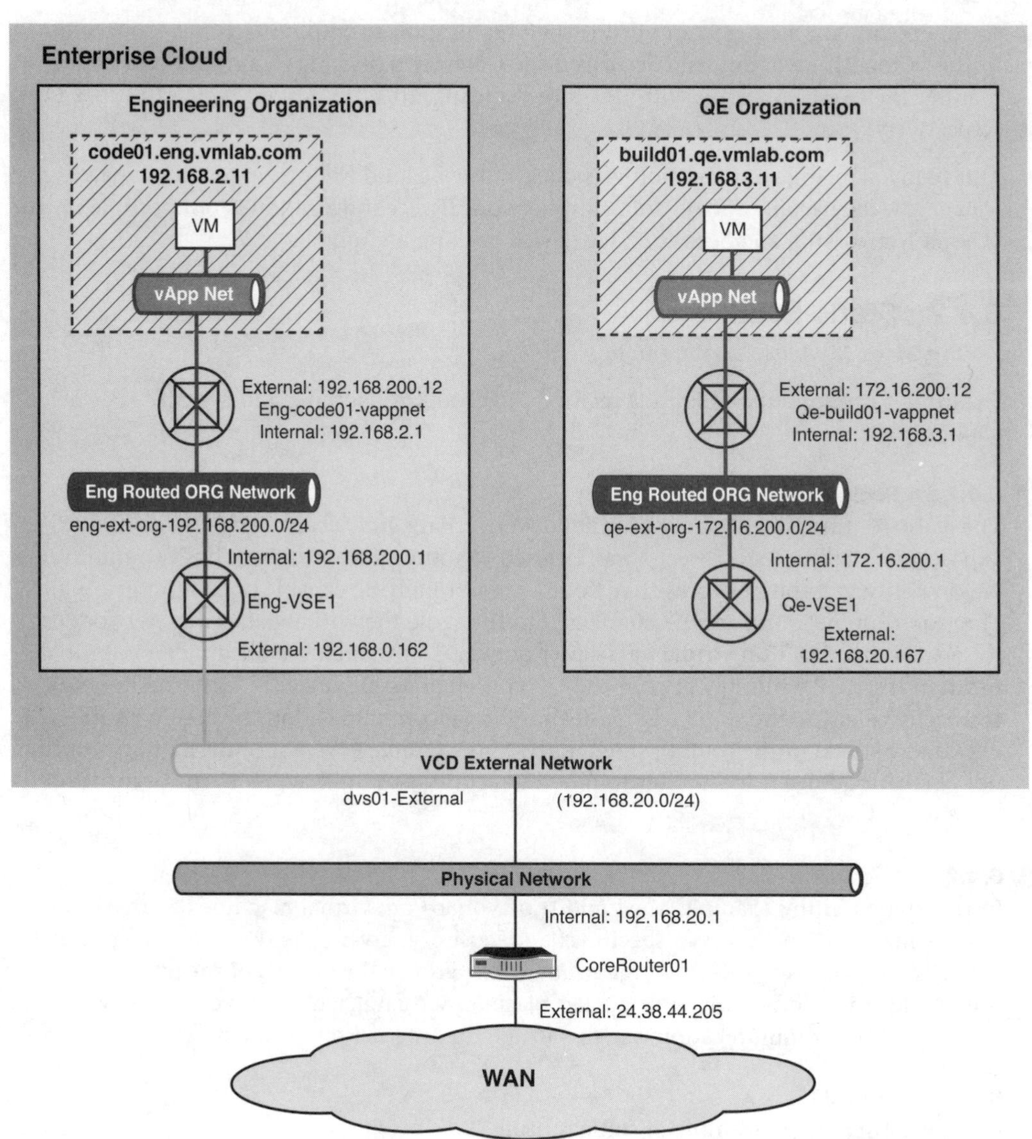

FIGURE 6.24 Routing example logical architecture

NOTE

- The implementation steps assume that both the Engineering and QE organizations have been provisioned with a single external routed organization virtual datacenter network in each organization. The creation of these two organization networks creates two vCloud Networking and Security Edge (Edge) devices in the System-virtual datacenter.
- Disable the firewall service in all four Edge devices shown in Table 6.12, to allow for testing of communication between vApp networks. Normally, you would enable the firewalls and use the Default Deny policy coupled with Allow policies for the specific traffic patterns that are required.

TABLE 6.12 Network Device Information

Device	Location	IP Address	Notes
Corerouter01	Physical network perimeter	192.168.20.1 24.38.44.205	Cisco ASR No static routes defined Gateway for physical network to Internet
QE-vse1	vCloud Director system virtual datacenter	Internal: 172.16.200.1 External: 192.168.20.167	vCloud Networking and Security Edge 5.1 QE external organization network
Eng-vse1	vCloud Director system virtual datacenter	Internal: 192.168.200.1 External: 192.168.20.162	vCloud Networking and Security Edge 5.1 Engineering External organization network
QE-build01-vappnet	vCloud Director system virtual datacenter	Internal: 192.168.3.1 External: 172.16.200.12	vCloud Networking and Security Edge 5.1 qe-build01 routed vApp network
Eng-code01-vappnet	vCloud Director system virtual datacenter	Internal: 192.168.2.1 External: 192.168.200.12	vCloud Networking and Security Edge 5.1 eng-code01 routed vApp network
Build01.qe.vmlab.com	QE organization	172.16.200.11	Ubuntu 11.10
Code01.eng.vmlab.com	Engineering organization	192.168.200.11	Ubuntu 11.10

6.4.2.3.1 Organization Virtual Datacenter Network Configurations

The configuration of static routes is performed on the Gateway Services tab of both the QE and Engineering organization virtual datacenter networks. A SNAT rule is created, as shown in Figures 6.25–6.28, if it doesn't already exist on both the QE and Engineering organization virtual datacenter networks. Two static routes are created on both organization virtual datacenter networks. These two routes correspond to the destination or external vApp network and the source or internal vApp network.

To configure static routes:

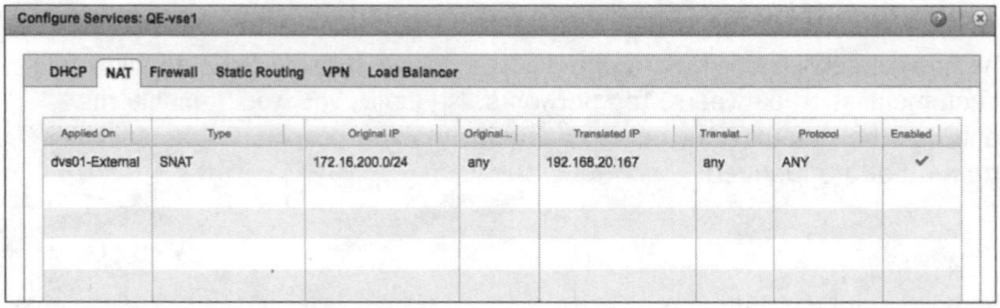

Configure Services: QE-vse1

DHCP NAT Firewall Static Routing VPN Load Balancer

Applied On	Type	Original IP	Original...	Translated IP	Translat...	Protocol	Enabled
dvs01-External	SNAT	172.16.200.0/24	any	192.168.20.167	any	ANY	✓

FIGURE 6.25 QE organization virtual datacenter network Gateway Services—NAT

Configure Services: QE-vse1

DHCP NAT Firewall Static Routing VPN Load Balancer

Static routes allow traffic between networks. Ensure that the firewall rules are configured appropriately.

☑ Enable static routing

Name	Network	Next Hop IP	Applied On
To Eng vApp .2 Net	192.168.2.0/24	192.168.20.162	dvs01-External
To QE vApp .3 Net	192.168.3.0/24	172.16.200.12	qe-org-ext

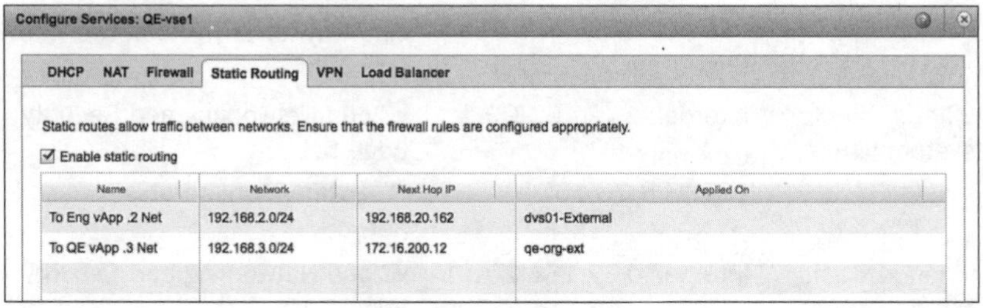

FIGURE 6.26 QE organization virtual datacenter network Gateway Services—static routing

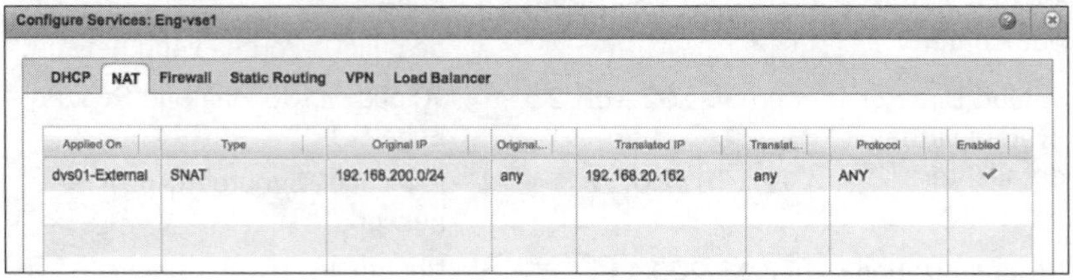

Configure Services: Eng-vse1

DHCP NAT Firewall Static Routing VPN Load Balancer

Applied On	Type	Original IP	Original...	Translated IP	Translat...	Protocol	Enabled
dvs01-External	SNAT	192.168.200.0/24	any	192.168.20.162	any	ANY	✓

FIGURE 6.27 Engineering organization virtual datacenter network Gateway Services—NAT

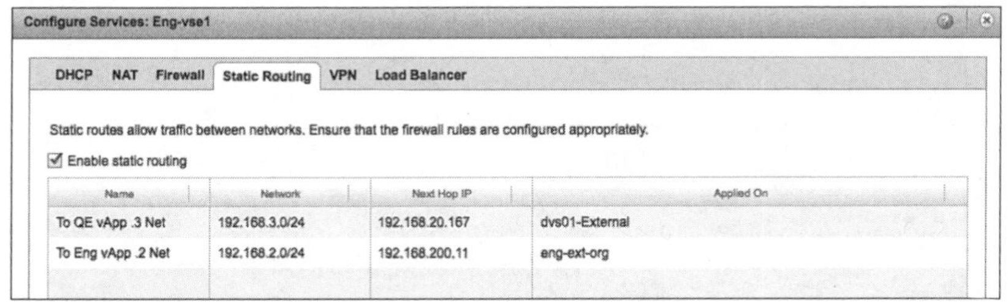

FIGURE 6.28 Engineering organization virtual datacenter network Gateway Services—static routing

6.4.2.3.2 vApp Network Configurations

For both of the vApps, create a routed vApp network connected to the parent external organization network, and then disable the firewall for testing. vCloud Director deploys a vCloud Networking and Security Edge device for these networks. No further configuration is needed on these vApp networks because the routing configuration is all performed on the external routed organization networks in the previous steps.

To create a routed vApp network:

Figures 6.29 and 6.30 show the steps to create a routed vApp network.

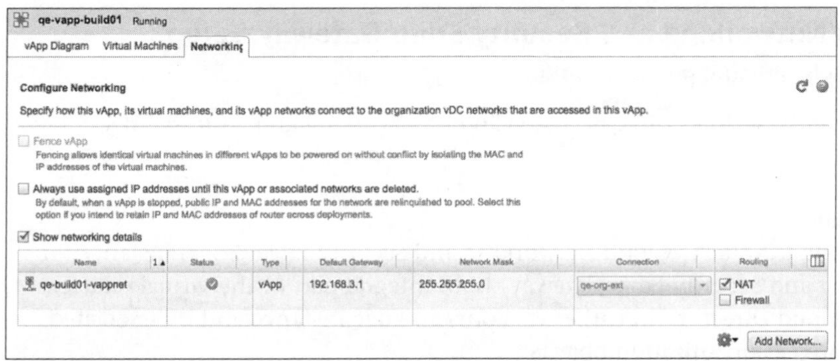

FIGURE 6.29 qe-vapp-build01 vApp networking

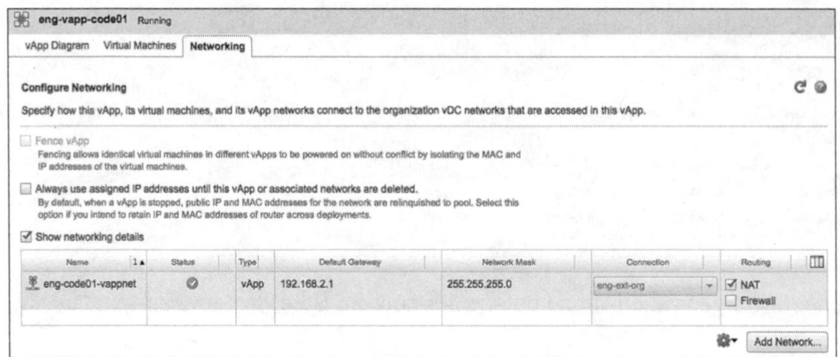

FIGURE 6.30 eng-vapp-code01 vApp networking

6.4.2.4 Design Implications

- Use static routing when you need a specific connection between vApp NAT networks.
- Configure a static route in vCloud Director when there is an existing IPsec VPN. The VPN handles this automatically because the target subnet is deemed "Interesting Traffic" and is automatically sent over the VPN to the target network.

6.4.3 vCloud Networking and Security Edge Gateway Setup

Deployment Models: Private, public, hybrid

Example Components: vCloud Director 5.1, vCloud Networking and Security Edge 5.1, vSphere 5.1

6.4.3.1 Background

As of version 5.1, the CIS stack vCloud Networking and Security Edge (Edge) instance (or vCloud Networking and Security Edge Gateway) is an integral part of the virtual datacenter construct in vCloud Director. (In earlier versions, an Edge instance and its associated networks were treated as organization objects.)

6.4.3.2 Example

In this example, a vCloud administrator provisions a vCloud Networking and Security Edge Gateway as part of an organization virtual datacenter provisioning process. This Edge instance is connected to an external network and an internal organization virtual datacenter network.

Later, this example demonstrates how an organization administrator can deploy an additional internal organization virtual datacenter network and connect it to the same vCloud Networking and Security Edge Gateway.

6.4.3.2.1 vCloud Networking and Security Edge Deployment and Configuration by the vCloud Administrator

The vCloud administrator can deploy a vCloud Networking and Security Edge Gateway at various stages. For example, a vCloud Networking and Security Edge Gateway can be provisioned while creating a new virtual datacenter (because the vCloud Networking and Security Edge object is part of the virtual datacenter). A vCloud Networking and Security Edge Gateway can also be added later to an existing virtual datacenter, but this case is out of scope for this example.

In the following procedure, the initial page of the wizard is used to create a virtual datacenter. The steps in the wizard are highlighted in red in the figures.

To use the wizard to create a virtual datacenter:

1. On the Allocate Resources screen, click Select Network Pool & Services. Click Next.

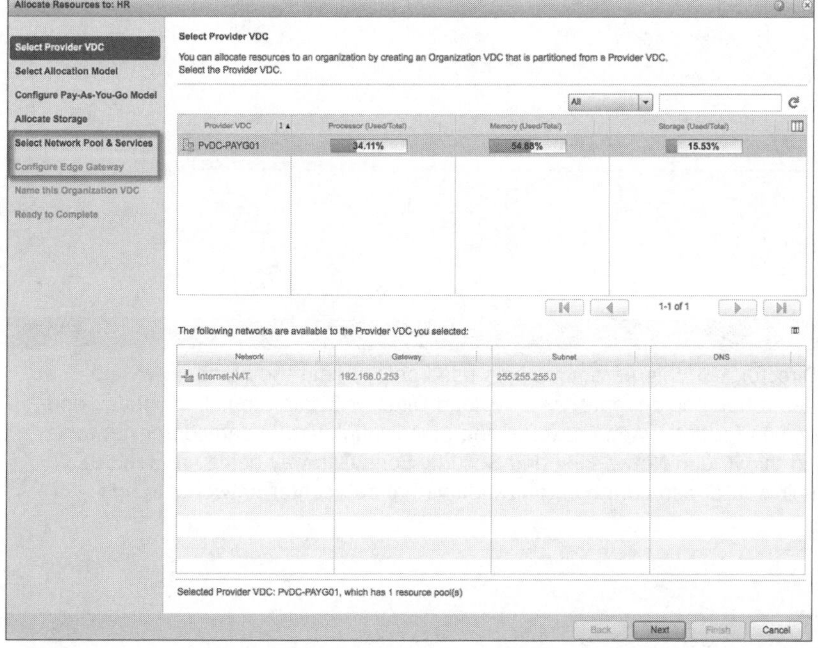

FIGURE 6.31

2. As part of this process the vCloud administrator entitles the organization for a number of networks. In the following example, the HR organization is entitled for 20 networks out of an existing VXLAN network pool.

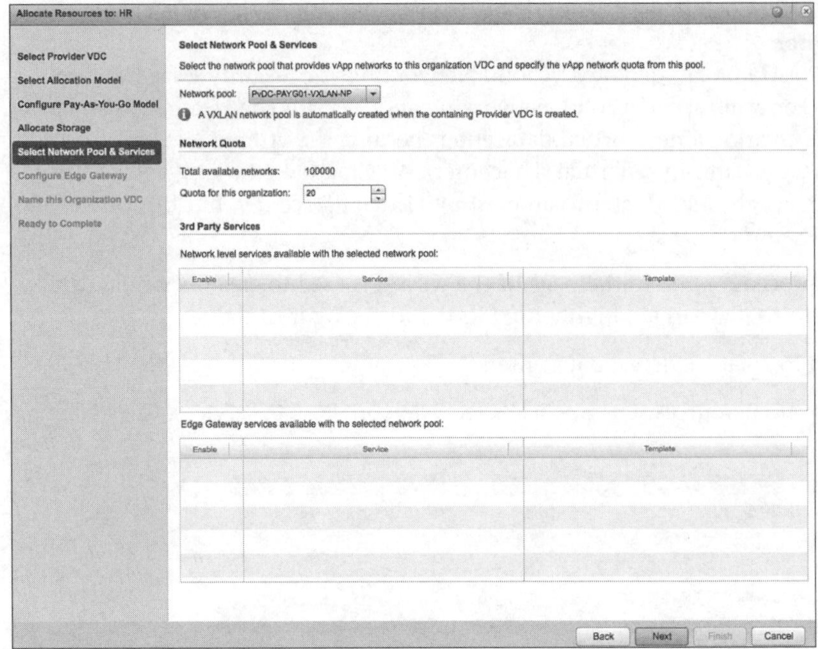

FIGURE 6.32

NOTE

Before vCloud Director 1.5, this parameter was used only to limit the number of vApp networks an organization could create. As of vCloud Director 5.1 this number entitles and limits an organization for both vApp networks and organization virtual datacenter networks to be attached to the vCloud Networking and Security Edge Gateway being created. An organization administrator can create organization virtual datacenter networks in self-service mode.

Click Next.

3. The vCloud Networking and Security Edge Gateway wizard page displays, and the vCloud administrator responds to whether an Edge Gateway must be deployed. If the vCloud administrator selects Create a New Edge Gateway, the Configure Edge Gateway screen appears.

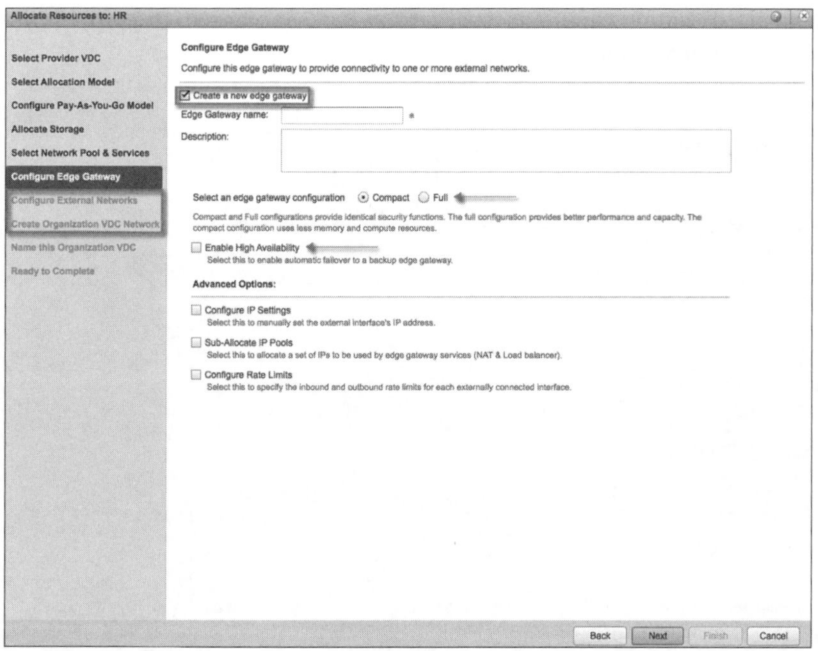

FIGURE 6.33

Note that the number of provisioning steps in the left pane has increased. This is because the provisioning process must accommodate additional information associated with the Edge.

Select your choices for Select an Edge Gateway Configuration (Compact or Full) and Enable High Availability (selected or deselected).

vCloud Director 5.1 introduced Compact Edge and Full Edge. These are two different vCloud Networking and Security Edge Gateway virtual machine configurations that provide different input/output throughput. These configurations are related to different virtual hardware configurations, as well as different parameters inside the vCloud Networking and Security Edge (Edge) software stack.

Similarly, *Edge HA* is a vCloud Director 5.1 resiliency feature. If HA is enabled, vCloud Director and vCloud Networking and Security Manager deploy two Edge devices in a clustered configuration. Edge previously leveraged traditional vSphere HA technology to provide resiliency. Previously, if the physical server running the single Edge instance failed, vSphere HA would restart the Edge virtual machine on another server. This means that the associated vCloud Director organization would not be able to communicate externally until the same Edge instance was restarted on a different physical server. With Edge HA, the two virtual machines work as a pair and can fail over immediately.

Additional advanced features can be selected on this page. If selected, the provisioning wizard adds a configuration page.

Click Next.

4. Choose an external network and click Next.

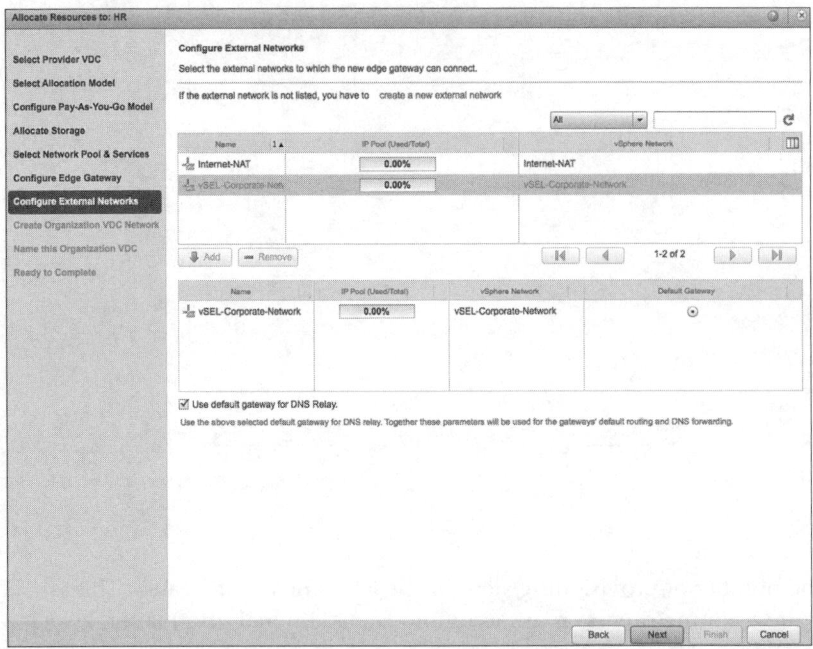

FIGURE 6.34

NOTE

As of vCloud Director 5.1, more than one external network can be selected. This is different from the earlier version, which permitted selecting only one external network and one organization network. This example has only one external network, so only one can be selected. At this point, the vCloud Networking and Security Edge Gateway can be set to act as a DNS relay.

5. Create an organization virtual datacenter network. If the vCloud administrator directs the wizard to create a network, the following page appears. After completing this screen, click Next.

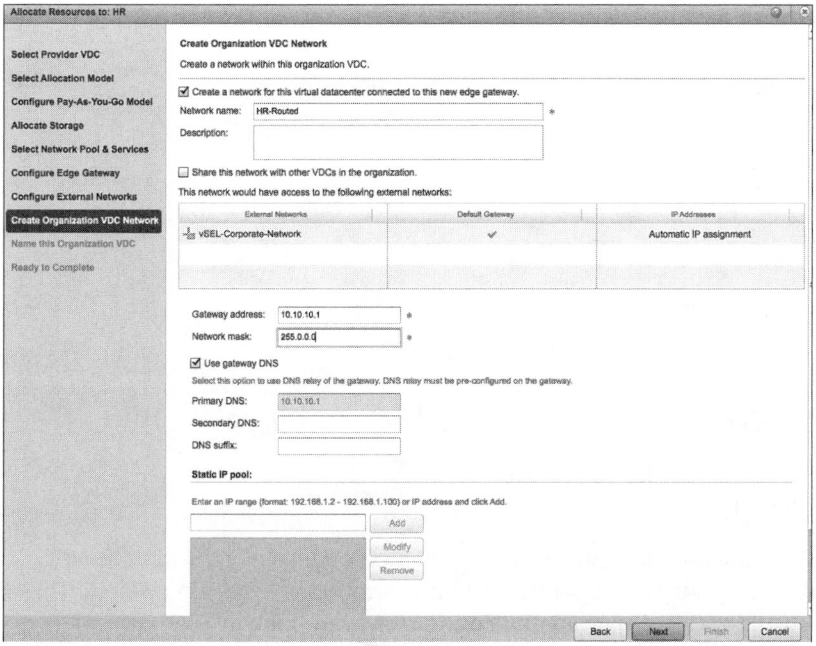

FIGURE 6.35

The network is named HR-Routed. It is the only network currently available in the organization.

Upon successful completion of the wizard, the resources are available to the organization. The vCloud Networking and Security Edge Gateway, along with the organization virtual datacenter networks, are all integral parts of the virtual datacenter.

Figure 6.36 shows the Edge Gateways tab.

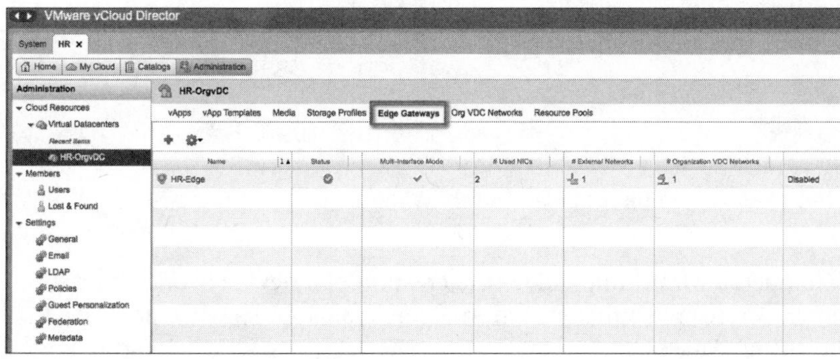

FIGURE 6.36 Edge Gateways tab

Figure 6.37 shows the Org VDC Networks tab.

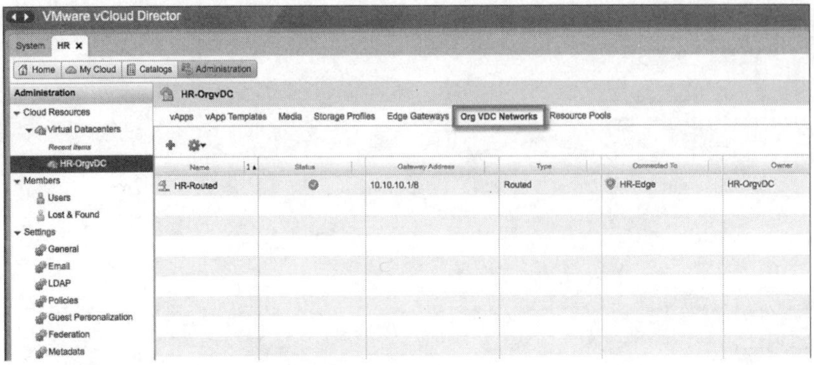

FIGURE 6.37 Org VDC Networks tab

What has been shown so far is how to provision a vCloud Networking and Security Edge Gateway (Edge Gateway) using the virtual datacenter provisioning wizard. The vCloud administrator can also create the Edge Gateway (or add an Edge Gateway) by clicking Add Gateway from the Edge Gateways tab of the organization virtual datacenter consolidated view.

6. Similarly, a vCloud administrator can add organization virtual datacenter networks in the organization virtual datacenter by clicking the green plus sign (Add Network) in the Org VDC Networks tab.

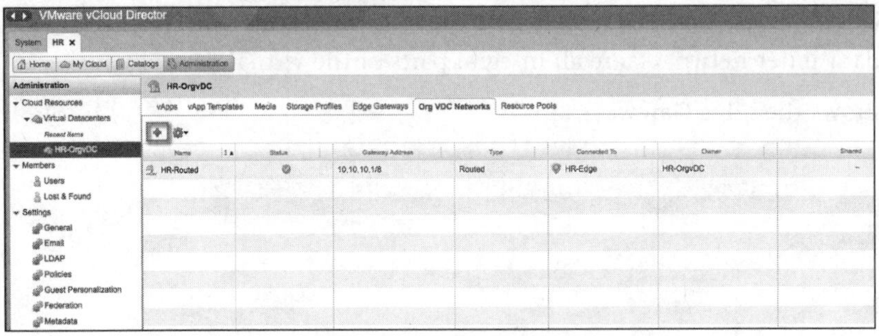

FIGURE 6.38 Add Networks icon in the Org VDC Networks tab

7. Click the link to open a wizard that guides the creation of a new network inside the virtual datacenter. A screen like that shown in Figure 6.39 appears when adding a network to the virtual datacenter.

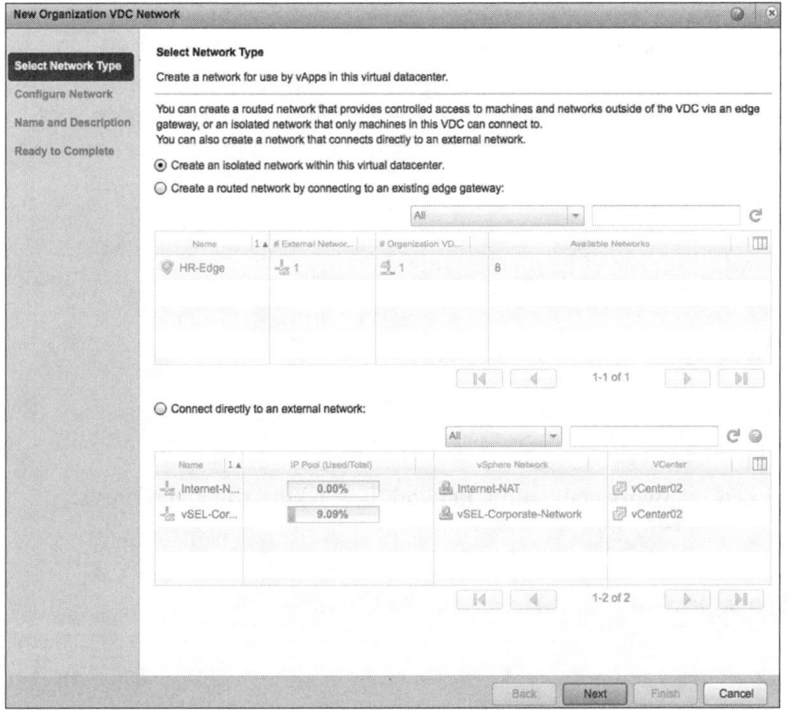

FIGURE 6.39

The vCloud administrator can create all three types of networks, including a direct connect to the external network (bypassing the Edge Gateway). This is not an option for the organization administrator. The organization administrator *cannot* deploy an additional vCloud Networking and Security Edge device from the Edge Gateways tab.

6.4.3.2.2 vCloud Networking and Security Edge Configuration and Deployment by the Organization Administrator

In this session, the HR organization administrator takes over where the vCloud administrator left off. The organization administrator's view of the organization virtual datacenter is similar to that of the vCloud administrator.

To configure and deploy the vCloud Networking and Security Edge instance:

1. On the HR screen, select HR-OrgvDC and click the Edge Gateways tab.

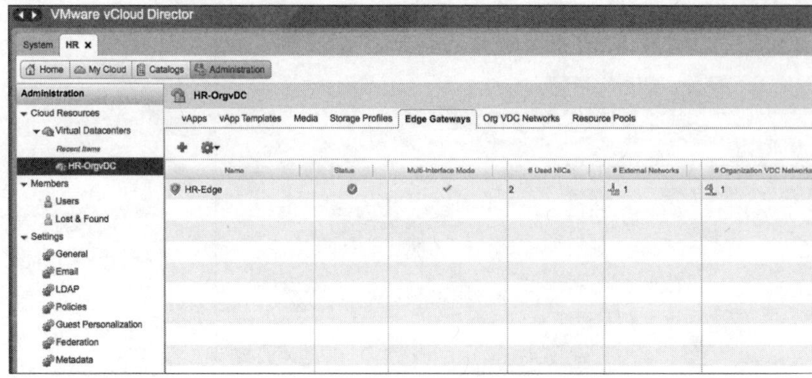

FIGURE 6.40

2. Under the Org VDC Networks tab, add a network by clicking the green plus sign (Add Network).

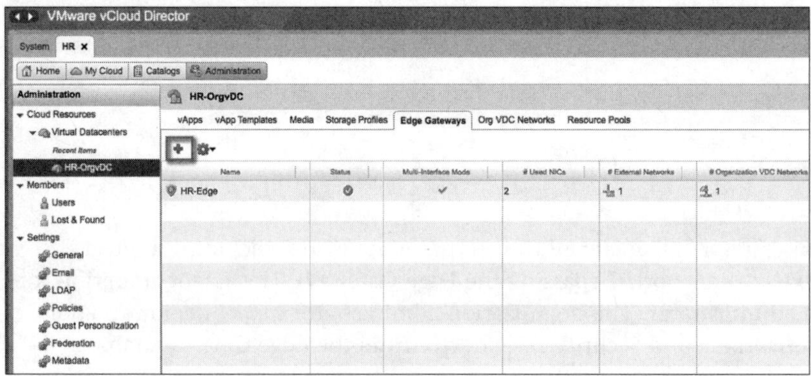

FIGURE 6.41

3. The New Organization VDC Network wizard appears. After completing this screen, click Next.

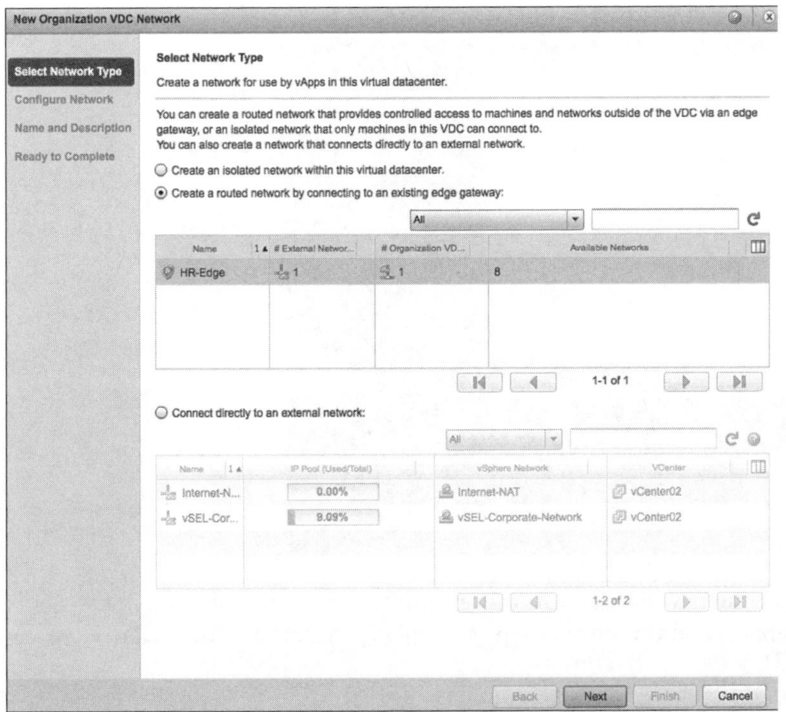

FIGURE 6.42

The organization administrator cannot create direct connections to external networks.

An organization administrator can create an isolated or routed network and connect it to an existing vCloud Networking and Security Edge Gateway. In this example, we have only one vCloud Networking and Security Edge (Edge) instance, so we will create a "temporary" network and connect it to this existing Edge instance.

4. On the Network Specification screen, define and personalize the new network. Click Next.

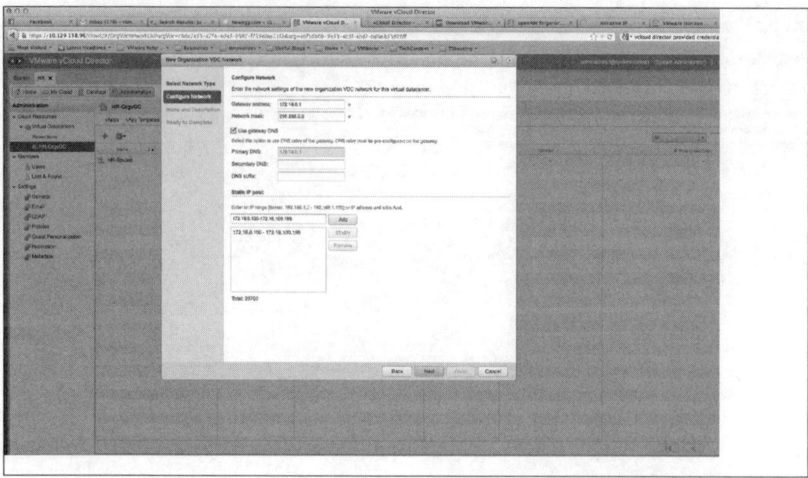

FIGURE 6.43

5. Set the name for the new network. In this example, it is named HR-temporary. The new network appears on the summary page of all organization virtual datacenter networks.

VMware vCloud Director

System HR

Home My Cloud Catalogs Administration

Administration

Cloud Resources
Virtual Datacenters
Recent Items
HR-OrgvDC
Members
Users
Lost & Found
Settings
General
Email
LDAP
Policies
Guest Personalization
Federation
Metadata

HR-OrgvDC

vApps vApp Templates Media Storage Profiles Edge Gateways Org VDC Networks Resource Pools

Name	Status	Gateway Address	Type	Connected To
HR-Routed		10.10.10.1/8	Routed	HR-Edge
HR-temporary		192.16.0.1/16	Routed	HR-Edge

FIGURE 6.44

At this point, users in the HR organization can attach virtual machines to both of these networks that are routed to the external network using the same Edge Gateway. The two organization virtual datacenter networks can also access each other using static routing configurations automatically defined on the single Edge Gateway.

A need to create an Edge device for each routed network deployed no longer exists. Also, as of vCloud Director 5.1 the organization administrator can create, in self-service mode, organization virtual datacenter networks.

Additionally, the organization administrator can configure all possible Edge Gateway services, such as DHCP, NAT, firewall, static routing, VPN, and load balancing.

6.4.3.3 Design Implications

A vCloud Networking and Security Edge Gateway (either compact or full) can support a maximum of 10 networks in any combination of external networks and organization virtual datacenter networks.

6.4.4 Public vCloud External Network

Deployment Models: Public

Example Components: vCloud Director 5.1, vCloud Networking and Security Edge 5.1, vSphere 5.1

6.4.4.1 Use Case

An external network is a method of providing communication to resources outside a vCloud. In vCloud Director, the external network is a logical representation that maps 1:1 to an existing vSphere port group on a standard or distributed virtual switch.

6.4.4.2 Example

In this external network example, the service provider uses existing network automation software to dynamically provision the vSphere and corresponding vCloud Director networks. The service provider uses an automation platform to dynamically automate the following tasks during customer onboarding:

- Provision a vSphere port group on the dvSwitch for each customer
- Assign an appropriate VLAN to this port group for each customer

NOTE

The external network can be differentiated through use of a separated physical network or VLAN. If using VLANs, only a single VLAN can be used on the port group.

- Provision a dedicated vCloud Director external network and map it to the port group created in step 1 for each customer
- Create a direct connect external organization network for each customer

Figure 6.45 shows a VLAN configuration that uses 802.1q VLAN trunk ports on the physical switches to the ESXi dvSwitch uplinks. This enables the physical switching infrastructure to allow all the VLANs configured in the infrastructure to communicate to the ESXi hosts while still keeping the VLANs separated and in separate broadcast domains. The dvSwitch delivers the appropriate Ethernet frames to the appropriate port group based on a match of the VLAN tag on the frame and the VLAN associated with the port group. The dvSwitch port groups remove the VLAN tag from the Ethernet frame and deliver it to the appropriate virtual machine. This architecture is commonly referred to as *virtual switch tagging* (VST).

6

In Figure 6.45, four organizations are shown: Two have vApps directly connected to the parent organization network, and two have a vApp network connected to the parent organization network.

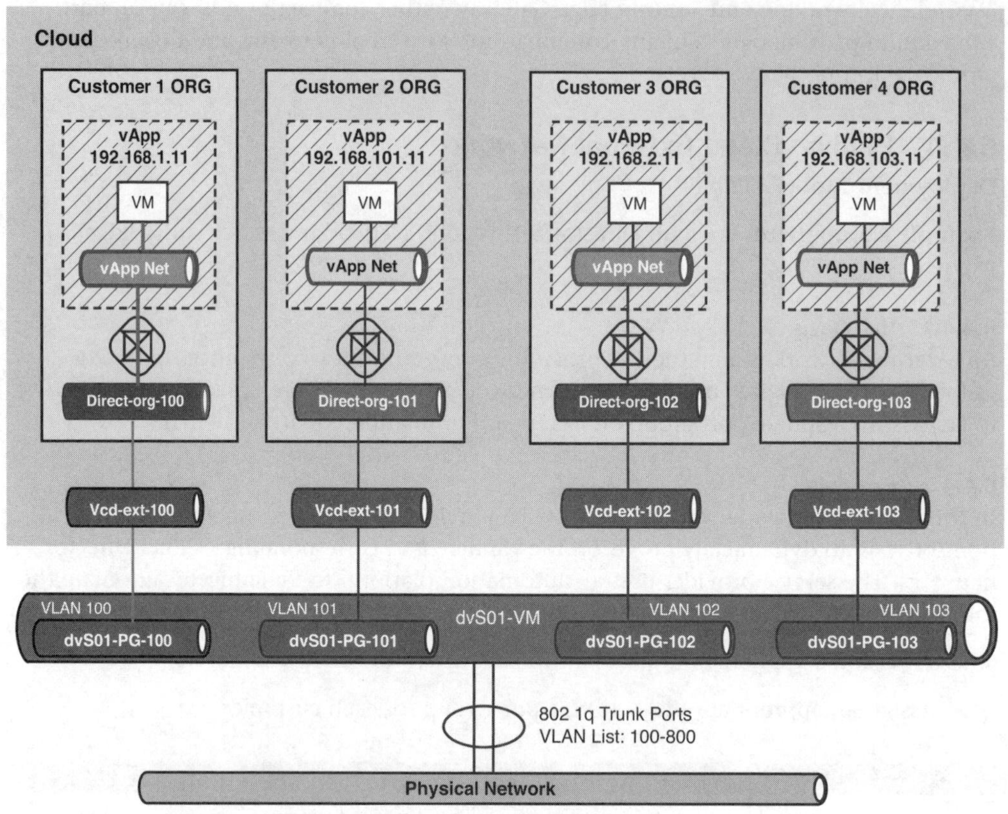

FIGURE 6.45 Service provider external network example

The vSphere configuration to support this architecture requires separate dvSwitch port groups for each customer and a VLAN provisioned for each. Figures 6.46 and 6.47 show four customers configured in this environment.

vcenter.t2.lab
Paris
none
dVS01
vCAT-DVUplinks-15
Internet-NAT
MGMT
vcd-ext-100
vcd-ext-101
vcd-ext-102
vcd-ext-103
vSEL-Corporate-Network
vxw-dvs-15-virtualwire-1-sid-5000-dvs.VCDVSOrgvDC_Net01-
vxw-dvs-15-virtualwire-2-sid-5001-dvs.VCDVSOrgvDC_Net02-
vxw-dvs-15-virtualwire-3-sid-5002-dvs.VCDVSHR-Routed-82c
vxw-dvs-15-virtualwire-4-sid-5003-dvs.VCDVSHR-temporary-a
vxw-vmknicPg-dvs-15-0-74ee9648-575c-4ac9-8021-ec268dfb

dVS01

Getting Started | Summary | Networks | Ports | Resource Allocation | Configuration | Virtual Machines | Hosts | Tasks & Events | Alarms

Name, Port binding, VLAN ID, Number of VMs, Number of ports or Alarm actions contains:

Name	Port binding	VLAN ID	Number of VMs	Number of ports	Alarm actions
vSEL-Corporate-Netwo...	Static binding	VLAN access : 1380	1	128	Enabled
vxw-dvs-15-virtualwire...	Static binding	VLAN access : 0	2	16	Enabled
vxw-dvs-15-virtualwire...	Static binding	VLAN access : 0	1	8	Enabled
Internet-NAT	Static binding	VLAN access : 0	0	128	Enabled
vxw-vmknicPg-dvs-15-...	Static binding	VLAN access : 0	0	8	Enabled
MGMT	Static binding	VLAN access : 0	0	128	Enabled
vxw-dvs-15-virtualwire...	Static binding	VLAN access : 0	1	8	Enabled
vxw-dvs-15-virtualwire...	Static binding	VLAN access : 0	2	16	Enabled
vCAT-DVUplinks-15	Static binding	VLAN Trunk : 0-4094	0	4	Enabled
vcd-ext-100	Static binding	VLAN access : 100	0	128	Enabled
vcd-ext-101	Static binding	VLAN access : 101	0	128	Enabled
vcd-ext-102	Static binding	VLAN access : 102	0	128	Enabled
vcd-ext-103	Static binding	VLAN access : 103	0	128	Enabled

FIGURE 6.46 vSphere port group configuration

External Networks

Name	Status	VLAN	IP Pool (Used/Total)	vSphere Network	
dvS01-External		1380	0.40%	vSEL-Corporate-Network	vCenter02
Internet-NAT		0	0.00%	Internet-NAT	vCenter02
vcd-ext-100		100	0.00%	vcd-ext-100	vCenter02
vcd-ext-101		101	0.00%	vcd-ext-101	vCenter02
vcd-ext-102		102	0.00%	vcd-ext-102	vCenter02
vcd-ext-103		103	0.00%	vcd-ext-103	vCenter02

FIGURE 6.47 vCloud external networks

Figures 6.48 and 6.49 show the network specification for one of the customer vCloud external networks (vcd-ext-101). A network specification represents a subnet and its associated configuration for the external network.

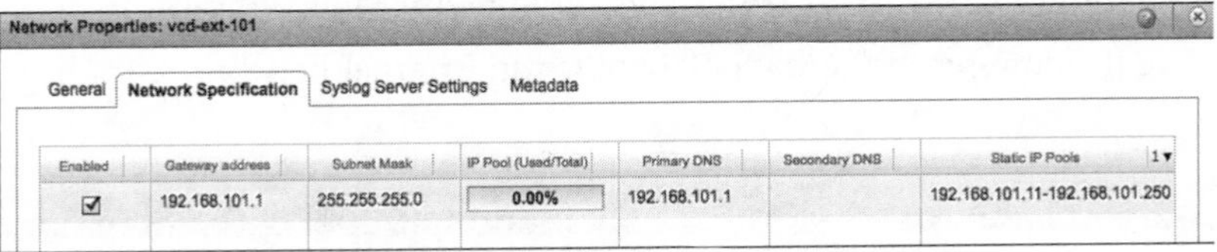

Network Properties: vcd-ext-101

General | Network Specification | Syslog Server Settings | Metadata

Enabled	Gateway address	Subnet Mask	IP Pool (Used/Total)	Primary DNS	Secondary DNS	Static IP Pools
☑	192.168.101.1	255.255.255.0	0.00%	192.168.101.1		192.168.101.11-192.168.101.250

FIGURE 6.48 vcd-ext-101 external network configuration

Modify Subnet

Gateway address: 192.168.101.1 *

Network mask: 255.255.255.0 *

Primary DNS: 192.168.101.1

Secondary DNS:

DNS suffix:

Static IP pool:

Enter an IP range (format: 192.168.1.2 - 192.168.1.100) or IP address and click Add.

Add *

192.168.101.11 - 192.168.101.250

Modify

Remove

Total: 240

OK Cancel

FIGURE 6.49 Network specification properties

In this example, a static IP pool was configured, providing a total of 240 IP addresses. vCloud Director allows multiple static IP pools for each external network. These addresses can be used for assignment by vCloud Director to virtual machines or external interfaces of the vCloud Networking and Security Edge devices. The gateway address in this configuration is 192.168.101.1, which is a logical interface on the Cisco Layer 3 switching infrastructure.

6.4.4.3 Management

As the vCloud Director environment grows, the service provider can modify the external network settings.

To modify external network settings:

1. Add a new network specification (subnet) to an existing external network.
2. Modify an existing network specification (DNS servers or suffix) for the external network. You cannot modify the network subnet mask or default gateway.
3. Add or remove IP addresses in the static IP pool for an external network.

NOTE

After you create a network specification (subnet) for an external network, you cannot delete it.

6.4.4.4 Design Implications

- This service provider has been providing managed compute and networking services for years, developing an established process for datacenter automation. The advantage for the service provider is that the established process and automation technology can be used as a foundation.
- Although external networks can be shared among multiple organizations and organization virtual datacenter networks, service providers are more likely to dedicate an external network for each customer.

By leveraging the existing investments and established process associated with datacenter automation, the service provider is automating what vCloud Director would typically handle at the networking layer. vCloud Director uses network pools to provide Layer 2 isolation of a tenant's virtual machines from the vApp through the physical network using VLANs, vCloud Director network isolation (VCDNI), or VXLAN.

6.4.5 VXLAN Implementation

Deployment Models: Private, public

Software Components: vCloud Director 5.1, vCloud Networking and Security Manager 5.1, vSphere 5.1

6.4.5.1 Background

Virtual Extensible LAN (VXLAN) is a technology that enables the expansion of isolated vCloud architectures across Layer 2 domains beyond the limits the IEEE 802.1Q standard imposes. By using a new MAC-in-UDP encapsulation technique, a VXLAN ID adds a 24-bit identifier, which allows networks to push beyond the IEEE 802.1Q limit to a possible 16 million logical networks.

Although the conventional IEEE 802.1Q standards can perform the function, when trying to adhere to greater scalability demands, VXLAN surpasses IEEE 802.1Q limitations by offering scalable capabilities of up to 16 million possible networks. Because of the scalable and flexible capabilities VXLAN offers, the technology can be used in local or stretched datacenters with a single vCloud/vSphere management domain. Figure 6.50 shows the VXLAN supported use cases.

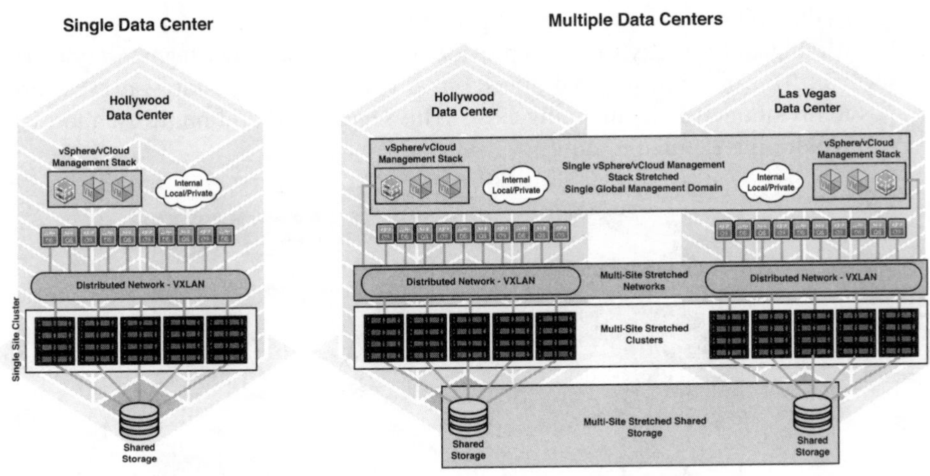

FIGURE 6.50 VXLAN supported use cases

6.4.5.2 Example

Configuring VXLAN for vCloud Director 5.1 requires the initial preparation of the vCloud Networking and Security network virtualization settings. This configuration is executed outside the vCloud Director 5.1 management interface.

Figure 6.51 shows the preparation and configuration of vCloud Networking and Security in a single cluster. The following procedure applies to any number of cluster configurations.

To prepare and configure vCloud Networking and Security in a single cluster:

1. Log into the vCloud Networking and Security management interface.
2. Select the Datacenter object.

3. Click the Network Virtualization tab, and click the Preparation link. This reveals the Connectivity and Segment ID configuration tabs.

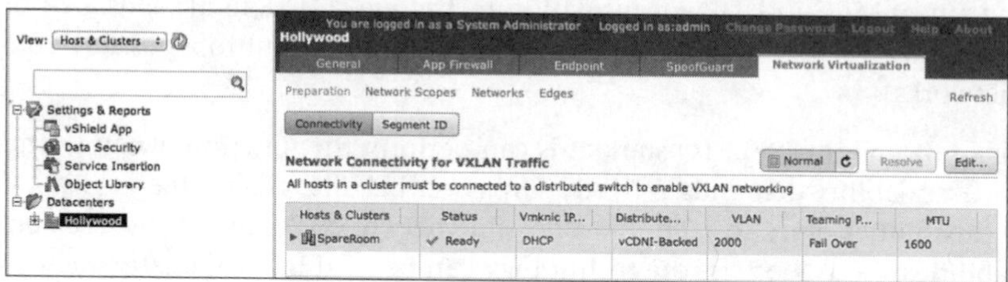

FIGURE 6.51

4. Click Edit, and enter the segment ID pool and multicast address for vCloud Networking and Security to use to provide the VXLAN network segmentation. The segment IDs cannot be mapped directly to any one multicast address because no possibility of one-to-one mapping exists. This segment ID and multicast address configuration is defined in ranges.

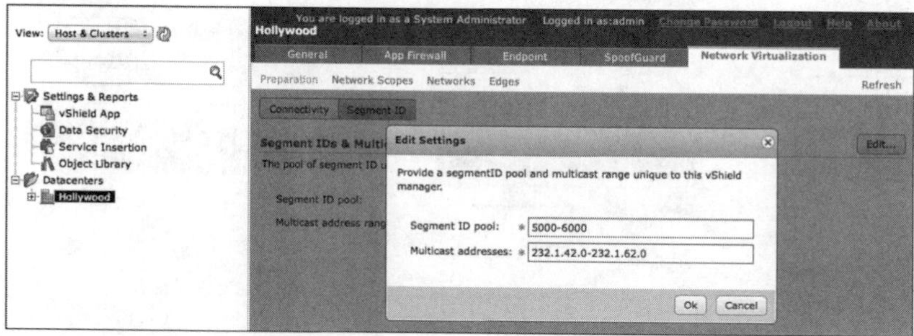

FIGURE 6.52

5. Click the Connectivity button under the Network Virtualization tab to prepare the resource clusters that will be part of the vCloud Director 5.1 VXLAN segments.

6. Choose the distributed switch that is to be associated with the resource cluster, and enter the VLAN ID for the network segment to use to overlay the VXLAN traffic coming from the distributed switches.

7. Perform the following configuration on the physical Layer 3 switches or routers:

    - Enable multicast routing on the routers.
    - Configure IGMP Snooping on the switches.

    If VXLAN is being used in a single VLAN, enable IGMP Querier and IGMP Snooping on the physical switches.

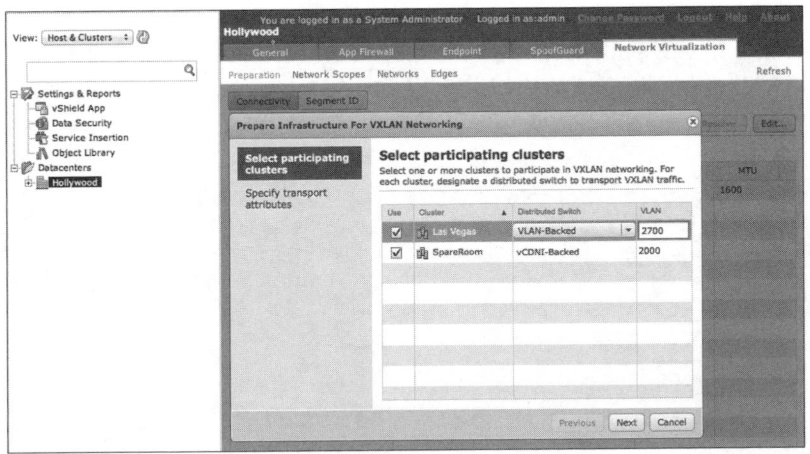

FIGURE 6.53

8. Specify the NIC teaming policy that applies to the respective distributed switch configuration, and MTU settings. The MTU settings for VXLAN default to 1600 bytes because of the VXLAN ID encapsulation technique, which increases the size of the packets. This behavior is similar to the VCDNI requirements in vCloud Director—VCDNI required a minimum MTU packet configuration of 1524. You must either use jumbo frames or increase the MTU across all network devices.

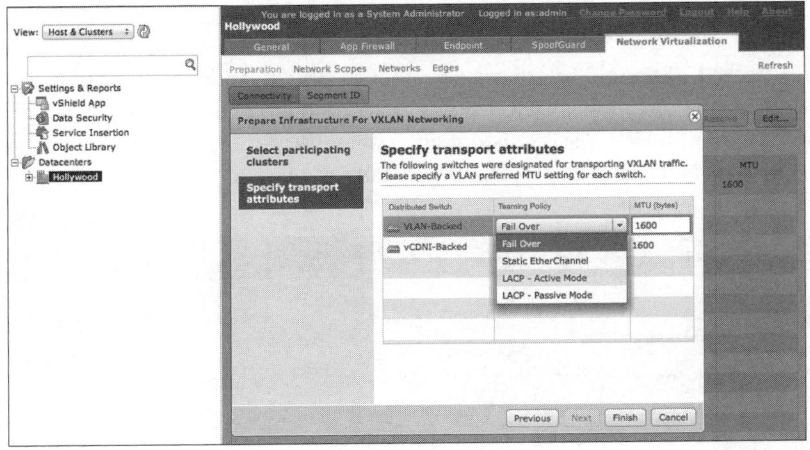

FIGURE 6.54

After configuring the settings for the distributed switches, the VXLAN VMkernel modules and VMkernel NICs are deployed and configured onto all members of the cluster. New dvPort groups are created and automatically added to the distributed switch associated with the VXLAN configuration.

The new dvPort group and VMkernel interface can be identified by their unique naming convention, vxw-vmknicPg-dvs-xx-xx-xx-xx. The deployed VMkernel modules and VMkernel NICs act as the Virtual Tunnel Endpoint (VTEP) that is used to perform VXLAN packet encapsulation and decapsulation.

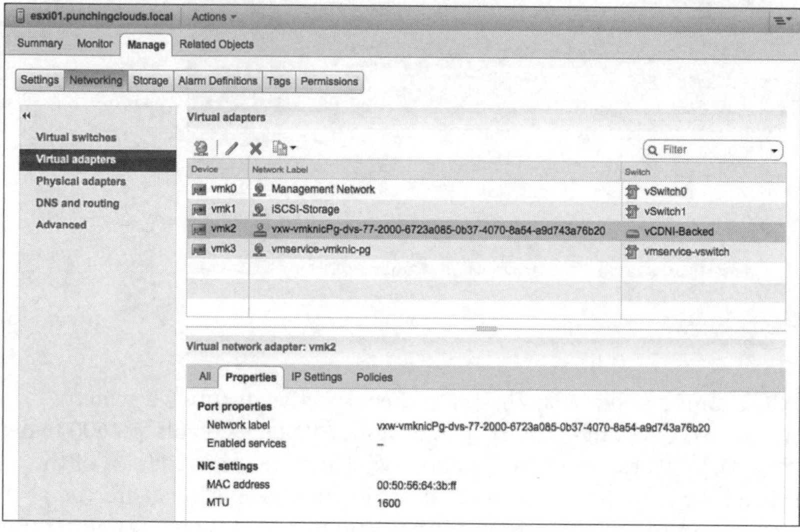

FIGURE 6.55

9. Apply IP addresses to the newly created VMkernel interfaces with DHCP.

 All the newly created VMkernel interfaces receive IPv4 private addresses within a 169.254.X.X/16 segment, unless a DHCP server is accessible on the network segment used for the VXLAN. If a DHCP server is not accessible, the configuration status of the hosts displays as Not Ready in the Status column.

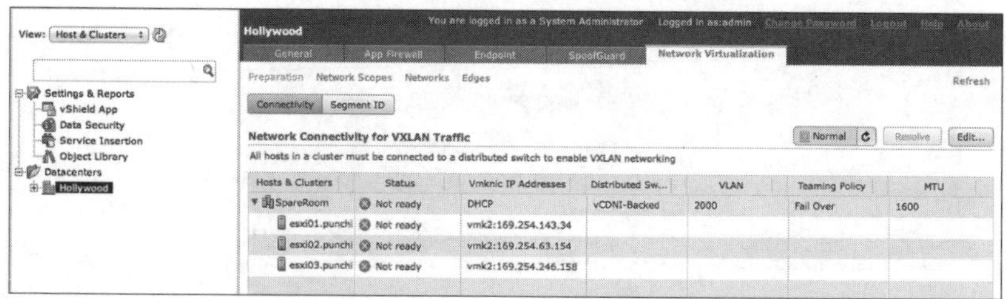

FIGURE 6.56

 If the configuration is correct, Status displays as Ready.

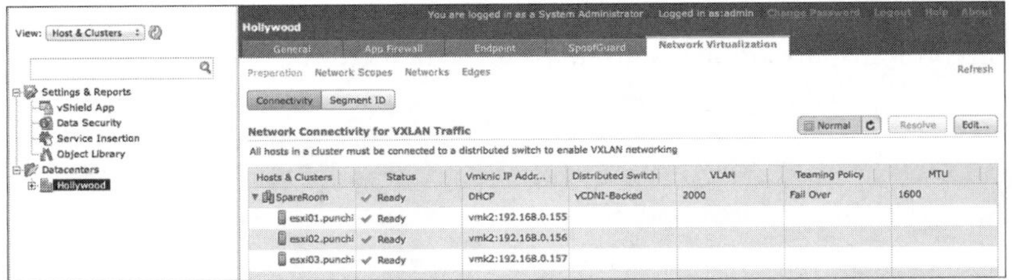

FIGURE 6.57

10. Click the Network Scopes link to define the network scope. Provide a name and description, and choose clusters to be part of the segment

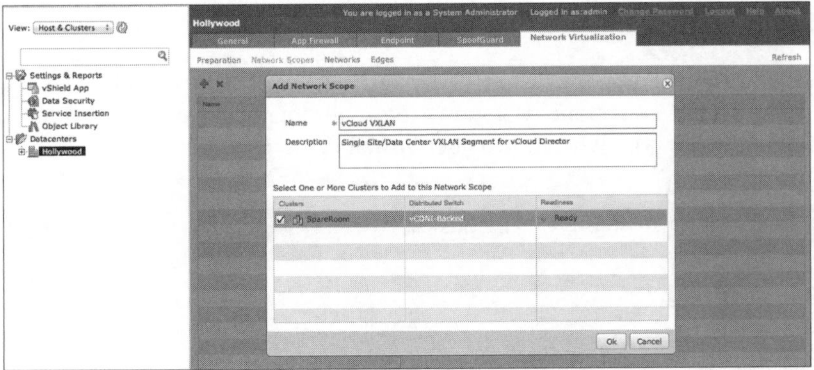

FIGURE 6.58

11. Create the logical network to be consumed beyond IEEE 802.1Q standards restrictions. Click the network link to create logical networks (also known as *virtual wires*). Provide a name and description, and choose the desired network segment.

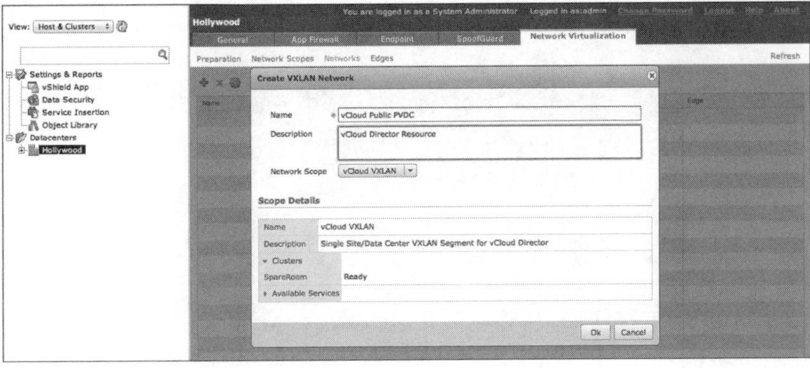

FIGURE 6.59

12. At this point, you can identify the segment IDs and multicast address of the created logical network. A new port group is automatically created for every logical network.

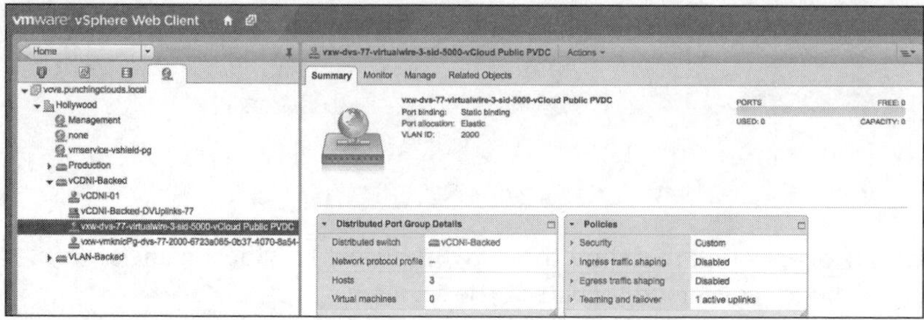

FIGURE 6.60

All the required vCloud Networking and Security Manager network preparation to use VXLAN with vCloud Director 5.1 is done. vCloud Director automatically enables VXLAN and creates a VXLAN network pool when a provider virtual datacenter is created.

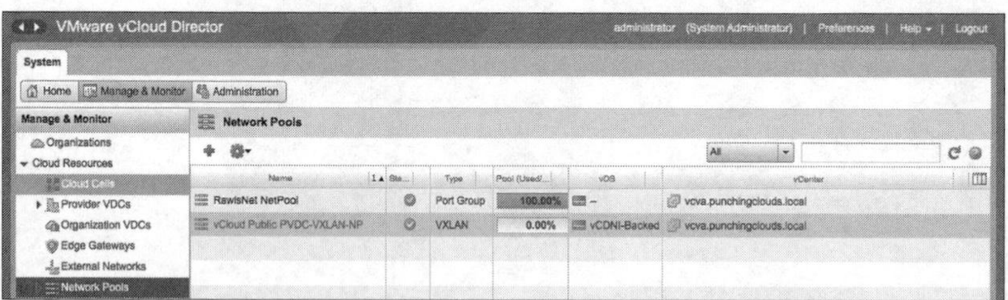

FIGURE 6.61

To see the configured options for a VXLAN network pool, go to an organization virtual datacenter's properties and, under the Network Pool & Services tab, select the VXLAN network pool.

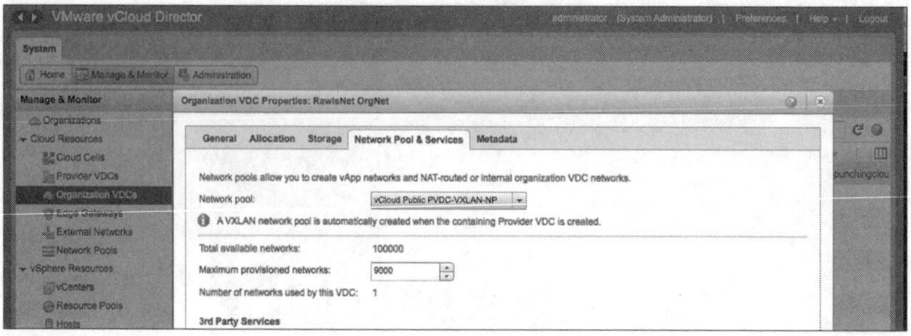

FIGURE 6.62

6.4.6 VXLAN ORG Network for Disaster Recovery

Deployment Models: Private, hybrid

Software Components: vCloud Director 5.1, vCloud Networking and Security Manager 5.1, vSphere 5.1

Hardware Components: NETGEAR GS724T Switch, Sophos UTM Router

6.4.6.1 Background

The process of failing over the management components or vApps from a primary vCloud to a disaster recovery site is documented in the VMware vCloud Director Infrastructure Resiliency Case Study (www.vmware.com/files/pdf/techpaper/vcloud-director-infrastructure-resiliency.pdf).

The presence of stretched Layer 2 networks greatly simplifies the recovery of vApps because vApps can remain connected to the same logically defined virtual networks regardless of the physical location in which the vApps are running. In the absence of a stretched Layer 2 network, VXLAN enables simplified DR and implementations of vCloud Director that span multiple locations. This is achieved by creating a Layer 2 overlay network without changing the Layer 3 interconnects already in place. This example illustrates failover of a VMware vCenter Site Recovery Manager (SRM)–based vCloud Director implementation without the need to reassign IP addresses to the virtual machines or the scripted changes that would need to be done to simplify the process.

6.4.6.2 Example

In keeping with the reference infrastructure and methodology defined in the VMware vCloud Director Infrastructure Resiliency Case Study, this example uses a cluster that has ESXi hosts at both the primary site and the recovery site. Workloads run in the primary site where the ESXi hosts are Connected. At the recovery site, the ESXi hosts are in maintenance mode but are configured in the same cluster and attached to the same VMware vSphere Distributed Switches™. The solution approach is developed on the basis of the VMware vCloud Director Infrastructure Resiliency Case Study, and the prerequisites it defines apply to this solution. The failover of a management cluster for a vCloud infrastructure in the absence of stretched Layer 2 networking is covered under separate design considerations in this chapter.

Figure 6.63 shows the logical architecture for this example.

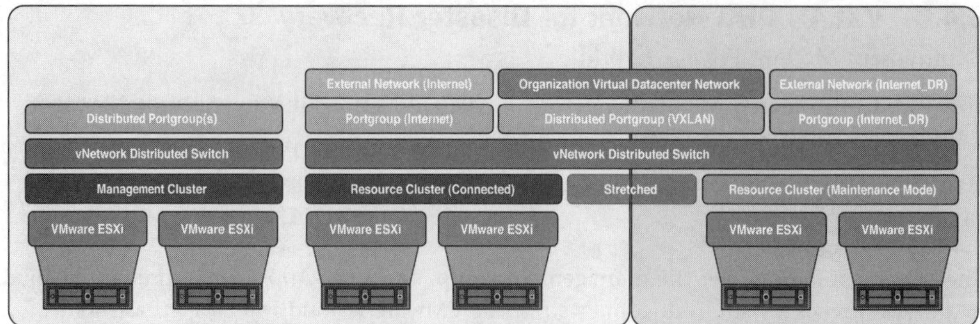

FIGURE 6.63 Example logical architecture

All ESXi hosts in the resource cluster are connected to a common vSphere Distributed Switch with defined site-specific port groups for external networks, Internet and Internet_DR. In conjunction with this, an organization virtual datacenter network is defined and results in a port group from the VXLAN-backed network pool being deployed. Figure 6.64 shows the physical architecture for this example.

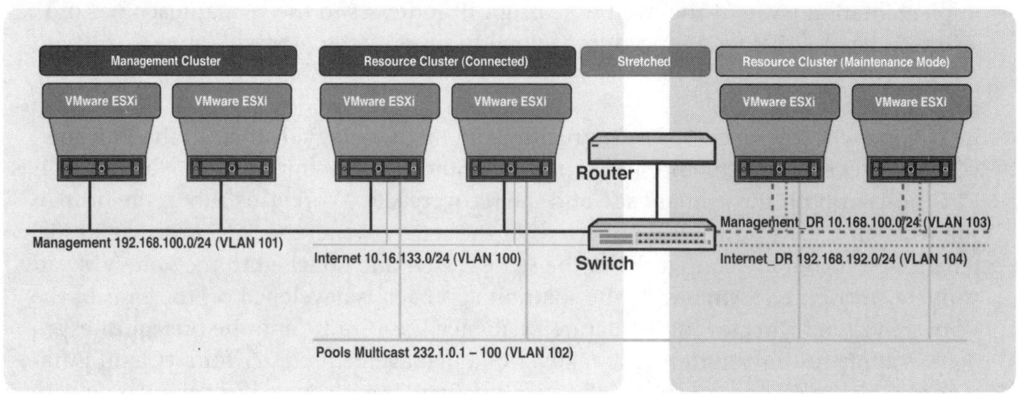

FIGURE 6.64 Example physical architecture

NOTE

For testing, a single switch and router/firewall were deployed to simulate the separate networks for the primary and recovery sites. Although this is not entirely consistent with a real-world deployment, this configuration is representative for lab testing. The router shown provides routing capability among all networks, with the exception of the pools network.

The ESXi hosts deployed in the production site are connected to a common Layer 3 management network. Similarly, the ESXi hosts deployed in the recovery site are connected to a common Layer 3 management network, but in a different Layer 3 than that of the network for the production site. In addition, the Internet external networks are the primary networks that will be used for vApp connectivity and are also in a different Layer 3 than the Internet network available at the recovery site. These are attached to vCloud Director as two different external networks.

vCloud Networking and Security Edge firewall rules, NAT translations, load balancer configurations, and VPN configurations must be reproduced on the DR side to maintain consistent configurations and make sure that everything will work after recovery. As shown in Figure 6.65, the example uses the vCloud API upon failover to duplicate the primary site configuration to the failover site. This eliminates much of the manual reconfiguration that would otherwise be required on the recovery side.

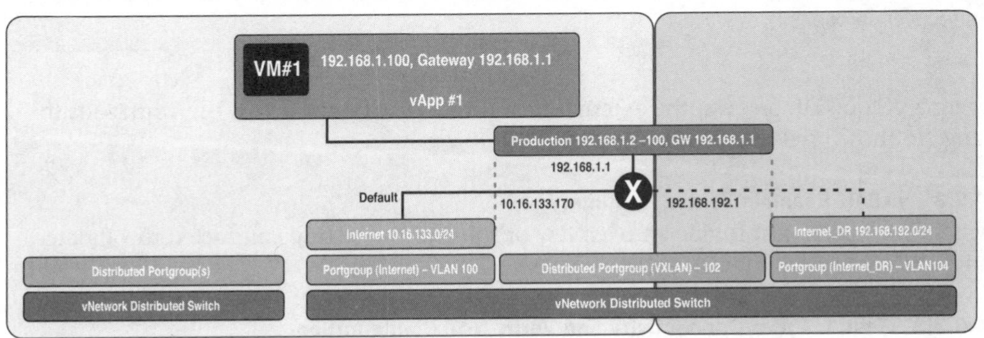

FIGURE 6.65 vCloud Director network configuration

The two Internet networks (Internet and Internet_DR) have been defined as external networks, along with their respective IP configurations. In conjunction with this, a new organization virtual datacenter network (VXLAN-backed) called Production is defined. Finally, an Edge Gateway device is deployed (note that the appliance is deployed in the Production site) with connectivity between the organization network and the two external networks. To facilitate virtual machine connectivity between the production organization virtual datacenter network and the external network, a number of destination NAT (DNAT) and source NAT (SNAT) rules are required. Table 6.13 shows an example of these rules.

NOTE

Although there is no technical reason for the Internet_DR DNAT rule to be disabled, the SNAT rule must be disabled so that network traffic is not inadvertently passed over the wrong interface to the Internet_DR network because it is not available in the production site.

TABLE 6.13 Sample NAT Rules

Applied On	Type	Original IP Address	Original Port	Translated IP Address	Translated Port	Protocol	Enabled
Internet	SNAT	192.168.1.0/24	*	10.16.133.171	*	TCP/UDP	Yes
Internet_DR	SNAT	192.168.1.0/24	*	192.168.192.2	*	TCP/UDP	No
Internet	DNAT	10.16.133.171	*	192.168.1.100	*	TCP/UDP	Yes
Internet_DR	DNAT	192.168.192.2	*	192.168.1.100	*	TCP/UDP	No

NOTE

An alternative to the chosen configuration is to implement a solution in which the vCloud Networking and Security Edge Gateway is connected only to the active external network. It was decided to predefine the connections because this enables options for preconfiguring rules for the recovery site and thereby reduces the number of reconfiguration steps during a recovery process.

During a vCloud DR process, the external IP addresses used must access the workloads to change to those used in the recovery site.

6.4.6.3 VXLAN Example Testing Summary

The following sections provide an overview of some of the testing conducted to validate using VXLAN to simplify vCloud DR recovery.

6.4.6.3.1 Test 1: Prove Connectivity and Verify NAT Configuration

The purpose of this test is to verify that predefining connections to both the production and recovery sites is viable and that following a disaster recovery scenario can establish the required connectivity to a recovered vApp. The following is the high-level test procedure.

To prove connectivity and verify the NAT configuration:

1. Validate connection to the vApp from a client device on the production external network 10.16.133.0/24 (SSH was used).
2. Change the default route defined on the vCloud Networking and Security Edge Gateway from the Internet network to the Internet_DR network, and validate connectivity to the vApp. This uses the directly attached network, to maintain connectivity.
3. Fail over the vApp to the recovery site.
4. Validate connection to the vApp from a client device on the production external network 10.16.133.0/24. It fails because the NAT addressing of the vApp is no longer connected to the directly attached vCloud Networking and Security Edge interface on the 10.16.133.0/24 network.

5. Enable the previously disabled SNAT/DNAT rules and validated connectivity from a client device on the failover external network 192.168.192.0/24 (Internet_DR) to the new address translated with NAT.
6. Remove the original Internet external network so that all connectivity is forced through the desired Internet_DR external interface on the vCloud Networking and Security Edge Gateway.
7. Validate connectivity from the vApp to the original client device on the 10.16.133.0/24 network (Internet) to the original client device (global routing between Internet and Internet_DR network should permit this to take place). This works because the Sophos UTM performs a NAT translation of the 192.168.192.0/24 network to the 10.16.1333.0/24 network on behalf of the vCloud Networking and Security Edge device.

During testing, the first three steps behave entirely as expected. Network traffic from the Internet network can successfully pass to the virtual machine defined in the vApp. Similarly, if the appropriate DNAT rule is enabled, network traffic can pass from the Internet_DR network.

When attempting to validate Step 4, despite reconfiguring the connection to the Internet_DR network as the default route, connections are still attempting to leave the vCloud Networking and Security Edge Gateway device over the original locally attached Internet interface. If the client device is then connected to the Internet_DR network with an appropriate IP address, network connections can be established as expected. Figure 6.66 illustrates the end result of this test.

6

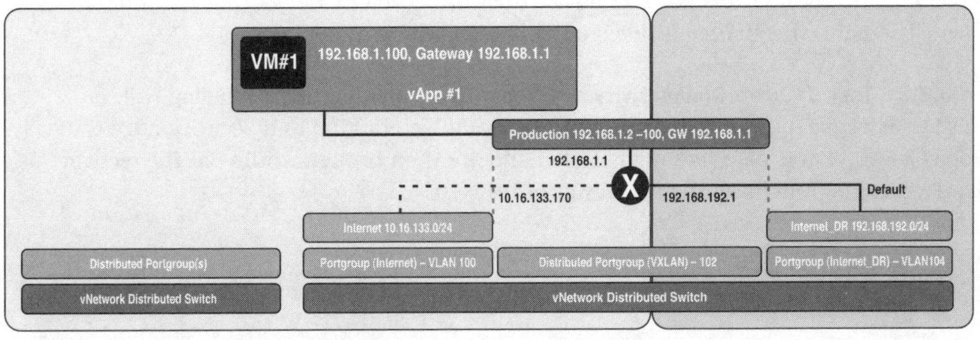

FIGURE 6.66 Removed external network

To make sure that network connections are directed over the correct interfaces on the vCloud Networking and Security Edge Gateway, the only "fail-safe" option is to remove the Internet external network, forcing all network traffic over the interface connected to the Internet_DR network.

NOTE

When an external network is removed from an Edge Gateway, any rules associated with it are deleted. In this scenario, all predefined SNAT/DNAT rules were deleted.

6.4.6.3.2 Test 2: Disable vCloud Networking and Security Edge Gateway vNICs

The purpose of this test is to investigate alternative methods to make sure network traffic is routed over a specific interface on an Edge Gateway. The approach verifies that disconnecting a virtual adapter takes down the interface. This prevents network traffic from being passed to the incorrect interface. The following is the high-level test procedure.

To verify lack of network connectivity:

1. Attempt to connect to vCenter Server, navigate the inventory, and edit the Connected status of the virtual machine settings. In vCenter Server, the option to edit the configuration of the vCloud Networking and Security Edge (Edge) appliance is disabled.
2. Repeat Step 1 on the ESXi host on which the Edge device is running. In ESXi, the option to edit the configuration of the Edge appliance is enabled.
3. Repeat the network connectivity steps defined in Test 1, Step 4. Despite disabling the network adapter, the Edge device continues to try to route packets over the original interface.

Although the capability to update the Edge device settings is disabled within vCenter Server, it is still accessible by connecting directly to the ESXi host on which the appliance is running. The key observation is that, despite disabling the virtual adapter for the Edge appliance, the guest OS of the Edge device does not correctly detect that the interface is down. The hardware change is detected as "protocol down, device up."

6.4.6.3.3 Test 3: Prove Connectivity and Verify NAT Configuration, Including Failover

This test is a repeat of Test 1, but both the vCloud Networking and Security Edge Gateway (Edge Gateway) and vApp are made to fail and are then brought online at the recovery site. Figure 6.67 illustrates the end result of this test.

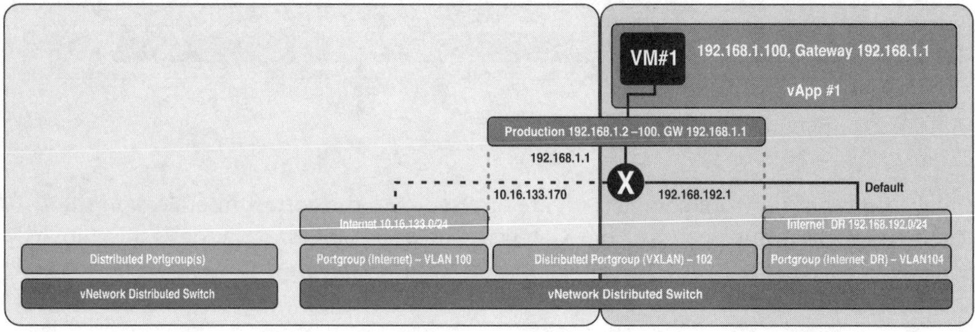

FIGURE 6.67 Test 3 end result

The result of this test is consistent with the Test 1 result, even with the added changes of failing over the vApp and Edge Gateway device.

Testing and validation results in a solution that can help simplify the deployment of vCloud Director DR solutions in the absence of stretched Layer 2 networking. Furthermore, this solution is complementary to the solution already defined in the VMware vCloud Director Infrastructure Resiliency Case Study (www.vmware.com/files/pdf/techpaper/vcloud-director-infrastructure-resiliency.pdf) and can be implemented with relatively few additions to the existing vCloud DR recovery process.

6.4.6.4 Updated vCloud DR Recovery Process

In the updated vCloud DR recovery process, following the successful recovery of a vCloud Director management cluster, some additional steps must be included during the recovery of resource clusters to facilitate the recovery of vCloud Networking and Security Edge Gateway (Edge Gateway) appliances and vApps. The following is the high-level procedure.

To facilitate the recovery of Edge Gateway appliances and vApps:

1. Restart all the virtual machines (Edge devices) in the systems folders, one at a time.
2. For each vCloud Networking and Security Manager, retrieve the current configurations and apply the site-specific networking mapping updates.
3. Remove the primary interface from the Edge devices to allow all traffic to flow through the recovery interface.
4. Bring up the virtual machines protected by the Edge devices.

NOTE

Consider using the metadata property of objects to define site-specific configuration information that can be applied during the recovery process. The use of metadata is discussed in the automation examples of the VMware vCloud Director Infrastructure Resiliency Case Study.

Table 6.14 provides a high-level overview of the existing vCloud DR recovery process and an updated vCloud DR process that incorporates the solution described in this example.

TABLE 6.14 Existing Versus Updated vCloud DR Process

Existing vCloud DR Process	Updated vCloud DR Process
1. Mount replicated VMFS volumes. 2. Bring recovery ESXi hosts online. 3. Power on vCloud Director workload virtual machines.	1. Mount replicated VMFS volumes. 2. Bring recovery ESXi hosts online. 3. Bring Edge Gateway device online. a Power on affected Edge Gateway devices. b Enable predefined services configurations for recovery site. c Remove interface connected to production site. 4. Power on vCloud Director workload virtual machines.

6.4.6.4.1 Updated vCloud DR Recovery Process—API Example

Automation is required for the updated vCloud DR process. Although this solution offers additional simplicity and reduced configuration, it is still necessary to update the configuration of multiple vCloud Networking and Security Edge Gateway (Edge Gateway) devices, which, in turn, can have multiple NAT or firewall rules.

This example addresses automation of Steps 3.b and 3.c. Step 3.a is not covered because it is only a case of identifying vCloud Networking and Security Edge devices (easily identified by their location in the system virtual datacenter resource pools) and issuing a Power On request. (This was covered previously in the automation examples for the existing vCloud DR solution.)

> **NOTE**
>
> In vCloud Director 1.x, network services such as firewall, static routing, DHCP, and so on, were all associated with the organization network. In vCloud Director 5.1 all network services are associated with the Edge Gateway instead of the organization virtual datacenter network.

6.4.6.4.2 Enable Predefined Services Configurations for Recovery Site

The following high-level procedure uses the vCloud Director API to get information about the vCloud Networking and Security Edge Gateway (Edge Gateway) devices, modifies that information, and updates the device configuration.

To use the vCloud Director API to get and modify information for the Edge Gateway devices:

1. Authenticate to vCloud Director (see Section 6.4.6.4.4).
2. Get and return the Edge Gateway devices (see Section 6.4.6.4.5).
3. Get and return the specific Edge Gateway device current configuration (see Section 6.4.6.4.6).
4. Modify the XML to reflect the new configuration (see Section 6.4.6.4.8).
5. Update the Edge Gateway device configuration (see Section 6.4.6.4.8).

The example updates a given Edge Gateway device to change the HA status. In a full recovery scenario, all configuration elements can be updated by editing or adding the correct section in the XML document that represents the Edge Gateway service configuration.

After you have successfully implemented your vCloud DR solution, you can look at how to use and implement this solution using the vCloud API. This section of the document introduces you to the VMware vCloud™ API and, in particular, the Edge Gateway API and Query Service API.

The vCloud API uses HTTP requests (which are often executed by a script or other higher-level language) as a way of making what are essentially remote procedure calls that create, modify, or delete the objects defined by the API. This vCloud REST API is defined by a collection of XML documents that represent the objects on which the API operates. The operations themselves (HTTP requests) are generic to all HTTP clients.

The vCloud REST API workflows fall into a pattern that includes only two fundamental operations:

- Make an HTTP request (typically `GET`, `PUT`, `POST`, or `DELETE`). The target of this request is either a well-known URL (such as the vCloud Director URL) or a link obtained from the response to a previous request.
- Examine the response, which can be an XML document or an HTTP response code:
    - If the response is an XML document, it can contain links or other information about the state of an object.
    - If the response is an HTTP response code, it indicates whether the request succeeded or failed, and it can be accompanied by a URL that points to a location from which additional information can be retrieved.

6.4.6.4.3 Using cURL

Using tools such as cURL, we can consume the vCloud Networking and Security REST API. Document descriptions are unnecessary because touching each URL with the appropriate method and data causes an immediate response.

cURL, sometimes written as *curl*, is a set of C-based libraries in PHP that supports HTTP `GET`. cURL supports the following command-line options:

- `-i` (HTTP): Includes the HTTP-header in the output. The HTTP-header includes the server-name, date of the document, HTTP-version, and so on.
- `-k`: Allows connections to SSL sites without certificates.
- `-H`: Specifies a custom HTTP header to pass to the server.
- `-X`: Specifies a custom request method to use when communicating with the HTTP server. The specified request is used instead of the method that would otherwise be used (which defaults to `GET`). Read the HTTP 1.1 specification for details and explanations. Common additional HTTP requests include `POST` and `DELETE`.

6.4.6.4.4 Authenticate to vCloud Director

The following example shows how to authenticate to vCloud Director.

Request

```
POST https://vcloud.cloudlab.com/api/sessions
```

FIGURE 6.68

```
$ curl -k -v -c cookie.txt -u "administrator@System:akimbi" -H
"Accept:application/*+xml;version=5.1" -d "" https://<VCD-IP>/api/sessions
```

Response

```
* About to connect() to <VCD-IP> port 443 (#0)
*   Trying <VCD-IP>... connected
* Connected to <VCD-IP> (<VCD-IP>) port 443 (#0)
* SSLv3, TLS handshake, Client hello (1):
* SSLv3, TLS handshake, Server hello (2):
* SSLv3, TLS handshake, CERT (11):
* SSLv3, TLS handshake, Server key exchange (12):
* SSLv3, TLS handshake, Server finished (14):
* SSLv3, TLS handshake, Client key exchange (16):
* SSLv3, TLS change cipher, Client hello (1):
* SSLv3, TLS handshake, Finished (20):
* SSLv3, TLS change cipher, Client hello (1):
* SSLv3, TLS handshake, Finished (20):
* SSL connection using DHE-RSA-AES256-SHA
* Server certificate:
*      subject: C=US; ST=California; L=Palo Alto; O=VMware, Inc.; CN=*.eng.vmware.
  com
*       start date: 2009-11-17 00:00:00 GMT
*       expire date: 2012-11-20 23:59:59 GMT
*       common name: *.example.vmware.com (does not match '<VCD-IP>')
*       issuer: C=US; O=DigiCert Inc; OU=www.digicert.com; CN=DigiCert High
  Assurance CA-3
*       SSL certificate verify ok.
* Server auth using Basic with user 'administrator@System'
> POST /api/sessions HTTP/1.1
> Authorization: Basic YWRtaW5pc3RyYXRvckBTeXN0ZW06YWtpbWJp
> User-Agent: curl/7.21.4 (universal-apple-darwin11.0) libcurl/7.21.4 OpenSSL/0.9.8r
  zlib/1.2.5
> Host: <VCD-IP>
> Accept:application/*+xml;version=5.1
> Content-Length: 0
> Content-Type: application/x-www-form-urlencoded
>
< HTTP/1.1 200 OK
< Date: Tue, 24 Jul 2012 18:11:38 GMT
< x-vcloud-authorization: +UDXmIeKSZ9QnPpg9OPNEhtC5QgTUzvNmyJ6IZgx6hI=
```

```
* Added cookie vcloud-token="+UDXmIeKSZ9QnPpg9OPNEhtC5QgTUzvNmyJ6IZgx6hI=" for
  domain <VCD-IP>, path /, expire 0
< Set-Cookie: vcloud-token=+UDXmIeKSZ9QnPpg9OPNEhtC5QgTUzvNmyJ6IZgx6hI=; Secure;
  Path=/
< Content-Type: application/vnd.vmware.vcloud.session+xml;version=5.1
< Date: Tue, 24 Jul 2012 18:11:39 GMT
< Content-Length: 1259
<
<?xml version="1.0" encoding="UTF-8"?>
<Session xmlns="http://www.vmware.com/vcloud/v1.5" user="administrator" org="System"
type="application/vnd.vmware.vcloud.session+xml"
href="https://10.147.50.34/api/session/" xmlns:xsi="http://www.w3.org/2001/
XMLSchema-instance" xsi:schema-
Location="http://www.vmware.com/vcloud/v1.5 http://<VCD-IP> /api/v1.5/schema/master.
xsd">
    <Link rel="down" type="application/vnd.vmware.vcloud.orgList+xml"
href="https://<VCD-IP> /api/org/"/>
    <Link rel="down" type="application/vnd.vmware.admin.vcloud+xml"
href="https://<VCD-
IP> /api/admin/"/>
    <Link rel="down" type="application/vnd.vmware.admin.vmwExtension+xml"
href="https://<VCD-IP>/api/admin/extension"/>
    <Link rel="down" type="application/vnd.vmware.vcloud.org+xml" name="System"
href="https://<VCD-IP>/api/org/a93c9db9-7471-3192-8d09-a8f7eeda85f9"/>
    <Link rel="down" type="application/vnd.vmware.vcloud.query.queryList+xml"
href="https://<VCD-IP>/api/query"/>
    <Link rel="entityResolver" type="application/vnd.vmware.vcloud.entity+xml"
href="https://<VCD-IP>/api/entity/"/>
    <Link rel="down:extensibility" type="application/vnd.vmware.vcloud.
apiextensibility+xml" href="https://<VCD-
IP>/api/extensibility"/>
</Session>
* Connection #0 to host <VCD-IP> left intact
* Closing connection #0
* SSLv3, TLS alert, Client hello (1):
```

(Optional) Return the vCloud Director metadata.

Request

```
POST https://vcloud.cloudlab.com/api/query
```

FIGURE 6.69

```
$ curl -k -v -b cookie.txt -H "Accept:application/*+xml;version=5.1" https://<VCD-
  IP>/api/query
```

This presents a list of many elements, such as `organization`, `adminOrgNetwork`, `providerVdc`, `externalNetwork`, and `edgeGateway`.

```
Response (Modified to separate the vCloud Director objects.)

Organization:

<Link rel="down" type="application/vnd.vmware.vcloud.query.records+xml"
name="organization" href="https://<VCD-
IP>/api/query?type=organization&amp;format=records"/>

adminOrgNetwork:

<Link rel="down" type="application/vnd.vmware.vcloud.query.references+xml"
name="adminOrgNetwork" href="https://<VCD-
IP>/api/query?type=adminOrgNetwork&amp;format=references"/>

providerVdc:

<Link rel="down" type="application/vnd.vmware.vcloud.query.references+xml"
name="providerVdc" href="https://<VCD-
IP>/api/query?type=providerVdc&amp;format=references"/>

externalNetwork:

<Link rel="down" type="application/vnd.vmware.vcloud.query.references+xml"
name="externalNetwork" href="https://<VCD-
IP>/api/query?type=externalNetwork&amp;format=references"/>

edgeGateway:

<Link rel="down" type="application/vnd.vmware.vcloud.query.references+xml"
name="edgeGateway" href="https://<VCD
-IP>/api/query?type=edgeGateway&amp;format=references"/>
```

6.4.6.4.5 Get and Return the vCloud Networking and Security Edge Gateways

The following example shows how to get information about the vCloud Networking and Security Edge Gateway (Edge Gateway).

Request

```
GET https://vcloud.cloudlab.com/api/query?type=edgeGateway
```

FIGURE 6.70

```
$ curl -k -v -b cookie.txt -H "Accept:application/*+xml;version=5.1"
https://<VCD-IP>/api/query?type=edgeGateway
```

Response

The following is a condensed format to show one Edge Gateway for this example—in this case, Edge-Gateway-01.

```
<EdgeGatewayRecord vdc="https://<VCD-IP>/api/vdc/1d7f9e91-ef16-48ad-bae8-
  299bfe56a54c"
numberOfOrgNetworks="1" numberOfExtNetworks="1" name="Edge-Gateway-01"
  isBusy="false"
haStatus="UP" gatewayStatus="READY" href="https://<VCD-
  IP>/api/admin/edgeGateway/0cf71e84-fdf6-4fa0-ae85-bdd688a64963"
isSyslogServerSettingInSync="true"
taskStatus="success" taskOperation="networkEdgeGatewayCreate"
task="https://<VCD-IP>/api/task/62928cf9-937b-
  4f06-ba55-01f032a32ace" taskDetails=" "/>
```

6.4.6.4.6 Get and Return a Specific vCloud Networking and Security Edge Gateway

The following example shows how to get information about a specific vCloud Networking and Security Edge Gateway.

Request

```
GET https://<VCD-IP>/api/admin/edgeGateway/0cf71e84-fdf6-4fa0-ae85-bdd688a64963
```

```
$ curl -k -v -b cookie.txt -H "Accept:application/*+xml;version=5.1"
https://10.147.50.33/api/admin/edgeGateway/0cf71e84-fdf6-4fa0-ae85-bdd688a64963
```

Response

```
<EdgeGateway xmlns="http://www.vmware.com/vcloud/v1.5" status="1" name="Edge-
  Gateway-01"
id="urn:vcloud:gateway:0cf71e84-fdf6-4fa0-ae85-bdd688a64963"
type="application/vnd.vmware.admin.edgeGateway+xml" href="https://<VCD-
  IP>/api/admin/edgeGateway/0cf71e84-fdf6-4fa0-ae85-bdd688a64963"
xmlns:xsi="http://www.w3.org/2001/XMLSchema-instance"
xsi:schemaLocation="http://www.vmware.com/vcloud/v1.5
http://10.147.50.33/api/v1.5/schema/master.xsd">
    <Link rel="edit" type="application/vnd.vmware.admin.edgeGateway+xml"
href="https://<VCD-IP>/api/admin/edgeGateway/0cf71e84-fdf6-4fa0-
```

```
ae85-bdd688a64963"/>
    <Link rel="remove" href="https://<VCD-IP>/api/admin/edgeGateway/0cf71e84-fdf6-
4fa0-ae85-bdd688a64963"/>
    <Link rel="up" type="application/vnd.vmware.admin.vdc+xml" href="https://<VCD-
IP>/api/admin/vdc/1d7f9e91-ef16-48ad-bae8-299bfe56a54c"/>
    <Link rel="edgeGateway:redeploy" href="https://<VCD-
IP>/api/admin/edgeGateway/0cf71e84-fdf6-4fa0-ae85-bdd688a64963/action/redeploy"/>
    <Link rel="edgeGateway:configureServices"
type="application/vnd.vmware.admin.edgeGatewayServiceConfiguration+xml"
href="https://<VCD-IP>/api/admin/edgeGateway/0cf71e84-fdf6-4fa0-ae85-
bdd688a64963/action/configureServices"/>
    <Link rel="edgeGateway:reapplyServices" href="https://<VCD-
IP>/api/admin/edgeGateway/0cf71e84-fdf6-4fa0-ae85-bdd688a64963/action/
reapplyServices"/>
    <Link rel="edgeGateway:syncSyslogSettings" href="https://<VCD-
IP>/api/admin/edgeGateway/0cf71e84-fdf6-4fa0-ae85-bdd688a64963/action/
syncSyslogServerSettings"/>
    <Link rel="edgeGateway:upgrade" href="https://<VCD-
IP>/api/admin/edgeGateway/0cf71e84-fdf6-4fa0-ae85-bdd688a64963/action/
upgradeConfig"/>
    <Description/>
    <Configuration>
        <GatewayBackingConfig>compact</GatewayBackingConfig>
        <GatewayInterfaces>
            <GatewayInterface>
                <Name>TestBed-VC1</Name>
                <DisplayName>TestBed-VC1</DisplayName>
                <Network type="application/vnd.vmware.admin.network+xml"
name="TestBed-
VC1" href="https://<VCD-IP>/api/admin/network/3ddab120-7d66-40d3-9536-
  af94f23e1361"/>
                <InterfaceType>uplink</InterfaceType>
                <SubnetParticipation>
                    <Gateway>192.168.1.1</Gateway>
                    <Netmask>255.255.255.0</Netmask>
                    <IpAddress>192.168.1.8</IpAddress>
                </SubnetParticipation>
                <SubnetParticipation>
                    <Gateway>192.168.2.1</Gateway>
                    <Netmask>255.255.255.0</Netmask>
                    <IpAddress>192.168.2.7</IpAddress>
                </SubnetParticipation>
                <SubnetParticipation>
                    <Gateway>198.125.2.6</Gateway>
                    <Netmask>255.255.0.0</Netmask>
                    <IpAddress>198.125.2.12</IpAddress>
```

```
            </SubnetParticipation>
            <SubnetParticipation>
                <Gateway>10.147.80.253</Gateway>
                <Netmask>255.255.255.0</Netmask>
                <IpAddress>10.147.80.217</IpAddress>
            </SubnetParticipation>
            <ApplyRateLimit>false</ApplyRateLimit>
            <InRateLimit>100.0</InRateLimit>
            <OutRateLimit>100.0</OutRateLimit>
            <UseForDefaultRoute>true</UseForDefaultRoute>
        </GatewayInterface>
        <GatewayInterface>
            <Name>MAH-VDC-Network</Name>
            <DisplayName>MAH-VDC-Network</DisplayName>
            <Network type="application/vnd.vmware.admin.network+xml" name="MAH-
VDC-Network" href="https://<VCD-IP>/api/admin/network/
  2d6b1a79-a249-4ba3-b863-e3649661801f"/>
            <InterfaceType>internal</InterfaceType>
            <SubnetParticipation>
                <Gateway>192.176.100.1</Gateway>
                <Netmask>255.255.255.0</Netmask>
                <IpAddress>192.176.100.1</IpAddress>
            </SubnetParticipation>
            <ApplyRateLimit>false</ApplyRateLimit>
            <UseForDefaultRoute>false</UseForDefaultRoute>
        </GatewayInterface>
    </GatewayInterfaces>
    <EdgeGatewayServiceConfiguration>
        <FirewallService>
            <IsEnabled>true</IsEnabled>
            <DefaultAction>drop</DefaultAction>
            <LogDefaultAction>false</LogDefaultAction>
        </FirewallService>
    </EdgeGatewayServiceConfiguration>
    <HaEnabled>false</HaEnabled>
    <UseDefaultRouteForDnsRelay>true</UseDefaultRouteForDnsRelay>
  </Configuration>
</EdgeGateway>
```

6.4.6.4.7 Modify the XML to Reflect the New Configuration

The entire body from the GET response in Step 3 in section 6.4.6.4.1 is used to make the required changes. This example shows the change of <HaEnabled> to true.

To automate the reconfiguration of the vCloud Networking and Security Edge Gateway devices:

1. Create a file and copy the contents of <EdgeGateway> ..... </EdgeGateway> into this file (for example, `EdgeGateway.xml`).
2. Change `<HaEnabled>false</HaEnabled>` to `<HaEnabled>true</HaEnabled>`.
3. Copy and paste the contents of this file into the http `PUT` or `cURL` command in Step 5.

6.4.6.4.8 Update the vCloud Networking and Security Edge Gateway Device Configuration

After making the preceding changes, you can update the vCloud Networking and Security Edge Gateway device using the vCloud API, as in the following example.

Request

```
PUT https://<VCD-IP>/api/admin/edgeGateway/0cf71e84-fdf6-4fa0-ae85-bdd688a64963
(this is the UUID 0cf71e84-fdf6-4fa0-ae85-bdd688a64963)
$ curl -k -v -b cookie.txt -H "Accept:application/*+xml;version=5.1" -X PUT --
header "Content-Type:application/vnd.vmware.admin.edgeGateway+xml" --data
@EdgeGateway.xml https://<VCD-IP>/api/admin/edgeGateway/0cf71e84-fdf6-4fa0-ae85-
bdd688a64963
```

Response

```
* About to connect() to <VCD-IP> port 443 (#0)
*   Trying <VCD-IP>... connected
* Connected to <VCD-IP> (<VCD-IP>) port 443 (#0)
* SSLv3, TLS handshake, Client hello (1):
* SSLv3, TLS handshake, Server hello (2):
* SSLv3, TLS handshake, CERT (11):
* SSLv3, TLS handshake, Server key exchange (12):
* SSLv3, TLS handshake, Server finished (14):
* SSLv3, TLS handshake, Client key exchange (16):
* SSLv3, TLS change cipher, Client hello (1):
* SSLv3, TLS handshake, Finished (20):
* SSLv3, TLS change cipher, Client hello (1):
* SSLv3, TLS handshake, Finished (20):
* SSL connection using DHE-RSA-AES256-SHA
* Server certificate:
*      subject: C=US; ST=California; L=Palo Alto; O=VMware, Inc.; CN=*.eng.vmware.com
*      start date: 2009-11-17 00:00:00 GMT
*      expire date: 2012-11-20 23:59:59 GMT
*      common name: *.eng.vmware.com (does not match <VCD-IP>)
*      issuer: C=US; O=DigiCert Inc; OU=www.digicert.com; CN=DigiCert High Assurance
       CA-3
*      SSL certificate verify ok.
```

```
> PUT /api/admin/edgeGateway/0cf71e84-fdf6-4fa0-ae85-bdd688a64963 HTTP/1.1
> User-Agent: curl/7.21.4 (universal-apple-darwin11.0) libcurl/7.21.4 OpenSSL/0.9.8r
  zlib/1.2.5
> Host: <VCD-IP>
> Cookie: vcloud-token=1hi8kZ4tNOnSnv3aq6/gSrDHlTPyYrBXQ5a2CdmX8C4=
> Accept:application/*+xml;version=5.1
> Content-Type:application/vnd.vmware.admin.edgeGateway+xml
> Content-Length: 4631
> Expect: 100-continue
>
< HTTP/1.1 100 Continue
< HTTP/1.1 202 Accepted
< Date: Fri, 24 Jul 2012 10:08:13 GMT
< Date: Fri, 24 Jul 2012 10:08:15 GMT
< Location: https://<VCD-IP>/api/task/e0c73c28-2d5b-4e9d-a304-bc6b3667f18a
< Content-Type: application/vnd.vmware.vcloud.task+xml;version=5.1
< Content-Length: 1331
<
<?xml version="1.0" encoding="UTF-8"?>
<Task xmlns="http://www.vmware.com/vcloud/v1.5" status="running" startTime="2012-07-
20T03:08:15.571-07:00" serviceNamespace="com.vmware.vcloud"
operationName="edgeGatewayUpdate" operation="Updating EdgeGateway (0cf71e84-fdf6-
4fa0-
ae85-bdd688a64963)" expiryTime="2012-10-18T03:08:15.571-07:00"
cancelRequested="false"
name="task" id="urn:vcloud:task:e0c73c28-2d5b-4e9d-a304-bc6b3667f18a"
type="application/vnd.vmware.vcloud.task+xml" href="https://<VCD-IP>/api/task/
e0c73c28-
2d5b-4e9d-a304-bc6b3667f18a" xmlns:xsi="http://www.w3.org/2001/XMLSchema-instance"
xsi:schemaLocation="http://www.vmware.com/vcloud/v1.5 http://<VCD-
IP>/api/v1.5/schema/master.xsd">
    <Link rel="task:cancel" href="https://<VCD-IP>/api/task/e0c73c28-2d5b-4e9d-a304-
bc6b3667f18a/action/cancel"/>
    <Owner type="application/vnd.vmware.admin.edgeGateway+xml" name=""
href="https://<VCD-IP>/api/admin/edgeGateway/0cf71e84-fdf6-4fa0-ae85-bdd688a64963"/>
    <User type="application/vnd.vmware.admin.user+xml" name="system"
href="https://<VCD-
IP>/api/admin/user/55c1d771-b2e2-4255-8387-7f6da1e0e3f1"/>
    <Organization type="application/vnd.vmware.vcloud.org+xml" name="MAH"
href="https://<VCD-IP>/api/org/60b44eb5-0e98-45bc-b96b-25549ce03033"/>
    <Progress>0</Progress>
    <Details/>
</Task>
* Connection #0 to host <VCD-IP> left intact
* Closing connection #0
```

6.4.6.5 Design Considerations

- The vCloud Networking and Security Edge (Edge) devices can be available in only one site at a time. Having the hosts in maintenance mode on the recovery side enforces this and also keeps them in sync with all the changes that happen at the primary site.
- Removing the primary interface after failover avoids loss of traffic for the primary site to a nonexistent interface in the case of partial environment recovery. This is because Edge always prefers the locally attached interface for sending traffic instead of sending all traffic out the default interface. Designating a default interface is used only when no locally attached networks exist. The Edge device uses this interface to send all unknown destination traffic to its designated default router. When the environment might be failing back to its primary site, it is prudent to save all interface-based rules and configurations before removal. This is because all configurations associated with the interface are removed as soon as an interface is removed.
- vCloud primary sites that have direct organization networks do not use VXLAN, so the recovery process is identical to the existing vCloud DR recovery process. All the vApps on that network must have IP addresses reassigned to the correct addressing used in the recovery site Layer 3 network.
- vCloud primary sites that use isolated networks that are VLAN backed must be re-created at the recovery site using the associated VLAN IDs available at the recovery site and the vApps reconnected to the new network. If the isolated networks were port group backed, the port groups would still exist in the recovery site, but their definitions must be revisited to verify that their configurations remain valid.
- vCloud primary sites that use routed or isolated VXLAN-backed networks are relatively easy to recover because of VXLAN technology.

6.4.6.6 References

- vCloud Director Infrastructure Resiliency Case Study (www.vmware.com/files/pdf/techpaper/vcloud-director-infrastructure-resiliency.pdf)
- *vCloud Director API Programming Guide* (www.vmware.com/pdf/vcd_15_api_guide.pdf)

6.4.7 VCDNI-Backed Organization Network

Deployment Models: Private, public, hybrid

Example Components: vCloud Director 5.1, vCloud Networking and Security Edge 5.1, vSphere 5.1

6.4.7.1 Background

A network pool is an object in vCloud that creates and manages isolated networks using vSphere port groups. The vSphere port groups can be preprovisioned in vSphere or created dynamically by vCloud as needed for organization or vApp networks.

The following types of network pools are available in vCloud Director:

- VXLAN (dynamically created vSphere port groups)
- VLAN backed (dynamically created vSphere port groups)
- vCloud network isolation backed (dynamically created vSphere port groups)
- vSphere port group backed (manually created vSphere port groups)

6.4.7.2 Example

This example documents the VCDNI-backed network pool.

The VCDNI-backed network pool example (see Figure 6.71) demonstrates how VCDNI networks are created automatically in vSphere and used in vCloud Director.

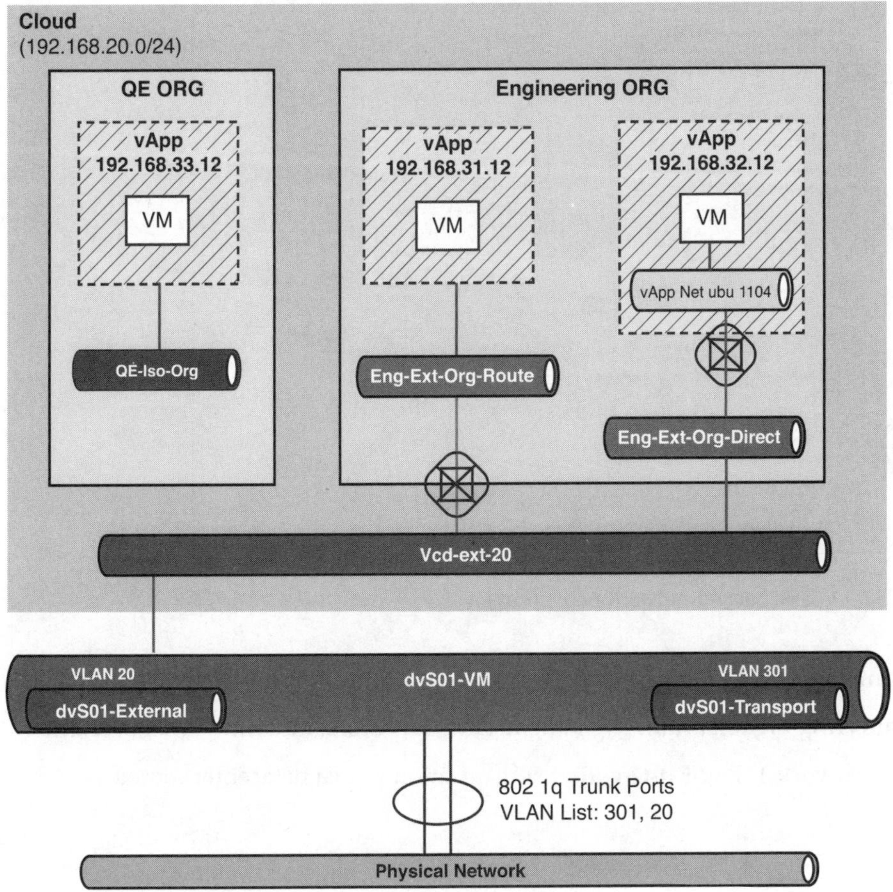

FIGURE 6.71 VCDNI network pool example configuration

The following are prerequisites used for the form in Figure 6.72:

- **vSphere Administrator:** A virtual distributed vSwitch that is connected to all vSphere (ESXi) hosts in the cluster for the underlying provider virtual datacenter
- **Network Administrator:** All physical switch port uplinks to the distributed vSwitch configured as 802.1Q VLAN trunk ports and configured to allow VLAN 20 and VLAN 301
- **Cloud Administrator:** vCloud Director VCDNI-backed network pool created with VLAN ID 301
- **Cloud Administrator:** (Optional) A vCloud Director external network (vcd-ext-20), if external connectivity is needed

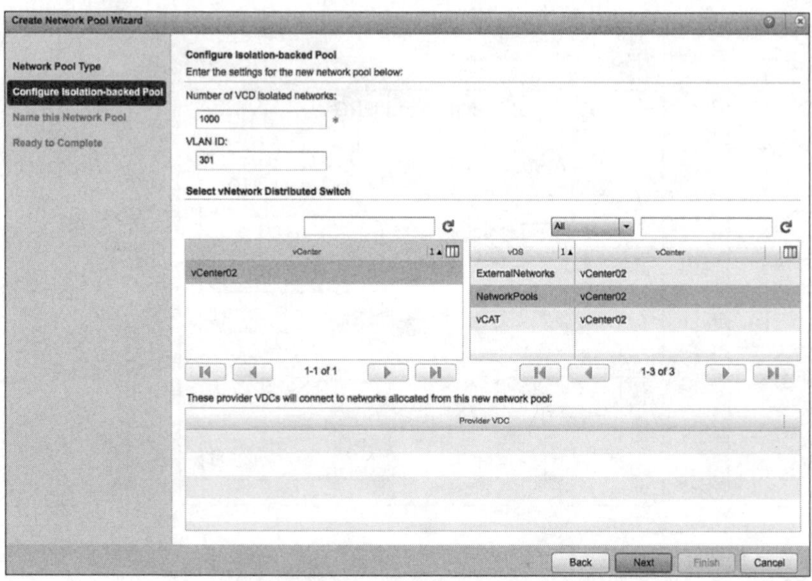

FIGURE 6.72 VCDNI-backed network pool creation

Cloud Administrator: Two organizations (Engineering and QE) provisioned.

- **Engineering organization:** High Engineering PAYG organization virtual datacenter
    - **Network 1:** Eng-Ext-Org-Route organization virtual datacenter routed

- **Engineering organization:** Default Engineering PAYG organization virtual datacenter
  - **Network 2:** Eng-Ext-Org-Direct organization virtual datacenter direct network
  - **Network 3:** vAppNet-ubu1104 vApp network
  - **QE organization:** High QE PAYG organization virtual datacenter
  - **Network 4:** QE-Iso-Org organization virtual datacenter isolated network

During the creation of an organization virtual datacenter, you can choose the network pool (the VCDNI pool created in Figure 6.72) to associate with this virtual datacenter. Multiple organizations and different virtual datacenters within an organization can share the same network pool, as shown in Table 6.15, but they are assigned separate and isolated networks from the pool.

TABLE 6.15 vCloud Director Networks

Network	Network Type	Organization	Organization Virtual Datacenter	Network Pool	Subnet
Eng-Ext-Org-Route	Organization virtual data-center routed	Engineering	High engineer-ing PAYG	VCDNI pool	192.168.31.0/24
Eng-Ext-Org-Direct	Organization direct	Engineering	Default engi-neering PAYG	—	192.168.20.0/24
vAppNet_ ubu1104	vApp NAT	Engineering	Default engi-neering PAYG	VCDNI pool	192.168.32.0/24
QE-Iso-Org	Organization isolated	QE	High QE PAYG	VCDNI pool	192.168.33.0/24

Table 6.15 shows that only the direct connect organization virtual datacenter network does not use a network from the network pool. Organization direct-connected networks use a bridged connection from the external network, requiring IP configuration on the virtual machines that matches the physical network IP configuration.

After the network pool is created and associated with an organization virtual datacenter, the network pools can be consumed. Whenever a routed or isolated organization virtual datacenter or vApp network is created, vCloud Director automatically provisions a port group on dvS01. These port groups are created automatically and do not share the same VLAN (301). However, each port group is treated as a separate Layer 2 network by virtue of the VCDNI technology. The administrator must define only the IP address settings for this network (see Figure 6.73).

6

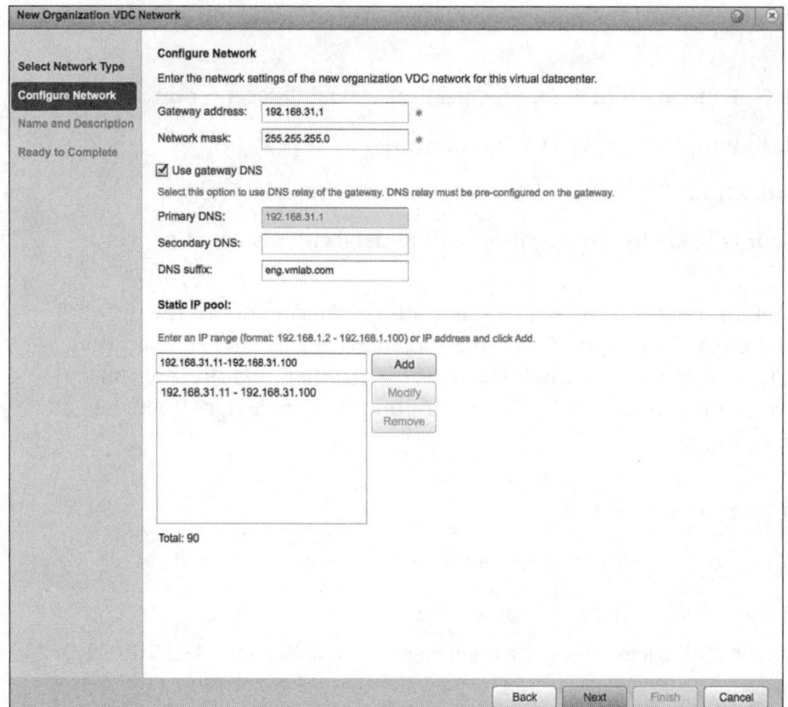

FIGURE 6.73 Organization virtual datacenter network—IP address settings

The VCDNI-backed network pool example uses the VMware VCDNI filter driver to multiplex an individual VLAN into many separate broadcast domains. The dvSwitch delivers the appropriate Ethernet frames to the appropriate port group based on the match of which vNIC belongs to which port group. For example, a broadcast from a particular vNIC is delivered only to the other vNICs connected to the same port group, even though the other port groups share the same VLAN (301), which is the transport VLAN configured for the VCDNI network pool.

This isolation persists only inside the vSphere boundaries. However, it allows isolated communication between vApps connected to the same network pool, even if they are on different ESXi hosts in the vSphere cluster.

6.4.7.3 Design Implications

- Only the following vCloud network types consume network pools:
    - Organization virtual datacenter routed networks
    - Organization virtual datacenter isolated networks
    - vApp networks

- Although the VCDNI-backed network pool provides Layer 2 (Ethernet) isolation, the use of routing or NAT capabilities at the vCloud Networking and Security Edge device can provide connectivity to externally connected networks at Layer 3.
- VCDNI uses encapsulation technology and, therefore, requires a larger Ethernet frame to be sent over the wire. To eliminate fragmentation of Ethernet frames, increase the MTU size on the physical network and network pool.
  - It is recommended to increase the MTU size on the physical devices backing the VCDNI network pool to 1524 bytes.
  - It is also recommended to increase the MTU size on the network pool itself to 1524 bytes.

See the vCloud Director documentation for more information.

6.4.8 VLAN ORG Network

Deployment Models: Private, public, hybrid

Example Components: vCloud Director 5.1, vCloud Networking and Security Edge 5.1, vSphere 5.1

6.4.8.1 Background

A network pool is an object in vCloud that creates and manages isolated networks using vSphere port groups. The vSphere port groups can be preprovisioned in vSphere or created dynamically by vCloud as needed for organization or vApp networks.

The following types of network pools are available in vCloud Director:

- VXLAN (dynamically created vSphere port groups)
- VLAN backed (dynamically created vSphere port groups)
- vCloud network isolation backed (dynamically created vSphere port groups)
- vSphere port group backed (manually created vSphere port groups)

This example uses the VLAN-backed network pool.

6.4.8.2 Example

The VLAN-backed network pool example demonstrates how the VLAN networks are created automatically in vSphere and used in vCloud Director. Figure 6.74 shows the configuration.

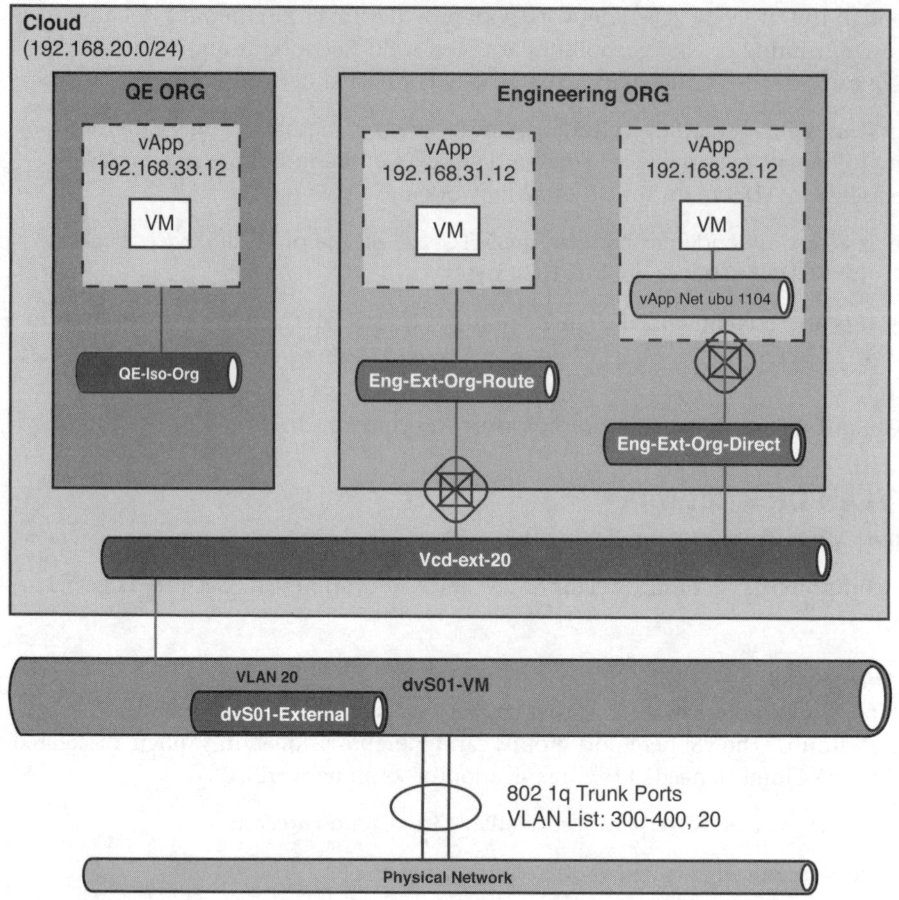

FIGURE 6.74 VLAN network pool example configuration

The following are the prerequisites for this configuration:

- **vSphere Administrator:** A virtual distributed vSwitch that is connected to all vSphere (ESXi) hosts that are in the cluster for the underlying provider virtual datacenter
- **Network Administrator:** All physical switch port uplinks to the distributed vSwitch configured as 802.1Q VLAN trunk ports and configured to allow VLANs 300–400 and VLAN 20 for the external network (vcd-ext-20)
- **Cloud Administrator:** vCloud Director VLAN-backed network pool created with a VLAN ID range of 300–400
- **Cloud Administrator:** (Optional) A vCloud Director external network (vcd-ext-20), if external connectivity is needed

Figure 6.75 shows the VLAN-backed network pool settings.

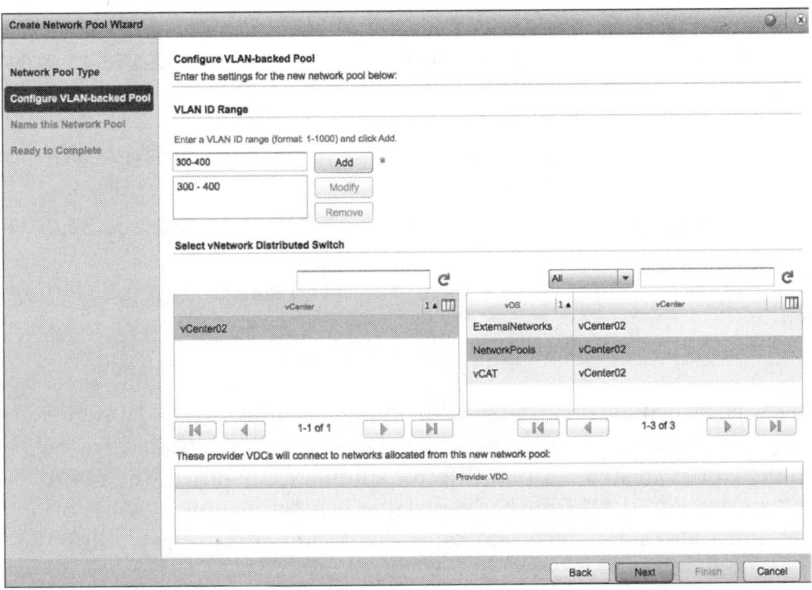

FIGURE 6.75 VLAN-backed network pool settings

- **Cloud Administrator:** Two organizations (Engineering and QE) provisioned.
- **Engineering organization:** High Engineering PAYG organization virtual datacenter
  - **Network 1:** Eng-Ext-Org-Route organization virtual datacenter routed network
- **Engineering organization:** Default Engineering PAYG organization virtual datacenter
  - **Network 2:** Eng-Ext-Org-Direct organization virtual datacenter direct network
  - **Network 3:** vAppNet-ubu1104 vApp network
  - **QE organization:** High QE PAYG organization virtual datacenter
  - **Network 4:** QE-Iso-Org organization virtual datacenter isolated network

During the creation of an organization virtual datacenter, you can choose the network pool (VLAN Pool 1) to associate with this virtual datacenter. Multiple and different virtual datacenters within an organization can share the same network pool, but they are assigned separate and isolated networks from the pool.

Table 6.16 shows that only the direct-connect organization virtual datacenter network does not use a network from the network pool. Organization direct-connected networks use a bridged connection from the external network, requiring IP configuration on the virtual machines that matches the physical network IP configuration.

TABLE 6.16 vCloud Director Networks

Network	Network Type	Org	Organization Virtual Datacenter	Network Pool	Subnet
Eng-Ext-Org-Route	Organization virtual data-center routed	Engineering	High engineering PAYG	VLAN Pool 1	192.168.31.0/24
Eng-Ext-Org-Direct	Organization direct	Engineering	Default engineer-ing PAYG	—	192.168.20.0/24
vAppNet_ubu1104	vApp NAT	Engineering	Default engineer-ing PAYG	VLAN Pool 1	192.168.32.0/24
QE-Iso-Org	Organization isolated	QE	High QE PAYG	VLAN Pool 1	192.168.33.0/24

After the network pool is created and associated with an organization virtual datacenter, the network pools can be consumed. Whenever a routed or isolated organization virtual datacenter or vApp network is created, vCloud Director automatically provisions a port group on dvS01 and assigns it a VLAN from the range that was defined for VLAN Pool 1 (300–400). The Administrator simply needs to define the IP address settings for this network (see Figure 6.76).

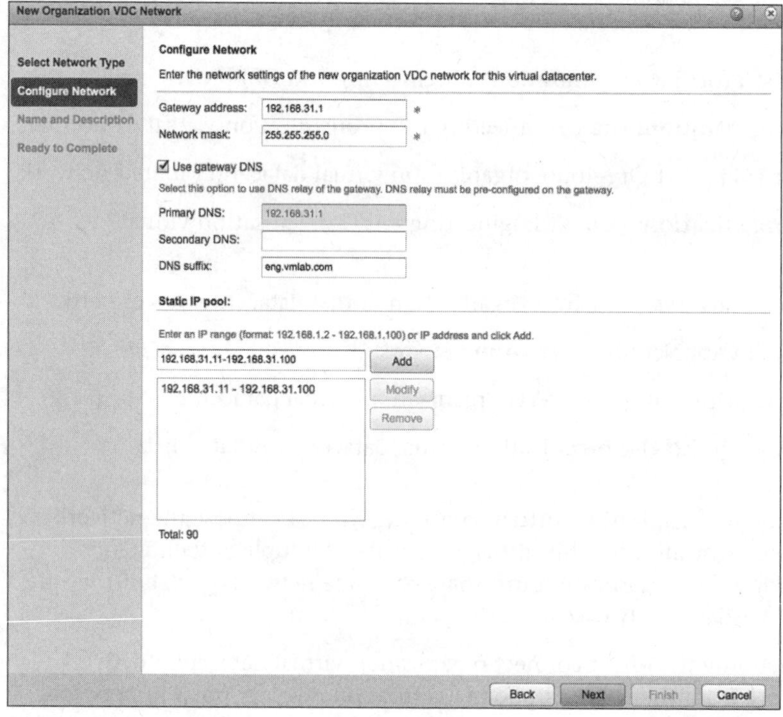

FIGURE 6.76 Organization virtual datacenter network—IP address settings

The VLAN-backed network pool (see Figure 6.77) leverages 802.1Q VLAN trunk ports to allow the physical switching infrastructure to pass all VLANs configured (300–400) to the ESXi hosts, while still keeping the individual VLANs separated and in separate broadcast domains. The dvSwitch delivers the appropriate Ethernet frames to the appropriate port group based on a match of the VLAN tag on the frame and the VLAN associated with the port group. The dvSwitch port groups remove the VLAN tag from the Ethernet frame and deliver it to the appropriate virtual machine. This architecture is commonly referred to as virtual switch tagging, or VST.

This isolation also persists across the physical switching infrastructure, allowing isolated communication between virtual machines connected to the same vCloud Director network even if they are on different ESXi hosts in the vSphere cluster.

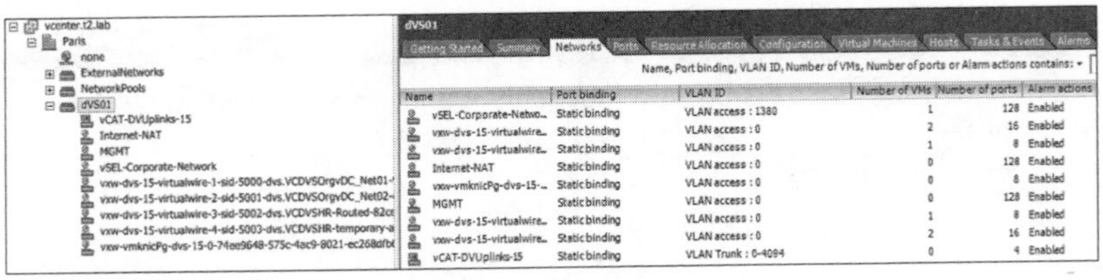

FIGURE 6.77 Network pool corresponding to vSphere port groups

6.4.8.3 Design Implications

- Only the following vCloud network types consume network pools:
  - Organization virtual datacenter routed network
  - Organization virtual datacenter isolated network
  - vApp networks
- A limit of 4,094 VLANs (1–4094) allowed in the 802.1Q standard.
- VLAN 0 and VLAN 4095 are reserved in the 802.1Q standard.
- Although the VLAN-backed network pool provides Layer 2 (Ethernet) isolation, the use of routing or NAT capabilities at the vCloud Networking and Security Edge instance can provide connectivity to externally connected networks at Layer 3.

6.5 Storage Design Examples

The following are examples used to help in storage design for a VMware vCloud.

6.5.1 vApp Snapshot

Deployment Models: Public

Example Components: vCloud Director 5.1, vCloud Networking and Security Edge 5.1, vSphere 5.1

6.5.1.1 Background

As of vCloud Director 5.1, vApp Users and vApp Authors can create, revert, and delete snapshots from the vCloud Director user interface or from the vCloud APIs.

6.5.1.2 Use Case

This example shows how a consumer of public vCloud resources who is responsible for a two-tiered application can manipulate snapshots at both the virtual machine level and the vApp level. This is especially useful for patching and testing where a rollback might be needed.

NOTE

Snapshots are not intended for use as a backup mechanism and generally should not be kept for long periods of time.

6.5.1.3 Example

Figure 6.78 shows the basic structure of the two-tiered vApp. It contains a web virtual machine and a database virtual machine. Both virtual machines are running.

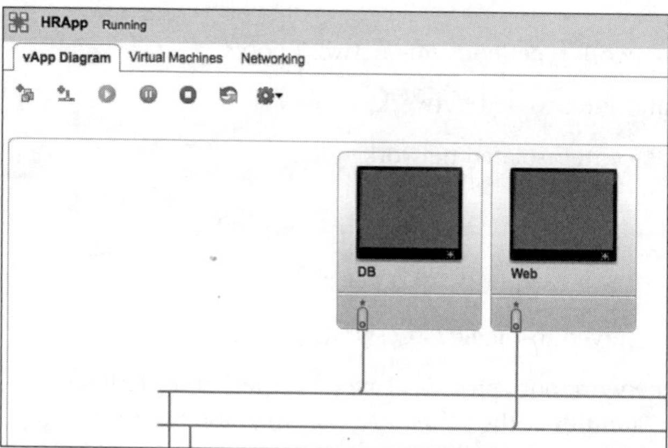

FIGURE 6.78 Two-tiered vApp

These virtual machines display in the vSphere Client as shown in Figure 6.79. The vSphere Client is used here only for illustration—it is the vCloud Director UI that is used to create, revert, and delete the snapshots.

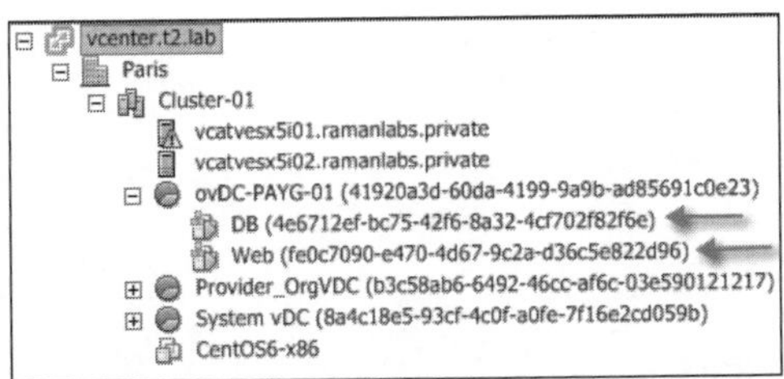

FIGURE 6.79 Two-tiered vApp as seen in vCenter

To take a snapshot of the entire vApp while the vApp is running:

1. In the vCloud Director UI, click the My Cloud tab; then right-click the vApp and select Create Snapshot. All virtual machines in the vApp have snapshots.

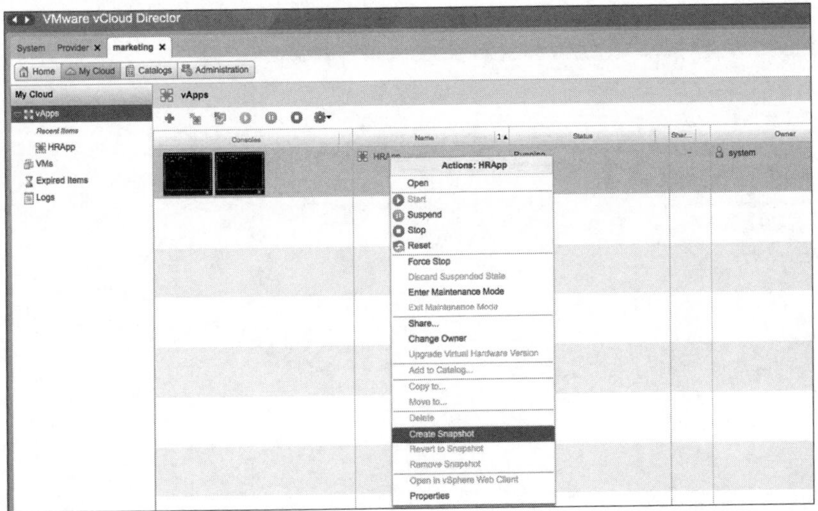

FIGURE 6.80

2. Select the snapshot options you want and click OK. While the vApp is running, vCloud Director can take a snapshot of its memory and/or quiesce its file system. Quiescing the file system requires that both virtual machines have VMware Tools installed.

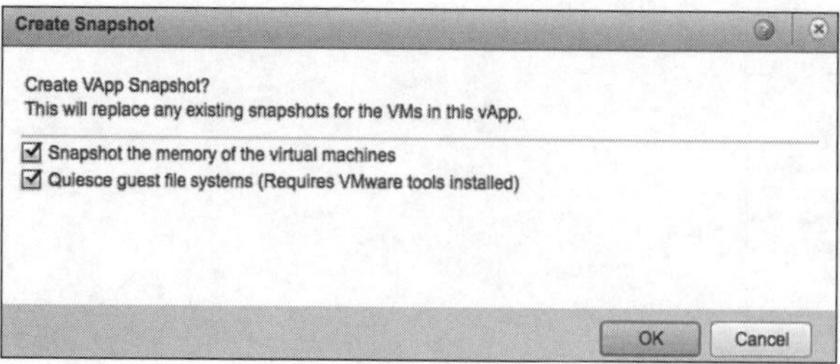

FIGURE 6.81

3. In the vSphere Client, see the Recent Tasks section to monitor progress. The snapshots for the two virtual machines contained in the vApp are created in vSphere. In Figure 6.82, the database virtual machine snapshot has just been taken and the web virtual machine snapshot is about to complete.

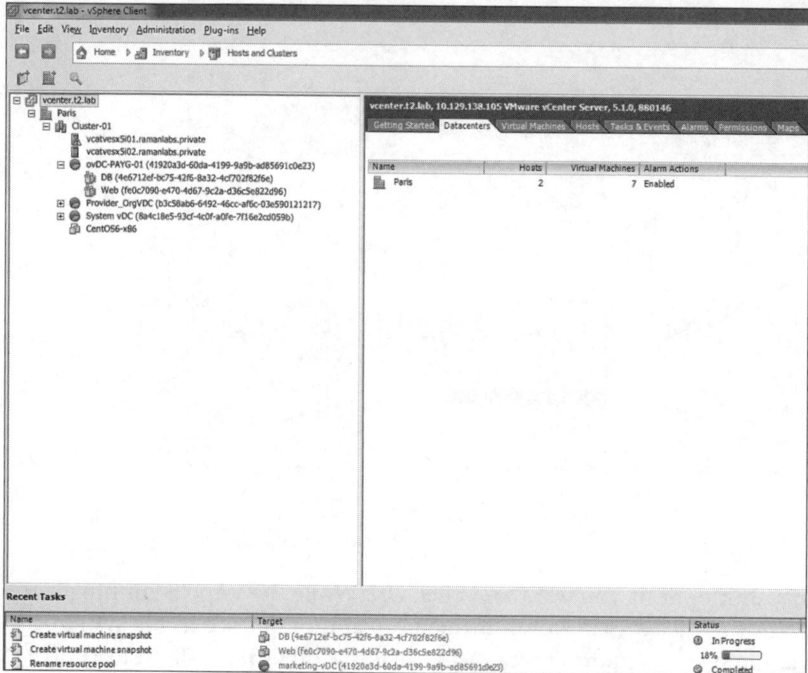

FIGURE 6.82

4. The virtual machines are in snapshot mode, and the consumer can start making changes to those virtual machines. If the consumer determines during testing that an additional snapshot should be taken for the web virtual machine, the consumer can select the single virtual machine in vCloud Director, right-click, and again select Create Snapshot.

Name	Target	Status
Create virtual machine snapshot	Web (fe0c7090-e470-4d67-9c2a-d36c5e822d96)	17%
Remove snapshot	Web (fe0c7090-e470-4d67-9c2a-d36c5e822d96)	Completed
Create virtual machine snapshot	DB (4e6712ef-bc75-42f6-8a32-4cf702f82f6e)	Completed
Create virtual machine snapshot	Web (fe0c7090-e470-4d67-9c2a-d36c5e822d96)	Completed

FIGURE 6.83

NOTE

vCloud Director supports only a single snapshot for each virtual machine. If you create a snapshot for a virtual machine that already has an existing snapshot, it deletes the existing snapshot and creates a new one. This commits the changes from the first snapshot to the guest OS image or VMDK.

5. When the tests are completed and the consumer determines that the web virtual machine is working, the snapshots can be deleted. This process saves and consolidates all the post-snapshot changes to the guest OS in the VMDK. In vCloud Director, as in vSphere, deleting a snapshot commits the changes and removes the virtual machine from snapshot mode.

Alternatively, the consumer might determine that the database virtual machine must be rolled back to its original state at the time the snapshot was created. To roll back the snapshot, the consumer right-clicks the database virtual machine and selects Revert to Snapshot (see Figure 6.84). Rolling back removes the virtual machine from snapshot mode, bringing the virtual machine back to the point in time of the snapshot, and starts a new snapshot file. To completely leave snapshot mode, you must delete the snapshot.

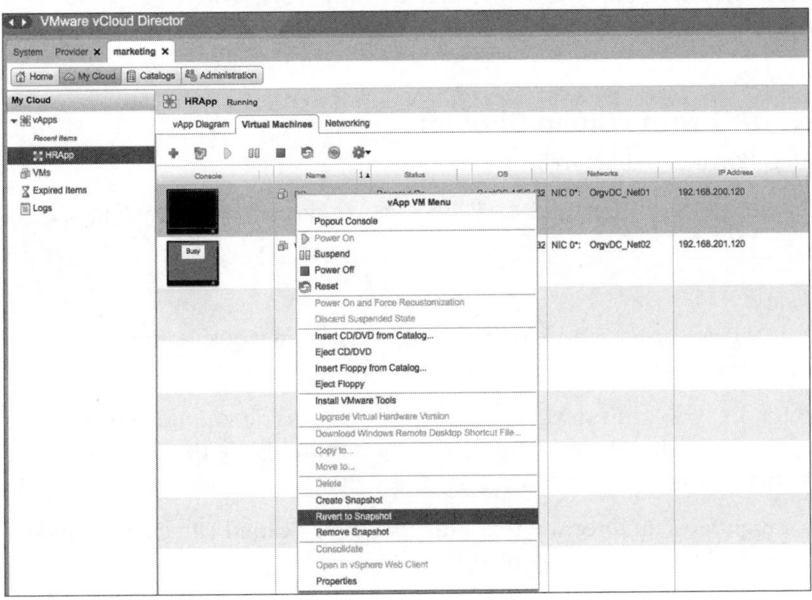

FIGURE 6.84

To roll back or revert a running virtual machine, vSphere must power it off, remove the snapshot, and restart the virtual machine from the original VMDK file, but with a new snapshot disk to which changes are logged. Figure 6.85 shows the tasks performed in vSphere when reverting a snapshot.

Name	Target	Status
Power On virtual machine	DB (4e6712ef-bc75-42f6-8a32-4cf702f82f6e)	Completed
Reconfigure virtual machine	DB (4e6712ef-bc75-42f6-8a32-4cf702f82f6e)	Completed
Revert snapshot	DB (4e6712ef-bc75-42f6-8a32-4cf702f82f6e)	Completed
Reconfigure virtual machine	DB (4e6712ef-bc75-42f6-8a32-4cf702f82f6e)	Completed
Power Off virtual machine	DB (4e6712ef-bc75-42f6-8a32-4cf702f82f6e)	Completed
Create virtual machine snapshot	Web (fe0c7090-e470-4d67-9c2a-d36c5e822d96)	Completed
Remove snapshot	Web (fe0c7090-e470-4d67-9c2a-d36c5e822d96)	Completed

FIGURE 6.85

The consumer can issue the snapshot command at either the vApp level or the virtual machine level from within vCloud Director.

In this example, the consumer took a vApp-level snapshot and then updated the individual virtual machines because each virtual machine required different operations. If a vApp-level snapshot command is issued, the same command is propagated to all the virtual machines that comprise the vApp.

6.5.1.4 Design Implications

- Snapshots can be managed at both the vApp and individual virtual machine level.
- Reverting an individual virtual machine to a snapshot does not restore vApp level constructs such as OVF properties or network mappings/properties.
- vCloud Director snapshots apply to vApps that are thin-provisioned or fast-provisioned.

6.5.2 Storage DRS with vCloud Director

Deployment Models: Private, public, hybrid

Example Components: vCloud Director 5.1, vCloud Networking and Security Edge 5.1, vSphere 5.1

6.5.2.1 Background

VMware introduced storage clusters and VM Storage Profiles in previous versions of vSphere, but vCloud Director could not consume them.

As of vCloud Director 5.1, you can expose VM Storage Profiles inside vCloud Director virtual datacenters, thus allowing the end user to choose from multiple tiers of storage within the same virtual datacenter.

Figure 6.86 shows a high-level architecture that illustrates how vCloud Director can map these features that are available in the core platform.

6.5.2.2 Use Case

The vCloud admin wants to provision a virtual datacenter to an organization and configure two storage profiles to be able to deploy vApp workloads in the proper storage class according to specific requirements. The admin also wants to create storage profiles that leverage datastore grouping features at the platform level so that the platform can automatically choose the best datastore in a cluster of datastores that belong to the same profile.

6.5.2.3 Example

At a high level, Figure 6.86 illustrates the procedure for a vCloud administrator to produce and expose to the consumer different profiles of storage.

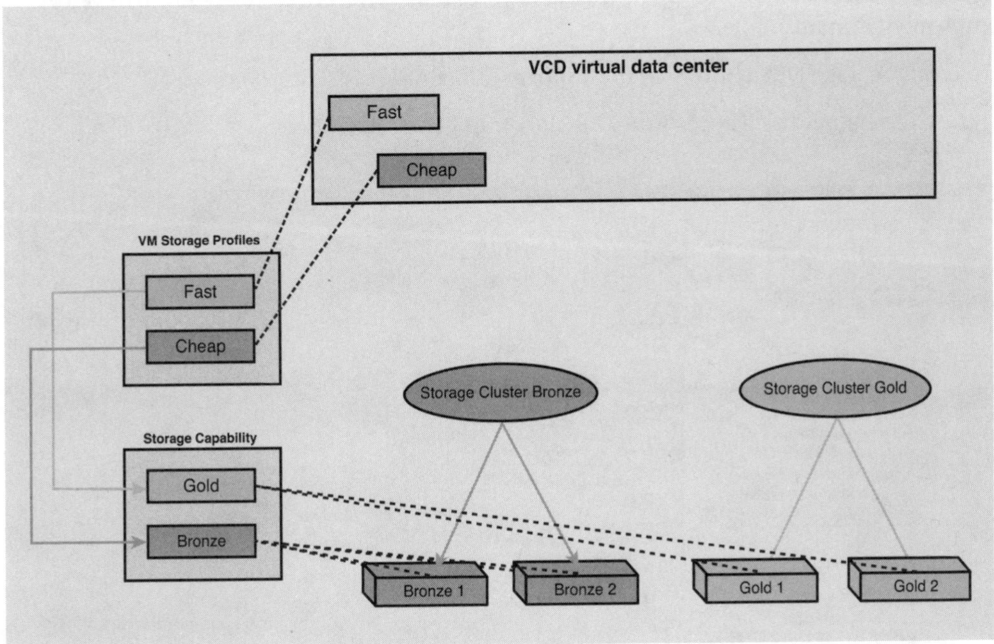

FIGURE 6.86 Overview of Storage Profiles architecture

To produce and expose storage profiles to the consumer:

1. Perform the following steps in the vSphere Web Client as administrator:
   a. Create datastore clusters and select the datastores.
   b. Assign proper storage capabilities to the datastores.
   c. Create VM Storage Profiles.
   d. Declare which storage capability is associated to the VM Storage Profiles.

6

2. Perform the following steps in vCloud Director as administrator:
   a. Assign the desired VM Storage Profile to the provider virtual datacenter.
   b. Create an organization virtual datacenter.
   c. Determine a default Storage Profile for the organization virtual datacenter.

The user can consume these classes at vApp deployment time.

6.5.2.3.1 Implementation

As an example, create Storage DRS clusters in the vSphere domain. In this scenario, two datastores (bronze1, bronze2) are backed by SATA storage, and two datastores (gold1, gold2) are backed by FC storage. Other datastores also exist, but they are not part of this implementation example.

To create Storage DRS clusters in the vSphere domain:

1. Create a new datastore cluster, as shown in Figure 6.87.

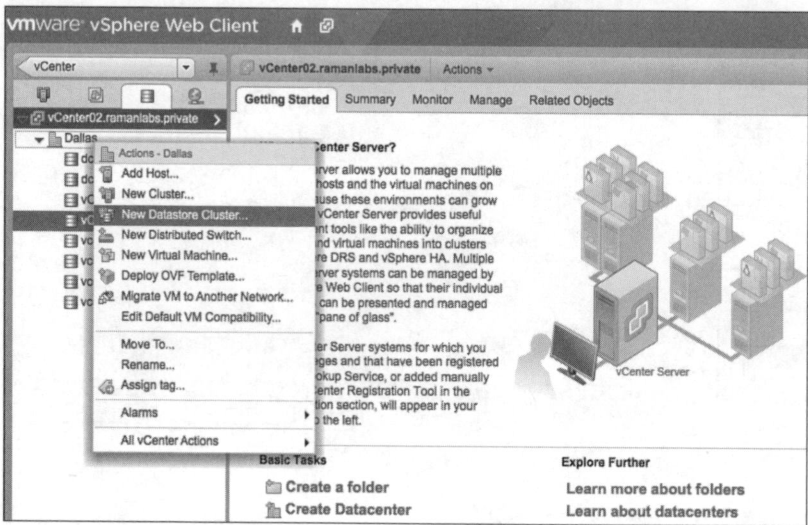

FIGURE 6.87

2. Move existing datastores into the cluster, highlighted in Figure 6.88.

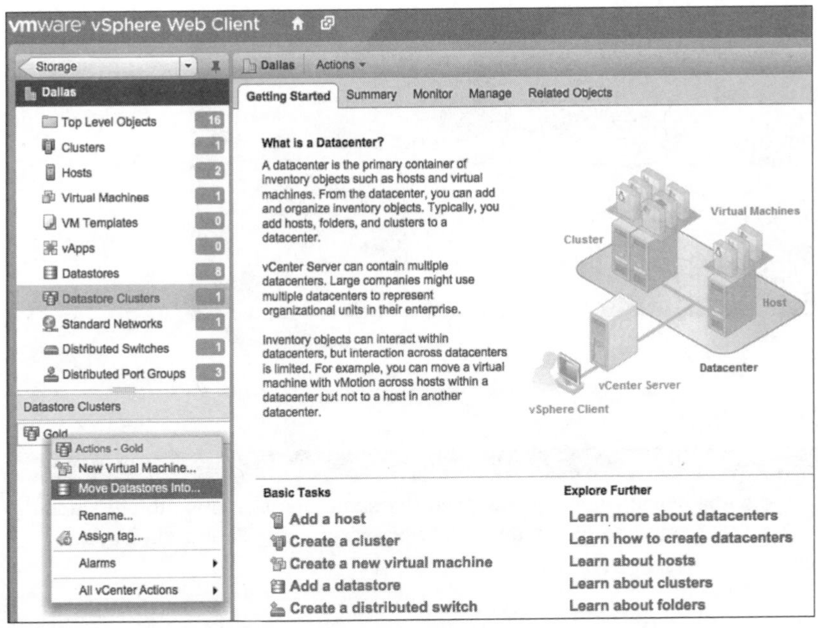

FIGURE 6.88

3. For each of the four datastores, click the datastore and assign a storage capability (see Figure 6.89).

6

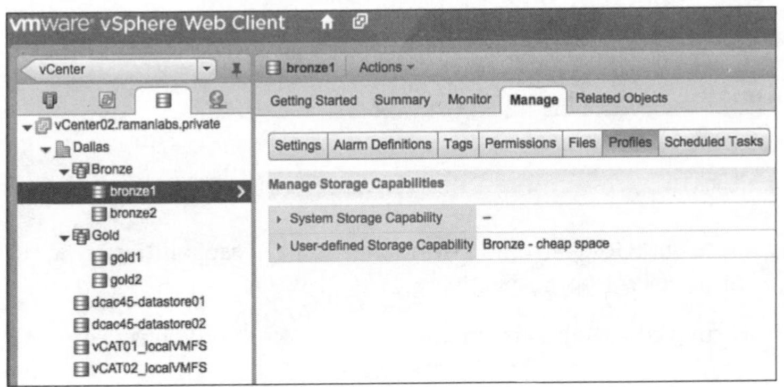

FIGURE 6.89

4. If you have not defined a storage capability, create a new one (see Figure 6.90). Assign the storage capability. In this example, the storage capabilities are named Bronze—Cheap Space and Gold—High Performance.

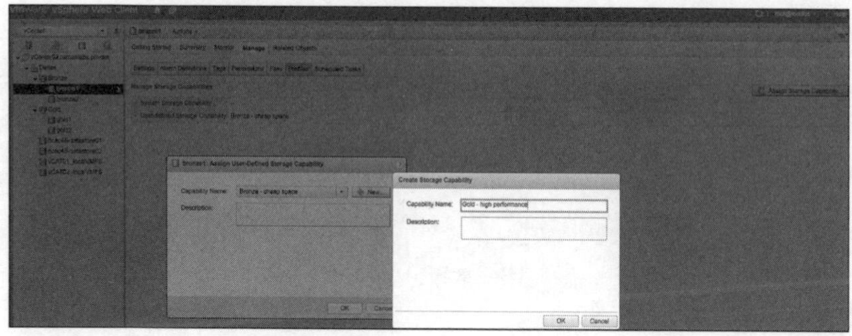

FIGURE 6.90

NOTE

All datastores in the same cluster must be assigned the same homogenous storage capability. Otherwise, the proper storage profile does not appear as available in the vCloud Director interface.

5. Create VM Storage Profiles. Each VM Storage Profile can have one or more storage capabilities. Figure 6.91 shows two VM Storage Profiles (vcd Economy Space and vcd High Performance).

vmware vSphere Web Client

Rules and Profiles

VM Storage Profiles 3

vcd cheap space
vcd high performance
vcd NFS storage

VM Storage Profiles

Name	Virtual Center	Associated VMs	Associated Virtual Disks
vcd cheap space	vCenter02.ramanlabs.private	0	0
vcd high performance	vCenter02.ramanlabs.private	0	0
vcd NFS storage	vCenter02.ramanlabs.private	0	0

FIGURE 6.91

The Bronze—Cheap Space and Gold—High Performance storage capabilities are assigned to these VM Storage Profiles, respectively.

Figure 6.92 shows how the vcd—High Performance VM Storage Profile has been configured.

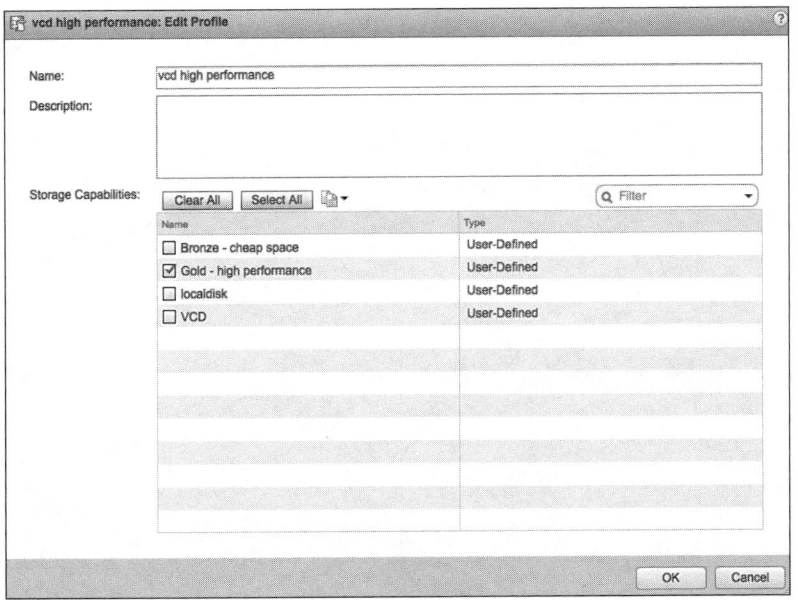

FIGURE 6.92

6. Switch to the vCloud Director management portal and configure these VM Storage Profiles in the provider virtual datacenter (see Figure 6.93).

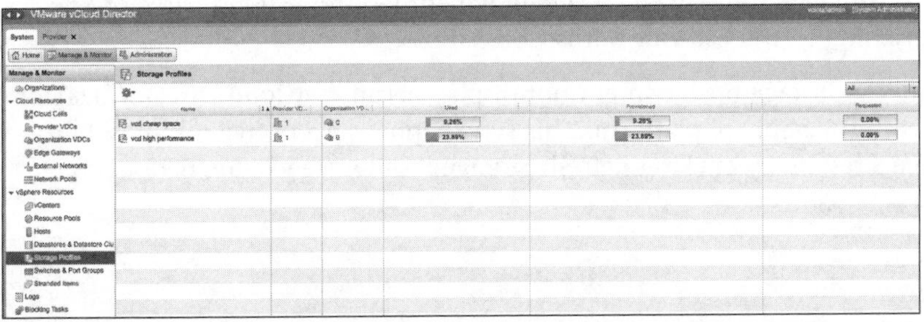

FIGURE 6.93

Additional VM Storage Profiles, if available, appear in the Add Storage Profile window (see Figure 6.94).

FIGURE 6.94

If the list does not display a configured VM Storage Profile, verify that the proper storage capability has been consistently configured for each datastore in the datastore cluster. Although vSphere marks a cluster as Incompatible when you select a particular VM Storage Profile in the VM deployment wizard, vCloud Director does not show anything in the list unless it is Compatible.

7. A configured VM Storage profile might not display because vCloud Director has not yet synced with the vSphere platform. This sync happens every five minutes, but you can force a resync by clicking Refresh Storage Profiles (see Figure 6.95).

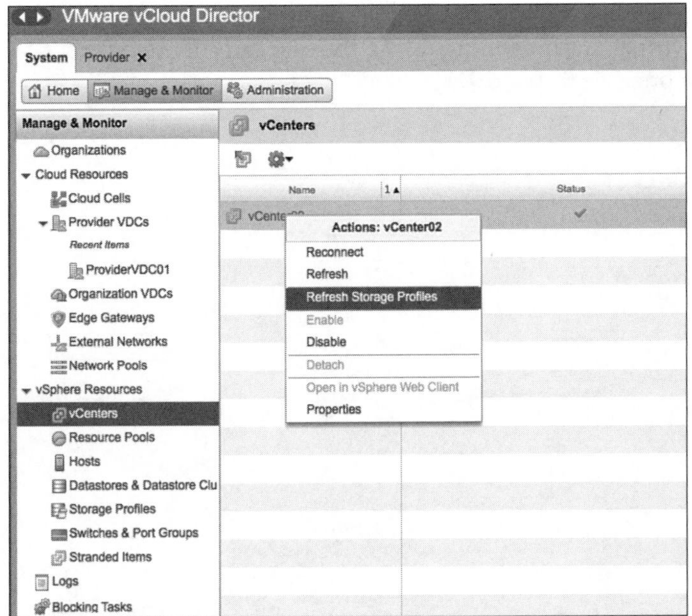

FIGURE 6.95

8. Create an organization virtual datacenter for the organization (see Figure 6.96).

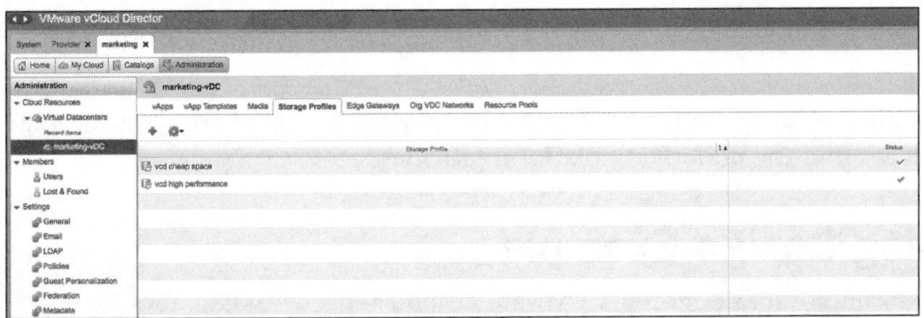

FIGURE 6.96

NOTE

This organization virtual datacenter was created for the marketing organization. A default storage profile is defined for the organization virtual datacenter. This is the default selection for virtual machines when vApp Authors and vApp Users deploy virtual machines. Being able to change the default settings of a storage profile is a privilege that you can use when defining user roles. By default, this privilege is assigned to organization administrators.

9. When a vApp Author deploys a two-tiered vApp that requires different storage characteristics for each virtual machine in the vApp, the user can choose different storage profiles for each one (see Figure 6.97).

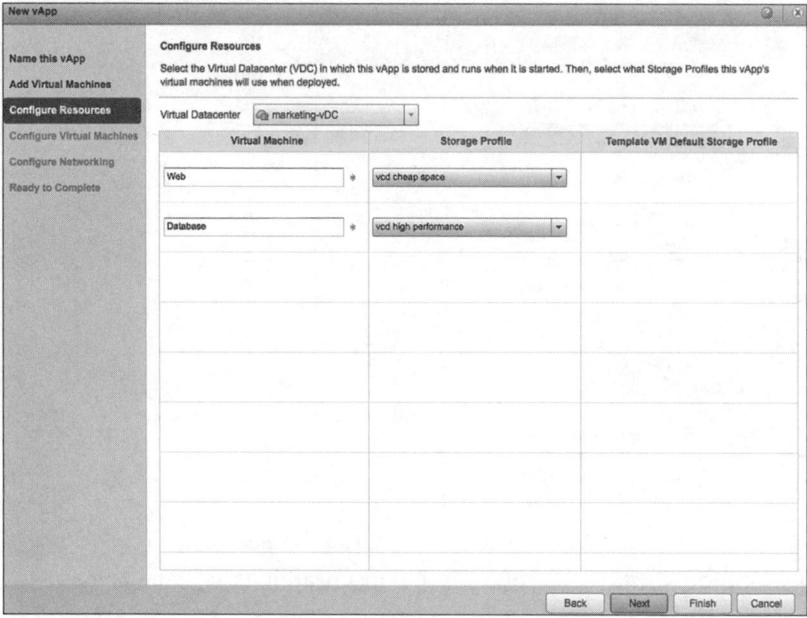

FIGURE 6.97

These virtual machines reside on a cluster of datastores managed by vSphere, thus leveraging all the advantages that the underlying platform provides.

6.6 Catalog Design Example

The following are examples for designing a VMware vCloud Service Catalog.

6.6.1 vCloud Public Catalog

Deployment Models: Public

Example Components: vCloud Director 5.1, vCloud Networking and Security Edge 5.1, vSphere 5.1

6.6.1.1 Background

Using vCloud Director, a public service provider can build and offer prepackaged vApps to its tenants through a public catalog. These vApps can vary from basic single virtual machines with only an operating system installed to more complex multitier vApps with application software preinstalled.

6.6.1.2 Use Case

A public service provider wants to offer to tenants, through a public catalog, a Linux distribution preinstalled in a virtual machine.

This will enable users in any organization to deploy a Linux image in minutes instead of having to create a vApp from scratch and installing the operating system themselves. This is usually a long process, with no value-add for the tenants. By providing a basic prebuilt operating system, the provider's customers can move quickly to adding applications.

Alternatively, the service provider can offer prebuilt middleware and application stacks on top of the basic operating system. However, this is beyond the scope of this example.

This example shows how to install a Ubuntu server distribution in the virtual machine to be posted in the catalog.

6.6.1.3 Example

The service provider uses the following procedure to create a vApp with the Ubuntu Server Linux distribution.

To create an Ubuntu Linux vApp:

1. Create a vCloud Director service organization whose goal is to export the catalog to all the actual tenants within the vCloud offering. A new catalog in this service organization is created and set to Publish to All Organizations (see Figure 6.98).

NOTE

Although not shown, the service organization must be configured to enable catalog publishing from within the organization.

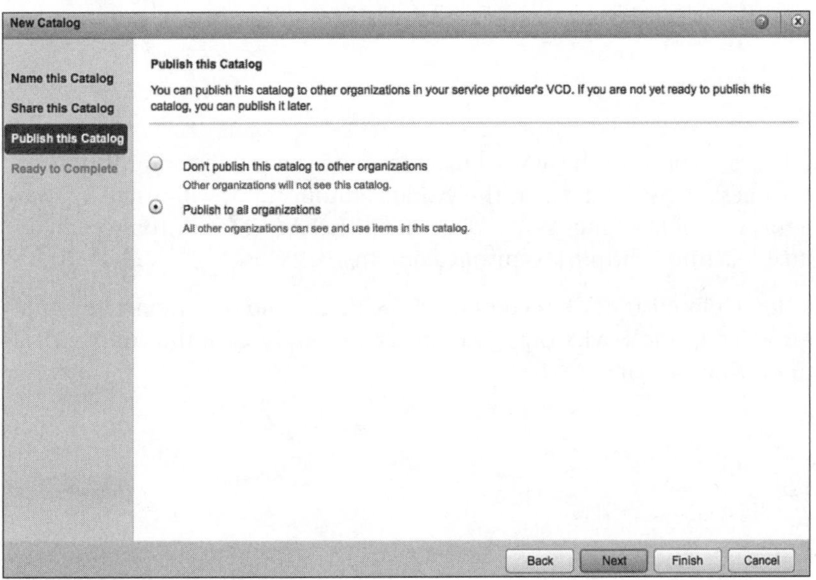

FIGURE 6.98

2. Upload the Ubuntu Server 12.04 x64 ISO file. This displays on the Media tab of the catalog.

3. Inside this service organization, create a new vApp that contains a single virtual machine.

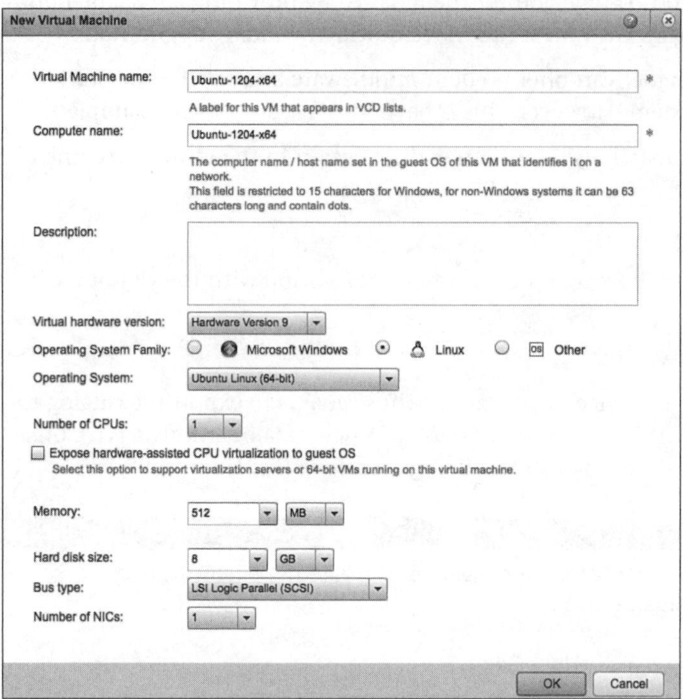

FIGURE 6.99

The Ubuntu ISO is mapped to this virtual machine, and the vCloud administrator can install the operating system. Later, the vCloud administrator will install VMware Tools inside this virtual machine, as described in "Installing VMware Tools in an Ubuntu Virtual Machine" (http://kb.vmware.com/kb/1022525).

4. When the vCloud administrator has completed the basic build operation, the vApp is ready to be added to the service organization catalog. Right-click the vApp and select Add to Catalog (see Figure 6.100).

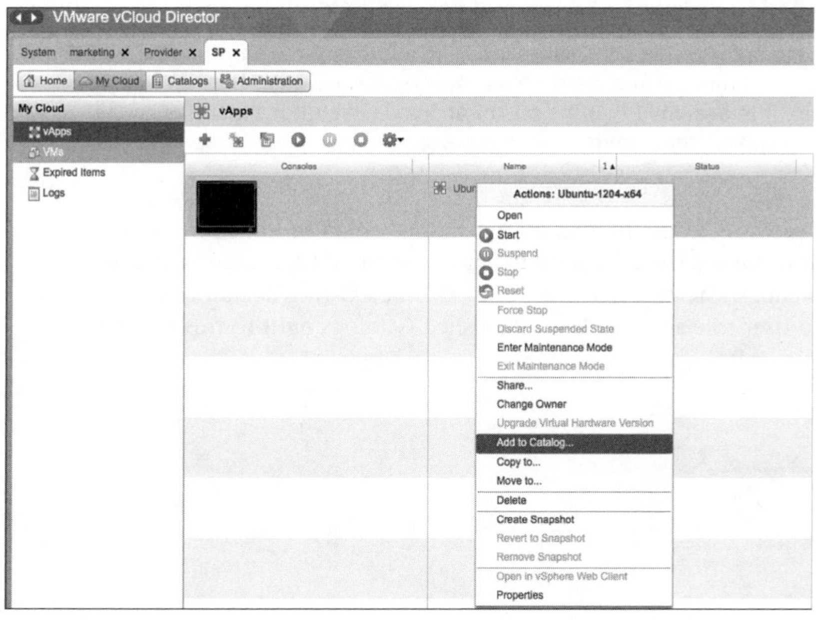

FIGURE 6.100

5. Verify that this vApp is set to Customize VM Settings. This enables each user deployment to be unique; the name of the guest operating system (along with its IP address0 is customized for each deployment from the catalog.

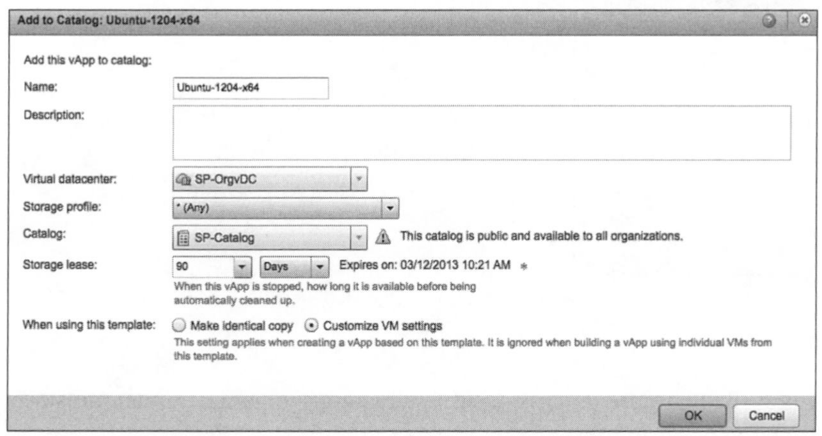

FIGURE 6.101

NOTE

By default, only the organization administrator built-in role has the right to deploy from published catalogs. Other built-in roles such as vApp Author and vApp User do not have this right enabled. It is assumed that the organization administrator goes through the public catalog and copies items from it into the private catalog for its users to consume.

6. This service provider wants to offer all the various organization administrators in their vCloud instances the capability to control some of their users' access to the published catalogs. Create a new role on top of the existing default roles. Clone the default vApp User role and add View Published Catalogs right to this newly created role (see Figure 6.102).

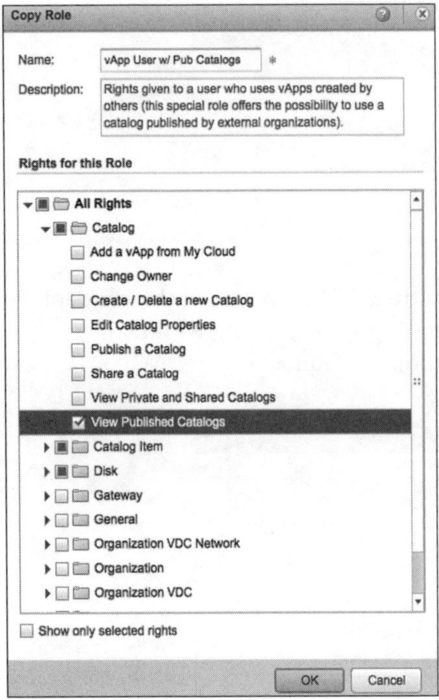

FIGURE 6.102

Now the new role is available to the tenants—specifically, to the organization administrators who are creating organization users.

6.6.1.4 Public Catalog Consumption Example

At this point, the service provider can start on-boarding tenants. In this example, an organization called Org1 represents a new customer that has subscribed to the IaaS cloud this service provider offers.

This organization does not yet have a local catalog. If desired, organization administrators can create local catalogs later that can be used as private repositories for their own templates after customization.

To create a local catalog:

1. Create a new user (called developer1) and assign the newly created custom role vApp user w/ Public Catalogs to this new user (see Figure 6.103).

FIGURE 6.103

This grants the developer1 user access to the templates the cloud provider has shared in the public catalog (see Figure 6.104).

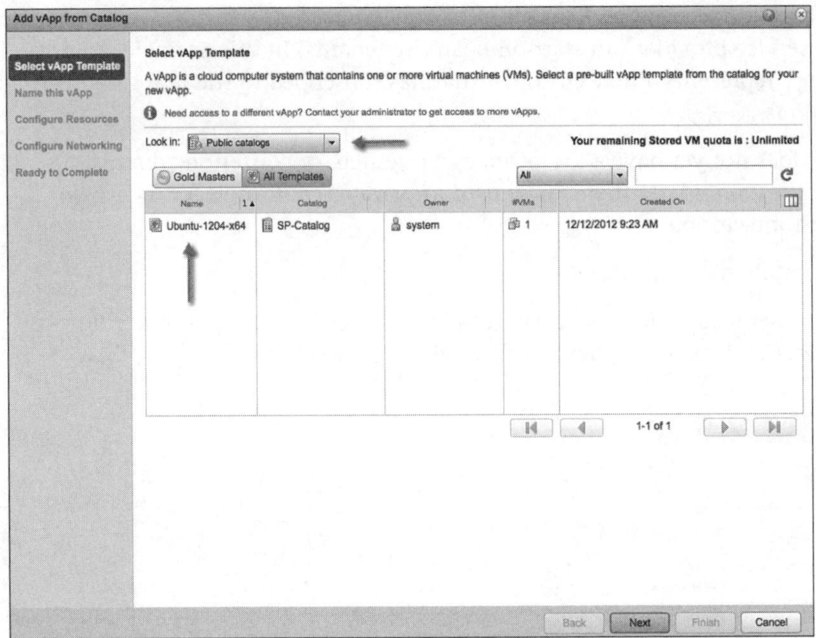

FIGURE 6.104

2. The user, developer1, can deploy this template to the user's cloud as a single virtual machine or as part of a multimachine vApp.

6.7 vCloud Security Examples

6.7.1 Single Sign-On (SSO)—Provider

Deployment Models: Private, public, hybrid

Example Components: vCloud Director 5.1, vCloud Networking and Security Edge 5.1, vSphere 5.1, SAML Compliant Identity Provider (IdP)

NOTE

The primary purpose and role of the IdP is to manage identity information and provide a central authentication service to trusted service providers.

6.7.1.1 Background

Support for Single Sign-On (SSO) in the vCloud environment is necessary because service providers and enterprise customers typically use many different management applications. Some of these applications are part of the platform; others are delivered by third parties but should be integrated in the vCloud solution.

The identity and federation market has moved from a closed, enterprise-centric view to an open, federated view. Not only do service providers and enterprise customers expect Single Sign-On across applications within the client environments, but they also want the same identity to work across security boundaries in public vCloud setups, as well as with SaaS applications. In a private and public vCloud setup, the authentication service must support multitenancy as well.

One of the cornerstones of achieving federation is the capability to make user identities transportable from one security domain to another relatively seamlessly. The industry has adopted standards such as WS-Trust and SAML to achieve this. VMware conforms to these standards and builds a Secure Token Service (STS) that generates SAML 2.0 tokens. These standards are also important for supporting multisite use cases because this allows for vCloud components such as vCenter to be passed a SAML token from a previously authenticated secure session. As long mutual trust exists between the vCloud environments, the same authenticated SAML token is respected.

6.7.1.2 Use Case

In this service provider SSO use case, a vCloud administrator provides credentials to the UI client only once, which validates the client against the SSO server. If the validation is successful, the SSO server issues a SAML token, which the UI client can then use to access both vCenter and vCloud Director without having to enter credentials multiple times. Figure 6.105 shows the logical architecture for this.

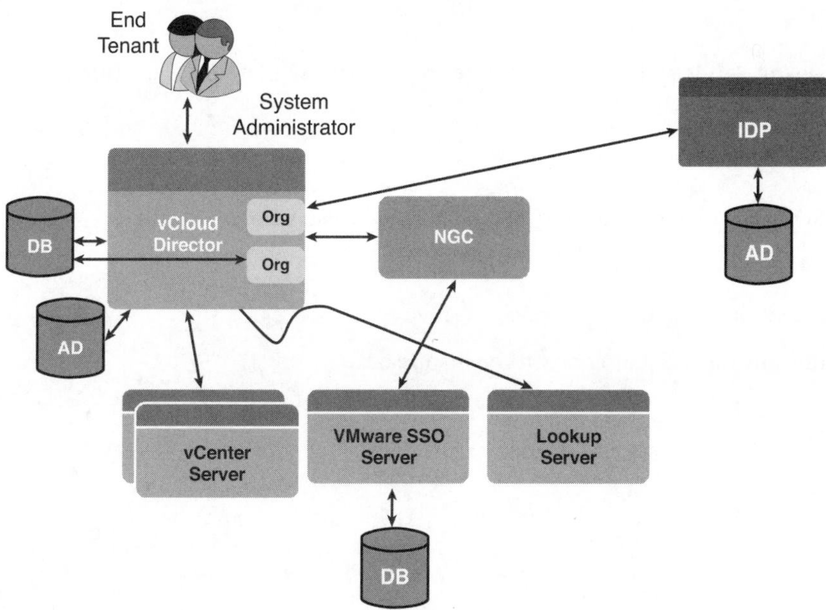

FIGURE 6.105 Cloud provider SSO logical architecture

6.7.1.3 Example

This example shows how vCloud Director administrators who are already authenticated to the vCenter Server through the vSphere Web Client do not have to separately authenticate to vCloud Director.

To authenticate through vCloud Director with Single Sign-On (see Figure 6.106):

1. Log into vCloud Director as the administrator.
2. Register vCloud Director with the Lookup Service. Click Administration > System Settings > Federation tab, and click the Register button under vSphere Services.

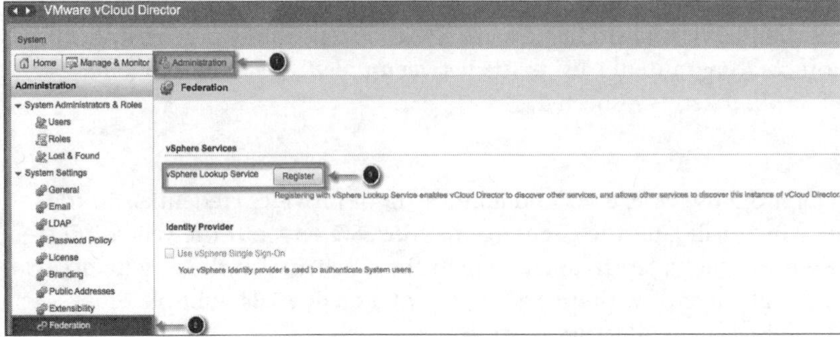

FIGURE 6.106

3. Enter the Lookup Service URL for the vCenter server with which you want this vCloud Director to use with SSO:

```
<qualified domain name of vCenter-server>:7444/lookupservice/sdk
```

4. Enter the SSO Admin User Name and SSO Admin User Password.
5. Enter the vCloud Director URL:

```
<qualified domain name of vcd-server>/cloud
```

6. Click OK and wait for the dialog box to be dismissed.

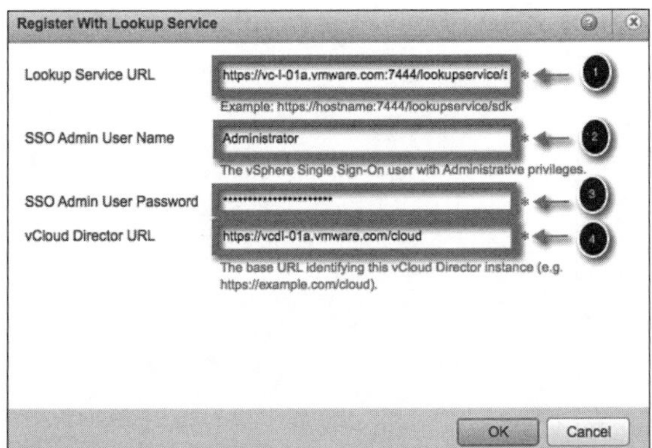

FIGURE 6.107

7. Select Use vSphere Single Sign-On and click Apply.

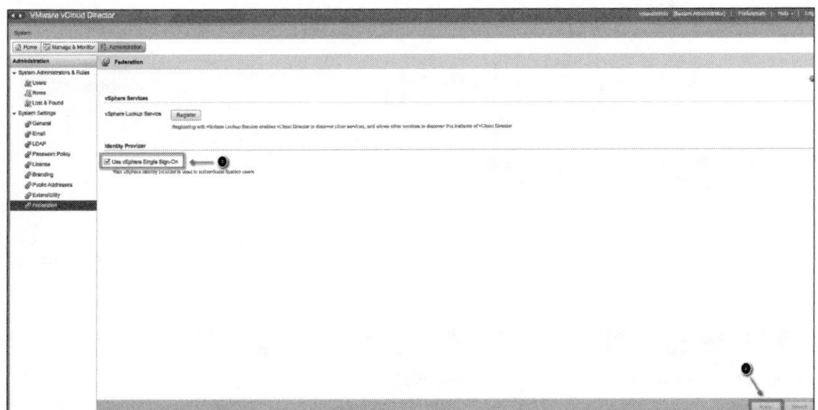

FIGURE 6.108

8. Click Users and import a vSphere SSO user into vCloud Director.

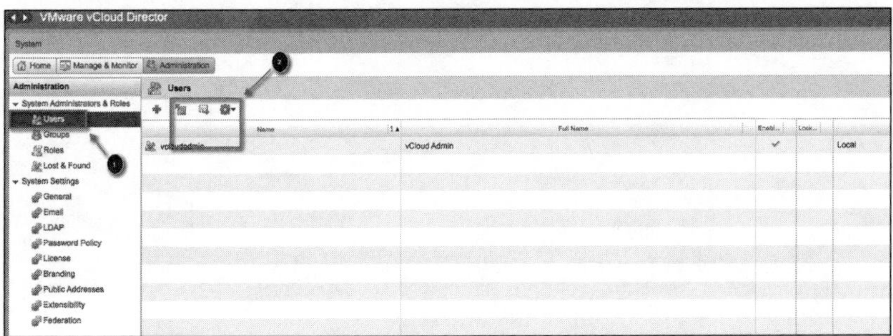

FIGURE 6.109

9. As an example, import the Administrator@System-Domain user from vCenter SSO server.

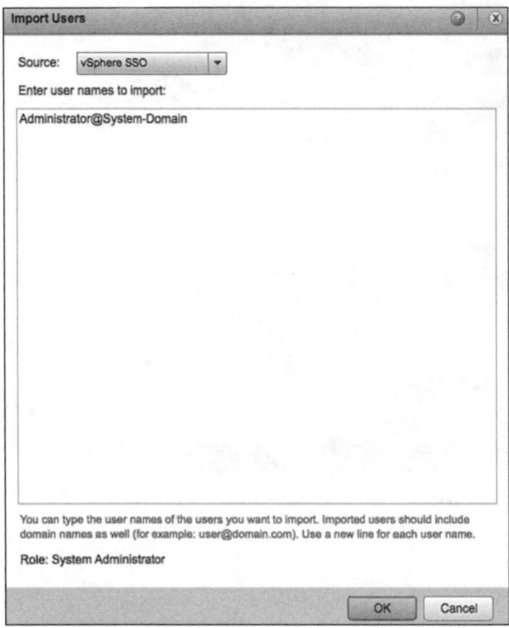

FIGURE 6.110

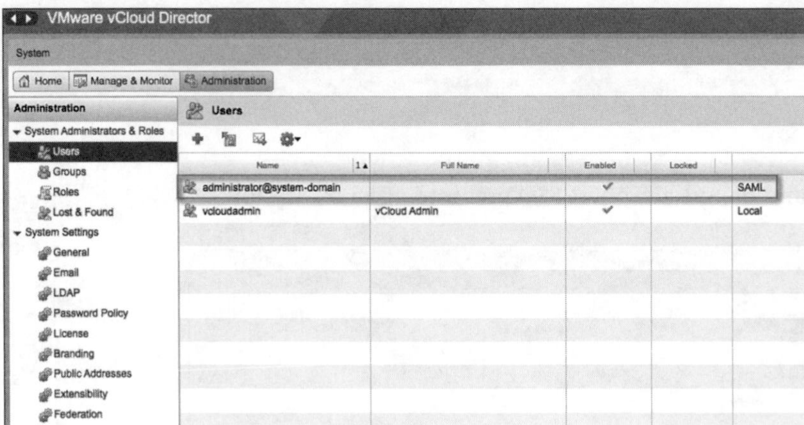

FIGURE 6.111

10. Log out of vCloud Director.

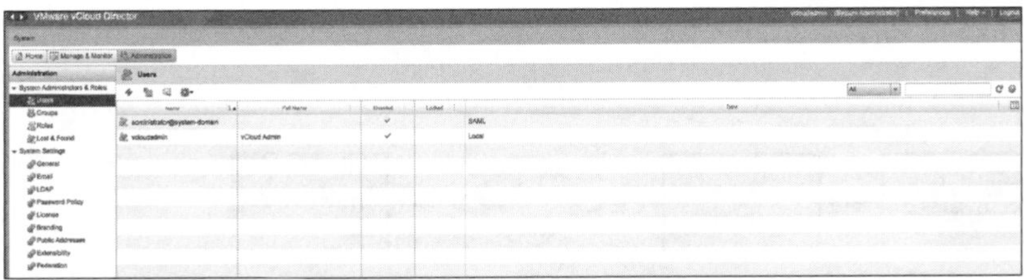

FIGURE 6.112

11. Go to the vCenter Sever and log in as the user that was imported in a preceding step.

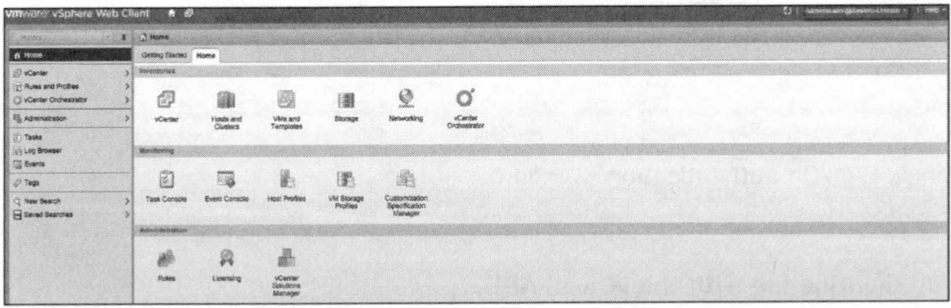

FIGURE 6.113

12. Open a new browser tab and go to vCloud Director. You are logged in without requiring further authentication.

13. To log in as a vCloud Director local user, type the following:

    https://<vcd-server>/cloud/login.jsp

14. Using RDP, access the virtual machine where the vSphere Web Client is running.

    a. Open a new browser tab and go to vCloud Director.

    b. You are redirected to the vSphere Web Client, where you can log in as Administrator@System-Domain.

    c. Upon successful authentication, you are redirected to vCloud Director.

6.7.1.4 Single Sign-On Authentication Workflow

Figure 6.114 illustrates the workflow for a Single Sign-On session using vCloud Director and the identity provider.

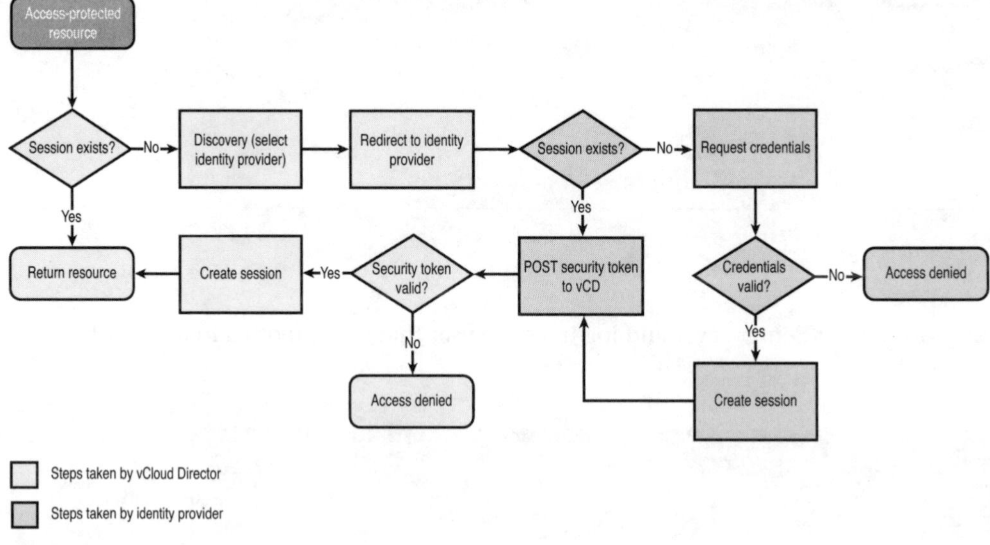

FIGURE 6.114 Single Sign-On authentication workflow

6.7.1.5 SSO and Authenticating with the vCloud API

Use the `POST/sessions` vCloud API, which accepts security tokens as the request body:

- **HTTP-Basic authentication:** Logs in using the username and password to the integrated identity provider for backward compatibility with vCloud Director 1.5
- **SAML assertion:** Verifies that the assertion is trusted
- **Proprietary token:** Verifies that the token from the integrated identity provider is valid

Use the vCloud API `GET /org/{id}/hostedIdentityProvider/token` to return the security token for the integrated identity provider:

- **HTTP-Basic authentication:** Logs in using the username and password
- **Kerberos:** Verifies a Kerberos token using Active Directory settings

Use the vCloud API `GET /org/{id}/identityProviders` to return a list of IdPs federated with vCloud (the currently integrated identity provider and possibly an external identity provider), which can be called anonymously.

Use the vCloud API `GET /org/{id}/saml/authnRequest` to return the signed SAML `AuthnRequest`.

6.7.1.6 Design Implications

- Use Single Sign-On (SSO) to provide a common service, both internally and externally.

- Single Sign-On (SSO) can be combined with the use of smart cards or common access cards (CACs) for initial authentication to a directory service.
- You must use a supported identity provider (IdP):
  - **Identity sources:** OpenAM, Active Directory Federation Services, Shibboleth
- **Deployment models:** Single mode (one node), HA mode (multiple nodes), Replication mode
- Use a high availability architecture to provide a highly available Single Sign-On (SSO) service.

Deploying vCenter Single Sign-On as a cluster means that two or more instances of vCenter Single Sign-On are installed in high availability (HA) mode. vCenter Single Sign-On HA mode is not the same as vSphere HA. All instances of vCenter Single Sign-On use the same database and should point to the same identity sources. When connected to vCenter Server through the vSphere Web Client, Single Sign-On administrator users see the primary Single Sign-On instance. In this deployment scenario, the installation process grants admin@System-Domain vCenter Server privileges by default. In addition, the installation process creates the user admin@System-Domain to manage vCenter Single Sign-On.

6.7.2 Single Sign-On (SSO): Consumer

Deployment Models: Private, public, hybrid

Example Components: vCloud Director 5.1, vCloud Networking and Security Edge 5.1, vSphere 5.1

6.7.2.1 Background

The security and identity infrastructure in the cloud has become an important management platform component. Without support for Single Sign-On (SSO) in the vCloud infrastructure or the capability to support federation, every vCloud solution would need to create its own user identities to participate in the management process. This would dramatically increase the administrative overhead.

6.7.2.2 Use Case

The web Single Sign-On (SSO) feature and configuration are exposed through vCloud Director and can be used in both service provider and consumer architecture. The following are several use cases that can be used:

- Between a single client and multiple back-end servers
- Solution-to-solution authentication
- Delegation
- Delegation and renew

The following sections further explore these use cases.

6.7.2.2.1 Between a Single Client and Multiple Back-End Servers

The classic Single Sign-On (SSO) use case is the single sign-on between a single client and multiple back-end services. A user accesses multiple back-end servers through a single UI client. The user provides credentials to the UI client only once, which validates them against the SSO server. If the validation is successful, the SSO server issues a SAML token that the UI client then can use to access other back-end servers. Figure 6.115 illustrates this use case.

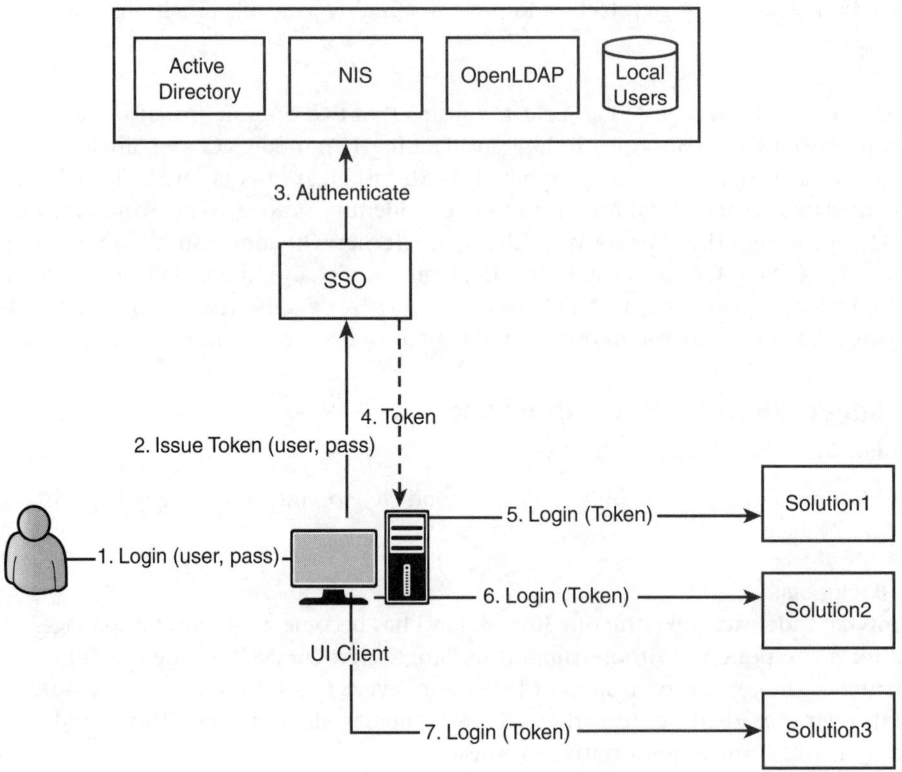

FIGURE 6.115 Single Sign-On (SSO) between a client and multiple back-end services

6.7.2.2.2 Solution-to-Solution Authentication

With solution-to-solution authentication, the goal is to assign an SSO user to each of the solutions. In this use case, two solutions communicate with each other. Before they start to communicate, they must prove each other's identity. The solution that initiates communication requests from the SSO server issues a SAML token that asserts its identity. As part of this request, the solution proves its identity using its own private key. After the SSO server has issued a token, the solution can use that token to access any other solution as if it is a normal user. For this use case to work, each solution must be registered with its public key in the SSO server. Figure 6.116 illustrates this use case.

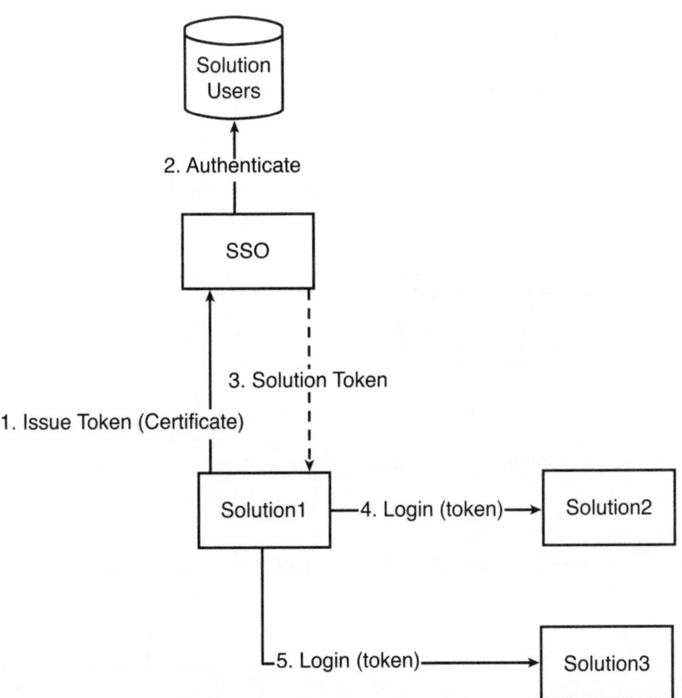

FIGURE 6.116 SSO Solution-to-solution authentication

6.7.2.2.3 Delegation

Executing tasks on behalf of a user is referred to as *delegation*. In this example use case, some workflows, which an end user initiates, might require multiple solutions to communicate with each other. This use case shows the SSO support for such workflows. Before the user can initiate the workflow through a given UI, the user must provide credentials. The UI then validates those credentials against the SSO server, which issues a SAML token. Then the user decides to initiate a workflow, which requires Solution-1 to access Solution-2 and Solution-3 on behalf of the end user. As part of this process, the UI requests from the SSO server a so-called "delegated" token for Solution-1 by providing the SAML token of the end user. The delegated token asserts that the user has granted Solution-1 the privileges to execute tasks on the user's behalf. When the UI has the delegated token, it gives it to Solution-1, which then can use it to log into Solution-2 and Solution-3. Figure 6.117 illustrates this use case.

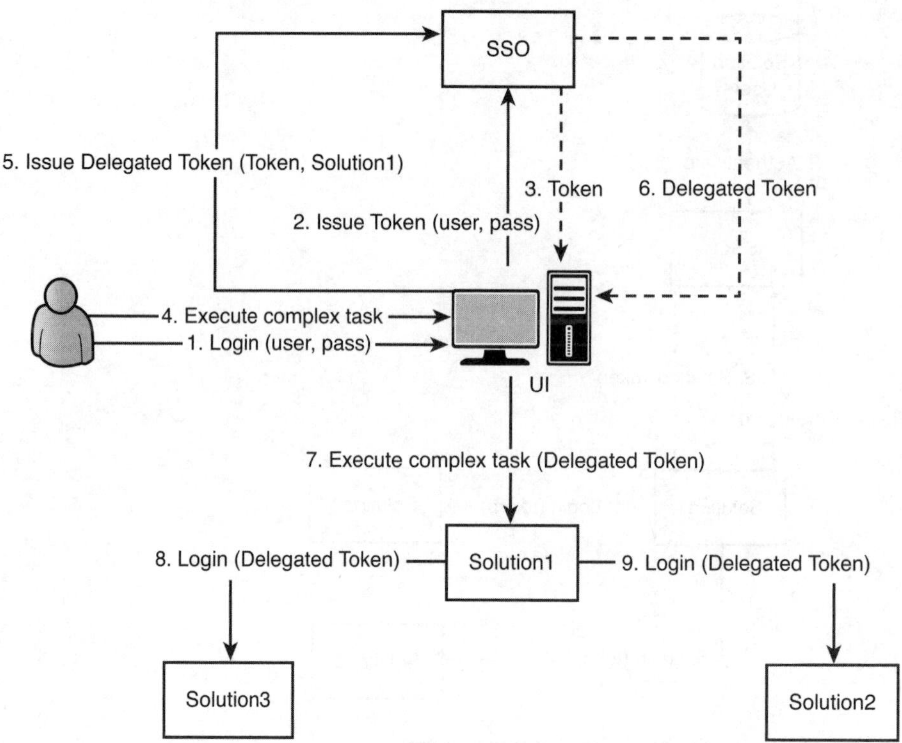

FIGURE 6.117 Task execution on behalf of a user

6.7.2.2.4 Delegation and Renew

Delegation and renew defines scheduling a long-lived task. Some long-running operations in the infrastructure require long-running tasks to be executed in the absence of the end user who has initiated them. The SSO server supports such tasks using delegated and renewable tokens. After a long-running task has been identified, the UI obtains from the SSO server a delegated and renewable token. It passes that token to the solution, which performs that long-running task. The solution persists the token in a nonsecured way as the token is self-secured. Each time the task gets activated, the solution reads the token from the disk and goes to the SSO server to renew it. By going to the SSO server for the renewal, the solution has the guarantee that the user has not previously deleted it from the system. Figure 6.118 illustrates this use case.

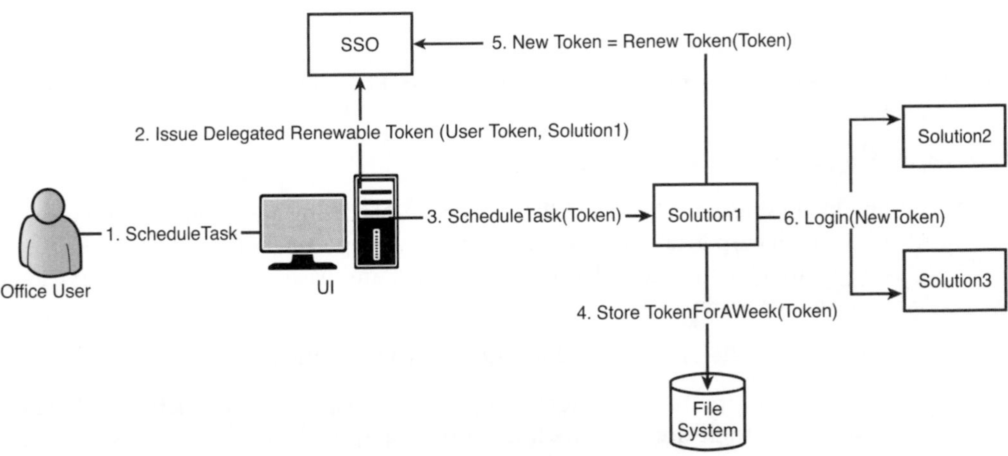

FIGURE 6.118 Single Sign-On for long-lived tasks

6.7.2.3 Example

This example covers a consumer Single Sign-On deployment architecture, as illustrated in Figure 6.119.

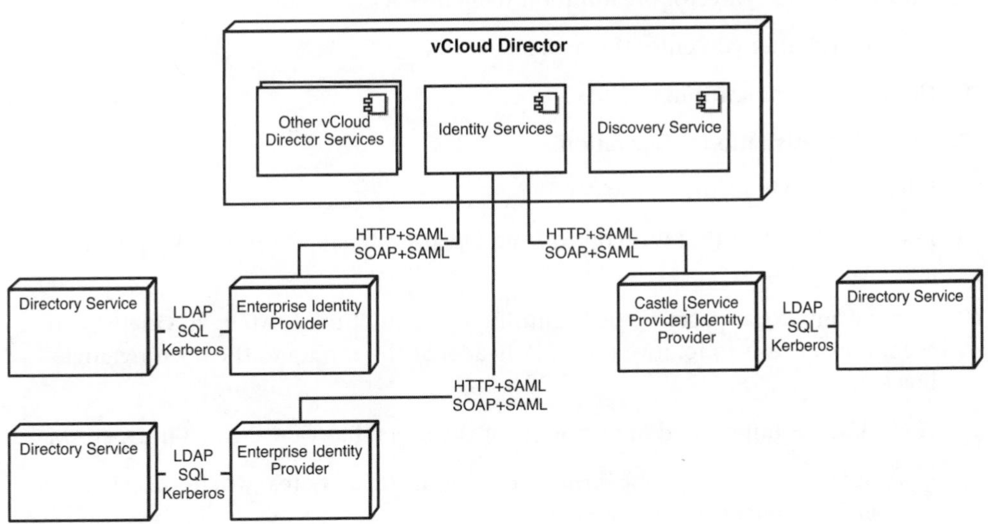

FIGURE 6.119 Consumer logical Single Sign-On deployment architecture

This example shows how enterprise customers can log into vCloud Director with their existing identity-management software, whether they are connecting to an internal cloud or to a vCloud Director–powered service provider. To demonstrate this behavior, you must set up a separate identity provider (IdP) using either OpenAM or ADFS. This example uses vCloud Director to create an organization named vCAT and sets the OpenAM IdP as the IdP of that organization. Thereafter, when you log into your organization, you are redirected to OpenAM, where you can authenticate and be directed back to the vCloud Director portal.

To set up Single Sign-On with OpenAM IdP:

1. Set up OpenAM as an enterprise IdP. As an example, using a web browser, go to http://openam.corp.local:8080/openam/saml2/jsp/exportmetadata.jsp?realm=labs. This page provides XML text that must be copied and pasted to a text area in vCloud Director in a later step.

    a. Right-click the browser window and select View Source.

    b. Select and copy the entire text and paste it into a text editor such as Notepad. Make sure there are no blank lines at the top or bottom of the text. Keep this information easily available; you will need it in step 9 (where it is pasted in the organization's Federation settings under the Administration section).

2. Create a vCloud Director organization named vCAT, and set up the IdP configuration to point to the OpenAM IDP server.
3. Log into vCloud Director as administrator.
4. Create a vCloud Director organization named vCAT.
5. Click Finish after you enter the name.
6. Go to your organization.
7. Go to Administration > Federation.
8. Select Use SAML Identity Provider.
9. Paste the XML text that was copied from OpenAM in step 1, and click Apply to apply the changes.
10. Remove any extra spaces at the beginning and end of the SAML text. One way to accomplish this is to remove the XML header at the top up to the opening angle bracket.
11. Go to Users > Import and import some of the users that were created in OpenAM.

    a. Specify `<username>@<domain name>.com` in the text area, where `<username>` is either `orguser` or `orgadmin`.

    b. Assign an organization administrator role to orgadmin and a vAppuser role to orguser.

    c. Log out from vCloud Director.

12. Open another browser tab and go to: https://<vcd-server>/cloud/org/Lab/saml/metadata/alias/vcd. This downloads a file called `vcd`. Perform the following steps:

   a. Access `openam.corp.local:8080/openam` from your browser.

   b. Log in as amadmin, password `<password>`.

   c. Go to the Federation tab.

   d. Under the Entity Providers list, click Import Entity.

   e. Select labs as the realm name.

   f. Upload the `vcd` file. (Click the first upload button.)

   g. Under the Circle of Trust list, click the name of the realm with which you are federating (labs).

   h. Under the list of available entity providers, locate the vCloud Director entity. Click Add and then Save.

   i. Log out from OpenAM.

   j. Log out from vCloud Director.

13. Type the vCloud Director organization URL: C:\Users\drichey\Documents\SharePoint Drafts\vmshare.vmware.com\gts\InitiativeIP\vCAT\vCAT 3.1\Delivery IP\Source\https://<vCloud Director server>/cloud/org/Lab.

You are redirected to the OpenAM IdP, where you can log in as one of the following users:

- orgadmin (password: `<password>`).
- orguser (password: `<password>`).

The user is redirected to vCloud Director after a successful authentication.

6.7.2.4 Consumer Workflow Example

The following shows what happens when you log in as an end tenant.

To log in as an end tenant:

1. Log into vCloud Director, which redirects to the NGC client login.

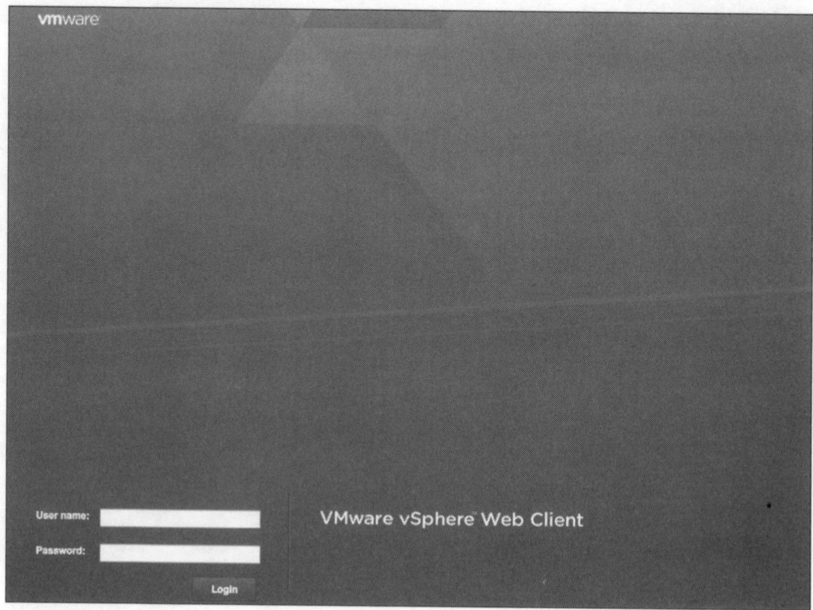

FIGURE 6.120

2. The login and authentication takes place on the NGC.

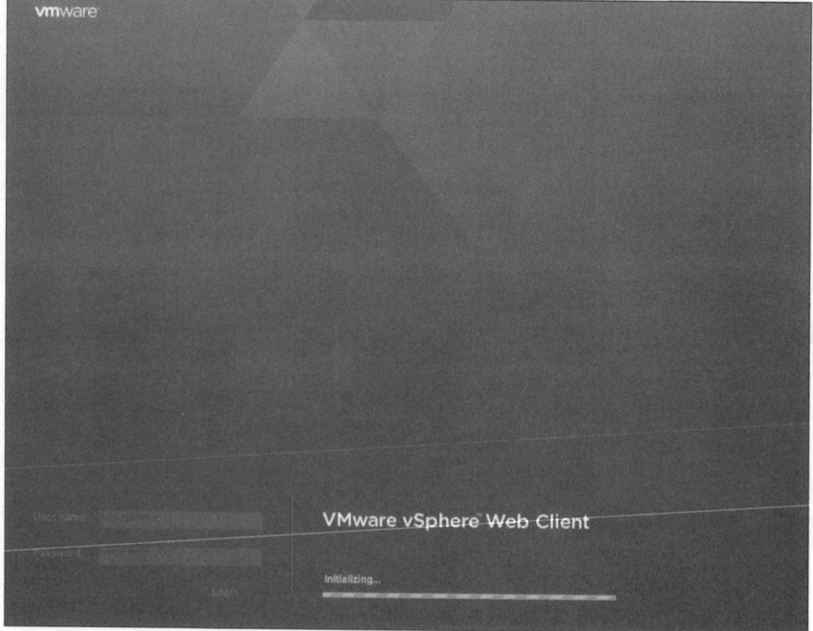

FIGURE 6.121

3. **Organization scope:** vCloud Director redirects to your IdP, which is OpenAM in this example.

FIGURE 6.122

4. **Organization scope:** OpenAM redirects back to vCloud Director, using the vCAT Organization in this example.

FIGURE 6.123

5. Install and configure the vCAT Organization Scope with a third-party IdP (which is OpenAM in this example).

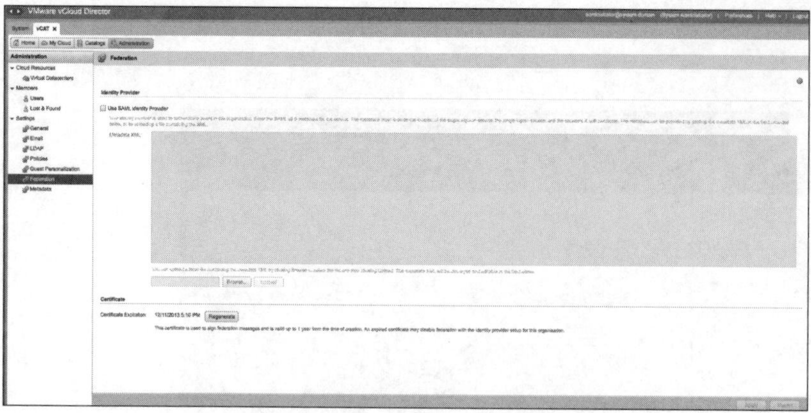

FIGURE 6.124

6. Apply the Use SAML Identity Provider option, paste the XML that you copied from OpenAM, and apply the changes.

   A Certificate Expiration option also appears. You can ignore the certificate generation because this is required only if your certificate is about to expire (in one year).

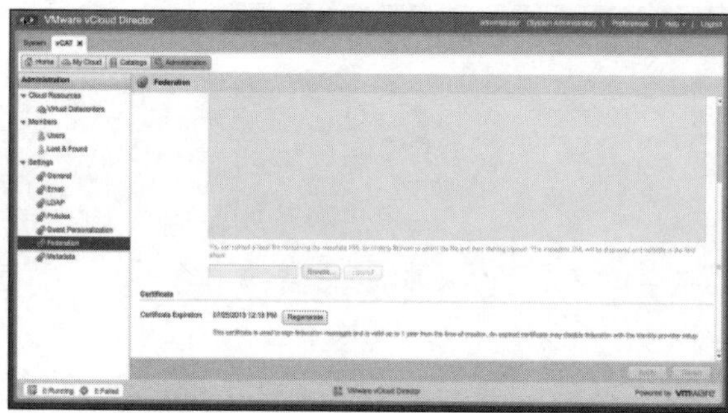

FIGURE 6.125

Figure 6.126 shows this procedure.

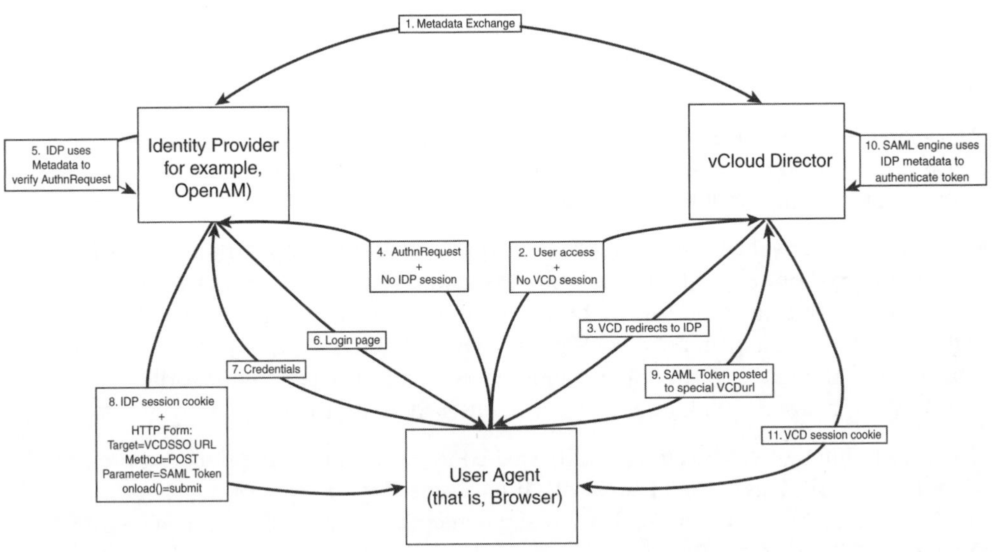

FIGURE 6.126 Consumer workflow detail

6.7.2.5 Design Implications

- Use Single Sign-On (SSO) to provide a common service, both internally and externally.
- You must use a supported identity provider (IdP).
- Make sure the SAML assertion contains attributes that vCloud Director understands.
- Make sure vCloud Director and the IdP are time-synchronized to within a few seconds.
- Make sure vCloud Director and the IdP have valid endpoint certificates.
- Use consistent hostnames or IP addresses while registering with the LookupService.

6.7.3 Implementing Signed Certificates from a Certificate Authority

Deployment Models: Private, public

Example Components: vCloud Director 5.1

6.7.3.1 Background

Network security leverages numerous techniques to help protect transmitted information. Traditionally, it relies on the principles of cryptology for the security foundation. This involves converting information into a form that is usable only to selected recipients capable of transforming the information back into a usable form. Transport Layer Security (TLS) and its predecessor, Secure Sockets Layer (SSL), are cryptographic protocols commonly used today in network security. Complex infrastructures such as vCloud computing involve multiple connections between various hosts and external communication channels. The use of SSL certificates is an important tool to encrypt connections to provide data privacy.

SSL certificates also provide for two-way authentication. This enables a host to validate that it is connected to the intended recipient. This decreases the capability of an imposter to intercept the information transmitted.

Moreover, "higher-value" SSL certificates, such as organization validation (OV) SSL and extended validation (EV) SSL, which name the actual certificate owner, are beneficial for connections with actual end users. The end user can view the certificate details to verify that the legitimate and intended website or device is being used and is not an imposter. With EV SSL, the name of the SSL owner appears next to the favicon (favorites icon) in most desktop browsers, making it easy for the user to verify this.

In the past, different certificate authorities (CAs) followed different validation procedures when issuing SSL. This caused issues with interoperability and ease of use. The CA and Browser Forum, of which QuoVadis is an active member, created common standards for OV and EV SSL to create consistency across providers and regions and to eliminate problems previously experienced. Browsers for all CAs in their root distribution programs have adopted these standards.

The white paper *VMware vCloud Director and Certificate Authority Issuance: Leveraging QuoVadis Certificate Authority with VMware vCloud Director* (www.vmware.com/resources/techresources/10332) provides insight into the requirements for using signed certificates and provides implementation guidance on how to achieve this.

6.8 vCloud Integration Examples

The following are examples of integrating vCloud Director with other technologies.

6.8.1 vCenter Operations Manager

Deployment Models: Private

Example Components: vCloud Director 1.5, vSphere 5.0, vCenter Operations Manager Enterprise 5.0.1, vFabric Hyperic 4.6.5

6.8.1.1 Background

Understanding and managing the unique operational challenges of the vCloud is the key to success for any vCloud provider. VMware vCenter Operations Manager and VMware vFabric™ Hyperic® can be used proactively to monitor both the service provider cloud resources and the management environment. The vCloud resources are the VMware clusters that provide the compute, storage, and network resources to the customers or consumers. The management environment handles the vCloud management components.

Using vCenter Operations Manager, the service provider can monitor the resource cluster for overall health and capacity. Health information includes metrics for CPU, memory, disk and network workloads, events, and anomalies. Capacity reflects the resources and capacity available for future client deployments.

Using Hyperic, the service provider can monitor the management components down to the application level. This includes SQL, vCenter, and vCloud Director database- and operating system–specific metrics.

6.8.1.2 Use Case

A vCloud-powered service provider has deployed two vSphere HA/DRS clusters. The first cluster hosts their management stack. The second cluster hosts the customer's actual vCloud workloads and maps directly to a provider virtual datacenter. The service provider agreed to SLAs and wants a dashboard interface to display the data.

The service provider needs custom alerting if SLAs are not met.

The service provider must monitor the following key metrics related to a virtual environment:

- Resource cluster
    - CPU, memory, storage, and network
    - External network switches
    - Capacity (consumed and remaining)
- Management cluster:
    - Specific SQL databases (vCenter and vCloud Director)
    - vCloud Director cell transfer disk space

6.8.1.3 vCenter Operations Manager Example

vCenter Operations Manager can be configured for different types of workload scenarios. For this scenario, vCenter Operations Manager is deployed as a medium-type deployment that is appropriate for supporting an environment of approximately 3,000 virtual machines.

The vCenter Operations Manager vApp consists of two virtual machines, one for the UI and the other for analytics (see Figure 6.127).

The UI VM is responsible for the following:

- vSphere web application
- Custom web application
- Administration web application

The Analytics virtual machine is responsible for collecting the data from the endpoints. In this example, data is collected from vCenter and Hyperic. Both of these endpoints have software adapters installed that will be configured to collect data. The analytics virtual machine is responsible for the following (see Figure 6.127):

- Capacity and performance analytics
- Capacity collector
- File system database
- PostgeSQL database

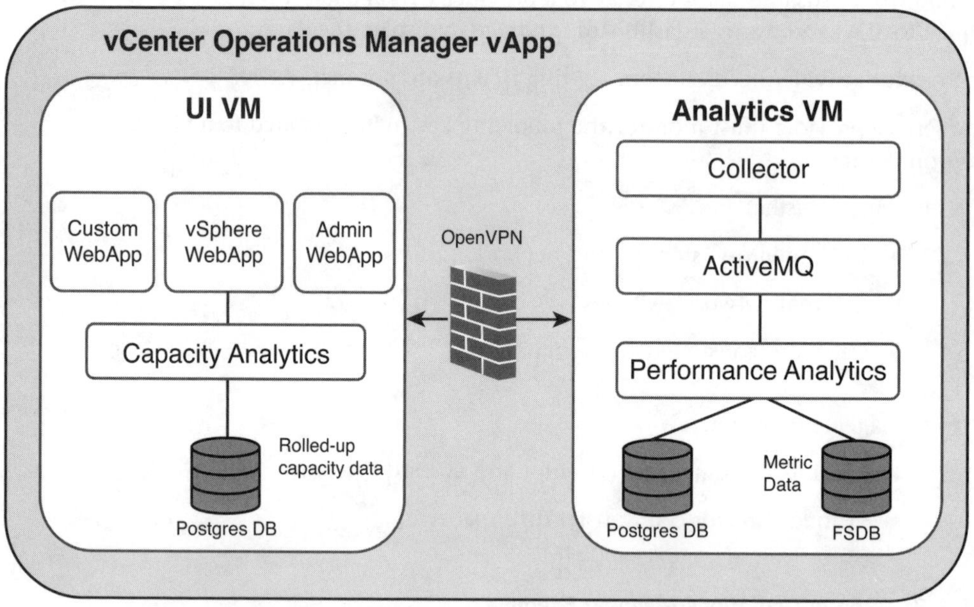

FIGURE 6.127 vCenter Operations Manager vApp components

6.8.1.3.1 vFabric Hyperic

The Hyperic component is used primarily to relay data to the vCenter Operations Manager system from individual, key vCloud infrastructure servers in the Management cluster. Hyperic obtains metrics and information about services and processes that are not reported through the vCenter integration with vCenter Operations Manager. Although vCenter can report virtual and physical hardware usage, Hyperic provides granular metrics for the operating systems and their various software components.

For example, Hyperic provides metrics relating to the status of the processes and services that are critical to the functioning of the vCloud Director cells.

The main components of VMware Hyperic include Hyperic Server, agent, and database, and the Hyperic user interface, also known as the *Hyperic Portal*. Figure 6.128 illustrates these components.

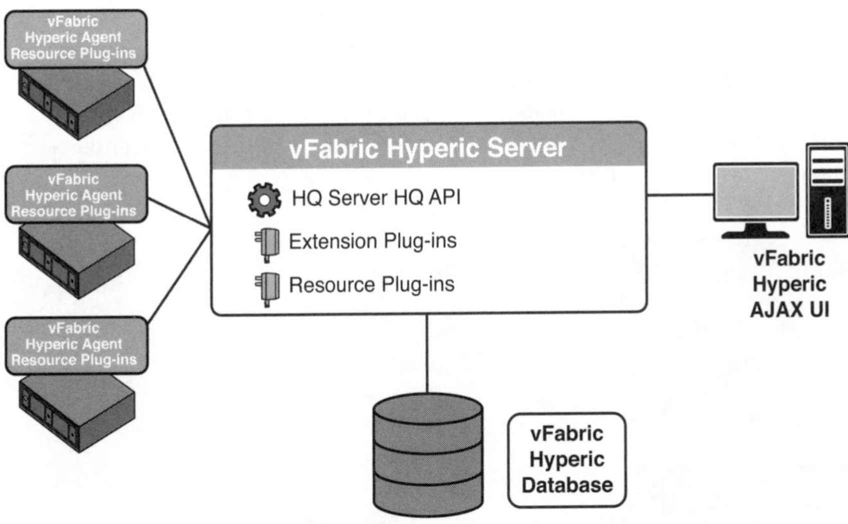

FIGURE 6.128 Hyperic configuration

6.8.1.3.2 vFabric Hyperic Agent

A Hyperic agent is installed on each physical or virtual machine that you want to manage with Hyperic. Agents autodiscover the software components running on the machine and periodically rescan the platform for changes in its configuration. Hyperic agents gather performance and availability metrics, perform log and event tracking, and enable you to perform control functions such as starting and stopping servers. Agents send the inventory and performance data they collect to the Hyperic server.

6.8.1.3.3 vFabric Hyperic Server and vFabric Hyperic Database

The Hyperic server receives inventory and metric data from the Hyperic agents and stores that data in the Hyperic database. The server provides facilities for managing your software inventory. It implements the Hyperic inventory and access model, which enables you to group your software assets in useful ways that ease the process of monitoring and management. The Hyperic server detects alerts and performs the notifications or escalation processes that you define. It also processes actions that you initiate through the Hyperic portal or Hyperic web services API. Hyperic server provides authentication services, using an internal engine or an external authentication service.

6.8.1.3.4 vFabric Hyperic User Interface (Hyperic Portal)

The Hyperic browser-based user interface, sometimes referred to as the *Hyperic Portal,* is a configurable, extendable user interface for monitoring and analyzing performance and availability.

See the VMware vFabric Hyperic documentation (www.vmware.com/support/pubs/vfabric-hyperic.html) for additional information on using vFabric Hyperic.

6.8.1.4 vCenter Operations Manager and vFabric Hyperic Integration

As detailed in the previous section, Hyperic is a source of data for vCenter Operations Manager from individual, key vCloud infrastructure-management servers. This proxy functions as a result of the vCenter Operations Manager Hyperic adapter that is installed and enables the required process and service information to be presented to vCenter Operations Manager (see Figure 6.129).

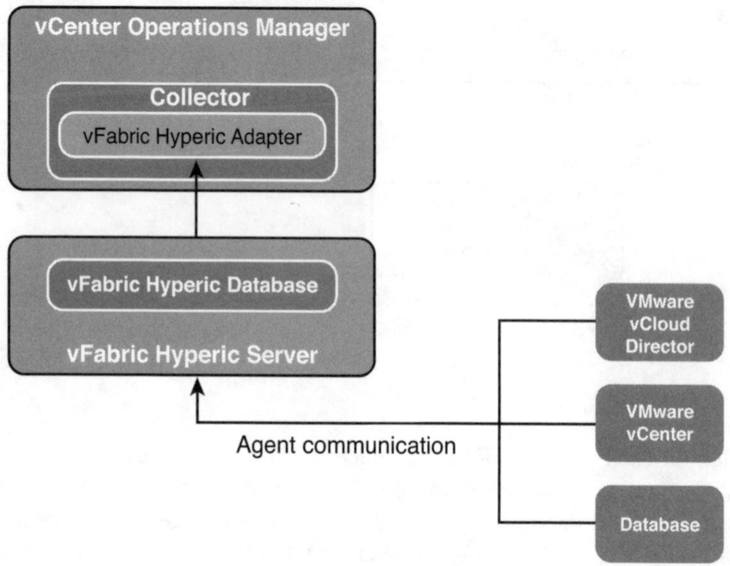

FIGURE 6.129 vCenter Operations Manager and Hyperic integration

As Figure 6.129 shows, vCenter Operations Manager Enterprise supports the Hyperic Adapter, which enables the exchange of information between vCenter Operations Manager Enterprise and Hyperic HQ data. The adapter provides the following functionality:

- Connects to and collects data from Hyperic HQ
- Transforms the collected data into the format vCenter Operations Enterprise is designed to consume
- Passes the data to the vCenter Operations Enterprise collector for final processing

In addition to the standard adapter functions, the adapter supports manual discovery and autodiscovery, as well as the capability to create relationships based on the associations found in Hyperic HQ.

6.8.1.4.1 How Data Is Retrieved

The Hyperic adapter's data source is the Hyperic HQ database. The adapter uses standard JDBC access to the database for running SQL queries. The adapter uses the vCenter Operations API to communicate and deliver data to vCenter Operations.

6.8.1.4.2 Retrieved Data

The vCenter Operations Manager Hyperic adapter can collect data from different resources and creates resource kinds dynamically according to platform types and server types in Hyperic. Resources in vCenter Operations represent Hyperic platforms and servers.

Resources in Hyperic are one of the following kinds:

- A platform, which is either an operating system platform such as Linux, Solaris, Windows 32-bit, or UNIX; or a virtual and network platform, such as Cisco IOS, VMware vFabric GemFire® Distributed System, NetApp Filer, vSphere Host, or a vSphere virtual machine.
- A server, which is a software product that runs on a platform such as Tomcat, JBoss, Exchange, SQL, or Oracle.
- Services and platform services, which are software components that run on either a server or a platform. Server services can be either internal server components such as database tables or .NET applications, or they can be a deployed item such as *CustomerEntityEJB*. Examples of platform services include DHCP, DNS, and CPU and network interfaces.

The Hyperic adapter can also collect data for Hyperic services. Service metrics are stored under a specific instance and group, and the service name is used as the instance name.

Sources map to vCenter Operations resources using resource names in vCenter Operations to match the names from the `eam_resource` table in the Hyperic HQ database. All available types of resources in the source system can be collected.

The adapter can import relationships between Hyperic platforms and servers. Relationships are based on the `platform_id` column value in the `eam_server` table. Relationships are imported during manual discovery only.

6.8.1.4.3 Metrics

The adapter can collect all metrics for Hyperic platforms, servers, and services. Use a single query for each adapter instance to retrieve the metric data for children instances. Metrics are collected using a query to the `HQ_METRIC_DATA` tables and viewed using a time filter.

- Availability metrics are collected from the `HQ_AVAIL_DATA_RLE` table. The system current time is used as the time stamp of the collected Availability metric.
- The collection interval used is assigned to the adapter instance resource and attribute package.

6.8.1.4.4 Events

No events are collected from Hyperic HQ.

6.8.1.4.5 Prerequisites

The adapter supports Hyperic HQ versions 3.x and 4.0.

6.8.1.4.6 Database Connection Configuration

Table 6.17 lists the default vCenter Operations Enterprise port connections for supported databases. You must specify the port number when you configure the adapter instance resource.

TABLE 6.17 vCenter Operations Enterprise Port Access Requirements

Database	Port Number
MySQL	3306 TCP
Oracle	1521 TCP

Table 6.18 lists the default vCenter Operations Enterprise URLs used to connect to data sources. The Hyperic adapter requires a standard JDBC connection URL.

TABLE 6.18 vCenter Operations Manager Data Source URLs

Database	URL
MySQL	jdbc:mysql://<db_host>:<db_port>/<hqdb_name>
Oracle	jdbc:oracle://<db_host>:<db_port>/<hqdb_name>

6.8.1.5 vCenter Operations Manager Dashboards

To get the full value from vCenter Operations Manager to monitor a vCloud environment, it is recommended that you configure vCenter Operations Manager dashboards. These dashboards provide a view of the health of the various vCloud constructs.

Dashboards can be shared between Admin groups. Examples of this are the disk and network dashboards. The storage administrators can have a dashboard that is related only to storage metrics from the cluster. This dashboard can include metrics such as cluster disk I/Os or read/write latency. At the same time, the network administrators can have a dashboard that is related to the cluster networking metric. These metrics can include physical switches that are connected to the vSphere cluster to give the network administrator visibility into statistics from the virtual and physical environment on one dashboard.

For this example, a dashboard has been created to display the following statistics on the resource cluster:

- Capacity remaining
- Alerts and events

- Network
- Storage
- Memory
- CPU

A second dashboard gives statistics on the management cluster. The dashboard has been configured with the following metrics:

- vCenter SQL database transactions/database size
- vCloud Director SQL database transactions/database size
- SQL Server operating system drive space remaining
- vCenter Server operating system drive space remaining
- vCloud Director mount point space remaining

6.8.1.5.1 vCenter Operations Manager Widget Configuration

The custom UI of vCenter Operations Manager uses widgets to display information about objects that are being monitored. Some widgets display only data, but others can be configured to display data and set thresholds that display different colors when thresholds are exceeded. The following are two examples of how to configure widgets.

6.8.1.5.2 Generic Scoreboard

Table 6.19 shows the widget configuration settings.

TABLE 6.19 Widget Configuration Settings

Setting	Value
Widget Title	Displayed title of widget
Self Provider	On
Refresh Widget Content	On
Widget Refresh Interval	300 (seconds)

After the widget settings have been set, the relevant objects and metrics must be selected. This example uses a filter for *cluster*. Then the cluster for which we want to display statistics and metrics is selected. After all the desired metrics are listed in Selected Metrics, the thresholds can be configured.

Table 6.20 shows the thresholds that can be set.

TABLE 6.20 Threshold Settings

Threshold	Range
Green	Up to 10
Yellow	10–20
Orange	20–30
Red	30 and higher

Figure 6.130 shows the completed widget.

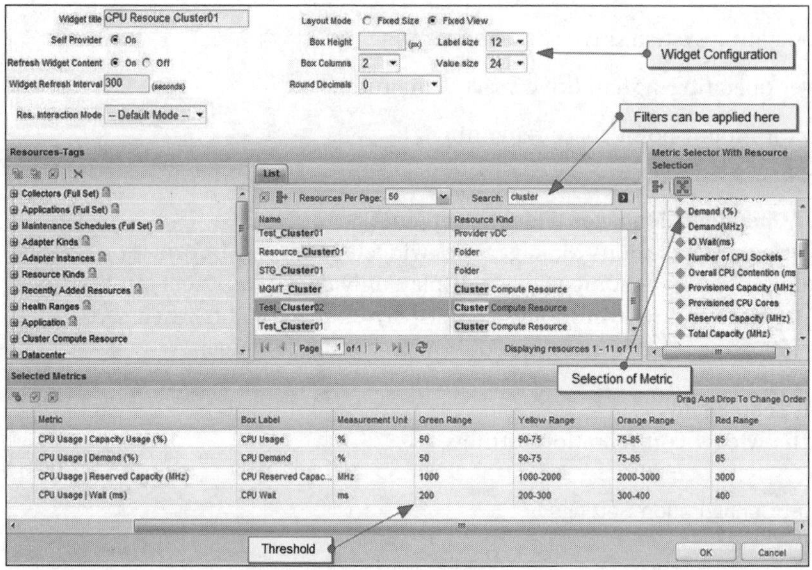

FIGURE 6.130 Generic cluster CPU scoreboard

6.8.1.5.3 Heat Map

The Heat Map widget can be used when a few objects (such as datastores and cluster physical CPU cores) must be displayed in comparison with each other. For example, physical CPU cores can be displayed for all hosts in a cluster, and those over a certain threshold can be displayed as red to indicate hot spots.

Table 6.21 shows the widget configuration settings.

TABLE 6.21 Widget Configuration Settings

Setting	Value
Widget Title	Displayed title of widget
Self Provider	On

Setting	Value
Refresh Widget Content	On
Widget Refresh Interval	300 (data collection is every 300 seconds)
Group By	Select object to group by
Resource Kind	Heat map data displayed for which type of resource

After the resource kind has been selected, choose the reported metric by selecting the attribute kind. Then select the tag from which the data will be reported.

After selecting metrics and tags, save the configuration. Click the green plus sign to give the configuration a name and save it. You can save multiple configurations and then select them to be displayed on the same widget.

Figure 6.131 shows the completed heat map widget.

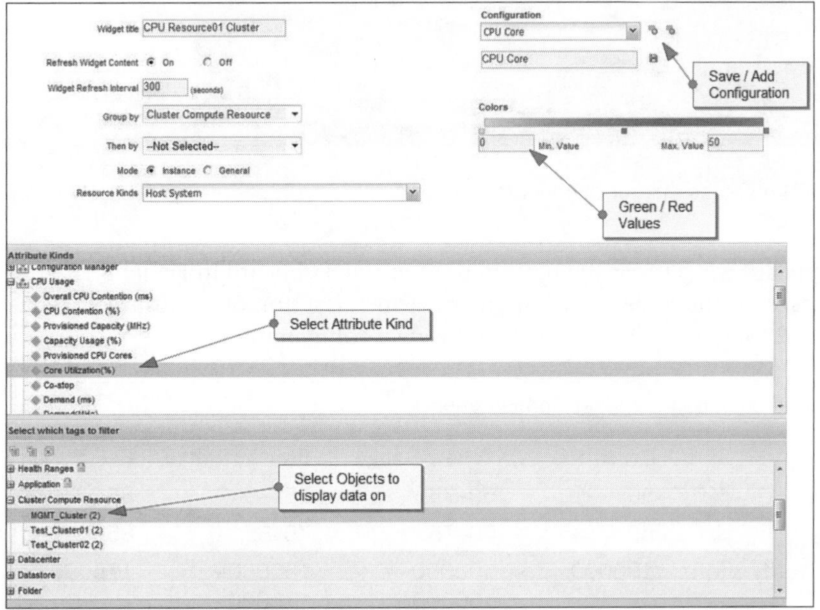

FIGURE 6.131 Management cluster CPU core utilization heat map

6.8.1.5.4 Physical CPU Resource Monitoring of Resource Clusters

The CPU Dashboard monitors the physical CPU performance of the resource cluster. Figure 6.132 shows a sample dashboard that was built using the following widgets:

- Generic Scoreboard (see Figure 6.133)
- Heat Map (see Figure 6.134)

- Metric Graph (see Figure 6.135)
- Health Status (see Figure 6.136)

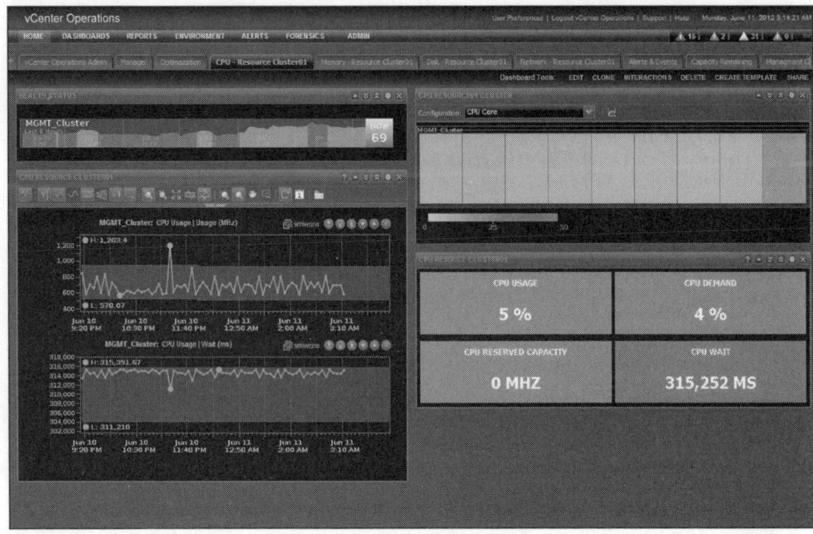

FIGURE 6.132 CPU resource cluster dashboard

The Generic Scoreboard widget is at the bottom right of the dashboard in Figure 6.132. The selection is based on the resource cluster metric, which is a sum of all host metrics in the cluster. Table 6.22 shows a generic scoreboard widget configuration.

TABLE 6.22 Generic Scoreboard Widget Configuration

Metric	Unit	Green Range	Yellow Range	Orange Range	Red Range
Capacity Usage %	%	50	50–75	75–85	85
Demand	%	50	50–75	75–85	85
CPU Reserved Capacity	MHz	100000	100000–150000	150000–175000	175000
Wait	ms	100	100–200	200–300	300

NOTE

These threshold/ranges are only examples. These values should be based on the cluster design threshold values and the customer requirements.

6 %

5 %

0 MHZ

314,751 MS

FIGURE 6.133 Resource cluster CPU Scoreboard widget

The Heat Map widget shows the resource cluster physical CPU core utilization. This displays all the ESXi physical CPUs and cores in the resource cluster to identify hot spots on the physical CPUs. This configuration uses the core utilization metric and resource cluster tag to display the heat map data.

FIGURE 6.134 Resource cluster physical CPU core Heat Map widget

The Metric Graph widget gives a graph view of some of the CPU metrics. The view is customizable to display from *last hour* to *last year*. The graph can also display the dynamic thresholds for certain metrics. As an example, this widget displays the cluster CPU usage and cluster CPU wait.

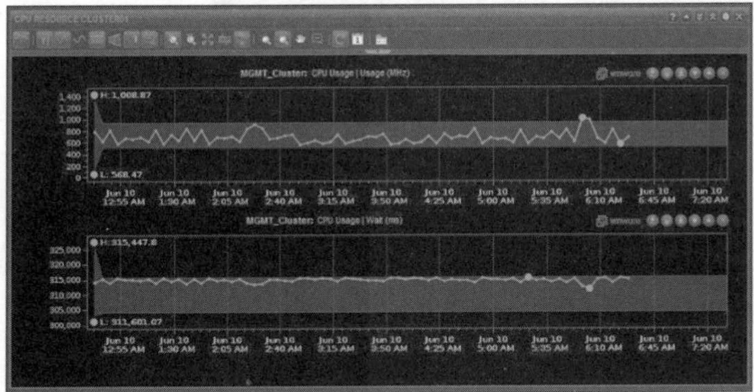

FIGURE 6.135 Resource cluster CPU Metric Graph widget

The Health widget displays overall resource cluster health. The widget can be configured to display data from the *last hour* to the *last month*.

FIGURE 6.136 Cluster Health widget

6.8.1.5.5 Memory Dashboard

The Memory Dashboard monitors the cluster memory usage and demand. Figure 6.137 shows a sample dashboard that was built using the following widgets:

- Generic Scoreboard (see Figure 6.138)
- Heat Map (see Figure 6.139)
- Metric Graph (see Figure 6.140)
- Health Status (see Figure 6.136)

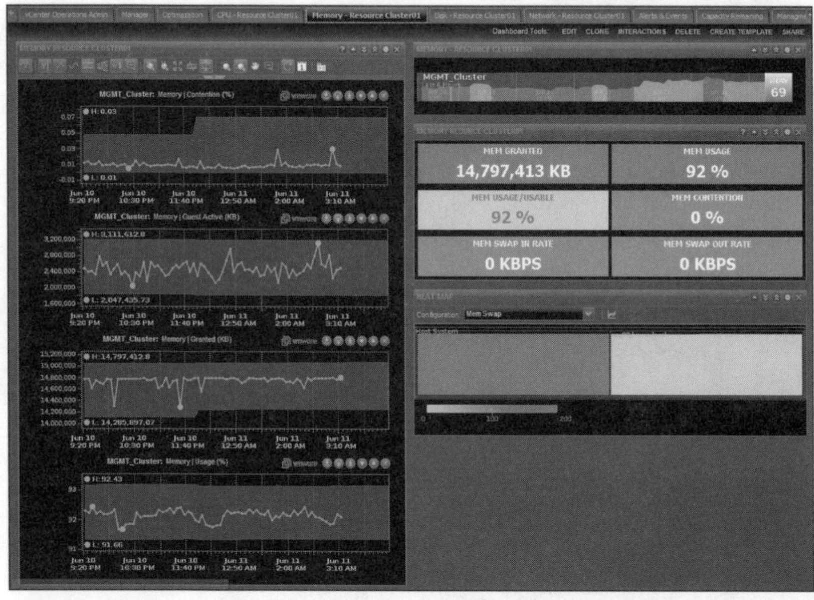

FIGURE 6.137 Cluster Memory Dashboard

The Generic Scoreboard widget was configured with these metrics defined at the cluster level. The resource cluster is used for memory metric selections. Table 6.23 shows a generic scoreboard configuration.

TABLE 6.23 Generic Scoreboard Configuration

Metric	Unit	Green Range	Yellow Range	Orange Range	Red Range
Memory Granted	KB	8000	8000–12000	12000–13000	13000
Usage	%	50	50–75	75–80	80
Usage/Usable	%	50	50–75	75–80	80
Contention	%	50	50–75	75–80	80
Swap In Rate	KBps	300	300–400	400–500	500
Swap Out Rate	KBps	5	5–10	10–20	20

NOTE

These threshold/ranges are only examples. These values should be based on the cluster design threshold values and the customer requirements.

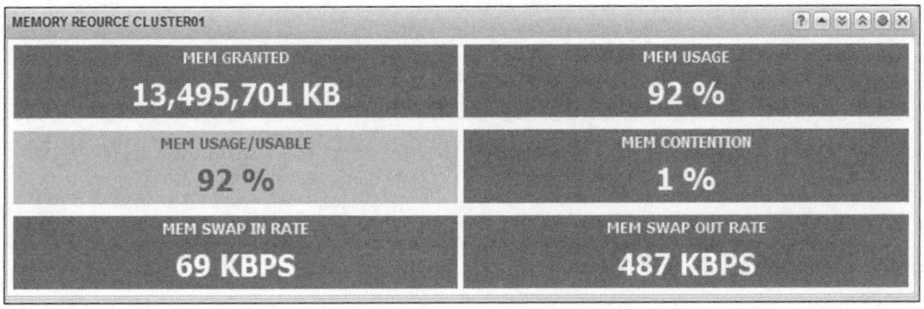

FIGURE 6.138 Cluster Memory Scoreboard widget

The Heat Map is configured with three metrics, created from the cluster resource, as follows:

- Swap Out Rate (KBps)
- Swap In Rate (KBps)
- Mem Swap Used (KB)

Table 6.24 shows settings for the Heat Map widget.

TABLE 6.24 Settings for the Heat Map Widget

Metric	Value
Attribute Kinds	Memory
Tags to Filter	Cluster compute resource (select the correct cluster)
Minimum Value	(Custom setting to environment)
Maximum Value	(Custom setting to environment)

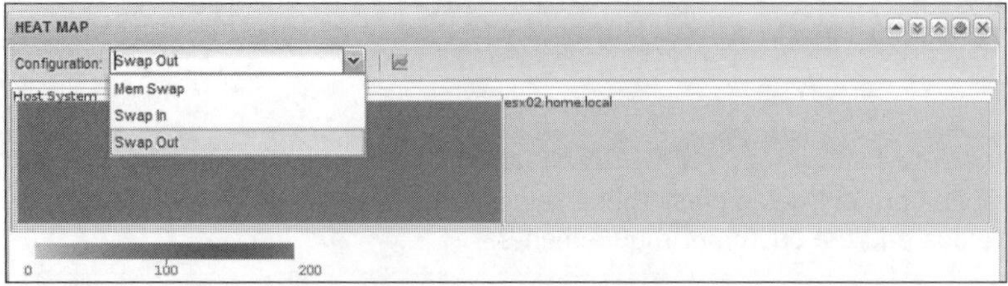

FIGURE 6.139 Cluster Memory Heat Map widget

The Metric Graph widget can display line graphs of historical memory statistics. This example (see Table 6.25) selects the memory metrics to be displayed over a 24-hour period. Note that the historical time can be changed to up to one year and can also indicate the DT (dynamic threshold) values.

TABLE 6.25 Cluster Memory Metric Graph Settings

Metric
Memory | Contention (%)
Memory | Guest Active (KB)
Memory | Granted (KB)
Memory | Usage (%)

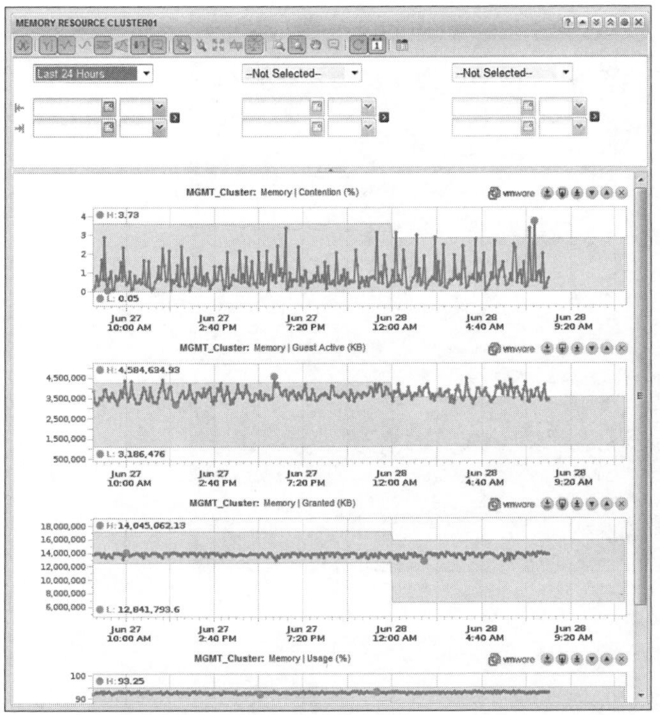

FIGURE 6.140 Cluster Memory Metric Graph widget

6.8.1.5.6 Storage Dashboard

The Storage Dashboard widget can help with troubleshooting at the cluster or host levels and can be used by the virtual infrastructure admins and the storage administrators. Figure 6.141 shows this dashboard, which is built using four widgets:

- Disk Scoreboard (see Figure 6.142)
- Disk Capacity Scoreboard (see Figure 6.143)
- Cluster Storage Metric Graph (see Figure 6.144)
- Health Status (see Figure 6.136)

This dashboard focuses on cluster statistics and datastore hot spots. Hot spots in this example relate to latency to the datastore as detected by the ESXi host. Heat maps can also identify datastores with low capacity remaining, which is done using a super metric.

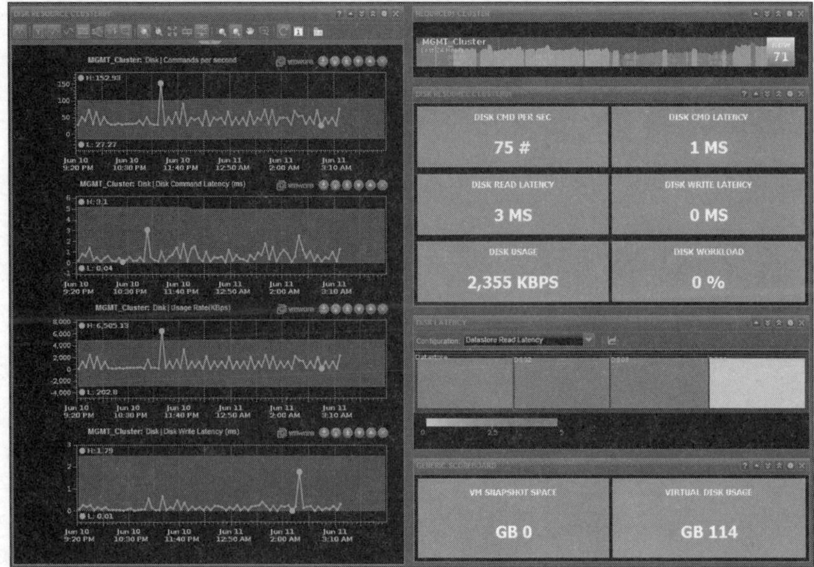

FIGURE 6.141 Storage Dashboard

This dashboard uses two Scoreboard widgets. The first widget displays statistics related to the cluster I/O usage. The second widget displays information about virtual memory snapshot space and virtual disk usage. Table 6.26 shows example cluster storage usage widget settings.

TABLE 6.26 Cluster Storage Usage Widget Settings

Metric	Unit	Green Range	Yellow Range	Orange Range	Red Range
Disk CMD Per Sec	#	200	200–300	300–400	400
Disk CMD Latency	ms	20	20–30	30–40	40
Disk Read Latency	ms	20	20–30	30–40	40
Disk Write Latency	ms	20	20–30	30–40	40
Disk Usage	KBps	10000	1000–2000	2000–3000	3000
Disk Workload	%	50	50–60	60–70	70

NOTE

These threshold/ranges are only examples. These values should be based on the cluster design threshold values and the customer requirements.

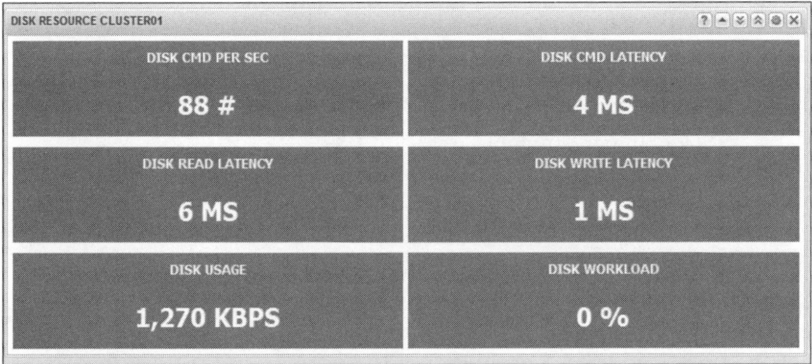

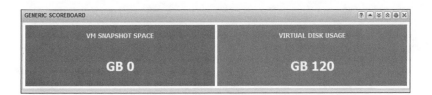

FIGURE 6.142 Cluster Disk Scoreboard widget

The second generic scoreboard widget displays virtual machine disk space information. This example (see Table 6.27) shows how much snapshot space is used and the total amount of virtual disk space used.

TABLE 6.27 Cluster Disk Capacity Scoreboard Settings

Metric	Unit	Green Range	Yellow Range	Orange Range	Red Range
Virtual Machine Snapshot Space	GB	1	1–10	10–20	20
Virtual Disk Usage	GB	90	90–200	200–500	500

NOTE

These threshold/ranges are only examples. These values should be based on the cluster design threshold values and the customer requirements.

FIGURE 6.143 Cluster Disk Capacity Scoreboard widget

The Metric Graph widget displays historical disk statistics that include the DT values. The DT values are also displayed for the next number of hours, depending on the Date Control selection). Figure 6.144 shows the Anomalies view enabled (all the yellow spikes). For the example, we are displaying historical stats for the metrics shown in Table 6.28.

TABLE 6.28 Example Metrics

Metric	Unit
Disk	Commands per second
Disk	Disk commands latency (ms)
Disk	Usage rate (KBps)
Disk	Disk write latency (ms)
Disk	I/O usage capacity

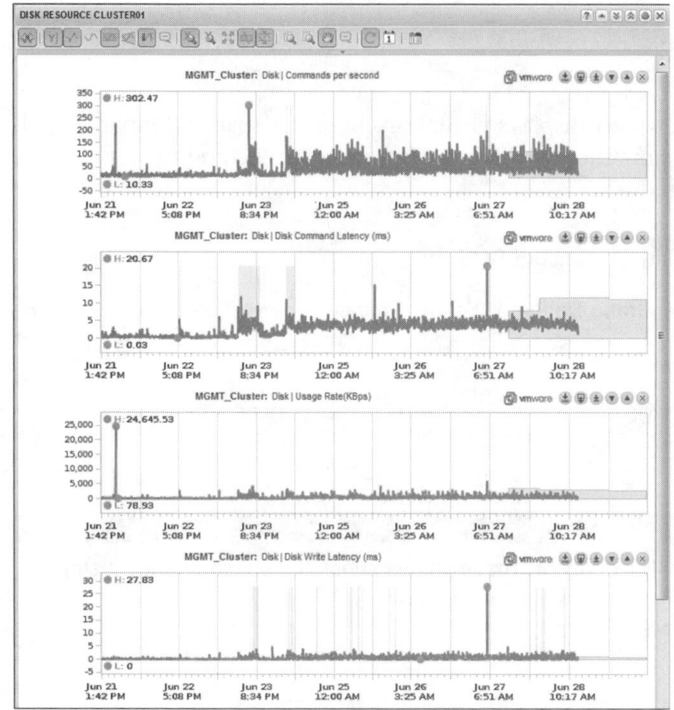

FIGURE 6.144 Cluster Storage Metric Graph widget

6.8.1.6 Network

The Network Dashboard uses vCenter Operations Manager data collected from vCenter and from Hyperic. The Hyperic server uses SNMP to collect data from a Cisco 3550 switch.

Figure 6.145 displays the completed Network Dashboard widget, which is built using the following four widgets:

- Outbound/Inbound Packet Rate Metric Graph (see Figure 6.146)
- Network Scoreboard (see Figure 6.147)

- Physical NIC Heat Map (see Figure 6.148)
- Network Performance Metric Graph (see Figure 6.149)

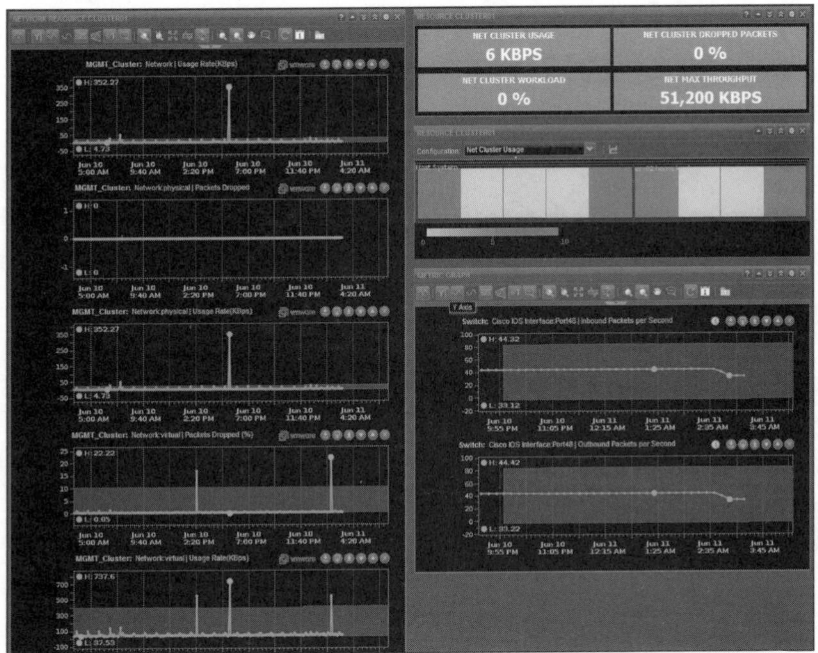

FIGURE 6.145 Network Dashboard widget

This example monitors port 48 on the switch for outbound and inbound packets. The metric graph displays these two metrics. Table 6.29 show the metric graph metrics and the units used.

TABLE 6.29 Metric Graph Metrics

Metric	Unit
Cisco IOS Interface:Port48	Outbound packets per second
Cisco IOS Interface:Port48	Inbound packets per second

Figure 6.146 shows the completed widget.

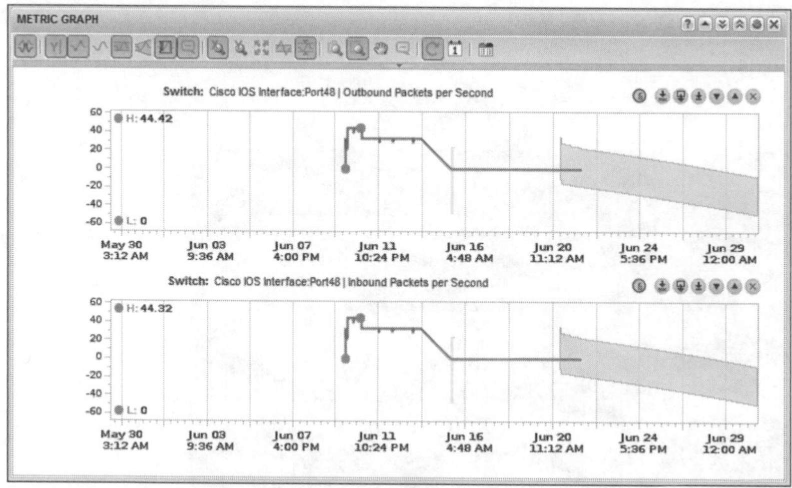

FIGURE 6.146 Outbound and inbound packet rate metric graph

Using the Scoreboard Widget and some cluster-wide statistics, the following widget can be created to show statistics on inbound packets per second, network bandwidth usage, and errors. This widget uses the metrics in Table 6.30.

TABLE 6.30 Example Scoreboard Widget Metrics

Metric	Unit	Green Range	Yellow Range	Orange Range	Red Range
Net Cluster Usage	KBps	100	100–1000	1000–5000	5000
Net Cluster Demand	%	50	50–60	60–70	70
Net Cluster Workload	%	50	50–60	60–70	70
Net Max Throughput	Kbps	6000	6000–6500	6500–7000	7000

NOTE

These threshold/ranges are only examples. These values should be based on the cluster design threshold values and the customer requirements.

Figure 6.147 shows the completed widget.

RESOURCE CLUSTER01

NET CLUSTER USAGE
22 KBPS

NET CLUSTER DROPPED PACKETS
0 %

NET CLUSTER WORKLOAD
0 %

NET MAX THROUGHPUT
169,472 KBPS

FIGURE 6.147 Completed Network Scoreboard widget

A Heat Map widget displays statistics for physical NIC usage in the ESXi host. Table 6.31 shows the heat map settings for this widget.

TABLE 6.31 Example Heat Map Settings

Metric	Value
Refresh Widget Content	On
Widget Refresh Interval	300
Group By	Resource kind
Mode	Instance
Resource Kinds	Host systems
Attribute Kinds	Network | usage rate (KBps)
Tags to Filter	Cluster compute resource | cluster

Figure 6.148 shows the completed Heat Map widget.

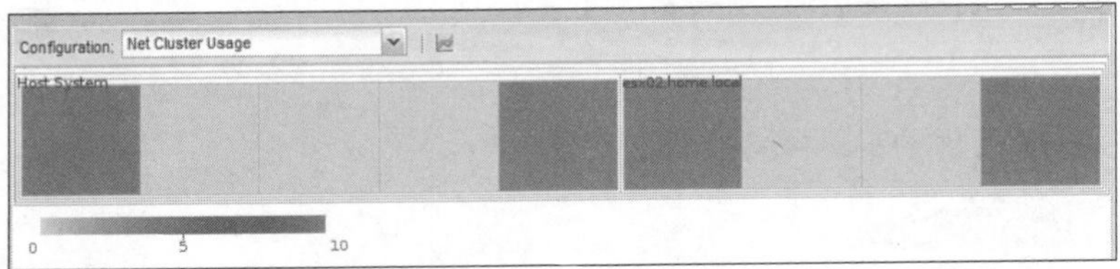

FIGURE 6.148 Physical NIC Heat Map widget

The Metric Graph widget displays historical network details regarding usage and errors. The widget displays information on both physical and virtual networking. The widget is configured with the metrics in Table 6.32.

TABLE 6.32 Example Metric Graph Widget Metrics

Metric	Units
Network	Usage rate (KBps)
Network:Physical	Packets dropped
Network:Physical	Usage rate (KBps)
Network:Virtual	Packets dropped (%)
Network:Virtual	Usage rate (KBps)

Figure 6.149 shows the completed widget.

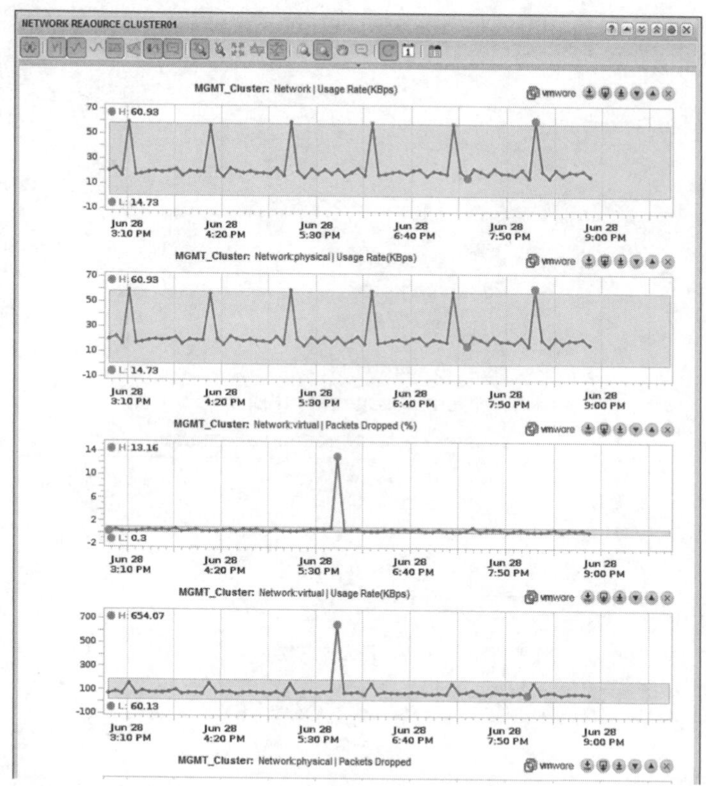

FIGURE 6.149 Network Performance Metric Graph Widget

6.8.1.7 Alerts, Events, and Health

Figure 6.150 shows the Health Status Dashboard, which is built using the following widgets:

- Cluster Health Bar (see Figure 6.151)
- Alerts (see Figure 6.152)

FIGURE 6.150 Health Status Dashboard

The Health widget displays management and resource cluster health information. Table 6.33 shows the widget configurations.

TABLE 6.33 Example Health Widget Configuration.

Metric	Value
Self Provider	On
Mode	Self
Refresh Widget	On
Widget Refresh Interval	300
Order By	Health (asc)
Period Length	Last 7 days
Tags to Filter By	Cluster compute resource (select clusters)

Figure 6.151 shows an example of the cluster health bar.

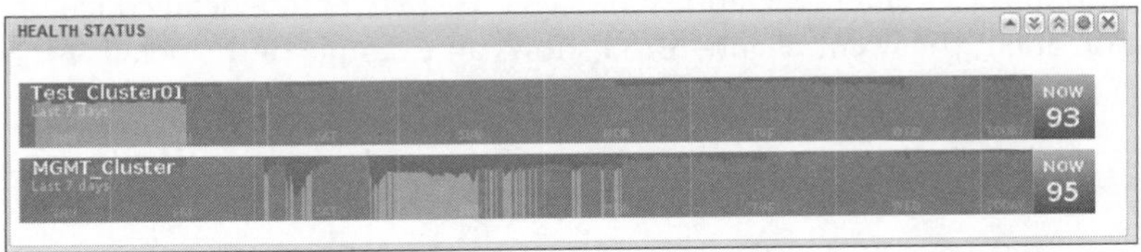

FIGURE 6.151 Cluster health bar

The Alerts widget can display alerts that have been generated. Alerts in this widget can be displayed for clusters or virtual machines. The correct filter must be applied. This widget displays alerts for the clusters. If needed, the *VM Entity Status* filter can be selected to include Powered:On or Powered:Off virtual machines.

This widget is configured as shown in Table 6.34.

TABLE 6.34 Example Alerts Widget Configuration

Metric	Value
Refresh Widget	On
Widget Refresh Interval	300
Tags to Filter	Cluster compute resource (select clusters)

Figure 6.152 shows the completed widget.

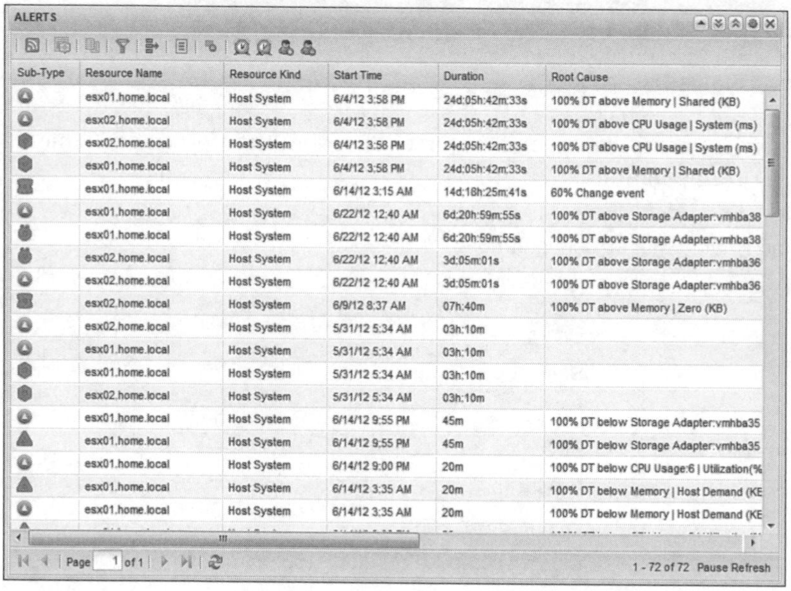

ALERTS

Sub-Type	Resource Name	Resource Kind	Start Time	Duration	Root Cause
	esx01.home.local	Host System	6/4/12 3:58 PM	24d:05h:42m:33s	100% DT above Memory | Shared (KB)
	esx02.home.local	Host System	6/4/12 3:58 PM	24d:05h:42m:33s	100% DT above CPU Usage | System (ms)
	esx02.home.local	Host System	6/4/12 3:58 PM	24d:05h:42m:33s	100% DT above CPU Usage | System (ms)
	esx01.home.local	Host System	6/4/12 3:58 PM	24d:05h:42m:33s	100% DT above Memory | Shared (KB)
	esx01.home.local	Host System	6/14/12 3:15 AM	14d:18h:25m:41s	60% Change event
	esx01.home.local	Host System	6/22/12 12:40 AM	6d:20h:59m:55s	100% DT above Storage Adapter:vmhba38
	esx01.home.local	Host System	6/22/12 12:40 AM	6d:20h:59m:55s	100% DT above Storage Adapter:vmhba38
	esx02.home.local	Host System	6/22/12 12:40 AM	3d:05m:01s	100% DT above Storage Adapter:vmhba36
	esx02.home.local	Host System	6/22/12 12:40 AM	3d:05m:01s	100% DT above Storage Adapter:vmhba36
	esx02.home.local	Host System	6/9/12 8:37 AM	07h:40m	100% DT above Memory | Zero (KB)
	esx02.home.local	Host System	5/31/12 5:34 AM	03h:10m	
	esx01.home.local	Host System	5/31/12 5:34 AM	03h:10m	
	esx01.home.local	Host System	5/31/12 5:34 AM	03h:10m	
	esx02.home.local	Host System	5/31/12 5:34 AM	03h:10m	
	esx01.home.local	Host System	6/14/12 9:55 PM	45m	100% DT below Storage Adapter:vmhba35
	esx01.home.local	Host System	6/14/12 9:55 PM	45m	100% DT below Storage Adapter:vmhba35
	esx01.home.local	Host System	6/14/12 9:00 PM	20m	100% DT below CPU Usage:6 | Utilization(%
	esx01.home.local	Host System	6/14/12 3:35 AM	20m	100% DT below Memory | Host Demand (KE
	esx01.home.local	Host System	6/14/12 3:35 AM	20m	100% DT below Memory | Host Demand (KE

Page 1 of 1 1 - 72 of 72 Pause Refresh

FIGURE 6.152 Alerts widget

Double-click an alert to direct vCenter Operations Manager to open a more detailed page displaying information about the event. Figure 6.153 shows an example of the details for an alert.

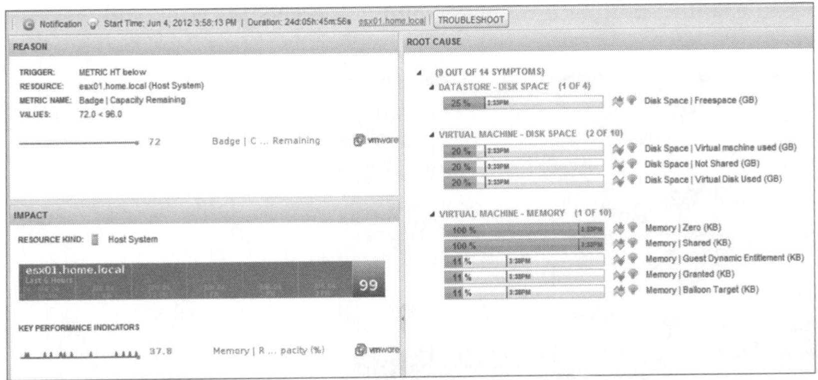

FIGURE 6.153 Alerts information detail

6.8.1.8 Capacity Remaining

Capacity remaining in a cluster is useful in determining available capacity for future virtual machine deployments. Public service providers provide the illusion of infinite capacity, so they must be able to proactively add capacity as needed on demand. As an example, this information can be used to gauge how many more virtual machines can be deployed on a resource cluster, based on the observed average workload profile in the environment. This example looks at the time left before running out of storage, network, and compute resources in a cluster.

The Scoreboard widget (see Figure 6.154) displays information about available time (days) left in the cluster for CPU, memory, disk, and network.

This example uses the Capacity Remaining metric. The Green threshold is high, and the Red threshold is low. Table 6.35 shows the metric resource selections used in the widget.

TABLE 6.35 Example Capacity Remaining Metric Resource Selections

Metric	Unit	Green Range	Yellow Range	Orange Range	Red Range
Count | VM	Days	90	60–90	30–60	30
Count | VM | Disk Space	Days	90	60–90	30–60	30
Count | VM | Disk I/O	Days	90	60–90	30–60	30
Count | VM | Memory	Days	90	60–90	30–60	30
Count | VM | Network	Days	90	60–90	30–60	30

NOTE

These threshold/ranges are only examples. These values should be based on the cluster design threshold values and the customer requirements.

Figure 6.154 shows an example of the Capacity Remaining Scoreboard Dashboard.

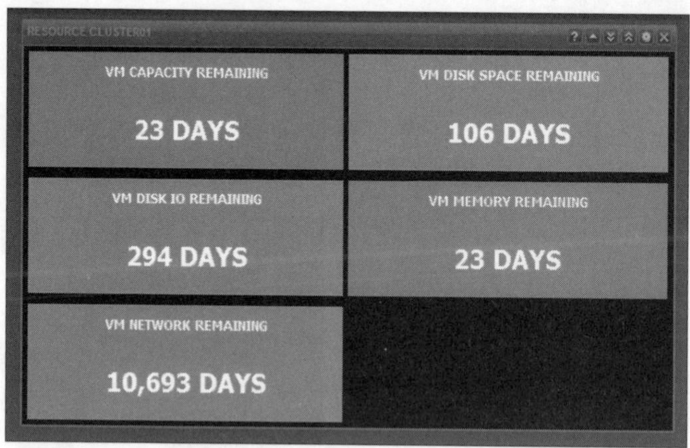

FIGURE 6.154 Capacity Remaining Scoreboard Dashboard

6.8.1.9 Management Cluster

The Management cluster has several different components that must be monitored for continued operation of the vCloud. Figure 6.155 shows a sample management dashboard. The dashboard in the example monitors the following vCloud management components:

- SQL Server (vCenter/vCloud Director databases)
- vCenter Server
- vCloud Director cell
- vCenter Operations Manager
- Chargeback
- vCloud Networking and Security Manager

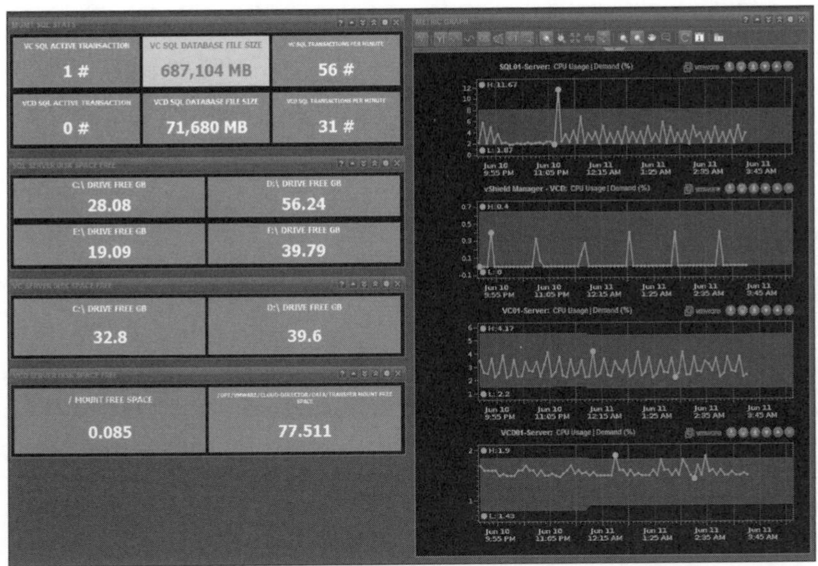

FIGURE 6.155 Management cluster dashboard

The first widget monitors the SQL database for database size and transactions metrics. The Hyperic agent collects these metrics and displays them in a scoreboard widget.

The following metrics are used for this widget:

- **Metric used:** Microsoft SQL Server 2008 (`database SQL01-Server MSSQLSERVER`)
- **Databases:** vCloud Director and vCenter (the SQL databases)

TABLE 6.36 Example Metrics

Metric	Unit	Green Range	Yellow Range	Orange Range	Red Range
vCenter SQL Active Transactions	#	100	100–200	200–300	300
vCenter SQL Database File Size	MB	60000–70000	70000–80000	80000–90000	900000
vCenter SQL Transactions per Minute	#	100	100–200	200–300	300
vCloud Director SQL Active Transactions	#	100	100–200	200–300	300
vCloud Director SQL Database File Size	MB	10000	10000–20000	20000–30000	30000
vCloud Director SQL Transactions per Minute	#	100	100–200	200–300	300

NOTE

These threshold/ranges are only examples. These values should be based on the cluster design threshold values and the customer requirements.

Figure 6.156 shows the completed widget.

FIGURE 6.156 Completed widget showing VC SQL Database File Size in Red Range and VC SQL Transactions Per Minutes in Yellow Range.

The following widget monitors the SQL Server free space on each logical operating system drive. This example uses the following drive letters:

`C:\` Operating system drive

`D:\` SQL database files

`E:\` SQL log files

`F:\` SQL backup

This example monitors free space available on each of the drives and configures alerts based on thresholds. The metric used is for the resource kind Virtual Machine, and data is collected using VMware Tools. This example uses the Scoreboard widget, as shown in the Table 6.37.

TABLE 6.37 Example Scoreboard Widget Configuration

Metric	Unit	Green Range	Yellow Range	Orange Range	Red Range
Guest File System `C:\` Guest File System Free	GB	15	10–15	8–10	8
Guest File System `D:\` Guest File System Free	GB	15	10–15	8–10	8
Guest File System `E:\` Guest File System Free	GB	15	10–15	8–10	8
Guest File System `F:\` Guest File System Free	GB	15	10–15	8–10	8

NOTE

These threshold/ranges are only examples. These values should be based on the cluster design threshold values and the customer requirements.

Figure 6.157 shows the completed widget.

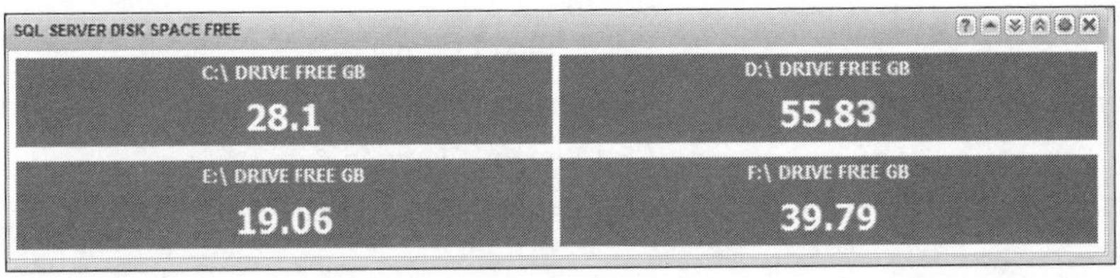

SQL SERVER DISK SPACE FREE
C:\ DRIVE FREE GB
28.1
D:\ DRIVE FREE GB
55.83
E:\ DRIVE FREE GB
19.06
F:\ DRIVE FREE GB
39.79

FIGURE 6.157 Completed widget showing all free drive space areas in Green Range.

The same metric can create a widget that monitors the vCenter and vCloud Director cells for free space. Monitor the transfer folder free space of the vCloud Director cells. Using a Scoreboard widget, you can create a widget as shown in Figures 6.158 and 6.159. Note that the transfer folder mount point is monitored. The default mount point is `/opt/vmware/cloud-director/data/transfer` in the Linux operating system (vCloud Director cell).

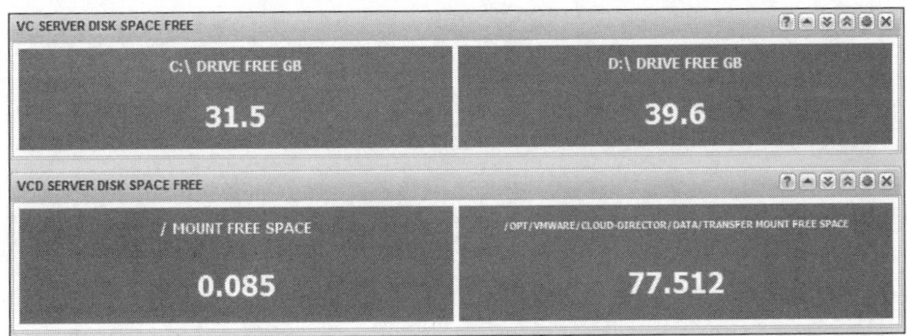

FIGURE 6.158 Example: Free Space widget showing the '/ Mount Free Space' in the Red Range.

You can use a Metric Graph widget to monitor historical CPU demand on the following infrastructure objects:

- SQL Server
- vCloud Networking and Security Manager
- vCloud Director cells
- vCenter Server

The metrics shown in Table 6.38 are used to create the widget.

TABLE 6.38 Example Metric Graph Widget Metrics

Resource	Metric
SQL Server	CPU Usage | Demand (%)
vCloud Networking and Security Manager	CPU Usage | Demand (%)
vCenter Server	CPU Usage | Demand (%)
vCloud Director Cell	CPU Usage | Demand (%)

Figure 6.159 shows the completed widget.

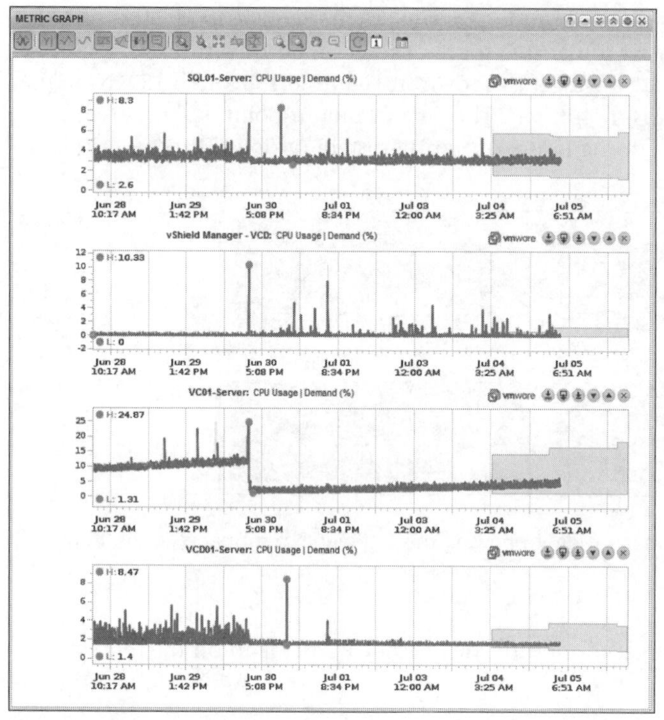

FIGURE 6.159 Completed widget showing the metric graph for cell management resources.

6.8.2 AMQP Messages

Deployment Models: Private

Example Components: vCloud Director 5.1, vCloud Networking and Security Edge 5.1, vSphere 5.1, RabbitMQ 2.8.4

6.8.2.1 Background

vCloud Director uses a message bus architecture for communicating vCloud Director events with third-party systems or services. Events fall into two classes, nonblocking and blocking. In the case of nonblocking events, vCloud Director publishes every action taken as a message to the configured exchange queue. Nonblocking messages do not halt the generating task; the task continues, regardless of what processing or acknowledgment is done on the event message.

Nonblocking and blocking event messages are not multitenant in nature and are not exposed to the tenant layer of the cloud. They are inherently intended for use by the cloud provider, not the tenant.

6.8.2.2 Example

The Enterprise vCloud administrator wants to collect all events generated by vCloud Director, to store them for searching later so that it can support troubleshooting or audit activities within the environment.

A nonblocking messages or notifications configuration consists of the following components (see Figure 6.160):

- vCloud Director cell (message producer)
- AMQP 0.9 or later message bus (message queue)
- AMQP client (message consumer)

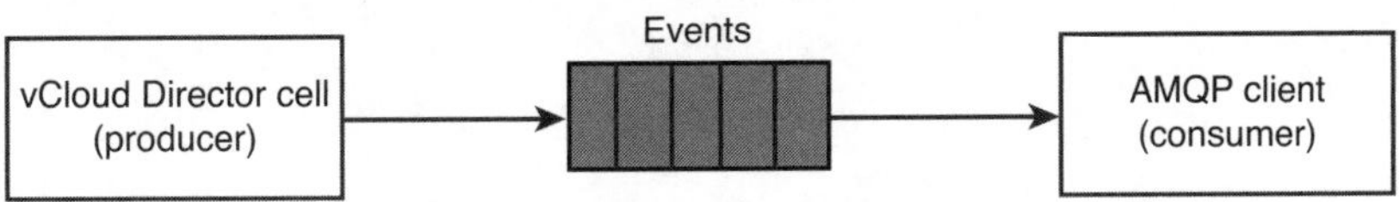

FIGURE 6.160 Nonblocking messages or notifications configuration

The producer (vCloud Director) sends messages to the *events* queue. The client (consumer) receives messages from the queue.

The queue type is defined in several ways, based on the use case for the messages being delivered. Message queues can be defined as direct, topic, fan out, system, or header.

For information on the exchange types and how to configure binding/routing of messages, see the RabbitMQ Tutorials (www.rabbitmq.com/getstarted.html).

6.8.2.2.1 AMQP Server Exchange Configuration

For detailed AMQP configuration with RabbitMQ, see "Downloading and Installing RabbitMQ" (www.rabbitmq.com/download.html).

vCloud Director requires an AMQP 0.9 (or later)–compatible message bus. This example uses RabbitMQ as the message bus. RabbitMQ provides a polyglot messaging infrastructure, with clients for all the latest development languages and generic APIs such as HTTP.

TABLE 6.39 RabbitMQ Server Exchange Configuration

Configuration Item	Value
AMQP Host	192.168.1.100
AMQP Port	5672
Exchange	vcdExchange
Exchange Type	topic
Durability	durable
Auto Delete	no
Internal	no
vHost	/
Prefix	vcd

6.8.2.2.2 AMQP Server Queue Configuration

This example (see Table 6.40) creates a queue bound to this exchange for the messages to be routed into.

TABLE 6.40 RabbitMQ Server Queue Configuration

Configuration Item	Value
Queue	notificationQueue
Durability	Durable
Auto Delete	No
Exchange	vcdExchange
Routing Key	#

6.8.2.2.3 Exchange Routing

The AMQP broker uses routing as a way to filter vCloud Director notification messages and send them to the appropriate queue for multiple consumers. For example, a public vCloud provider can filter messages based on organization and send each customer's notifications to a separate queue for isolation of logging information. The vCloud Director routing key syntax follows:

```
<operationSuccess>.<entityUUID>.<orgUUID>.<userUUID>.<subType1>.<subType2>....
  <subtypeN>.taskName
```

For example, to route only VM `create` messages to a queue, the routing key would be:

```
true.#.com.vmware.vcloud.event.vm.create
```

vCloud Director sets sane routing keys in the messages that are generated. This example uses the `#` (hash) routing key because this is a wildcard match on one or more segments of a routing key. This effectively routes all messages generated by vCloud Director of type `vm.create` to a notificationQueue. If you are interested in specific messages being routed to the appropriate queue, you can use a nonwildcard or selective wildcard (*) routing key.

Blocking tasks messages have similar identifiers, with the object being the blocking task. The blocking task references the following:

- **Its parent task:** The suspended task referencing the object and the task parameters attributes it was set with in the original request
- **TaskOwner:** The object on which the task operates
- **The actions that can be taken on this blocking task:** Resume, abort, fail, updateProgress

Receiving and acting upon on the blockings task is accomplished with the vCloud Director API callbacks. System admin privileges are required to perform these operations.

6.8.2.2.4 vCloud Director Configuration

To configure vCloud Director:

1. Under the System > Administration > Extensibility section of the admin user interface, enter the appropriate configuration details for your AMQP message bus.
2. Select Enable Notifications.

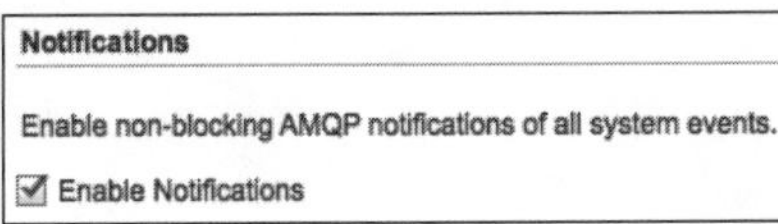

FIGURE 6.161

3. Configure vCloud Director with the message bus settings so that it knows where to send event messages. This is a system task and must be done by a vCloud provider administrator user.

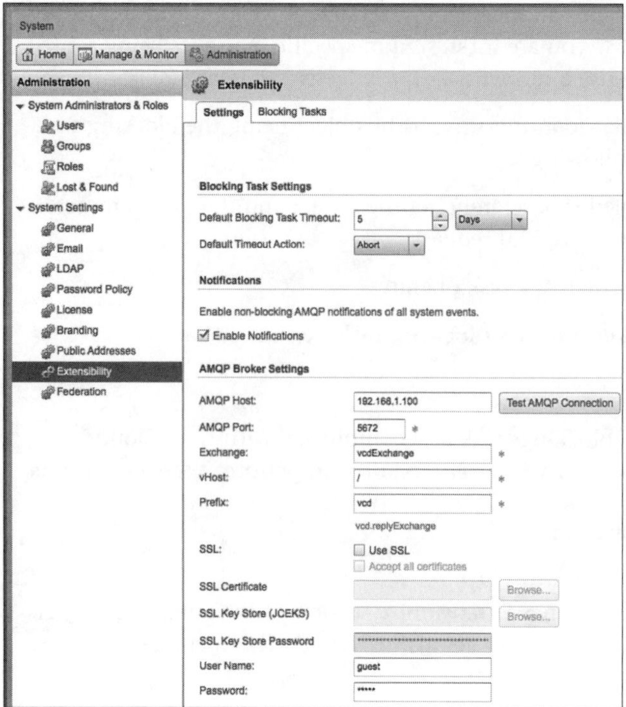

FIGURE 6.162

4. Click Apply.

vCloud Director begins to send nonblocking notification events to the configured exchange. Regardless of whether the notification message is delivered successfully or acknowledged, the task within vCloud Director that generated the message continues uninterrupted.

6.8.2.2.5 AMQP Client Configuration

Because AMQP messaging is a polyglot messaging system, the client configuration is implementation specific. Several options exist for consuming the AMQP Exchange for nonblocking messages, including using the AMQP plug-in for vCenter Orchestrator or the vCloud Director API. When consuming messages, if your queue is not configured for autodelete, you must acknowledge the messages sent to the queue when consuming them. The payload of the message is an XML document as a UTF-8 encoded string.

The following simple (Java) example (see Figure 6.163) loops over a queue, waiting on the delivery of the next message. `ackMessage` is a Boolean variable setting that deals with whether to acknowledge the message when it is retrieved from the queue.

```
@SuppressWarnings("unchecked")
public void retrieveMessages() throws IOException, InterruptedException {
    Channel channel = connection.createChannel();
    QueueingConsumer consumer = new QueueingConsumer(channel);
    channel.basicConsume(amqpConnection.getQueue(), ackMessage, consumer);

    while (true) {
        QueueingConsumer.Delivery delivery = consumer.nextDelivery();
        Map headers = delivery.getProperties().getHeaders();
        String payload = new String(delivery.getBody(), "UTF8");
```

FIGURE 6.163 Simple example Java code for looping over a queue awaiting next message delivery

This example performs the basic steps to acknowledge and process the AMQP messages to obtain the message headers and message body from a single message queue and set the message body to a String for subsequent processing. Additional logic could be used to take action based on the message header or message body.

6.8.3 AMQP Blocking Tasks

Deployment Models: Private, public, hybrid

Example Components: vCloud Director 5.1, vCloud Networking and Security Edge 5.1, vSphere 5.1, RabbitMQ 2.8.4

6.8.3.1 Background

vCloud Director uses a message bus architecture to communicate vCloud Director events with third-party systems or services. Events fall into two classes, nonblocking and blocking. In the case of blocking events, vCloud Director publishes messages to the configured exchange queue for the tasks that are configured as blocking tasks. Blocking tasks halt the generating task, and the task waits for acknowledgment that it is allowed to continue.

6.8.3.2 Example

In this example, the private cloud provider wants to configure approvals for the instantiation of vApps by cloud consumers in their private clouds. When a user attempts to instantiate a vApp from a template, vCloud Director sends a notification of the request to the appropriate AMQP exchange and waits on acknowledgment and approval of the request before continuing.

The blocking task example configuration in Figure 6.164 consists of the following components:

- vCloud Director 5.1 cell (message producer)
- AMQP 0.9 or later message bus (message queue)
- AMQP client (message consumer)
- REST client or vCloud SDK

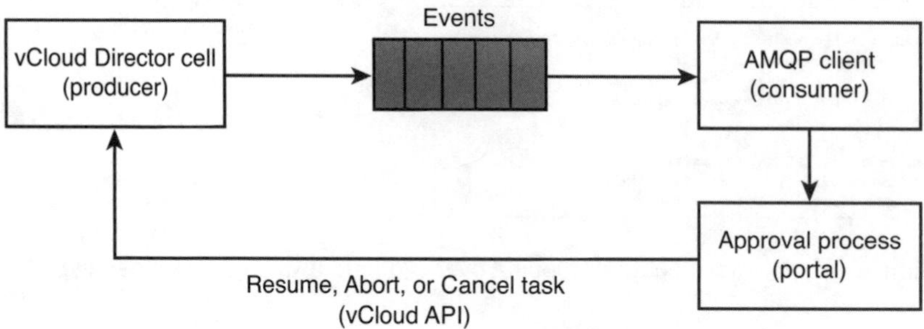

FIGURE 6.164 AMQP blocking task architecture

The producer (vCloud Director) sends messages to the *events* queue. The client (consumer) receives messages from the queue. The client triggers the approval process. The result of the approval step (resume, abort, cancel) is submitted to vCloud Director for completion of the task within vCloud Director. At this point, the task completes its processing or is terminated with the appropriate state.

The queue type is defined in several ways, based on the use case for the messages being delivered. Message queues can be defined as direct, topic, fan out, system, or header.

For information on the exchange types and how to configure binding/routing of messages, see the RabbitMQ Tutorials (www.rabbitmq.com/getstarted.html).

6.8.3.2.1 Exchange Configuration

vCloud Director requires an AMQP 0.9 or later compatible message bus. This example uses RabbitMQ as the message bus. RabbitMQ provides a polyglot messaging infrastructure, with clients for all the latest development languages, as well as generic APIs like HTTP.

For detailed AMQP configuration with RabbitMQ, see "Downloading and Installing RabbitMQ" (www.rabbitmq.com/download.html).

Table 6.41 shows an example of the RabbitMQ Server Exchange configuration settings.

TABLE 6.41 RabbitMQ Server Exchange Configuration

Configuration Item	Value
AMQP Host	192.168.1.100
AMQP Port	5672
Exchange	vcdExchange
Exchange Type	topic
Durability	durable
Auto Delete	no
Internal	no
vHost	/
Prefix	vcd

6.8.3.2.2 RabbitMQ Queue Configuration

This example (see Table 6.42) creates a queue bound to this exchange for the messages to be routed into.

TABLE 6.42 AMQP Queue Configuration

Configuration Item	Value
Queue	notificationQueue
Durability	Durable
Auto Delete	No
Exchange	vcdExchange
Routing Key	#

6.8.3.2.3 Exchange Routing

The AMQP broker uses routing as a way to filter vCloud Director notification messages and send them to the appropriate queue for multiple consumers. The vCloud Director routing key syntax follows:

```
<operationSuccess>.<entityUUID>.<orgUUID>.<userUUID>.<subType1>.<subType2>....
  <subtypeN>.taskName
```

For example, to route only VM `create` messages to a queue, the routing key would be as follows:

```
true.#.com.vmware.vcloud.event.vm.create
```

vCloud Director sets sane routing keys in the messages that are generated. This example uses the `#` (hash) routing key because this is a wildcard match on one or more segments of a routing key. This effectively routes all messages generated by vCloud Director of type `vm.create` to the notificationQueue. If you are interested in specific messages being routed to the appropriate queue, you can use a nonwildcard or selective wildcard (*) routing key.

Blocking tasks messages have similar identifiers, with the object being the blocking task. The blocking task references the following:

- **Its parent task:** The suspended task referencing the object and the task parameters attributes it was set with in the original request
- **TaskOwner:** The object on which the task operates
- **The actions that can be taken on this blocking task:** Resume, abort, fail, updateProgress

Receiving and acting upon on the blockings task is accomplished with the vCloud Director API callbacks. System admin privileges are required to perform these operations.

6.8.3.2.4 vCloud Director Configuration

Under the System > Administration > Extensibility section of the admin user interface, enter the appropriate configuration details for your AMQP message bus.

6.8.3.2.5 Enable Blocking Tasks

Click the Blocking Tasks tab and, from the folder tree, select the blocking tasks you want to enable. In this example, select the Instantiate vApp from Template option and click Apply (see Figure 6.165).

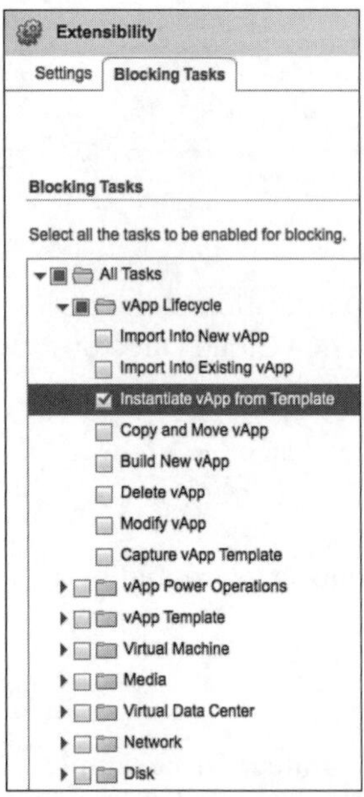

FIGURE 6.165 Enable a task for blocking in vCloud Director

6.8.3.2.6 Message Bus Configuration

Configure vCloud Director with the message bus settings so that it knows where to send event messages, and click Apply. Figure 6.166 shows the configuration panel. This is a system task and must be done by a cloud system administrator.

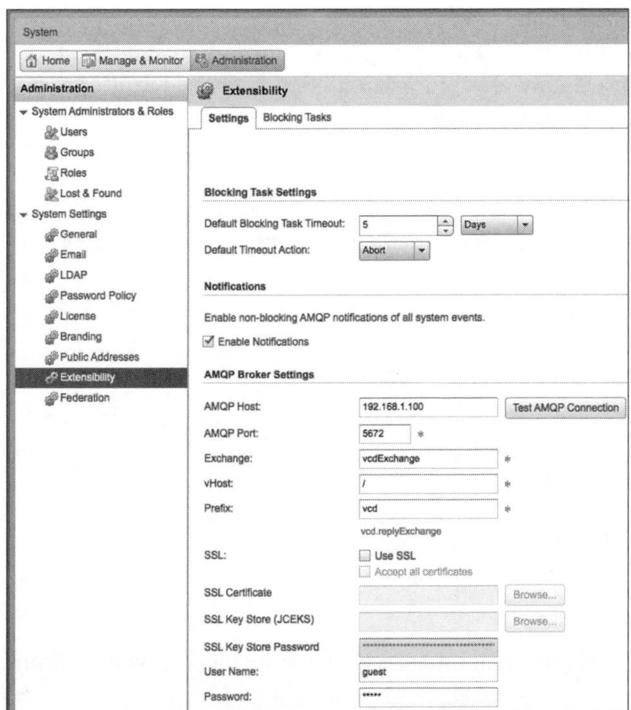

FIGURE 6.166 vCloud Director AMQP configuration

6.8.3.2.7 Blocking Message

The blocking message contains a reference to the task submitted so that the approver process can locate the task to interact with it.

```
    <vmext:Link rel="entityResolver" href="https://192.168.1.44/api/entity/"/>
    <vmext:EntityLink rel="entity" type="vcloud:blockingTask"
name="vdcInstantiateVapp"
id="urn:vcloud:blockingTask:9f4b1051-7c44-40e7-b0da-49e611b551be"/>
    <vmext:EntityLink rel="down" type="vcloud:user" name="system"
id="urn:vcloud:user:8b209f7f-052f-41e0-bba3-063aab1d7b04"/>
    <vmext:EntityLink rel="up" type="vcloud:org" name="nuvemo"
id="urn:vcloud:org:1f6de3ed-aad9-418e-95ef-ac93bcf2b774"/>
    <vmext:EntityLink rel="task" type="vcloud:task" name="vdcInstantiateVapp"
id="urn:vcloud:task:5f1a2884-fac0-4b3d-ae50-8cd8bd7090e7"/>
    <vmext:EntityLink rel="task:owner" type="vcloud:vapp"
id="urn:vcloud:vapp:f12509a8-71d1-4484-8062-b444c7aae6e2"/>
```

6.8.3.2.8 Approval Process Implementation

The approval process consists of sending a blocking message, performing the approval action (such as sending an email or creating a webform), and, based on the result of that action, resuming or failing the task that was blocked.

6.8.3.2.9 Deploying a vApp

When the vApp is initially deployed, because we have configured a blocking task for Instantiate vApp from Template, the vApp enters into a Pending Processing state upon deployment (see Figure 6.167).

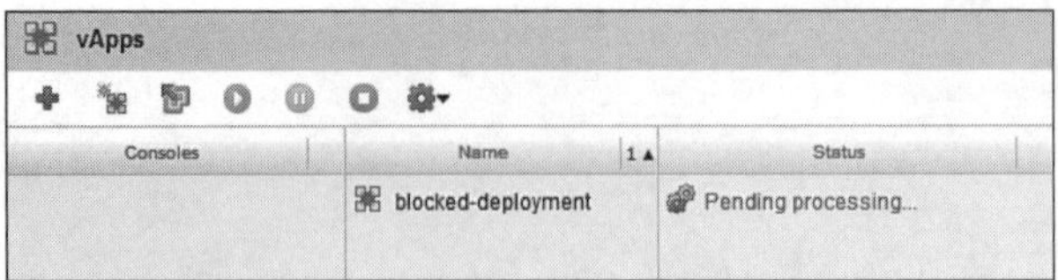

FIGURE 6.167 vApp Pending Processing status

6.8.3.2.10 Resuming a Blocked Task

Blocked tasks can be resumed either via the vCloud Director UI as a cloud provider administrator or programmatically using the vCloud API.

6.8.3.2.11 Administrator Resume

In the System > Blocking Tasks window, the vCloud administrator has a list of blocking tasks and their statuses.

1. Right-click the task, or highlight the task and click the Options icon, to give the administrator the options to resume, abort, or fail the blocked task.
2. Enter a reason for the status change to the blocked task.

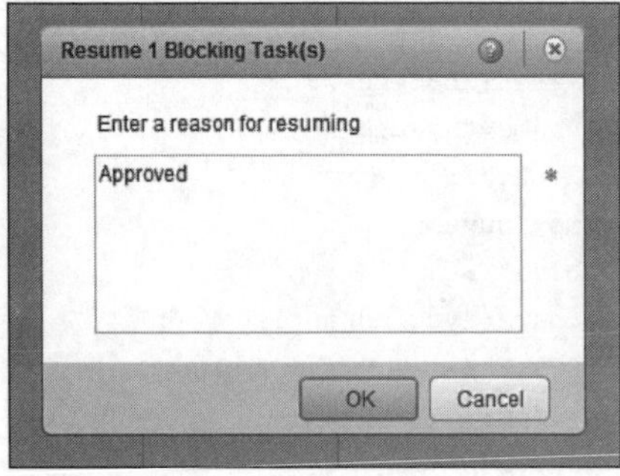

FIGURE 6.168

3. After being resumed, the vApp continues deployment and will complete unless any additional blocked tasks relevant to other deployment steps halt the process.

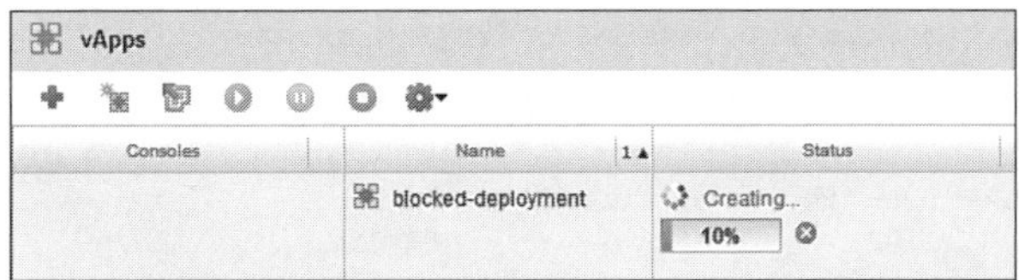

FIGURE 6.169

6.8.3.2.12 vCloud API Resume

To use the API:

1. Find the blocked task from the message with the entity resolver using the following command:

```
GET https://vcd51-01.corp.nuvemo.com/api/entity/
urn:vcloud:blockingTask:9f4b1051-7c44-40e7-b0da-49e611b551be
```

The data returned is the blocking task entity:

```
<Entity xmlns="http://www.vmware.com/vcloud/v1.5"
name="urn:vcloud:blockingTask:9f4b1051-7c44-40e7-b0da-49e611b551be"
id="urn:vcloud:blockingTask:9f4b1051-7c44-40e7-b0da-49e611b551be"
type="application/vnd.vmware.vcloud.entity+xml" href="https://vcd51-
01.corp.nuvemo.com/api/entity/urn:vcloud:blockingTask:9f4b1051-7c44-40e7-b0da-
49e611b551be" xmlns:xsi="http://www.w3.org/2001/XMLSchema-instance"
xsi:schemaLocation="http://www.vmware.com/vcloud/v1.5
http://192.168.1.44/api/v1.5/schema/master.xsd">
    <Link rel="alternate" type="application/vnd.vmware.admin.blockingTask+xml"
href="https://vcd51-01.corp.nuvemo.com/api/admin/extensionblockingTask/
  9f4b1051-7c44-40e7-b0da-49e611b551be"/>
</Entity>
```

2. Get the blocking task from the resolved entity:

```
GET https://vcd51-01.corp.nuvemo.com/api/admin/extension/blockingTask/9f4b1051-
  7c44-40e7-b0da-49e611b551be
```

This returns the blocking task and methods that can be performed against it:

```
HTTP/1.1 200 OK
Date: Tue, 03 Jul 2012 16:30:33 GMT
Date: Tue, 03 Jul 2012 16:30:33 GMT
Content-Type: application/vnd.vmware.admin.blockingtask+xml;version=1.5
Content-Length: 2428

<?xml version="1.0" encoding="UTF-8"?>
```

```
<vmext:BlockingTask xmlns:vmext="http://www.vmware.com/vcloud/extension/v1.5"
xmlns:vcloud="http://www.vmware.com/vcloud/v1.5" status="active"
timeoutDate="2012-07-
08T09:06:33.757-07:00" timeoutAction="abort" createdTime="2012-07-
03T09:06:33.757-07:00"
name="vdcInstantiateVapp" id="urn:vcloud:blockingTask:9f4b1051-7c44-40e7-b0da-
49e611b551be" type="application/vnd.vmware.admin.blockingTask+xml"
href="https://vcd51-
01.corp.nuvemo.com/api/admin/extension/blockingTask/9f4b1051-7c44-40e7-b0da-
49e611b551be" xmlns:xsi="http://www.w3.org/2001/XMLSchema-instance"
xsi:schemaLocation="http://www.vmware.com/vcloud/extension/v1.5
http://192.168.1.44/api/v1.5/schema/vmwextensions.xsd http://www.vmware.com/
vcloud/v1.5
http://192.168.1.44/api/v1.5/schema/master.xsd">
    <vcloud:Link rel="resume"
type="application/vnd.vmware.admin.blockingTaskOperationParams+xml"
href="https://vcd51-
01.corp.nuvemo.com/api/admin/extension/blockingTask/9f4b1051-7c44-40e7-b0da-
49e611b551be/action/resume"/>
    <vcloud:Link rel="abort"
type="application/vnd.vmware.admin.blockingTaskOperationParams+xml"
href="https://vcd51-
01.corp.nuvemo.com/api/admin/extension/blockingTask/9f4b1051-7c44-40e7-b0da-
49e611b551be/action/abort"/>
    <vcloud:Link rel="fail"
type="application/vnd.vmware.admin.blockingTaskOperationParams+xml"
href="https://vcd51-
01.corp.nuvemo.com/api/admin/extension/blockingTask/9f4b1051-7c44-40e7-b0da-
49e611b551be/action/fail"/>
    <vcloud:Link rel="updateProgress"
type="application/vnd.vmware.admin.blockingTaskUpdateProgressOperationParams+
xml" href="https://vcd51-
01.corp.nuvemo.com/api/admin/extension/blockingTask/9f4b1051-7c44-
40e7-b0da-49e611b551be/action/updateProgress"/>
    <vcloud:Link rel="up" type="application/vnd.vmware.vcloud.task+xml"
href="https://vcd51-01.corp.nuvemo.com/api/task/5f1a2884-fac0-4b3d-ae50-
8cd8bd7090e7"/>
    <vcloud:Organization type="application/vnd.vmware.admin.organization+xml"
name="nuvemo" href="https://vcd51-01.corp.nuvemo.com/api/admin/org/1f6de3ed-
aad9-418e-
95ef-ac93bcf2b774"/>
    <vcloud:User type="application/vnd.vmware.admin.user+xml" name="system"
href="https://vcd51-01.corp.nuvemo.com/api/admin/user/8b209f7f-052f-41e0-bba3-
063aab1d7b04"/>
    <vcloud:TaskOwner type="application/vnd.vmware.vcloud.vApp+xml" name=""
href="https://vcd51-01.corp.nuvemo.com/api/vApp/vapp-f12509a8-71d1-4484-8062-
```

```
b444c7aae6e2"/>
</vmext:BlockingTask>
```

3. Resume the blocked task:

```
POST https://vcd51-01.corp.nuvemo.com/api/admin/extension/
blockingTask/9f4b1051-7c44-40e7-b0da-49e611b551be/action/resume
Content-Type: application/vnd.vmware.admin.blockingTaskOperationParams+xml
Pass in this content as the post to the resume request:
<?xml version="1.0" encoding="UTF-8"?>
<BlockingTaskOperationParams
  xmlns=http://www.vmware.com/vcloud/extension/v1.5
  <Message>Approved task. </Message>
</BlockingTaskOperationParams>
```

6.8.3.2.13 Failed/Aborted Task

The end user (tenant) is notified through the vCloud Director UI that the deployment has failed or has been aborted (see Figure 6.170). Click into the details of the failure message to find the provider-entered reason for failing.

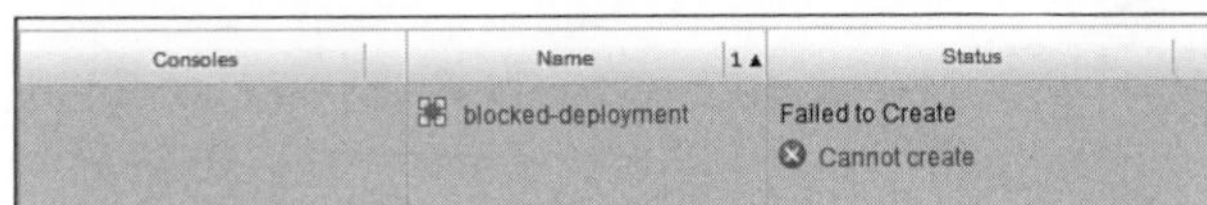

FIGURE 6.170 Status showing the end-user notification of a failed or aborted deployment

Failing or aborting tasks is carried out in the same manner, via the vCloud API as a resume task. Looking at the XML returned when performing a `GET` on the blocking task, methods are returned for Resume, Abort, and Fail, as follows:

```
    <vcloud:Link rel="abort"
type="application/vnd.vmware.admin.blockingTaskOperationParams+xml" href="https://
  vcd51-01.corp.nuvemo.com/api/admin/extension/blockingTask/9f4b1051-7c44-40e7-b0da-
  49e611b551be/action/abort"/>
```

You can fail or abort a task as part of a provisioning process that requires an external approval to complete. If you have a provisioning portal or workflow executing the task of deploying and approving vApps, when an approval is declined, the portal fails the blocked task with an appropriate message to the user. If a user submits a deploy request for a vApp and then decides to cancel the deployment before the approval, the portal can issue an abort on the blocking task with the appropriate message. An abort and a fail both result in termination of the vApp deployment, but contextually, they are different.

CHAPTER 7
Workflow Examples

IN THIS CHAPTER

7.1 Overview

In a VMware® vCloud® environment, sometimes a mechanism is required to consistently complete tasks outside the scope of VMware vCloud Director®. As an example, it might be necessary to coordinate a sequence of tasks among multiple products or to communicate with external systems. VMware vCenter™ Orchestrator™ is useful in these cases.

vCenter Orchestrator can automate tasks across VMware products, including many of those in the VMware vCloud Suite. vCenter Orchestrator provides a large library of workflows and actions in its base configuration, and its library grows with each newly installed plug-in. You can build powerful workflows with little or no knowledge of an API.

The following sections provide example workflows that complement vCloud deployments and enable the orchestration of multiple products through tight integration at the API level. Although VMware offers other products with workflow capabilities, these examples are specific to vCenter Orchestrator.

7.1.1 Audience

This chapter is primarily intended for people involved in designing, implementing, and operating a VMware vCloud environment. These can include workflow developers and testers, vCloud operators, system administrators, and architects who need to understand automation and integration capabilities.

You should be familiar with the configuration, administration, and architecture of the following products:

- VMware vCloud Director
- VMware vSphere®
- VMware vCenter Orchestrator

7.1.2 Scope

The examples in this chapter provide a starting point to demonstrate some of the capabilities possible when leveraging workflows in a vCloud environment. Many of the examples provided require additional configuration, customization, and testing before use in a production environment.

These workflows demonstrate the use of provided library content, along with custom scripting and workflows. VMware supports the plug-ins and their library content, but the custom content is provided only as examples and is not officially supported.

Packages for the workflow examples in this chapter are available for download from VMware Communities (http://communities.vmware.com/docs/DOC-20230).

7.1.3 Launching Workflows

vCenter Orchestrator workflows can be started from any of the following interfaces:

- vCenter Orchestrator Client
- VMware vSphere Web Client
- SOAP API
- REST API

7.1.3.1 vCenter Orchestrator Client

With the vCenter Orchestrator client application, you can start workflows manually or automatically by setting a schedule or task. Workflow developers and testers usually start a workflow from the client.

To execute a workflow manually from the client while in Run or Design mode, select the workflow to run and use one of the following methods:

- Right-click the desired workflow and select Start Workflow.
- From the toolbar, click the Start Workflow icon (green triangle).
- Use a keyboard shortcut—Ctrl+R on Windows or Cmd+R on Mac OS X.

Similarly, to schedule a workflow from the vCenter Orchestrator client, select the workflow and use one of the following methods:

- Right-click the desired workflow and select Schedule Workflow.
- From the toolbar, click the Schedule Workflow icon (clock).

- Use a keyboard shortcut—Ctrl+S on Windows or Cmd+S on Mac OS X.
- Use the Scheduler tab in the left pane of the client to add a new scheduled execution.
- Use the Policies tab in the left pane of the client to create a new policy that executes the workflow (see Figure 7.1).

FIGURE 7.1 vCenter Orchestrator client workflow toolbar

Policies provide powerful options for starting workflows, using triggers from plug-ins. The following scenarios show how workflows are started from policy triggers:

Simple Network Management Protocol (SNMP) plug-in:

1. The plug-in receives a trap.
2. A plug-in trigger activates an active policy.
3. The policy starts a preconfigured workflow.

Advanced Message Queuing Protocol (AMQP) plug-in:

1. A notification is received.
2. A plug-in trigger activates an active policy.
3. The policy starts a preconfigured workflow.

You can also launch a workflow directly from an item in the vCenter Orchestrator inventory. For this option to be available, the workflow developer must set the show in inventory property as a variable in the presentation section of a workflow, and the type of the variable must match the type of the selected inventory item.

To launch a workflow directly from an item in the vCenter Orchestrator inventory:

1. Browse the inventory for your object.
2. Right-click an inventory item.
3. Select Run Workflow. Alternatively, if Use Contextual Menu in Inventory is selected under the Inventory tab in the client preferences dialog box, select a workflow from the list that is displayed.
4. Complete the workflow normally.

7.1.3.2 vSphere Web Client

As of vSphere 5.1, you can launch vCenter Orchestrator workflows directly from vSphere inventory objects in the vSphere Web Client. You can access available workflows for an object by right-clicking a vSphere inventory object and selecting the All vCenter Orchestrator Actions submenu. The list of available workflows is context aware and is based on the type of object selected. By default, the workflows included in the vCenter Server plug-in's workflow library are displayed. You can display additional workflows for a particular object by associating workflows with a vSphere object type. For information on the configuration of these options, see the VMware vSphere documentation (www.vmware.com/support/pubs/vsphere-esxi-vcenter-server-pubs.html).

7.1.3.3 SOAP API

The SOAP API presented by the vCenter Orchestrator server enables external systems to start workflows. Integration developers, service-management applications, and web portals use this interface. To learn more about this API, see the VMware vCenter Orchestrator documentation (www.vmware.com/support/pubs/orchestrator_pubs.html).

7.1.3.4 REST API

In vCenter Orchestrator 5.1, a REST API is presented in addition to the SOAP API. The REST API enables the execution of workflows and provides additional functionality that is not available in the SOAP API. The vSphere Web Client, for example, includes integration with vCenter Orchestrator through the REST API. For more information on the capabilities of this API, see the VMware vCenter Orchestrator documentation (www.vmware.com/support/pubs/orchestrator_pubs.html).

7.2 Triggering Workflows with vCloud Notifications

vCenter Orchestrator fully supports responding to blocked tasks and notification messages with callbacks and callouts to external systems through vCloud Director, AMQP, and other product-specific plug-ins. This can be implemented using a combination of library building block workflows and custom workflows to accomplish the following tasks (see Figure 7.2):

1. Configure the AMQP broker to route messages to a given queue.
2. Listen for incoming messages.
3. Consume the messages and extract relevant information.
4. Trigger workflows using the extracted information.

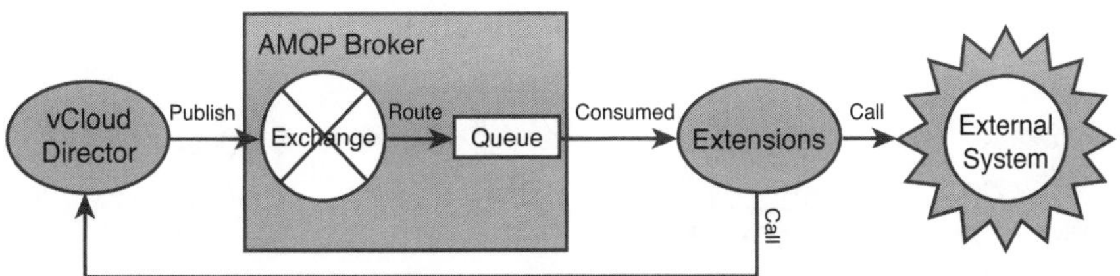

FIGURE 7.2 vCenter Orchestrator as a vCloud Director extension

The vCloud Director notification package implements this mechanism, using workflows and policies that serve as a base that you can expand upon.

7.2.1 Prerequisites

The notification package uses the following components:

- vCenter Orchestrator 5.1 Server
- vCenter Orchestrator 5.1 Client
- vCloud Director 5.1
- vCenter Orchestrator vCloud Director 5.1 plug-in
- vCenter Orchestrator AMQP 1.01 plug-in
- vCenter Orchestrator Microsoft Active Directory 1.01 plug-in
- vCenter Orchestrator Mail plug-in
- Compatible AMQP Serve, such as VMware vFabric™ RabbitMQ™ 2.0 and later
- vSphere 5.1 Server (optional—UI alternative)
- vCenter Orchestrator Perspective plug-in (optional—UI alternative)

7.2.2 Workflow Folders

The content for this example is contained in the com.vmware.coe.vcd51.notifications.package file.

The end-user-facing workflows are located in the PSO/vCloud Director notifications folder. Sections 7.2.3 and 7.2.4 discuss these workflows.

7.2.3 Workflow: Create a vCloud Director Notification Subscription

The Create a vCloud Director Notification Subscription workflow, shown in Figure 7.3, is the main workflow that creates the necessary configurations and integration among vCloud Director, AMQP, vCenter Orchestrator, and the systems it orchestrates. This workflow should be used to fill a queue with messages that match specific properties to start a specified workflow.

The end user of the workflow is the vCloud System administrator.

FIGURE 7.3 Workflow Schema: Create a vCloud Director Notification Subscription

7.2.3.1 Workflow Inputs

The Create a vCloud Director Notification Subscription workflow has a set of reduced inputs to configure AMQP and a set of necessary inputs to create all possible combinations of message filtering.

Table 7.1 provides information about the inputs used to configure AMQP.

TABLE 7.1 AMQP Setup Inputs: Create a vCloud Director Notification Subscription

Input Name	Detail
Queue and subscription name	The name for the queue and the subscription, such as vApp Deletion Approval
vCloud Director Host	The vCloud Director host providing messages to the AMQP server
AMQP password	The password used for authentication to the AMQP server
Create broker/Choose broker	Option to add an AMQP broker in the vCenter Orchestrator inventory or choose an existing broker

The username and other AMQP configuration items are gathered from the AMQP settings on the specified vCloud Director host. To be able read these settings, you must have configured the specified vCloud Director host object with System Administrator level access. For more information on configuring AMQP in vCloud Director, see "vCloud Managing and Monitoring Examples" in Chapter 6, "*Implementation Examples*".

The filter policy inputs determine which messages published by vCloud Director to include in the subscription and to use to trigger a specified workflow. Each filter type can be enabled or disabled.

- Enabled filter types allow the selection of a specific value. This indicates that only messages that match the value for that type should be included.
- Disabled filter types indicate that all messages matching that type should be included.

Table 7.2 describes the inputs used to generate the filter policy.

TABLE 7.2 Filter Policy Inputs: Create a vCloud Director Notification Subscription

Input Name	Detail
Operation success	Filter messages on operation success (true/false).
Organization	Filter messages on the organization. (Select an organization from the inventory.)
User	Filter messages on the user who started the event that generated the message. (Select a user from the inventory.)
Blocking task operation type	Filter messages that apply to a given blocking task operation type. (Select a blocking task type from the ones that have been enabled in the vCloud Director blocking tasks configuration.)
Event type	Filter messages that apply to a given event type. Select an event type from the list of supported event types, such as com/vmware/vcloud/event/catalog/create. If a blocking task operation type is selected, the list includes only events related to blocking tasks.
Entity type	Filter messages that apply to a given entity type. Table 7.3 provides the list of supported entity types.
Entity	Filter messages that apply to the selected entity object.

TABLE 7.3 Filter Policy Input Entity Types

Entity Type	Description
vcloud:blockingTask	A blocking task
vcloud:catalog	An organization virtual datacenter catalog attached to an organization
vcloud:catalogitem	A catalog item (linking to a media or a vApp template)
vcloud:datastore	A datastore attached to a vSphere host (Admin extension object)
vcloud:disk	A disk attached to a vApp virtual machine
vcloud:gateway	A gateway attached to an admin virtual datacenter (Admin object)
vcloud:group	A group attached to an admin organization (Admin object)
vcloud:host	A vSphere host (Admin extension object)
vcloud:licenseReport	A licensing report (Admin extension object)
vcloud:media	An ISO or floppy image attached to a virtual datacenter
vcloud:network	A vApp network, or an organization virtual datacenter network or an external network (Admin object)
vcloud:networkpool	A network pool attached to a provider virtual datacenter (Admin object)
vcloud:organization	An organization
vcloud:providervdc	A provider virtual datacenter (Admin object)
vcloud:lr.providervdcstorageclass	A storage profile attached to a provider virtual datacenter (Admin object)
vcloud:right	A user right (Admin object)

Entity Type	Description
vcloud:role	A user role (Admin object)
vcloud:strandedItem	A stranded item (Admin extension object)
vcloud:task	A task attached to its parent object
vcloud:user	A user attached to an organization (Admin object)
vcloud:vapp	A vApp attached to a virtual datacenter
vcloud:vapptemplate	A vApp template attached to a virtual datacenter
vcloud:vdc	A virtual datacenter attached to an organization
vcloud:lr. vdcstorageClass	A storage profile attached to a virtual datacenter
vcloud:vimserver	A vSphere server (Admin extension object)
vcloud:vm	A virtual machine attached to a vApp

Table 7.4 shows the workflow input for creating a vCloud Director notification subscription.

TABLE 7.4 Workflow Input: Create a vCloud Director Notification Subscription

Input Name	Detail
Workflow	The workflow to start when getting a message that matches all the previous filters

If the workflow has input parameters that match the name or type of the objects referenced in the message, the input parameter is assigned when the workflow is started. This functionality is provided by the Workflow Runner workflow described in Section 7.2.5, "Process Notifications and Trigger Workflows."

7.2.3.2 Workflow Overview

The workflow contains the following elements:

- Create Routing Key
- Configure vCloud Director AMQP Subscription (workflow)
- Set Custom Properties

7.2.3.2.1 Create Routing Key

The filter policy inputs generate a routing key. Routing keys define which messages received by an exchange to route to the queue. The routing key is used when the queue is bound to the exchange. It is a required parameter for the Configure vCloud Director AMQP Subscription workflow. The vCloud notification messages routing key has the following format:

```
<operationSuccess>.<entityUUID>.<orgUUID>.<userUUID>.<subType1>.<subType2>...
  <subTypeN>.
[taskName]
```

Depending on the chosen filter policy inputs, each segment in the routing key generated by the createRoutingKey action can include either a specific type or # as a wildcard character. For additional information on routing keys and exchange routing, see "vCloud Managing and Monitoring Examples" in Chapter 6 and the RabbitMQ Documentation (www.rabbitmq.com/documentation.html).

7.2.3.2.2 Workflow: Configure vCloud Director AMQP Subscription

This workflow configures the AMQP server to handle a given message type. Table 7.5 shows the steps to do this.

TABLE 7.5 Workflow Steps: Configure vCloud Director AMQP Subscription

Step	Detail
1. Get the AMQP configuration.	Get the AMQP configuration from the specified vCloud Director host, including AMQP hostname, port, virtual host, username, exchange name, and SSL setting.
2. Add a broker.	Add an AMQP broker or use an existing one.
3. Declare an exchange.	Declare an exchange for the configured broker. The exchange type is topic, to match the vCloud Director routing format. New exchanges are set to be durable and to not autodelete.
4. Declare a queue.	Declare a queue using the provided queue name. New queues are set to be durable, not exclusive, and to not autodelete.
5. Bind.	Bind the declared queue to the exchange by providing the routing key generated from the input filter policy.
6. Subscribe to queues.	Allows the AMQP plug-in to receive message updates on new messages.

This workflow creates broker and subscription inventory objects that are saved and reloaded automatically when the vCenter Orchestrator server is restarted.

7.2.3.2.3 Set Custom Properties

The subscription object is set with custom properties that match all the input parameter settings. These are used to view the properties of a subscription in a human-readable form and also to pass required parameters to the workflow that the AMQP policy uses.

7.2.4 Workflow: Create a vCloud Director Notification Policy

The Create a vCloud Director Notification Policy workflow (see Figure 7.4) creates a policy listening for new messages of a given subscription.

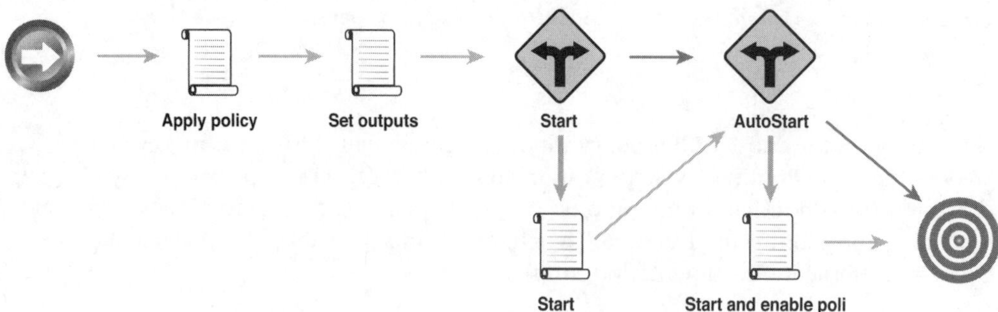

FIGURE 7.4 Workflow Schema: Create a vCloud Director Notification Policy

7.2.4.1 Workflow Inputs

Table 7.6 lists inputs for the Create a vCloud Director Notification Policy workflow.

TABLE 7.6 Workflow Inputs: Create a vCloud Director Notification Policy

Input Name	Detail
Subscription	The subscription that was created with the Create a vCloud Director Notification Subscription workflow
Start right away	Enables the policy to receive messages when submitting the workflow
Autostart	Automatically starts the policy when the vCenter Operations service is started

7.2.4.2 Workflow Steps

1. Create a policy from the Handle vCloud Director Message Notifications policy template included in the package, and set the subscription to which this policy should apply. The policy has the same name as the subscription name.
2. Start the policy if the Start Right Away option was selected.
3. Set the policy to start automatically when the server starts if the Autostart option was selected.

After it is submitted, the policy is displayed in the Policy tab, where it can be stopped or started. The policy also provides logs of the messages received for that subscription.

7.2.5 Process Notifications and Trigger Workflows

The Handle vCloud Director Message Notifications policy (see Figure 7.5) and the Workflow Runner workflow (see Figure 7.6) elements from the package process incoming messages and trigger workflows.

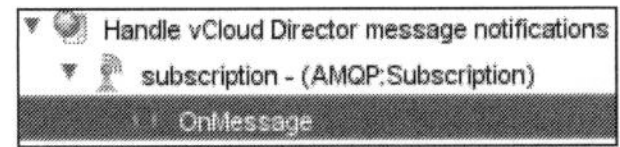

FIGURE 7.5 Policy Element: Handle vCloud Director Message Notifications

The AMQP plug-in provides the capability to add a policy element to a policy with a type of AMQP:subscription and an OnMessage trigger event. The Handle vCloud Director Message Notifications policy is set up to start a workflow that processes a received message. The policy uses a script to start the Workflow Runner workflow (see Figure 7.6), with the subscription object that received the message and the message body passed in as input parameters.

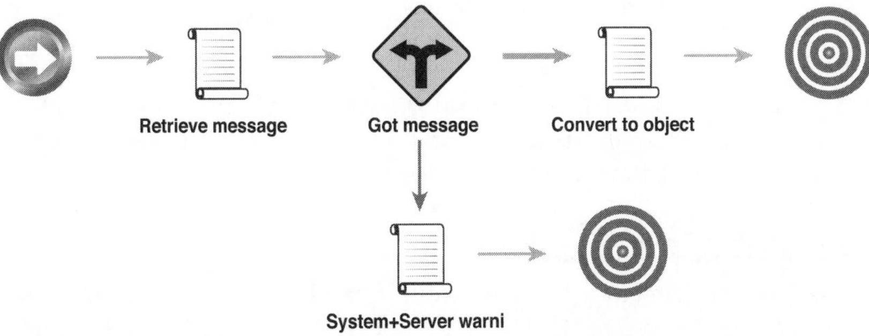

FIGURE 7.6 Workflow Schema: Workflow Runner

The Workflow Runner workflow has the following main steps:

1. Read properties of the subscription.
2. Convert message contents into objects.

One parameter passed to this workflow is the subscription object that received the message. The Create a vCloud Director Notification Subscription workflow sets custom properties on the subscription objects that it creates. One custom property set on the subscription is the workflow to trigger. Another custom property is the vCloud Director host that published the message.

The Workflow Runner workflow reads these custom properties to determine which workflow to trigger in response to the received message and which parameters to pass in to the workflow. Using the vCloud Director host custom property, the Workflow Runner converts the references in the message received by the subscription into objects that match input parameters for the workflow. Finally, the Workflow Runner triggers the workflow.

Because the Workflow Runner can process any type of message, it can set various input parameters. Table 7.7 describes the input parameter types that the Workflow Runner can set.

TABLE 7.7 Input Parameter Types Set by Workflow Runner

Parameter Type	Requirement
Organization	Input must be of type vcloud:Organization.
Notification type	Input must to be of type vcloud:EventType.
Operation success	Input must be specifically named operationSuccess.
User	Input must be of type vcloud:User.
Entity	Input must be of one of the types listed in Table 7.3 for the example named entityCatalog and/or with a type of vcloud:Catalog.
TaskOwner	Input must be of one of the types listed in Table 7.3, for the example named taskOwnerCatalog and/or with a type of vcloud:Catalog.
BlockingTask	Input must be of type vcloud:BlockingTask.
Task	Input must be of type vcloud:Task.

The consumed message can be produced by a vCloud Director notification or a vCloud Director blocking task. The notification triggers a workflow after an event happens. The blocking task triggers a workflow before an event happens.

7.2.6 Triggered Workflow Examples

Examples of workflows to be triggered by the notifications and blocking tasks are provided as part of the package and are located in the PSO/vCloud Director notifications/Workflow samples to be triggered by the policies folder. Table 7.8 shows these workflow samples.

TABLE 7.8 Workflow Samples to Be Triggered

Workflow	Description
Log All	Log all the output parameters passed by Workflow Runner. This is useful to check what information can be obtained from a given event, to create a workflow with the matching inputs.
Approve vApp (Simple)	Used for handling the Instantiate vApp from Template blocking task.
Approve vApp (AD)	Used for handling the Instantiate vApp from Template blocking task. (Supplies the capability to add a computer account to an organization unit in Active Directory that matches the vCloud Director organization name.).
Customize VM Names and IP	Upon deployment of a new vApp, sets custom vApp virtual machine names and IP address. Used for handling the Instantiate vApp from Template blocking task.
Approve Build vApp	Used for handling the Build New vApp blocking task.
Approve Add Move or Delete VM from vApp	Used for handling the Add, Move, or Delete Virtual Machine from vApp blocking task.
Approve Modify VM Configuration	Used for handling the Modify Virtual Machine Configuration blocking task.
Approve Delete vApp	Used for handling the Delete vApp blocking task.

To use the approval workflows, you must first run the Customization Config workflow in the PSO/vCloud Director notifications/Install – Config folder. This workflow creates or updates a configuration element named vCloud Director vApp approval. It provides the following configuration settings:

- General settings: Rejects email template content.
- Approval information:
  - Option to have organization administrators be the approvers
  - LDAP group for the approvers
  - Organizations that do not require approval
- Workflow settings:
  - Number of hours before sending the last notice
  - Blocking task default timeout (in days)
- Active Directory Organization Unit: Parent organization units for creating new organization units

7.2.6.1 Example of a Workflow Approval: Approve vApp (Simple)

The Approve vApp (Simple) workflow (see Figure 7.7) is a good example of the different mechanisms involved in gathering information from blocking tasks, making decisions, and then taking action.

The Workflow Runner workflow automatically populates the input parameters listed in Table 7.9.

TABLE 7.9 Workflow Inputs: Approve vApp (Simple)

Parameter	Detail
vApp	The vApp to be approved
user	The user who provisioned the vApp
blockingTask	The blocking task for the vApp instantiation

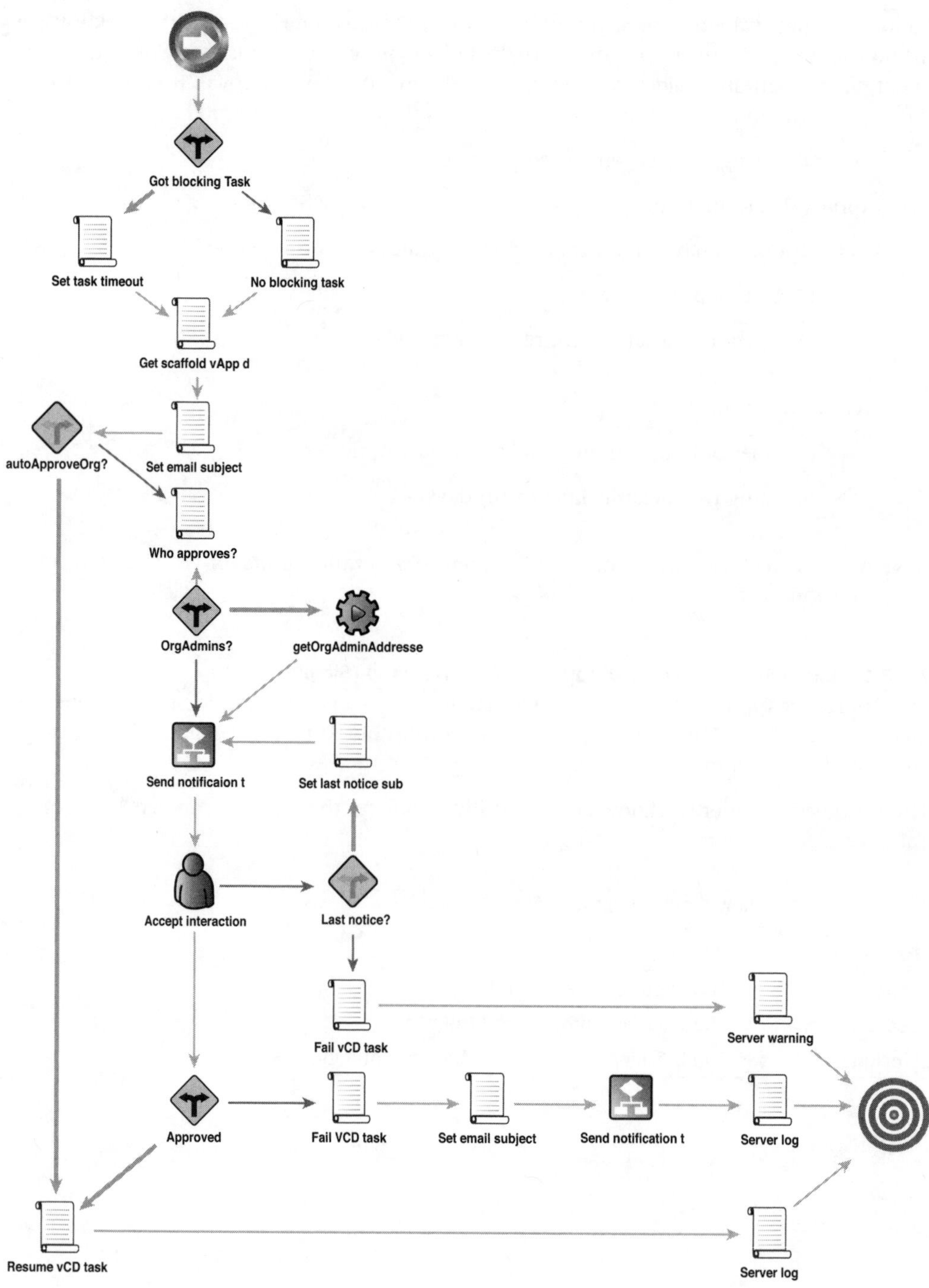

FIGURE 7.7 Workflow Schema: Approve vApp (Simple)

7.2.6.1.1 Workflow Steps

1. Change the blocking task timeout to the one set in the configuration (to avoid the blocking task timing out before it can be handled).
2. Get as much information as possible on the vApp and its child virtual machines. Because the vApp does not yet exist, its object might not contain all the expected information. This information is compiled in a content attribute.
3. Set an email subject to "vApp Request [vAppName] has been requested by user [username]".
4. Determine whether this organization was set for autoapproval. If so, resume the blocking task.
5. If the organization is not set for autoapproval, set the approvers (either a single email, or set it to use the organization administrators, and get their email addresses).
6. Send a notification email for the approval. The approval can be done from the vCenter Orchestrator client or the vSphere Web Client.
7. Generate a user interaction waiting for approval.
8. Send a last notice email if the user interaction times out. Fail the blocking task if the last notice email was previously sent.
9. If the user interaction is approved, resume the blocking task. Otherwise, fail the blocking task.

The other approval workflows are built on the same base.

7.2.6.1.2 Error Handling

Avoid a looping situation in which the triggered workflow generates a message that triggers the workflow again. Different techniques can help in avoiding this problem:

- The workflow might have started the vCloud operation using a different user, so the triggered workflow should resume the blocking task when the user configured for vCenter Orchestrator in vCloud Director is used.
- Use metadata to set a defined key/value pair on the task that should be resumed if blocked, and check incoming tasks for it.

The package also contains a helper category that contains the following useful workflows:

- **Abort, fail, or resume all blocking tasks:** Allows unblocking of all tasks for a given vCloud Director host at the same time
- **Remove all AMQP brokers:** Removes all brokers that have been added in the vCenter Orchestrator inventory
- **Remove a vCloud Director notification subscription:** Deletes a subscription and all its queues

7.3 Automated Import of Virtual Machines to vCloud Director

The vCloud Director UI allows the import of vSphere virtual machines as a vApp to an organization virtual datacenter. After importing, additional configuration tasks are required for these virtual machines to operate, such as connecting them to the appropriate networks. This process involves several steps for each virtual machine. In the private vCloud context, importing many virtual machines in a short time is not possible without providing some automation.

The following implementation of workflows enables the processing of many imports and configuration:

- Selecting a vCenter resource pool or virtual machine folder that contains virtual machines
- Creating vCloud Director external networks and organization virtual datacenter networks required for the virtual machines that the resource pool or virtual machine folder contains
- Importing each virtual machine as a vApp
- Configuring the virtual machine network cards with a network directly connected to the created organization virtual datacenter network
- Powering on the vApp

7.3.1 Prerequisites

The Mass VM Import package leverages the following components:

- vCenter Orchestrator 5.1 Server
- vCenter Orchestrator 5.1 Client
- vCloud Director 5.1
- vSphere 5.1 Server
- vCenter Orchestrator vCloud Director 5.1 plug-in

Before being imported, the source virtual machines must be powered off.

vCloud Director has specific configuration requirements to support the use of this package:

- The vCenter managing the virtual machines to be imported must be attached only to the vCloud host in which the virtual machines are to be imported.
- A provider virtual datacenter must be created in the same vCenter, to enable virtual machines to be reconnected to their original networks.
- The provider virtual datacenter should be linked to a resource pool from the same cluster as the one where the virtual machines are hosted, to avoid cluster-to-cluster migrations and provide network consistency. Preferably, it should also use a storage profile containing the datastores used by the virtual machines, to avoid datastore-to-datastore migrations.
- vCloud Director should be configured with at least one organization, and its organization virtual datacenter should be partitioned from the created provider virtual datacenter. Optionally, the organization virtual datacenter can have organization virtual datacenter networks of type Direct connected to external networks using the same vCenter networks and distributed virtual port groups as the one connected to the virtual machines being imported.

7.3.2 Usage

Because these workflows can potentially be used on a very large number of virtual machines, it is recommended to perform import tests on a small number of test virtual machines, to confirm that the import process is working as expected and tune the parameters.

For example, moving the virtual machines can improve the process time dramatically if the virtual machines do not need to be migrated, but it mitigates recoverability. The optimum number of concurrent imports changes depending on the vSphere infrastructure.

7.3.3 Workflow Folders

The content for this example is in the com.vmware.coe.vcd51.import.vcenterVMs.package file.

The end-user-facing workflows are located in the PSO/Import VMs in vCloud folder.

The technical workflows started by the end-user workflows are located in the PSO/Import VMs in vCloud/Helpers folder.

7.3.4 Choose Virtual Machines to Import

The Import a Resource Pool VMs to a Virtual Datacenter (see Figure 7.8) and Import a Folder Virtual Machines to a Virtual Datacenter (see Figure 7.9) workflows are the two end-user-facing workflows that import virtual machines as vApps. They can be started from the vCenter Orchestrator client or from the vSphere Web Client. It is also possible to configure the vSphere Web Client to make these workflows display in a contextual menu on a resource pool or virtual machine folder directly in the vSphere inventory.

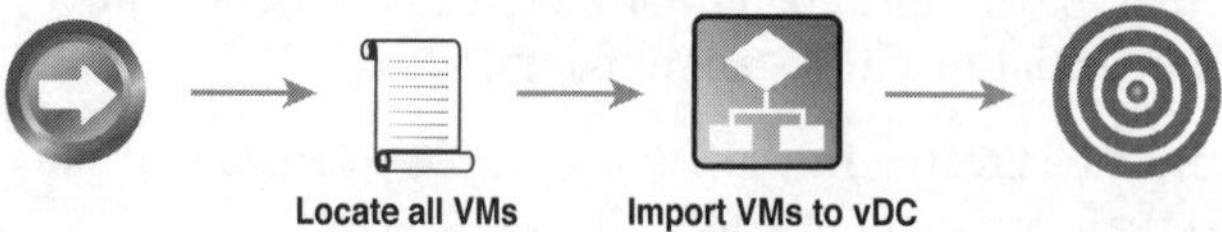

FIGURE 7.8 Workflow Schema: Import a Resource Pool VMs to a virtual data center

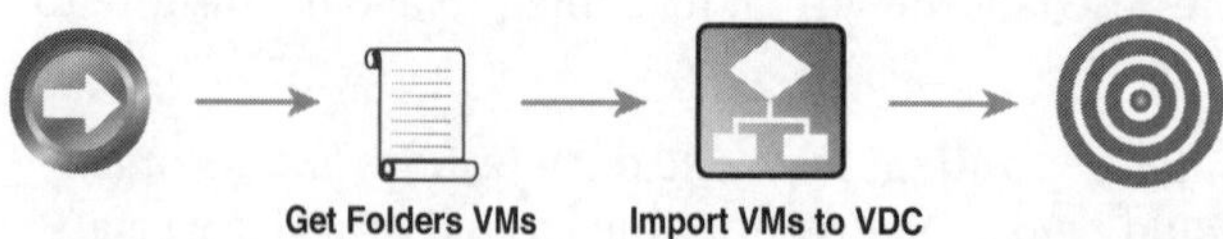

FIGURE 7.9 Workflow Schema: Import a Folder Virtual Machines to a Virtual Datacenter

7.3.4.1 Workflow Inputs and Outputs

The Import a Resource Pool VMs to a Virtual Datacenter and Import a Folder Virtual Machines to a Virtual Datacenter workflows have nearly identical inputs. The destination and options sections are identical, and the source section varies based on the selected workflow, as follows:

- Source:
  - **Virtual Machine folder or resource pool:** The vCenter container for the virtual machines to be imported (mandatory input).
  - **Include Subfolders or Include VMs from Child Resource Pools:** Include virtual machines in subcontainers recursively.
- Destination:
  - **Virtual datacenter:** The created vApp is placed in this datacenter (mandatory input)
  - **Storage profile:** If set, the vApp is placed on the datastores defined in the specified storage profile.

- Options:
  - **Import VMs with Networks That Cannot Be Reconnected:** If set to No, the virtual machines that have networks with no organization virtual datacenter network mapping to an external network are not imported. If set to Yes, these virtual machines are imported and have network cards that are not connected to any network.
  - **Deploy the vApp:** Configure the virtual machines to be powered on.
  - **Power On the vApp:** Start the virtual machines in the vApp.
  - **Move VMs:** Migrate virtual machines instead of making a copy. Setting this option to Yes dramatically reduces the duration of the import when the virtual machine is not moving to a new datastore. Setting this option to No makes a copy of the original virtual machine, enabling you to revert back using the original virtual machine in case an issue arises with the imported one.
  - **Number of Concurrent Imports:** Involves the number of imports started from vCloud Director in parallel. Because vCenter can run a number of tasks issued from different imports, this can speed up the overall import process. If the value is set too high, it either slows disk accesses or does not make any changes because vCenter queues the additional operations.

The workflow outputs are vApps; the vCloud vApps result from the import of the vCenter virtual machines.

7.3.4.2 Workflow Steps

The workflows are mainly wrappers that simplify the virtual machine selection. They have nearly identical steps:

- Get all the virtual machines from the resource pool or virtual machine folder (including child virtual machines, if the option was set).
- Start the Import VMs to VDC workflow, with all the inputs passed in as parameters—with the exception of the virtual machine container (virtual machine folder or resource pool), which is replaced by the list of virtual machines.

7.3.5 Workflow: Import VMs to VDC

The Import VMs to VDC workflow (see Figure 7.10) prepares the inputs, starts the imports in parallel, and reports on the imports when finished.

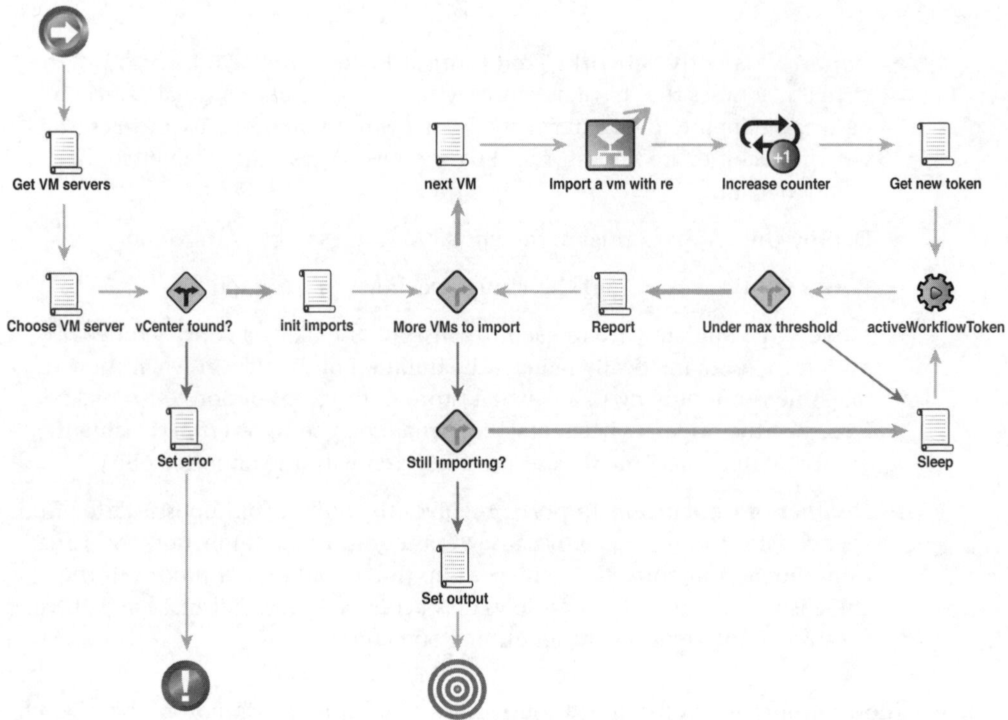

FIGURE 7.10 Workflow Schema: Import VMs to VDC

7.3.5.1 Workflow Inputs

The Import VMs to VDC workflow has the same inputs as the wrapper workflows in Section 7.3.4 but has a list of virtual machines in the source section instead of a resource pool or a virtual machine folder.

7.3.5.2 Workflow Steps

1. Get all the vCloud host's vCenter Server systems.
2. Find the vCenter Server system that hosts the virtual machines to import.
3. Prepare the main loop for starting individual virtual machine import.
4. For each virtual machine, start the Import a VM with Remapping Networks workflow.
5. Check on the number of concurrent workflows started. If less than or equal to the number of concurrent import, determine whether any have completed, and report on the status. If there are more virtual machines to import, import a new virtual machine. If not, sleep 10 seconds before checking again on the number of concurrent workflows started.
6. After all imports have been started, wait until they are all completed.
7. Set the vApps output.

7.3.5.3 Error Handling and Logs

If the vCenter hosting the virtual machines to be imported is not found, fail the workflow with the error "vCenter [vCenter name] must be added to vCloud Director [vCloud url]".

- When a virtual machine import completes successfully: "Import of VM [VM name] completed".
- When a virtual machine import fails: "Import of VM [VM name] failed".
- When a virtual machine import is cancelled: "Import of VM [VM name] cancelled".

Errors and reported information are written in the workflow's events for logging purposes.

7.3.6 Workflow: Import a VM with Remapping Networks

The Import a VM with Remapping Networks workflow (see Figure 7.11) is the core workflow that does the import and network reconfiguration. This workflow's executions provide technical details on the import operations.

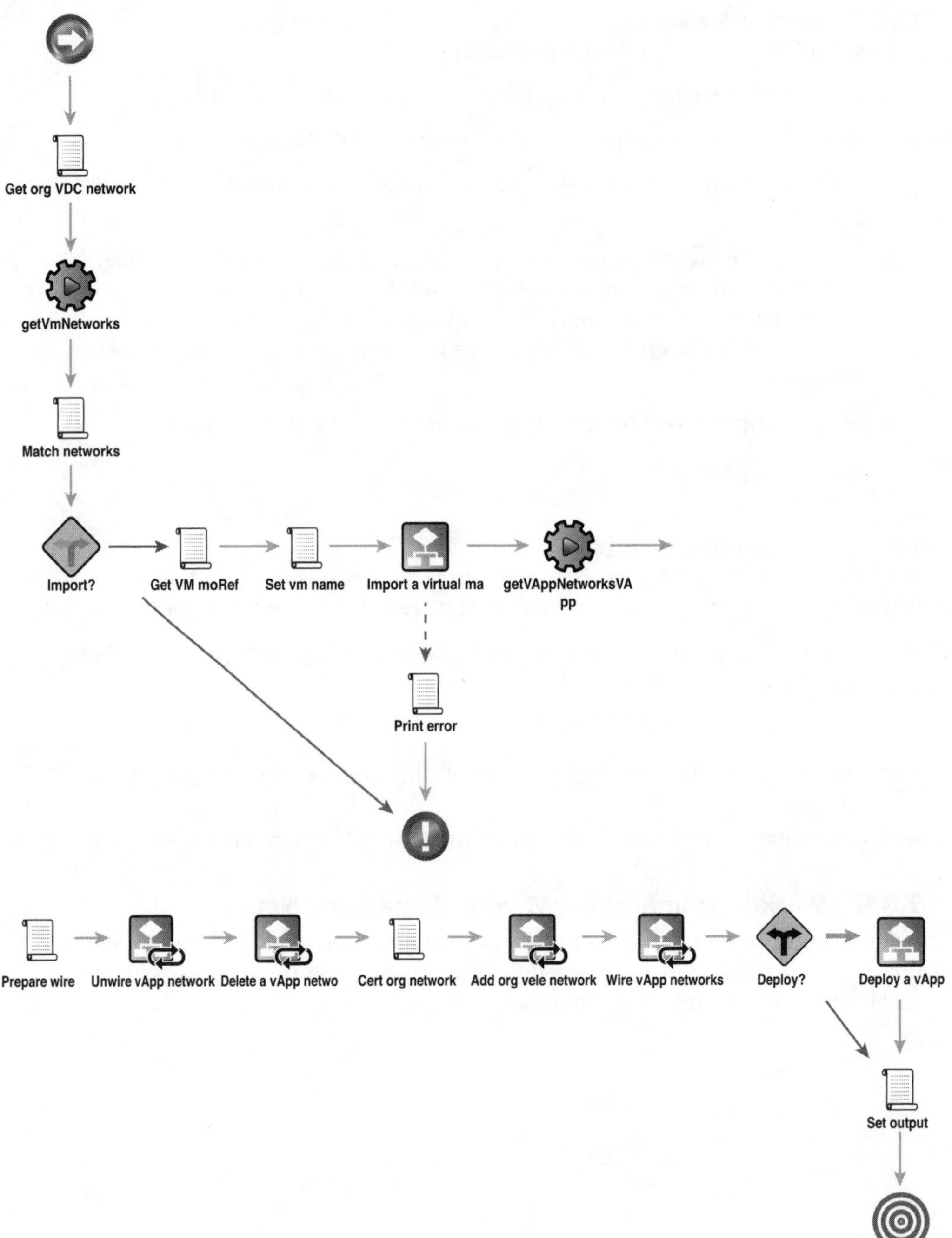

FIGURE 7.11 Workflow Schema: Import a VM with Remapping Networks

NOTE

The Prepare Wire element follows the getVAppNetworksVApp element in the workflow schema.

7.3.6.1 Workflow Inputs

Table 7.10 shows the workflow inputs to import a VM with a remapping of networks.

TABLE 7.10 Workflow Inputs: Import a VM with Remapping Networks

Parameter	Description
server	The vCenter Server system that was found hosting these virtual machines
vdc	The destination virtual datacenter
storageProfile	The storage profile, if any was selected
powerOn	Power on the vApp
deploy	Deploy the vApp to be powered on
moveSource	Move the virtual machine or clone it
vCenterVm	The virtual machine to be imported
importWithoutNetworkMapping	Import the virtual machine if some of its networks have no organization virtual datacenter network connected to the external network that matches the virtual machine network

7.3.6.2 Workflow Steps

1. Create a mapping to associate organization virtual datacenter networks to external network references.
2. Create a mapping to associate virtual machine network references to a network adapter number.
3. Create a mapping to associate virtual machine networks references to the organization virtual datacenter networks, using the mappings in the first two steps.
4. If all the virtual machine networks are not successfully mapped to an organization virtual datacenter network, and if the importWithoutNetworkMapping option is not set, the workflow fails. Otherwise, it continues.
5. Get the vCenter virtual machine reference.
6. Set the vApp name, virtual machine name as the same as the imported virtual machine. Set the description as Imported by vCO [Date and Time].
7. Run the library workflow Import a Virtual Machine As a vApp.
8. Get the vApp networks.
9. Get the virtual machine in the vApp, and get the network card adapters and the name of the organization virtual datacenter networks to which it should be linked.

10. For each network adapter, disconnect the virtual machine from the vApp networks created by vCloud Director during import by running a simplified version of the library workflow Wire a Virtual Machine Network.

11. Delete existing vApp networks by running the Delete a vApp Network library workflow.

12. Get the list of unique organization networks that need to be added to the vApp as vApp networks from the virtual machine networks references to the organization virtual datacenter networks mapping.

13. Add these vApp networks by running a simplified version of the library workflow Add a vApp network.

14. For each network adapter, connect the virtual machine to the newly created vApp networks by running a simplified version of the library workflow Wire a Virtual Machine Network.

15. If the Deploy option was set to Yes, deploy the vApp by passing the powerOn parameter. Otherwise, skip the deploy process.

16. Set the vApp output.

7.3.7 Create vCloud Director Networks Workflows

The Create External Networks and Organization VDC Networks from Resource Pool VMs (see Figure 7.12) and Create External Networks and Organization VDC Networks from a VM Folder (see Figure 7.13) workflows create network objects in vCloud Director.

Reconnecting the virtual machines to their networks requires creating an external network and a virtual datacenter network. These two end-user-facing workflows require user interaction to configure specific external network settings.

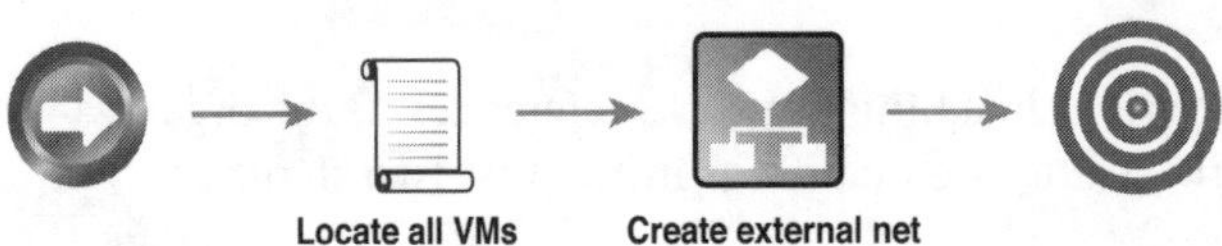

FIGURE 7.12 Workflow Schema: Create External Networks and Organization VDC Networks from Resource Pool VMs

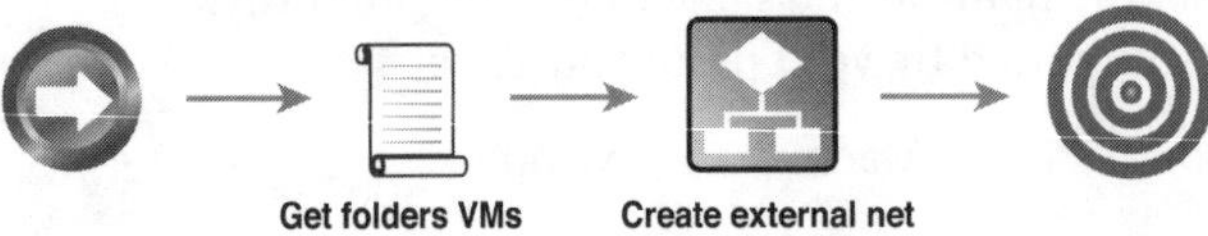

FIGURE 7.13 Workflow Schema: Create External Networks and Organization VDC Networks from a VM Folder

7.3.7.1 Workflow Inputs

These workflows have a nearly identical set of inputs. The destination section is identical, and the source section varies based on the selected workflow:

- Source:
  - **Virtual Machine folder or Resource pool:** This is the vCenter container for the virtual machines to be imported (mandatory input)
  - **Include Subfolders or Include VMs from Child Resource Pools:** Include virtual machines in subcontainers recursively.
- Destination:
  - **Virtual Data Center:** The created vApp is placed in this datacenter (mandatory input).

7.3.7.2 Workflow Steps

These workflows are mainly wrappers that simplify the selection of virtual machines. They have the same steps:

1. Get all the virtual machines—including child virtual machines, if the option was set—from the resource pool or virtual machine folder.
2. Start the Create External Networks and Organization VDC Networks from VMs List workflow, and pass all the inputs except the VM container parameter as input parameters.
3. Replace the VM container parameter with a list of virtual machines.

7.3.8 Workflow: Create External Networks and Organization VDC Networks from VMs List

The Create External Networks and Organization VDC Networks from VMs List workflow (see Figure 7.14) prepares the inputs and starts the workflow that creates the external networks and matching organization virtual datacenter networks.

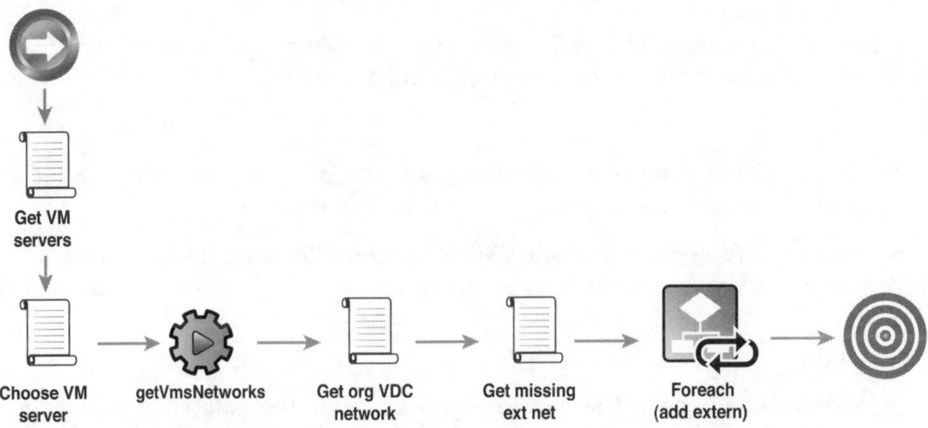

FIGURE 7.14 Workflow Schema: Create External Networks and Organization VDC Networks from VMs List

7.3.8.1 Workflow Inputs

Table 7.11 shows the workflow inputs for creating external networks and organization VCDC networks from the list of virtual machines.

TABLE 7.11 Workflow Inputs: Create External Networks and Organization VDC Networks from VMs List

Parameter	Description
vdc	The destination virtual datacenter
vCenterVmsToImport	The list of virtual machines

7.3.8.2 Workflow Steps

1. Get all the vCloud host's vCenter Server systems.
2. Find the vCenter Server system that hosts the virtual machines to import.
3. Get the list of all virtual machines network references.
4. Get the list of the external networks references that back the organization virtual datacenter networks.
5. Match the two lists to find the external networks that should be created.
6. For each of these, run the Add External Network and Organization Virtual Datacenter Network workflow.

7.3.9 Workflow: Add External Network and Org VDC Network

Add External Network and Org VDC Network (see Figure 7.15) is the core workflow that creates the external networks and matching organization virtual datacenter networks. This workflow is started by the Create External Networks and Org VDC Networks from VMs List workflow.

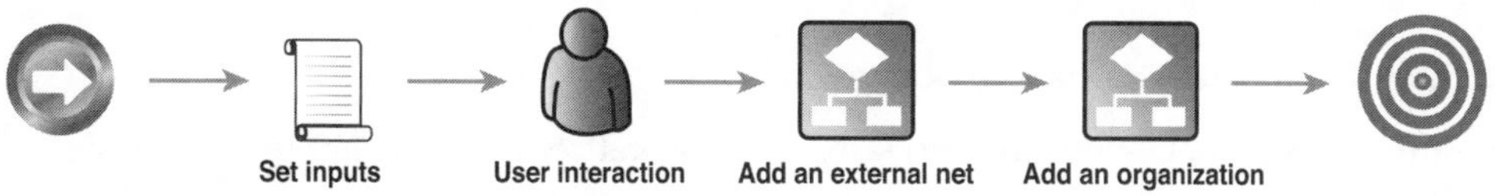

FIGURE 7.15 Workflow Schema: Add External Network and Org VDC Network

7.3.9.1 Workflow Inputs

Table 7.12 shows the workflow inputs for adding an external network and an organization VDC network.

TABLE 7.12 Workflow Inputs: Add External Network and Org VDC Network

Parameter	Description
networkName	The name for the external network
vdc	The destination virtual datacenter
vimServer	The vCenter Server system managing the network to be used for the external network
networkPortgroupMoRef	The reference to the vCenter network or DV port group to create the external network

7.3.9.2 Workflow Steps

1. Set the inputs for the library workflows, such as vCloud Director host, network names, and descriptions, and set whether the network is port group based.
2. Invoke a user interaction with the following inputs:
   - External network name and description (default name and description provided, but names can be edited).
   - External network specification, including:
   - Network mask (mandatory)
   - Default gateway (mandatory)
   - Primary DNS
   - Secondary DNS
   - DNS suffix

- Address pool for static IP allocation (mandatory)
- Organization virtual datacenter network:
- Name
- Description
- Whether to share this network with other virtual datacenters

3. Run the Add an External Network workflow from the library.
4. Run the Add an Organization VDC Network workflow from the library.

User interaction is needed because some of the parameters, such as the IP address pool, cannot be determined automatically.

7.4 vCloud vApp Provisioning

The Custom Deploy vApp workflow is an example of a custom workflow built from library items and additional scripting. It provides a single-call workflow that is capable of instantiating a vApp template from vCloud Director and performing a number of operations on the resulting vApp before actually deploying and powering it on.

These operations include the following:

1. Check the organization for a vApp name to see if it already exists in any virtual datacenters. If so, append the number until it is unique.
2. Instantiate, but do not deploy or power on immediately.
3. Add an organization virtual datacenter network, if needed.
4. Apply a custom naming convention to each virtual machine in the vApp.
5. Base the virtual machine name on the vApp name.
6. Customize the guest OS customization script.
7. Specify an IP address for the virtual machine.
8. Create a computer account in a specific organization unit (OU) of Active Directory.
9. Add a specified domain/user to the local administrators group.
10. Connect the virtual machine to the network.
11. Change the system hard disk size.
12. Add an extra disk to the virtual machine.
13. Modify the virtual machine CPU count.
14. Modify the virtual machine memory.
15. Deploy the vApp.

Figure 7.16 illustrates the Custom Deploy vApp workflow.

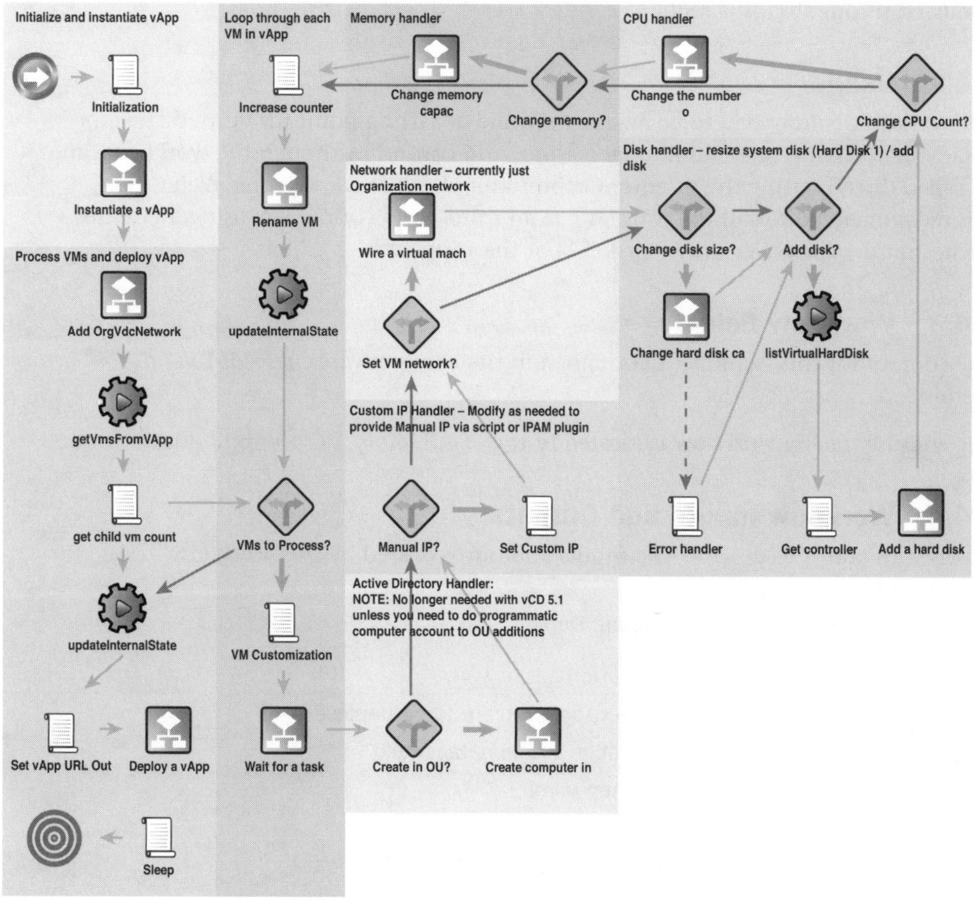

FIGURE 7.16 Workflow Schema: Custom Deploy vApp

7.4.1 Prerequisites

The Custom Deploy vApp package uses the following components:

- vCenter Orchestrator 5.1
- vCloud Director 5.1
- vCloud Director 5.1 plug-in for vCenter Orchestrator
- Active Directory plug-in for vCenter Orchestrator

A functional vCloud Director environment should be available with one or more vApp templates that contain at least one Windows virtual machine. All should be configured as discussed throughout this section.

7.4.2 Usage

The workflow is intended to be an example and a starting point for vCloud Director deployments that require additional features and control. Although the workflow can be called directly using the vCenter Orchestrator client or the vCenter Web Client, it is recommended to call the workflow from third-party connectors using a vCenter Orchestrator web service (SOAP or REST) or the vSphere Web Client.

7.4.3 Workflow Folders

The content for this example is contained in the com.vmware.coe.vcd51.vapp.customdeploy.package file.

The end-user-facing workflow is located in the PSO/Library/VCD/vApp folder.

7.4.4 Workflow Inputs and Outputs

Tables 7.13 and 7.14 describe the inputs and outputs used by this workflow.

TABLE 7.13 Workflow Inputs: Custom Deploy vApp

Parameter	Description
vappTemplate	Source vApp template to be deployed.
vdc	Destination virtual datacenter.
name	New vApp name.
description	vApp description.
runtimeLeaseHours	Number of hours for the runtime lease.
storageLeaseHours	Number of hours for the storage lease.
connectVMtoNetwork	Whether to connect the virtual machine(s) to a network.
vmNetwork	Network to which virtual machines should be connected.
ipAddressAllocationMode	IP address allocation type, such as manual, DHCP, or pool.
vmIP	Static IP address manually assigned if IP address allocation mode is set to Manual and a programmatic method of assigning addresses is not coded.
ou	Organizational unit to which new Windows virtual machine(s) should be added. The ou parameter lets you associate the new virtual machines with an OU domain. This input field is hidden because vCloud Director 5.1 lets you specify an OU in which computer accounts can be created. The input and supporting code is not removed, though, because it can be beneficial for use cases that require programmatically determining the OU for computer accounts.

Parameter	Description
domainName	Domain name of the user account to be added as local administrator of the Windows virtual machine.
username	Username to be added as local administrator of the Windows virtual machine.
postDeployWaitTime	Sleep time at the end of the workflow, to allow for guest OS customization to complete.
changeSystemDiskSize	Whether to change the system disk size. (*Note:* This requires that fast provisioning be disabled on the target virtual datacenter.)
newSystemDiskSize	The new size (in megabytes) if the system disk is to be resized.
addDataDisk	Whether to add another disk.
dataDiskSize	If addDataDisk is true, size of new disk in megabytes.
setCPUCount	Whether to set a new CPU count.
newCPUCount	If setCPUCount is true, the new CPU count.
changeMemory	Whether to set new memory.
newMemorySize	If changeMemory is true, the new memory size in megabytes.
vmnamesAsvappName	Whether virtual machine names should be based on the vApp name. If not, a custom naming convention is used.

TABLE 7.14 Workflow Outputs: Custom Deploy vApp

Parameter	Description
vAppOut	The new vApp created by the workflow
vAppURL	The vCloud Director API URL (or HREF) of the newly created vApp

7.4.5 Workflow Overview

The following sections describe the main steps performed by the Custom Deploy vApp workflow.

7.4.5.1 Initialize and Instantiate

As part of the initialization process, the vApp name is checked for uniqueness. Each vApp must have a unique name within an organization. The Initialization scriptable task builds a list of vApp names that already exist in the organization. The requested vApp name is checked against this list to see whether it is unique. If the name already exists, a numeric value is appended and incremented until a unique variant of the requested name is obtained. After a unique vApp name has been identified, the vApp is instantiated.

When the vApp is instantiated, access to the child virtual machines becomes available. Access to virtual machine objects allows properties and settings of each virtual machine to be modified as desired. Keeping the virtual machines undeployed and powered off allows custom modifications to take place before the vCloud Director Deploy process applies customizations. This piece of the custom workflow uses the vCloud Directory Library workflow Instantiate a vApp Template.

7.4.5.2 Process VMs and Deploy vApp

This section starts by checking whether the organization virtual datacenter network has been added to the vApp and adds it if necessary. This allows for a later step to connect the virtual machine to the network.

Next, the workflow retrieves all the virtual machines from the newly instantiated vApp and prepares a loop to process the virtual machines. After the loop has completed, the internal state of the vApp is updated and the outputs are set. Finally, the vApp is deployed.

The final step of the workflow is to deploy the customized vApp. This last part of the workflow uses the vCloud Director Library workflow named Deploy a vApp. Deploying and powering on the vApp applies the customizations to the guest OS as specified throughout the earlier parts of the workflow. This process can take 10 to 20 minutes to fully complete, so a Sleep box has been added to the end of the workflow to prevent the workflow from actually completing until the specified amount of time (15 minutes, by default) has lapsed. This delay time is available as an input option to the workflow.

7.4.5.3 Loop Through Each VM in the vApp

This section processes the loop through each virtual machine. It checks to see if there are additional virtual machines to process. If there are, it sets the current virtual machine, performs custom naming operations, and passes on to the Active Directory Handler.

7.4.5.3.1 Apply Custom Naming Convention to Each VM in the vApp

At the start of the workflow, especially when being called from the API, the number of child virtual machines is unknown. This makes it quite challenging to provide user-supplied names or other per-VM properties to the virtual machines before deployment. A programmatic method of generating virtual machine names can be developed that matches client requirements. For demonstration purposes, the custom naming convention applied in the example workflow is as follows:

```
<OS Initial><4 digit number><First initial of organization name><First initial of
  virtual datacenter name>
```

In this naming convention, <OS Initial> is either W for Windows or L for non-Windows. The four-digit number begins at 0001 and is incremented if the final virtual machine name is discovered to already exist in the target organization. The final two parts of the name are the upper-case first initial of the organization and the virtual datacenter, respectively. For relevant scripting, see the VM Customization scriptable task of the sample workflow.

7.4.5.3.2 Base VM Name on vApp Name

In many cases when a single virtual machine is all that each vApp contains, it is desirable to give the virtual machine the same name as the vApp. This allows for user-specified names upon request, an option not easily available for multivirtual machine vApps. The example workflow autoadds a numeric suffix to the virtual machine name if the name is found to already exist in the organization. For relevant scripting, see the VM Customization scriptable task of the sample workflow.)

7.4.5.3.3 Customize the Guest OS Customization Script

vCloud Director lets you specify a guest OS customization script on each virtual machine. The custom script runs on the virtual machine upon deployment, after the general Sysprep and hardware customization have taken place. This is similar to the RunOnce commands of a Windows Sysprep operation. Using vCenter Orchestrator, you can establish variables in this customization script to be substituted at workflow runtime. An example of this is demonstrated in Section 7.4.5.3.4, "Add Specified Domain/User to Local Administrators Group." For relevant scripting, see the VM Customization scriptable task of the sample workflow.

7.4.5.3.4 Add Specified Domain/User to Local Administrators Group

You can use the guest OS customization script to add a domain/user account to the Local Administrators group of Windows virtual machines that are joined to a domain.

To add a domain/user account to the Local Administrators group of Windows virtual machines that are joined to a domain:

1. Configure the vCloud Director organizations to Enable Domain Join for Virtual Machines in This Organization, specifying the appropriate domain and credentials.
2. Specify the domain in full format, such as vmware.com, instead of in the NetBIOS form of vmware. This setting is located under the Organization > Administration > Settings > Guest Personalization page of the vCloud Director UI.
3. Prepare the vApp template with one or more Windows virtual machines that have had the Guest OS Customization tab of their properties properly populated. Use the following settings:
   - **Enable Guest Customization:** Selected.
   - **Change SID:** Selected.
   - **Password Reset:** As desired.
   - **Join Domain:** Populated as desired using either the domain configured for the organization or the specified domain and credentials.
   - **An appropriately formatted customization script:** The following is a sample used in a custom workflow:

```
if '%1%' == 'postcustomization' (net localgroup administrators @domain@\\@username@
  /add)
```

The variables @domain@ and @username@ are replaced at workflow execution time. For scripting details, see the VM Customization scriptable task of the sample workflow.

7.4.5.4 Active Directory Handler

Many organizations are looking at vCloud Director for corporate uses where Active Directory is in place and used to apply group policies and permissions. In most cases, the organizations prefer to have new computer accounts created in specific organizational units (OU) instead of the default Computers container to which newly joined computers are added. This piece of the sample workflow uses the Create Computer in Organizational Unit Active Directory plug-in library workflow if an OU is specified and the virtual machine being processed is a Windows virtual machine.

7.4.5.5 Custom IP Handler

When you deploy a single virtual machine with MANUAL IP Addressing Mode, the workflow enables you to specify the static IP address to use. It often is desirable simply to use POOL or DHCP because those methods are safe to use both with virtual machine vApps that use single virtual machines and with those that use multiple virtual machines. The sample workflow codes IP handling for user-specified IP addresses at this time, but you can replace or modify the Scriptable Task handling manual assignment to call a third-party script or IPAM plug-in to retrieve and assign a managed IP address. For scripting details, see the Set Custom IP scriptable task of the sample workflow.

7.4.5.6 Network Handler

The sample workflow provides the option of connecting a virtual machine to an organization network. For demonstration purposes, the first NIC of the virtual machine is connected to the specified network. All virtual machines should have at least one NIC when captured to template. Additionally, when preparing the vApp template for this custom workflow demo, set the network connection to None, and remove any networks in the vApp so that the resulting vApp has a clean networking diagram after the custom deploy. This piece of the sample workflow uses the Wire a Virtual Machine Network vCloud Director Library workflow.

7.4.5.7 Disk Handler

Many organizations require the capability to change their system disk size at deployment time. Although the vCloud Director API does allow for this, and a workflow exists and is incorporated into the sample provided here, it might not be ideal because of the vCloud Director fast provisioning option, which uses linked clones. If fast provisioning is enabled on the virtual datacenter where a vApp is being deployed, and the request specifies resizing the system disk, the workflow is configured to catch the exception generated by the failure to resize the disk, log it, and continue with the next step of the workflow. This piece of the sample workflow uses the Change Hard Disk Capacity vCloud Director Library workflow.

Most virtual machines used as vApp templates have a limited number of base hard disks, where the operating system and base applications are installed. A common request has been the capability to add a disk at the time of request. The sample workflow has this feature built-in. This piece of the sample workflow uses the Add a Hard Disk vCloud

Director Library workflow. The disk, however, is only *presented* to the guest operating system—it is not *partitioned* or *formatted*. This in-guest operation requires additional scripting for the requester to partition and format the new disk as desired.

7.4.5.8 CPU Handler

Base virtual machines might have only one or two CPUs while stored as templates. A common requirement is the capability to modify the CPU count upon initial vApp request. This piece of the sample workflow uses the Change the Number of CPUs vCloud Director Library workflow.

7.4.5.9 Memory Handler

Base virtual machines might have limited memory while stored as templates. A common requirement is the capability to modify the memory upon initial vApp request. This piece of the sample workflow uses the Change Memory Capacity vCloud Director Library workflow.

7.5 Additional Resources

The examples in this chapter are intended to demonstrate some of the capabilities of using orchestration in a vCloud environment. Although they provide a starting point, further exploration and maturation of orchestration within your environment are important elements in its evolution.

The following resources are useful to further explore the capabilities and benefits of orchestration and to facilitate the automation of processes within your environment.

- vCenter Orchestrator Community (http://communities.vmware.com/community/vmtn/server/vcenter/orchestrator).

vCenter Orchestrator has a robust and active online community that can be a helpful resource for additional workflow examples and community-based support for custom workflows that you develop for your environment.

Packages for the workflow examples contained in this document are available for download from http://communities.vmware.com/docs/DOC-20230.

- VMware Solution Exchange (https://solutionexchange.vmware.com/store/category_groups/datacenter/categories/vmware-vcenter-orchestrator)

The VMware Solution Exchange (VSX) is a virtualization and cloud infrastructure marketplace that provides a variety of resources, including vCloud Orchestrator plug-ins. The plug-ins described in this chapter, as well as additional plug-ins that might be useful in your environment, are available for download from the VMware Solution Exchange.

- VMware vCenter Orchestrator Blog (http://blogs.vmware.com/orchestrator)

The official blog for vCenter Orchestrator provides useful information on product releases and usage, including new and updated plug-ins. See the VMware vCenter Orchestrator Blog.

CHAPTER 8
Software Tools

IN THIS CHAPTER

8.1 Overview

V*Mware vCloud Architecture Toolkit Software Tools* provides information about software tools that can be used to support VMware® vCloud® planning, implementation, testing, and maintenance.

- The VMware vCloud Director™ Server Resource Kit software tools are applications developed by VMware engineering teams. You can use them in your vCloud test and development environments to test, automate, and maintain vCloud Director servers. These tools are freely available and can be used by anyone.
- Services automation tools, such as VMware Capacity Planner™, VMware HealthAnalyzer, and VMware Migration Manager™, support delivery of various VMware services by automating aspects of service delivery. These services and tools, which are useful for working with a vCloud solution, are not directly available to customers, but customers can engage VMware Professional Services or partner companies for services that employ the tools. Eligible VMware partners who meet certain criteria, or who purchase a VMware Services Software Solutions subscription (SKU: CON-SSS), can use the services automation tools.

8.1.1 Audience

This document is written for vCloud IT administrators and software developers who are implementing a vCloud computing solution, typically for testing and automating the process of implementing the vCloud software stack. VMware partner consultants who deliver services that employ the use of VMware Services Software Solutions service automation tools should also find it useful.

Administrators should understand how to administer the vCloud Director server and its components, including the following technologies:

- VMware vCenter Server™
- VMware vCloud Director™
- Java
- HyperText Markup Language (HTML)
- eXtensible Markup Language (XML)

In addition, administrators and developers should be familiar with vCloud Director and associated products that comprise the vCloud stack. These include supported data repositories and command-line syntax for the particular shell and platform on which the server is installed. Knowledge of the basic vCloud Director architectural concepts needed to successfully design and deploy a vCloud Director architecture and service is also helpful.

8.1.2 Scope

This reference guide documents only vCloud Director Server Resource Kit and services automation tools. See the VMware product documentation for detailed information about vCloud and vCloud Director.

8.2 VMware vCloud Director Server Resource Kit

The VMware vCloud Director Server Resource Kit includes the following tools:

- vCloud Director Audit
- vCloud Provisioner
- CloudCleaner

8.2.1 vCloud Director Audit

vCloud Director users need to be able to report on vCloud Director infrastructure, producing audit reports on their vCloud Director deployments and returning data in a centralized, easy-to-read report. vCloud Director Audit, based on the vCheck 6 framework from virtu-al.net (http://www.virtu-al.net/featured-scripts/vcheck/), provides vCloud Director audit capabilities as an extensible, plug-in driven solution. vCloud Director Audit works with vCloud Director 1.5.

8.2.1.1 Prerequisites

- VMware vSphere® PowerShell™ 2.0
- vCloud PowerCLI 5.0.1 (or later)

When you install PowerCLI 5.0.1, verify that the vCloud Director PowerCLI option is selected, otherwise the `cmdlets` required by the vCloud Director Audit tool are not made available. This option is not selected by default. The custom setup screen is shown in Figure 8.1.

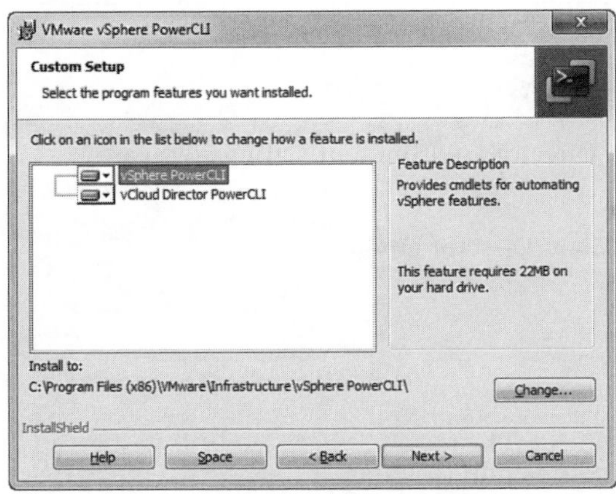

FIGURE 8.1 vSphere PowerCLI Custom Setup screen

8.2.1.2 Setup, Configuration, and Use

To set up, configure, and use vCloud Director Audit:

1. Download vCloud Director Audit from http://www.virtu-al.net/2012/03/13/vcdaudit-for-vcloud-director/.
2. Unzip to a folder. There is no installation process.
3. Edit the `00 Connection Plugin for VCD.ps1` file to set the appropriate credentials for your vCloud environment (see line 19).

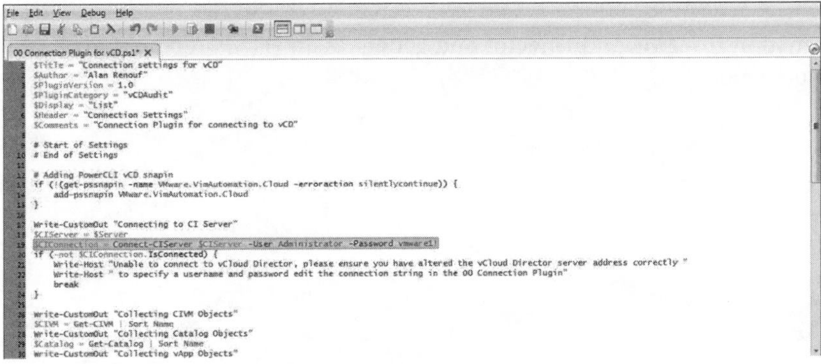

FIGURE 8.2 '00 Connection Plugin for VCD.psl' file

4. From PowerCLI, execute the following command:

```
.\VCDAudit.ps1
```

5. If it is your first time running the application, you are prompted to configure vCloud Director Audit. If you want to reconfigure after the initial setup, add the `-configure` flag to the command-line argument.

```
PS C:\Users\Downloads\vCDAudit> .\vCDAudit.ps1
```

6. Configure the script with your vCloud Director environment settings. You are prompted for the following:

   - IP address or hostname of the vCloud Director environment
   - SMTP server address
   - Email address to which to send reports
   - Subject line for report emails
   - Whether to display reports after completion (true/false)
   - Whether to send an email after the report is completed (true/false)
   - Whether to include the report attachment as an HTML file (true/false)
   - Report title color (HTML RGB)
   - Report heading color (HTML RGB)
   - Report title text color (HTML RGB)
   - Whether to include plug-in runtimes in report (true/false)
   - Whether any plug-ins take longer than n seconds (integer, seconds)

7. From PowerCLI, run vCloud Director Audit:

```
.\VCDAudit.ps1
```

This collects information from vCloud Director and generates an HTML report similar to the following sample report:

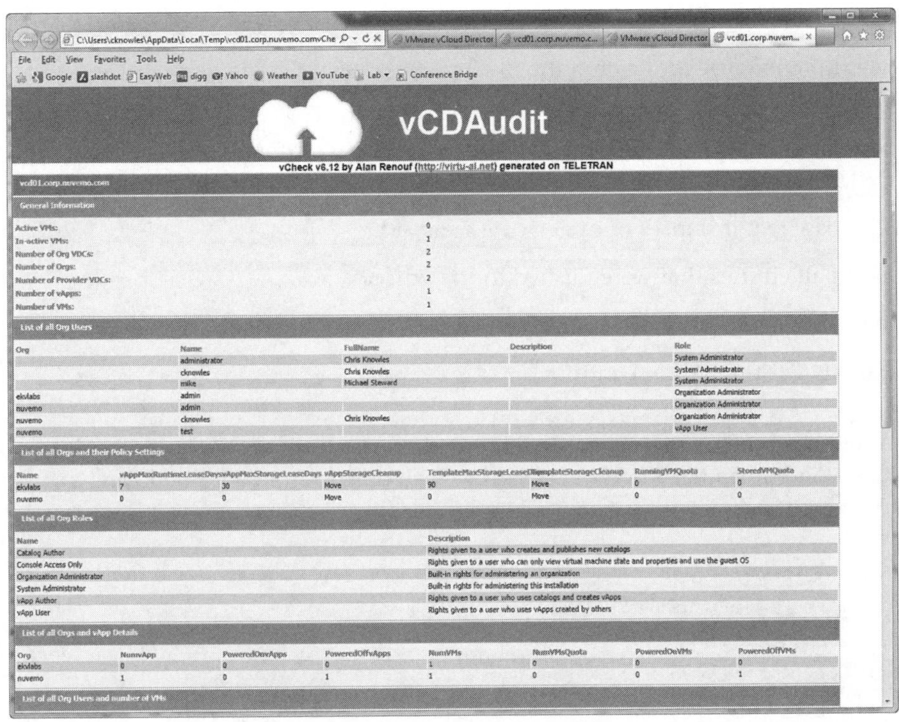

FIGURE 8.3 vCloud Director sample HTML report

8.2.2 vCloud Provisioner

vCloud Provisioner acts as a middle layer that conveys data to and from its business objects model and to and from a vCloud Director instance. An abstraction layer enables a choice between implementations of the communication protocol between the vCloud Provisioner and vCloud Director.

vCloud Provisioner provides a solution for the following problems and tasks:

- Data-driven vCloud provisioning
- Externalization of the vCloud object specifications in provision files
- Abstraction between object specifications and the framework used for communicating with the vCloud
- Loading of object specifications from an active vCloud Director setup
- Comparison of two states of object specifications

vCloud Provisioner includes the following features:

- Provides an interface for vCloud operations so that test cases do not have to be modified when the communication layer is replaced or modified.

- Provides a container for vCloud entities (`CloudProvisionData`).
- Provides functionality for loading the `CloudProvisionData` container, whether from an XML file or directly from a running vCloud.
- Provides functionality for flushing a `CloudProvisionData` container to a vCloud or to an XML format.
- Can compare two instances of `CloudProvisionData`.
- Can clean all entities that were flushed to the vCloud.
- Can append one instance of `CloudProvisionData` to another one.
- Can modify existing vCloud entities.

Figure 8.4 shows a workflow that uses vCloud Provisioner to flush an XML object specification to a vCloud. A similar workflow is used to load objects from a vCloud Director instance into a container.

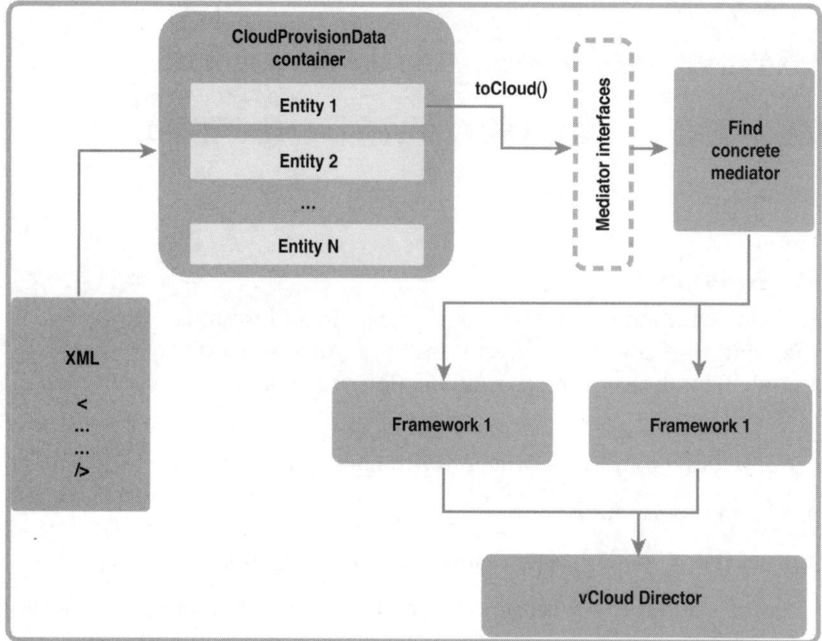

FIGURE 8.4 Workflow for flushing an XML object specification to the vCloud

8.2.2.1 vCloud Provisioner Requirements

- vCloud Provisioner runs on any operating system that has a JRE (Java Runtime Environment) 5.x or later installed.
- vCloud Provisioner depends on the following external JAR files:

  - vcloud-test-backend
  - vcloud-test-util
- To make sure that you have covered all of the dependencies, download the entire vmware-redwood-test.tar.gz archive.

8.2.2.2 Installing vCloud Provisioner

The source code for the vCloud Provisioner framework is part of the `test\qa\vcloud-test-iuc` project in the `com.vmware.vcd.provisioner` package.

You can also use a ready-to-use binary. The `vcloud-test-iuc` JAR file is part of the `vcloud-redwood-test.tar.gz` archive, which also includes all the dependency JAR files.

8.2.2.3 Basic Use of vCloud Provisioner

Example 8.1:

```
<org-network org="org1"
    name="yellow"
    desc="yellow routed network"
    net-pool="network pool 1"
    external-net="external network 1"
    net-config="org-yellow"
    allowed-external-ips="" />
```

Loading object specifications from XML:

```
CloudProvisionData prerequisites = CloudProvisionData.fromXml("network-
prequisities.xml", restServiceBundle);
```

Flushing the object specifications to the cloud:

```
prerequisites.toCloud();
```

8

8.2.2.4 Advanced Use of vCloud Provisioner

Advanced use includes cleaning, comparing two instances of the `CloudProvisionData` container, appending, and modifying.

8.2.2.4.1 Cleaning

You can clean up all entities that were flushed to the vCloud using the following method:

```
CloudProvisionData.cleanUp(boolean onlyOwnedEntities);
```

Use the `onlyOwnedEntities` argument if only the entities that were created from this `CloudProvisionData` should be cleaned.

Example 8.2:

```
// Provision some networks and vApps
```

```
CloudProvisionData pdNewEntities = CloudProvisionData.fromXml("network-new.xml",
restServiceBundle);
try {
  pdNewEntities.toCloud();
  // Verify it works OK
  ....
} finally {
  pdNewEntities.cleanUp();
}
```

8.2.2.4.2 Comparing Two Instances of the CloudProvisionDataContainer

Comparing two instances is useful for tests that need to verify the state of the two vCloud instances, such as before and after an upgrade.

Example 8.3:

```
CloudProvisionData pdBefore = CloudProvisionData.fromXml("network-prequisities.xml",
restServiceBundle);
upgradeToT2(ssh);
CloudProvisionData pdAfter = CloudProvisionData.fromCloud(restServiceBundle);
if (pdAfter.equals(pdBefore) {
// Success
} else {
// FAILURE!
}
```

8.2.2.4.3 Appending Entities

You can append the entities from one `CloudProvisionData` container to another and then operate on the latter.

```
pdFirst.append(pdSecond);
```

8.2.2.4.5 Modifying Entities

You can modify existing entities by using the `modify()` method of individual entities, or the `modify()` method of the `CloudProvisionData` container.

8.2.3 CloudCleaner

VMware vCloud Director works in tandem with vCenter Server to deliver a reliable and efficient vCloud experience for users. Starting with the bottom layer, virtual machines are deployed on VMware ESXi™ hosts. vCenter Server manages the hosts and monitors their usage and capacity. vCloud Director, in turn, manages and abstracts vCenter hardware concepts and concerns so that the user can request resources without concern about where or how they are acquired from the vCloud.

vCloud Director is the layer where organizations, users, vCenter instances, hosts, and other components come together in a vCloud. vCloud Director manages these resources well, and the system administrator can create, add, edit, remove, and destroy vCloud Director entities as needed. However, if you uninstall a vCloud Director, unneeded entities may be left on you vCenter Servers. Use CloudCleaner to clean up these unneeded entities.

CloudCleaner is a Java application, so it runs on Windows, Mac OS X, and any UNIX or Linux platforms that supports Java. When you use the CloudCleaner User Interface (UI) to enter your vCenter IP and credentials, CloudCleaner examines the state of your vCenter and provides a list of entities to be cleaned.

8.2.3.1 CloudCleaner Requirements

- CloudCleaner requires an installed vCloud Director instance.
- Administrator access to at least one of the vCenter Servers.
- CloudCleaner will run on any operating system that has a JRE (Java Runtime Environment) 5.x or later installed.
- CloudCleaner uses the following open source libraries:
- JSch -- Java Secure Channel (http://www.jcraft.com/jsch/)
- VMware VI Java API (vijava) (http://vijava.sourceforge.net/)

8.2.3.2 How CloudCleaner Works

CloudCleaner talks directly to vCenter Server and its ESXi hosts, so it can be run at any time, regardless of the state of vCloud Director. (In fact, CloudCleaner could be used by a vCenter Administrator as an easy way to clean up vCenter servers). It only uses secure connections, and will try to validate host credentials upon first connection.

CloudCleaner uses entity naming and placement on vCenter as the primary means of identifying which items were created by vCloud Director, as opposed to items created on vCenter directly by users. Specifically, it targets:

- Virtual machines
- Resource pools
- Orphaned datastore folders
- Networks
- vCloud Director ESXi host agents

Due to the enormous number of entities potentially needing to be cleaned, CloudCleaner runs up to 2000 simultaneous tasks.

CloudCleaner is safe to use. It displays a preview of the items it selected for removal before making any changes to your systems. CloudCleaner is used internally by VMware development and QA teams to clean hundreds of systems every week.

8.2.3.3 Leftover Entities

The following vCloud Director and vCenter screens illustrate the problem with leftover entities after vCloud Director is removed.

To view leftover entities:

1. Display the vCloud Director UI.

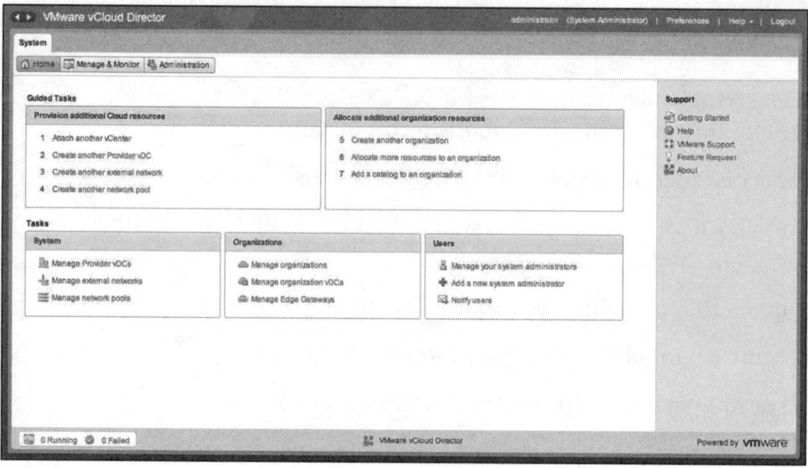

FIGURE 8.5 vCloud Director user interface

2. Go to your organization. In this example, there are four vApps and a few virtual machines in the organization.

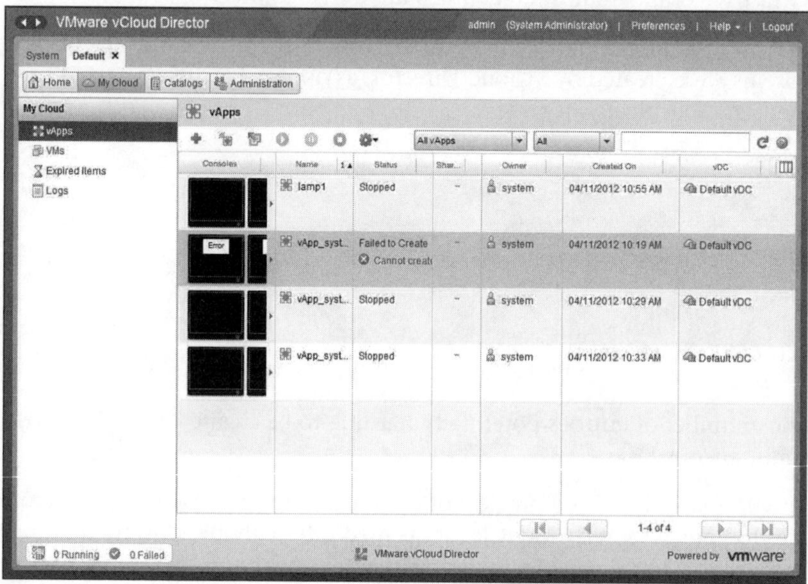

FIGURE 8.6 vCloud Director user interface showing vApps

3. On the **Manage & Monitor** tab, there are entities such as external networks, network pools, and so on.

   If you uninstall and remove vCloud Director, and remove all of the settings and database, your vCenter Servers are left with of all these unneeded artifacts.

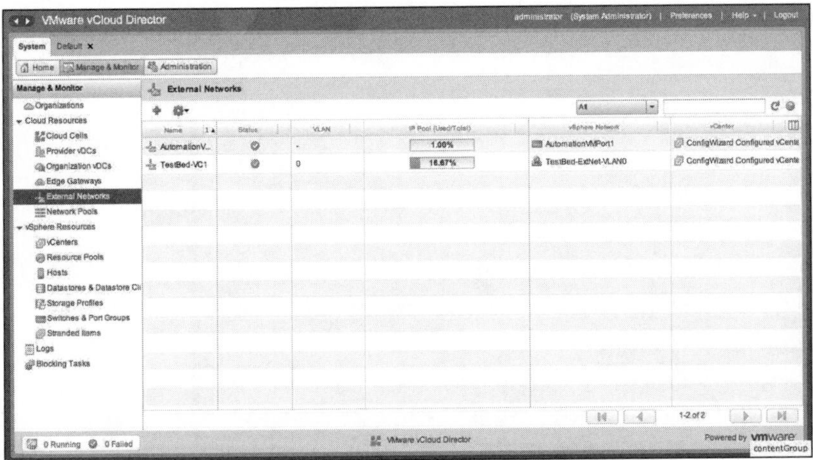

FIGURE 8.7 Manage & Monitor screen showing external networks

4. These entities remain in your vCenter instances even after you have uninstalled and removed vCloud Director.

CloudCleaner cleans up these entities and puts your vCenter Servers back to a clean state. Then, the vCenter Servers can be used with; for example, a new version of vCloud Director, as shown in Figure 8.8.

8

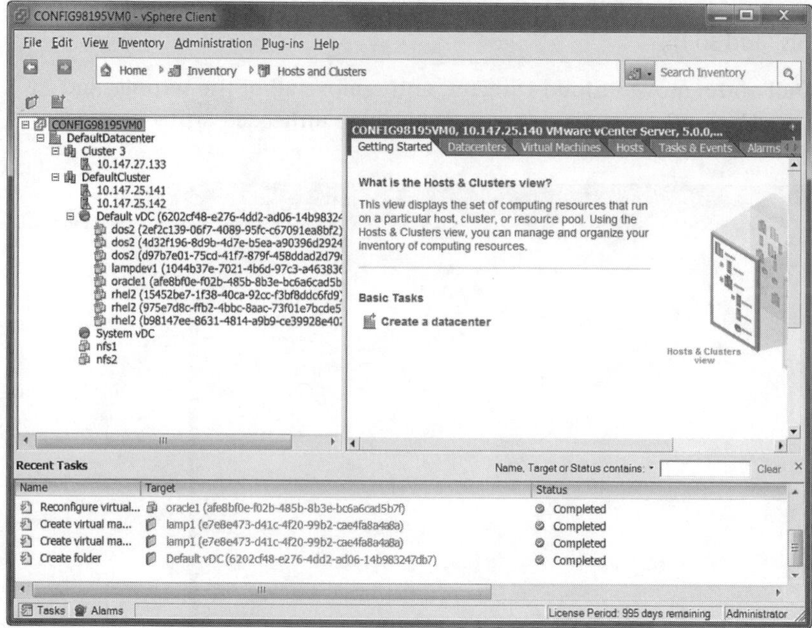

FIGURE 8.8 vSphere client interface after CloudCleaner run

8.2.3.4 Installing CloudCleaner

To install CloudCleaner:

1. Download CloudCleaner from the VMware Labs Flings website:

   http://labs.vmware.com/flings/cloudcleaner

2. Accept the Technical Preview Agreement and click **Download**, as shown in Figure 8.9.

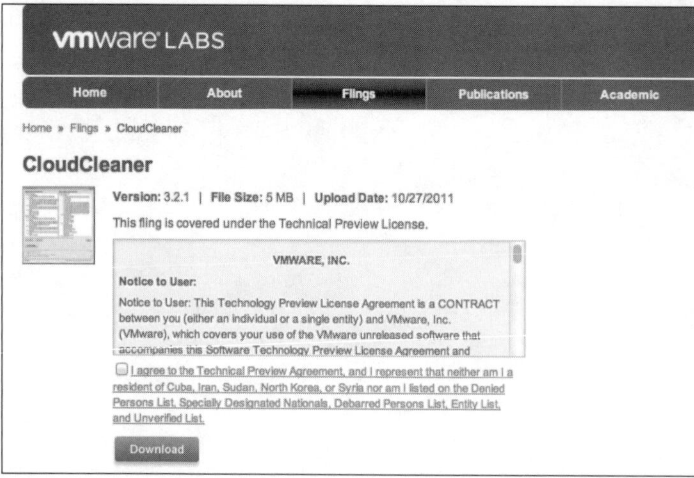

FIGURE 8.9 Technical Preview agreement and Download button

3. After CloudCleaner finishes downloading, the CloudCleaner JAR file is displayed:

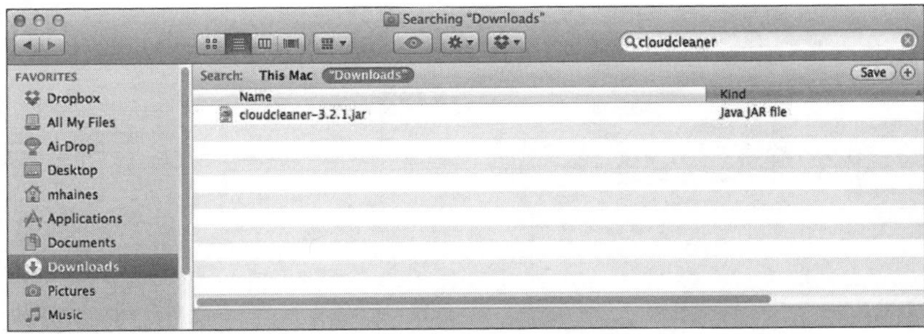

FIGURE 8.10 Download director showing CloudCleaner JAR file

8.2.3.5 Basic Use of CloudCleaner

To use CloudCleaner to clean one or more vCenter Servers:

1. Verify that you downloaded and saved CloudCleaner as a JAR file (*not* a ZIP file).
2. Run CloudCleaner.
3. You can run CloudCleaner from the UI, or in Basic or Advanced mode from the command line.
   - To invoke CloudCleaner from the UI in Windows or Mac OS X, double-click the `cloudcleaner-3.2.1.jar` file. The vCenter Credentials screen is shown in Figure 8.11.

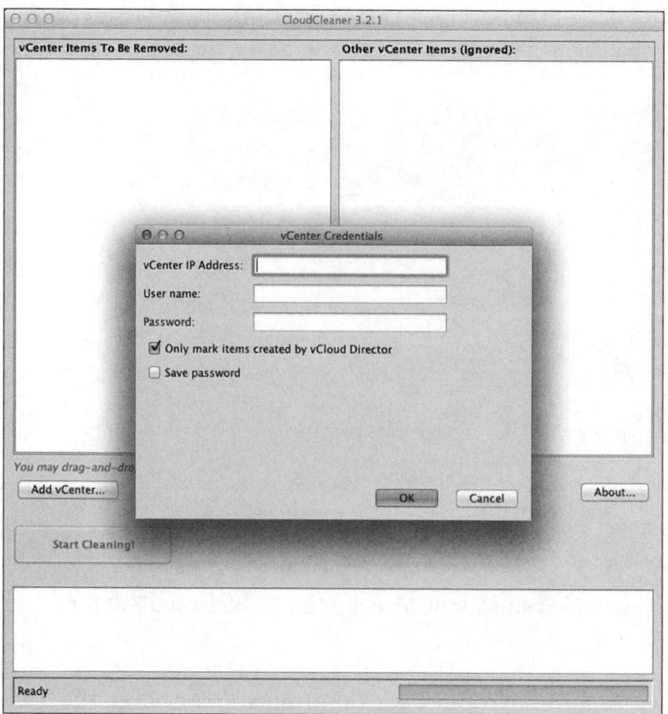

FIGURE 8.11 vCenter Credentials entry screen

- To invoke CloudCleaner for basic use from a command line, run the `cloud-cleaner-3.2.1.jar` command, as shown in the following command output:

```
$ pwd
/Users/mhaines/Downloads/Cloudcleaner
$ ls -l
total 9192
-rw-r—r--@ 1 mhaines  staff  4704257  9 Nov 18:32 cloudcleaner-3.2.1.jar
$ java -jar cloudcleaner-3.2.1.jar
```

For information about advanced command-line options, see Section 8.2.3.6, "Use with Advanced Options."

4. Provide your vCenter credentials. An example is shown in Figure 8.12.
   - Deselect **Only mark items created by vCloud Director** if you want to remove *all* items from your vCenter Server.
   - The default setting marks and removes only items that were created by vCloud Director.
5. Click **OK**.

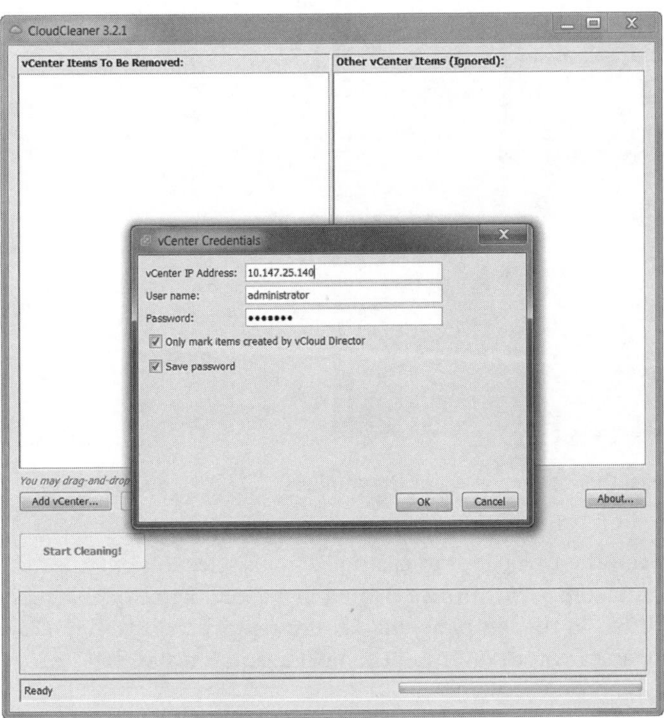

FIGURE 8.12 Example entry for vCenter Credentials

6. After authenticating, the dialog is displayed in Figure 8.13.

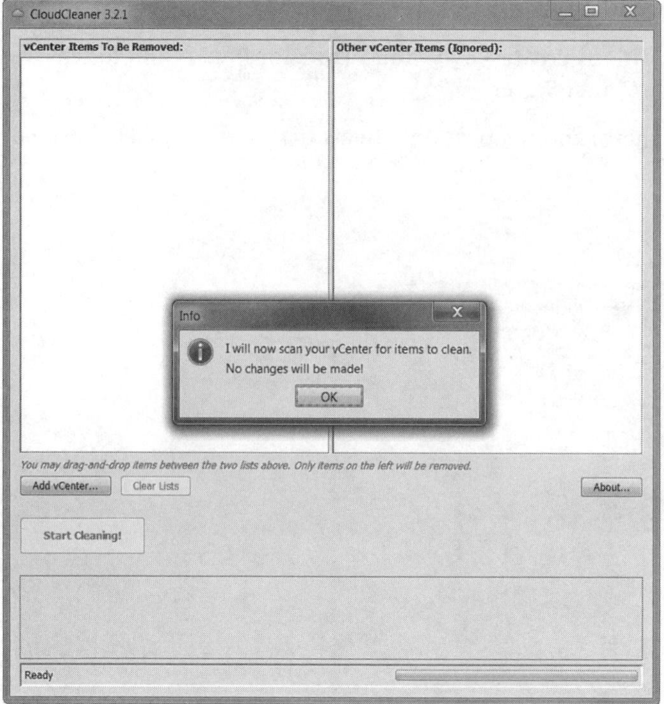

FIGURE 8.13 Confirmation after authenticating vCenter Credentials

7. Drag-and-drop items between the two panes to customize your selection of entities to remove, as shown in Figure 8.16. Entities created by vCloud Director that CloudCleaner detects are listed in the left pane, marked for removal. Hosts may also be displayed, which enables you to uninstall the host agent. Entities that CloudCleaner ignores are listed on the right.

8. Optionally, click **Add vCenter** to add multiple vCenter Servers that have been used with vCloud Director. This option is shown in Figure 8.14. If you add multiple vCenter Servers, CloudCleaner cleans them all at the same time. CloudCleaner can use up to 5000 simultaneous threads, so it can handle large loads of vCenter Servers and their entities.

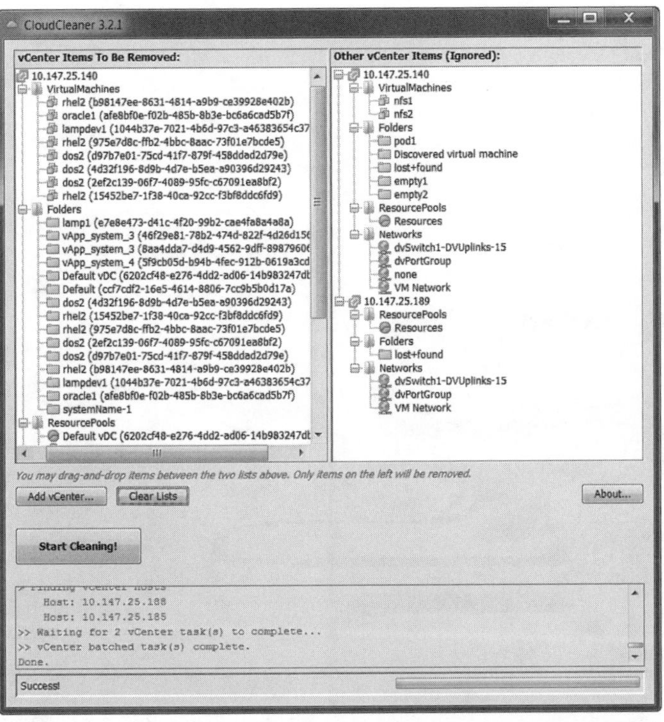

FIGURE 8.14 Control pane for removal of vCenter Items and to add additional vCenter servers

9. Click **Start Cleaning**. Before CloudCleaner starts the cleaning process, you are again asked for your vCenter Server credentials, as shown in Figure 8.15. Following successful authentication, a confirmation dialog is displayed. This is your final chance to cancel this process, which cannot be undone.

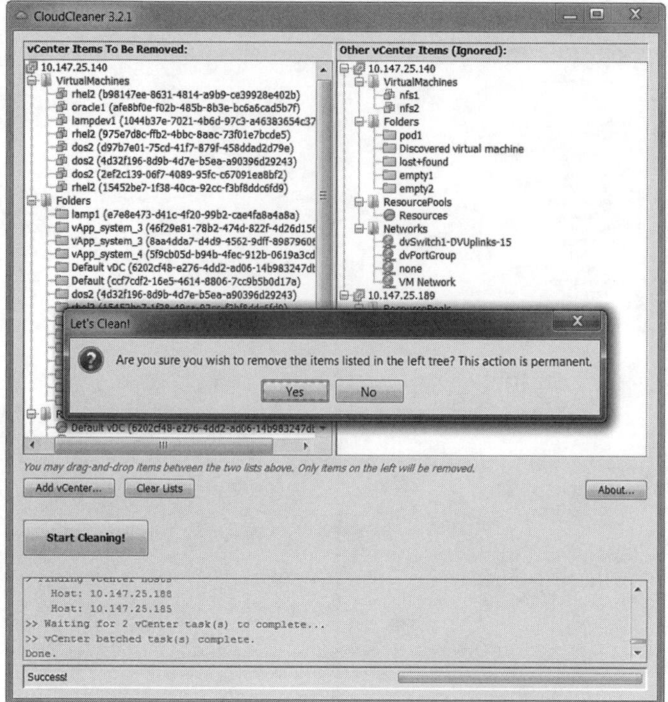

FIGURE 8.15 CloudCleaner confirmation to start removal of vCenter items

8.2.3.6 Use with Advanced Options

Command-line options can be used with CloudCleaner. Running CloudCleaner with advanced options enables you to run the application "headless," meaning you can run it from the command line. This is useful when using CloudCleaner in a testing or automated environment where vCenter cleaning needs to occur on a regular basis. It is also useful when using CloudCleaner on a Linux machine from the shell.

The following is a basic command-line example:

```
$ java -jar cloudcleaner.jar -vcIpAddress=10.10.10.1 -vcLogin=administrator -
  vcPwd=secret -hostLogin=root -hostPwd=password
```

This runs CloudCleaner and automatically removes all vCloud Director-detected entities from the vCenter Server at IP Address 10.10.10.1. It uses a single username and password to connect to all of the vCenter hosts. When run in this mode, you cannot preview the items CloudCleaner selects to remove—it is assumed that you accept the default assessment of what should and should not be deleted.

The following command output shows the CloudCleaner advanced options.

```
$ pwd
/Users/mhaines/Downloads/Cloudcleaner
$ ls-1
total 9192
-rw-r—r--@ 1 mhaines  staff  4784257  9 Nov 18:32 cloudcleaner-3.2.1.jar
$ java -jar cloucleaner-3.2.1.jar -help

Usage: java -jar cloudcleaner.jar -vcIpAddress=10.0.0.0 -vcLogin=admin -
  vcPwd=yourpwd -
hostLogin=root -hostP

-vcIpAddress=<yourVcIpAddress. - the IP address of the VC to clean.
-vcLogin=<login> - your VC administrator username.
-vcPwd=<pwd> - your VC administrator password.
-hostLogin=<login> - the administrator username for your host machines.
-hostPwd=<pwd> - the administrator password for your host machines.

Additional optional flags:

-skipVerify=true - disable SSL certificate verification.
-slowCleanMode=true - when run from cmd-line we do a faster, single-pass clean.
Setting this does the 'normal' multi-pass cleaning.
-scanOnly=ture - only scan VC, don't clean! Good for testing. Only works with -
slowCleanMode=true
$
```

8.2.3.7 Additional CloudCleaner Flags

- `-skipVerify=true`

  CloudCleaner checks a vCenter Server's security certificate the first time it accesses it. In UI mode, you can choose to ignore invalid certificates. You cannot elect to ignore security certificates in command-line mode, so CloudCleaner fails if it accesses a vCenter instance that it has not previously detected in UI mode. If you use this flag, CloudCleaner automatically ignores unknown and invalid security certificates.

- `-slowCleanMode=true`

  When run from the UI, CloudCleaner first scans your vCenter instances and then shows you the results. After you are satisfied, the actual cleaning begins. CloudCleaner does two full passes through your vCenter instances and their entities. When run from the command line, CloudCleaner skips the scan and goes directly to the clean phase, doubling its speed. Although these two modes clean identically, you can pass this flag if you want to emulate CloudCleaner's scan-then-clean behavior.

- `-scanOnly=true`

If you want to test your command-line parameters without actually cleaning your vCenter instances, you can pass this flag. You must also pass the `-slowCleanMode=true` flag.

8.2.3.7.1 Examples

Run and skip certificate verification (recommended usage):

```
$ java -jar cloudcleaner.jar -vcIpAddress=10.10.10.1 -vcLogin=administrator -
  vcPwd=secret -hostLogin=root -hostPwd=password -skipVerify=true
```

Do a test run (only scan, do not actually remove anything):

```
$ java -jar cloudcleaner.jar -vcIpAddress=10.10.10.1 -vcLogin=administrator -
  vcPwd=secret -hostLogin=root -hostPwd=password -slowCleanMode=true -scanOnly=true
```

8.3 Services Automation Tools

VMware Services Software Solutions services automation tools support various VMware services and are available to eligible VMware partners who meet certain criteria or purchase a VMware Services Software Solutions subscription (SKU: CON-SSS). This subscription provides access to and support for VMware Capacity Planner, VMware HealthAnalyzer, VMware Migration Manager, and more.

For information about services automation tools partners can visit VMware Partner Central. Services automation tools are not directly available to customers, but customers can engage with VMware Professional Services or VMware partners for services that employ these tools. Customers who have a VMware TAM may also purchase a subscription.

Services automation tools that provide support for vCloud include the following:

- VMware Capacity Planner
- VMware HealthAnalyzer
- VMware Migration Manager

All services automation tools are fully supported by VMware Partner Support team.

8.3.1 Assessments and Capacity Planner

VMware Capacity Planner can help to successfully plan and estimate the size of the foundation infrastructure required for a scalable vCloud deployment. Capacity Planner provides the following benefits:

- Increased productivity with server consolidation and capacity optimization.
- Reduced complexity through IT standardization and hardware containment.
- Improved predictability with capacity utilization trends and virtualization benchmarks.

See the VMware Capacity Planner datasheet for additional information (http://www.vmware.com/products/capacity-planner/overview.html).

VMware Capacity Planner software is typically used during a Virtualization Assessment service delivered by VMware Professional Services or a VMware partner.

8.3.1.1 What Is Capacity Planner?

VMware Capacity Planner is an agentless and robust capacity planning tool that provides an integrated set of analysis, planning, and decision support functionality that accelerates the delivery of accurate and benchmarked infrastructure assessment services for vCloud workloads. It is an integrated platform for analysis, planning, and decision making that enables comprehensive capacity planning, virtualization, and consolidation assessments. These assessments help to virtualize and consolidate datacenter vCloud infrastructure, redeploy strategic IT assets, and optimize vCloud workload planned capacity utilization.

Capacity Planner enables not only current state analysis of the existing infrastructure landscape, but also "what-if analysis" of the preferred vCloud end state. It includes a rich set of components that deliver integrated capacity planning functionality including:

- Data collection
- Data analysis
- Decision engine based on industry benchmarks
- Monitoring capabilities

The following are key components of Capacity Planner:

- **Data Collector:** The data collector is installed at the customer site and uses an agentless implementation to quickly discover systems. It collects detailed hardware and software inventory data, as well as key performance metrics required for optimal capacity utilization analysis. The data collector can gather information from heterogeneous environments based on multiple platforms.
- **Data Manager:** The data manager manages the data collection process. It provides an organized view of the collected information and administrative control for the data collector including setting up the job schedules, and starting, monitoring, and stopping various data collection tasks. The data manager also manages the process by which the collected data is sent to the information warehouse.
- **Information Warehouse:** The information warehouse is a central hosted data warehouse where the data collected from the client environment is sent, scrubbed, aggregated, and prepared for analysis. The information warehouse also includes valuable industry benchmark data that can be leveraged for benchmarking, scenario modeling, and for setting utilization thresholds.
- **Data Analyzer:** The data analyzer serves as the core analytical engine that performs all the analysis required for intelligent capacity planning. It includes advanced algorithms that resolve capacity optimization challenges and support analysis capabilities such as aggregation, trending, and benchmarking. Scenario modeling and the

what-if analysis help to model and test various planning scenarios including virtualization, hardware procurement and server consolidation scenarios.

- **Capacity Planner Dashboard Portal:** The dashboard portal is a web-based, hosted application portal that delivers capacity analysis and planning capabilities to users through a browser interface. Users can access a rich set of prebuilt analyses, order and examine data, and create custom reports. Planning capabilities allow users to set objectives and constraints, also model and test scenarios to arrive at informed capacity decisions. The monitoring capabilities of Capacity Planner dashboard enable proactive anomaly detection and alerts.

Figure 8.16 shows all the Capacity Planner components.

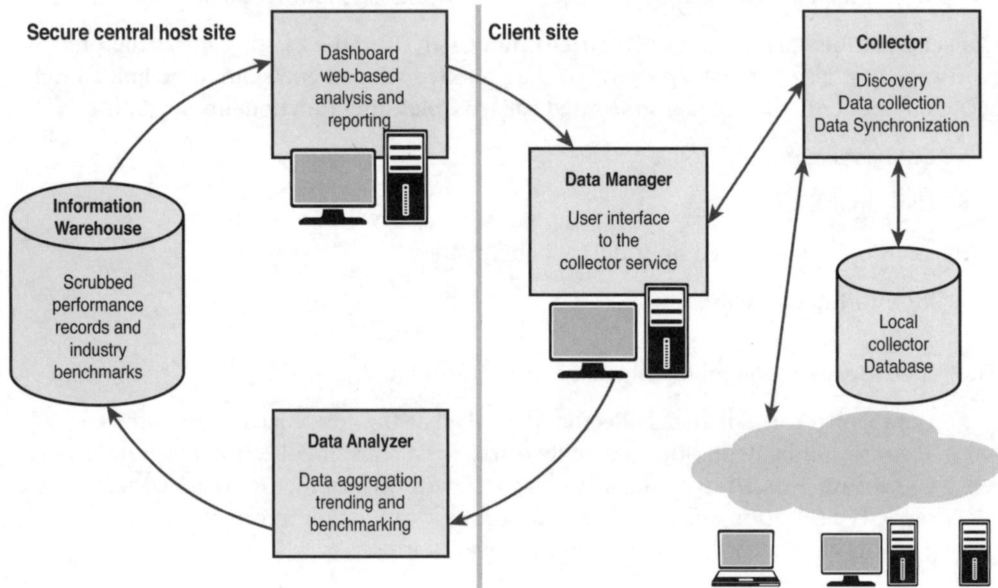

FIGURE 8.16 Capacity Planner Components

8.3.1.1.1 When Should Capacity Planner Be Used?

The vCloud delivery methodology is conducted in phases, as shown in Figure 8.17.

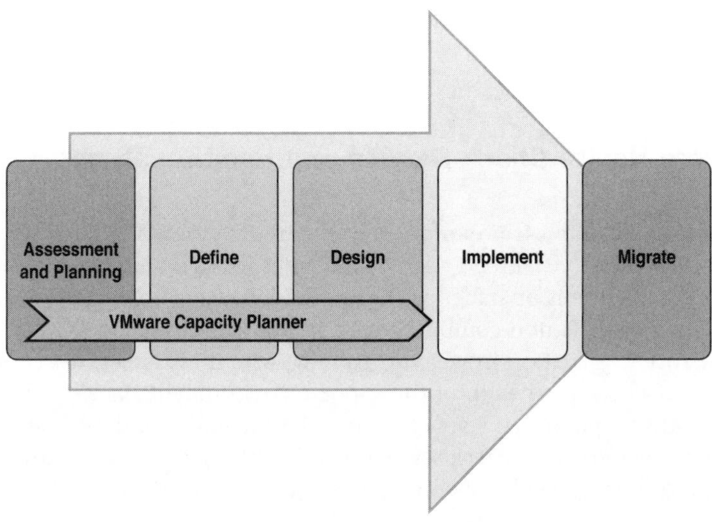

FIGURE 8.17 Capacity Planner Agile vCloud Delivery Methodology

Capacity Planner is typically used during the first three phases:

1. Assessment and planning
2. Define
3. Design

8.3.1.1.2 Capacity Planner Alignment with Agile vCloud Delivery Methodology

VMware Capacity Planner is aligned with the phases of the Agile vCloud delivery methodology.

- **Assess and Plan:**
  - *Assess* the current state of an infrastructure's workload capacity through comprehensive discovery and inventory of IT assets. Measure server loads and capacity utilization across various elements of the IT infrastructure by function, location, and environment.
  - *Plan* for capacity optimization through detailed utilization analysis, benchmarking, trending, and identification of capacity optimization alternatives. Identify resources and establish plan for vCloud-based virtualization, hardware purchase, or redeployment.
- **Define and Design:** Gather requirements and decide on the optimal solution by evaluating various alternatives through scenario modeling and "what-if" analyses. Determine which alternative best meets the predefined criteria. Monitor resource utilization through anomaly detection and alerts based on benchmarked thresholds. Help generate design recommendations for ongoing vCloud capacity optimization.

The effective use of Capacity Planner enables optimal design and construction of robust vApps that are published in the private or public catalogs in the vCloud Director, resulting in a scalable vCloud deployment.

8.3.2 VMware vSphere Health Check Service and HealthAnalyzer Tool

VMware vCloud is built on vSphere and it is important that the underlying infrastructure for a vCloud complies with the industry standard design guidelines for optimal performance. Over time, as the infrastructure is upgraded with new hardware and software versions, the infrastructure may become non-compliant with standard best practices, which can result in performance degradation in vCloud. To remediate these issues, it is recommended to periodically check the health of the vSphere environment against VMware design guidelines. VMware published a set of vSphere best practices and made them available through the vSphere Health Check service. The HealthAnalyzer tool automates data collection and parts of the analysis of compliance with best practices.

VMware HealthAnalyzer is fully supported by the VMware Partner Support team and is periodically updated with the latest best practice catalog, new features, and maintenance releases. A complete set of VMware HealthAnalyzer documentation is available from VMware Partner Central.

NOTE

A new version of HealthAnalyzer that supports a Health Check service for VMware View® environments is also available.

8.3.2.1 Health Check Service

During a Health Check service a VMware-certified consultant works with the customer vSphere infrastructure team to understand the customer environment, provide guidance on current best practices for configuring and managing vSphere, identify gaps between the current environment and design guidelines, and make recommendations to optimize the environment.

The Health Check service offers the following benefits:

- Optimize VMware vSphere performance.
- Maximize resources through efficiencies and roadmap for future improvements.
- Mitigate risks by leveraging experienced consultants and proven best practices.
- Interactive workshop to facilitate knowledge transfer on VMware vSphere best practices.

The Health Check service is sold and delivered by VMware and eligible VMware partners.

8.3.2.2 VMware HealthAnalyzer

VMware HealthAnalyzer is a software tool used during a Health Check service. Although HealthAnalyzer is usually used during a Health Check service, it can also be used at other times.

VMware HealthAnalyzer automates the collection of VMware vSphere inventory, configuration, and utilization data, analyzes data against best practices, recommends grades, and generates a report card that presents observations, findings, and data categorized by VMware Health Check best practices. The workflow is shown in Figure 8.18. VMware and partner consultants use the HealthAnalyzer web UI to review collected data, findings, and observations, assign grades, make recommendations, and generate a Health Check Report.

VMware HealthAnalyzer is a Java web application also available as a virtual appliance (OVF). It can be configured and run on VMware Workstation, VMware Fusion, and VMware vSphere. At a high level, using HealthAnalyzer involves the following high-level steps:

1. Collect data from a VMware vCenter Server or ESXi host.
2. Create a report card where the tool analyzes data for a majority of the best practices.
3. Validate the recommendations provided by HealthAnalyzer.
4. Generate a final report.

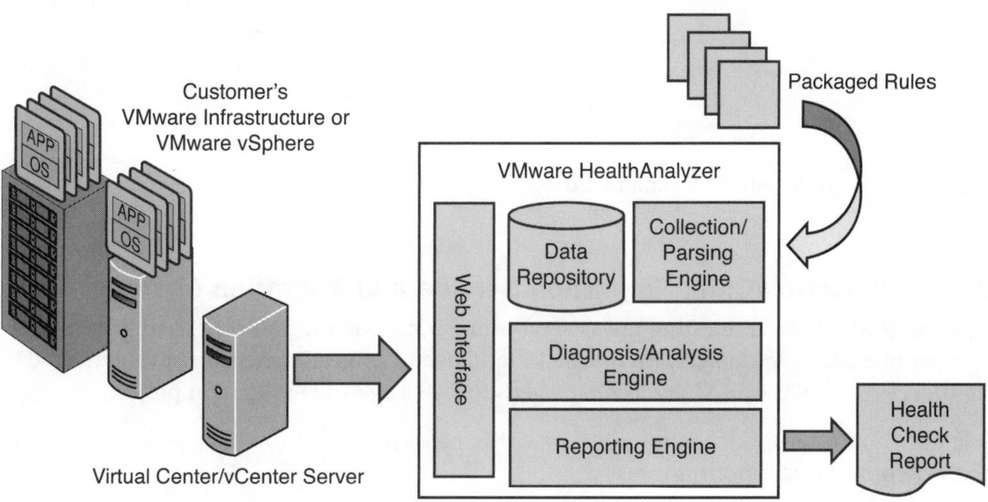

FIGURE 8.18 VMware HealthAnalyzer processing

8.3.2.3 VMware HealthAnalyzer Requirements

HealthAnalyzer is distributed as a virtual appliance (OVF) or Java app, and requires the following:

- VMware vSphere (4.0 or later), VMware Player™ (2.5 or later), VMware Workstation™ (6.5 or later)
- Web browser – Mozilla Firefox (3.0 or later), Microsoft Internet Explorer (7.0 or later)
- Adobe Flash Player (10.0.12 or later)
- Microsoft Word (2007 or later), Microsoft Excel (2007 or later)
- A vCenter account with read-only permissions for all objects and permissions to read diagnostics and license information

Figure 8.19 shows a sample HealthAnalyzer report card screen.

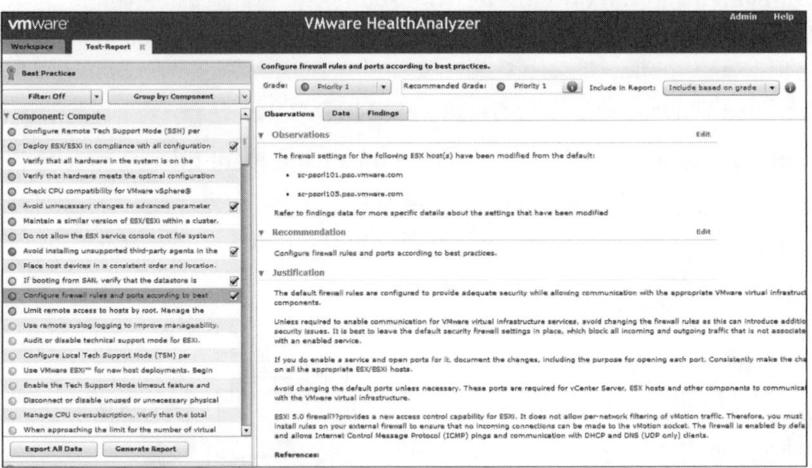

FIGURE 8.19 HealthAnalyzer report card

8.3.3 VMware vCloud Migration Service and Migration Manager Tool

Customers who have an existing physical or virtual infrastructure and plan to migrate a large number of existing workloads to a private vCloud need a project management tool designed for that purpose. VMware Migration Manager supports large-scale migration projects.

Migrating existing workloads (physical or virtual) to a private vCloud is a process comprised of several important tasks:

- Identifying resources to migrate.
- Scheduling migration to fit resource availability.
- Defining workflow steps to get approval from various workload owners, project managers, and resource owners.
- Documenting steps to migrate workloads.
- Updating and communicating status of migration of workloads to project personnel.

There can be other processes involved during the migration of a workload to a vCloud. When there are hundreds of workloads to be migrated managing these tasks is not trivial and requires a project management tool. Based on years of experience with P2V (physical to virtual) projects, VMware defined a methodology and a service for performing workload migration. This service uses a project management tool, VMware Migration Manager, that uses the P2V methodology and helps manage the migration process flow. You can find more information about the P2V service from the datasheet (http://www.vmware.com/files/pdf/services/consserv-p2v-accelerator-datasheet.pdf).

8.3.3.1 What is VMware Migration Manager?

VMware Migration Manager is a web-based application migration management application. It helps to manage the process of physical to virtual migration (P2V), or virtual to virtual migration (V2V) when there are many migrations involved. Migration Manager provides a collaboration platform, a workbench, and a series of dashboards to facilitate end-to-end migration management from initial candidate load to migration workbench and tracking. It also provides a centralized project management workbench with complete control over the migration process as well as comprehensive reporting including migration history and status.

The following high-level diagram (see Figure 8.20) illustrates a typical workflow when using Migration Manager for a migration project and the tasks associated with each part of the workflow.

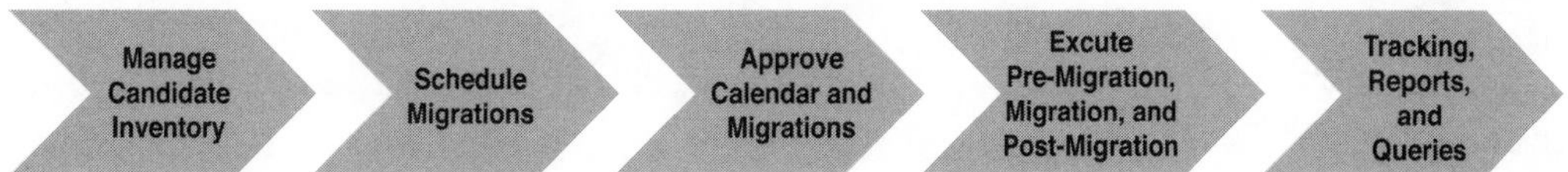

FIGURE 8.20 Migration Manager workflow

8.3.3.2 Migration Manager System Requirements

VMware Migration Manager installs on Microsoft Windows and requires the following:

- Windows 2003 or Windows 2008
- Microsoft .NET 4.0
- MS SQL Server 2005 or later
- MS IIS 6.0 or higher
- MS Internet Explorer 8 or later, Google Chrome 13 or later, or Mozilla Firefox 3.0 or later

8.3.3.3 VMware Migration Manager Sample Screens

The following sample screens (Figures 8.21 through 8.27) show Migration Manager features and capabilities.

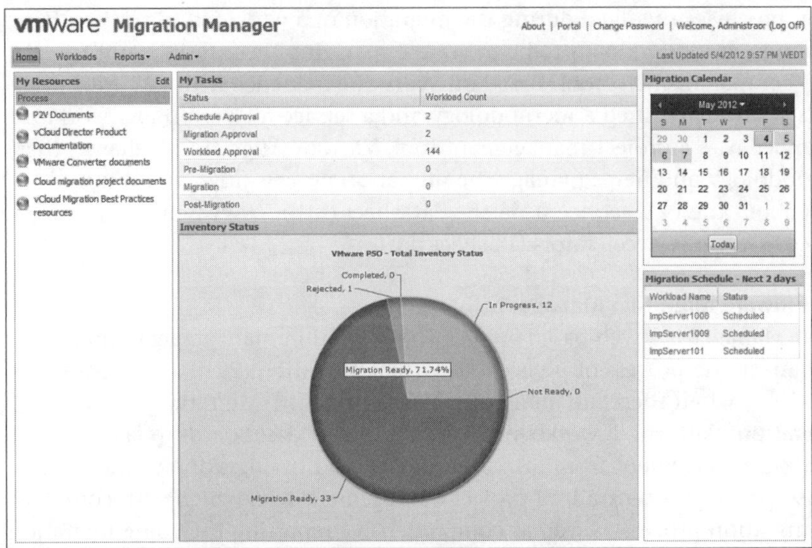

FIGURE 8.21 Home screen (view depends on role)

vmware® Migration Manager

About | Portal | Change Password | Welcome, Administraor (Log Off)

Home | Workloads | Reports | Admin — Last Updated 5/4/2012 10:01 PM WEDT

Search: Name or IP Address... | View: Default | Datacenter: All | Schedule Date: All | My Assigned

Name	IP Address	Status	Schedule Date	Primary Owner	Next Task	Next Task Assigned	Progress	Migration Engineer	Pend Wor
aaa		Migration In-Progress	3/8/2012	Administraor	Migration	me		me	
atest		Post-Migration Comp...	9/28/2011	Administraor	Validation	user		me	
autoserver1	10.2.23.1	Migration Ready		Administraor	Schedule	Administraor			Adm
autoserver11	10.2.23.1	Migration Ready		Administraor	Schedule	Administraor			Adm
autoserver2	10.2.23.2	Migration Ready		Administraor	Schedule	Administraor			Adm
autoserver21	10.2.23.2	Migration Ready		Administraor	Schedule	Administraor			Adm
autoserver3	10.2.23.3	Migration Ready		Administraor	Schedule	Administraor			Adm
autoserver31	10.2.23.3	Migration Ready		Administraor	Schedule	Administraor			Adm
ImpServer004	10.2.23.4	Scheduled	9/26/2011	Administraor	Release Migration	Administraor		me	Adm
ImpServer005	10.2.23.5	Scheduled	9/26/2011	Administraor	Schedule Approval	Administraor		me	Adm
ImpServer006	10.2.23.6	Scheduled	5/7/2012	Administraor	Release Migration	Administraor		*Unassigned	Adm
ImpServer007	10.2.23.7	Migration Ready		Administraor	Schedule	Administraor			Adm
ImpServer008	10.2.23.8	Migration Ready		Administraor	Schedule	Administraor			Adm
ImpServer009	10.2.23.9	Migration Ready		Administraor	Schedule	Administraor			Adm
ImpServer010	10.2.23.10	Migration Ready		Administraor	Schedule	Administraor			Adm
ImpServer1001	10.3.23.1	Scheduled	10/2/2011	Administraor	Release Migration	Administraor		me	
ImpServer1002	10.3.23.891	Scheduled	10/2/2011	Administraor	Schedule Approval	Administraor		me	

Page 1 of 3 | Page size 17 | Visible size 17 — Displaying 1 - 17 of 45

Tasks | Schedule | Multiple Update | Clear Selections | Add | Import | Export

FIGURE 8.22 Workloads screen showing all workloads and their migration status

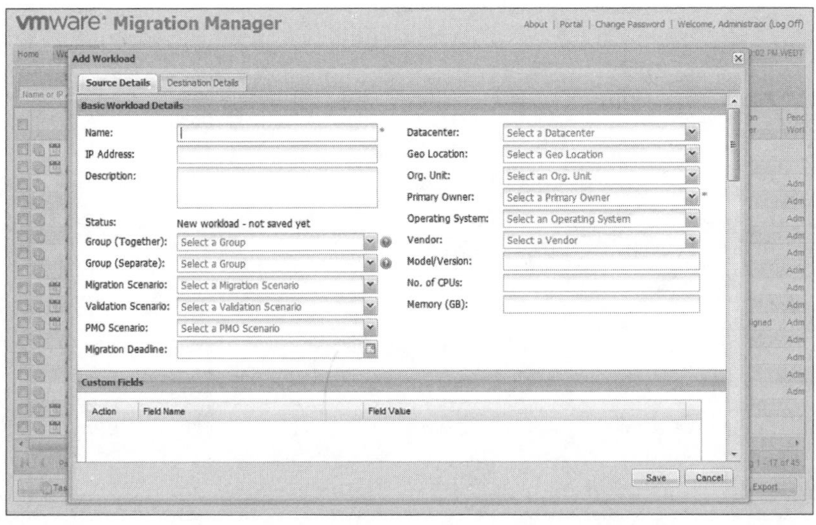

FIGURE 8.23 Add Workload screen to add a new workload for migration (Source Details)

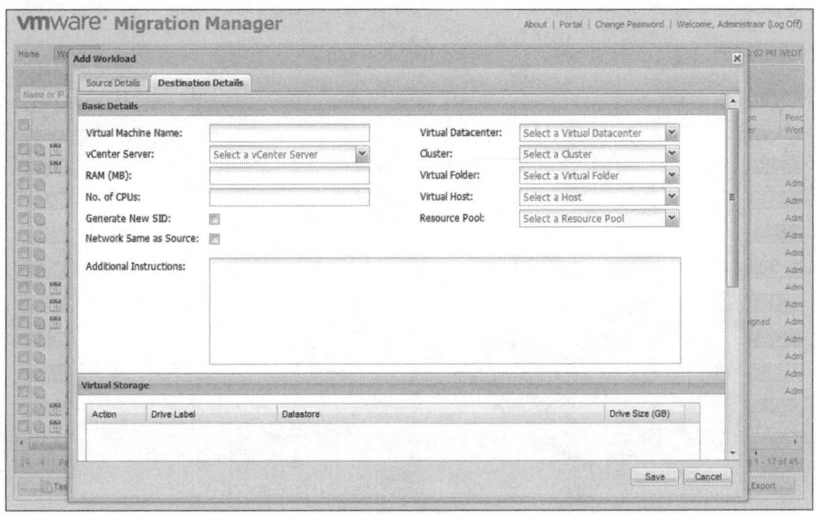

FIGURE 8.24 Add Workload screen to add a new workload for migration (Destination Details)

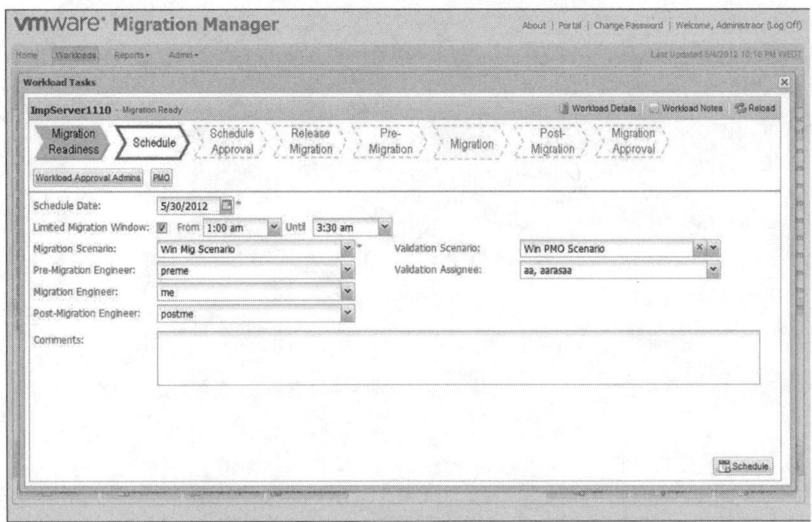

FIGURE 8.25 Workflow screen listing all steps in the migration workflow

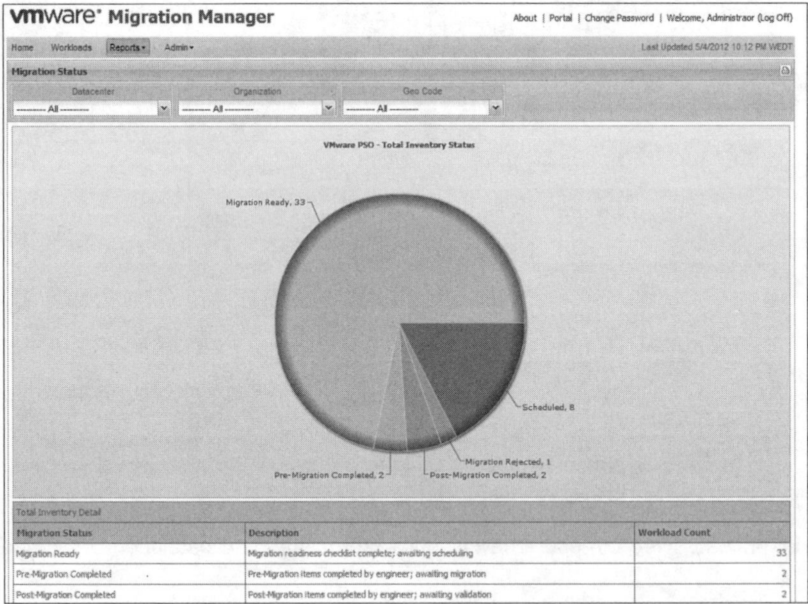

FIGURE 8.26 Report: Migration status of different workloads by migration stage

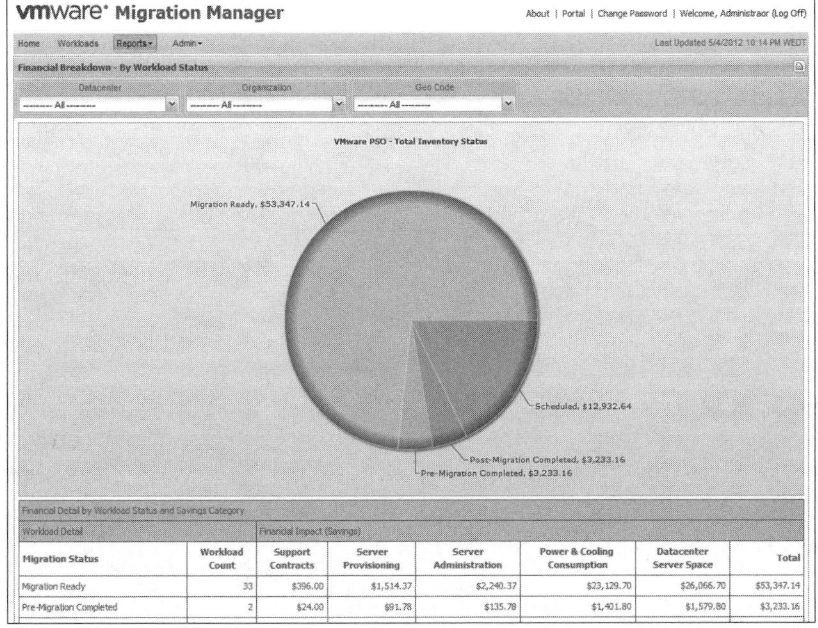

FIGURE 8.27 Report: Financial breakdown of savings by migration status

CHAPTER 9
Cloud Bursting

IN THIS CHAPTER

9.1 Overview

Cloud bursting is the act of dynamically leveraging off-premises private or public computing resources in response to an increase in demand. *Autoscaling* is the act of dynamically adding local resources to a service in response to an increase in demand. Cloud bursting and autoscaling are *bursting modes* that an increase in demand can trigger. The resources consumed during cloud bursting or autoscaling are not explicitly dedicated to the service and are deallocated when the increase in workload normalizes.

Cloud bursting is an advanced topic that is rapidly evolving. This guide examines design guidelines, theory, and early technical insights developed to help address emerging use cases related to building an autoscaling infrastructure. The focus of this guide is specifically on the infrastructure components of autoscaling, so it does not address the application and end-user layer implications of an autoscaling infrastructure.

9.1.1 The Autoscaling Process

Autoscaling or cloud bursting allows the infrastructure to consume resources when they are needed and return them to the pool of available resources when they are not. This serves the end user by providing the following benefits:

- Automatic response to performance or capacity incidents
- Reduced service delivery cost
- Reduced outages due to human error

The automatic or dynamic scaling of an application requires that the infrastructure provide the following components:

- Monitoring
- Orchestration
- A programmable API-driven infrastructure

Each of these components can be implemented using various technologies, all providing the same function for each component. The implementation used determines how the autoscaling process is triggered and carried out, but the end result is the same. The goal of the system is to allow the application or service to autonomously remain within compliance of a service-level agreement (SLA). If necessary, additional resources are added to remain in compliance and meet increased demand.

9.1.2 Open-Loop and Closed-Loop Implementation Models

The dynamic Infrastructure as a Service (IaaS) infrastructure can be thought of in terms of two implementation models: *open loop* or *closed loop*. Regardless of the approach, a monitoring system is required to track the critical metrics used to trigger a scale-out event and instruct the orchestrator to perform the scaling task.

9.1.2.1 Closed-Loop Systems

Closed-loop control systems provide feedback on the actual state of the system and compare it to the desired state of the system in order to adjust the system.

9.1.2.1.1 Control Theory

The closed-loop control system (see Figure 9.1) is a system that senses the actual behavior of the system, feeds it back to the controller, and mixes it with the *reference* or desired state of the system to adjust the system to its desired state. The objective of the control system is to calculate solutions for the proper corrective action to the system so that it can hold the set point (reference) and not oscillate around it.

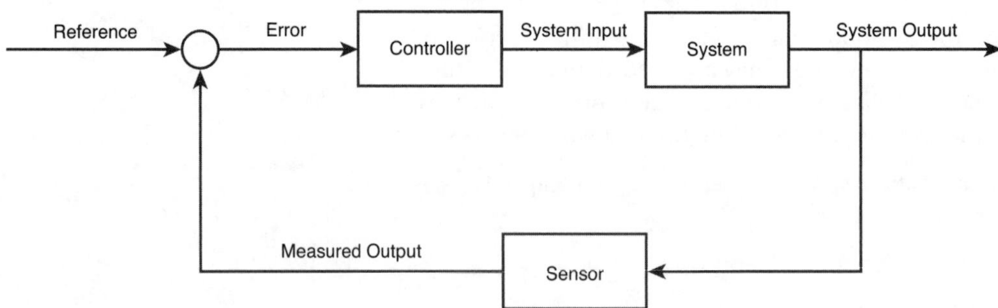

FIGURE 9.1 Closed-loop control system

9.1.2.1.2 Closed-Loop Dynamic IaaS

When a scale-out triggering event occurs, the input parameter that triggers the event is monitored around its set point. The system increases and decreases capacity on demand to stay as close as possible to the set point for the triggering parameter.

With closed-loop systems, you can evaluate the system near the set point using a PID control algorithm or similar control scheme. A simpler approach, such as *hysteresis*, can be very effective and can be implemented with less complexity and tuning.

Hysteresis is the dependence of a system not only on its current state, but also on its past state. For example, a thermostat controlling a heater might turn the heater on when the temperature drops below *x* degrees but not turn it off until the temperature rises above *y* degrees.

An example of a closed-loop dynamic IaaS system (see Figure 9.2) is one in which the infrastructure is constantly monitoring the end-user experience. When an end-user experience measure drops below a desired threshold (for example, transactions taking >n milliseconds), the controller scales out the environment to compensate. The experience is checked with the new resources, and if it still is below the desired state, the controller continues to scale out the service. When the transaction time drops below the desired *n* milliseconds, the controller scales back the environment to reduce the resources consumed and continues to monitor whether the user experience is within the acceptable range.

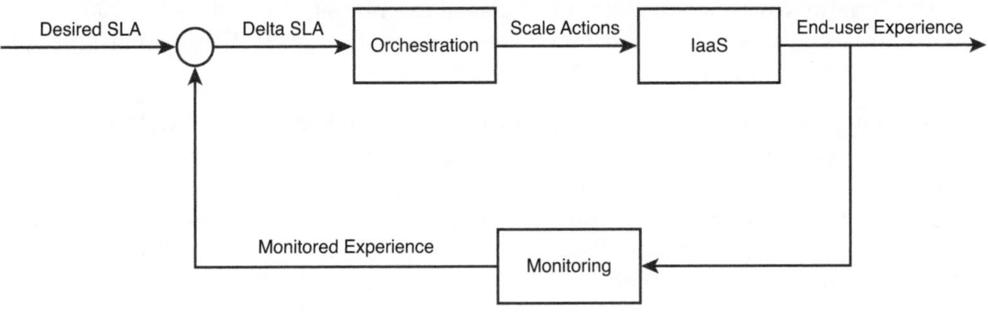

FIGURE 9.2 Closed-loop dynamic IaaS

9.1.2.2 Open-Loop Systems

Open-loop control systems do not provide feedback on the actual state of the system in order to adjust the system.

9.1.2.2.1 Control Theory

The open-loop control system (see Figure 9.3) is a nonfeedback system in which the control input to the system is determined using only the current state of the system and a model of the system. No feedback determines whether the system is achieving the desired output based on the reference input or set point. The system does not observe itself to correct itself; as such, it is more prone to errors and cannot compensate for disturbances to the system.

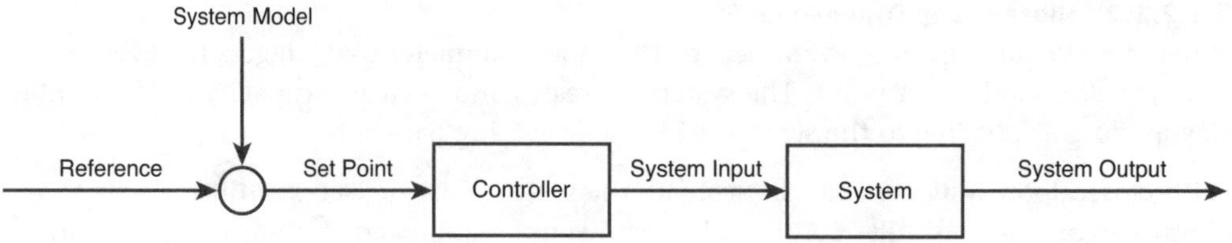

FIGURE 9.3 Open-loop control system

9.1.2.2.2 Open-Loop Dynamic IaaS

When a scale-out triggering event occurs, the infrastructure expands its capacity through the appropriate bursting mode, either autoscaling or cloud bursting. (See Figure 9.4.)

The system has no feedback from the usage of the new capacity to tightly control the amount of resources added or decommissioned from the service based on real-world service utilization. A model of the service determines the appropriate scaling activities.

For example, a basic model of this service shows that, for every 100 active sessions, one virtual machine in the web tier is required to provide a 100ms transaction time. Capacity planning data indicates that 1,000 active sessions must be supported during weekdays and 250 active sessions on weekends.

On weekdays, the environment scales to 10 virtual machines in the web tier (1,000 sessions/100 sessions per virtual machine); on weekends, it scales to 3 virtual machines in the web tier (250 sessions).

The model describes the number of virtual machines per 100 sessions, but it does not account for rogue sessions that might consume significantly more resources than the typical session. It also does not account for transient spikes in resource consumption that might occur, which makes the 100 sessions per virtual machine model incorrect. In this scenario, the open-loop control method does not account for the real-world state of the system, and the end-user experience degrades.

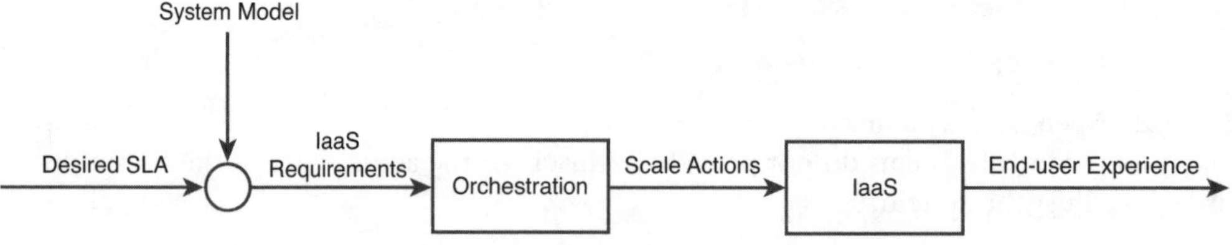

FIGURE 9.4 Open-loop dynamic IaaS

9.1.2.3 Closed Loop Versus Open Loop

Open-loop systems have many disadvantages because of their lack of feedback from the system. With feedback in a closed-loop system, you can more closely manage the state of the system relative to preferred goals, such as staying within an SLA or providing an appropriate end-user experience. Closed-loop systems provide several advantages over open-loop systems:

- Disturbance rejection from unforeseen increases in user load
- Predictable performance with uncertain service models when a user does not know exactly how the service scales relative to user workload
- Improved reference tracking so that resource allocation can closely track what is needed to provide SLA compliance without overprovisioning

Closed-loop systems are recommended because of these benefits.

9.2 Sensing (Monitoring) the Service State

To be implemented, the control system must be capable of sensing (monitoring) the state of the service.

9.2.1 Monitoring Approaches

Polled monitoring and *stream monitoring* are approaches to monitoring the service state. Figure 9.5 shows a typical monitoring process.

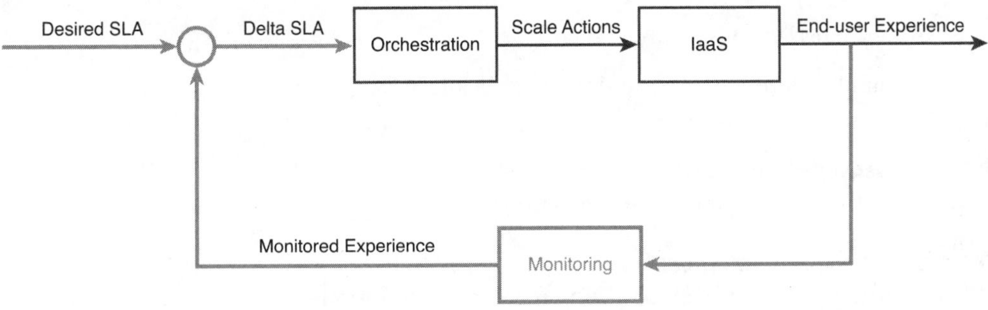

FIGURE 9.5 Monitoring process

The observable service state is critical in implementing an effective, dynamic IaaS architecture. *Observability* is related to the possibility of observing the state of the service through measurement. If you have no way of understanding what the service is providing to the end users, you cannot dynamically react to that state. The fidelity of the monitoring is important because monitoring provides the information that makes it possible for the system to respond.

9.2.1.1 Polled Monitoring

In *polled monitoring*, the application performing the monitoring task queries the service at a set interval and evaluates the state of the service at that moment. Polled monitoring is relatively simple to implement and typically far less costly than real-time or stream monitoring in terms of overhead and dollars. Although it is simpler and less costly than stream monitoring, polled monitoring has the following negative issues:

- Potentially long event-detection periods
- Missed events (architecture dependent)

If a polled monitoring solution has an interval of five minutes (300 seconds), the worst-case response time to an event is 300 seconds—the worst-case response time is the polling interval. This is the response time to determine that something must be done and includes the time the system takes to actually respond to the event, in addition to the possible 300 seconds it took to detect the event.

9.2.1.2 Stream Monitoring

Stream monitoring is passively monitoring the service by "listening" to streams of data between the application and the end-user or application components. This is typically done at the network packet layer and introduces little or no overhead on the service itself. Stream monitoring provides benefits over polled monitoring. Every session is observed as it occurs, so events should not go unnoticed. However, stream monitoring is typically far more complex and costly than polled monitoring.

Although it provides the benefits of real-time visibility, stream monitoring has the following negative issues:

- It has increased complexity and cost.
- It is application specific, and not all applications support it.

9.2.1.3 Derived Metrics

Derived metrics include *composite metrics* and *forecast metrics*.

9.2.1.3.1 Composite Metrics

Whether using polled, stream, or a combination of both monitoring techniques to observe the system, more fidelity can be provided to the results by creating macro metrics that are a function of several metrics to derive a composite metric that describes the system state.

9.2.1.3.2 Forecast Metrics

By using simple or complex statistical and signal analysis techniques, data can be taken from polled, streamed, or derived metrics, and it can predict what the future metrics might be. This supplies the capability to provide data to the controller to make decisions ahead of the event and to proactively take action on the system, to reduce the chance of end-user impact from slow controller response.

9.2.1.4 Monitoring Criteria

When monitoring the delivered service to understand its current behavior, the need to scale out or scale back can arise across several main categories. Each category has its own benefits and drawbacks. The ideal system considers metrics from multiple sources to make the best decisions regarding how to adapt the system to provide the preferred service level for the end user. Table 9.1 describes each category of monitoring criteria.

TABLE 9.1 Monitoring Criteria Categories

Category	Description	Example
Infrastructure	Utilization of specific infrastructure resources such as the following: ▶ CPU or memory utilization. ▶ Disk latency and bandwidth. ▶ Any metric that describes the health or utilization of the infrastructure.	CPU utilization greater than 80% on web tier virtual machines
Application	Consumption of application-specific resources such as active sessions.	Active sessions per web server > 200
End User (Real)	The response time of a live user transaction that exceeds acceptable levels. Measured from the perspective of real users. Can be real time.	▶ Load time on a specific object > 250ms ▶ Page latency > 100ms
End User (Synthetic)	The response time of a synthetic user transaction. Measured by executing synthetic transactions against an application.	▶ Load time on a specific object > 250ms ▶ Complete synthetic session > 5s

9.2.1.5 End-User Monitoring

Of all the metrics that a service generates at all layers, *end-user experience* is a single metric that serves as an overall indicator of service health. If the end-user experience falls below a given threshold mandated by an SLA, the service does not have sufficient capacity to deliver the required SLA, and capacity must be added.

This approach monitors the service and uses this measure as a trigger for scaling out and scaling back dynamic infrastructure. Whenever the end-user experience falls below a threshold, capacity is added; as the measure increases above the threshold, capacity is decreased. Increasing and decreasing capacity are equally important: You do not want to overspend on infrastructure to provide a service that exceeds your SLA beyond where it provides business value based on the cost.

The drawback of using only an end-user monitoring approach is that it only indicates some problem with the performance for end users; it does not give the system any information on where the problem is or what is causing the problem. To create a truly intelligent dynamic IaaS service, you must consider end-user experience as the key performance indicator (KPI), but infrastructure and application metrics provide the causal analysis data.

9.2.1.6 Infrastructure and Application Monitoring: Causal Analysis

When creating a dynamic infrastructure, end-user experience is almost always the most important KPI. For example, if CPU utilization on virtual machines is a constant 90%, paid resources are being used efficiently. As long as the end-user experience is where it should be, high CPU or memory usage is not a critical metric. This is the target in this control model—you want to drive resource consumption on a given virtual machine as high as possible without requiring additional virtual machines, as long as the end-user experience does not degrade.

When the KPI falls outside an acceptable range, a scaling event must be investigated. This does not explicitly mean that the incident requires scaling out; an actual problem instead of a capacity issue might be causing the KPI degradation.

You must perform a causal analysis on the environment to determine whether to scale out or whether the event should trigger a fault alert that requires intervention.

9.2.1.7 Triggering the Scale Event

Scaling can be uncontrolled, controlled, or controlled with hysteresis.

9.2.1.7.1 Uncontrolled Scaling

When triggering a scale event, you cannot determine whether to increase capacity when the threshold exceeds or falls below the set point. This causes a *ping-pong* effect in which the infrastructure constantly scales out and scales back as it seeks the set point for the triggering metric. Depending on the instability of the system, this can result in significant *overshoot* while seeking the set point. The system then goes back and forth between increasingly overprovisioning resources and then decreasing them, resulting in an ever-increasing problem. Figure 9.6 illustrates uncontrolled scaling.

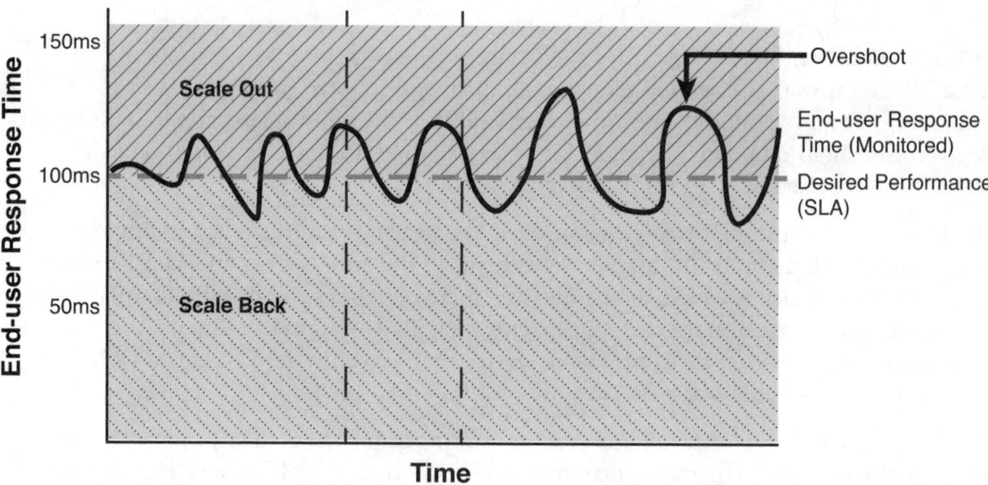

FIGURE 9.6 Uncontrolled scaling

This constant expansion and contraction of resources with today's technology places an undesirable load on the infrastructure and can ultimately result in further degradation of the service.

9.2.1.7.2 Controlled Scaling

The scaling process must be controlled to provide the overall stability of the application and its underlying infrastructure (see Figure 9.7).

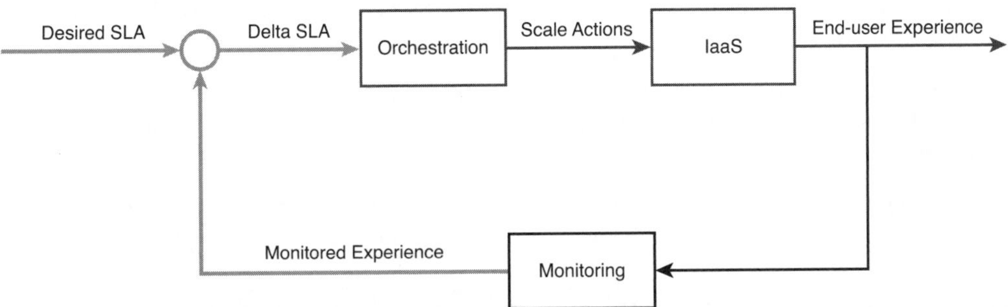

FIGURE 9.7 Scaling controller

The overall system must control the monitoring information, in conjunction with the preferred performance of the system (set point), to prevent the constant seeking of the set point. This allows the infrastructure to operate more efficiently and in a far more stable manner. The simplest control scheme for dynamic IaaS is to add hysteresis to the system (see Figure 9.8).

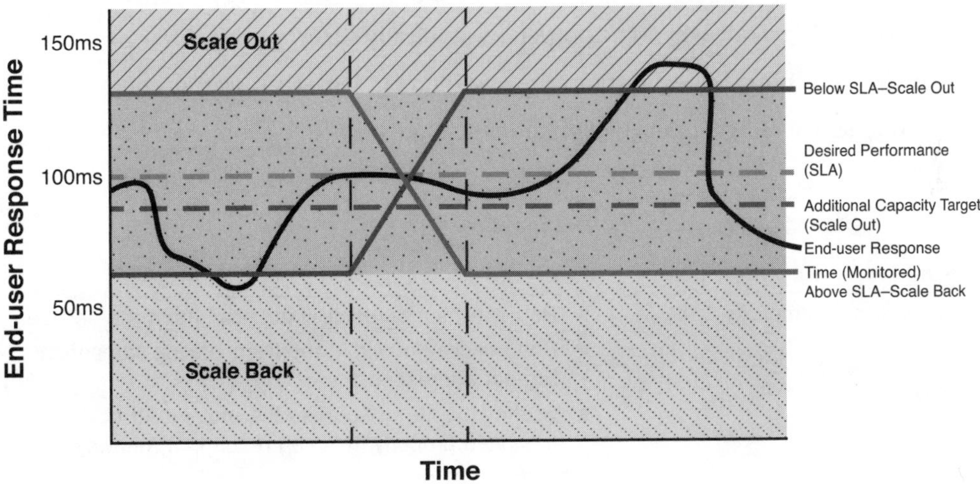

FIGURE 9.8 Controlled scaling using hysteresis

With this method of control, rather than aggressively seeking the set point for the end-user experience, a band can be created around it. Action is taken only when the performance falls outside this band.

9

In the preceding example, as end-user experience improves in the form of decreased response time, a higher-than-necessary service is provided and too much capacity is consumed. This results in spending too much on the service and the controller scaling back resources to get as close as possible to the SLA (set point). When response time increases and a reduction in service quality occurs, the SLA scale out threshold is reached and resources are added to bring the service level to the set point.

You can bring the service level slightly above or below the preferred set point, based on your understanding of the service, how it responds to additional resources, and the cause of the increase.

Creating a dead band within the scaling model enables service performance to fluctuate around the set point and not aggressively seek it, which can result in the ping-pong effect.

9.3 Orchestration (Infrastructure Scaling)

The service orchestrator performs the task of scaling the infrastructure. The orchestrator of the service is responsible for executing the scaling task after the monitoring party deems it necessary. When scaling infrastructure, you must understand what to scale and how to scale it.

9.3.1 Scaling Localization

Depending on the complexity and architecture of the application service, scaling uses several approaches (see Table 9.2).

- **Fixed scaling:** Scale where the bottlenecks typically occur.
- **Scale everything:** Scale out the entire environment with each scale event.
- **Intelligent scaling:** Scale where the resources are needed.

TABLE 9.2 Scaling Modality Benefits and Drawbacks

Scaling Mode	Benefits	Drawbacks
Fixed Scaling	Simplicity	▶ Bottlenecks can result in other areas of the service. ▶ Bottlenecks not within the fixed scaling components are not addressed. ▶ Scaling might not address the problem. If not managed properly, this can result in a runaway scaling event.
Scale everything	Simplicity	▶ This mode can result in overprovisioning in some tiers of the service. ▶ This mode can be far more time-consuming during the orchestration phase of scaling out. ▶ This mode can be more complicated than a fixed scaling approach because of database configuration and synchronization challenges.

Scaling Mode	Benefits	Drawbacks
Intelligent scaling	▶ Capacity added where it is needed every time ▶ Scaling out across tiers and components, to dynamically avoid creating new bottlenecks ▶ Excess capacity not added where it is not required	More complexity is involved.

In the context of scaling, the scale remediation can scale out, scale up, or do a combination of both, depending on the level of complexity within the system. Make scaling design decisions based on prior knowledge of the application or services scaling characteristics.

9.3.1.1 Fixed Scaling

In fixed scaling mode (see Figure 9.9) in a two-tier web application (with *n* web servers and a database server), we add web servers to the environment as user load increases. For the scaling model, assume that the database is infinitely scalable to support the increase in web servers. Scaling the database server is a separate exercise and is addressed outside automated scaling.

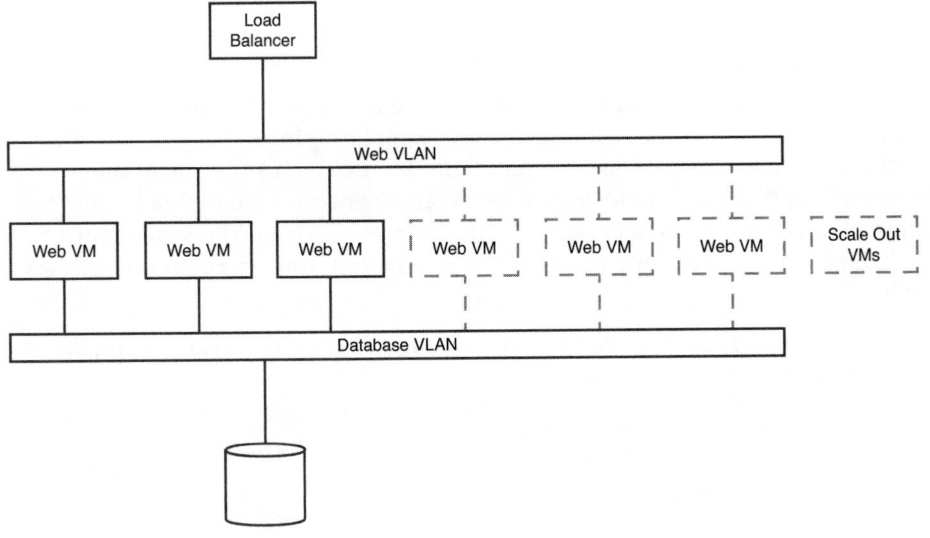

FIGURE 9.9 Fixed scaling

9

9.3.1.2 Scale Everything

In the two-tier web application, instead of considering the database as an infinite resource, the database is more closely sized to the number of web servers within the initial deployment architecture. The entire environment is then scaled whenever a scale-out event occurs. This maintains database resource alignment with the web server resources that are placing load on the database. The scale everything model replicates the entire application service, as Figure 9.10 shows.

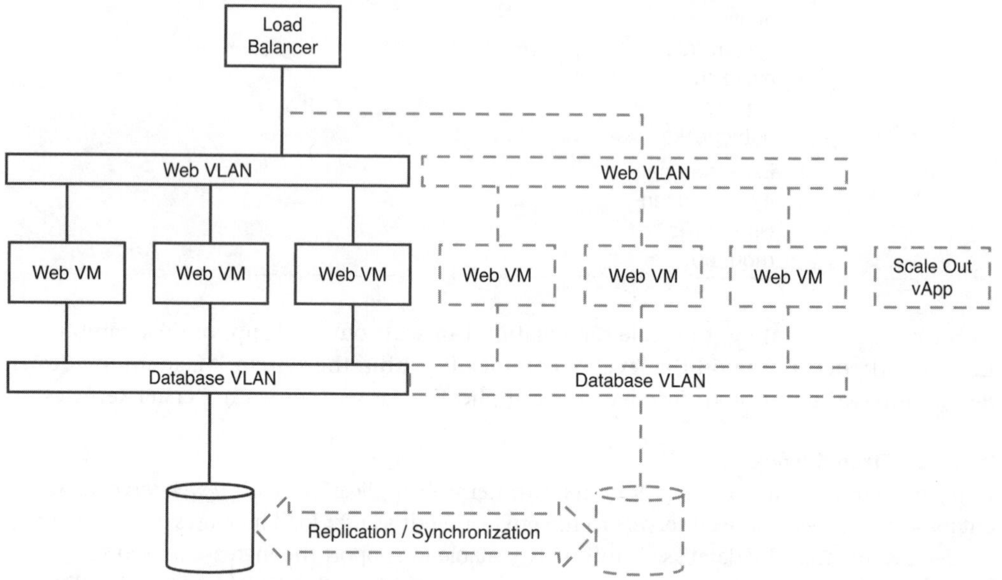

FIGURE 9.10 Scale everything

9.3.1.3 Intelligent Scaling

Intelligent scaling eliminates the drawbacks of the fixed and scale everything dynamic infrastructures. This comes at the cost of increasing complexity in the system. An infrastructure that performs intelligent scaling must consider the current state of all the components within the system to identify which components are responsible for the degradation of KPI or where the service is currently overprovisioned. The system must monitor the KPI (set point) and the details of the system itself (infrastructure and application monitoring).

When a KPI event occurs, the system performs an analysis to determine next steps; Figure 9.11 shows a flowchart of this analysis.

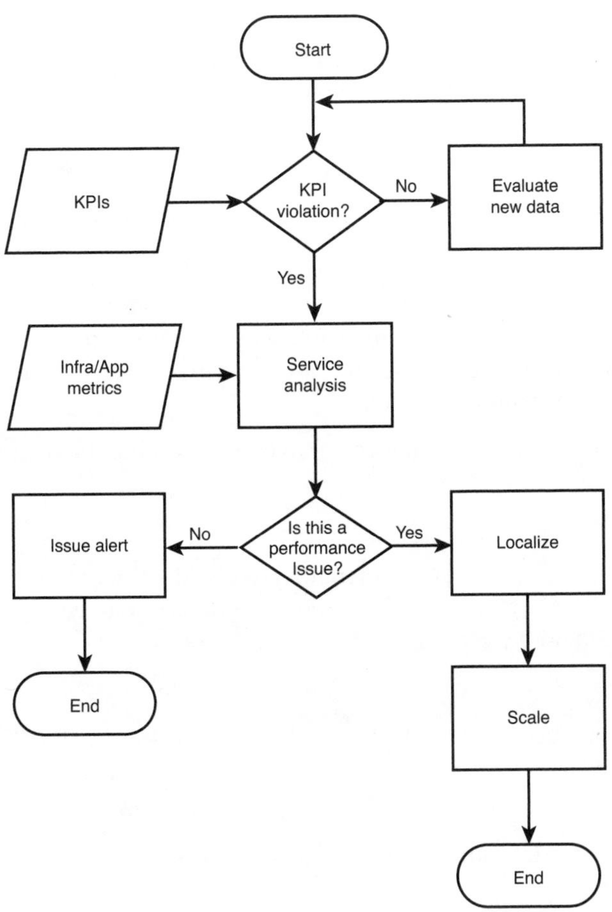

FIGURE 9.11 Intelligent scaling flowchart

The decision flowchart for intelligent scaling must perform the following tasks:

1. Identify a KPI violation.
2. Determine whether the violation is caused by an infrastructure performance/capacity issue.
3. Localize the performance/capacity issue.
4. Issue the appropriate scaling request and scale.

9.3.1.3.1 Identify a KPI Violation

Identifying a KPI violation is a common requirement of all the scale-out modes. However, in all other modes, the violation triggers the scaling event. In the intelligent scaling model, the KPI violation triggers a second-phase analysis or causal analysis to determine the cause of the KPI violation.

9.3.1.3.2 Determine KPI Violation Cause

To determine the KPI violation root cause and decide whether to scale the service, you must analyze the infrastructure and application metrics. This can be done using the following techniques:

- Trend analysis
- Historical or baseline comparison
- Pattern matching

The analysis results in one of two outcomes. The violation is related to performance or capacity, or it is related to a problem with the service. In the case of a service problem, an alert is issued; the scaling tasks need take no further action.

If the analysis determines that the root cause is a bottleneck or overprovisioning, the next task is to localize the cause.

9.3.1.3.3 Localize the Cause

During the localization phase, the service metrics are further analyzed to identify the root cause of the capacity issue. Identify the tier that requires additional resources, and determine which type of resource those should be.

Are the following required?

- Additional web servers
- More database throughput

Identify the location of the capacity issue by using techniques such as the following:

- Correlation
- Anomaly detection

9.3.1.3.4 Issue the Scaling Request

When the system knows there is a performance- or capacity-related issue and has determined where the issue is located, it can issue a scaling request to the orchestrator to resolve the issue. The solution might be to add web servers or another database node to a cluster. It might also be to remove capacity from the service to bring costs back in line. Figure 9.12 shows an example.

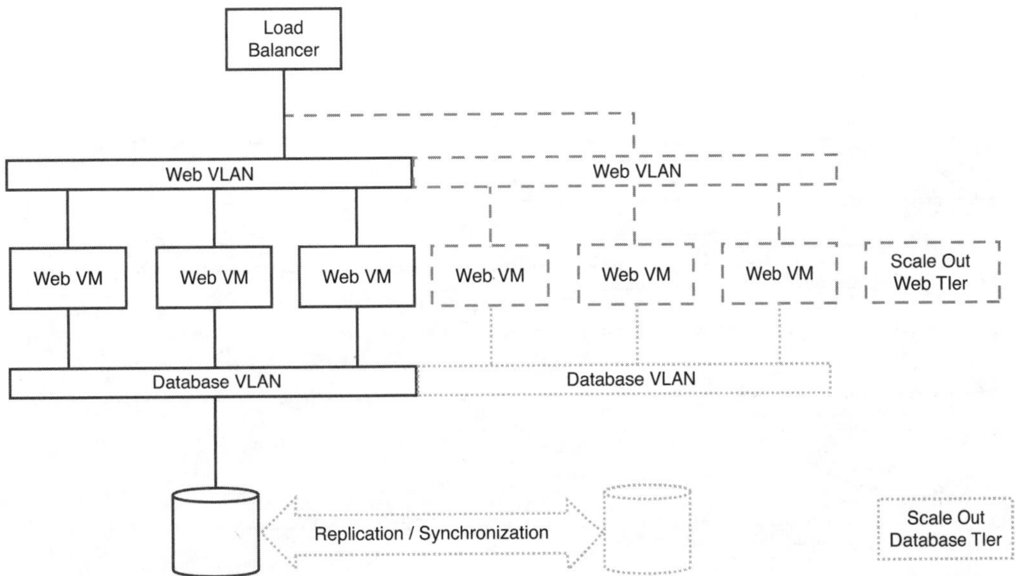

FIGURE 9.12 Intelligent scaling

9.3.2 Scaling Orchestration

Application infrastructure scaling requires orchestrating multiple changes to the application and underlying infrastructure. The orchestration engine does this within the dynamic infrastructure.

9.3.2.1 Foundational Requirements

All scaling activities have a fundamental set of required tasks to scale any application. Figure 9.13 shows the scaling resources workflow.

- Scaling management
- Addition/removal of resources:
  - Connectivity
  - Customization
  - Starting/stopping

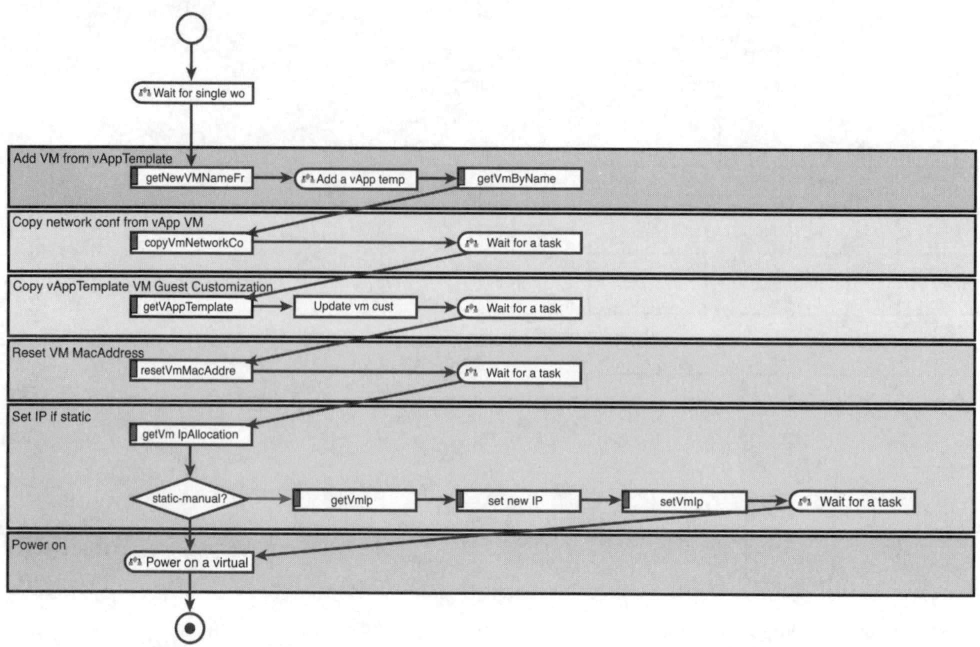

FIGURE 9.13 Scaling resources workflow

Scaling Management

When scaling out, orchestrating the scaling process not only must configure the resources, but also must manage the scaling task. This includes activities such as the following:

- Verifying available capacity before consuming additional resources
- Coordinating or restricting parallel scaling activities on the same application

Generally, scaling activities should be serialized to avoid issues that can arise from the parallel execution. For example, in a parallel operation, you must manage name and IP assignment across tasks to prevent duplicate names or IP addresses from being assigned to the new resources. Additionally, parallel deployment across tiers can overshoot the KPI goal, resulting in the immediate triggering of a scale-back activity. Parallel scaling can be implemented, but because of the complexity, it should be implemented after serial scaling has proven stable. Figure 9.14 shows the scaling management workflow.

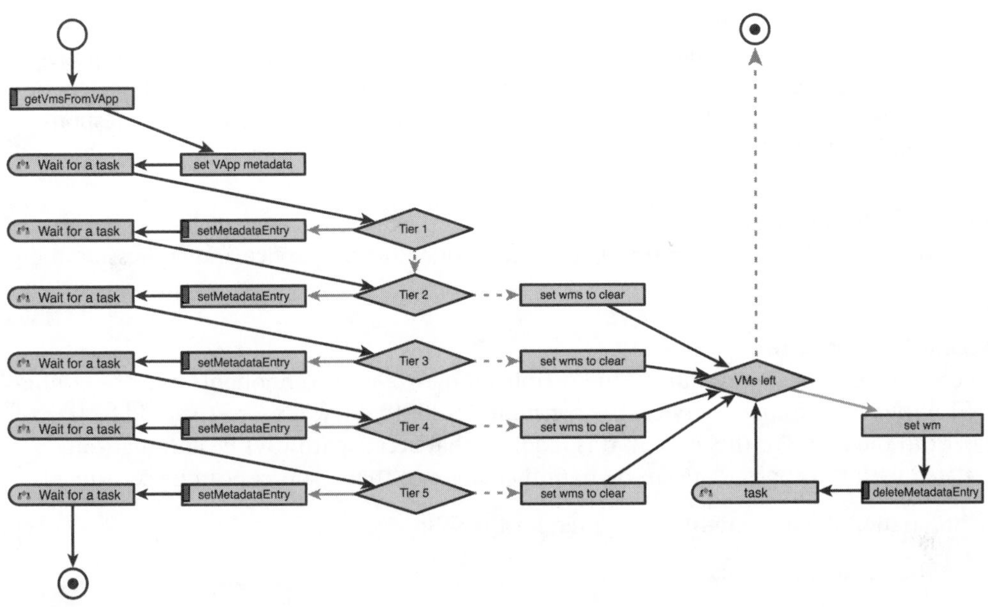

FIGURE 9.14 Scaling management

The scaling management process is driven by directives contained within the application metadata, or by information contained within the scaling workflow. In the following example, several directives are contained as XML data within the OVF descriptor:

```
<ns2:Property ns2:value="4" ns2:userConfigurable="true" ns2:type="string" ns2:key=
  "autoscaleMinTier1Instances">
<ns2:Label/>
<ns2:Description>Minimum number of instances for tier 1 VMs</ns2:Description>
</ns2:Property>
```

9.3.2.3 Adding/Removing Resources

When adding resources, identify whether they are new or existing resources and what must be done with the resources.

9.3.2.3.1 Adding Resources

There are several means by which to allocate and configure new resources for a service being scaled out.

- In the *fixed scaling model*, the same type of resource is always added to the service, such as additional web servers. This information can be a configuration parameter to the orchestration workflow that the administrator sets in advance.
- In the *scale everything* model, the application itself scales out, and it requires the location of the application in the service catalog from which it is derived.

- With *intelligent scaling*, the localization process identifies the resource to be scaled and passes that information to the orchestration workflow to scale that component. Depending on the application requirements, the scaling workflow might be generic enough to address all components of the application as a single workflow responsible for the scaling execution.

Because of the application complexities at each layer (web, business logic, data), a separate workflow is developed for scaling each component of the service and addressing the configuration.

9.3.2.3.2 Connectivity

To use the newly added resources, the peripheral networking components must be configured. When autoscaling a service, the consumption of the new resources should be transparent to the user. For this reason, it is required that access pathways be automatically updated with the appropriate configuration changes so that resources can be consumed.

Configuration updates might be required for the following:

- Local load balancing
- Global load balancing
- Firewalls
- Authentication
- VPN gateways

APPENDIX A
Availability Considerations

vCloud availability depends on eliminating single points of failure (SPOF) in the underlying infrastructure, ensuring availability of personnel with appropriate skills, and establishing suitable operational processes.

Table A.1 provides availability considerations for vCloud components and considers the impact of component failure.

TABLE A.1 vCloud Availability Considerations

Component	Availability	Failure Impact
Maintaining Running Workload		
vSphere hosts	Configure all vSphere hosts in highly available clusters with a minimum of n+1 redundancy. This provides protection for the customer's virtual machines, the virtual machines hosting the platform portal/management applications, and all the vCloud Networking and Security Edge gateways.	In the event of a host failure, vSphere HA detects the failure within 13 seconds and begins to power on the host's virtual machines on other hosts within the cluster. vSphere HA Admission Control makes sure sufficient resources are available in the cluster to restart the virtual machines. VMware recommends the admission control policy Percentage of Cluster Resources because it is flexible and also provides resource availability. For a description of design guidelines about increasing availability and resiliency, see the white paper *VMware High Availability: Deployment Best Practices: VMware vSphere 5.0* (http://www.vmware.com/files/pdf/techpaper/vmw-vsphere-high-availability.pdf) VMware also recommends configuring vCenter to proactively migrate virtual machines off a host if the host's health becomes unstable. Rules can be defined in vCenter to monitor host system health.
Virtual machine resource consumption	vSphere DRS and vSphere Storage DRS migrate virtual machines between hosts to balance the cluster and reduce the risk of a "noisy neighbor" virtual machine monopolizing CPU, memory, and storage resources within a host at the expense of other virtual machines running on the same host. vSphere Storage I/O Control automatically throttles hosts and virtual machines when detecting I/O contention and preserves fairness of disk shares across virtual machines in a data store. This makes sure that a noisy neighbor virtual machine does not monopolize storage I/O resources. Storage I/O Control makes sure that each virtual machine receives the resources it is entitled to by leveraging the shares mechanism.	No impact. Virtual machines are migrated between hosts with no downtime by vSphere DRS or vSphere Storage DRS. No impact. Virtual machines and vSphere hosts are throttled by Storage I/O Control based on their entitlement relative to the amount of shares or the maximum amount of IOPS configured. For more information on Storage I/O Control, see the white paper *Storage I/O Control Technical Overview and Considerations for Deployment* (www.vmware.com/files/pdf/techpaper/VMW-vSphere41-SIOC.pdf).

Component	Availability	Failure Impact
vSphere host network connectivity	Configure port groups with a minimum of two physical paths to prevent a single link failure from impacting platform or virtual machine connectivity. This includes management and vMotion networks. Use the load-based teaming mechanism to avoid oversubscribed network links.	No impact. Failover occurs with no interruption to service. Configuration of failover and failback, as well as corresponding physical settings such as PortFast, are required.
vSphere host storage connectivity	vSphere hosts are configured with a minimum of two physical paths to each LUN or NFS share, to prevent a single storage path failure from resulting in an impact to service. Path selection plug-in is selected based on the storage vendor's design guidelines.	No impact. Failover occurs with no interruption to service.
Maintaining Workload Accessibility		
VMware vCenter Server	vCenter Server runs as a virtual machine and makes use of vCenter Server Heartbeat.	vCenter Server Heartbeat provides a clustered solution for vCenter Server with fully automated failover between nodes, providing near-zero downtime.
VMware vCenter Database	VMware vCenter Database resiliency is provided with vCenter Heartbeat if MS SQL or Oracle RAC is used.	vCenter Heartbeat or Oracle RAC provides a clustered solution for a vCenter database, with fully automated failover between nodes providing zero downtime.
vCloud component databases (vCloud Director and Chargeback)	VMware vCloud component database resiliency is provided through database clustering. Microsoft Cluster Service for SQL and Oracle RAC are supported.	Microsoft Cluster Service and Oracle RAC support the resiliency of the vCloud Director and Chargeback databases as they maintain vCloud Director state information and the critical Chargeback data required for customer billing, respectively. Though not required to maintain workload accessibility, clustering the chargeback database protects the capability to collect chargeback transactions so that providers can accurately produce customer billing information.
VMware vCenter Chargeback	Multiple Chargeback, vCloud, and vCloud Networking and Security Manager data collectors are installed for active/passive protection.	If one of the data collectors goes offline, the other picks up the load so that vCenter Chargeback continues to capture transactions.

Component	Availability	Failure Impact
vCloud Infrastructure Protection		
vCloud Networking and Security Manager	VM Monitoring is enabled on a cluster level within HA and uses the VMware Tools heartbeat to verify that virtual machines are alive. When a virtual machine fails and the VMware Tools heartbeat is not updated, VM Monitoring checks whether any storage or networking I/O has occurred in the last 120 seconds before restarting the virtual machine. VMware highly recommends scheduling backups of vCloud Networking and Security Manager to an external FTP or SFTP server.	Infrastructure availability is impacted, but service availability is not. vCloud Networking and Security Edge devices continue to run without management control, but no additional Edge gateways can be added and no modifications can occur until the service comes back online.
vCenter Chargeback	vCenter Chargeback virtual machines can be deployed in a cluster configuration. Multiple Chargeback data collectors can be deployed to avoid a single point of failure.	No impact affects infrastructure availability or customer virtual machines. However, it is important to keep vCenter Chargeback available to preserve all resource metering data. Clustering the vCenter Chargeback servers protects the capability to collect chargeback transactions so that providers can accurately produce customer billing information and usage reports.
vCloud Director	The vCloud Director cell virtual machines are deployed as a load-balanced, highly available clustered pair in an n+1 redundancy set up, with the option to scale out when needed.	▶ Session state of users connected via the portal to failed instance is lost. Users can reconnect immediately. ▶ Customer virtual machines are not affected.

Component	Availability	Failure Impact
vCloud Networking and Security Edge	vCloud Networking and Security Edge can be deployed through the vCloud API and vCloud Director web console. To provide network reliability, VM Monitoring is enabled. In case of an Edge guest OS failure, VM Monitoring restarts the Edge device. vCloud Networking and Security Edge Gateway use a custom version of VMware Tools and are not monitored by vSphere HA guest OS monitoring. vCloud Networking and Security Edge Gateway 5.1 provides the following HA capabilities: ▶ Network HA: Customers can choose to deploy two gateways working in an active/passive configuration. A stateful failover occurs if the active gateway dies. Then a second gateway is deployed, and it becomes the new passive gateway. ▶ VMware HA: If the vSphere host dies, taking a gateway down with it, the gateway is restarted on another vSphere host. ▶ Application HA: The gateway internals are monitored for process lock-up and other issues, and VMware HA failover is triggered if problems are detected.	▶ Partial temporary loss of service occurs. vCloud Networking and Security Edge is a possible connection into organization. ▶ Neither customer virtual machines nor Virtual Machine Remote Console (VMRC) access is affected. ▶ All external network routed connectivity is lost if the corresponding Edge gateway is lost.
vCenter Orchestrator	Plan for high availability of all systems involved in the orchestration workflow. Design the workflows to remediate the unavailability of orchestrated systems (for example, by alerting and retrying periodically). vSphere HA and vSphere FT can provide high availability for vCenter Orchestrator, in addition to application-based clustering If a copy of the database is available, a vCenter Orchestrator Application Server with the appropriate configuration can resume workflow operations. An active/passive node configuration best suits vCenter Orchestrator.	End users interacting directly with vCenter Orchestrator experience a temporary loss of access. Workflows executed by vCenter Orchestrator experience disruption. This includes workflows started by vCenter Orchestrator and workflows started by external applications.

vCloud Director Cell Load Balancing

A load-balanced, multicell vCloud Director architecture provides the following benefits:

- Scalability by distributing session load across cells
- Improved availability by monitoring cell server health and adding or removing cells from service based on status
- Nondisruptive operating system patching and maintenance of the cell servers
- Reduced impact to vCloud Director application upgrades

Load balancing improves scalability in the following areas:

- Number of concurrent operations
- Number of active and concurrent console sessions via the console proxy service
- Number of concurrent users
- Number of vCenter Server operations (when multiple vCenter servers are attached to the vCloud Director instance)

vCloud Networking and Security Edge can be used to load-balance vCloud Director cells, in addition to third-party external hardware or virtual gateways as load balancers.

Table A.2 lists the design considerations for load balancing of vCloud Director cells.

TABLE A.2 Load Balancer Considerations

Consideration	Detail
Security	A front-end firewall is typically deployed in front of the load balancer. In some environments, additional firewalls can be located between vCloud Director cells and the resource tiers vCenter manages. Load balancers can also provide NAT/SNAT (source network address translation) for the clustered cells. VMware recommends securing access between cells and the other management and resource group components. Refer to the *vCloud Director Installation and Configuration Guide* for ports that must be opened.
Single vCloud Director site and scope	This architecture covers load balancing of a single vCloud Director site or instance. It does not cover client application load balancing or global load balancing.

Consideration	Detail
Sizing recommendations for number of cells	VMware recommends the number of vCloud Director cell instances = n+1, where *n* is the number of vCenter Server instances providing computing resources for vCloud consumption. Based on the service definition *requirements*, two vCloud Director cell instances are sufficient to increase availability and upgradeability (first upgrade one vCloud Director cell, then upgrade the other).
Requirements for multicell configurations	Multiple vCloud Director cells require NTP (Network Time Protocol), which is a design guideline for all elements of the vCloud infrastructure. See the white paper *Timekeeping in VMware Virtual Machines* (www.vmware.com/files/pdf/Timekeeping-In-VirtualMachines.pdf) for more information on how to set up NTP.
Load balancer availability	Use at least two load balancers in an HA configuration to reduce single points of failure. Multiple strategies for this are used, depending on the vendor or software used.
Proxy configuration	Each load-balanced vCloud Director cell requires setting a proxy console IP address that the load balancer typically provides.
Rest API URL configuration	Map the vCloud service URL to the address that the load balancer provides. This is configured in the vCloud Director administrator GUI and in the load balancer configuration. Use this address to check the health status of the vCloud Director cell.
Awareness of multicell roles	Some vCloud Director cell tasks (such as image transfer) can consume significant resources. All cells can perform the same set of tasks, but it is possible to set policies that affect which ones are used.
Load balancer session persistence	Sessions are generally provided in secure methods and are terminated at the cells. Because of this, session persistence should be enabled using SSL.
Load-balancing algorithm	Least connections or round robin is generally acceptable.
vCloud Director cell status health checks	▶ Configure the load balancer service to check the health of individual vCloud Director cells. Because each cell responds by way of HTTPS, this can be configured through the IP and API endpoint URL. Load balancers might support other types of health checks. An example UI URL is https://my.cloud.com/cloud/ ▶ An example is to use a well known URL such as the https://my.cloud.com/api/versions vCloud API URL. In the second example, the versions this endpoint supports are returned as XML. Check services periodically based on load. A good starting point is to check every five seconds.

Consideration	Detail
Public IP/port	Specify the service IP appropriately before adding cells to the service group. Typically, port 443 (standard HTTPS) is the only port exposed.
Web Application Firewall	This can be used to apply URL restrictions on vCloud Director access to admin or organization portals based on source address. It requires SSL sessions to be terminated on the load balancer.
SSL Initiation	This is used when SSL is terminated on the load balancer to initiate an SSL session to the vCloud Director cells (which accept only HTTPS).
Advanced configurations	Load balancers can also provide Layer 7 content switching or direction, which can allow a vCloud Director configuration to send certain types of client traffic to dedicated cells. Although each cell can perform any function, it is possible to separate functions by directing certain types of requests to specific cells.
Connection mapping	When a cell joins an existing vCloud Director server group, it might try to load-balance sessions. This can affect connection mapping through the load balancer because it is unaware of the balancing that is occurring within the server group.

APPENDIX B
Security

This appendix provides security guidance relating to VMware security certifications, network access, Single Sign-On (SSO), and demilitarized zone (DMZ).

VMware Security Certifications

Third-party certifications such as Common Criteria (CC), Federal Information Processing Standards (FIPS), the National Institute of Standards and Technology (NIST), Security Content Automation Protocol (SCAP) provide independent validation of the security of VMware products.

The Common Criteria (CC) certification is an industry-recognized standard for computer security certification that provides a set of requirements used to evaluate and certify the security of a system.

Federal Information Processing Standards (FIPS) is a standard for U.S. government computer systems used by all nonmilitary agencies. The Federal Information Processing Standards (FIPS) 140 series specifies hardware and software requirements for cryptographic modules.

The Security Content Automation Protocol (SCAP) certification determines the capability of a product to implement SCAP for configuration, vulnerability scanning, and remediation.

Organizations across a variety of verticals either require or recommend the use of products adhering to validation under Common Criteria, FIPS, and SCAP.

For the latest information on the state of VMware security certifications, go to https://www.vmware.com/support/support-resources/certifications.html.

Common Criteria

The National Institute of Standards and Technology (NIST) and the National Security Agency (NSA) established a program under the National Information Assurance Partnership (NIAP) to evaluate IT product conformance to international standards.

Characteristics of the Common Criteria certification include the following:

- Internationally recognized standard (among 26 member nations)
- Mutually recognized by all nations (up to EAL4)
- ISO standard (ISO15408)

The Common Criteria program, officially known as the NIAP Common Criteria Evaluation and Validation Scheme for IT Security (CCEVS), is a partnership between the public and private sectors. This program is intended to help consumers select commercial off-the-shelf information technology (IT) products that meet necessary security requirements and to help manufacturers of those products gain acceptance in the global marketplace. VMware has participated in Common Criteria evaluation of products beginning with VMware ESX Server 2.5 and VMware VirtualCenter 1.2 in March 2006.

As of August 2012, the NIAP has instituted multiple changes to the Common Criteria certification processes, including making changes to the certification levels offered and eliminating the In Evaluation List. The highest level of certification now available is EAL 2+ (Evaluation Assurance Level 2). This new designation is more robust than the previous EAL4+ certification level, which was the highest level attainable. Each successive level of the Common Criteria is harder to achieve and requires additional validation, testing, and documentation.

vSphere 5.1, including the new Single Sign-On components, is currently under evaluation as part of the new EAL2+ certification. The Common Criteria certification of vSphere 5.1 at EAL2+ demonstrates VMware's continued commitment to the evolving standards and validation of the latest VMware platform that provides assurance to our customers.

Other Common Criteria evaluations are as follows:

- VMware vCloud Networking and Security v5.1.2 is undergoing Common Criteria Certification evaluation for EAL4+ under the old program.
- VMware vFabric™ tc Server 2.8.2 is going through Common Criteria certification under the new EAL2+ scheme.

Federal Information Processing Standards

The Federal Information Processing Standards (FIPS) publications are guidelines that set best practices for software and hardware computer security products.

FIPS 140-2 is the standard for Security Requirements for Cryptographic Modules. It is important to understand that while FIPS 140-2 does not require Common Criteria as they are completely separate validations, there is a connection between them.

With a Common Criteria evaluation, if security claims are being made that depend on cryptography to enforce security, the cryptography must be FIPS 140 validated cryptography, unless the data being protecting is considered management data and not user data. For management data, only algorithm validations are required through the Cryptographic Algorithm Validation Program (CAVP).

For the vSphere Common Criteria certifications, VMware only claimed protection of the management data and performed algorithm validations different from a FIPS 140 validation. Therefore, vSphere does not currently have FIPS 140 validated cryptography.

Security Content Automation Protocol

NIST has validated that both VMware vCenter Configuration Manager and vCenter Protect Essentials Government Edition (with SCAP Processor) conform to the Security Content Automation Protocol (SCAP) standards. The following depicts the VMware product and SCAP validations:

- VMware vCenter Configuration Manager v5.5
    - **FDCC Scanner:** The capability to audit and assess a target system to determine its compliance with the FDCC requirements.
    - **USGCB Scanner:** The capability to audit and assess a target system to determine its compliance using USGCB content.
    - **Authenticated Configuration Scanner:** The capability to audit and assess a target system to determine its compliance with a defined set of configuration requirements using target system logon privileges.
    - **Authenticated Vulnerability and Patch Scanner:** The capability to scan a target system to locate and identify the presence of known vulnerabilities and evaluate the software patch status to determine compliance with a defined patch policy using target system logon privileges.
- vCenter Protect Essentials Government Edition (with SCAP Processor) v8.0
    - FDCC Scanner: The capability to audit and assess a target system to determine its compliance with the FDCC requirements.

For more information on SCAP validated products, go to http://nvd.nist.gov/scapproducts.cfm.

Network Access Security

vCloud Networking and Security Edge VPN functionality facilitates the creation of site-to-site tunnels using IPsec. It supports NAT-T traversal for using IPsec through network address translation (NAT) devices.

vCloud Networking and Security Edge exposes three VPN services. Consider the following terminology:

- IPsec is the first service provided by Edge. This facilitates Layer 3 site-to-site connectivity.

SSL VPN-Plus exposes two additional VPN services:

- Remote access
- Layer 2 site-to-site connectivity

The two site-to-site mechanisms solve different problems. Layer 2 site-to-site connectivity extends a network across boundaries so that the virtual machines being extended are not aware of it and do not require changes to their routing, MAC addresses, and so forth. vCloud Connector typically uses this for datacenter extensions. Layer 3 site-to-site connectivity is a typical site-to-site solution that interconnects two networks.

vCloud Networking and Security Edge supports NAT traversal (NAT-T). NAT-T addresses the use case in which, when terminating the remote IPsec client, the client is often located behind a device that performs SNAT (source network address translation). In this case, the SNAT on the IPsec traffic can modify the source address and UDP port in the packet, which makes the original packet invalid.

Table B.1 provides the use cases tied to network access.

TABLE B.1 Network Access Security Use Cases

Category	Description
Multisite vCloud deployment	The vCloud Networking and Security VPN can connect multiple vCloud deployments. For example, an organization's virtual datacenter at a public vCloud provider can be securely connected with the organization's internal private vCloud. Or virtual datacenters hosted at a vCloud service provider in Europe can be connected to a vCloud service in Asia. Because vCloud Networking and Security also provides address translation, it is possible to deploy multiple organization virtual datacenters at different providers using the same RFC 1918 address space, as long as unique subnets are used.
Single-site vCloud deployment	vCloud Networking and Security VPNs can be created between different organizations in the same vCloud Director instance or different networks within the same organization. For these deployments, the site-to-site VPN is used to secure sensitive traffic between networks over shared infrastructure.

Category	Description
Remote site to vCloud VPN	A permanent secure connection from a router- or firewall-based VPN, for example, from Cisco or Juniper devices at a remote site to a vCloud environment with vCloud Networking and Security Edge. vCloud Networking and Security VPN uses a standards-based IPsec implementation, which enables a wide range of devices to be used at the remote site (commercial or open source).
Client to vCloud VPN	Client software is generally not used with IPsec VPNs (an IPsec VPN is typically a permanent network-to-network tunnel), although clients with static IP addresses that implement preshared key authentication are supported.

Site-to-site IPsec VPN configuration is available to organization administrators directly from the vCloud Director web console. VPN functionality is implemented using integration with the vCloud Networking and Security Edge Gateway Services, which provides per-tenant Layer 3 network security and routing. Preshared key mode, IP unicast traffic, and NAT-T traversal with no dynamic routing protocols are supported between the vCloud Networking and Security Edge device and peers. Behind each remote VPN endpoint, multiple subnets can be configured to connect to the network behind a vCloud Networking and Security Edge device over IPsec tunnels. These networks must have nonoverlapping address ranges.

When configuring a site-to-site VPN between different organization virtual datacenter networks in a vCloud environment (across different vCloud environments or within an organization), much of the configuration complexity is abstracted from the vCloud consumer. After the appropriate networks are selected, both ends of the VPN tunnel are configured to provide compatibility between the edge peers. In comparison, configuring remote devices to connect to a VPN based on vCloud Networking and Security Edge requires understanding IPsec and the supported policies to successfully establish an encrypted tunnel.

The vCloud Networking and Security Edge VPN uses the following IKE Phase 1 parameters:

- Main mode
- Preshared key authentication mode
- AES-256 (Default), AES or 3DES
- SHA1 authentication
- MODP Group 2 (1024 bits)
- SA lifetime of 28800 seconds (8 hours)
- Disabled ISAKMP aggressive mode

The following additional parameters for IKE Phase 2 are supported:

- Quick Mode
- Diffie-Helman Group 2/5 (1024 bit/1536 bit, respectively)
- Perfect Forward Secrecy (PFS)
- ESP tunnel mode
- SA lifetime of 3600 seconds (1 hour)

vCloud Networking and Security Edge VPN proposes a policy that requires AES-256 (Default), AES or 3DES (configurable, although AES-256 is recommended), SHA1, PSK, and DH Group 2/5.

To allow IPsec VPN traffic, the following ports must be open on firewalls between the two endpoints:

- Protocol 50 ESP
- Protocol 51 AH
- UDP port 500 IKE
- UDP port 4500

The external IP address for the vCloud Networking and Security Edge device must be accessible to the remote endpoint, either directly or using NAT. In a NAT deployment, the external address of the vCloud Networking and Security Edge device must be translated into a publicly accessible address. Remote VPN endpoints then use this public address to access the vCloud Networking and Security Edge device.

It is also possible for the remote VPN endpoints to be located behind an NAT device, although on both ends a static one-to-one NAT is required for the external IP address.

VPNs provide secure access to an organization's remote networks, and consumers should be aware of any security implications. A guideline for VPN configuration is to filter and restrict VPN traffic to necessary destinations. vCloud Director 1.5 (and later) can also apply firewall rules to VPN traffic (filtering was previously restricted to only the remote end of a VPN tunnel).

The vCloud Director IPsec VPN has a maximum of 10 sites per vCloud Networking and Security Edge device.

Figure B.1 shows a sample configuration for site-to-site VPN connectivity.

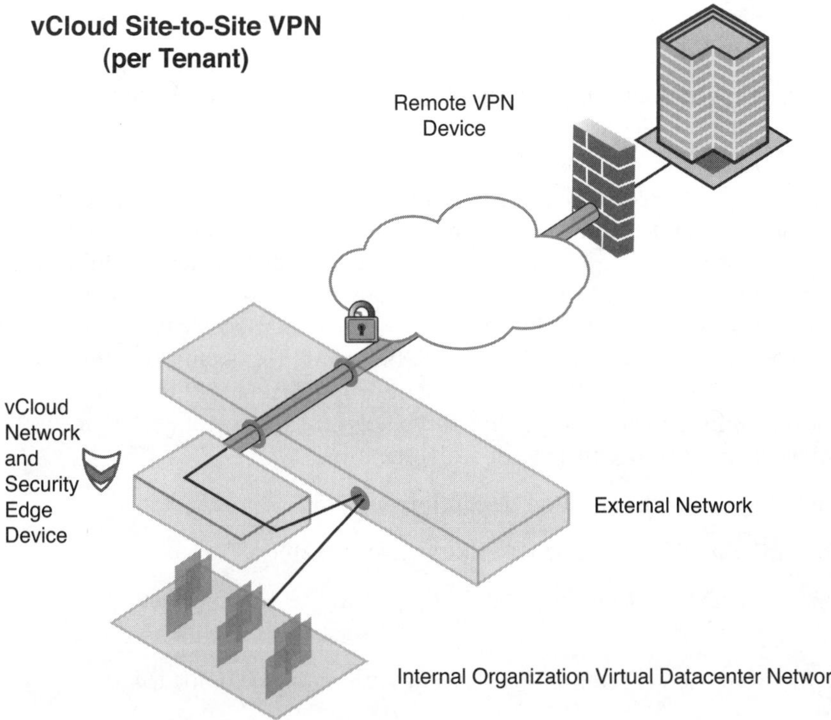

FIGURE B.1 Site-to-site VPN connectivity

The following features are not currently supported in any Edge VPN implementation:

- Remote endpoints with dynamic IP addresses.
- Site-to-site VPNs at the vApp network level (available only to organization virtual datacenter networks).
- SSL VPNs. These typically support per-user tunnels instead of network tunnels with IPsec VPNs, work over HTTPS, and are based on vendor-specific implementations.
- IPv6 support.
- Authentication types other than preshared keys (for example, certificates).
- Fenced vApps (VPN can be enabled only on routed networks).

Two-Factor Authentication

The following are options for providing two-factor authentication to a vCloud Solution:

- Enable SSPI support in vCloud Director 5.1 and delegate authentication to Active Directory, which has a number of two-factor solutions.

- Implement SAML with vCloud Director 5.1, and configure the SAML Identity Provider (IdP) to use SSPI.
- Implement a third-party solution [for example, RSA SecurID, HyTrust Cloud Control, or Safenet Authentication Service (SAS)].

Note : Both SSPI and SAML do not relate directly to two-factor authentication, but rather refer to a technology that abstracts away authentication systems that may or may not use two-factor authentication. SSPI is most appropriate for enterprise deployments, whilst in general VMware recommend SAML as the way to go for any new vCloud deployments. vCloud Director 5.1 adds support for Security Support Provider Interface (SSPI), which is Microsoft's proprietary implementation of GSSAPI. SSPI is an API for obtaining numerous security services, including integrated Windows authentication. Using SSPI to delegate identity verification to Windows and Active Directory allows for the use of authentication mechanisms such as secure token or two-factor authentication.

The following are two-factor authentication design implications:

- The authentication method must be set to Kerberos to enable SSPI.
- The Organizations LDAP settings must be configured to use Active Directory with Kerberos.
- The keytab file from the Kerberos authentication server must be uploaded.
- The keytab upload is the only step required beyond a normal vCloud Director with Kerberos setup.
- The Service Principal Name (SPN) must be specified. A client uses the SPN to uniquely identify an instance of a service.
- A keytab file is needed to enable authentication for the SPN.
- Using SSPI implies that the workstation must be a member of an Active Directory domain.
- By using SSPI, vCloud Director is allowing a trust relationship to Active Directory to perform the authentication on behalf of vCloud Director.
- Using native support for two-factor authentication solutions through SSPI enables service providers and enterprise organizations to achieve strong authentication without requiring manual configuration or integration of each individual virtualization host.
- Combining technologies from VMware and third parties such as RSA, Symantec, and HyTrust enables end-to-end security of vCloud infrastructure and accelerates time to market.
- VMware is continually evolving and adding new security components to its security framework, including capabilities such as controlling identities enterprise-wide, supporting more secure authentication methods, and providing interoperability with future vCloud Director releases.

Secure Certificates

To provide security for a vCloud service based on VMware vCloud Director, VMware requires the implementation of certificates and key management for secure access and authentication to the vCloud Director server during its installation.

vCloud Director uses symmetric encryption to protect sensitive data from eavesdroppers and unwanted guests, uses public key encryption to exchange keys securely over an insecure transport, and supports certificates and their digital signatures to establish a trust relationship. This makes it possible to create a secure protocol and channel between the vCloud Director service and end tenant that functions over an insecure connection without any previous interaction between the parties. This enables secure data transmission in a shared, multitenant environment.

Secure Certificates Example

Deployment models are private, public, and hybrid.

In the vCloud environment, Secure Sockets Layer (SSL) and Transport Layer Security (TLS) protocols provide secure communication between the end tenant (client) and vCloud Director cell (server). The secure communication includes confidentiality and privacy of communication, message integrity and hashing, and authentication.

Web browsers display a warning message indicating that a site's identity cannot be trusted if a certificate has expired or if the certificate was issued by a certificate authority that is not trusted. The primary role of SSL/TLS is to provide confidentiality and privacy of the communication and to prevent MITM (man-in-the-middle) attacks, side channel attacks, and attacks intended to compromise your privacy and security. Figure B.2 shows an example security message generated when the preceding conditions occur.

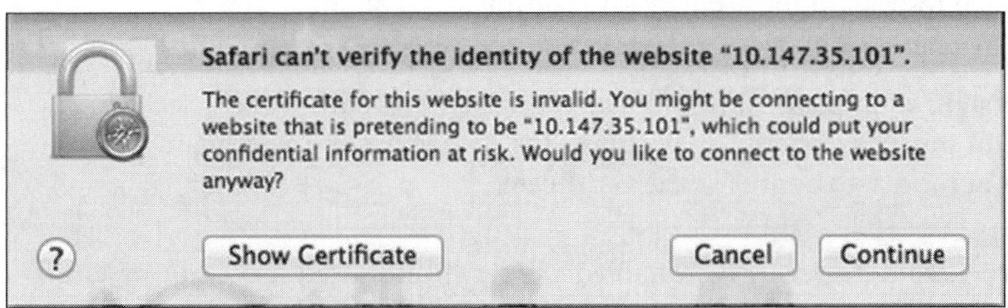
Safari can't verify the identity of the website "10.147.35.101".
The certificate for this website is invalid. You might be connecting to a website that is pretending to be "10.147.35.101", which could put your confidential information at risk. Would you like to connect to the website anyway?
?
Show Certificate
Cancel
Continue

FIGURE B.2 Example error message

Message integrity and hashing is the capability to guarantee that the data has not been modified during the protocol exchange and transmission.

Using *certificates for authentication* is a process of confirming identity. In the context of network interactions, authentication involves one party identifying another party. Certificates are one way of supporting authentication.

Certificates or digital certificates are collections of data that uniquely identify and verify an individual, company, or other entity on the Internet. Certificates also enable secure, confidential communication between two entities. In the context of vCloud Director, server certificates establish secure sessions between the cell server and clients using SSL and TLS.

Figure B.3 shows the address bar for a website that has been secured using SSL/TLS. The URL begins with https, and a padlock symbol appears in the top-right corner of the browser.

FIGURE B.3 Website address bar

Types of SSL certificates are the following:

- Self-signed certificate: Generated for internal purposes, and not issued by a certificate authority (CA).
- Domain-signed certificate:
  - An entry-level SSL certificate that can be issued quickly.
  - The only check performed is to verify that the applicant owns the domain where the certificate will be used.
  - No additional checks are done to confirm that the owner of the domain is a valid business entity.
- Fully authenticated SSL certificate:
  - First step to true online security and confidence building.
  - Takes slightly longer to issue because these certificates are granted only after the organization passes a number of validation procedures and checks to confirm the existence of the business, the ownership of the domain, and the user's authority to apply for the certificate.
- Server Gated Cryptography (SGC)–enabled SSL certificate: Used for old browsers or clients that do not support 128/256-bit encryption.
- Wildcard certificate: Applies full SSL security to any host in domain.
- SAN (Subject Alternative Name) SSL certificate: Allows more than one domain to be added to a single SSL certificate.
- Code signing certificate: Specifically designed to make sure that downloaded software was not tampered with during the download.
- Extended Validation (EV) SSL certificates: Offers the highest industry standard for authentication and the highest level of customer trust.

For a private, hybrid, or public vCloud provider, VMware recommends implementing SSL certificates from a trusted CA.

The following process flow, shown in Figure B.4, outlines all the steps to request, configure, obtain, and install an SSL certificate from a CA that can be used as for a CA for vCloud Director.

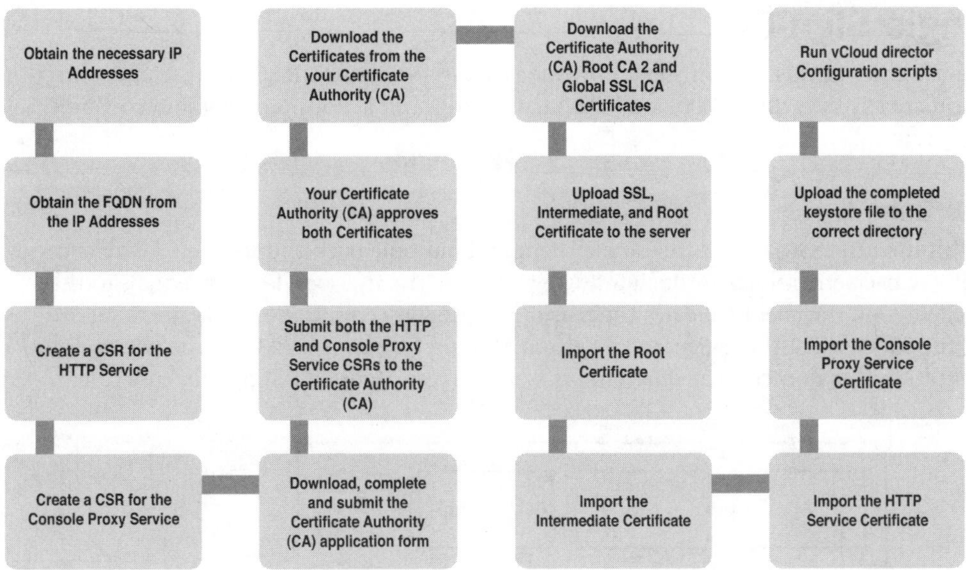

FIGURE B.4 Requesting, configuring, obtaining, and installing an SSL certificate from a CA

The following guidelines apply when considering SSL certificates:

- Understand and evaluate the different types of SSL certificates that are available, and use one that matches your requirements.
- In a production environment, do not configure vCloud Director to use self-signed certificates. This is an insecure practice. Self-signed certificates are certificates that are digitally signed by the private key corresponding to the public key included in the certificate. This is done in place of having a CA signing the certificate. By self-signing a certificate, you are attesting that you are who you say you are. No trusted third-party validation is involved.
- Self-signed certificates do not have a valid chain of signatures leading to a trusted root certificate and provide a weaker form of security. Although you can verify that such a certificate is internally consistent, anyone can create one, so examining the certificate does not confirm that it is safe to trust the issuer or the site from which the certificate is coming. Nevertheless, self-signed certificates are common. For example, vCenter installations use a self-signed certificate by default.

- The server keystore is highly sensitive because a compromise of the server key allows impersonation of the server and/or access to the encrypted traffic. Java keystores provide a password-protected method of securely storing private keys and their associated certificates. vCloud Director supports only the JCEKS format for keystore files. (Other formats that Java supports include PKCS12 and JKS. JKS is less secure and is not recommended).

Single Sign-On

The use cases in this section show how the web Single Sign-On (SSO) feature and configuration are exposed through vCloud Director 5.1 for both service provider and consumer architectures.

Use Case 1

In this use case, SSO applies to a single client and multiple back-end services. A user accesses multiple back-end servers through a single UI client. The user provides credentials to the UI client, and the client validates them against the SSO server. If the validation is successful, the SSO server issues a Security Assertion Markup Language (SAML) token, which the UI client then uses to access the different back-end servers. Figure B.5 shows this use case.

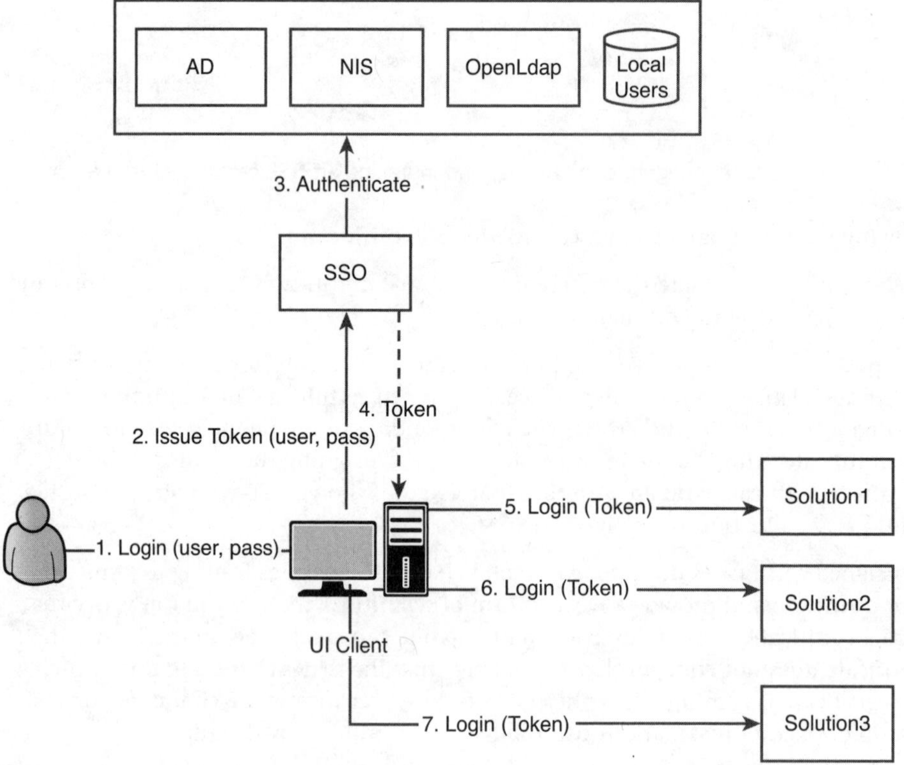

FIGURE B.5 SSO Between a single client and multiple back-end services

Use Case 2

This use case illustrates solution-to-solution authentication in which an SSO user is assigned to each solutions. In Figure B.6, two solutions need to communicate with each other. Before they start to communicate, they must verify each other's identity. To do so, each solution initiates a request from the SSO server to issue a SAML token that asserts its identity. As part of this request, the solution proves its identity using its own private key. After the SSO server has issued a token, the solution can use that token to access any other solution as if it were a normal user. For this use case to work, each solution must be registered with its public key in the SSO server.

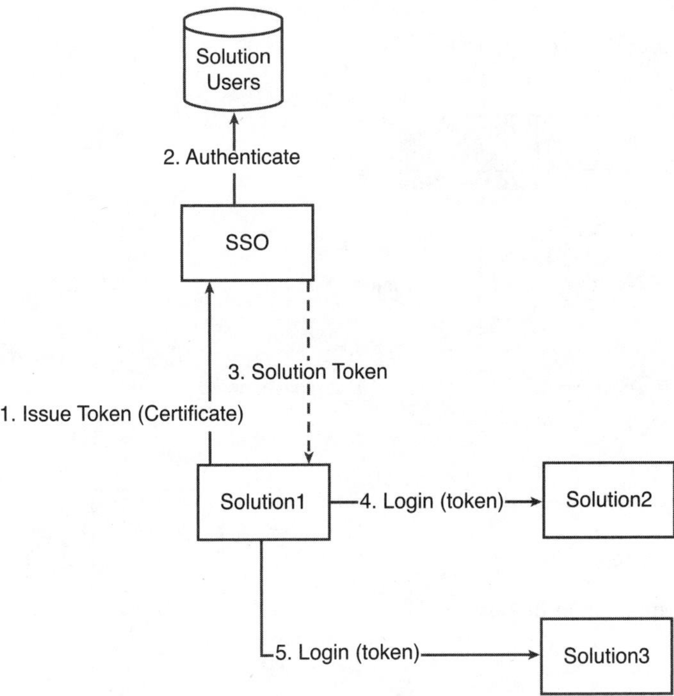

FIGURE B.6 SSO solution-to-solution authentication

Use Case 3

In this use case, tasks are executed on behalf of a user (referred to as *delegation*). Some workflows that an end user initiates might require multiple solutions to communicate with each other, and SSO can support such workflows. Before the user can initiate the workflow through a given UI, the user must provide credentials. The UI validates the credentials against the SSO server, which issues a SAML token. The user then initiates a workflow.

In Figure B.7, the workflow requires Solution-1 to access Solution-2 and Solution-3 on behalf of the end user. As part of this process, the UI requests a *delegated* token from the

SSO server for Solution-1 by providing the SAML token of the end user. The delegated token asserts that the user has granted Solution-1 the privileges to execute tasks on the user's behalf. After the UI has the delegated token, it gives it to Solution-1 to use to log into Solution-2 and Solution-3.

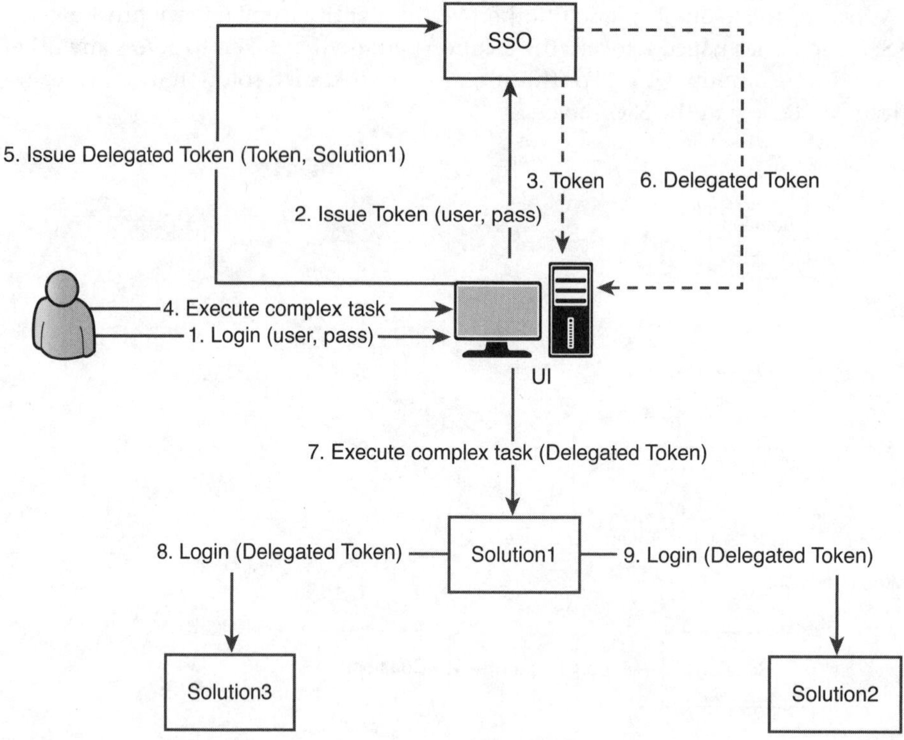

FIGURE B.7 Executing tasks on behalf of a user

Use Case 4

This use case involves scheduling long-lived tasks and is referred to as *delegation and renew*. Some long-running operations in the infrastructure require executing long-running tasks in the absence of the end user who initiated them. The SSO server supports such tasks by means of delegated and renewable tokens.

After a long-running task is identified, the UI obtains a delegated and renewable token from the SSO server. It then passes the token to the solution, which performs the long-running task. The solution persists the token in a nonsecured way because the token is self-secured. Every time the task is activated, the solution reads the token from the disk and makes a request to the SSO server to renew it. The user is not deleted from the system during this process. Figure B.8 shows this workflow.

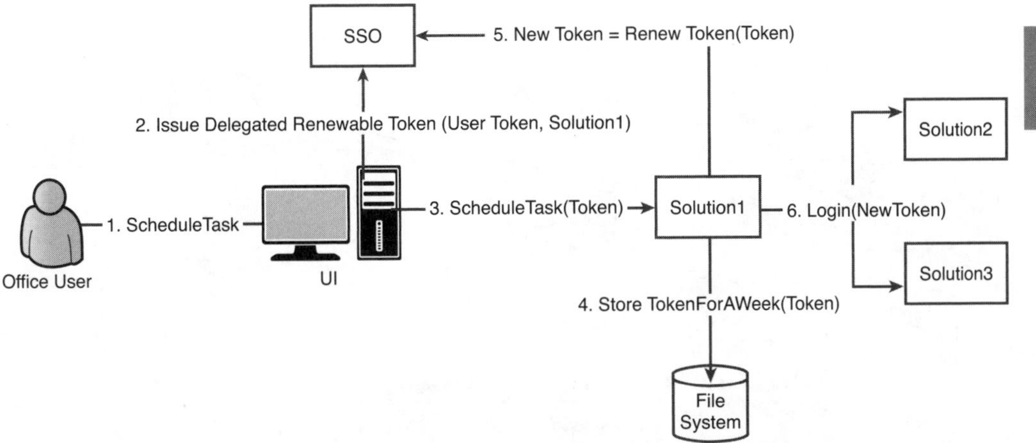

FIGURE B.8 Scheduling long-lived tasks

Consumer SSO Architecture Example

Figure B.9 shows a consumer logical SSO deployment architecture.

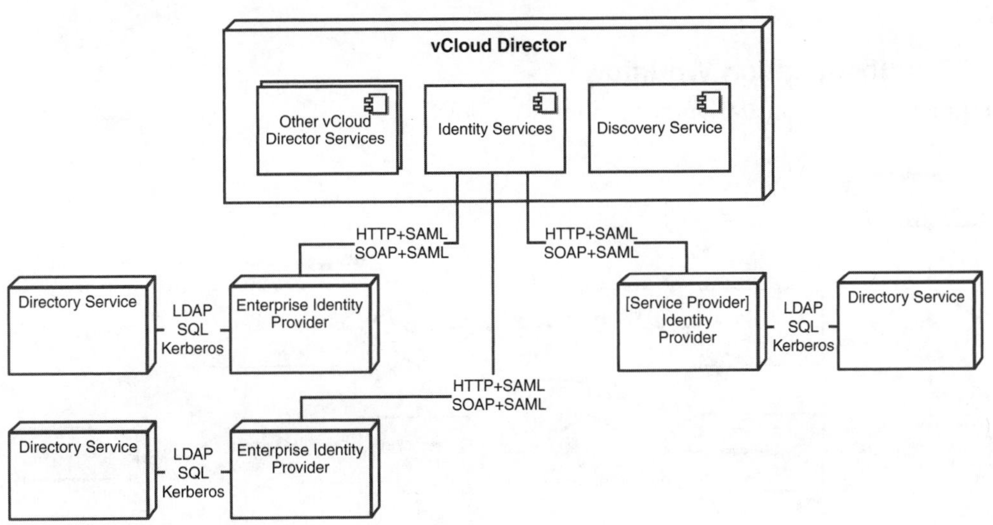

FIGURE B.9 Consumer logical SSO deployment architecture

vCloud Provider SSO Architecture Example

Figure B.10 shows a vCloud provider SSO architecture example.

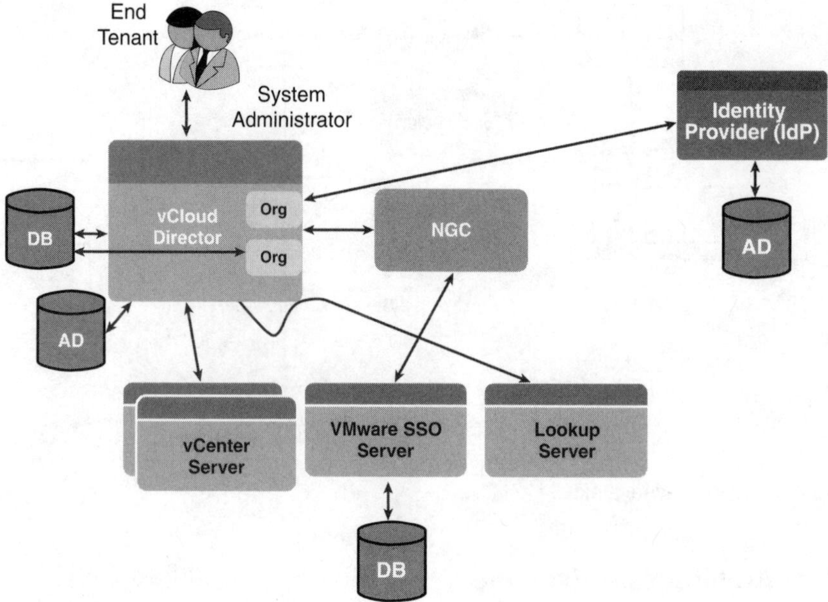

FIGURE B.10 vCloud provider SSO architecture example

SSO Authentication Workflow

Figure B.11 shows an SSO authentication workflow.

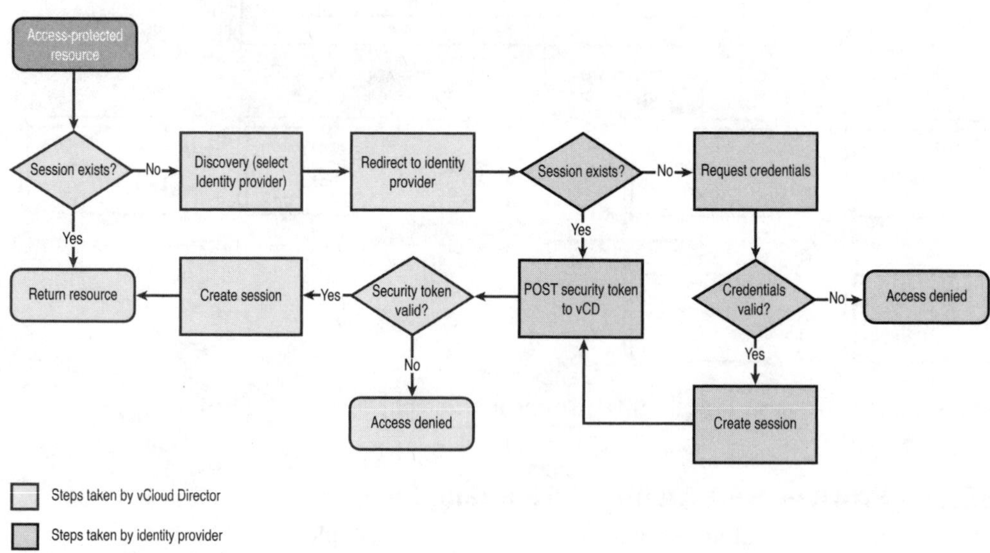

FIGURE B.11 SSO authentication workflow

You can use SSO to authenticate with the vCloud API in the following ways:

- Use the POST/sessions vCloud API, which accepts security tokens as the request body. The following URL in the vCloud API Programming Guide provides an example of how to log in with a SAML assertion. More details can be found on-line here:

  http://pubs.vmware.com/vcd-51/topic/com.vmware.vcloud.api.doc_51/GUID-335CFC35-7AD8-40E5-91BE-53971937A2BB.html:

  - **HTTP-Basic authentication:** Logs in using a username and password to an integrated identity provider for backward compatibility with vCloud Director v1.5. The integrated identity provider basically provides local user management. More details can be found on-line here:

    http://pubs.vmware.com/vcd-51/topic/com.vmware.vcloud.api.doc_51/GUID-536ED934-ECE3-4B17-B7E5-F8D0765C9ECB.html.

  - **SAML assertion:** You are required to have a SAML assertion from a registered Identity Provider (IdP).

- **SAML User and Group Administration:** It is possible to import users and groups from an external Identity Provider (IdP) that supports SAML. More details can be found on-line here:

  http://pubs.vmware.com/vcd-51/topic/com.vmware.vcloud.api.doc_51/GUID-4E0DF041-CC29-4327-9E58-E62D55716CE0.html

SSO Design Considerations

The following are SSO design considerations recommended for deployment.

- Use SSO to provide a common service, both internally and externally.
- Use a supported Identity Provider (IdP) from VMware.
- To federate with vCloud Director you need to get the metadata for the realm you will be federating with.
- vCloud Director and the Identity Provider (IdP) must be time-synchronized to within a few seconds.
- vCloud Director and the Identity Provider (IdP) must have valid endpoint certificates.
- Use a consistent hostname (or IP address) when registering with the LookupService.
- If the SSO Server is not accessible and the accessibility issue cannot be resolved, use the SSO repoint tools that are that are packaged with SSO clients such as vCenter and the web client.
- VMware officially support OpenAM, OpenSSO, and Active Directory Federation Services 2.0. However, in theory we support any other SAML 2.0 compliant Identity Provider (IdP), but VMware does not QA or test them.

- Provide a highly available SSO service.
- Deploying vCenter Single Sign-On as a cluster means that two or more instances of vCenter Single Sign-On are installed in high availability (HA) mode. vCenter Single Sign-On HA mode is not the same as vSphere HA. All instances of vCenter Single Sign-On use the same database and must point to the same identity sources. When connected to vCenter Server through the VMware vSphere Web Client, vCenter Single Sign-On administrator users see the primary SSO instance. In this deployment scenario, the installation process grants admin@System-Domain vCenter Server privileges by default, and the installation process creates the user admin@System-Domain to manage vCenter Single Sign-On.
- ESXi 5.1 is not integrated with vCenter Single Sign-On, and you cannot create ESXi users with the vSphere Web Client. You must create and manage ESXi users with the vSphere Client. vCenter Server is not aware of users that are local to ESXi, and ESXi is not aware of vCenter Server users. However, you can configure vCenter Single Sign-On to use an Active Directory domain as an identity source, and configure ESXi to point to the same Active Directory domain to obtain user and group information.

DMZ Considerations

VMware recommends that you follow standard DMZ firewall design guidelines in a vCloud environment. However, the following aspects require special consideration. Some vCloud Director operations involve sessions that remain open to management infrastructure, which is protected by the back-end firewall, for an extended period.

- **Idle session timeouts:** Depending on the level of activity within the vCloud environment, some connections, such as sessions to vSphere hosts to retrieve thumbnails by way of the vslad agent and to vCenter Server for inventory, might require adjustment to default TCP timeout policies. This also applies to the Oracle Notification Service (ONS) connections needed for fast connection failover support in Oracle RAC environments.
- **Dead connection detection or equivalent:** Many firewalls support functionality to allow idle but still valid connections to persist. This modifies the idle timeout behavior by probing endpoints of the connection and verifying that the session is not terminated.
- **Logging:** Send firewall logs to a centralized syslog server.
- **SMTP filtering:** Many firewalls filter email connections, restricting ESMTP commands. Disabling this capability might be necessary to permit vCloud Director to send mail notifications.
- **Bandwidth:** Some vCloud operations require either high throughput or low latency (examples of this are NFS transfer access and database access). The firewall must be correctly specified so that it does not become a performance bottleneck.

- **Availability:** Deploy firewalls and load balancers in highly available pairs, where possible.
- **Secure administrative access:** Tightly control access to the management networks using strong authentication, logging, and encryption.
- **Scalability:** vCloud environments are typically architected to scale and support a large number of workloads and users. Scale firewalls along with the vCloud to help avoid future downtime.

Port Requirements

Table B.2 provides a mapping of vCloud Director port requirements that the networking and security teams can use to enable access.

TABLE B.2 vCloud Director Port Requirements

Description	Ports	Protocol	Direction
vCloud Director portal and console proxy access	443	TCP	Inbound
SSH (back-end management access only)	22	TCP	Inbound
JDBC access to Oracle database	1521 (default)	TCP	Outbound
ONS connections for Oracle RAC	6200 (default)	TCP	Outbound
Microsoft SQL database port	1433 (default)	TCP	Outbound
vSphere web access to vCenter Server	443	TCP	Outbound
Virtual machine console to vCenter Server	902, 903	TCP	Outbound
vSphere web access to ESX/vSphere host	443	TCP	Outbound
Virtual machine console to vSphere host	902	TCP	Outbound
REST API access to vCloud Networking and Security Manager	443	TCP	Outbound
SMTP	25	TCP	Outbound
DNS client	53	TCP, UDP	Outbound
NTP client	123	TCP, UDP	Outbound
LDAP	389	TCP	Outbound
LDAPS	636	TCP	Outbound
Syslog	514	UDP	Outbound
NFS portmapper (optional)	111	TCP, UDP	Inbound and outbound
NFS rpc.statd (optional)	920	TCP, UDP	Inbound and outbound
ActiveMQ	61611, 61616	TCP	Inbound and outbound

Figure B.12 provides a mapping between vCloud components by showing the vCloud Director port requirements.

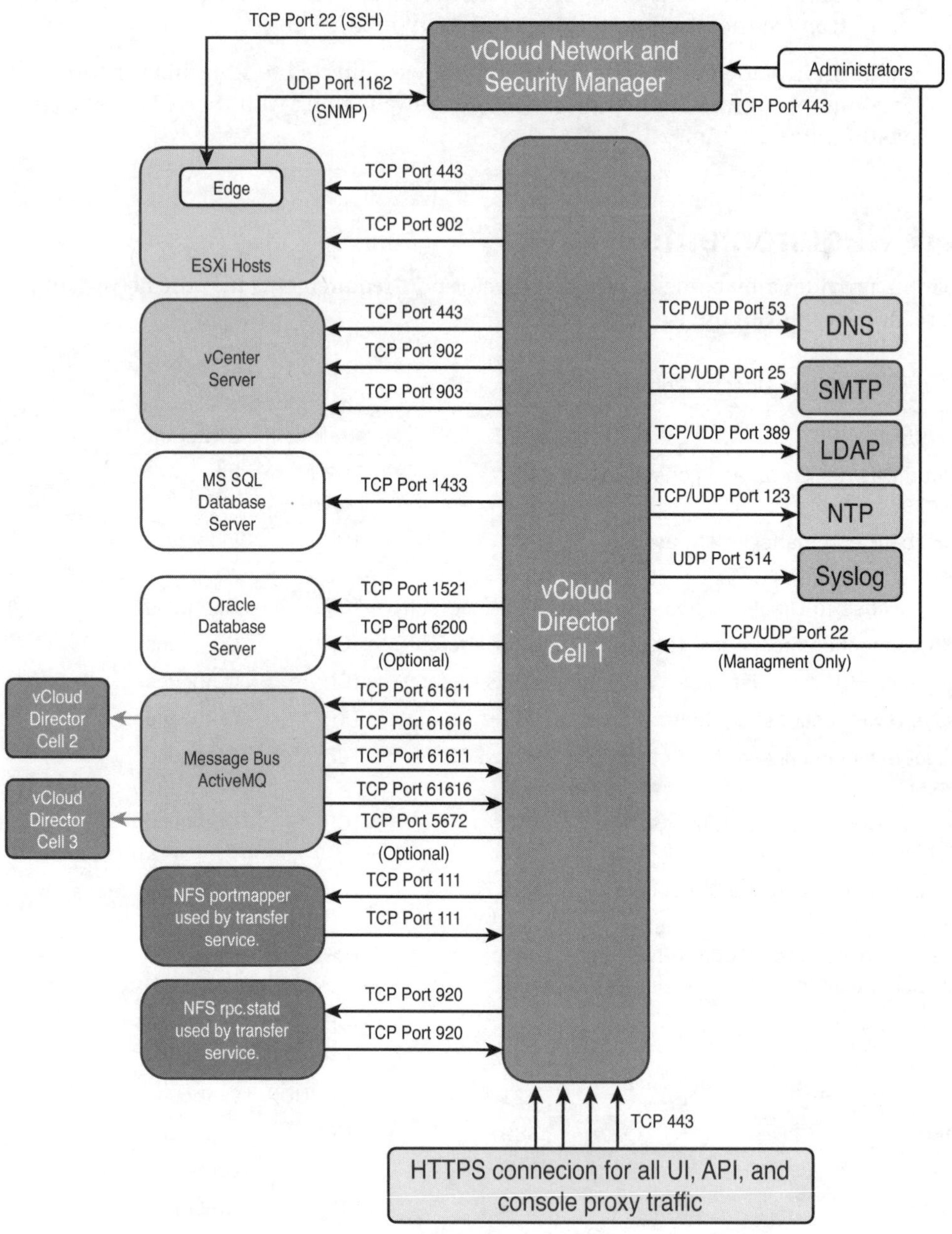

FIGURE B.12 vCloud Director port requirements

Table B.3 provides the vCenter Orchestrator port requirements.

TABLE B.3 vCenter Orchestrator Port Requirements

Name	Protocol	Hostname	Default Port
Database	Oracle	Oracle Database Server	1521
	MSSQL	Microsoft SQL Server	1433
Directory Service	LDAP/LDAP SSL/GC	Microsoft Active Directory Server	389/636/3268
	LDAP/LDAP SSL	Novell eDirectory	389/636
	LDAP/LDAP SSL	Sun Java Directory Server	389/636
Domain Name System	DNS	DNS Server	53
vCenter Server	HTTPS	vCenter Server	443
vCloud	HTTPS	vCloud Server or vCloud load balancer, if configured	443
SSH	SSH	SSH Server	22
Mail	SMTP	SMTP Server	25
Net	POP3	POP3 Server	110
JDBC	Oracle	Oracle Database Server	1521
	MSSQL	Microsoft SQL Server	1433
Cisco UCS Manager	HTTP	UCS Manager Server	80
SOAP	HTTP	SOAP Server	80
	HTTPS		443
REST	HTTP	Rest Server	80
	HTTPS		443
Microsoft Active Directory	LDAP msft-gc	Active Directory Domain Controller Server	3268
		Active Directory Global Catalog Domain Controller Server	389
VIX	HTTPS	vCenter Server	443

APPENDIX C
vCloud Suite Disaster Recovery

Disaster recovery for vCloud Director is described as "DR of the Cloud." It is full-site-based failover and recovery of the entire vCloud infrastructure, including associated vApps.

Because vCloud Director does not currently integrate with vCenter Site Recovery Manager, there is no obvious way to use vCenter Site Recovery Manager to protect a vCloud environment from a disaster scenario by failing over the site to a recovery site.

The VMware vCloud Suite assembles existing products to facilitate disaster recovery of the vCloud from one site to another. See the following for more information about how this architecture supports disaster recovery:

- *Overview of Disaster Recovery in vCloud Director* http://blogs.vmware.com/vcloud/2012/02/overview-of-disaster-recovery-in-vcloud-director.html
- *VMware vCloud Director Infrastructure Resiliency Case Study* www.vmware.com/files/pdf/techpaper/vcloud-director-infrastructure-resiliency.pdf

The following are the most important considerations:

- Stretched Layer 2 networking (see *Using VXLAN to Simplify vCloud Disaster Recovery*)
- IP address changes to applications
- Force-mounting of LUNs
- Order of management startup after vCenter Site Recovery Manager failover
- vApp startup with HA

- Failover process steps, order of operations
- Manual versus automated steps

This vCloud solution as described covers only the main use case of complete site-based failover. It also requires the configuration to handle the failover of an entire provider virtual datacenter. It does not prevent a provider from having unprotected virtual datacenters.

Dealing with vCloud disaster recovery has some design implications. Refer to your internal architecture documentation to understand vCloud disaster recovery design implications. If a vCloud design already exists, the design might require changes to support the current disaster recovery solution.

Using VXLAN to Simplify vCloud Disaster Recovery

When architecting a resilient multisite VMware virtual infrastructure, always consider the use of stretched Layer 2 networks to simplify solution design and the associated recovery process. The following are the main benefits of implementing stretched Layer 2 networks:

- Capability to run workloads in more than one geographical location
- Migration of virtual machine workloads between geographic locations
- No need for virtual machine IP address changes when migrating between environments
- Simplified disaster recovery when not using VMware vCenter Site Recovery Manager
- When used with vCenter Site Recovery Manager, simplified disaster recovery by not having to change IP addresses

Even with the simplification afforded by stretched Layer 2 networks, people tend to avoid them. The reason for this has to do with the network instability that is introduced when there is a lot of latency between switching nodes on the network. Stretched Layer 2 networks also increase the failure domain radius by encompassing multiple locations. Most people do not opt for stretched Layer 2 because of the higher cost usually associated with implementation.

Background

It has been demonstrated that vCenter Site Recovery Manager, in conjunction with some complementary custom automation, can offer a vCloud DR solution that enables recovery of a vCloud Director solution at a recovery site.

When stretched Layer 2 networks are present, the recovery of vApps is greatly simplified because vApps can remain connected to the same logically defined virtual networks, regardless of the physical location in which the vApps are running.

Although the existing vCloud disaster recovery process is theoretically capable of supporting designs that do not include stretched Layer 2 networks, it does not lend itself well to this configuration. The primary issue is the requirement to update the network configuration of all vApps. Several factors influence the complexity associated with the reconfiguration of vApp networking, including these:

- Type of networks to which a vApp is connected (organization virtual datacenter, organization external, or vApp)
- Routing configuration of the networks to which the vApp is connected (NAT routed or direct)
- Firewall and/or NAT configuration defined on vCloud Networking and Security Edge devices (NAT routed)
- Quantity of networks to which the vApp is connected

When connected to an organization virtual datacenter network, there is little or no impact. The vApp can retain its initial configuration because there are no dependencies upon the physical network. This is not the case for organization external networks.

In the case of vApps connected to an organization external network that is directly connected, the current vCloud disaster recovery process involves disconnecting vApps from the network for the production site and connecting them to an equivalent network for the recovery site. For this to work, site-specific network configuration parameters such as netmask, gateway, and DNS must be defined. Following reconfiguration, external references to the vApps also need updating. This situation is further complicated when an organization external network has a routed connection. The complication arises from the multiple IP address changes taking place:

1. The vApp is allocated a new IP address from the new organization virtual datacenter network.
2. The associated external network has a different IP address.

The introduction of vApp networks can further complicate the process.

VXLAN makes the disaster recovery and multilocation implementation of vCloud Director possible. This is achieved by creating a Layer 2 overlay network without changing the Layer 3 interconnects that are already in place.

This section describes a test scenario in which a vCloud Director implementation based on vCenter Site Recovery Manager fails over without needing to reassign IP addresses to the virtual machines and describes the scripted changes that must be done to simplify the process.

VXLAN for DR Architecture

To conduct the required testing, a sample architecture was deployed to simulate the process. In keeping with the reference infrastructure and methodology defined in the *vCloud DR Solution Tech Guide,* the test infrastructure constitutes a cluster that has ESXi members in both the primary and the recovery site. The premise is that the workloads run in the primary site where the vSphere hosts are connected.

At the recovery site, the vSphere hosts are in maintenance mode but are configured in the same cluster and attached to all the same vSphere Distributed Switches. The solution approach considered in the following sections is developed based on *Overview of Disaster Recovery in vCloud Director* (http://communities.vmware.com/docs/DOC-18861). All prerequisites for this solution continue to apply.

Logical Infrastructure

To address the complexities of recovering a vApp from the production site to the recovery site in the absence of stretched Layer 2 networking, a mechanism is required to abstract the underlying IP address changes from the recovered vApps. Figure C.1 provides a logical overview of the deployment infrastructure.

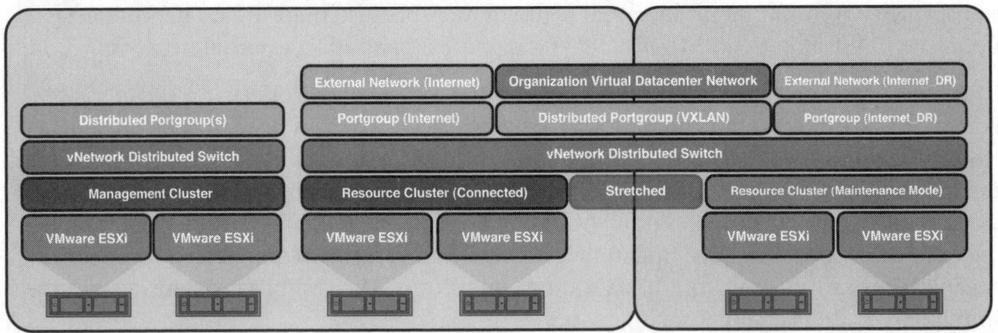

FIGURE C.1 Logical view of infrastructure

In the resource cluster, all vSphere hosts are connected to a common vSphere Distributed Switch with site-specific port groups defined for the Internet and Internet_DR networks. In vCloud Director, the Internet and Internet_DR port groups are defined as external networks. An organization virtual datacenter network is defined in conjunction with this, and a port group from the VXLAN network pool is deployed.

The vSphere hosts deployed in the production site are connected to a common Layer 3 management network. Similarly, the vSphere hosts deployed in the recovery site are connected to a common Layer 3 management network, albeit in a different Layer 3 than that of the network for the production site. The Internet external networks are the primary networks that will be used for vApp connectivity, and they are also in a different Layer 3 than the Internet network available in the recovery site. These are attached to vCloud Director as two distinct external networks.

vCloud Networking and Security Edge firewall rules, NAT translations, load balancer configurations, and VPN configurations must be duplicated to cover the disparate production and failover address spaces. Two options exist for keeping the configurations in sync:

Option 1: Maintain the configuration for both sites at the same time.

- Advantage: Simplifies failover because configurations are already in place.
- Disadvantages:
  - Requires the organization administrator to be diligent in maintaining the configurations
  - Is difficult to troubleshoot if there is a configuration mismatch
  - Requires removal of the primary interface if hosts on the original Layer 2 primary network need to be reachable

Option 2: Use the API upon failover to duplicate the primary site configuration to the failover site.

- Advantages:
  - Requires no maintenance after the initial failover address space metadata has been populated
  - Enables address mapping to be done and allocated in advance
- Disadvantages:
  - Must have failover address metadata specified to work
  - Requires that the address size match to simplify mapping
  - Requires that the address pool size match to simplify mapping

Leveraging VXLAN can greatly simplify the deployment of vCloud Director DR solutions in the absence of stretched Layer 2 networking. Furthermore, this type of networking topology is complementary to the solution defined in the *vCloud DR Solution Tech Guide* and can be implemented with relatively few additions to the existing vCloud DR recovery process.

Following the successful recovery of a vCloud Director management cluster, some additional steps need to be included in the recovery of resource clusters to facilitate the recovery of edge gateway appliances and vApps. See the VXLAN example in *Implementation Examples*.

VXLAN for DR Design Implications

Recovery hosts must be in maintenance mode so that virtual machines do not end up running in the recovery site and generating traffic between the recovery site and the primary site. The reason for this is that the vCloud Networking and Security Edge device is available in only one site at a time. Having the hosts in maintenance mode also keeps them in sync with all the changes that happen in the primary set.

If an organization has organization virtual datacenter networks that are directly attached, the process is as outlined in the existing vCloud DR recovery process. All the vApps on that network need to change their IP addresses with the correct addressing used in the recovery site Layer 3 network.

However, if the organization is using isolated networks that are VLAN backed, they need to be re-created on the recovery site using the associated VLAN IDs available in the recovery site and the vApps that are reconnected to the new network. If they were port group backed, the port groups still exist in the recovery site, but their definitions need to be revisited to verify that they are valid from a configuration point of view. Ease of recovery is afforded by using VXLAN-backed networks outlined in this scenario, whether they are NAT-routed or isolated.

Reference

vCloud Director 5.1 Documentation Center, http://tpub-review.eng.vmware.com:8080/vcd-20/index.jsp

APPENDIX D

vCloud Director Upgrade Considerations

The upgrade process from vCloud Director 1.5.x to 5.1 requires thorough planning. This document focuses on the impact, considerations, and advantages when performing a phased upgrade of vCloud Director. Several upgrade phases are described, with guidance on Phase 1 of the upgrade process. For further guidance on all upgrade phases, see the vCloud Suite 5.1 product documentation.

Background

The upgrade process can be divided into four phases. After completing a phase, the next phase can begin immediately or can be deferred without having a major effect on the vCloud infrastructure. However, new features are not available until all components in each phase are fully upgraded.

This document focuses on the considerations for Phase 1, upgrade considerations for moving from VMware vCloud Director 1.5 to 5.1.2.

Table D.1 lists the steps for each phase.

TABLE D.1 Upgrade Phases

Phase	Steps
1	▶ Upgrade vCloud Director cells from 1.5.x to 5.1.2 ▶ Upgrade vCloud Networking and Security Manager, and deploy vCloud Networking and Security Edge from 5.0 to 5.1.2a ▶ Upgrade Chargeback from 2.0.1 to 2.5.1. ▶ (Optional) Upgrade the Oracle/SQL Database versions on database servers.
Deferring next phase effect	vCloud Director 5.1 can manage existing vSphere 5.0, but new features are not available until the components in Phases 2, 3, and 4 are upgraded.
2	▶ Upgrade vCenter Server from 5.0 to 5.1 Update 1a. ▶ Upgrade vCenter Orchestrator 5.0 to 5.1.1.
Deferring next phase effect	vCenter Server 5.1 and vCenter Orchestrator 5.1 can manage vSphere ESXi 5.0, but new features are not available until the necessary components are upgraded.
3	Upgrade vSphere hosts from 5.0 to 5.1 Update 1.
Deferring next phase effect	New features are not available until the necessary components are upgraded.
4	▶ Upgrade vSphere Distributed Switches. ▶ Update vCloud Director configuration. ▶ Upgrade vApp hardware levels to hardware version 9. ▶ Upgrade VMware Tools.

Phase 1 Impact

Phase 1 requires downtime of the following components:

- **vCenter Chargeback Manager:** Version 2.5.1 is required for vCloud Director 5.1.2. vCenter Chargeback Manager 2.5 is backward compatible with VMware vCloud Director v1.5, v1.5.1 and v1.5.2. VMware recommends stopping vCenter Chargeback Manager services and upgrading only after vCloud Director is fully upgraded.
- **vCloud Networking and Security Manager:** This usually requires a specific build to work with vCloud Director. vCloud Director 5.1 supports vCloud Networking and Security Manager 5.1 but does not support vCloud Networking and Security Manager 5.0 when deploying new vCloud Networking and Security Edge devices.
- **vCloud Networking and Security Manager:** Although vCloud Networking and Security Manager 5.0 will continue to work with older edge devices after vCloud Director is upgraded, new vCloud Networking and Security Edge devices cannot be deployed until vCloud Networking and Security Manager is upgraded from 5.0 to 5.1.

- **vCloud Portal and vCloud APIs:** The vCloud portal and vCloud APIs are not available during this phase. Determining specific downtime is difficult, because downtime depends on the number of cells and size of each customer's database. The Virtual Machine Remote Console (VMRC) is also not available to users in this phase.
- **vCloud Director database:** The upgrade changes the schema, so a database backup is important. vCloud Director 5.1.2 does not support Oracle 10 (all release versions). vCloud Director 5.1.2 provides support for Microsoft SQL Server 2008 SP3 Standard/Enterprise. For a full listing of the Oracle and Microsoft SQL Server databases that are supported by vCloud Director 5.1.2 please go to:

  http://partnerweb.vmware.com/comp_guide/sim/interop_matrix.php
- **Rollback:** Rollback is complex because the database changes are irreversible.
  - Back up the database after stopping the vCloud Director Services before proceeding.
  - Back up the vCloud Networking and Security Manager database using the UI, which provides support for both the ftp and sftp transfer protocols. This is the only method of possibly restoring the vCloud Networking and Security Manager for a redeployment.
  - Perform a backup of the vCenter database at this time, as well as during future steps. The vCloud Director services get started multiple times throughout the process and can affect the vCenter and vCloud Networking and Security Manager databases.

Upgrade Considerations

Tables D.2 through D.4 list some general considerations before starting an upgrade of vCloud Director components.

Back up the following components of vCloud before making any changes. VMware recommends that all backups occur at the same time while all vCloud components are shut down. This has a major impact on availability but maintains data consistency among all components in the event of a rollback.

TABLE D.2 Components to Back Up

Component	Backup Considerations	Resources
vCloud Director database	Create a full backup of the vCloud Director database after all cells are shut down.	Database administrator
vCloud Networking and Security Manager database	Create a full backup of the vCloud Networking and Security Manager database.	vCloud administrator
vCenter Chargeback database	Create a full backup of the vCenter Chargeback Database after all vCenter Chargeback servers are shut down.	Database administrator

VMware strongly recommends performing a full virtual machine backup. If this is not possible, take a snapshot while the virtual machine is powered off or while creating a full clone of the virtual machine.

TABLE D.3 Backup or Snapshot Considerations

Virtual Machine	Backup and/or Snapshot Considerations	Resources
vCloud Director cells	Suspend vCloud Director scheduler, stop the vCloud Director services, and shut down the cells. Then take a backup, snapshot, or full clone of the virtual machine.	vCloud administrator
vCloud Networking and Security Manager	After creating a full backup of the vCloud Networking and Security Manager Database, shut down the virtual machine and take a backup, snapshot, or full clone of the virtual machine.	vSphere administrator
Chargeback Managers	Shut down the virtual machines, and then take a backup, snapshot, or full clone of the virtual machine.	vSphere administrator

For non-vCloud components, consider the following guidelines.

TABLE D.4 Non-vCloud Considerations

Component	Consideration	Resources
Red Hat patches	Run Red Hat patch updates before running the vCloud Director installer. The package dependencies have updates that vCloud Director 5.1 might require. Do not update kernel or other packages that would bring the system to an unsupported version of RHEL. vCloud Director 5.1 supports the following Red Hat releases: ▶ Red Hat Enterprise Linux 5 (64 bit) Updates 4,5,6, and 8 ▶ Red Hat Enterprise Linux 6 (64 bit) Updates 1 and 2 Update the packages only when necessary, as detailed in the *vCloud Director Installation and Configuration Guide* (www.vmware.com/support/pubs/vcd_pubs.html).	Linux administrator
DNS for load balancer VIPs	Consider lowering the TTL (Time to live) on the DNS for the load-balanced VIPs for HTTP and console proxy a day or two before upgrading. Lowering these enables clients to update their DNS cache quicker when resolving the portal name. Because the DNS name is directed to temporary maintenance pages and then back to the original pages, a lower TTL prevents the need for users to manually flush their DNS cache for updates. Redirect the DNS before upgrading to a custom maintenance page on a completely separate web server outside the vCloud Director cells. Verify that all users are redirected to the maintenance page before shutting down cells.	DNS administrator

Phase 1 Process

The following sections cover upgrade preparation and execution.

Preupgrade Considerations

The following process assumes that all vCloud components are turned off so that backups and snapshots are data consistent before any upgrade work. Table D.5 includes the steps with the components, considerations, and resource roles.

TABLE D.5 Preupgrade Considerations

#	Component	Consideration	Resource
1	DNS	▶ Lower TTL on DNS. ▶ Redirect to maintenance page.	DNS administrator
2	vCloud Director Cells	▶ Suspend vCloud Director scheduler and shut down first cell. ▶ Repeat for subsequent cells. ▶ Back up or take a snapshot of virtual machines.	vCloud administrator vSphere administrator
3	vCloud Director database	Back up the vCloud Director database.	Database administrator
4	Chargeback Managers	Shut down vCenter Chargeback servers and perform a backup or take a snapshot of virtual machines.	vSphere administrator
5	Chargeback database	Back up the Chargeback database.	Database administrator

Upgrade Considerations

The guidelines outlined in Table D.6 list the key steps to perform during an upgrade.

TABLE D.6 Upgrade Procedure

#	Component	Consideration	Resource
1	vCloud Director Cells	▶ Suspend vCloud Director scheduler and stop the vCloud Director service. ▶ Repeat for subsequent cells. ▶ Perform Red Hat patches. ▶ Unmount the NFS transfer share on each cell. ▶ Run the vCloud Director installer but do not start the services. ▶ Run the database upgrade script on the first cell only. Do not repeat this on the other cells. ▶ Run the vCloud Director installer on the other cells. ▶ Reboot each vCloud Director cell one at a time to make sure that all services start up correctly and that the NFS transfer volume is successfully mounted on the first cell before rebooting subsequent cells. ▶ Validate that vCloud Director has started by checking `/opt/vmware/vcloud-director/logs/cell.log`. ▶ Validate that the portal is working on each cell by connecting directly to the cell's HTTP interface. ▶ Do not redirect the load balancer or allow users back onto the system yet.	vCloud administrator Linux administrator vCloud administrator
2	Update vCloud Director Agent on vSphere hosts	Update the host agent on all connected hosts. Check that connected hosts are still showing Available and Prepared.	vCloud administrator
3	vCloud Director Validation 1	▶ Validate basic functionality of vCloud Director by deploying a new vApp. ▶ Validate basic functionality by deploying a NAT-routed network (either a routed organization network or through fencing a vApp that is deployed). ▶ Troubleshoot any issues before moving on. ▶ Rollback is possible at this stage by restoring the vCloud Director database and restoring the vCloud Director cells virtual machine backup or deleting the virtual machine snapshot.	vCloud administrator vCloud administrator vSphere administrator or database administrator

#	Component	Consideration	Resource
4	vCloud Networking and Security Manager Server	Upgrading the vCloud Networking and Security Manager Server requires using an upgrade package. This file is usually named `VMware-vShield-Manager-upgrade-bundle-5.1.2-943471.tar.gz`. Do not deploy a new Service Manager appliance (OVA). Removing the existing Service Manager appliance breaks all connections and management to any deployed vCloud Networking and Security Manager Edge devices, resulting in errors. After a Service Manager is deployed, upgrade it only using a `tar.gz` file (*in-place upgrade*). This preserves the local Service Manager database.	vCloud administrator
5	Edge devices	After vCloud Networking and Security Manager is upgraded, wait at least 15 minutes for it to update information with vCloud Director. Upgrade any organization vCloud Networking and Security Manager devices that are connected to an organization network that is routed. These devices are identified in vCloud Director 5.1 as *edge gateways* and can be upgraded by performing a redeploy. Upgrade any vApp network vCloud Networking and Security Manager devices connected to an vApp network that is routed. These devices are identified in vCloud Director 5.1 as *edge gateways* and can be upgraded by performing Re-Deploy.	vCloud administrator vCloud administrator or organization administrator
6	vCloud Director Validation 2	▶ Validate basic functionality of vCloud Director by deploying a new vApp. ▶ Validate basic functionality by deploying a NAT-routed network (either a routed organization network or through fencing a vApp that is deployed). ▶ Troubleshoot any issues before proceeding. ▶ Rollback is not possible at this stage because the vCloud Networking and Security Edge devices have been upgraded to the latest compatible versions.	vCloud administrator vCloud administrator
7	Chargeback Managers	The installer requires uninstallation of the previous version. Select Do Not Empty the Database.	vCloud administrator

Post-Upgrade Considerations

Table D.7 lists post-upgrade considerations that apply after a successful upgrade of the vCloud environment.

TABLE D.7 Post-Upgrade Considerations

#	Component	Consideration	Resource
1	Local datastores	vCloud Director 5.1 automatically adds local datastores currently presented to ESXi hosts. Disable these datastores from vCloud Director to prevent vCloud Director from using local datastores.	vCloud administrator
2	Storage profiles	All datastores that vCloud Director 1.5 used are placed into the * (Any) storage profile. VMware recommends not changing these at this stage. Storage profiles must be configured in vCenter 5.1 before they can be used in vCloud Director.	vCloud administrator vSphere administrator
3	Upgrade VMRC	vCloud Director 5.1 requires a reinstallation of the VMRC plug-in.	vCloud VMRC users

Upgrade Advantages

The following is a list of advantages that customers have cited as their main reasons for upgrading to vCloud Director 5.1. However, not all new features are available upon completing Phase 1.

- **User/tenant usability improvements:** The user/tenant usability improvements in vCloud Director 5.1 are targeted at enabling enterprises and service providers to appeal to less tech-savvy vCloud consumers, and expand to users who might not necessarily work in traditional infrastructure management roles.
- **Elastic virtual datacenter:** Customers can purchase a virtual datacenter of arbitrary size from a robust set of offerings and grow it at will. vCloud Director and vSphere intelligently manage capacity below a robust virtual datacenter abstraction and prevent virtual datacenters from hitting boundaries unless physical capacity is exhausted.
- **Multiple classes of capacity:** vApps can be deployed as multitier applications with differing infrastructure performance requirements across different tiers (for example, DB on fast storage, web tier on standard storage) within a single application construct.
- New features enabled by upgrade to vCloud Director 5.1 include the following:
  - vSphere Storage DRS
  - Storage profiles
  - Virtual hardware version 9
  - Windows 8 guest OS support
  - Snapshot and revert

- Multi-interface vCloud Networking and Security Edge support for 10 interfaces that can be configured as either uplinks (external networks) or internal interfaces (facing internal networks)
- Fast provisioning support for more than eight hosts
- Support for the Google Chrome browser

This is not an exhaustive list. All four upgrade phases must be completed to enable all new features.

APPENDIX E

vCloud Director Cell Monitoring

Table E.1 represents a subset of MBeans that can improve the monitoring performance of a vCloud instance.

TABLE E.1 MBeans Used to Monitor vCloud Cells

Local User Sessions	
MBean	`com.vmware.vcloud.diagnostics.UserSessions`
Description	Local (cell) user session statistics
Cardinality	1
Instance ID	—
Attribute	Description
`totalSessions`	Total number of sessions created on this cell
`successfulLogins`	Total number of successful logins to this cell
`failedLogins`	Total number of failed login requests to this cell
Global User Sessions	
MBean	`com.vmware.vcloud.GlobalUserSessionStatistics`
Description	List of active user sessions by organization
Cardinality	1
Instance ID	—
Attribute	Description
`Organization`	Database ID of the organization
`Active`	Number of active sessions
`Open_Session`	Number of open sessions
Data Access Diagnostics	
MBean	`com.vmware.vcloud.diagnostics.DataAccess`
Description	Local (cell) user session statistics
Cardinality	1
Instance ID	Conversation
Attribute	Description
`lastAccessInfo`.objectType	Object type of the last database object accessed
`lastAccessInfo`.accessTime	Time taken to access the last database object accessed
`worstAccessInfo`.objectType	Object type of the worst (slowest) database object access
`worstAccessInfo`.accessTime	Time taken by the worst (slowest) database object access
Database Connection Pool	
MBean	`com.vmware.vcloud.datasource.globalDataSource`
Description	Statistics and configuration information about the database connection pool. This information is currently specific to the database JDBC driver being used (Oracle).
Cardinality	1
Instance ID	
Attribute	Description
`abandonedConnectionTimeout`	
`availableConnectionsCount`	

Local User Sessions	
borrowedConnectionsCount	
connectionHarvestMaxCount	
connectionHarvestTrigger-Count	
connectionPoolName	
connectionWaitTimeout	
databaseName	Database connection database name (SID)
dataSourceName	
fastConnectionFailoverEn-abled	
inactiveConnectionTimeout	
initialPoolSize	
loginTimeout	
maxConnectionReuseCount	
maxIdleTime	
maxPoolSize	Maximum number of connections allowed in the pool
maxStatements	
minPoolSize	Minimum number of connections in the pool
networkProtocol	Network protocol used by the JDBC driver
ONSConfiguration	
portNumber	Database connection port number
SQLForValidateConnection	
timeoutCheckInterval	
timeToLiveConnectionTimeout	
URL	Database connection URL
user	Database connection username
validateConnectionOnBorrow	
VIM Operations	
MBean	com.vmware.vcloud.diagnostics.VlsiOperations
Description	Local (cell) user session statistics
Cardinality	1 per VIM endpoint (VC or host agent)
Instance ID	VIM endpoint URL
Attribute	Description
ObjectType.MethodName.httpTime	The total network round-trip time taken to make the MethodName call on an object of type ObjectType in the VIM endpoint.

Local User Sessions	
Presentation API Methods	
MBean	`com.vmware.vcloud.diagnostics.VlsiOperations`
Description	Local (cell) user session statistics
Cardinality	1 per presentation layer method
Instance ID	method name
Attribute	Description
`currentInvocations`	Currently active invocations
`totalFailed`	Total number of failed executions
`totalInvocations`	Total number of invocations over time
`executionTime`	Total time taken to execute
Jetty	
MBean	`com.vmware.vcloud.diagnostics.Jetty`
Description	Web server request statistics
Cardinality	2:1 for REST API and 1 for UI
Instance ID	`UI Requests` for UI, `REST API Requests` for REST API
Attribute	Description
`Active`	Number of web requests currently being handled
REST API	
MBean	`com.vmware.vcloud.diagnostics.VlsiOperations`
Description	Local (cell) user session statistics
Cardinality	1 per operation stage/granularity: `RoundTrip`, `BasicLogin`, `Logout`, `Authentication`, `SecurityFilter`, `ConversationFilter`, `JAXRSServlet`. `RoundTrip` is the most interesting because it represents the overall REST API performance.
Instance ID	One of `RoundTrip`, `BasicLogin`, `Logout`, `Authentication`, `SecurityFilter`, `ConversationFilter`, or `JAXRSServlet`
Attribute	Description
`currentInvocations`	Currently active invocations
`totalFailed`	Total number of failed executions
`totalInvocations`	Total number of invocations over time
`executionTime`	Total time taken to execute
Task Execution	
MBean	`com.vmware.vcloud.diagnostics.TaskExecutionJobs`
Description	Statistics about long-running tasks
Cardinality	1 per task
Instance ID	Name of task
Attribute	Description

Local User Sessions	
`currentInvocations`	Currently active invocations
`totalFailed`	Total number of failed executions
`totalInvocations`	Total number of invocations over time
`executionTime`	Total time taken to execute

Query Service (UI)

MBean	`com.vmware.vcloud.diagnostics.QueryService`
Description	Presentation layer query service statistics
Cardinality	1 per query
Instance ID	Query name
Attribute	Description
`currentInvocations`	Currently active invocations
`totalFailed`	Total number of failed executions
`totalInvocations`	Total number of invocations over time
`executionTime`	Total time taken to execute
`returnedItems`	Number of items returned by successful query executions

VC Task Manager

MBean	`com.vmware.vcloud.diagnostics.VcTasks`
Description	VC task-management statistics
Cardinality	1
Instance ID	
Attribute	Description
`successfulTasksCount`	Total successful tasks
`failedTasksCount`	Total failed tasks
`waitForTaskInvocationsCount`	Total invocations of VIM "wait for task"
`completedWaitForTasksCount`	Total completed task waits
`historicalTasksCount`	Total historical task updates received
`vcRetrievedTaskCompletionsCount`	Total task completions received
`taskCompletionMessagesPublishedCount`	Total task completion messages published on the message bus
`taskCompletionMessagesReceivedCount`	Total task completion messages received on the message bus
`success_elapsedTaskWaitTime`	Time elapsed for successful tasks
`failed_elapsedTaskWaitTIme`	Time elapsed for failed tasks

VIM Inventory Update Processing: Object Update Statistics

MBean	`com.vmware.vcloud.diagnostics.VimInventoryUpdates`
Description	Inventory processing statistics

Local User Sessions	
Cardinality	3: one for `ObjectUpdate`, one for `PropertyCollector`, and one for `UpdateSets`
Instance ID	`ObjectUpdate`
Attribute	Description
`totalUpdates`	Total number of object updates received
`totalFailed`	Total number of object updates failed to be processed
`executionTime`	Time taken for updates
VIM Inventory Events	
MBean	`com.vmware.vcloud.diagnostics.VimInventoryEvents`
Description	VIM inventory event manager statistics. Tracks the frequency of common vCenter events.
Cardinality	1 per folder per VC URL, 1 MBean per event name
Instance ID	Event name
Attribute	Description
`totalInvocations`	Total number of VIM inventory events dispatched since that vCloud Director cell started
`totalFailed`	Total number of VIM inventory events that failed to be handled
`executionTime`	Total time to handle VIM inventory events
VC Object Validations	
MBean	`com.vmware.vcloud.diagnostics.VcValidation`
Description	VC object validation statistics
Cardinality	1 global plus 1 per validator
Instance ID	null = global, validator name = per validator
Attribute	Description
`totalInvocations`	Total number of validation executions
`executionTime`	Total time spent in validator
`totalItemsInQueue`	Total items currently queued for validation (global)
`objectsInQueue`	Total items currently queued for validation (per validator)
`objectBusyRequeueCount`	Total number of objects requeued for validation because of busy objects
`loadValidationObjectTime`	Time taken to load a validation object
`duplicatesDiscarded`	Total number of discarded duplicate validations
VC Object Validation Reactions	
MBean	`com.vmware.vcloud.diagnostics.Reactions`
Description	Validation reaction statistics
Cardinality	1 global plus 1 per reaction
Instance ID	null = global, reaction name = per reaction
Attribute	Description

Local User Sessions	
`totalReactionsFired`	Total number of reaction executions
`requeueCount`	Total number of reactions requeued because of busy objects
`totalInvocations`	Total number of executions of this reaction
`executionTime`	Total time spent in reaction
`failedReactions`	Total number of failed reactions
`objectRequeueCount`	Number of times this reaction was requeued because of busy objects

VC Connections

MBean	`com.vmware.vcloud.diagnostics.VimConnection`
Description	Local (cell) user session statistics
Cardinality	1 per VC
Instance ID	`VC-VcInstanceId`, where `VcInstanceId` is an integer identifying the vCenter instance

Attribute	Description
`Connected Count`	Total successful connections
`Disconnected Count`	Total disconnections
`Start Count`	Total number of times the VC listener was started
`UI Vim Reconnect Count`	Total number of times the VC was reconnected through the UI

ActiveMQ

MBean	`com.vmware.vcloud.diagnostics.ActiveMQ`
Description	ActiveMQ (message bus) statistics
Cardinality	1 global and 1 per peer vCloud Director cell (each cell other than the current one)
Instance ID	`Global` = global statistics `to_cellName_cellPrimaryIp_cellUUID` = per cell

Attribute	Description
`lastHealthCheckDate`	Last time a health check was performed (date/time)
`messageRoundTripDurationMs`	Time taken for an echo message to be sent and returned (ms)
`isHealthy`	Health of connection to a peer cell in the case of the per-cell MBean; overall message bus connection health in the case of the global MBean (true/false)
`timedOutMessages`	Total number of echo messages for which no reply was received within the timeout (controlled by the `activeMonitorCheckDelayMs` config parameter, with a default of 10 minutes)
`sendErrors`	Total number of failed echo message sends (messages)
`corruptedOrBadEchoMessages`	Total number of corrupted/bad echo messages received (starts)_ (messages)

Local User Sessions	
Transfer Server	
MBean	`com.vmware.vcloud.diagnostics.VlsiOperations`
Description	Transfer server statistics
Cardinality	1
Instance ID	
Attribute	Description
`successfulPuts`	Number of items successfully transferred (transfer items)
`failedPuts`	Number of items that failed to be transferred (transfer items)
`successfulUploads`	Number of successful upload operations (uploads)
`acceptedQuarantinedTransferSessions`	Number of accepted quarantined transfers (quarantined items)
`rejectedQuarantinedTransferSessions`	Number of rejected quarantined transfers (quarantined items)
`expiredTransferSessions`	Number of transfer sessions that timed out (transfer sessions)

APPENDIX F
Compliance Considerations

Audit concepts such as segmentation and monitoring applied to a vCloud environment reveal new challenges. Elasticity might break old segmentation controls and the capability to isolate sensitive data in a rapidly growing environment. Role-based access controls and virtual firewalls must also demonstrate compatibility with audit requirements for segmentation, including detailed audit trails and logs. Can a provider guarantee that an offline image with sensitive data in memory is accessible only by authorized users? Can a log indicate who accessed it and when? vCloud resource management requires multiple admin-level roles.

The complexity of vCloud environments, coupled with new and different technology, requires careful audits to document and detail compliance. Table F.1 lists common audit concerns in the vCloud.

TABLE F.1 vCloud Audit Concerns

Concern	Detail
Hypervisor	An additional layer of technology is present in every vCloud and could present an attack surface. The hypervisor introduces a layer between the traditional processing environment and the physical layer, which brings a new level of communication with layers above and below it.
Segmentation and isolation	Any environment can expose sensitive data when not configured and monitored properly—physical and logical isolation has always been an audit concern. The ease and speed of change to a virtualized environment within vCloud computing, often called *elasticity*, makes the setup and review of segmentation controls even more relevant to compliance through isolation.
Different/multiple primary functions per host	The vCloud environment can make more efficient use of hardware, but it increases the proximity of information in transit and at rest. Some compliance standards explicitly require one primary function per server (or virtual server), as Figure F.1 illustrates.
Enforcement of least privilege	In a vCloud environment, remote network access is the only available path offered to customers to manage their environment. Instead of physical access audits for equipment installation and modification, virtual system management software must be audited.
Machine state and migration	The capability of systems to quickly change and move in a vCloud environment gives auditors a need to track authorization and related change controls. Separate and isolated networks should be used for data migration that is in the clear, to avoid exposing sensitive information.
Data is much less permanent	Cloud environments make extensive use of short-lived instances. Virtual machines might have a lifecycle far shorter than physical systems because they are easy to provision and repurpose. Systems also share data across large arrays in swap space. Permanence of data is also affected by environments that push as much storage as possible through high-speed memory to avoid the latency of spinning disks.
Immaturity of monitoring solutions in vCloud environments	Customers need audit trails and views unique to their own use of the vCloud environment, which also supports incident response and investigations. Providers must extend and develop log management and monitoring solutions to meet regulatory and client requirements for the vCloud environment.

Figure F.1 shows how specific applications use business drivers that require the underlying servers to have a primary function, such as support for regulated data.

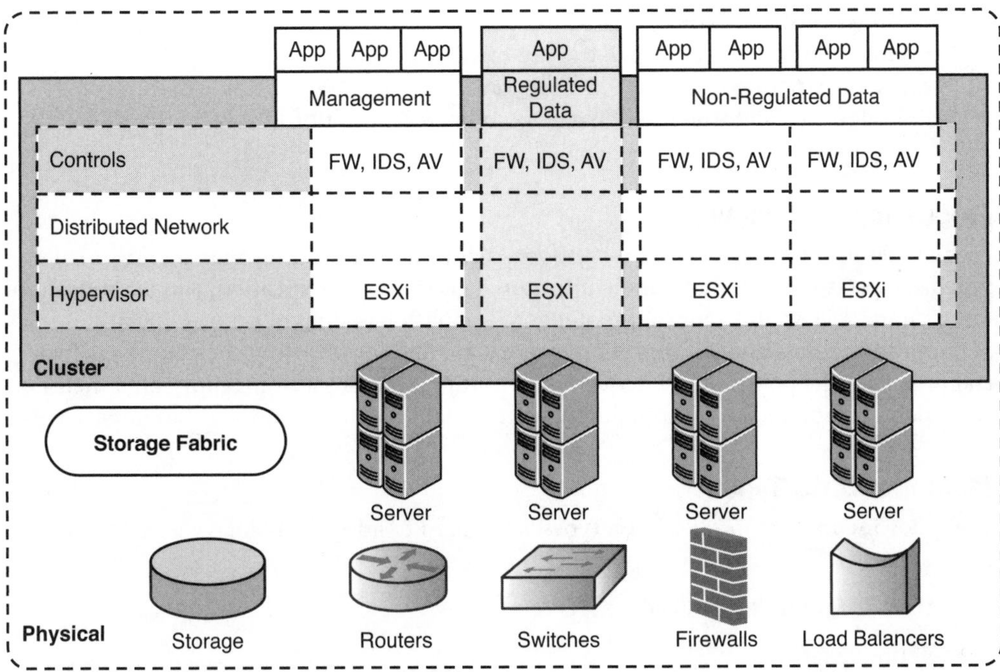

FIGURE F.1 One primary function per server

Use Cases: Why Logs Should Be Available

Monitoring and recording events is important in mitigating damage and preventing future attacks. An audit log enables an organization to verify compliance, detect violations, and initiate remediation activities. It can help detect attempts (whether successful or not) for unauthorized access, information probes, or disruption.

Log Purposes

Logs are the foundation of many controls used to achieve internal requirements and regulatory compliance. They track and record changes and incidents as they form an audit trail. Logs offer the following benefits:

- **Compliance requirements:** Logs are required for all compliance regulations, to assist with control auditing, breach review, analysis, and response. Specific types of logs often can be matched with specific compliance controls. For example, the authentication log can show the access controls that are allowed for only authorized users.
- **Customer requirements:** End customers can retrieve logs that pertain to their environment to meet their own requirements.
- **Operational integrity:** Operational alerts should be defined for logs to trigger notifications for remediation. This is frequently set up as a backup alert, secondary to monitoring. A storage array that goes offline generates error messages in the logs, which can alert administrators.

- **Troubleshooting:** Closely related to operational integrity, logs are essential for troubleshooting. For example, the use of vCloud Networking and Security Edge logs can show whether a specific external connection request is being passed through a firewall or through the use of Network Address Translation (NAT) by the firewall.

Frequency of Review

Logs should be reviewed daily for unauthorized or unusual and suspicious activity on all systems, especially those that handle intrusion detection, authentication, and authorization. This requires review and verification of logs to establish baselines of normal operations, such as monitoring access and authorization (every login and logout) from the console, network, and remote access points. More frequent and routine log analysis for security often helps in early identification of system configuration errors, failures, and issues that can impact SLAs.

Minimum Data Types

The following minimum set of data types is required to adequately log vCloud environment activity for regulatory compliance:

- User (including system account) access
- Action taken
- Use of identification and authentication mechanisms
- Start and stop of audit logs
- Creation or deletion of system-level objects

The audit trail entries recorded for each event must include the following details:

- Identification (ID)
- Type of event
- Date and time
- Success or failure
- Origination of event
- ID of affected data or component

Retention

Daily review of logs alone might not be sufficient to detect incidents—they also must be retained for a period consistent with effective use and legal regulations. The laws for log retention range from 1 year to more than 20 years. Therefore, log archives should always be able for at least one year of history, scheduled to match financial calendar cycles, and with a minimum of three months available for immediate response and review in case of an incident.

Example Compliance Use Cases for Logs

The following use cases exemplify events that benefit from careful logging and monitoring in the vCloud environment. Other examples include unauthorized services or protocols, remote login success, and certificate changes.

- **Shared accounts:** An investigation is initiated to review network outages and finds multiple instances in which an administrator account logged into critical servers before failure. Shared accounts make it difficult to trace fault to one individual—determining from the logs on that system which person was logged into the user account that made the error is impossible. Therefore, to aid in investigations, usage must be tied to an individual user ID and unique password with correct time. Systems also should be configured to detect use of generic IDs, such as an administrator or root account, and trace them to unique identities.
- **User account changes:** A malicious user finds an unpatched flaw in an environment that allows elevation of privileges. The user then uses system-level privileges to create a new bogus user object from which to launch further attacks. A user object might be a Microsoft Windows domain or local user account. User object logs can determine when a name was changed or an account added. This assists in detecting actions without authorization or identifying users trying to hide attacks.
- **Unauthorized software:** System object logs can find malware or a new virtual machine instance in the vCloud. A system must track system objects that are added, removed, or modified. This can be helpful during installation in monitoring system changes caused by software.

VMware vCloud Log Sources for Compliance

Customers should be able to retrieve logs from all areas that are relevant and unique to their organization. Programmatic retrieval, such as an API to allow for automated queries, should be possible. Log collection nodes must be added to a vCloud environment, as Figure F.2 illustrates.

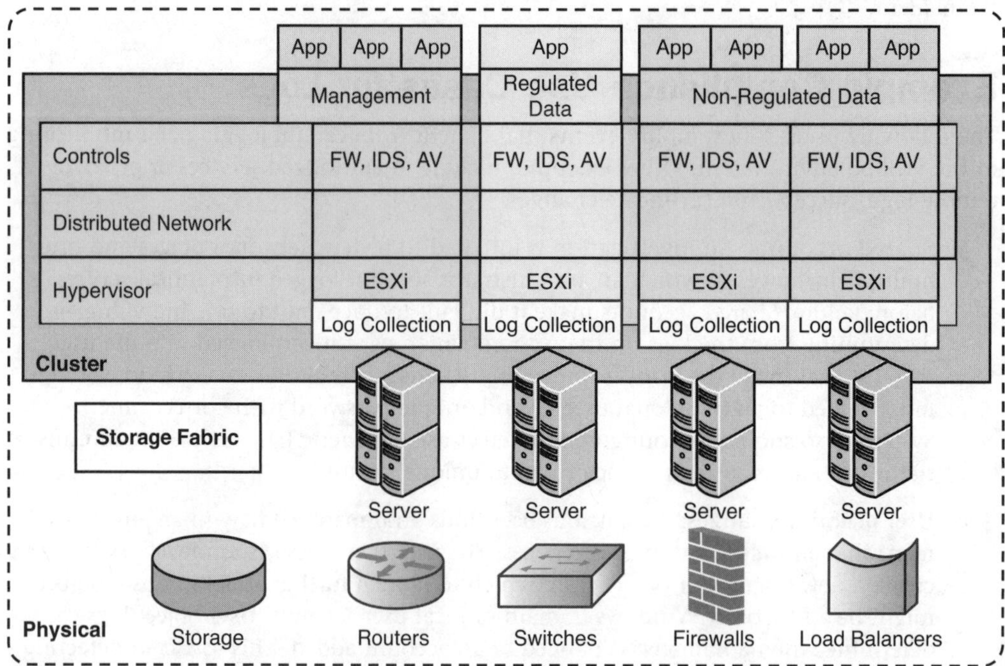

FIGURE F.2 Log collection in the vCloud environment

Logs that VMware components generate must be maintained by the provider but also available to tenants. Tenants should be able to download in raw format all vCloud Director and vCloud Networking and Security Edge logs that pertain to their organizations and networks. Logs with customer identifiers should be flagged or indexed for retrieval.

Figure F.3 illustrates the architecture of vCloud components and log collection.

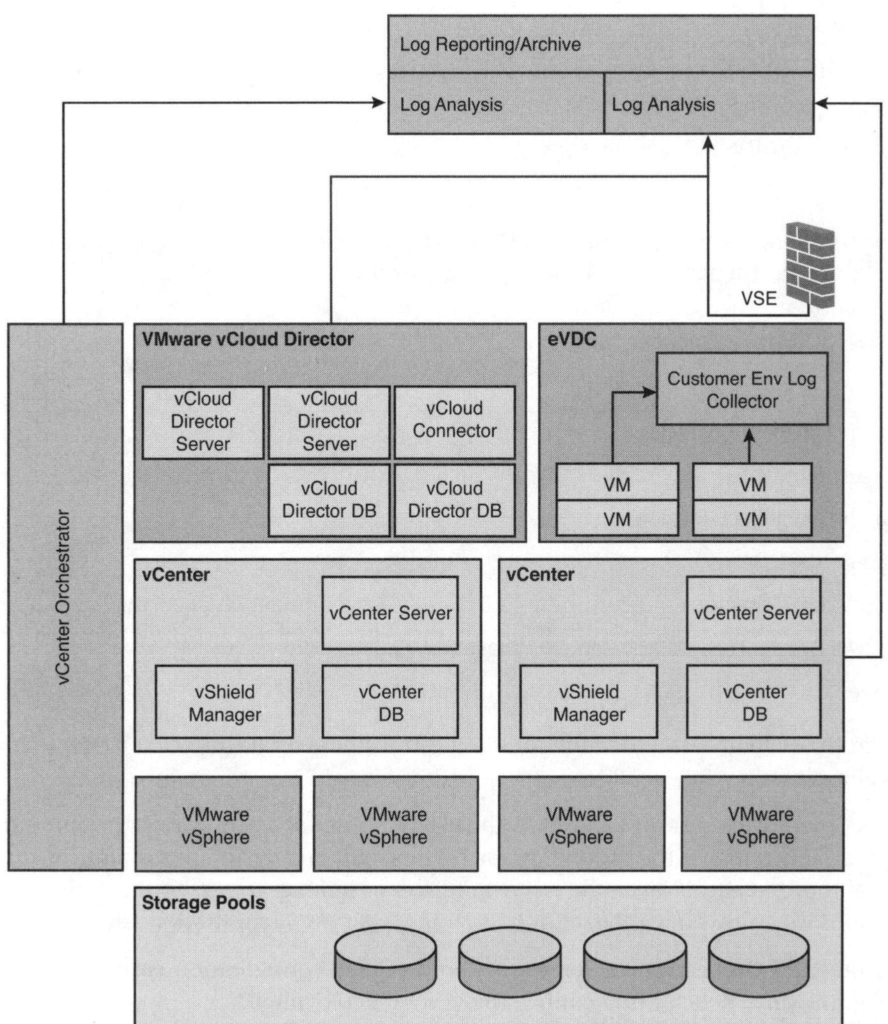

FIGURE F.3 Architecture of vCloud components and log collection

Table F.2 lists the logs to which the vCloud tenant must have access.

TABLE F.2 vCloud Component Logs

VMware Component	Provider Logs	Tenant Logs
VMware vCloud Director	X	X
vCenter Server	X	
vSphere Server (ESXi)		
vCenter Chargeback Manager	X	

VMware Component	Provider Logs	Tenant Logs
vCenter Orchestrator	X	
vCloud Networking and Security Manager	X	
vCloud Networking and Security Edge	X	X

Other components also generate logs in the vCloud environment that the provider must maintain. Direct tenant access is not required for the logs in Table F.3.

TABLE F.3 Other Component Logs

Other Component	Provider Logs	Tenant Logs
vCloud Director DB (Oracle)	X	
vCenter Database	X	
vCenter Chargeback Database	X	
Microsoft SQL Server	X	
Linux (vCloud Director)	X	
Windows System Logs (CBM, vCenter Orchestrator, vCenter Server)	X	

Logs in the vCloud datacenter environment can further be categorized into the following logical business layers:

- **vCloud Application:** Represents the external interface with which the enterprise administrators of the vCloud interact. These administrators are authenticated and authorized at this layer and have no (direct or indirect) access to the underlying infrastructure. They interact only with the Business Orchestration Layer.
- **Business Orchestration:** Represents both vCloud configuration entities and the governance policies that control the vCloud deployment:
    - **Service catalog:** Presents the different service levels available and their configuration elements.
    - **Service design:** Represents the service level and specific configuration elements, along with any defined policies.
    - **Configuration Management Database (CMDB):** Represents the system of record, which can be federated with an enterprise CMDB.
    - **Service provision:** Represents the final configuration specification.
- **Service Orchestration:** Represents the provisioning logic for the vCloud infrastructure. This layer consists of an orchestration director system and automation elements for network, storage, security, and server/compute—vCenter Server, VMware vCloud Director (vCloud Director), and vCenter Orchestrator.

- **Infrastructure Layer:** Represents the physical and virtual compute, network, storage, hypervisor, security, and management components—vSphere Server (ESXi), vCloud Networking and Security Manager, and vCloud Networking and Security Edge.

The abstraction of these layers and their security controls in Figure F.4 helps illustrate audit and compliance requirements for proper authentication and segregation.

For example, vCloud provider administrator accounts should be maintained in a central repository integrated with two-factor authentication. Different tiers of vCloud deployments (provider virtual datacenters) would be made available to enterprise users.

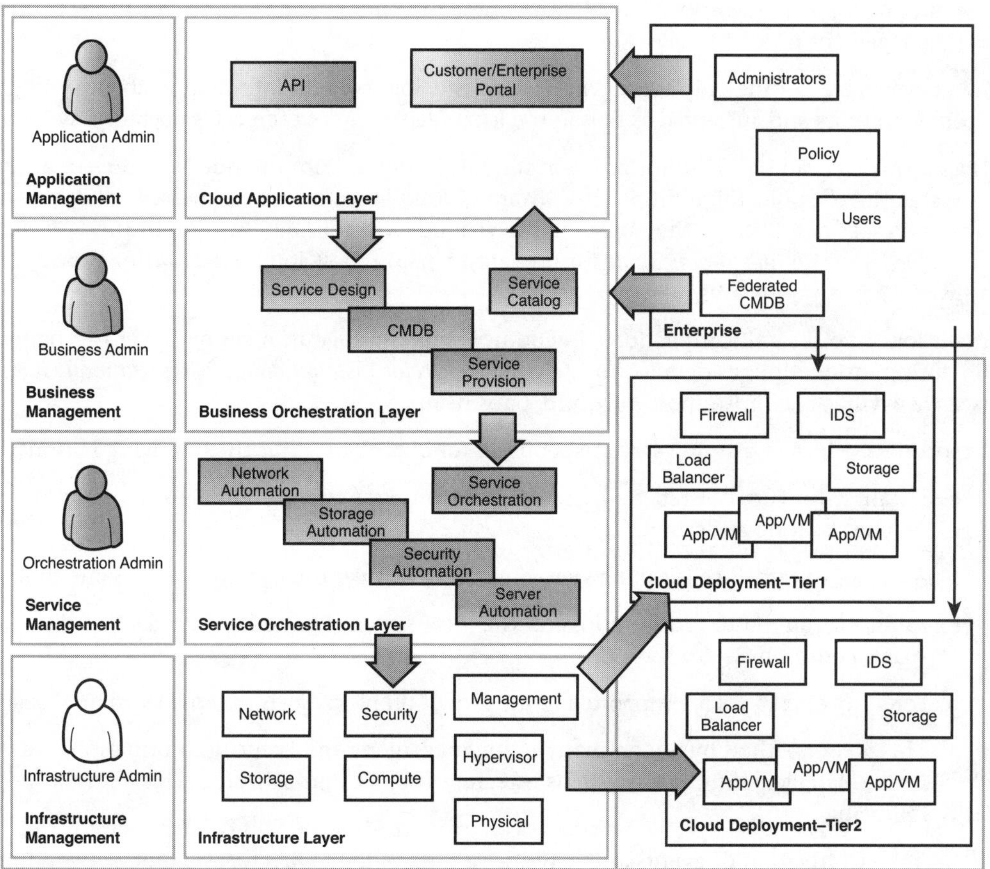

FIGURE F.4 Infrastructure layers

F

vCloud Director Diagnostic and Audit Logs

VMware vCloud Director includes the following types of logs:

- Audit logs that are maintained in the database and, optionally, in a syslog server
- Diagnostic logs that are maintained in each vCloud Director cell's log directory

The VMware vCloud Director system audit log is maintained in the Oracle database and can be monitored through the Web UI. Each organization administrator and the system administrator have a view into the log, scoped to their specific area of control. A more comprehensive view of the audit log (and long-term persistence) is achieved through the use of remote syslog (described shortly). A variety of vendors and open source projects offer log-management products.

Audit events are not the only event types. Diagnostic logs contain information about system operation events and are stored as files in the local file system of each cell's operating system.

Diagnostic logs can be useful for problem resolution but are not intended to preserve a trail of system interactions for audit. Each VMware vCloud Director cell creates several diagnostic log files, as described in the "Viewing the vCloud Director Logs" section of the *VMware vCloud Director Administration Guide* for the latest version of vCloud Director (see www.vmware.com/support/pubs/vcd_pubs.html).

Audit logs record significant actions, including login and logout. A syslog server can be set up during installation, as detailed in the *vCloud Director Installation and Configuration Guide* (see www.vmware.com/support/pubs/vcd_pubs.html).

Exporting the logs to a syslog server is required for compliance, for the following reasons:

- Database logs are not retained after 90 days, but logs transmitted via syslog can be retained as long as desired.
- Audit logs from all cells can be viewed together in a central location at the same time.
- Audit logs are protected from loss on the local system due to failure, a lack of disk space, compromise, and so on.
- Forensics operations are supported in the face of problems such as those listed previously.
- This is the method by which many log-management and Security Information and Event Management (SIEM) systems integrate with vCloud Director. This allows the following:
    - Correlation of events and activities across vCloud Director, vCloud Networking and Security, vSphere, and even the physical hardware layers of the stack
    - Integration of vCloud security operations with the rest of the vCloud provider or enterprise's security operations, cutting across physical, virtual, and vCloud infrastructures
- Logging to a remote system, instead of the system the cell is deployed on, provides data integrity by inhibiting tampering. Even if the cell is compromised, it does not necessarily enable access to or alteration of the audit log.

APPENDIX G
Capacity Planning

Capacity forecasting provides an efficient way to acquire the appropriate amount of physical resources to support the increased demand for the vCloud. This allows for the growth of vCloud to be planned and included in the service providers' budgetary process and reduces the likelihood of "panic buying," which generally increases costs dramatically and undermines standardization efforts. Capacity planning also reduces the likelihood of last-minute surprises, such as a lack of available space or power to support the new vCloud infrastructure components.

From a vCloud perspective, the provider virtual datacenter and organization virtual datacenter constructs simplify capacity management, but it is potentially complicated by the three models of consumption: pay as you go, allocation pool (committed), and reservation pool (dedicated). All of these capacity management aspects must address both the vCloud (service provider) administrator and the customer (organization) administrator perspectives.

Sizing for workload resource group clusters can be difficult to predict because the provider is not in charge of what the consumer runs. The provider is also not aware of existing usage statistics for virtual machines that are run in the vCloud. The following information should assist in initially sizing the vCloud environment and is based on information from *service definitions*. This information is provided in the form of examples. A local VMware representative can assist with detailed sizing of the environment.

vCloud Administrator (Service Provider) Perspective

The primary capacity management concerns of the vCloud administrator are as follows:

- Capacity management of provider virtual datacenters and the service offerings backed by each provider virtual datacenter
- Network capacity management (network bandwidth capacity management is beyond the scope of this book)
- Capacity forecasting
- Capacity monitoring and triggers

The VMware vCloud solution makes extensive use of reservations. As such, previous approaches to capacity management used in vSphere are not as applicable to a vCloud. For example, CPU and memory overcommitment cannot be applied as extensively as in a multitenant environment.

Unlike managing capacity for vSphere, in a vCloud, the virtual machine is no longer the basis for resource consumption from a service provider perspective. The organization virtual datacenter is the basis for resource consumption in a vCloud.

Capacity management is further impacted by multiple consumption models in the vCloud model. Each model requires its own capacity management approach. As a result, this appendix provides guidance for capacity management from a service provider vCloud administrator perspective as it applies to each of the consumption models: pay as you go, allocation pool, and reservation pool.

Regardless of the particular consumption model applied in a provider virtual datacenter, the common starting point of vCloud Capacity Management is to calculate the total amount of CPU and memory resources available for consumption. Because the underlying infrastructure provisioning unit of a provider virtual datacenter is an ESXi host, the first step is to determine the total CPU and memory at the vSphere host level.

Table G.1 shows the key vSphere host variables needed to calculate capacity, along with example values.

TABLE G.1 vSphere Host Variables

Item	Variable	Value	Units
Processor sockets	`Nsocket,1`	2	Integer
Processor cores	`Ncores,1`	4	Integer
Processor speed	`Sproc,1`	2.4	GHz
Host memory	`Mhost,1`	64	GB

Calculating the total available memory is straightforward: It is the total amount of RAM for the vSphere host. Total CPU resources are calculated using the following formula:

$$P_{host} > N_{socket} N_{cores} S_{proc}$$

Using the example values from the table, the total CPU resource equals 19.2GHz.

After defining the vSphere host capacity model, the next step is to determine the provider virtual datacenter (vSphere cluster) capacity. Determining the provider virtual datacenter capacity is critical: vCloud Capacity Management should be performed at the provider virtual datacenter level, not the vSphere host level.

When considering vCloud provider virtual datacenter capacity, an additional step is required to account for redundancy. The provider virtual datacenter cluster redundancy varies, depending on service levels offered. For the next example, we assume n+2 cluster redundancy. This means that the provider virtual datacenter can absorb up to two vSphere host failures and continue to support all hosted virtual machines at the same level of performance. To accomplish this, enough capacity must be available on the remaining vSphere hosts to take over all workloads.

Based on a requirement for provider virtual datacenter cluster redundancy, the overall number of memory and CPU consumption units for the provider virtual datacenter (cluster) must be reduced. To determine the redundancy overhead, the number of vSphere hosts in the cluster and the desired number of redundant vSphere hosts need to be considered. Table G.2 describes this.

G

TABLE G.2 Determining Redundancy Overhead

Redundancy Variables	Description
`Nnodes`	Represents the number of nodes in a cluster.
`Nredundant`	Represents the minimum number of redundant nodes.
`Rredundancy,HA`	Represents a targeted ratio of redundancy as indicated by a real number greater than 1. This ratio (such as 1.10) indicates that a 10% overhead is committed to availability. For example, a 10-node provider virtual datacenter with a 1.10 redundancy ratio requires 11 nodes to deliver the appropriate capacity. This level of redundancy can vary, depending on the class of service offering being delivered on that provider virtual datacenter. The following equation determines redundancy variables.

Calculating Redundancy Ratio from Minimal Level of Redundancy

$$\left(\frac{N_{nodes} + N_{redundant}}{N_{nodes}} \right) = R_{redundancy}$$

For example, the level of redundancy is calculated here for a cluster size of 10 nodes containing 2 redundant nodes.

$$\left(\frac{N_{nodes} + N_{redundant}}{N_{nodes}}\right) = \left(\frac{8+2}{8}\right) = 1.25 = R_{redundancy}$$

After the ratio of redundancy is calculated, the number of units of consumption per provider virtual datacenter can be determined using the following equation:

CPU Resources Per Cluster

$$N_{CPU,\ cluster} = \frac{N_{hosts,\ cluster} P_{CPU,host}}{R_{redundancy,\ HA}}$$

For the example where:

$$P_{CPU,\ host} = 19.2GHz$$

This results in:

$$N_{CPU,\ cluster} = \frac{8 \times 19.2}{1.25} = 122.88GHz$$

The number of memory units of consumption is calculated in the following equation.

For the example where:

$$N_{mem,\ host} = 64GB$$

This results in:

$$N_{mem,\ cluster} = \frac{N_{hosts,\ cluster} M_{mem,\ host}}{1.25} = \frac{8 \times 64}{1.25} = 409.6GB$$

Based on the calculations, the example provider virtual datacenter has 122.88GHz of available CPU and 409.6GB of available memory, taking a vSphere cluster redundancy of n+2 into account. The next section provides guidance for capacity management as it applies to each of the consumption models.

Pay As You Go Model

When an organization virtual datacenter is created in the pay as you go model, a resource pool is instantiated with expandable reservations. As such, the customer organization virtual datacenters contained on that provider virtual datacenter can grow to consume all the available provider virtual datacenter resources. Although this could be true in any vSphere environment, the added challenge in a vCloud is the use of reservations at the vApp level. When an organization virtual datacenter is created out of a provider virtual datacenter using the pay as you go consumption model, a `%guarantee` is configured for CPU and memory. This is applied to each vApp or virtual machine within a vApp. For example, if the service provider configures the organization virtual datacenter with a 50% guarantee for CPU and 75% guarantee for memory, the customer creates a virtual machine consuming 1 vCPU of 1GHz and 1GB of memory, a reservation for that virtual machine is set at 50% of 1GHz, or 0.5 GHz and 75% of 1GB, or 0.75GB of memory.

Because there is no way of knowing how a customer will define virtual machine templates in private customer catalogs—and because an organization's virtual datacenters can expand on demand—VMware recommends the following:

- Calculate the total available CPU and memory resources (minus an amount reserved for global catalog templates), adjusted by the cluster redundancy ratio, at the provider virtual datacenter level.
- Establish a CPU and memory `%RESERVED` threshold at the provider virtual datacenter level.
- Initially establish the `%RESERVED` for the provider virtual datacenter at a number in the 60% range.
- As the total amount of reserved CPU or reserved memory approaches the `%RESERVED` threshold, do not deploy new organization virtual datacenters in that provider virtual datacenter without adding resources. If the corresponding vSphere cluster has reached its maximum point of expansion, a new provider virtual datacenter should be deployed and any new organization virtual datacenter should be assigned to the new provider virtual datacenter. In this way, when the provider virtual datacenter has reached its maximum point of expansion, there is still 40% of expansion capacity for the existing organization virtual.
- CPU and memory overcommitment can be applied. If so, the `%RESERVED` value should be set lower than if no overcommitment is applied because of the unpredictability of the virtual machine sizes being deployed (and, hence, reservations being established).
- Monitor the `%RESERVED` on a regular basis, and adjust the value according to historical usage as well as project demand.

Allocation Pool Model

When an organization virtual datacenter is created in the allocation pool model, a nonexpandable resource pool is instantiated with a `%guaranteed` value for CPU and memory that was specified. Using a `%guaranteed` value of 75%, this means that if an organization virtual datacenter is created specifying 100GHz of CPU and 100GB of memory, a resource pool is created for that organization virtual datacenter with a reservation of 75GHz and limit of 100GHz for CPU and a reservation of 75GB with a limit of 100GB for memory.

The additional 25%, in this example, is not guaranteed and can be accessed only if it's available across the provider virtual datacenter. In other words, the 25% can be overcommitted by the provider at the provider virtual datacenter level and, therefore, might not be available, depending on how *all* the organization virtual datacenters in that provider virtual datacenter are using it.

At the virtual machine level, when a virtual machine is deployed, it is instantiated with no CPU reservation, but with a memory reservation equal to the virtual machine's memory allocation multiplied by the `%guaranteed`. Despite the fact that no CPU reservation is set at the virtual machine level, the total amount of CPU allocated across all virtual machines in that organization virtual datacenter is still subject to the overall CPU reservation of the organization virtual datacenter established by the `%guarantee` value.

Based on this use of reservations in the allocation pool model, VMware recommends the following:

- Calculate the total available CPU and memory resources (minus an amount reserved for global catalog templates), adjusted by the cluster redundancy ratio, at the provider virtual datacenter level.
- Determine how much resources, at the provider virtual datacenter level, you want to make available for expanding organization virtual datacenters that are deployed to that provider virtual datacenter.
- Establish a CPU and memory `%RESERVED` (guaranteed, not allocated) threshold at the provider virtual datacenter level, based on the `%guaranteed` minus the amount reserved for growth. The remaining unreserved resources are available to all organization virtual datacenters for bursting.
- As the total amount of reserved CPU or reserved memory approaches the `%RESERVED` threshold, do not deploy new organization virtual datacenters in that provider virtual datacenter without adding resources. If the corresponding vSphere cluster has reached its maximum point of expansion, a new provider virtual datacenter should be deployed and any new organization virtual datacenters should be assigned to the new provider virtual datacenter. This gives some predetermined amount of capacity available for expanding the existing organization virtual datacenters when the provider virtual datacenter has reached its maximum point of expansion.
- CPU and memory overcommitment can be applied, but it should be based only on the amount of unreserved resources at the provider virtual datacenter level, allowing for overcommitting the resources available for organization virtual datacenter bursting.
- Monitor the `%RESERVED` on a regular basis, and adjust the value according to historical usage as well as project demand.

Reservation Pool Model

When an organization virtual datacenter is created in the reservation pool model, a nonexpandable resource pool is instantiated with the reservation and limit values equivalent to the amount of resources allocated. This means that if an organization virtual datacenter is created allocating 100GHz of CPU and 100GB of memory, a reservation pool is created for that organization virtual datacenter with a reservation and limit of 100GHz for CPU and a reservation and limit of 100GB for memory.

At the virtual machine level, when a virtual machine is deployed, it is instantiated with no reservation or limit for either CPU or memory.

Based on this use of reservations in the reservation pool model, VMware recommends the following:

- Calculate the total available CPU and memory resources (minus an amount reserved for global catalog templates), adjusted by the cluster redundancy ratio, at the provider virtual datacenter level.
- Determine how much resources, at the provider virtual datacenter level, you want to make available for expanding organization virtual datacenters that are deployed to that provider virtual datacenter.
- Establish a CPU and memory `%RESERVED` threshold at the provider virtual datacenter level equivalent to the capacity of the underlying vSphere cluster, taking into account HA redundancy.
- As the total amount of reserved CPU or reserved memory approaches the `%RESERVED` threshold, do not deploy new organization virtual datacenters in that provider virtual datacenter without adding resources. If the corresponding vSphere cluster has reached its maximum point of expansion, a new provider virtual datacenter should be deployed and any new organization virtual datacenters should be assigned to the new provider virtual datacenter. In this way, some predetermined amount of capacity is available for expanding the existing organization virtual datacenters after the provider virtual datacenter has reached its maximum point of expansion.
- No overcommitment can be applied to the provider virtual datacenter in the reservation pool model because the reservation is at the resource pool level.
- Monitor the `%RESERVED` on a regular basis, and adjust the value according to historical usage as well as project demand.

Storage

VMware vCloud Director uses a largest available capacity algorithm for deploying virtual machines to datastores. Storage capacity must be managed both on an individual datastore basis and in the aggregate for a provider virtual datacenter.

In addition to considering VMware storage allocation design guidelines, manage capacity at the datastore level using the largest virtual machine storage configuration, in terms of units of consumption, offered in the service catalog when determining the amount of spare capacity to reserve. For example, if 1TB datastores are used (100 storage units of consumption, based on a 10GB unit of consumption) and the largest virtual machine storage configuration is six storage units of consumption (60GB), applying the VMware design guideline of approximately 80% datastore utilization implies managing to 82 storage units of consumption. This results in 82% datastore utilization and reserves capacity equivalent to three of the largest virtual machines offered in the service catalog in terms of storage.

Network Capacity Planning

A vCloud also brings network capacity planning to the forefront. Providers must consider IP address, VLAN, and ephemeral port capacity. Table G.3 describes what must be managed from a capacity perspective and its impact.

TABLE G.3 Network Capacity Planning Items

Item to Manage	Impact
IP addresses	▶ Available IP addresses need to be assigned in support of a dedicated external network for an organization, such as for Internet access or hardware-based firewall rules. ▶ IP addresses assigned to specific organizations must be tracked to determine what is available for a shared external organization network.
VLANs	▶ VLANs are available for VLAN-backed pool assignment, if required. ▶ VLANs are available for vCloud Director Network Isolation transport networks, one per vCloud Director Network Isolation pool.
Expandable static port bindings	▶ Expandable static port bindings are the Default vCloud Director network pool type. ▶ Overall number of static ports expands in increments of 10, as needed. Unused but allocated static port bindings do not increase the total number of static port bindings available.

APPENDIX H
Capacity Management

Capacity Forecasting Specific to vCloud—Demand Management

Capacity forecasting consists of determining how many organization virtual datacenters are expected to be provisioned during a specific time period. Capacity provisioning is concerned with determining when vCloud infrastructure components must be purchased to maintain capacity. From a financial budget perspective, the procurement of the vCloud infrastructure requires more planning and an understanding of customer future requirements.

VMware recommends performing two forecasting functions over time:

- **Capacity trending:** Historical organization virtual datacenter capacity and utilization data can help predict future capacity requirements.
- **Demand pipeline:** Understanding future customer requirements through the sales pipeline provides the necessary information to understand future capacity requirements, as well as knowledge of marketing/business development functions bringing new service offerings to market.

Initially, no historical utilization metrics are available, so performing capacity trending for some period of time is not possible. During this initial period, a good understanding of the customer demand pipeline needs to be established. Over time, this pipeline can be combined with trending analysis to more accurately predict capacity requirements.

The customer demand pipeline must be established in conjunction with the service provider's sales teams (or lines of business [LOB] in a private vCloud) to determine future vCloud capacity requirements. This demand pipeline must contain information on all known new customers, expansion of existing customer organization virtual datacenters, projected sizing metrics, plus any new service offerings that are in development. The forecasting plan must fit both the budgetary cycle and the procurement and provisioning timeframes. For example, if a quarterly budgetary cycle exists and the procurement and provisioning timeframe is one month, a pipeline of *at least four months* is needed to make sure all requests in the pipeline can be fulfilled.

Over time, capacity trending can assist in forecasting organization virtual datacenter provisioning needs. It uses historical information to determine trends and validates the organization virtual datacenter forecast based on demand pipeline data.

Capacity Monitoring and Establishing Triggers

The metrics in Table H.1 must be carefully monitored to warn of approaching or exceeding consumption thresholds. These metrics should be measured against each vCloud provider virtual datacenter and for each organization virtual datacenter within it. To monitor for threshold breaches, and possible subsequent violation of service level commitments to the vCloud consumer, the appropriate tools and triggers are needed for proper notification.

TABLE H.1 Capacity-Monitoring Metrics

Attribute	Monitored Per
`%RESERVED CPU`	Provider virtual datacenter, organization virtual datacenter. For the pay as you go allocation model, this is the aggregation of reservations values for the contained virtual machines.
`%RESERVED Memory`	Provider virtual datacenter, organization virtual datacenter.
CPU utilization	Provider virtual datacenter, organization virtual datacenter.
Memory utilization	Provider virtual datacenter, organization virtual datacenter.
Datastore utilization	Provider virtual datacenter.
Transfer store utilization	vCloud.
Network IP addresses available	vCloud.
Network IP addresses consumed	Organization.
Network VLANs available	vCloud.
Network ephemeral ports consumed	vNetwork distributed switch.

If thresholds are exceeded, the group responsible for capacity management of the vCloud should be notified to add capacity. Take into account the time required to add the physical components necessary to increase the capacity of a provider virtual datacenter. A vCloud-aware capacity-management tool should be deployed. Whichever tool is chosen, the capacity model can forecast new provider virtual datacenter capacity usage, as well as ongoing capacity management of existing provider virtual datacenters. It should also account for expansion triggers based on provisioning timeframes.

After the total amount of available resources has been calculated for a provider virtual datacenter, no adjustments to that provider virtual datacenter (such as adding or removing hosts) should be made without updating the calculated value. This model can be altered if long-term CPU and memory reservations are not at the levels for which they were designed. An increase in the resources allocated to an organization virtual datacenter can affect the remaining capacity of a *full* provider virtual datacenter. Full provider virtual datacenters should be monitored weekly. The resource consumption of virtual machines within an organization's virtual datacenter should be reviewed to identify trends that indicate the resources purchased are insufficient.

Although VMware vCenter CapacityIQ™ is not vCloud Director aware, it offers insight into provider virtual datacenter utilization and trends.

Capacity Management Manual Processes—Provider Virtual Datacenter

The following vCloud administrator capacity-management activities include periodic planning activities supported by day-to-day operational activities. Periodic continuous improvement activities are critical to extracting the most value from your vCloud infrastructure.

Planning activities (initially monthly, then quarterly):

- Determining usable capacity by provider virtual datacenter and organization virtual datacenter (taking into account vSphere overhead)
- Reviewing current utilization
- Reviewing provisioning timeframes for new provider virtual datacenter components (hosts, network, storage)
- Forecasting growth over the coming period (preferably based on the actual pipeline, validated with historical trending)
- Planning for procurement and implementation of additional capacity over the coming period, including bills of materials and budgets
- Reviewing capacity alert threshold levels and setting alerts for capacity warnings

Operational activities (daily):

- Monitoring for alerts
- Investigating performance issues to determine whether capacity is the root cause
- Initiating and managing the procurement and provisioning of additional provider virtual datacenter capacity

Continuous improvement activities (quarterly/yearly):

- Comparing capacity model utilization levels to observed levels and tuning the model to drive greater utilization without sacrificing reliability
- Optimizing provisioning timeframes (shortening them and making them more predictable)

Customer (Organization) Administrator Perspective

The primary capacity-management concern of the organization administrator is capacity management of the organization's organization virtual datacenters.

VMware recommends that all organizations establish a capacity-management process based on a standard unit of consumption. Table H.2 shows the recommended base unit of consumption for each resource important for capacity management from an organization administrator perspective.

TABLE H.2 Organization Virtual Datacenter Units of Consumption

Attribute	Variable	Value
vCPU	`PUC`	1GHz
Memory	`MUC`	1GB
Storage	`DUC`	10GB

This approach enables more efficient capacity management because the vApp component virtual machine resource allocations are predefined in the service catalog, resulting in a more accurately predicted vCloud infrastructure resource consumption.

Each organization has a finite quantity of resources (in the cases of the allocation pool and reservation pool consumption models) from one or more provider virtual datacenters in the form of organization virtual datacenters. This means that, as the organization consumes the organization virtual datacenter resources, a trigger point needs to be defined to prompt actions to expand the organization virtual datacenter.

First, the resource consumption limits for an organization's organization virtual datacenters need to be defined, with these limits defining when action needs to be taken to remove the potential capacity issue. Table H.3 provides recommendations.

TABLE H.3 Recommended Organization Virtual Datacenter Capacity Thresholds

Attribute	Variable	Limit	Description
Organization virtual datacenter CPU peak utilization	`CCPULimit`	80%	The limit for allocating CPU resources within the organization virtual datacenter before expansion is required. This value varies, depending on the consumption model used. From an organization virtual datacenter perspective, reservation values should be considered equal to the amount of CPU allocated because reservation values are not available to the organization administrator.
Organization virtual datacenter memory allocation limit	`CmemLimit`	80%	The limit for allocating memory resources within the organization virtual datacenter before expansion is required. This value varies, depending on the consumption model used. From an organization virtual datacenter perspective, reservation values should be considered equal to the amount of memory allocated because reservation values are not available to the organization administrator.

The CPU and memory resources vary, depending on the size of the contracted organization virtual datacenter. Table H.4 provides an example of the resources needed to calculate the organization virtual datacenter's capacity.

TABLE H.4 Sample Organization Virtual Datacenter Resource Allocation

Item	Variable	Value	Units
Total organization virtual datacenter vCPU units of consumption	`Sorgvirtual datacenter`	`50`	GHz
Organization virtual datacenter memory allocation in units of consumption	`Morgvirtual datacenter`	`64`	GB

The following equations determine the number of capacity units available within this organization virtual datacenter.

Determining organization virtual datacenter memory units of consumption:

$$M_{UC,orgVDC} = \left(\frac{C_{memLimit} M_{orgVDC}}{M_{UC}} \right)$$

Based on the information from the previous tables, the total memory unit of consumption for the organization virtual datacenter is calculated:

$$M_{UC,orgVDC} = \left(\frac{C_{memLimit} M_{orgVDC}}{M_{UC}} \right) = \left(\frac{0.8 \times 64}{1} \right) = 51.2GB$$

This results in 51.2 memory units of consumption for the sample organization virtual datacenter.

Determining organization virtual datacenter CPU units of consumption:

$$P_{UC,orgVDC} = \left(\frac{S_{orgVDC} C_{CPULimit}}{P_{UC}} \right)$$

Based on the information from the previous tables, the CPU units of consumption per organization virtual datacenter are calculated:

$$P_{UC,orgVDC} = \left(\frac{S_{orgVDC} S_{CPULimit}}{P_{UC}} \right) = \left(\frac{50 \times 0.8}{1} \right) = 40GHz$$

This results in 40 CPU units of consumption for this sample organization virtual datacenter.

Organization Virtual Datacenter-Specific Capacity Forecasting

Capacity forecasting consists of determining how many virtual machines are expected to be deployed during a specific time period of the organization's choosing. The time period used for the virtual machine forecast should correspond to the budgetary process. Capacity provisioning is concerned with determining when an organization virtual datacenter must be expanded to maintain capacity.

VMware recommends that organizations perform two forecasting functions over time:

- **Capacity trending:** Using historical virtual machine capacity and utilization data can predict future capacity requirements.
- **Capacity pipeline:** Understanding future user resource requirements for virtual machines through IT and LOB projects provides the necessary information for understanding future capacity requirements.

Over time, capacity trending can assist in forecasting virtual machine provisioning needs. It uses historical information to determine trends and validates the virtual machine forecast based on pipeline data.

Capacity provisioning depends on determining the point of expansion for the organization virtual datacenter. This is based on determining a point of resource consumption at which the process of procuring and expanding the organization virtual datacenter must begin so that reserve capacity is not exhausted before the additional capacity is available. In the vCloud context, this can be considered to depend on the time it takes to process the purchase request for additional organization virtual datacenter resources. Provisioning time can be assumed to be zero but depends on specific contractual agreements with the service provider.

The next sections describe recommended steps to perform capacity trending and determine a point of organization virtual datacenter expansion.

Collect Organization Virtual Datacenter Consumption Information Regularly

The primary issue with the trending of organization virtual datacenter consumption is identifying the point of record for all new virtual machines. This can then determine the capacity trends and, therefore, the overall need for purchasing additional organization virtual datacenter capacity. To establish the point of record for new virtual machines, the items listed in Table H.5 should be tracked, ideally in a configuration management or capacity planning database as virtual machine attributes.

TABLE H.5 Organization Virtual Datacenter Trending Information

Variable	Name	Description	Units
`orgvirtual datacenter`	Organization virtual datacenter	Organization virtual datacenter in which the virtual machine resides	Identifier
`Dbuild`	Build date	Date the virtual machine was built	Date
`NUC,cpu`	CPU units of consumption	Number of CPU units of consumption allocated to the virtual machine	CPU units of consumption
`NUC,mem`	Memory units of consumption	Number of memory units of consumption allocated to the virtual machine	Memory units of consumption
`NVGB`	Storage	Amount of storage (GB) allocated to the virtual machine	GB

Determine Trending Variables

With the information recorded as described in Table H.6, determining the rate of organization virtual datacenter consumption is possible.

TABLE H.6 Organization Virtual Datacenter Capacity Trending Variables

Variable	Name	Description	Units
T	Time	Time between points of observation	Weeks
NcpuUC	New CPU units	Total number of CPU units of consumption required for the forecast virtual machines	CPU units of consumption
NmemUC	New memory units	Total number of memory units of consumption required for the forecast virtual machines	Memory units of consumption
NVGB	New storage (GB)	Total amount of storage required for the forecast virtual machines	GB
Tpurchase	Organization virtual datacenter expansion purchase time	Amount of time to procure additional organization virtual datacenter resources	Weeks

Determining the Trended Growth Rate

$$\Delta N_{cpuUC} = \frac{N_{cpuUC}}{\Delta T}$$

$$\Delta N_{memUC} = \frac{N_{memUC}}{\Delta T}$$

$$\Delta N_{VGB} = \frac{N_{VGB}}{\Delta T}$$

Determining the Trend

The rate of increase dictates how far in advance additional organization virtual datacenter resources need to be purchased. Table H.7 presents a sample virtual machine forecast for a quarter, along with sample time-to-purchase value.

TABLE H.7 Sample Organization Virtual Datacenter Trending Information

Attribute	Value
ΔNcpuUC	12
ΔNmemUC	12
ΔNVGB	360GB
Tpurchase	2 weeks
NcpuUC,cluster	320
NmemUC,cluster	717

In the following example, `NcpuUC,free` and `NmemUC,free` represent the number of free resources within an organization virtual datacenter. At this point, additional organization virtual datacenter resources should be ordered.

To determine the trigger point for ordering, use the following equation if no pipeline data exists.

Determining Trigger Point for Ordering Capacity Using Trends

$$N_{UC,\,free} = \Delta N_{CU} \times T_{purchase}$$

For example, from the following data, one can calculate the needed free consumption units as listed in the following equation, or 24 units.

$$N_{cpuUC,\,free} = \Delta N_{cpuUC} \times T_{purchase} = 12 \times 2 = 24GHz$$

$$N_{memUC,\,free} = \Delta N_{memUC} \times T_{purchase} = 12 \times 2 = 24GB$$

For storage, in this example, the trigger point is calculated at 720GB:

$$N_{VGB,\,free} = \Delta N_{VGB} \times \left(T_{purchase}\right) = 360 \times 2 = 720GB$$

Determine the Automatic Point of Expansion

Based on the previous example, additional organization virtual datacenter resources need to be ordered when the available units of CPU or memory fall to 24GHz or 24GB, respectively, or when storage capacity falls to 720GB. The additional capacity needs to be on order when described for the capacity to be available in time to meet demand.

Currently, no tools are available to assist in organization virtual datacenter capacity management. However, it is possible to develop scripts to gather pertinent information using languages such as PowerCLI.

Capacity Management Manual Processes—Organization Virtual Datacenter

The following organization administrator capacity-management activities include periodic planning activities supported by day-to-day operational activities. Periodic continuous improvement activities are critical to extracting the most value from your vCloud.

- Planning activities (initially monthly, then quarterly):
    - Determining usable capacity by organization virtual datacenter
    - Reviewing current utilization (and performance, where possible)

    - Reviewing purchasing timeframes for expanding an organization virtual datacenter
    - Forecasting utilization growth over the coming period (preferably based on actual pipeline validated by historical trending)
    - Reviewing capacity alert threshold levels and setting alerts for capacity warnings

- Operational activities (daily):
    - Monitoring for alerts
    - Investigating performance issues to determine whether capacity is the root cause
    - Initiating and managing the procurement and provisioning of additional capacity

- Continuous improvement activities (quarterly/yearly): Comparing capacity model utilization levels to observed levels

APPENDIX I

Integrating with Existing Enterprise System Management

Several mechanisms are available for integrating vCloud with existing enterprise system management tools. These range from the vCloud Director notification capabilities to vCenter Orchestrator, the vCloud API, and, for providers, the VIX API. This appendix addresses the vCloud Director notification capability using vCenter Orchestrator and the VIX API. For more information about the vCloud API, see the *vCloud API Specification* (www.vmware.com/pdf/vcd_10_api_spec.pdf) and the *vCloud API Programming Guide* (www.vmware.com/support/pubs/vcd_pubs.html).

vCloud Director Notifications and Blocking Tasks Messages

vCloud Director supports notifications and blocking tasks features that enable it to extend its capabilities by interoperating with applications. Figure I.1 illustrates how these extensions fit between vCloud Director, the vFabric RabbitMQ message bus broker, and external systems.

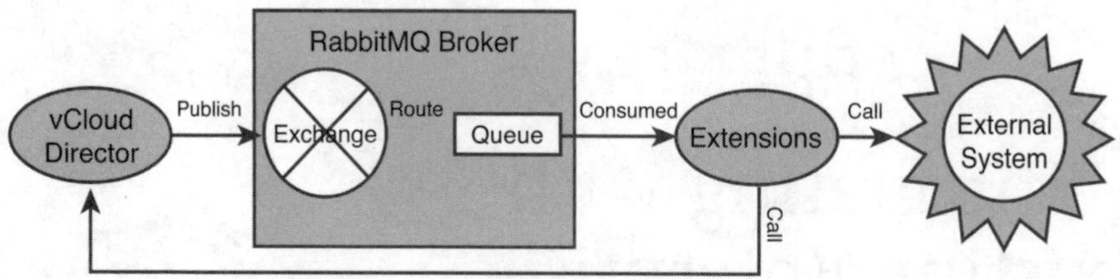

FIGURE I.1 vCloud Director extension overview

Message Publication

The system administrator can configure vCloud Director to enable the publication of messages for all event notifications and/or for specific blocking tasks:

- The notifications indicate the new state of the corresponding vCloud Director entity and are published upon user-initiated events (for example, creation, deployment, and deletion of a vApp) and system-initiated events (for example, vApp lease expiration).
- The blocking tasks suspend long-running operations started as tasks before publishing messages and wait until a system administrator takes action.

The message publication is enabled for operations started in both the vCloud Director UI and the vCloud API, either of which can be used to act upon a message.

The notification messages are published to an Advanced Message Queuing Protocol (AMQP) exchange (AMQP version 0.9.1, supported by RabbitMQ version 2.0 and later).

Routing

The AMQP broker uses routing as an effective way to filter vCloud director notification messages and dispatch them to different queues for one or more extensions.

The exchange routes notifications to its bound queues according to their queue routing key and exchange type. The vCloud notification messages routing key has the following syntax format:

```
<operationSuccess>.<entityUUID>.<orgUUID>.<userUUID>.<subType1>.<subType2>...
<subTypeN>.[taskName]
```

Extension

An extension is a script or application with the following capabilities:

- Subscribes to an AMQP queue for receiving new messages
- Triages the received messages
- Processes messages into operations (internal or external calls)
- Calls back the vCloud Director API to get more information on the objects involved in an operation and take action on a blocked task

Subscribe to an AMQP Queue

Subscribing to queues involves declaring a queue, binding with a routing key, and then subscribing to the declared queue.

The queue routing key supports the `*` and `#` wildcard characters to match a single segment and zero or more segments. For example, `true.*.*.*. com.vmware.vcloud.event.vm.create` or `true.#.com.vmware.vcloud.event.vm.create` routes a notification to the queue with this binding key every time any user from any organization successfully creates a virtual machine).

Declaring asserts the existence of the object. If the object does not exist, declaring it creates it.

Triage the Consumed Messages

When a message is consumed, the extension can use the message header that contains all the routing components to further filter and act upon. For example, some notifications might be ignored.

Separate the notifications messages from the blocking tasks because the blocking tasks must be handled differently.

Handling the Notification Messages

The notification messages contain the operation triggering the event, the object type, and identifiers and names for the organization, user, and object.

These can be used as markers for applications such as audit logging, change management, and incident management. If the application cannot correlate the IDs to present the object properties in a user-consumable form, the extension application must call back the vCloud API to extract these.

Use notification messages to start an operation that must follow another one (for example, enabling the public IPs of a vApp in a load balancer).

Handling Blocking Tasks Messages

Blocking tasks messages have similar identifiers, with the object being the blocking task. The blocking task references include the following:

- **Its parent task:** The suspended task referencing the object and the task parameter attributes it was set with in the original request.
- **TaskOwner:** The object on which the task operates.
- **Actions that can be taken on this blocking task:** Resume, abort, fail, and `updateProgress`.

Receiving and acting upon on the blockings task is accomplished with the vCloud director API callbacks. System admin privileges are required to perform these operations.

Aborting a task returns a success status. It should be done only under the following conditions:

- The requested vApp went through automatic approval logic and was disapproved.
- It is necessary to replace an operation to be carried out by another one (for example, to start a preprovisioned vApp instead of provisioning a vApp)
- Parameters for a requested task must be replaced (for example, when determining a specific virtual datacenter for a vApp based on placement logic).
- When calling the same operation as the one that triggered, the notification routing and filtering must be properly configured to avoid creating a loop.

A task should be failed when the operation occurring before the task is determined to fail. An example is when an operation required before running the task failed (for example, the CMDB was not reachable).

The task must be resumed for operations that must complete before the next task starts. Examples include the following:

- OVF user information must be added to a vApp before adding a vApp to catalog.
- The requested vApp goes through automatic approval logic and was approved before being added to vCloud.
- The change request must record the object state in the CMDB system before making the change.

Task progress should be updated to avoid having the task time out, or to log a status message to the user.

Blocking Tasks and Notifications Use Cases

This section covers the messages published during the use case: App Author adds a vApp from catalog. Notifications and blocking task for Instantiate vApp from vApp Template are enabled.

- Notification message: "vApp creation requested." (`true.#.com.vmware.vcloud.event.vapp.create_request - # is used as a placeholder`)
- Notification message: "VM creation requested—a scaffold object is created and resources are locked." (`true.#.com.vmware.vcloud.event.vm.create_request`)
- Notification message: "A task to instantiate a vApp is created." (`true.#.com.vmware.vcloud.event.task.create.vdcInstantiateVapp`)
- Blocking tasks message: "vApp instantiation has been blocked." (`true.#.com.vmware.vcloud.event.blockingtask.create.vdcInstantiateVapp`)
- vCloud Director User Interface shows the task as "Pending processing...."

Case 1: The system admin calls an abort on the blocked task.

- Blocking tasks message: "The blocking task has been aborted." (`true.#.com.vmware.vcloud.event.blockingtask.abort.vdcInstantiateVapp`)

- Notification message: "The vApp is modified as per the next operation." (`true.#.com.vmware.vcloud.event.vapp.modify`)
- Notification message: "The scaffold object is deleted. Resources are unlocked." (`true.#.com.vmware.vcloud.event.vm.delete`)
- Notification message: "The vApp instantiation is aborted." (`true.#.com.vmware.vcloud.event.task.abort.vdcInstantiateVapp`)
- The newly created object is no longer displayed from the vCloud Director user interface. The task can be seen in Logs/Tasks.

Case 2: The system admin fails the blocked task.

- Blocking tasks message: "The blocking task has been failed." (`true.#.com.vmware.vcloud.event.blockingtask.fail.vdcInstantiateVapp`)
- Notification message: "The VM is not created." (`false.#.com.vmware.vcloud.event.vm.create`)
- Notification message: "The vApp instantiation task has been failed." (`true.#.com.vmware.vcloud.event.task.fail.vdcInstantiateVapp`)
- The vCloud Director user interface shows that the task is having an error on the object grid and in Logs/Tasks.

Case 3: The system admin resumes the task.

- Blocking tasks message: "The blocking task has been resumed." (`true.#.com.vmware.vcloud.event.blockingtask.resume.vdcInstantiateVapp`)
- Notification message: "The vApp is instantiated." (`true.#.com.vmware.vcloud.event.task.start.vdcInstantiateVapp`)
- Notification message: "The vApp is created." (`true.#.com.vmware.vcloud.event.vapp.create`)
- Notification message: "The VM is created." (`true.#.com.vmware.vcloud.event.vm.create`)

Case 3a: The vApp instantiation is successful or aborted. (`true.#.com.vmware.vcloud.event.task.complete.vdcInstantiateVapp`)

Case 3b: The vApp instantiation fails. (`false.#.com.vmware.vcloud.event.task.complete.vdcInstantiateVapp`)

Using vCenter Orchestrator As a vCloud Director Extension

VMware vCenter Orchestrator fully supports the consumption of blocked tasks and notifications messages, callbacks, and calls to external systems via the vCloud Director, AMQP, and other product plug-ins. Figure I.2 illustrates this using vFabric RabbitMQ as the message bus broker integrated with vCenter Orchestrator.

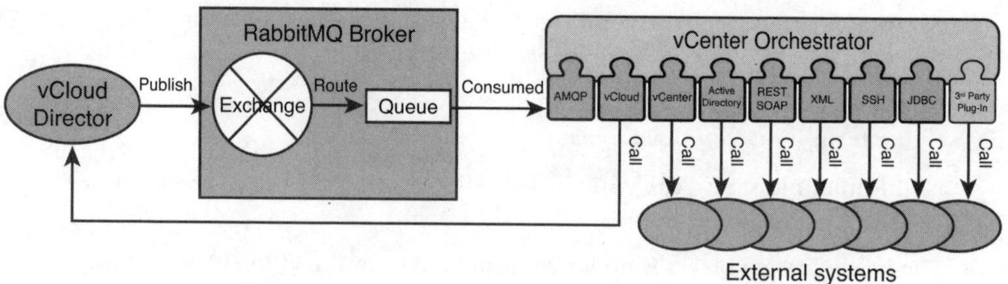

FIGURE I.2 vCenter Orchestrator as a vCloud Director extension

The AMQP plug-in comes with workflows and requires a one-time setup.

1. Add an AMQP broker with hostname and credentials.
2. Declare an exchange for the configured broker.
3. Declare a queue.
4. Bind a queue to an exchange by providing a routing key.
5. Subscribe to queues, enabling message updates on new messages.

This configuration is saved and reloaded automatically when the vCenter Orchestrator server is restarted.

The plug-in supports adding a policy element of type subscription that has an `OnMessage` trigger event. A policy can be set up to start a workflow that processes new messages.

Workflows are provided to triage and process the message to output vCloud Director objects. These can provide all the information necessary for audit purposes and for designing custom logic before calling external systems. External systems are called using specific vCenter Orchestrator plug-in adapters such as vCloud Director, vCenter, Update Manager, or Active Directory, or generic plug-ins adapters such as REST, SOAP, XML, SSH, and JDBC. Blocked tasks objects can then be aborted, resumed, or failed by calling vCloud Director Workflows.

vCenter Orchestrator As an Extension Example

This section shows a simple example leveraging the blocked tasks as a trigger mechanism for starting extension workflows using different vCenter Orchestrator plug-ins.

As a prerequisite, a subscription to an AMQP queue, bound to the exchange used by vCloud Director, was created using the workflows listed in the previous section. As part of this, the routing key is set to filter on vApp creation (`#.blockingtask.create.vdcInstantiateVapp`).

Next, an Approve New vApp policy is created to listen on new messages. It is set to start the Approve a vApp workflow.

The Approve a vApp workflow is designed as shown in Table I.1.

TABLE I.1 Approve a vApp Workflow

Workflow	Description	Plug-In in Use
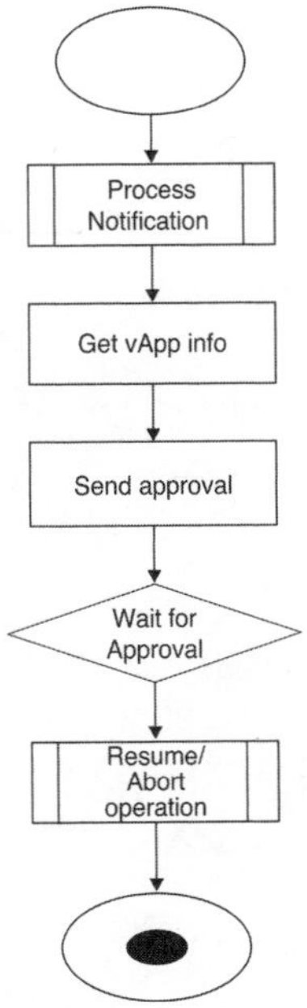 Process Notification	Important information is extracted from the subscription message, such as the name of the vApp requester and the scaffold object of the vApp being requested.	AMQP
Get vApp info	The detailed properties of the requested vApp are gathered.	vCloud Director
Send approval	The vApp requester's manager name and email are found in Active Directory, and an email is sent to approve the vApp. It contains all the details gathered previously.	Active Directory and mail
Wait for Approval	The workflow is stopped until the approver follows the link in his or her email, authenticates using the Active Directory credential, and approves or rejects the vApp.	
Resume/ Abort operation	Depending on whether the vApp was approved, the aborted task is resumed or aborted. An email message is sent to the requester.	vCloud Director and mail

APPENDIX J
Business Continuity

Backing up and restoring the entire vCloud infrastructure involves coordinating numerous components. Consider what is necessary to recover from a service disruption. What components are most critical and complex to restore? What types of failures would be the most catastrophic? The biggest threat to data loss is not hardware failure, but people accidentally deleting or incorrectly configuring their vApps.

vApp Backup/Restore

Currently, most backup products lack integration with vCloud Director. Without visibility into the vApp metadata stored in the vCloud Director database, recovery involves manual steps to restore data and re-establish configuration attributes. Some of the configuration attributes include the owner, network, and organization; these can be manually configured or reassigned through the vCloud API.

The following sections examine how a vCloud backup product can back up and restore a vApp in the vCloud environment.

Use the following high-level procedure to back up and restore a vCloud vApp:

1. Manage credentials.
2. Protect vApps and create backup jobs.
3. Execute the backup job.
4. Recover the vApp to a new vApp or overwrite the existing vApp.

Manage Credentials

Without credentials, no systems are accessible. Because vCloud Director and vSphere components have separate sets of credentials, the backup product either requests that the user enter both sets of credentials at runtime or harvests the credentials for later use. Figure J.1 illustrates the workflow for credential management.

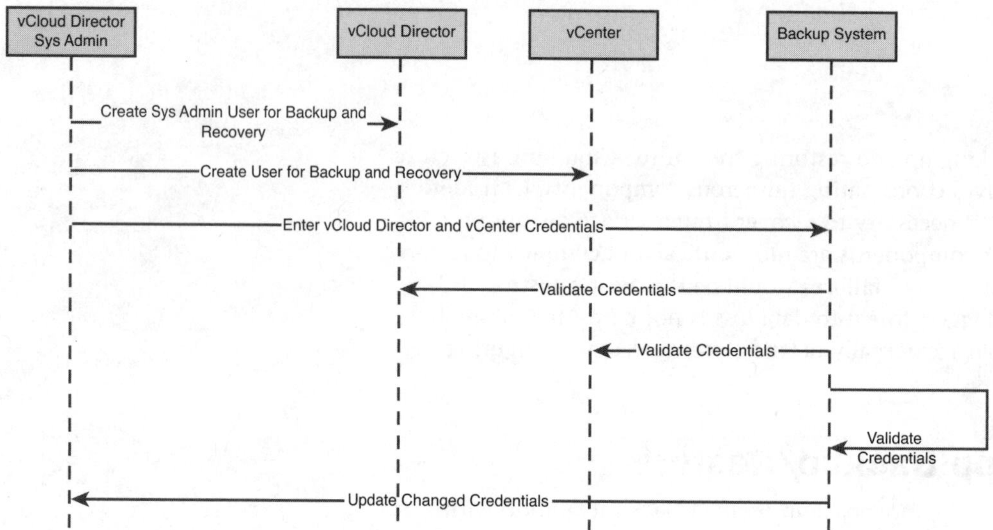

FIGURE J.1 Credential management workflow

Protect vApps and Create Backup Jobs

With valid credentials, the backup product can connect to vCloud Director and vSphere components, extract the data hierarchy, and list the UUIDs of the vApps available for backup. Use the vCloud API or the vCloud Director web console to perform this task. Then find the location of the virtual machines to back up.

If using REST code, the logic is as follows:

1. Start at the top level of the inventory by getting a list of the vCenter Servers that are attached to vCloud Director and all the organizations.

2. Build a map of the vCenter Servers keyed on their ID for easy lookup later.

3. Browse to the appropriate level. When browsing to an organization virtual datacenter, all the vApps in that organization virtual datacenter are visible, as are all the datastores accessible to the organization virtual datacenter (through the parent provider virtual datacenter). When browsing to a vApp, all virtual machines in that vApp are visible.

4. The following data should be captured by the end of the process:
   - Organization.
   - Organization virtual datacenters.
   - Datastores.
   - vApp network configuration (vApp networks; organization networks; and NAT, firewall, and DHCP settings).
   - Virtual machines belonging to that vApp. For each virtual machine, retrieve the same virtual machine properties needed to perform vSphere backups (such as managed object reference, network, and description).

Execute Backup Jobs

After locating the virtual machines to back up, the backup product can execute the backup job using the appropriate information. The APIs used are the vCloud API, vSphere API, and VMware Virtual Disk Development Kit (VDDK). The VDDK is a subset of the VMware vSphere Storage APIs—Data Protection (VADP).

Most customers no longer use agent-based backups, opting instead for more efficient and tightly integrated products that leverage VADP. Agent-based backups can be used in a vCloud environment to overcome some of the challenges vApp networks pose.

Recovery

Before recovery, place the vApp in maintenance mode, to prohibit users from performing operations that change the state of the vApp. After recovering the vApp, make the vApp available by exiting maintenance mode.

To restore vApps to a previous state, shut down the vApp and use the backup product to overwrite existing virtual disk files in the vApp.

Recovering a deleted vApp requires reimporting virtual machines into vCloud Director as follows:

1. Import the first virtual machine into a new vApp, thereby creating the vApp.
2. Import the rest of the virtual machines belonging to the vApp.
3. Configure each virtual machine with the appropriate properties (organization virtual datacenter, newly restored name, vApp network, and so on).
4. After all virtual machines have been imported, validate that the correct properties are in place (network connections, ownership, and so on).

Infrastructure Backup/Restore

Synchronize the backup of all vCloud infrastructure components—for instance, with snapshots, VADP, or other backup tools. Quiesce all databases at the same time before taking snapshots or creating backups. A database that is out of sync can cause a recovery nightmare. See Table J.1 for recommended protection policies.

TABLE J.1 Recommended Protection Policies

Data	Type	Description	Data Protection Policy
vCloud Director installation files	Infrastructure	Static information that consists of product binaries for each cell.	VM snapshot Frequency—once
vCloud Director log files	Infrastructure	Dynamic information generated by each cell. Located in `$VCLOUD_HOME/logs`. Multicell installations can use a syslog server to centralize log files.	File-level backup Frequency—periodic
vCloud Director configuration file	Infrastructure	Dynamic information for each cell. The file is `$VCLOUD_HOME/etc/global.properties`.	File-level backup Frequency—on change, periodic
vCloud Director VC Proxy	Infrastructure	Stateless.	None
vCloud Director Console Proxy	Infrastructure	Stateless.	None
vCloud Director Database Server	Infrastructure	Dynamic information shared by all cells. The database instance may be shared with other applications.	vCloud database schema-level backup Frequency—periodic
vCenter Server installation files	Infrastructure	Static information that consists of product binaries and configuration files. See the backup vCenter Chargeback database and configuration files (http://kb.vmware.com/kb/1026796).	VM snapshot Frequency—once
vCenter Server log files	Infrastructure	Dynamic generation generated by each vCenter Server.	File-level backup Frequency—periodic
vCenter Database Server	Infrastructure	Dynamic information shared by all cells. Multiple database servers can exist in a multi-VC configuration.	vCenter database schema-level backup Frequency—periodic
vCloud organizations	Content	Dynamic information, virtual datacenter, networks, vApps, virtual machines, users, and catalogs.	vCloud REST API Frequency—periodic

Data	Type	Description	Data Protection Policy
vCloud provider resources	Content	Provider virtual datacenters, provider networks, and network pools.	vCloud REST API Frequency—periodic
Orchestrator application database	Orchestration	Contains the workflow engine library (workflows, actions, policy templates, configuration elements, resource elements, web views) and the workflow engine current state (workflows status, events).	Very frequently
Orchestrator plug-ins databases	Orchestration	Contains plug-ins database objects.	Very frequently
Orchestrator application and plug-ins configuration	Orchestration	Contains the configuration.	Upon configuration change
Orchestrator application and plug-ins	Orchestration	Contains the vCenter Orchestrator Server application.	Upon application or plug-ins upgrade
Orchestrator application logs	Orchestration	Contains the vCenter Orchestrator Server logs.	Very frequently

APPENDIX K
Upgrade Checklists

The following checklists cover the upgrade of vCloud Director and associated components. Review all applicable product documentation before upgrading.

Phase 1

Upgrade vCloud Director Cells

- Verify operating system, database, and other component compatibility with target vCloud Director version. See the online *VMware Compatibility Guide* (www.vmware.com/resources/compatibility/search.php).
- Obtain the updated vCloud Director installation package.
- Back up vCloud Director configuration and response files.
- Perform a backup of the vCloud Director database and vCenter database(s).
- If multiple cells exist, use a cell-management tool to quiesce and shut down services on each server (see the *vCloud Director Installation and Configuration Guide*).
- Upgrade vCloud Director software on all servers, but do not start the services yet. See the *vCloud Director Installation and Configuration Guide* for recommendations on minimizing the interruption of vCloud Director portal service.
- Upgrade the vCloud Director database with scripts included in vCloud Director installation.
- Restart the vCloud Director services on upgraded vCloud Director servers.

CAUTION

If Chargeback is in use, upgrade to Chargeback 1.6.2 or later before continuing, to minimize disruption of metering service. Versions earlier than Chargeback 1.6.2 cannot collect data from vCloud Director. For details, refer to the *vCloud Director Installation and Configuration Guide* (www.vmware.com/support/pubs/vcd_pubs.html).

Upgrade vCloud Networking and Security Manager and Edge Devices

- Obtain the vCloud Networking and Security Manager update package. Do *not* deploy a new appliance.
- Perform an upgrade of vCloud Networking and Security Manager servers.
- Update vCloud Networking and Security Manager authentication settings within the vCloud Director portal for each configured vCenter and vCloud Networking and Security Manager, to utilize directory-based service accounts with appropriate permissions within vCenter.
- Reset organization and vApp networks within the vCloud Director portal to redeploy the updated vCloud Networking and Security Edge devices.

For details, refer to the *vShield Administration Guide* (www.vmware.com/support/pubs/vshield_pubs.html).

Upgrade Validation

- Verify the vCloud Director version on each cell.
- In vCloud Director portal, confirm that vCenter and hosts are available.
- Verify the version of vCloud Networking and Security Manager.
- Verify the version of each deployed vCloud Networking and Security Edge device.
- If in use, verify that the load balancer accurately detects the status of all cells.
- Validate service availability through access to vCloud Director organization portals.
- Validate usage metering collection within vCenter Chargeback.

For details, refer to the *vShield Administration Guide* (www.vmware.com/support/pubs/vshield_pubs.html).

Phase 2

Upgrade vCenter Server

- Verify operating system, database, and other component compatibility with the target vCenter version.
- Perform a backup of vCenter Server configuration files.

- Back up the vCenter database using a method appropriate for configured databases.
- Disable the vCenter server within the vCloud Director system portal.
- Perform an upgrade installation of vCenter Server.
- Enable the vCenter server in the vCloud Director system portal.
- Install VMware Update Manager and register with vCenter Server.

vCenter Upgrade Validation

- Validate vCenter version and availability status within the vCloud Director system portal.
- Validate usage metering collection within vCenter Chargeback.

Phase 3

Upgrade Hosts

- Back up host configurations.
- Place the host in maintenance mode and confirm that vCloud Director detects that the host is unavailable.
- Perform an upgrade to ESXi 5, removing any incompatible third-party packages that are installed.
- Reconnect the upgraded host within vCenter to upgrade vCenter agents.
- Disable maintenance mode.

Host Upgrade Validation

- Within the vCloud Director portal, refresh the status to verify that new agents are installed and hosts are listed as available.
- Verify the detected ESXi version in the vCloud Director system portal.

Phase 4

Additional Upgrades

- Upgrade all hosts that are connected to datastores and vSphere distributed switches.
- Upgrade VMFS datastores to VMFS-5.
- Upgrade vSphere distributed switches.
- Modify provider virtual datacenters to support virtual hardware version 8, if desired.
- Modify organization virtual datacenters.

APPENDIX L
Custom Workflow Development Guidelines

Providing customized workflows to an internal or external customer follows a typical software development lifecycle, with specific vCloud orchestration requirements and design guidelines for setting up the environments and managing the content lifecycle.

Workflow Development Lifecycle

The workflow development lifecycle provides a custom workflow solution based on the customer's requirements.

Requirements Gathering

Requirements gathering involves interviewing the customer about project characteristics such as planning, budget, scope, prioritization, and constraints. It also includes some vCloud specific technical requirements, such as the following:

- The operations to automate, which must be defined, documented, reliable, and repeatable
- The system environment, including the external system to integrate and the relevant interfaces
- The data flows
- The users and roles

Functional Specifications and Effort Estimate

The functional specifications and level of effort estimate consist of restating the requirements, matched to a high-level, workflows-based implementation and an effort estimate for each resulting task. You can break down the tasks into milestones to fit the project's characteristics. All of this must be documented, and the customer must sign off on it. For external customers, translate effort to cost and include the estimate with the functional specifications in a statement of work (SOW).

Design

Upon agreement between the customer and the delivery team, the delivery team designs the solution following the high-level implementation defined in the functional specification. This consists of architecting how the different elements of the solution work together with the external systems, the use of existing components such as plug-ins and workflows, and the development of custom components.

Development

Development consists of breaking down the different development tasks and assigning them to available development resources who create the elements of the solution.

Test

Testing involves verifying that the solution is reliable and conforms to the functional specifications. Testing requires setting up an environment that simulates the target environment.

Implementation

The solution implementation consists of installing and configuring the solution in a preproduction or production environment (or both) and demonstrating that it works as expected.

Support

The solution support consists of handling support requests, verifying that the solution conforms to the specification, and, if not, troubleshooting and providing bug fixes to the customer.

Orchestration Content Lifecycle

The orchestration content lifecycle, shown in Figure L.1, is the process of staging the elements of the solution from development to test, test to preproduction, and preproduction to production.

FIGURE L.1 Orchestration content lifecycle

Packages are used for exporting content from one Orchestrator server to another. Packages can contain workflows, policies, actions, web views, configurations, and resources. Packages or their individual elements (or both) can also be synchronized directly from one server to another, as long as the servers are interconnected.

At creation time, packages manage dependencies between package elements by automatically adding missing elements. During a package import, the server analyzes and displays differences and lets the administrator choose which elements to import. Packages use X509 certificates to monitor which users export and redistribute elements.

After a package meets the required quality criteria for a release, export and store it, either on a backed-up file system or on a repository vCenter Orchestrator server (that is, a server used specifically for storing packages). At export time to the file system, the following options exist:

- Encrypt the package.
- Set digital rights management to prevent the customer who imports the package from seeing the JavaScript code or modifying or repackaging elements.
- Do not export the element's version history

Use vCenter Orchestrator configuration elements for all the attributes that have dependencies on the environment, to allow orchestration content to be moved from one Orchestrator server to another without requiring that the workflows be edited or the attribute values be modified. It is recommended that you provide configuration workflows with the solution, set the configuration, and update the configuration attribute values, if needed.

Orchestrated vCloud Environments

Some parts of the solution development lifecycle have specific environments, as Figure L.2 shows.

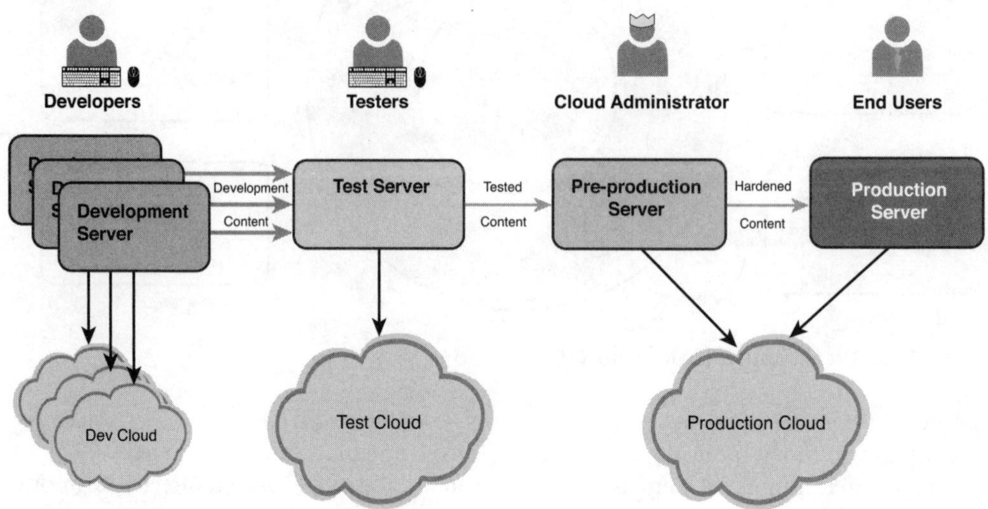

FIGURE L.2 Orchestrated vCloud environments

Developer Environment

The recommended development environment is as follows:

- Allocate one development server per developer. Sharing a single development server among different developers is not recommended for the following reasons:
  - The server might have to be restarted to install or upgrade plug-ins under development, thus creating downtime.
  - The server might have to be configured for a particular environment for a given developer.
  - Two or more developers editing the same element (for example, editing a workflow) at the same time is not supported and can result in data being overwritten.
- Use the developer workstation as the vCenter Orchestrator development server:
  - Provides integration within the development tool chain. For example, consider the plug-in development environment.
  - The vCenter Orchestrator client used to develop the workflows relies on its connection to the server. If the network connection is lost, the changes since the last save are lost.

- For unit testing purposes, the developer server should be configured in a vCloud development environment, with the components defined in the reference architecture plus additional integrations as required. This can be a simple, small environment for each developer or a shared one among developers. Ideally, this environment should be local, but it can be remote. For example, a vCenter Orchestrator client and server can be installed on a laptop and used to connect to vCloud Director over a WAN.
- The vCenter Orchestrator client is not optimized for connecting to a vCenter Orchestrator server over a WAN or through a firewall. If remote access to a vCenter Orchestrator server is required, use Remote Desktop Connection (RDC) to start a vCenter Orchestrator client installed on the same server as the vCenter Orchestrator server.

Test Environment

At least one vCenter Orchestrator server should be dedicated to testing the solution and reporting bugs back to the development team. This server should be a newly installed vCenter Orchestrator server with the same specifications as the target production vCenter Orchestrator server. It can be deployed by using a template, by reverting to a snapshot when decommissioning an existing test environment, or by creating a new vCenter Orchestrator database.

The vCloud environment should differ from the developer environment and use a configuration that resembles the production environment as closely as possible.

Preproduction Environment

To validate the solution with the customer, use a vCenter Orchestrator test server in a preproduction environment (that is, connected to the production environment, but not orchestrating business-critical items or copies of them). Use this server for final validation testing and demonstration to the customer.

Production Environment

If the customer is a vCloud provider and the orchestration solution applies to multiple organizations, use workflows as a vCloud back-end extension while respecting the organization multitenancy.

If the customer is an organization tenant and the orchestration solution is to automate and integrate with a specific environment, deploy a vCenter Orchestrator in the customer's organization and connect it to an external network with access to the vCloud API.

Support Environment

To provide support in a timely manner, it is necessary to stand up the customer environment quickly. Although the customer environment can be rebuilt from the customer-delivered packages and plug-in archives, keeping a copy of it as a vApp enables quick resumption of the specific environment.

Index

B

C

D

E

F

G-H

I

J-K

L

M

N

O

P

Q

R

S

T

U

W-Z

How can we make this index more useful? Email us at indexes@samspublishing.com